Women in the Mosque

Women in the Mosque

A HISTORY OF LEGAL THOUGHT AND LOCAL PRACTICE

Marion Holmes Katz

The American University in Cairo Press

This edition published in Egypt in 2015 by
The American University in Cairo Press
113 Sharia Kasr el Aini, Cairo, Egypt
www.aucpress.com

Exclusive distribution in the Middle East outside Egypt by I.B.Tauris & Co Ltd., 6 Salem Road, London, W4 2BU

Dar el Kutub No. 25794/14
ISBN 978 977 416 722 5

Dar el Kutub Cataloging-in-Publication Data

Katz, Marion
Women in the Mosque: A History of Legal Thought and Local Practice / Marion Katz.—Cairo: The American University in Cairo Press, 2015

p. cm.
ISBN 978 977 416 722 5
1. Women (Islamic Law)
2. Mosques (Islamic Law)
3. Women in Islam

297.351082

1 2 3 4 5 19 18 17 16 15

Printed in Egypt

CONTENTS

Acknowledgments *vii*

INTRODUCTION 1

1. WOMEN'S MOSQUE ATTENDANCE AS A LEGAL PROBLEM 17

2. RECONSTRUCTING PRACTICE 111

3. DEBATING WOMEN'S MOSQUE ACCESS IN SIXTEENTH-CENTURY MECCA 199

4. MODERN DEVELOPMENTS 259

Notes *295*

Bibliography *373*

Index *405*

ACKNOWLEDGMENTS

The research for this book was made possible by a generous grant from the Carnegie Corporation for my project "Contesting the Mosque: Debates over Muslim Women's Ritual Access" in 2006–2008. I presented my first efforts to make sense of the juristic discussion of women's mosque access at the conference "Text, Tradition and Reason in Comparative Perspective" at the Benjamin N. Cardozo School of Law, October 10–12, 2004. Various parts and versions of chapter 3 were presented at the Islamic Studies Program and Interdisciplinary Seminar for Islamic Studies, University of Michigan, November 10, 2011; at the International Society for Islamic Legal Studies VII Conference, "Islamic Law and the State," Ankara, Turkey, May 31, 2012; and at the Institute for the Transregional Study of the Contemporary Middle East, North Africa, and Central Asia, Princeton University, February 19, 2013. I thank the organizers of all of these events for the opportunity to present my work and the other participants for their feedback. I owe a debt of gratitude to Kevin Reinhart, Jonathan A. C. Brown, Intisar Rabb, and anonymous Reader Number One from Columbia University Press for their helpful comments on various stages and versions of the manuscript; this is a far better book than it would have been without their help. My particular gratitude goes out to those who read it in its far lengthier and more unruly earlier stages, which were (I hope) significantly tamed with the help of their advice. All remaining errors of fact and interpretation are, of course, purely my own. I also thank Susan Graham, Professor Nadia Lachiri, Dr. Khader Salameh of the al-Aqsa Mosque Library, Robert Dankoff, Justin Stearns, and Guy Burak for identifying sources or helping to make them available to me.

This book was a labor of love, and it depended on both the labor and the love of the members of my family. My mother, Adria Katz, is an unsung genius of editing, and this is not the first of my books to benefit from her keen eye. My father, Stanley Katz, borrowed books for me to consult on lightning visits to Princeton; he is the world's most overqualified research assistant, and my thanks are inadequate for his help. My husband, Bradley McCormick, cheerfully put up with my precarious piles of books and irrepressible urge to share the wonders of Islamic law and history.

This book is dedicated to the memory of Aḥmad ibn ʿAbd al-Ghaffār al-Mālikī, whose humane faith remains humbling five centuries later. May we all use our learning with his justice and integrity.

Women in the Mosque

INTRODUCTION

In the mid-1830s, the Englishwoman Julia Pardoe (then resident in Istanbul) visited the mosque of Hagia Sophia with a group of more recently arrived visitors. She writes, "A group of Ulemas were engaged in prayer as we entered . . . and almost in the centre of the floor knelt a party of women similarly engaged, while a couple of children, who had accompanied them, were chasing each other over the rich carpets." The sight of women worshipping in a mosque was one for which she had not been prepared when she began her sojourn in Turkey; as she observes, "An erroneous impression has obtained in Europe that females do not attend, or rather, I should perhaps say, are not permitted to enter, the mosques; this, as I have just shewn, is by no means the case." Other members of the party, however, had yet to correct their misconceptions. Pardoe comments,

> Those who were lately from Europe could scarcely believe their eyes; and when, in reply to the remark of a person who stood near me, expressing his astonishment at such an apparition, I explained to him that the presence of females in the different mosques was of constant and hourly occurrence, he looked so exceedingly annoyed at the sweeping away of his ancient prejudices, that I verily believe he thought the deficiency of the whole female Empire of Turkey must be transferred to my own little person.[1]

The assumption that women have been largely excluded from mosques for much of Islamic history is one that that has long prevailed in academic scholarship, as well as in more popular circles. Although acknowledging some exceptions and variations, scholars have emphasized the early emergence of a broad and effective consensus against women's mosque attendance among Muslim jurists and its persistence until the modern period. In Leila Ahmed's influential survey *Women and Gender in Islam*, the decline in women's mosque access serves as an index of the erosion of their status in Islamic society after the time of the Prophet. She writes that the second caliph, ʿUmar ibn al-Khaṭṭāb, sought (although, for the moment, unsuccessfully) to exclude women from mosques and that in the ʿAbbasid period (starting in the mid-eighth century CE) women "are not to be found, as they were in the previous era, either on [the] battlefield or in mosques."[2] In contrast, modern Muslim women are "reclaiming the right, not enjoyed for centuries, to attend mosque."[3] Other authors similarly emphasize the broad and durable Islamic scholarly sentiment against women's attendance at public worship (and the consequent marginalization of women from mosque space), which is contrasted both with women's participation in mosque activities in the time of the Prophet and with the resurgence of mosque-based activities among Islamist (and other) women since the 1970s.[4]

A number of authors have observed that, historically, neither scholarly disapproval of women's mosque attendance nor the absence of women from mosques was uniform or monolithic. Johannes Pedersen has noted the presence of designated women's space in important mosques over the centuries, and Christopher Melchert and Behnam Sadeghi have demonstrated a degree of diversity in legal doctrines, as well as change (largely in the direction of greater restrictions on women) over time.[5] Scholars have also noted both anecdotal accounts and visual images of women's presence in premodern mosques.[6] As Asma Sayeed has observed, "legal prescriptions . . . did not always determine historical realities," and "women's mosque attendance and participation is characterized by tremendous diversity across time and place and dependent on numerous factors."[7] Nevertheless, there has as yet been no significant effort to gather and evaluate the evidence for women's activities in (or their absence from) mosques in the period between the generation of the Prophet and the modern Islamic revival or to analyze the relationship between such practices and the evolving juristic debates over the legal status of women's presence in mosques.

The significance of the legal discourse on women's mosque attendance lies largely in what it reveals about the evolution of normative assumptions about gender. Because mosque-going was a paradigmatic case of women's mobility and visibility outside of the home, discussion of its permissibility or merit was an occasion for the expression of fundamental ideas about women as wives, community members, and ritual actors. Logically prior to the articulation of concrete doctrines about women's mosque attendance—rarely overtly debated, but underlying the very terminology used in discussing the issue—was the question of whether women constituted a monolithic category at all. Early jurists universally presumed that women of different ages or statuses were subject to significantly different standards of behavior; there was no assumption that a consistent rule could be applied to "women" as a group. Women might also be divided in terms of physical allure, religious learning, or personal propriety. A central factor in the development of legal doctrines in this area is the progressive ascent of the concept of *fitna* (a multivalent term whose semantic range embraces sexual temptation and social disorder). Although the centrality of *fitna* to *fiqh* discourses on women has been widely recognized, the history of this concept has yet to be written; this study tells one central aspect of that story.

Jurists debating women's mosque access also grappled with questions about the authority structure of the family and the limits of governmental power: If it was undesirable for some or all women to go to mosques, who (if anyone) was empowered to prevent them? Finally, changing attitudes toward women's mosque attendance raised significant issues of legal theory: Did the practice of the community in the time of the Prophet establish a concrete and detailed model for the interaction of men and women for all future times, or must standards of conduct be revised as society changes (perhaps pursuing the early community's standards of piety and propriety by quite different means)? Although the long-term constriction of the latitude afforded to women is an important element of this story (one that Sadeghi has eloquently illustrated for the Ḥanafī case), the history of the debate over women's mosque access is not a linear progression from freedom to oppression for Muslim women. Instead, it manifests lively competition among alternative approaches to women as social and religious actors, one in which restrictive or misogynistic trends were by no means always victorious.

On a concrete, behavioral level, the question of women's access to mosques is significant for several reasons. One is that assumptions about women's exclusion from mosques may, tacitly or overtly, inform our understanding of the motivations and constraints conditioning Muslim women's religious choices. Numerous studies emphasize the historical prevalence of Muslim women's rituals that are neither performed within the mosque nor mandated by Islamic law.[8] To the extent that this emphasis reflects the realities of many times and places, it raises several questions. Have women historically sought religious fellowship and fulfillment in other venues (and often in normatively problematic ritual activities) because they have been marginalized or excluded from mosques?[9] If so, does their (relative or absolute) avoidance of mosques reflect their acceptance and internalization of restrictive legal norms or simply their inability to defy male authorities? Alternatively, to the extent that women have, in fact, avoided mosques in favor of other religious venues, might this largely reflect their own religious priorities and agendas? The question of women's access to mosques is relevant to wider issues of power, authority, and agency.

Although mosques have never been the exclusive venues of Islamic religious instruction, reconstructing the history of women's mosque attendance also helps us determine the degree to which women were exposed (through preaching, teaching, and shared ritual performance) to the ideas and practices familiar from the normative Islamic sources or (alternatively) the extent to which their religious lives were separate and autonomous from those of men. Medieval scholars sometimes explicitly expressed their awareness that women suffered from a religious ignorance (that is, of the forms of Islam favored by the scholars themselves) that arose directly from their relative seclusion. However, the same authors often discouraged women from frequenting mosques even when this limited their exposure to the religious norms that the scholars themselves sought to instill.

For instance, the twelfth-century Baghdadi scholar and preacher Ibn al-Jawzī laments that "a girl ordinarily grows up in her inner chamber (*mukhdaʿ*); she is not taught the Qur'an, and does not know how to purify herself from menstruation; she is also not taught the obligatory components of prayer (*ṣalāt*), and no one talks to her before marriage about her husband's rights."[10] Nevertheless, even as he acknowledges the lawfulness of a woman's attending the mosque, in the same work he strongly emphasizes the superior merit of her remaining at home and praying in her inner chamber.[11] The fourteenth-century Cairene scholar Ibn al-Ḥājj notes that "men have more frequent contact with religious scholars than women"; in contrast, "women are secluded and have been reared in ignorance, hence they are more prone to adopt innumerable vile habits contrary to the shari'a."[12] Nevertheless, as we shall see, he emphatically prefers that women pray at home and expresses a deep dismay at women's presence in sessions of public teaching at mosques and madrasas.[13] Reconstruction of the degree to which women attended mosques—and of the activities in which they engaged when they were there—adds to our understanding of the kinds of religious knowledge and practice to which women were exposed and the extent to which these overlapped with those cultivated by men.

Furthermore, the belief that women have historically been excluded from mosques in part reflects an implicit equation between presence in the mosque and performance of specific normative rituals. Shampa and Sanjoy Mazumdar have noted that "the non-presence of women in mosques, referred to in the literature, is contextual and is primarily associated with *Jumma* (Friday) prayers"; thus, descriptions of women's relative exclusion do not "address the diversity of mosques and the multifaceted roles they play in the lives of Muslim men and women."[14] Although these authors are primarily referring to the contemporary period, their observation also applies to premodern contexts. People have used (and continue to use) mosques for many purposes, both sacred and profane; the question of women's presence or absence in mosques should not be conflated with that of their participation in specific activities, such as Friday prayer.

Although mosques always varied widely in size, in the range of functions performed in them, and in the numbers of people that they served, they were rare public spaces in the urban fabric of premodern Middle Eastern cities. (Village mosques and small neighborhood mosques, although they will appear fleetingly in this study, are generally outside of the scope of our textual sources.) The great mosques were often places where ordinary people took naps, ate meals, peddled wares, sought legal redress for their grievances, and sometimes took up temporary or long-term residence.[15] With the exception of the marketplace, before the rise of the coffeehouse in the sixteenth century the mosque was one of the few places where an adult could tarry and socialize outside of the domestic courtyard or the neighborhood cul-de-sac.[16] When European travelers and colonialists began to visit mosques, they were sometimes shocked (and in other cases impressed) by the wide variety of sacred and profane activities mosques embraced and the diverse social strata they accommodated.[17]

However, mosques in the premodern Middle East were not only in some ways more profane than is often imagined but also more sacred. It is a widely stated fact that Muslims can validly perform *ṣalāt* (the prayer ritual) in any place that is free of ritually impure substances. There is no necessity to pray in a mosque; only the Friday congregational prayers must be performed in a formally designated public place of worship, although classical scholars unanimously exempted women from this duty. Nevertheless, the frequentation of mosques is far from religiously neutral. All Sunnī scholars hold it to be desirable for men to perform their obligatory prayers in the mosque, and Ḥanbalīs hold it to be obligatory in the absence of a valid excuse. Ibn al-Ḥājj enumerates a staggering ninety-two pious intents that may be framed by a man as he goes out to the mosque, yielding copious quantities of religious merit. The goals and benefits mentioned include gaining and imparting religious knowledge, correcting one's ritual practices through the example of learned and holy men, and learning and sympathizing with the fortunes of the Muslim polity.[18] Major mosques (and even minor ones) often contained physical features or locations that were credited with powerful blessings (*baraka*) or where it was believed prayers would be answered by God.[19] Mosques (and particularly pulpits) were believed to carry an aura of holiness that would deter false oaths by parties to legal cases.[20] The secondary literature has often sought to distinguish mosques (assumed to be neutral sites of communal prayer) from shrines (assumed to be sites characterized by contagious blessings, often conferred by the presence of holy remains); however, we shall see over the course of this study that the dichotomy between mosques and shrines is, in fact, as porous and questionable as the dichotomy between "normative" and "folk" Islam onto which it is often mapped. (This is not to deny that the distinction may be relevant in emic or functional terms in specific times and places, but merely to indicate that it is problematic as an analytic tool on a general level.)

One of the overall conclusions emerging from this study is that historically women's mosque usage often differed significantly from that of men. Scholars seeking evidence of women's presence in mosques have often taken male duties and activities as representative of mosque usage in general and simply examined the extent to which women did or did not partake of these same religious pursuits (most notably, attendance at Friday congregational prayers). However, to foreground activities that were obligatory or salient for men disregards the degree to which women's preferred usage of mosque space may have diverged in timing and nature. As we shall see, for instance, in the Ḥijāz over a period of centuries Thursday evening seems to have eclipsed Friday noon as a time for women to gather in the mosque, and postchildbirth rituals represented a major and locally respected mode of women's usage of the great mosques. Women's mosque-based activities were not simply more limited or constrained versions of men's.

In a study on the geography of gender in Renaissance Italy, Robert Davis writes that "the gendered valence of urban space was not only 'defined' through the edicts of male elites, but was also the result of an ongoing process, a continuing social interplay between the sexes and between social groups that helped maintain, extend, or challenge prevailing notions that certain areas of the city should be reserved for men and others for women."[21] Rather than framing women's usage of mosque space either as being dictated by male-generated legal norms or as ignoring or defying them, this study will similarly assume that the gendering of mosque space was subject to ongoing negotiation. The gendered allocation of space was not static, but temporally varied; as we shall see, mosque space that was dominated by men during Friday prayers might be dominated by women at other times of the day, week, or year. Fadwa El Guindi writes of "the Arab cultural construction of space that connects space to time and gender," noting that "Arab and Islamic space . . . is characterized by the spatial and temporal interweaving pattern. . . . Sacred space and rhythmic time are both public and private."[22] Rather than seeing this temporal fluidity as characterizing Arab or Islamic culture in binary opposition to Western others, however, this study posits that such fluidity and negotiability may potentially characterize the gendering and sacralization of space—and its construction as "public" or "private"—in any given context.

The scope of this study is broad, yet also limited. It deliberately brackets issues of historical reconstruction regarding the lifetime of the Prophet Muḥammad. The authenticity and dating of ḥadīth (reports recounting the statements and actions of the Prophet) are highly contested, and any detailed reconstruction of women's ritual practices during the Prophet's life would be contingent on hotly disputed methodological issues that this study does not attempt to resolve.[23] For our purposes, it is less important whether a ḥadīth is literally true (in the sense of recording words uttered or acts performed by the Prophet Muḥammad) than that it was held to be authoritative by scholars in the time and place in question or that a given scholar selected and emphasized ḥadīth texts reflecting one attitude rather than another from those available to him. Similarly, little attention will be given to the precise time or place where a given legal doctrine first appeared. Rather than assuming that a doctrine's significance can best be illuminated by identifying its point of origin, we will focus more centrally on the longer process by which certain ideas spread and prevailed.

Furthermore, the study is limited to the question of whether women were encouraged or discouraged to attend mosques; whether they, in fact, did so; and, if they did attend, what they did while they were there. It brackets a number of related questions that, although important, are too large to address here. Women's involvement in the foundation of mosques began very early and included some of the most important mosques in the Islamic world.[24] However, women's patronage of mosque construction is a separate issue that does not necessarily correlate with the magnitude and nature of their physical presence in mosques.[25] The important issues of women's religious learning and scholarly authority will be discussed here only in terms of women's participation in teaching and learning activities within mosques. Finally, the issue of women's ritual leadership (*imāma*) will not be addressed; it is treated separately from the question of women's mosque attendance in the legal sources and does not feature in the reports of women's activities in mosques examined here.[26]

The first chapter of this study examines legal texts associated with the four classical schools of Sunnī law (with the addition of the work of the Ẓāhirī scholar Ibn Ḥazm (d. 456/1064), both because he played a role as an interlocutor of the Andalusian Mālikīs and because his arguments were in part assimilated into those of the major schools). These were not historically the only schools of law even within the tradition that gradually crystallized as Sunnism, although they achieved almost exclusive domination of Sunnī legal discourses and institutions by the fifth century AH/eleventh century CE. Not only would the many schools of law that proliferated in the early period be worthy of investigation, but also other legal traditions (such as those of Imāmī Shī'ism and Ibāḍī Khārijism) that survived and prevailed in later centuries could offer examples fully as rich as those explored here. The four Sunnī schools have been selected not because they reflect the full breadth and diversity of Islamic legal thought, but because they are important sample cases that offer rich and accessible bodies of legal literature associated with specific geographical areas where recorded behavior can usefully be compared with prevailing doctrines.

The chapter traces the evolving debate over women's mosque attendance in these schools from their emergence in the eighth to ninth centuries CE approximately to the nineteenth century (although the seventeenth to nineteenth centuries are the least thoroughly examined and would merit further study). The broad chronological scope of this survey is made possible by the relative conservatism of the legal discourses in question. The authority structures of the schools ensured that even significant departures from earlier attitudes were framed in an idiom of deference to school precedent (*taqlīd*). Nevertheless, as we shall see, major trends and changes are discernible over time, and turning points in the debate are identifiable. In addition to tracking the development of legal doctrine on this point, the study seeks to discern and analyze the deeper assumptions underlying it.

In the past, Islamic legal texts have sometimes been studied as a proxy for social history. It was assumed (either tacitly or explicitly) that one can infer actual behavior from the dictates of legal manuals originating in the time and place in question.[27] This assumption, less often made in such relatively "profane" areas as economic or sexual behavior, is more tempting in the field of ritual, where people's activity might be imagined to be more consistently aimed at satisfying pious standards. However, copious evidence (such as the many works denouncing religious "innovations," or *bidaʿ*) demonstrates that even in the area of religious ritual, scholars often strove in vain to recruit the broader population for their agendas. Furthermore, divergent ritual activities did not simply represent the unruly exuberance of "popular" piety; they also often represented—even among the unlearned—powerful alternative views of Islamic normativity.[28] The subtitle of Huda Lutfi's wonderful piece on Ibn al-Ḥājj, *Female Anarchy Versus Male Shar'i Order in Muslim Prescriptive Treatises*,[29] perfectly captures the tone of this austere jurist's laments; however, in our own analyses we must be careful not to accept uncritically male scholars' polemical depiction of women's religious activities as anarchic, even if their structuring logic is not directly available to us in the surviving sources. The meaning of women's ritual activities is not exhausted by their failure to conform to standards constructed by (some) male scholars. Furthermore, particularly in the case of ritual, the degree to which women adhered to—or were even aware of—the finer points of legal doctrine as expounded by male scholars is at least partially related to the very question we are examining, their access to the spaces where these doctrines were disseminated and modeled.

Nevertheless, we will not assume that normative discourses were completely divorced from social realities or that they existed in an abstract space unaffected by the scholars' interactions with the world around them. Rather, instead of presuming that scholars unilaterally dictated behavioral norms that were unquestioningly carried out (or even defiantly ignored) by ordinary women and men, we will argue that legal norms were in a more complex dialogic relationship with actual behavior. For instance, in several cases it is demonstrable that the most vehement and categorical prohibitions on women's mosque attendance were produced in contexts where women were highly visible in at least some mosques (a fact that was sometimes explicitly cited by the very authors who produced the prohibitions). This situation suggests less that women were oblivious to the dictates of scholars than that these scholars were deeply affected by the activities of women, if only in the sense that they were spurred to vigorous opposition.[30] Of course, it is also likely that scholars' norms had significant influence over the behavior of many women, even if those norms were themselves rarely unanimous.

This study does not assume that all Muslim women have naturally or necessarily desired to frequent mosques. As reflected in the work of scholars like Ibn al-Ḥājj, who exhorted men to attend prayers in the mosque while acknowledging that even religious scholars sometimes preferred not to, mosque-going was a cultivated desire (indeed, one among multiple alternatives, including pious seclusion) whose existence could not be taken for granted even among the devout.[31] However, it is notable that the premodern Islamic legal tradition quite consistently represents mosque-going as a female desire and a male concern, addressing questions such as "May a woman go to the mosque?" and "May her husband prevent her?" (rather than, for instance, "Should a husband encourage his wife to go to the mosque?"). It may be that this pattern reflects a genuine legacy of women's seeking access to mosques in the face of male opposition or that it is a convention of the legal discourse to treat all kinds of public mobility as female privileges that must be examined in light of male claims to control. In either case, it constrains our analysis. Thus, the first chapter of the study (which deals with legal discussions) will examine only whether a woman "may" go to the mosque, not whether (or why) she might or might not wish to do so. In contrast, the second chapter of the study (which examines descriptions of actual behavior) will start with the working assumption that women in a given time or place may or may not have sought to access mosque space. The absence of women cannot thus be assumed to be the result of effective male prohibition; rather, the possibility of alternative preferences on the part of women will also be considered.

The second chapter turns to nonlegal sources for reports of women's actual presence and behavior in mosques (or, alternatively, of their absence from mosques or their preference for other sites of religious activity) in a selection of specific locations. This chapter draws on an eclectic array of genres, including descriptions of mosques in geographical texts, accounts from travelers' narratives, and incidents recounted by chroniclers or (later) memoirists. It also draws from texts inveighing against the innovations (*bidaʿ*) being committed in mosques.[32] Although these texts certainly have normative agendas, they also provide more circumstantial detail about actual behavior in mosques than any comparable premodern genre. Given the paucity of premodern sources for women's religious conduct, they are indispensable to a study of this kind, even if their polemical force introduces an unmistakable bias into their descriptive accounts.

Historians of the Islamic Middle East are, in comparison with historians of Europe, hampered by a severe lack of archival sources before the Ottoman period. In this particular case, the lack of systematic archival data is not alleviated even by the advent of the Ottomans. Unlike premodern churches or synagogues, which historically sometimes rented pews or seats to individual congregants, mosques did not provide seats (assigned or otherwise) and ordinarily did not keep records of individual attendance.[33] Although there are instances of disciplinary action being taken against men who failed to attend Friday congregational prayers, all scholars agreed that women were never actually obligated to attend prayers in the mosque. Thus, unlike in some early modern Christian societies where women were disciplined for failing to attend church, Muslim women were never tried or disciplined for their nonattendance at mosques.[34] As a result, neither women's presence in mosques nor their absence from them generated documentation that could provide systematic evidence of their ritual behavior. For this reason, even Ottomanists (who enjoy a wealth of archival evidence in many other areas) have sometimes been forced to resort to the anecdotal accounts of Western travelers when trying to reconstruct women's attendance or nonattendance at mosques.[35]

Because accounts produced by Western travelers pose particular interpretive and ideological problems, an examination of this issue precedes the discussion of travelers' accounts of Ottoman mosques. However, texts produced by male Muslim scholars are in some sense also outsider descriptions of women's practices. We cannot always assume that the categories and assumptions of the preserved texts reflect the values, terminology, or underlying assumptions of the women involved. For instance, scholars consistently represent women's self-adornment as an issue of vanity and seductiveness. However, there are other dynamics that may have been relevant to women who adorned themselves for the mosque. On the one hand, men were encouraged to use fine dress and perfume when going to the mosque, honoring the sacredness of the place and time. Although the scholarly tradition inverted this model with respect to women (asserting that they should be plainly or even shabbily dressed and unperfumed), some women may well have believed that they, too, should honor sacred times and places with sweet smells and festive attire. Furthermore, self-adornment may have communicated important messages about wealth and status rather than simply expressing personal flirtatiousness. Women's possible motivations for displaying finery are suggested by a thirteenth-century report of a criminal whose wife-accomplice would tell their female victims that there was a wedding or feast in the neighborhood and that "a number of high-ranking women have gathered there, so don't leave off any adornment so you can show off well among them" (the unfortunate women were then robbed and murdered).[36] As we shall see in chapter 3, fine dress and jewelry seem to have played an important role in status maintenance—even, or perhaps especially, in the mosque—among women in sixteenth-century Mecca.

It should also be remembered that even formally nonnormative sources, which are overtly descriptive rather than prescriptive, often pursue agendas that complicate our effort to reconstruct the nature and extent of women's use of mosque space in the past. In all cases, observers were far more likely to record behavior that shocked, surprised, or (less often) delighted them than activities they found routine and unexceptionable. Collecting references to women's presence in mosques from such sources does correct the impression communicated by the legal manuals, which often deemphasize or deprecate women's presence in mosques to the point that one might assume that mosques were consistently empty of women. Recourse to other genres allows us glimpses of many women using many mosques for many different purposes, although (as we shall see) both the accessibility of mosques and women's interest in frequenting them seem to have varied widely over time and space. However, given the inevitable underrepresentation in our sources of behavior considered normal and unproblematic, there is a danger that we may replace the notion that mosques were always empty of women with an equally unbalanced notion that mosques teemed with unruly women engaged in normatively problematic activities. It is always necessary to remember that the routine participation of women in religiously uncontroversial activities such as congregational prayer is the kind of activity least likely to achieve salience in our sources; even observers who considered such behavior technically undesirable were presumably more likely to polemicize against more vivid instances of alleged misbehavior. Thus, our historical reconstruction will necessarily remain partial and provisional, despite attentiveness to the biases of our sources.

Information about women's usage of mosques is simultaneously everywhere and nowhere—scattered in the most diverse sources and yet rarely concentrated enough to provide a complete picture of practice in a given time and place. Because incidental (yet valuable) references to women's presence in mosques may emerge from the most unexpected contexts, it is not possible to conduct a thorough survey of all possible sources for such information—particularly when one takes into account the wide range of literary sources that may provide an evocative sense of people's assumptions about gendered behavior, even if they do not document concrete examples of mosque-based activities by actual women. Thus, the historical survey in the second chapter of this study is necessarily provisional and must be supplemented and corrected as new materials emerge. However, because the accumulation of anecdotal material is unlikely ever to be superseded by comprehensive archival data (if only because such data were usually never recorded in the first place), the present study provides a useful step toward a necessarily fragmentary assemblage of information about women's usage of mosques.

Although analyses of Islamic legal discourses have often drawn connections with social behavior and historical works have often invoked the norms of Islamic law, this study is centrally structured around the relationship between normative discourses and social practice. By attempting to reconstruct broad patterns of women's behavior, even in the face of limited data, it strives to recognize that this behavior may have been informed by broad and enduring patterns and objectives of its own. It strives to be attentive to the ways in which women's practice and scholars' legal constructs mutually influenced and informed each other. This juxtaposition of evolving legal discourses with the greatest currently practical collection of reports about women's behavior over time (and in several of the most important locations where the legal debates in question occurred) provides new insight into the dynamics of premodern Islamic law and society.

This study is in different ways both dauntingly broad and severely limited. Its chronological and geographical sweep will be disquieting to those who enjoy richer bodies of sources on specific times and places (such as Europeanists or people working on better-documented issues in Islamic history). It is the frustratingly low density of relevant data that has led me to bring together information about such a broad range of times and places, thus using the coherence of the overall patterns to compensate for the lacunae in our knowledge about specific contexts. Despite its sweep, this study is also limited in terms of both geography and language, covering only the Arabic-speaking Middle East, North Africa, and Andalusia. The final section of chapter 2 uses Western travelers' accounts to reconstruct some aspects of practice in Ottoman Istanbul, seeking some insight into practice in a context strongly dominated by Ḥanafīs. Other major regions of the Islamic world—including sub-Saharan Africa and South and Southeast Asia—are not covered. This limitation results from the nature of my own linguistic and historical training, as well as from the already unmanageable volume of sources involved. The degree to which the Middle Eastern patterns examined here were typical of the broader Islamic world can be clarified only by research on other regions.

The diffuse nature of the sources in the first and second chapters of the book is balanced by the specificity of the third chapter, which takes as a case study the best-documented instance of contestation of mosque space in the premodern Islamic world. This is an incident in which the authorities in Mecca decided, in 937 AH/1530 CE, to bar women from the Great Mosque of Mecca during the nighttime hours. This episode gave rise to a fierce, if short-lived, regional legal debate over the regulation of women's mosque access. A unique manuscript describing the sequence of events in Mecca, which appears never to have been discussed in the secondary literature, is the most extensive and circumstantial account of women's actual usage of a mosque—and its contestation by scholars and political authorities—before the twentieth century. Although the Great Mosque of Mecca is in many ways unique, it has also been paradigmatic for Muslims, and in this case it evoked serious reflection about women's mosque access in general (as well as about issues specific to Mecca, such as pilgrimage and circumambulation of the Kaʿba). By combining an account of women's active (and ultimately successful) resistance to the restriction of their mosque access with legal opinions that were generated in the immediate context of this debate, this remarkable account makes direct connections between social practice and normative discourse that can only be inferred in most other cases.

The final chapter of the book examines legal sources of the twentieth and early twenty-first centuries. Unlike in the earlier periods, for which it was useful to collate scattered evidence of women's presence and activities in mosques, for this period a wealth of evidence about actual practice is available and continues to be generated. Rather than attempting to construct an overall account of women's evolving presence in mosques, this chapter thus focuses on shifts and transformations in the legal discourses against the background of changing patterns of women's participation documented in other studies.

one

WOMEN'S MOSQUE ATTENDANCE AS A LEGAL PROBLEM

This chapter surveys the discussions of women's mosque access in the major Sunnī schools of Islamic law. Later chapters will examine connections between legal doctrine and social practice; this chapter approaches legal debate as an autonomous discursive field whose construction and disputation of gender ideologies are significant and revealing in themselves. Because legal manuals are often quite repetitive in their formulations over time and because important shifts in assumptions and categories can be signaled by quite subtle changes in terminology and argumentation, this chapter does not attempt to reproduce the rules on women's mosque attendance as presented in each of the major legal sources. Instead, the chronological survey of each school focuses on specific thematic nodes and temporal points of transition that illuminate the underlying issues under negotiation.

THE MĀLIKĪS

In a section titled "Chapter on women's going out to mosques," the *Muwaṭṭaʾ* of Mālik ibn Anas (d. 179 AH/796 CE) presents four reports. In the first, transmitted through ʿAbd Allāh ibn ʿUmar, the Prophet straightforwardly declares (presumably to the men of the community),

"Do not forbid the maidservants of God from [going to] the mosques of God" (*lā tamnaʿū imāʾ allāh masājid allāh*).[1] In the second, he admonishes women directly: "If one of you attends the evening prayers, let her not touch perfume."[2] The third report shifts the scene from an (at least imagined) encounter with the Prophet himself to the tensions experienced by his Companions in the years after his death. It recounts that ʿĀtika bint Zayd, the wife of ʿUmar ibn al-Khaṭṭāb, used to ask the latter's permission to go to the mosque. He would remain silent, upon which she would declare, "By God, I will go out, unless you forbid me"—and he would not forbid her.[3] In the fourth report, again clearly set after the Prophet's death, his widow ʿĀʾisha is said to have declared, "If the Messenger of God had lived to see what women have innovated, he would have forbidden them from visiting the mosque, as the women of the Israelites were forbidden."[4]

These four reports encapsulate, in a concentrated and rather perplexing form, the ideas about women's mosque attendance that informed Islamic juristic discussions of the issue. It was nearly universally assumed (even among those who later opposed the practice) both that women attended public prayers in the mosque in the Prophet's lifetime—an assumption supported by the wide range of ḥadīth reports that mention women's presence in incidental and nonpolemical ways[5]—and that the Prophet explicitly forbade the exclusion of women from mosques. More restrictive statements attributed to figures speaking after the Prophet's death quite consistently address this assumption and attempt to neutralize it in one way or another. Not only does the anecdote about ʿUmar and ʿĀtika assume the fact of women's attendance, but also the wording of the prophetic ḥadīth presented at the beginning of the section: ʿUmar's evidently reluctant refusal to "forbid" ʿĀtika implicitly reflects his awareness that he is himself forbidden to prohibit her attendance. The ʿĀʾisha report, destined to be the most widely cited authority statement condemning women's mosque attendance in later centuries, invokes the swiftly deteriorating moral standards of the women of the community as grounds for divergence from the assumed practice of the Prophet's time.

The text of the *Muwaṭṭaʾ* does not contain any statement about Medinian practice or any indication of Mālik's juristic preference. However, the early Mālikī tradition did attribute to him more than one statement on this subject, primarily in the *Mudawwana*, believed to be compiled by Saḥnūn ibn Saʿīd al-Tanūkhī (d. 240/854) chiefly from material transmitted by Mālik's disciple Ibn al-Qāsim (d. 191/806).[6] In a report suggesting a continuing female presence in the mosque in Medina, Mālik is asked about the situation of men who arrive at prayers to find that the mosque itself is full of men and the courtyard (*raḥba*) is full of women (he affirms that the men's prayers are valid even if they stand behind the women).[7] Indeed, visiting the mosque appears to be one of the most routine and acceptable reasons for a woman to leave her home; in the *Mudawwana*, early authorities mention the mosque as an acceptable destination even for a divorced woman awaiting the expiration of her waiting period (*ʿidda*), who is generally expected to remain in her home.[8]

The most programmatic and legally influential statement about women's mosque attendance in the *Mudawwana* is one in which the authorial voice (traditionally identified as Saḥnūn) asks his informant (traditionally identified as Ibn al-Qāsim), "Did Mālik disapprove of women going out to the mosque or to the two festival prayers or the prayer for rain [both of which would be held on an outdoor prayer ground, *muṣallā*]?" Ibn al-Qāsim replies, "As for going out to mosques, he used to say, 'They should not be forbidden to go out to mosques'; as for the prayer for rain and the two festival prayers, we are of the opinion that it is not a problem for any mature (*mutajālla*) woman to go out."[9] The first half of this statement reflects the distinctive wording of the first report presented in the *Muwaṭṭa*ʾ—although the saying is here not explicitly identified as a prophetic ḥadīth, Mālik knows the rule that women are not to be forbidden from attending mosques. The second half of the statement, which appears to be framed as a statement of juristic opinion from Ibn al-Qāsim, represents something new: a categorization of women in which only one type, the mature or elderly woman (*al-mutajālla*), is permitted without reservation to go out for public worship.[10]

Saḥnūn's somewhat younger contemporary Muḥammad al-ʿUtbī al-Qurṭubī (d. 255/869) transmitted in his work *al-Mustakhraja* (known as *al-ʿUtbīya*) another statement attributed to Mālik: "He was asked about women's going to attend prayers at mosques; he said, 'That varies with respect to the mature women (*al-mutajālla*) and the young woman (*al-shābba*). The *mutajālla* goes out to the mosque but does not frequent it often, and the young woman goes out to the mosque once in a while.'"[11] Here the distinction between old and young women is apparently attributed to Mālik himself. There is no reference to the prophetic ḥadīth or juristic dictum condemning women's exclusion from mosques, although there does seem to be some tension between an affirmation that both old and young women may go to mosques and a desire that they do so infrequently.

The word *mutajālla* is an odd and distinctive one, occurring very rarely outside of Mālikī legal discourse; there are several other words that would ordinarily be used to refer to a woman of advanced years. Indeed, outside the classical Mālikī legal context, both premodern manuscripts and modern editors not infrequently get it wrong.[12] Outside of Mālikī *fiqh*, the locus classicus (cited, for instance, by the lexicographer Ibn Manẓūr[13]) is a report in the *Kitāb al-ṭabaqāt al-kubrā* of Ibn Saʿd (d. 230/845). In it, the Companion of the Prophet Umm Ṣubayya Khawla bint Qays recounts,

> In the time of the Prophet, Abu Bakr, and the beginning of the caliphate of ʿUmar, we used to be in the mosque, women who had grown old (*niswa qad tajālalna*). Sometimes we would spin, and sometimes some of us would work braiding palm leaves in it [i.e., the mosque]. ʿUmar said, "I will surely make you into free/noble women again! (*la-arudannakunna ḥarāʾir*)," and he expelled us from it, except that we used to attend the [obligatory] prayers at the [set] time.[14]

The women in this anecdote appear to be enjoying a privilege of their seniority, engaging in productive labor in the public space of the mosque. It is unclear whether they have chosen this space for its commercial potential (conceivably, they hope to sell the products of their craft) or for its social pleasures. ʿUmar, in a recognizable (although not necessarily nonhistorical) trope,[15] asserts a different form of social differentiation among women: as free women, they should not linger in the mosque, although they may frequent it on a limited basis for obligatory prayers.

Even beyond the context of women's mosque attendance, the *mutajālla* is an important category in the gender discourse of early

Mālikī legal texts. In another report, Mālik declares that it is incumbent upon the ruler to instruct craftsmen not to allow young women (*al-shābba*) to sit with them (presumably to negotiate over their wares). "As for the mature woman (*al-mutajālla*) who does not arouse suspicion by sitting, and the low-ranking servant (*al-khādim al-dūn*) sitting with whom arouses no suspicion, there is no harm in that."[16] Like low social status (which was presumed to render subservient males either unattractive as sexual partners or unworthy of social concern), advanced age carried at least partial exemption from the social pressures and restrictions that applied to young women. Mālik is also said to have affirmed that a woman who is *mutajālla* may travel to Mecca for the pilgrimage without a male guardian (*walī*) as long as she is accompanied by a group of trustworthy people.[17]

The complex structure (and the disputed authenticity) of the earliest sources makes it difficult to determine whether the term *mutajālla*—and the fundamental age distinction among women that it signals—originates with Mālik himself or represents the terminology of the following generation. Sometimes the age division is clearly superimposed on Mālik's opinions. Thus, whereas Mālik affirms in the *Muwaṭṭa*ʾ that a woman may eat with an unrelated male within the limits of custom, Ibn al-Jahm (d. 323/934) "explains" that he is referring to the *mutajālla*.[18] Although it is difficult to date the usage of this term precisely, its meaning is clear; the *mutajālla* emerges as a woman who is nonsecluded by virtue of her age, one whose prescribed personal behavior (including public worship activities) diverges sharply from that envisioned for the young and nubile *shābba*.

The opinions attributed to Mālik also address one more scenario that might involve a woman's venturing forth to a mosque, this time in the context not of public worship, but of legal procedure. Mālik is reported to have recommended that a judge hold court in mosques, in part because this would make him accessible to "powerless persons and women" (*yaṣil ilayhi al-ḍaʿīf wa'l-marʾa*).[19] A judge might preside in any convenient public location; however, some specific procedures demanded the solemnity of the mosque setting. According to Mālik, judicial oaths in significant cases (in financial matters, only for cases involving at least one-fourth gold dinar) were to be taken in the mosque. The objective was to ensure an appropriate attitude of awe (and, presumably, of veracity).[20]

Of course, giving an oath at the mosque involved leaving the home and appearing in a public place, which raised the question of whether some women might decline to do so. In the *Mudawwana*, the voice identified as Ibn al-Qāsim reports, [Mālik] said, "As for any important matter, for it they are made to go out to the mosques. If she is a woman who goes out in the daytime, she is made to go out in the daytime and give her oath in the mosque. If she is one of those who do not go out, she is made to go out at night and give her oath there."[21] Other early authorities are similarly reported to have stated that "a woman who does not go out in the daytime, should go out at night [to swear in the mosque] regarding a quarter dinar or more."[22] These comments suggest that in the cultural milieu of early Mālikism, some women—implicitly, one assumes, elite women—secluded themselves by remaining at home in the daylight hours.

Interestingly, there is independent evidence that staying home during the day was a genuine cultural practice, at least in the Ḥijāz. In a report preserved in the *Muṣannaf* of ʿAbd al-Razzāq al-Ṣanʿānī, Ibn Jurayj (d. 149–51/766–68) asks the Meccan scholar ʿAṭāʾ ibn Abī Rabāḥ (d. 115/733–34) whether "a woman who goes out during the daytime" is obligated to go to congregational worship if she hears the call to prayer. (ʿAṭāʾ replies firmly that she is not, although she may do so if she wishes.[23]) A century later, the littérateur al-Jāḥiẓ remarks in passing that the women of Mecca and Medina exchange visits at night and are never seen in the daytime; in contrast, the women of Egypt exchange visits during the daytime and are never seen out at night.[24]

The reason women went out (to attend prayers at the mosque or for other purposes) only during the nighttime hours seems to have been that darkness would conceal them from the eyes of strangers, or at least obscure their individual identities. In a ḥadīth transmitted by al-Bukhārī, ʿĀʾisha recounts that the women of the Believers would wrap themselves in their outer garments to attend dawn prayers with the Prophet and then return to their homes while still unrecognizable in the gloaming.[25] Overall, ḥadīth reports mentioning women's mosque attendance in Medina during the Prophet's lifetime tend to suggest a preference for the dawn and nighttime prayers, the two times when congregational worship was not held during full daylight. Some versions of the anecdote about ʿĀtika bint Zayd specify that she used to frequent the mosque "at night."[26] A version of the same story transmitted by al-Bukhārī, where the woman involved remains unnamed, states that "a wife of ʿUmar's used to attend the dawn and nighttime prayers in congregation in the mosque."[27] Both al-Bukhārī and Muslim also transmit a ḥadīth in which the Prophet declares, "If your women ask your permission to go to the mosque at night, allow them."[28] Regardless of the ultimate authenticity of these ḥadīths (i.e., whether they represent actual statements by the Prophet or the practice of his lifetime), they reflect an image of Medinian practices that circulated during the early centuries of the Islamic era. A preference for attending the dawn and nighttime prayers in the mosque is also associated with Medinian women of a somewhat later generation.[29]

Although issues of status and timing played a role, the most significant category distinction in the minds of Mālikī scholars of subsequent generations remained that of age. Ibn Abī Zayd al-Qayrawānī (d. 386/996) notes in his *Risāla*, one of the central teaching texts of the Mālikī school, that "a young woman (*al-shābba*) should not go out to [Friday prayers],"[30] as well as noting that, for instance, a man could look at the face of an unrelated woman unrestrictedly if she was of mature years.[31] By the time of Ibn ʿAbd al-Barr (d. 463/1070), the division between mature and young women with respect to mosque attendance was so well established among jurists of all regions and schools that he was able to declare, "The scholars consider it unobjectionable for mature women (*al-mutajāllāt min al-nisāʾ*) to attend congregational and Friday prayers, and they consider it objectionable for young women to do so."[32] Sind ibn ʿInān al-Azdī (d. 541/1146) even speculated that the age distinction must have been followed in the time of the Companions of the Prophet: "It is not known that their virgins and those similar to them used to go out to the mosque. If all women had gone out, they would have filled the mosque and equaled the men in that respect." Certainly "customary practice proceeded in this way continuously (*wa-mithlu dhālika kān yattaṣil bihi al-ʿamal fīʾl-ʿāda*)"—that is, in his opinion only older women went to the mosque.[33]

By the fifth century AH/eleventh century CE, legal scholars were increasingly concerned with providing detailed textual rationales for the established doctrines of their schools. In particular, the distinction between older and younger women lacked strong textual support from the Qur'an or sunna. The Mālikī scholar most responsible for integrating distinctions among women of different age cohorts into a rigorous interpretation of the textual sources of the law was Abū'l-Walīd Ibn Rushd (d. 520/1126), a judge and imam of the Great Mosque of Cordoba. In his commentary on al-ʿUtbī's *Mustakhraja*, he makes a fresh attempt to harmonize and rationalize the received doctrines of Mālik both with each other and with the statements attributed to the Prophet Muḥammad. As we have seen, the *Mudawwana* quotes Mālik as stating that women "should not be forbidden from going to mosques," although the statement attributed to him in the *ʿUtbīya* specifies that a mature woman should not frequent the mosque excessively and a young one should go only on rare occasions. Though not strictly incompatible, the two statements certainly display a sharp contrast of emphasis, one stressing that women should not be denied access to mosques and the other insisting that their attendance should be sharply limited. Ibn Rushd explains,

> The rationale (*wajh*) for Mālik's statement that young women should not be forbidden to go out to mosques is the general meaning of the Prophet's statement, "Do not forbid the maidservants of God from [going to] the mosques of God." The rationale for his deeming it repugnant (*karāhīyatihi*) for them to go out frequently is the temptation (*fitna*) that it is feared they will cause for men. [The Prophet], may God bless him and grant him peace, said, "I have left no temptation after me that is more harmful to men than women."[34]

Having identified *fitna* as the implicit rationale behind Mālik's limitations on young women's mosque attendance, Ibn Rushd can use it as the basis for an entire taxonomy of women based on age.

> The summary of this issue, according to the most accurate view on it in my opinion, is that there are four kinds of women: [1] an old woman (*ʿajūz*) for whom men no longer have any desire; she is like a man in that respect; [2] a mature woman (*mutajālla*) for whom men's desire is not completely extinct; she may go out to the mosque but does not frequent

> it often, as [Mālik] said in the report; [3] a young woman (*shābba*), who goes out to the mosque on rare occasions and for the funerals of her parents and relatives; and [4] a young woman who is peerless in youth and portliness (*thakhāna*)[35]; for her, the preferred option is that she not go out at all.[36]

In his typology of women, Ibn Rushd makes overt and systematic a concern with sexual temptation that is at most implicit in earlier formulations of school doctrine. Although it is plausible to assume that the *mutajālla* was considered less sexually alluring than a youthful woman, issues of life cycle, social role, and mature moral development also seem to be implied in earlier discussions of her role. Early usage of the term *mutajālla* arguably suggests a stage of social life rather than a perceived degree of erotic magnetism. Similarly, the statements attributed to early figures such as Mālik and Ibn al-Qāsim make no reference to the woman's physical appearance or to the sexual desires of men. In specifying the mature woman who may appropriately deal with craftsmen, Mālik describes her as someone who "is not subject to accusations" (*lā tuttaham*). Such a statement, rather than focusing attention on the woman's physical allure, suggests implicit reliance on social conventions according to which young women were more vulnerable to gossip than mature matrons.

Ibn Rushd's overt invocation of the concept of *fitna*—a potent term designating the sexual temptation and chaos assumed to result from the interaction of unrelated men and women—thus reflects an innovative development in the Mālikī discussion of women's mosque access. The ḥadīth that he cites is well authenticated and widely attested,[37] but does not feature in legal discussions of women's mosque attendance before this time. Indeed, overall *fitna* does not serve as a central concept for the analysis of gender roles in the earliest Mālikī texts. In the *Mudawwana*, for instance, the term *fitna* refers either to political strife and religious schism or to the "testing of the grave" (*fitnat al-qabr*).[38] (Similarly, in al-Shāfiʿī's legal compilation *al-Umm* the word *fitna* refers overwhelmingly to political strife, temporal or otherworldly punishment, or general "testing."[39]) In contrast, *fitna* becomes the central concept in the Mālikī discussion of women's presence in mosques from the fifth/eleventh century. For instance, Ibn Rushd's contemporary Ibn Baṭṭāl remarks that the ḥadīth forbids a husband from preventing his wife from going to the mosque only "if he does not fear *fitna* to her or from her."[40] It is certainly the case that concerns with women's mobility and visibility figured in legal debates long before the time of Ibn Rushd. The early development of the concept of *fitna* among ḥadīth specialists will be discussed later in this chapter. Nevertheless, it would be rash to infer that by invoking the concept of *fitna*, Ibn Rushd was merely labeling the concern that had tacitly shaped the legal debate over women's mosque attendance all along. Ibn Rushd's typology of mosque-going women proved enormously influential in the Mālikī school, and one might see in it the increasing sway of a more sexualized, *fitna*-based, and perhaps essentializing attitude toward women, their mobility in general, and their public worship in particular.

Ibn Rushd also comments on another important issue related to women's mosque access. Were men—whether rulers or husbands—obligated to allow women to go to the mosque, or was it merely recommended that they do so? To phrase it somewhat differently, did women have a right to go to the mosque? Despite the Mālikī school's deeply rooted and ḥadīth-based affirmation that husbands should not forbid their wives to go to the mosque, most Mālikīs approached this as a moral exhortation rather than as an enforceable rule. The early Mālikī scholar Yaḥyā ibn Ibrāhīm ibn Muzayn (d. 260/874) wrote in a commentary on the *Muwaṭṭa*ʾ that "if a young woman (*al-mar*ʾ*a al-shābba*) asks permission from her husband to go out to the mosque, he is not legally obligated to let her go out; he is entitled to discipline her and detain her."[41] In fact, many questioned whether the wife had an enforceable right to go to the mosque even if she had a stipulation to this effect in her marriage contract. According to the *ʿUtbīya*, Mālik himself was asked about the scenario of a man who married a woman on the condition that he not forbid her from going to the mosque; he replied, "He ought to fulfill what he promised to her, but he is not legally compelled to do so (*lā yuqḍā bi-dhālika ʿalayhi*); if he declines to allow her he is entitled to do so, and he is entitled to prevent her."[42]

Some Mālikī scholars did ponder the possibility that women had an enforceable right to go to the mosque.[43] However, the comments of Sind ibn ʿInān suggest the extent to which some jurists placed moral responsibility for a wife's behavior upon the husband. He writes that "the situation depends on the nature of the woman; if the man knows her to be characterized by piety and propriety (*in ʿarafa minhā al-diyāna wa'l-ṣiḥḥa*), there is no harm in his permitting her to do that." The situation is different, however, "if he knows her to be characterized by deviousness and he is not sure it is true that she wants to go to the mosque until he verifies it."[44] Nevertheless, it is notable that the underlying fear in this passage appears to be not the disruptive potential of the woman's presence in the mosque, but the possibility that she will use a supposed trip to the mosque as a pretext for some less savory outing.

Ibn Rushd himself regards a woman's entitlement to go to the mosque as completely contingent on the permission of her husband. Even if her marriage contract contains a condition affirming her right to do so, in his view it constitutes a moral rather than a legal obligation upon the husband; it is preferable, but not mandatory, for him to allow her to go whether or not this is specified in the contract.[45] He supports his conclusions with the story of ʿĀtika bint Zayd and ʿUmar (apparently because the fact of her asking permission suggests his authority to make the choice).[46] He argues that Mālik's statement that women are not to be forbidden to go to mosques refers not to individual husbands, but to a general prohibition on women's mosque attendance (*al-manʿ al-ʿāmm*) imposed by the authorities. Basing his conclusion on Mālik's doctrine that young women should not go out to festival prayers or prayers for rain, Ibn Rushd holds that the authorities should prohibit them from doing so. In contrast, the ruler should not bar young women from the mosques because they are allowed to go there on some occasions. In contrast, with respect to the women themselves it was religiously undesirable (*yukrah*) to do so often, and then only with the permission of their husbands.[47] Despite Ibn Rushd's formal commitment to grounding legal doctrine in ḥadīth, it is notable that his arguments here consistently subvert the surface meanings of the relevant texts.

Another formative contribution to the Mālikī discussion of women's mosque access was provided by ʿIyāḍ ibn Mūsā al-Yaḥṣubī (al-Qāḍī ʿIyāḍ, d. 544/1149), who lived in North Africa and Spain. Commenting on the ḥadīth "Do not forbid the maidservants of God from [going to] the mosques of God," ʿIyāḍ comments that it is "an indication that it is permissible for them to go out, an exhortation that they not be forbidden [from doing so], and a proof that they may not go out except with the husband's permission." Rather than seeing women's mosque-going as completely at the discretion of individual husbands, however, ʿIyāḍ presented a set of criteria for the permissibility of a woman's venturing out to the mosque.

> The scholars (*al-ʿulamāʾ*) have set as conditions for [women's] going out that it be during the night, that [they] not be adorned or wearing perfume, that they not crowd close to men (*lā muzāḥimāt li'l-rijāl*), and that [the individual in question] not be a young woman from whom *fitna* is to be feared. Equivalent to perfume is displaying adornments and pretty jewelry. If any of these occurs, it is obligatory to prohibit them [from going out] for fear of *fitna*.

He adds, "If they are prohibited from going to mosques" (i.e., if they violate one or more of these conditions), "then *a fortiori* [they should be prohibited] from [going to] other places."[48]

Lists of conditions for women's mosque attendance appear to be a new element in the discussion of this issue. A later Mālikī scholar astutely observes that ʿIyāḍ's vague reference to "the scholars" avoids any implication that his list of conditions derives from the authorities of the Mālikī school;[49] rather, it appears to originate within the tradition of ḥadīth commentary. Furthermore, in his commentary on the *Mudawwana* (a more strictly legal work) ʿIyāḍ himself does not add any conditions or modifications to the *Mudawwana*'s statement that "women should not be forbidden from going out to mosques."[50] Thus, his interpretation of the relevant ḥadīth apparently did not shape his understanding of the established content of Mālikī legal doctrine. Nevertheless, lists of conditions like those presented in ʿIyāḍ's ḥadīth commentary were to appear in Mālikī works quite regularly in subsequent centuries.

Muḥammad ibn Khalīfa al-Ubbī (d. ca. 828/1425) regards the conditions enumerated by al-Qāḍī ʿIyāḍ as new limitations imposed in view of the decadence of women living after the time of the Prophet. He observes:

> It can be inferred from ʿĀʾisha's statement [that the Prophet would have barred women from mosques had he seen what they innovated after him] that these were not conditions at the beginning of Islam; they became conditions only when society became corrupt. This is what ʿUmar ibn ʿAbd al-ʿAzīz [reigned 99–101/717–720] was referring to when he said, "New judgments arise for people in proportion to the immorality they innovate (*yaḥduth li'l-nās aqḍiya bi-qadr mā aḥdathū min al-fujūr*)."[51]

Indeed, the early authorities of the school had not subjected women's mosque-going to specific conditions. Nevertheless, this development does not reflect growing reservations toward mosque attendance in particular; it is notable that among later Mālikīs the conditions for women's going out to the mosque were essentially identical to those for their leaving the home for any purpose. For example, ʿUmar al-Fākihānī (d. 731/1256) states that a woman should leave the home only on five conditions: first, that her going out should be in the early morning or late evening (lit., "at the two ends of the daytime," *ṭarafay al-nahār*) unless there is a pressing need to go out at some other time; second, that she wear her humblest clothing (*adwan thiyābihā*); third, that she walk at the edges of the path and not in the middle, in order to keep her distance from men; fourth, that she not smell of perfume; and fifth, that no part of her be visible that [unrelated] men are forbidden to look at.[52] Despite its completely independent wording, this list of conditions parallels that of al-Qāḍī ʿIyāḍ with remarkable fidelity—save the glaring omission of any reference to the woman's age, which completes the transition from an emphasis on age cohort to one on dress and behavior.

It is notable that both ʿIyāḍ and al-Fākihānī seek to limit women's public mobility to the hours of darkness or of dusk, one specifying that she may venture forth only "at night" and the other referring to the early morning and late evening (the "two ends of the daytime"). Whereas in the earliest Mālikī sources staying home during the day appears to be an elite practice or prerogative, by the fifth/eleventh century the limitation of mosque-going to the nighttime hours is held up as a normative ideal for all women. Ibn ʿAbd al-Barr argues that, although most versions of the ḥadīth in which the Prophet instructs, "Give women permission to go to mosques" do not add the specification "at night," as this is an addition to the text reported by a reliable transmitter (*ziyādat ḥāfiẓ*), it imposes a valid limitation on the Prophet's general command to allow women to attend mosques.[53] Ibn Baṭṭāl (d. 449/1057) makes similar arguments, further inferring that the Prophet's command to allow women to attend the mosque "at night" implies that "daytime is different from night" (i.e., women should not go to the mosque during the daytime). Ibn Baṭṭāl attributes this qualification of the permission for women to go to mosques directly to Mālik.[54]

The comments of Ibn ʿAbd al-Barr's contemporary Sulaymān ibn Khalaf al-Bājī (d. 474/1081) suggest that the limitation of women's mosque attendance primarily to the nighttime may have been not only a juristic preference but also a practical reality. He remarks that "in general the prayers that [women] attend [at the mosque] (*ghālib mā yaḥḍurna*) are those that are in the hours of darkness, like the evening and dawn [prayers], because that better covers them and better conceals their appearances (*aḥwālihinna*)."[55] However, the limitation of women's mosque attendance to the nighttime hours remained contested among later Mālikīs. Surveying the legal literature from the vantage point of a far later age, the Egyptian Mālikī ʿAlī al-ʿAdawī al-Ṣaʿīdī remarked that "the scholars have set the condition that her going out [to the mosque] be at night, and some [others] of them said that [women] should not go out at night, but only during the daytime; this is something that may differ with differences in the times."[56] As we shall see in chapter 3 of this study, the expectation that women should limit their public appearances either to the discreet darkness of night or to the decorous safety of day could be deeply entrenched in specific times and places.

Khalīl ibn Isḥāq al-Jundī (d. 767/1366), the most influential Mālikī jurist of the Middle Period, perpetuated both the standard legal doctrines rooted in the statements attributed to Mālik and the newer tradition of behavioral conditions for women's mosque attendance associated with al-Qāḍī ʿIyāḍ. In his *Mukhtaṣar*, which became the most important statement of school doctrine for later generations of Mālikīs, he states in the section on congregational prayer (*al-jamāʿa*) that it is permissible "for a mature woman (*mutajālla*) to go out to [prayers] for a festival or for rain, and a young woman (*shābba*) [to go out] to the mosque; and her husband is not legally compelled to [allow her to go]."[57] In the section on Friday prayers, he states that it is undesirable for a young woman to attend (*kuriha...ḥuḍūr shābba*).[58] In his work *al-Tawḍīḥ*, he enumerates the conditions established by "the ʿulamāʾ," concluding that "some of them have added to the conditions that it must occur at night."[59] In the same work, Khalīl expresses a surprising new conviction, declaring that "what is appropriate in our time is that [women] should be prevented [from going to mosques]; this is indicated by ʿĀʾisha's famous statement, 'If the Messenger of God had seen what women have innovated.'"[60] It is unclear what force or scope Khalīl intended for his statement that latter-day women should be prevented from going to the mosque; its juxtaposition with a list of conditions very similar to those of al-Qāḍī ʿIyāḍ suggests that he did not propose the exclusion of all women without exception. His terse formulations in the *Mukhtaṣar* are similar to the positions established by earlier authorities of the school and suggest no radical departures from school doctrine. Perhaps, then, the force of his statement that latter-day women should be forbidden from going to mosques is largely rhetorical.

In any case, Khalīl was neither the first nor the last Mālikī scholar to express the sentiment that his female contemporaries should be forbidden from going to mosques (although he may have been the first to incorporate it into a legal work). Ibn Abī Jamra, an Andalusian scholar and Sufi who settled in Egypt and died at the end of the seventh/thirteenth century, made a similar point in his commentary on the *Ṣaḥīh* of Bukhārī. The report in question states that if the Prophet heard a child crying while leading congregational prayers, he would make his recitation brief to avoid burdening the child's mother. Ibn Abī Jamra writes that the ḥadīth "contains an indication (*dalīl*) for the permissibility of women's praying with men; however, today that is forbidden. That was forbidden in the time of the [early] caliphs."[61] Another Mālikī authority who emphasized that contemporary women should be discouraged from going to mosques was Ibn al-Ḥājj al-ʿAbdarī (d. 737/1336), perhaps not coincidentally a devoted disciple of Ibn Abī Jamra (and also a resident of Egypt).[62] Having argued that it is acceptable for women to bring young children to the mosque, Ibn al-Ḥājj declares,

> That is, if necessity requires that a woman pray in congregation in the mosque; it is better for her to pray at home. If it were to be said, "The women used to go out to the mosque in the time of the Prophet and pray with him in congregation, and it is reported that the Prophet used to abbreviate his prayer if he heard a child crying, for fear that his mother would be distracted (*tuftan*)," the response to that is twofold. The first [response] is what ʿĀʾisha said: "If the Messenger of God knew what women have innovated, he would have forbidden them to go to the mosques as the Israelite women were forbidden." The second is that nothing equals prayer behind the Prophet.[63]

Ibrāhīm ibn ʿAlī ibn Farḥūn (d. 799/1397), a Mālikī qāḍī of Medina, endorses Khalīl's statement that women should be prevented from going to mosques. After enumerating the conditions for their doing so, he concludes, "Refraining from going out is more conducive to soundness in religion, even if [she] has correct intent and the conditions—or some of them—are met."[64] Another prominent Egyptian Mālikī authority, ʿAbd Allāh ibn Miqdād al-Aqfahsī (or al-Aqfāṣī, d. 823/1420), writes in his commentary on the *Mukhtaṣar* of Khalīl that "in our time neither an old woman nor a young one, whether beautiful or not, should go out because of what we have seen (*li-mā raʾaynāhu*)."[65] (Unfortunately, he does not appear to have elaborated on this ominous allusion.[66])

The sentiment that times had changed and that latter-day women ought to be discouraged from attending the mosque altogether clearly existed among prominent Mālikī scholars by the thirteenth century CE, although its force appears in context to be more exhortative than legal. Both the growing sentiment against women's public worship and the degree to which it diverged from existing practice are reflected in a fatwa by the North African Mālikī jurist Rāshid ibn Abī Rāshid al-Walīdī (d. 675/1228). He writes,

> As for zealous women's (*al-mujtahidāt*)[67] praying behind unrelated men at night or in the daytime, that is something that women ought not to do, because women are not among those who should pray in congregation (*lasna min ahl al-jamāʿa*) for the obligatory prayers, so how could that be appropriate for them in a supererogatory prayer? It is better for them to perform the obligatory prayers in the depths of their homes (*fī*

> *qaʿr buyūtihinna*), and it is better for them to sit at home at their spindles than to go out for any kind of public worship (*al-ʿibādāt al-ẓāhira*). If you know that, you must inform all of the zealous women of it; it is the sign[68] of their sincerity in their zeal that they refrain from going out for such a purpose.[69]

Al-Walīdī here opposes women's public worship, even during the nighttime—although he appears unable to state that it is legally impermissible. The clear implication of his remarks, of course, is that at least some women in his environment attended mosques to perform obligatory and supererogatory prayers—and, as emerges later in the passage, ṣūfī *dhikr*—along with men.

The evolution of Mālikī attitudes over time is particularly clear when one examines the relatively rare discussions of mosque-based activities other than canonical prayer. The great Mālikī jurist and theologian al-Bāqillānī (al-Qāḍī Abū Bakr ibn al-Ṭayyib, d. 403/1013), who spent most of his life in Baghdad, is reported to have stated that women

> may go out to hear preaching, to acquire knowledge (*taʿallum al-ʿilm*), and [to perform] a meritorious action such as prayer or the like. It is permissible for those from whom no temptation is feared, old women and those who are equivalent to them, to attend Friday and festival prayers while remaining apart from the men. As for the young women, it is obligatory to censure their mixing with men in mosques and in the gatherings of storytellers, unless they are behind a barrier (*ḥijāb*) so that the men cannot see them.[70]

It is notable both that al-Bāqillānī envisions a wide variety of mosque-based activities as accessible to women and that he advocates only that young women be prevented from mixing with men at the mosque (rather than from going there in the first place). In contrast, Ibn ʿArafa (d. 803/1401) held that young women should be forbidden to go out to sessions of study, *dhikr*, and preaching, even if they were separated from men, on the grounds that the dispensation for their attendance at the mosque applied only to prayer.[71] Once more, there appears to be a hardening of attitudes after the thirteenth century

CE—although here again it seems likely that Ibn ʿArafa addressed this behavior precisely because it was occurring.

Much of the subsequent Mālikī discussion on women's mosque attendance takes the form of commentary on the *Risāla* of Ibn Abī Zayd and the *Mukhtaṣar* of Khalīl. Although framed as glosses and commentaries on these authoritative manuals, however, the remarks of later scholars often significantly modified the apparent meaning of the texts. Because the authoritative early sources of the school usually did not explicitly assign women's mosque attendance to one of the five legal statuses (*aḥkām*)—obligatory, desirable, neutral, repugnant, or forbidden—commentators could superimpose these judgments on their remarks. It was often possible to interpret the same statement as establishing mosque attendance by a certain category of women as an absolute right or a limited dispensation, as a positive religious good or an undesirable alternative. For instance, Muḥammad ibn Ibrāhīm al-Tatāʾī (d. 937/1434) glosses Khalīl's text by stating that it is undesirable to attend Friday prayers for a young woman *who is not feared to cause fitna* (*ghayr makhshīyat al-fitna*); if it is feared that she will cause *fitna*, it is forbidden (*yaḥram*).[72] Here the threat of *fitna* escalates mere disapproval to actual prohibition. Although Khalīl implies that it is permissible for young women to go to mosques on occasions other than the Friday noon prayer, al-Zurqānī (d. 1099/1688) glosses the text to say that "it is permissible *as a sub-optimal alternative* (*jāza ʿalā khilāf al-awlā*)"—again on the condition that no *fitna* is to be feared.[73] Commenting on the *Risāla* of Ibn Abī Zayd al-Qayrawānī, Aḥmad ibn Ghunaym al-Nafrāwī (d. 1125/1713) writes of Friday prayers: "As for a woman, it is not desirable for her to attend them . . . even if she is mature (*mutajālla*); the legal status of attending is prohibition (*al-ḥurma*) for a tender young woman (*al-shābba al-nāʿima*), undesirability with respect to a young woman to whom people are generally not attracted (*lā tamīl ilayhā al-nufūs ghāliban*), and permissibility with respect to the mature woman; so there are three categories."[74]

However, the later commentarial tradition does not uniformly emphasize the negative aspects of women's mosque attendance. The Egyptian Muḥammad ibn ʿAbd Allāh al-Khurashī (d. 1101/1690) glosses Khalīl's statement that it is permissible for a mature woman to go out to festival prayers or prayers for rain by saying "meaning that it is permissible *and desirable* for an old, mature woman (*al-mutajālla al-musinna*) for whom men have no desire to go out to festival prayers or prayers for rain, and even more so to [daily] obligatory prayers (*wa-aḥrā li'l-farḍ*)."[75] This judgment was perpetuated by later scholars such as Aḥmad al-Ṣāwī (d. 1241/1825).[76]

Later Mālikī texts also bring up more regularly than their pre-sixteenth-century CE predecessors the issue of mosque-based activities other than prayer. Al-Khurashī states that a young woman may go out to the mosque "for obligatory prayers and the funerals of her family and relatives, but not for *dhikr* or teaching sessions (*majālis ʿilm*), even if she is located separately (*inʿazalat*)," attributing this opinion to Ibn ʿArafa.[77] Al-Khurashī's contemporary and fellow Egyptian Ibrāhīm ibn Marʿī al-Shabrakhītī (d. 1106/1694–95) elaborates somewhat that a young woman ought not to go out to the mosque for "sessions of teaching, *dhikr*, or preaching, even if she is far away [from the men], and even if she is separated,"[78] a statement that is produced verbatim by ʿAlī ibn Aḥmad al-ʿAdawī (d. 1189/1775–76).[79] Although these parallel statements express disapproval of women's presence in mosques for purposes of learning and *dhikr*, it is significant that they apply exclusively to young women; the tacit implication appears to be that these activities are acceptable reasons for mature women to frequent mosques.

This implication is made explicit by the Egyptian commentator Muḥammad al-Dasūqī (d. 1230/1815) in the context of a strikingly divergent rendition of Ibn Rushd's categorization of the different age cohorts of women. He quotes Ibn Rushd regarding the old woman who is no longer attractive to men:

> She is like a man; she goes out to the mosque for obligatory prayers (*al-farḍ*) and for sessions of *dhikr* and study, and goes out to the desert (*al-ṣaḥrāʾ*, that is, the prayer ground outside of town) for the prayers for the two festivals and for rain and the funerals of her family and relatives, and [she goes out] to take care of her affairs (*li-qaḍāʾ ḥawāʾijihā*).

As for the *mutajālla* who still retains some allure, "this one goes out to the mosque for obligatory prayers and for sessions of study and *dhikr*, but does not go out frequently (*tukthir al-taraddud*) to take care of her affairs—that is, that is undesireable (*yukrah*) for her." Here the reservation that "she does not go frequently" (attributed to Mālik in the *ʿUtbīya*) applies not to the woman's visits to the mosque, but to her excursions on personal errands. Finally, al-Dasūqī's citation of Ibn Rushd states that a young woman who is not distinguished either by her tender youth or by her nobility (*najāba*) can go out to perform obligatory prayers in congregation or to attend the funeral of a relative, but not to attendsessions of study or *dhikr* or to perform festival prayers or prayers for rain.[80] This more permissive rendition of Ibn Rushd's statement is also presented by al-Ṣāwī.[81]

It thus appears that among the Egyptian Mālikīs of the seventeenth to nineteenth centuries, there is a tendency not only explicitly to mention study and *dhikr* as activities that women might pursue in mosques, but also to accept them as legitimate for all but the youngest and most problematic category of women. As usual, it is difficult to determine the degree to which this trend in the legal manuals reflects the tendency to reproduce a statement once it has been introduced to the tradition rather than the practical mores of the surrounding society. Nevertheless, it is striking that this pattern is associated specifically with Egypt, a place with (as we shall see in the next chapter) a well-documented history of women's presence at sessions of teaching, preaching, and *dhikr* in mosques (although perhaps less so for this particular period). It contrasts with the overwhelming emphasis on congregational prayer in earlier Mālikī sources associated primarily with North Africa and Spain (although again this pattern may be largely an artifact of the conventions of legal writing).

Overall, one notable feature of the Mālikī discussion of women's mosque attendance as compared with other *madhhab*s is the pervasive (if muted) assumption that women's participation in public congregational prayers is inherently meritorious, even if other conditions make it inadvisable. Al-Bājī comments that ʿUmar ibn al-Khaṭṭāb's wife asked his permission to go to the mosque "because she wanted to earn the merit of going out [to the mosque] if she went, or even if she did not go, because of her intention (*nīya*)."[82] Sind ibn ʿInān argues that the Prophet had prohibited men from preventing their wives from going to the mosque "because reports [from the Prophet] state that performing the obligatory prayers in congregation has great merit (*faḍl kabīr*), as does walking to mosques; and women are in the greatest need of that [merit], as are men."[83] Ibn al-ʿArabī (d. 543/1148) writes disparagingly that femininity is a deficiency of the intellect (*al-unūtha nuqṣān mukhill bi'l-ʿaql*), which is why women are forbidden from mixing with men at congregational prayers. However, he goes on to say that God has permitted them to participate in congregational worship on a basis secondary to men "out of compassion to them and to provide them with more abundant reward." He proceeds to praise the regular attendance at Friday prayers of the women of Nablus.[84] Al-Ubbī questions whether it is merely neutral (*mubāḥ*) for a woman to go out to the mosque, on the grounds that attending congregational prayers is either a *sunna* (recommended action) or a *farḍ kifāya* (communal obligation), and it is unlikely that this applies only to men.[85]

The assumption that (in the absence of counterindications such as *fitna*) it was meritorious for a woman to pray in the mosque was not universal among Mālikīs. Ibn al-Ḥājj, who inveighs against women's presence in Cairene mosques, claims that the authorities of the school (*ʿulamāʾunā*) hold that "a woman's prayer at home by herself is superior to her prayer in congregation in the mosque, her prayer in an inner chamber in her home is superior to her prayer in [an exterior room of] her home, and whatever increases her coverage and concealment is superior for her prayer."[86] However, not even Mālikīs who fervently wished that women would stay home from the mosque necessarily agreed with him. Despite his hostility to women's presence in the mosque, Ibn Abī Jamra assumes that it would be the more meritorious place for a woman to pray in the absence of public corruption. He observes that when ʿUmar ibn al-Khaṭṭāb's wife chose to stay home because of the corruption of the people, "she refrained from the more perfect way of performing her prayers, which is to go out to the mosque" (*tarakat al-akmal fī ṣalātihā, wa-huwa al-khurūj ilā al-masjid*), because of the new rationale that had emerged.[87]

The prevalent Mālikī assumption of the underlying meritoriousness of women's prayer in the mosque is rooted in part in the fact that ḥadīth asserting the superior value of women's prayer within the home were largely transmitted by Iraqi authorities and were not included in the corpus preserved from Mālik. Also relevant is the Mālikī rejection of women's worship in single-sex groups, which left male-led prayer in the mosque as the primary opportunity to gain the merit of congregational worship—if one subject to many reservations and conditions.

THE ẒĀHIRĪS: IBN ḤAZM

One of the most potent and lastingly influential responses to Mālikī doctrines on women's mosque attendance was the product of Ẓāhirī thought. Characterized by a rejection of school authority (*taqlīd*) and an emphasis on direct reference to the texts of the Qur'an and ḥadīth, Ẓāhirism was most notably represented in Andalusia by Ibn Ḥazm (d. 456/1064). In the Andalusian context, overwhelmingly dominated by the Mālikī school of law, Ẓāhirism constituted not merely a neutral legal methodology but also "an effective means of opposing and of condemning the tyranny of the Mālikī jurists."[88] Ibn Ḥazm's discussion of women's mosque attendance, like that of many other legal issues, is not merely an example of independent hermeneutic activity but also a scathing critique of his fellow jurists' infidelity to the reported example of the Prophet. Ibn Ḥazm's textual formalism, although it could potentially render his reading of the law static or disconnect it from the evolving needs of the community, also insulated it from manipulation in light of allegedly changing social conditions; the pristine model of the Prophet's day, in his view, always remained valid.[89] The relevance of this latter point to the issue of women's mosque attendance is obvious. Whereas later Mālikī authorities would advocate further constricting women's mosque access in deference to the changing needs of the times, Ibn Ḥazm advocated radically expanding it based on the timelessness of the prophetic example.

In general, Ibn Ḥazm's principles tended to yield rulings that were favorable to the autonomy of women.[90] To what extent this reflects a positive attitude toward women or a critique of the gender ideology of Mālikism (as opposed to simply the logical outcome of his fundamental legal principles and of the relative freedom of action enjoyed by women in the Prophet's time) is not completely clear. Ibn Ḥazm himself represents his conclusions as the inevitable result of the content of the texts, declaring "We say, if [the Prophet] had forbidden [women from going to mosques], we would have forbidden them; since he did not forbid them, we do not forbid them [either]!"[91]

Ibn Ḥazm affirms that it is not mandatory for women to perform their prayers in congregation, a fact he states to be undisputed. However, "if a woman goes to pray with the men it is good (*ḥasan*), because of the well-authenticated fact that [women] used to attend [public] prayers with the Messenger of God with his knowledge."[92] He considers the ḥadīth "Do not forbid the maidservants of God from [going to] the mosques of God" to be a binding command as long as the woman's husband or guardian knows that she is actually intending to pray. If the woman in question is wearing perfume or is attractively dressed, however, he may forbid her.[93]

In contrast to most members of the established schools of law, Ibn Ḥazm explicitly and forcefully affirms that the ḥadīth setting out the greater merit of congregational prayer applies to women as well as men, whether they pray in single-sex or mixed-sex congregations.[94] He argues, "If it were more meritorious for women to pray at home [than in the mosque], the Messenger of God would not have let them wear themselves out with an exertion that yielded them no increase in merit, or that [even] detracted from their merit."[95] Going out to the mosque involves effort (*kulfa*), particularly when it involves facing unpleasant weather or other adverse conditions. If praying in the mosque yielded no additional merit for women, then their effort in going to the mosque would be frivolous and futile; it cannot be assumed that the Prophet allowed the female Companions to squander their energies in this way. What is more, any action that actually detracts from the merit of prayer must necessarily be forbidden. However, "all the people of the world agree that the Messenger of God never forbade women to pray with him in his mosque before he died, nor did the Rightly Guided caliphs after him."[96]

Ibn Ḥazm indignantly rejects the argument that women's public prayer was a temporary or strategic dispensation during the lifetime of the Prophet. As for ʿĀʾisha's statement that "If the Prophet had seen what the woman have innovated, he would have forbidden them to go to the mosque" Ibn Ḥazm argues that it is not legally relevant for a number of reasons. The first is that the Prophet did not, in fact, see what the women innovated and thus did not forbid them;

for anyone else to do so is an innovation (*bidʿa*) and an error. It is absurd to use a condition contrary to fact as the basis of a legal ruling. Second, even if the Prophet did not see what women innovated, God certainly knew about it; anyone who denies this is an unbeliever. Nevertheless, God did not reveal to the Prophet that he should forbid women to go to mosques for this reason. Third, women have innovated nothing in subsequent generations that they had not already innovated in the time of the Prophet. There is nothing more heinous than their innovation of fornication and adultery (*zinā*); the Prophet had women stoned and lashed for this, but he did not forbid women to go to the mosques. Furthermore, sexual misbehavior is forbidden to men as well; how could it be the rationale for women's exclusion from mosques, but not for men's?

Ibn Ḥazm's fourth reason is that the innovation undoubtedly occurred on the part of some women and not of others; it is absurd (*muḥāl*) to deny a good to someone who has not committed an innovation because of someone else who has—unless there were a text revealed by God to this effect, in which case we would hear and obey. On the contrary, however, in the Qur'an, God states that no soul will bear another's burden (verse 6:164). The fifth reason is that, if women's innovation were a reason to ban women from mosques, a fortiori it would be a reason to ban them from the markets and the roads; however, Ibn Ḥazm's opponents have barred them from mosques to the exclusion of other destinations. The sixth reason is that even ʿĀʾisha herself did not explicitly forbid women from going to mosques.[97]

Significantly, the term *fitna* in the sense of sexual temptation is strikingly absent not only from Ibn Ḥazm's analysis of women's public worship but also from his legal work in general.[98] It may be that, writing almost a century before Ibn Rushd, he is simply not aware of *fitna* as a central motif in legal argumentation about women's mosque attendance. (He does, however, clearly assume that the potential for sexual misbehavior underlies ʿĀʾisha's reference to "innovation.") It may also be that his refusal to scrutinize and define the rationales behind the commands and prohibitions in the Qur'an and ḥadīth (*taʿlīl*) prevents him from identifying *fitna* as the underlying issue informing the rules on women's mosque attendance. Unlike his Mālikī peers, as a Ẓāhirī he was also relieved both from the need to explain

Mālik's reluctance to encourage female mosque-going and from the inherited category distinctions between old and young women. Although he notes Mālikī age terminology in passing, he does not even see fit to refute it.[99]

The great Andalusian mystic Ibn ʿArabī (d. 638/1240), although not primarily a jurist, had some affinities with Ẓāhirī legal theory and was inspired by the work of Ibn Ḥazm.[100] He analyzes men's resistance to the divine decree allowing women to go to mosques as an instance of jealousy (*ghayra*), arguing that personal animus can lead humans to be jealous even of the rulings of God. Only full establishment of the authority of intellect and faith can prevent such feelings of resentment (*ḥaraj*) against God's decree.[101] Ibn ʿArabī here implicitly challenges the discourse of *fitna*. A man who forbids his wife to go to the mosque is not preventing other men from succumbing to her charms, but is himself succumbing to base sentiments of sexual possessiveness. Ibn ʿArabī thus combines a literalist commitment to the word of ḥadīth with a ṣūfī concern with the analysis of subtle egoistic obstacles to achieving harmony with the will of God.

THE SHĀFIʿĪS

The most substantial discussion of the issue of women's mosque access attributed to al-Shāfiʿī occurs in a short work titled "Book on Discrepancies Among Ḥadīth" (*Kitāb Ikhtilāf al-ḥadīth*), appended to his great work of substantive law *al-Umm*.[102] As suggested by its title, this piece deals most centrally with an issue of legal theory (the proper approach to apparent contradictions among statements transmitted from the Prophet) rather than with the substantive question of whether women should frequent mosques. The discussion opens with a challenge by al-Shāfiʿī's hypothetical interlocutors, who confront him with the legal implications of the ḥadīth "Do not forbid the maidservants of God from [going to] the mosques of God." They point out that "according to you, a negative command from the Prophet indicates that [the action] is forbidden (*taḥrīm*) unless there is an indication from the Messenger of God that he did not intend to signify that it is forbidden." Furthermore, the statement refers generally to the "mosques of God."[103] In short, the opponents claim that if al-Shāfiʿī applies his methodology consistently to this text, he is compelled to concede that a woman may never be denied the opportunity to go to any mosque. Implicit in this challenge is the assumption that this result would be unacceptable to both parties to the dispute.

However, al-Shāfiʿī unhesitatingly replies that the ḥadīth is, in fact, specific (*khāṣṣ*)—that is, it applies only to some (as yet unspecified) instances of women's mosque-going. In support of this contention, he cites another ḥadīth: "It is not permissible for a woman who believes in God and the Last Day to travel a day and night's journey except with a close male relative (*dhī maḥram*)." The relevance of this report becomes clear when al-Shāfiʿī applies it to a woman's desire to make the pilgrimage to Mecca—here defined as a visit to a mosque, albeit one that is distant and unique. By citing the ḥajj, al-Shāfiʿī selects the most extreme possible example, one in which a woman's entitlement to visit a mosque might entail a demand to make a long and costly journey. Al-Shāfiʿī adroitly argues that the position that the woman's guardian may not prevent her from going on the ḥajj entails unacceptable legal consequences, including the necessity of compelling a male relative to bear the expenses of the journey as her chaperone. Because any other position requires that the male guardian be entitled to forbid the woman access to one specific mosque (the Sacred Mosque of Mecca), the ḥadīth cannot be general; there is at least one exception.

Al-Shāfiʿī then shifts his argument to other grounds. He demands, "Do you know of anyone who disputes that a man is entitled to forbid his wife from going to the mosque of her clan (*ʿashīra*), even if it is next to her house, and to Friday prayers, which are the most obligatory prayers in a city?" The hypothetical opponent concedes, "I am not aware of any."[104] According to al-Shāfiʿī's principles, the agreement of the scholars constitutes binding evidence for the correct interpretation of a revealed text, particularly when this interpretation diverges from the apparent (*ẓāhir*) meaning.[105] In this case, al-Shāfiʿī holds that, because an overwhelming majority of scholars agree that men may indeed prevent their wives from going to mosques, the meaning of the Prophet's apparent statement to the contrary can refer only to specific cases.

Now that al-Shāfiʿī has demonstrated that the ḥadīth in question does not mean that men are categorically forbidden to prevent the women of their households from frequenting mosques, his opponents demand to know precisely what it does mean. Having just demonstrated the specific nature of the ḥadīth by arguing that men may sometimes forbid women to visit the Sacred Mosque of Mecca, al-Shāfiʿī executes a startling about-face to argue that the Sacred Mosque of Mecca is precisely the one mosque to which the ḥadīth specifically refers. The ḥadīth does not mean that men must allow their womenfolk to visit all mosques at all times; rather, it means that they must allow them to visit one mosque (the mosque of Mecca) one time (for the obligatory pilgrimage). Despite the myriad objections that he had earlier raised to the contention that a man must enable his wife or ward to make the pilgrimage, al-Shāfiʿī now sweeps aside all difficulties. Most men will willingly consent to accompany their female dependents on the ḥajj, and if they do not, the woman can go in the care of trustworthy female companions. Because one ḥajj in a lifetime is a legal obligation, the expenses can be disbursed from the woman's assets on her behalf if she is not legally independent. Despite appearances, al-Shāfiʿī is not being flagrantly inconsistent here (although he is certainly being creative). The argument that a woman may *sometimes* be prevented from making a pilgrimage to Mecca (which is all that is required, according to al-Shāfiʿī, to demonstrate that the ḥadīth is not general) is clearly distinct from the argument that she may not be prevented from making the pilgrimage once in her life.

By basing his argument on the obligatory status of the pilgrimage, al-Shāfiʿī is able to make a clear distinction from all other instances of women's mosque attendance. Since there is no other case where a woman is actually obligated to attend a mosque, there is no other case where her husband or guardian is forbidden to prevent her from doing so. Interestingly, al-Shāfiʿī bases his argument that women are not obligated to pray in mosques not only on the agreement of the scholars but also on the precedents set by the Prophet's wives and the other female members of his household. Al-Shāfiʿī declares,

> Attending Friday prayers is an obligation for men, unless they have a valid excuse, and we do not know of any woman among the Mothers

> of the Believers who went out to a Friday or congregational prayer in a mosque; the wives of the Messenger of God are most worthy to fulfill their ritual obligations by virtue of their relationship to the Messenger of God.

He reiterates and elaborates soon after:

> There were women with the Messenger of God, his female relatives (*ahl baytihi*), daughters, wives, freedwomen, and his servants, and the servants of his relatives; I do not know of any woman among them who went out to attend Friday prayers . . . or to any other congregational prayer in the day or the night. . . . I do not doubt that by virtue of their relationship with the Prophet they were more intent upon what was right and more knowledgeable about it than other women, and that the Prophet would not have failed to instruct them about what was obligatory for them . . . and what merit they would earn from it, even if it was not obligatory for them. . . . I do not know of any one of the early Muslims (*salaf al-muslimīn*) who instructed any one of his wives to attend the Friday or congregational prayers during the night or the day; if there were any merit for them in doing that, they would have instructed them to do it and allowed them to do it.[106]

This is an interesting point, given that a myriad of ḥadīth texts refer to the presence of women at congregational prayers in the mosque in the lifetime of the Prophet. It may be that these reports are unknown to al-Shāfiʿī or that he considers them poorly authenticated. It may also be that he is aware of such reports, but that they do not (in general) refer specifically to wives, daughters, or freedwomen of the Prophet. Given that the Prophet's wives had chambers opening into the mosque and could participate in congregational prayers without leaving their homes, it is conceivable that they did not "go to the mosque" in the technical sense. An early Mālikī source suggests that the Prophet's wives prayed along with the congregation within their own chambers, which adjoined the mosque.[107] Al-Shāfiʿī's statement that "by virtue of their relationship with the Prophet" the women of his household "were more intent upon what was right and more knowledgeable about it than other women" may implicitly suggest that al-Shāfiʿī was aware of reports affirming the presence of other women in the mosque during the lifetime of the Prophet. Al-Shāfiʿī is also perfectly aware that the women of the Prophet's household were subject to a standard of modesty and seclusion that did not apply to other female Believers; he responds to this objection by stating that when the ḥijāb was imposed on the Prophet's wives, "none of their ritual obligations were removed from them." Even though the women of the Prophet's family were subject to special constraints, these did not affect their ritual duties, which would have continued to include mosque attendance had this been incumbent upon them in the first place.

Al-Shāfiʿī's discussion in this passage suggests several things about the overall state of Muslim attitudes toward women's mosque attendance in his time. First, the ḥadīth "Do not forbid the maidservants of God from [going to] the mosques of God" seems to have been in sufficiently wide circulation that al-Shāfiʿī was compelled to take it into account. He makes no attempt to question its provenance and displays familiarity with several different versions of the report. He also knows a ḥadīth report establishing a hierarchy of merit culminating in the most private and secluded locations for women's prayer. It is notable that this ḥadīth is cited without an *isnād* and with the disclaimer that "God knows best"; al-Shāfiʿī appears to be using it as auxiliary support for his argument without actually endorsing its authenticity. Second, there seems to have been an overall consensus—according to al-Shāfiʿī, among both religious scholars and "common people" (*al-ʿāmma*)—that a man may, in fact, deny his wife or ward the opportunity to visit the mosque and that he allows her to do so at his own discretion.

It has been accurately observed that al-Shāfiʿī takes a relatively negative attitude toward women's mosque access in this passage.[108] However, we must be attentive to the precise points that he is making. His primary objective is to refute the contention that the ḥadīth in question is a telling counterexample to his hermeneutical principles; his opponents believe that they can force him to concede that he denies the legal force of a universally acknowledged prophetic report. To the extent that his discussion addresses behavioral norms rather than legal theory, his overriding concern here is with the authority of the husband or male guardian—and thus with the power structure of the Muslim family. Although al-Shāfiʿī believes that a man may restrict the mosque-going of his wife or ward and that a woman's prayer at home is more religiously valuable than her prayer in the mosque, he nevertheless says nothing to suggest that he believes women's mosque attendance is legally undesirable, let alone forbidden. It appears from his discussion that a man may indeed allow his wife or other female relative to go to the mosque, and (other than the possible loss of religious merit accruing to prayer at home) there seems to be nothing to prevent her from going if he does so. Al-Shāfiʿī's interpretive energies are expended to preserve male authority at home, not to empty mosques of women.

Indeed, even though al-Shāfiʿī offers no general discussion of the legal status of women's mosque attendance in the body of *al-Umm*, he does refer to it in passing at several points. It emerges clearly from his remarks that at least some women may go to mosques if they so desire (and perhaps implicitly that some actually do). Like Mālik, he holds that women and slaves need not attend Friday prayers, but that they can validly perform them if they do.[109] He then remarks, "I prefer that (*uḥibb*) aged women and those who do not have [attractive] appearances attend [congregational] prayers and festivals; I prefer more strongly that they attend the festival [prayers] than that they attend other obligatory prayers (*al-ṣalawāt al-maktūbāt*)."[110] Here al-Shāfiʿī indicates not only the permissibility but also the positive desirability of mosque attendance by old women (*al-ʿajāʾiz*). In another passage, discussing the Friday congregational prayers, al-Shāfiʿī notes that it is not incumbent upon women, slaves, or minors to attend, but that "I prefer (*uḥibb*) for slaves to perform Friday prayers if they are given permission, and for old women [to do so] if they are given permission."[111] Writing about the prayers performed on the occasion of an eclipse (*ṣalāt al-kusūf*), which al-Shāfiʿī holds should be performed in the Friday mosque, he states that "I do not consider it objectionable for a woman who does not have a splendid appearance (*lā hayʾa lahā bāriʿa*), or for an old woman or a young girl, to attend *ṣalāt al-kusūf* with the imam; rather, I consider it desirable for them (*uḥibbuhā lahunna*). I prefer that those women who have [attractive] appearances (*dhawāt al-hayʾa*) to perform it in their homes."[112]

Al-Shāfiʿī's second category of women who are encouraged to go to congregational prayers—literally, "women who do not have appearances" (*ghayr dhawāt al-hayʾa*)—is somewhat ambiguous. *Al-hayʾa* (form, appearance) is a word that is used to refer to dress and grooming, and particularly to the donning of fine clothes and the use of perfume. Thus, al-Shāfiʿī's chapter in *al-Umm* on Friday prayer includes a subsection on dress and grooming for Friday prayers (*al-hayʾa li'l-jumʿa*), in which he advises that men should bathe, trim their hair and nails, perfume themselves, and don white or undyed garments before attending Friday services. He notes that these recommendations also apply to youths and slaves (who are not obligated to attend Friday prayers). However, for women he recommends only that they cleanse themselves to remove any objectionable smells; he considers it undesirable (*akrah*) for them to perfume themselves or to make themselves conspicuous by wearing white clothes.[113]

The phrase "those who have appearances" (*dhawāt al-hayʾa*, which I am translating literally to preserve the ambiguity of the Arabic) was interpreted by some later commentators to refer to the women's inherent physical charms rather than to dress and grooming. Al-Nawawī (d. 676/1277) glosses women "who have appearances" (*dhawāt al-hayʾāt*) as "the ones who are desired because of their beauty."[114] Although the two interpretations of women "who have appearances"—as those who are attractively decked out and as those who are themselves attractive—address the same basic concern that women should not attend public worship while displaying excessive charms, they have significantly different concrete implications. If "women who have [attractive] appearances" are those adorned with festive clothing or perfumes, then this particular factor is subject to the control of any woman willing to observe appropriate limits in her self-presentation. (At least one later commentator discerned and rejected this possibility, stating that "the obvious meaning [*ẓāhir*] is that a beautiful woman may attend if she does not adorn herself. This is not the case."[115]) Yet another possibility, reflected in ḥadīth texts that circulated at an early date, is that "people of appearances" are persons of high rank or known public virtue.[116] In this case, the restriction on women's mosque attendance would apply not to women with nice appearances, but to women with appearances to keep up—an option that seems not to have been considered by the later commentators on al-Shāfiʿī's statement, but that would be a plausible usage for his own time. This would suggest a limitation on the public exposure of elite women—an interesting possibility, but one that cannot be confirmed.

Despite al-Shāfiʿī's famously passionate and insistent focus on the authority of ḥadīth, his positions on this issue are not directly derived from textual sources. He struggles mightily with a ḥadīth text whose authenticity he apparently cannot deny (the one in which the Prophet forbids men to prevent women from going to mosques) only to eviscerate it of most of its meaning. He rhetorically cites a ḥadīth emphasizing the greater value of women's prayer in secluded spots within the home, only to affirm that it is desirable for elderly and unadorned or unattractive women to pray in public. His attitudes toward women's mosque attendance are fundamentally shaped by what appears to be a prior social and scholarly consensus, to which he accords interpretive authority on the grounds that large sectors of the Muslim community cannot be ignorant of the Prophet's true intent. Most significantly, his two major category distinctions (between the old and the young and between the unattractive and the attractive) have no apparent textual basis. (However, in reiterating his denial that the women of the Prophet's household attended congregational prayers "in the day or night," he may be obliquely refuting a widespread cultural and legal distinction with scant textual basis.)

Building on Shāfiʿī's opinions, scholars of the *madhhab* in the following centuries broadly conformed to the patterns we have already encountered in the Mālikī school. The textually established prohibition on men's barring their womenfolk from the mosque was considered a nonbinding recommendation, and a fundamental distinction between older and younger women was assumed without any significant textual support. As in the case of the Mālikīs, these ideas were systematically rationalized around the criterion of sexual temptation (*fitna*) in the fifth/eleventh century. In this case, however, the implicit equation between age and physical desirability was not unquestioningly accepted.

The Shāfiʿī authority ʿAlī ibn Muḥammad al-Māwardī (d. 450/1058) writes regarding women's attendance at Friday prayers,

> As for women, whoever possesses [attractive] appearance and beauty should be prevented from going out to Friday prayers for her own protection (*ṣiyānatan lahā*), and out of fear that she will be a source of temptation. As for those who do not possess [attractive] appearances, they

> should not be prevented; they should go out unadorned and unperfumed, because of [the Prophet's] statement, "Do not prevent God's maidservants from [going to] God's mosques, and let them go out unperfumed."[117]

Here al-Māwardī preserves al-Shāfiʿī's terminology, to a quite different ultimate effect. Al-Shāfiʿī's concept of "[attractive] appearances" (here explicitly associated with personal beauty, *jamāl*) is now the sole criterion that determines the appropriateness of women's going out for public prayer; it presumably subsumes the distinction between old and young women, deemphasizing the older categories associated with the female life cycle. Al-Māwardī was not the only Shāfiʿī authority to elide the distinction between old and young women in favor of an exclusive focus on the capacity to excite physical desire.[118]

Whereas al-Shāfiʿī had explicitly stated the desirability of elderly and unadorned women's attendance at public worship, al-Māwardī does not mention the possibility that any woman's public worship could be positively desirable. Indeed, although at least one classical Shāfiʿī legal manual conscientiously records al-Shāfiʿī's opinion that elderly women's attendance at public prayers is positively to be encouraged, the overall doctrine of the school was simply to treat it as legally permissible (*lā yukrah, lā baʾs*).[119] It also seems that the attitude toward younger women's mosque attendance hardened. Although al-Shāfiʿī clearly denied that it was meritorious for a young and attractive woman to go out to public worship, he left it open whether such an action would be *mubāḥ* (neutral), or (more likely) *makrūh* (undesirable), or even *ḥarām* (forbidden). According to al-Māwardī, an attractive woman should be actively deterred from going to Friday prayers; although the unattractive one need not be deterred, he gives no indication that she should be encouraged.

The criterion of physical allure and the distinction between old and young women appeared both alternatively and in tandem in the classical manuals of the Shāfiʿī school. In his authoritative work *al-Muhadhdhab*, which was studied and commented upon for centuries, Abū Isḥāq al-Shīrāzī (d. 476/1083) writes,

> If a woman wants to attend the mosque with the men, if she is a young woman or an old woman the likes of whom is desired (*kabīra tushtahā*

> *mithluhā*), it is undesirable for her to attend; if she is an old woman who is no longer desirable, it is not objectionable (*lam yukrah*), because of [the report] that is transmitted that the Prophet (peace be upon him!) forbade women to go out except for an old woman in her boots.[120]

Here, rather than subsuming the distinction between old and young women, the criterion of physical desirability crosscuts it. Instead of assuming the undesirability of elderly women, al-Shīrāzī makes sexual undesirability an additional criterion for the acceptability of older women's presence at the mosque. Whereas al-Shāfiʿī states that both old women *and* unattractive or unadorned (presumably younger) women may attend, for al-Shīrāzī (and other later Shāfiʿīs) the requirement of being unattractive is an additional restriction placed on older women. Whereas al-Shāfiʿī had asserted that it was positively good for all old women to go to congregational prayers, al-Shīrāzī allows only that it is permissible for some of them. Perhaps because al-Shīrāzī is not using age as a proxy for the assumed motivating factor of physical desirability, he also feels obliged to provide textual support for the distinction between old and young women by citing a ḥadīth report. The ḥadīth in which the Prophet condones going out only for the crone became the locus classicus for the distinction between old and young women in Shāfiʿī discussions of women's mosque attendance, although it was sometimes admitted to be of questionable provenance.[121]

Shāfiʿī scholars' increasingly dubious attitude toward women's mosque-going culminated in the suggestion that most or all women should not attend in the changed conditions of latter-day Muslim societies. This view appears to have deeper roots in the Shāfiʿī than in the Mālikī school. The Shāfiʿī authority al-Qāsim ibn Muḥammad al-Qaffāl al-Shāshī (d. 400/1010)[122] is quoted as saying, "It is objectionable (*yukrah*) for [a woman] to go out to the [prayer] gatherings of the Muslims (*majmaʿ al-muslimīn*),[123] because people have changed (*liʾanna al-nās qad taghayyarū*)." He attributes this view to ʿAbd Allāh ibn al-Mubārak (d. 181/797) and Sufyān al-Thawrī (d. 161/778) and also cites the ʿĀʾisha report. He follows up with a version of the story (sometimes associated with ʿĀtika bint Zayd) in which a jealous husband discourages his wife from attending the mosque by tugging her clothing in the darkness when she goes there, prompting her to declare that "the times have changed and people have changed."[124]

The author who transmits this passage, ʿAbd al-Wāḥid ibn Ismāʿīl al-Rūyānī (d. 502/1025), comments succinctly: "That is good, but it is in contradiction to the doctrine of the school" (*wa-hādhā ḥasan, wa-lakinnahu khilāf al-madhhab*).[125] Indeed, al-Qaffāl's remarks represent a sharp departure from the teachings attributed to al-Shāfiʿī. What is at stake is no longer the authority of the husband to detain his wife at home, but the inadvisability of women's venturing out (even for prayer) for reasons of public order.

A tension between pious disapproval of women's presence in mosques and fidelity to school doctrine is evident in the work of al-Rūyānī's contemporary, the great jurist and ṣūfī Abū Ḥāmid al-Ghazālī (d. 505/1111). In his didactic work *Iḥyāʾ ʿulūm al-dīn*, which provides a comprehensive guide to Muslim piety extending far beyond the conventional parameters of a legal compilation, al-Ghazālī touches on the subject of women's mosque attendance in the context of a discussion of the various forms of corruption occurring in mosques. After lamenting the conduct of handsome young preachers who behave flirtatiously as they preach to mixed congregations, he advocates that a barrier be erected between men and women at preaching sessions to prevent them from seeing each other. (Interestingly, al-Ghazālī's Persian work *Kīmyā-ye saʿādat*, which largely represents a popularization of the teachings of the *Iḥyāʾ*, specifies that *young* men and *young* women should not sit in the mosque to hear preaching without a barrier between them.[126]) He continues,

> It is necessary to forbid women from attending mosques for prayers and sessions of pious invocation (*majālis al-dhikr*) if it is feared that they will be a cause of temptation (*fitna*). ʿĀʾisha forbade them; someone said to her that the Messenger of God did not forbid them from congregational prayers, and she said, "If the Messenger of God knew what they had innovated after his death, he would have forbidden them."[127]

In another passage of the same work, al-Ghazālī states that "the Prophet permitted women to attend the mosque, [but] what is correct now is to forbid [them], except for old women (*al-ʿajāʾiz*)." He then cites (and interpretively defuses) an anecdote that might seem to impugn the legal validity of ʿĀʾisha's statement. In it, the Prophet's Companion Ibn ʿUmar quotes the Prophet's statement that one should not forbid the maidservants of God from going to the mosques of God. One of his sons retorts, "Nay, by God, we will forbid them!" At this, Ibn ʿUmar becomes angry and strikes his son, exclaiming "You hear me say, 'The Messenger of God said: Do not forbid,' and you say, 'Nay, we will!'?"[128] Al-Ghazālī explains that Ibn ʿUmar's son said what he did because he was aware of the changed nature of the times; Ibn ʿUmar became angry because of the impertinent way in which he expressed his reservation, as an unqualified contradiction of the Prophet's injunction, rather than because of the content of his son's statement.

Although he does invoke the classical distinction between older and younger women, al-Ghazālī's comments in the first passage seem to imply that women in general have become a cause of temptation and should be excluded from mosques. Certainly he has been understood by some later Muslims as advocating general exclusion of women from mosques. However, his advocacy of barriers to separate the sexes at preaching sessions seems to reflect his recognition not simply that women do attend mosques, but also that they will continue to do so and must be accommodated—even if they are sufficiently young or attractive that they would prove alluring to the male gaze. In his strictly legal works, in contrast, al-Ghazālī does not suggest it is undesirable for women in general to attend mosques, but repeatedly emphasizes that it is legally neutral for shabbily dressed and unperfumed older women to do so[129]—which may be regarded as a somewhat negatively inflected reiteration of classical Shāfiʿī doctrine. If al-Ghazālī's remarks in the *Iḥyāʾ* are, in fact, intended as a broad condemnation of women's mosque attendance, the contrast with his legal works suggests that they are intended more as a moral exhortation than as a statement of the law.

Beginning in the seventh/thirteenth century, in tandem with the continued reiteration of the school's received *madhhab* doctrine, new elements entered the Shāfiʿī discussion on women's mosque attendance through the work of the great ḥadīth scholars of the school. Just as al-Ghazālī expressed distinctive ideas in his capacity as a spiritual counselor, while adhering to well-established school positions in his capacity as an expositor of legal doctrine, such authors might cleave to *madhhab* doctrine in their legal works, while exploring fresh perspectives in their exploration of ḥadīth. The earliest major contributor to this trend was the Damascene scholar Abū Zakarīyā al-Nawawī (d. 676/1277). In his legal compendia, he perpetuated standard school doctrine.[130] Most influential for later members of the school, however, are al-Nawawī's remarks on the ḥadīth "Do not prevent the maidservants of God from [going to] the mosques of God" in his commentary on the *Ṣaḥīḥ* of Muslim. He writes,

> The clear meaning of this and the other similar ḥadīth texts on the subject is that [a woman] should not be prevented from [going to] the mosque, but on conditions mentioned by the scholars that have been drawn from [other] ḥadīths. They are that she not be perfumed or adorned, nor be wearing ankle bracelets whose sound is audible, nor fancy clothes; that she not mix with men; that she not be a young woman (*shābba*) or the like, such that she would cause temptation; and that there not be anything along the way from which corruption or the like is to be feared. This prohibition on preventing them from going out is interpreted as [indicating] undesirability (*karāhat al-tanzīh*)[131] if the woman has a husband or master [presumably, if she is a slave] and the conditions mentioned are met. If she has neither a husband nor a master, it is impermissible to forbid her if the conditions are met.[132]

These comments are not necessarily in conflict with the doctrine of the school. However, the list of conditions as a whole is not derived from the Shāfiʿī legal tradition; it is similar to the list of conditions established by the Mālikī authority al-Qāḍī ʿIyāḍ a century and a half earlier (with the notable exception of the requirement that the woman go out only at night, which al-Nawawī omits). Rather than being distinctively Mālikī or Shāfiʿī, this list of conditions for a woman's proper attendance at the mosque appears to represent an approach to the problem typical of the *muḥaddithūn*. It is not coincidental that in this context (like al-Qāḍī ʿIyāḍ in the same context) al-Nawawī refers simply to "scholars" rather than to "the members of our school."

In some ways, al-Nawawī's list of conditions for women's mosque attendance could be regarded as more restrictive than the mainstream doctrine of the Shāfiʿī school. If each item on the list is regarded as a necessary condition for allowing the woman's attendance at the mosque, then it represents a more exacting standard for women's presentation and behavior than a simple endorsement of attendance by older and less attractive women. However, by shifting the focus away from the woman's age and personal appearance to standards of dress and comportment, al-Nawawī's list of requirements also suggests a new focus on women's good behavior rather than their physical characteristics. The first five conditions are all functions of the woman's self-presentation rather than her inherent qualities; a woman who pursued modesty as an expression of piety could easily fulfill them. Although the age terminology used by different scholars is both vague and elastic, it is also notable that, rather than requiring that the woman be old, al-Nawawī here simply excludes the young. If we assume that the *shābba* is genuinely youthful (and perhaps unmarried), in this passage al-Nawawī opens the mosque door to the modest matron.

Even though al-Nawawī confirms the long-standing Shāfiʿī interpretation that the ḥadīth "Do not prevent the maidservants of God . . ." does not represent a binding legal prohibition, he also makes the sovereign will of the husband or master subject to the conditions enumerated. Apparently, he is obligated to forbid her if these conditions are not fulfilled. If they are fulfilled, however, the woman's right to visit the mosque can be preempted only by a man with a personal right to control her mobility; if she is not individually a threat to public propriety, no one else can bar her access to the mosque.

This not the only passage where al-Nawawī implies the ability of Muslim women to preserve propriety in situations of public worship. In his commentary on the legal compendium of Abū Isḥāq al-Shīrāzī, al-Nawawī critiques the latter's statement that women are exempted from attending Friday prayers both on the basis of a ḥadīth and on the grounds that a woman who did so "would mix (*takhtaliṭ*) with the men; and that is not permissible." Al-Nawawī rejoins with some asperity, "It is not as he said, because her attendance of Friday prayers does not necessitate mixing [with men (*al-ikhtilāṭ*)]; rather, she will be behind them." He observes that ḥadīth texts overwhelmingly demonstrate that women prayed behind the men in the

Prophet's mosque during his lifetime and concludes that in any case "it is not forbidden (*ḥarām*) for women to mix with men if they do not do so alone (*khalwa*)."[133] Although al-Nawawī's remarks on this point are brief, his dismissal of al-Shīrāzī's statement is strikingly categorical. Furthermore, his (textually justified) assertion that it is merely private tête-á-têtes between unrelated men and women that are forbidden by the sunna, rather than all public mixing of men and women, is a sharp repudiation of the broad concerns about women's mobility and participation that had been expressed by many legal scholars for centuries before al-Nawawī.

Ibn Daqīq al-ʿĪd (d. 702/1302) presents a similar analysis in his *Iḥkām al-aḥkām*, a commentary on legally relevant ḥadīth. Like al-Nawawī, he was a jurist who also achieved distinction in the discipline of ḥadīth; he spent much of his career in Cairo. He was trained in both the Mālikī and the Shāfiʿī *madhhabs*, but was known for the independence of his legal thinking. He insisted on the primacy of ḥadīth in the derivation of legal norms and complained that *madhhab* loyalty led many scholars to conform their interpretation of ḥadīth to the doctrines of their schools rather than vice versa.[134]

The ḥadīth "Do not prevent the maidservants of God," Ibn Daqīq al-ʿĪd observes, is in itself a general statement applying to all women. However, the legal scholars (*al-fuqahāʾ*) have limited its application based on certain conditions and circumstances, including the requirement that the woman not be perfumed, which is stipulated by ḥadīth. Perfume was prohibited, he argues, because of its tendency to arouse sexual impulses. Anything else that creates the same effect is treated in the same way, including pretty clothes and visible jewelry.[135] The restrictions cited by Ibn Daqīq al-ʿĪd refer to the woman's self-presentation; the primary limiting factor on a woman's mosque attendance is her own behavior. Interestingly, he completely disregards any division among women on the basis of age. Commenting on another ḥadīth in which ʿĀʾisha recounts that women used to attend the dawn prayers in the mosque with the Prophet, he remarks that "it constitutes a proof for women's attending congregational prayers with men, and there is nothing in the ḥadīth to indicate that they were old or young," although "some [scholars] have disapproved of young women's going out."[136] The great Shāfiʿī traditionist Ibn Ḥajar al-ʿAsqalānī

(d. 807/1449) reproduces Ibn Daqīq al-ʿĪd's comment in a more expansive form (whether the elaboration originates with Ibn Ḥajar or with another recension of Ibn Daqīq al-ʿĪd's work is unclear):

> Many legal scholars, Mālikīs and others, have distinguished between the young woman and others; this is problematic (*wa-fīhi naẓar*), unless there is fear [of misbehavior] on her own part (*min jihatihā*), because if she is free from the things that have been mentioned [i.e., perfume, fine clothes, visible jewelry, etc.] and she is covered, her security is assured, especially if that is during the night.[137]

Ibn Daqīq al-ʿĪd also deals with one of the other major issues relating to women's mosque attendance: whether it is, under the right circumstances, actually meritorious for women to take part in congregational worship in mosques. The classical doctrine of the Shāfiʿī school held that it was preferable for women, like men, to pray in congregation rather than alone. However, mainstream doctrine also held that the preference was more confirmed (*ākad*) for men that for women.[138] Arguably this meant that women's congregational prayer was less meritorious than men's, although still more meritorious than individual prayer.[139] Simultaneously, Shāfiʿīs affirmed that it was more meritorious for a woman to pray at home; some ḥadīth texts widely cited by legal scholars affirmed the superiority of women's worship at home, preferably in a secluded spot. Unsurprisingly, the combination of these two positions resulted in the classical doctrine that it is best for women to pray at home in a group of women.[140]

However, a number of questions regarding the relative religious merit of various forms of prayer remained to be answered. What if praying at home meant praying alone, or at least in a much smaller group than that available in the mosque? (Shāfiʿī scholars tended to affirm that—at least for men—the larger the congregation, the greater the merit accruing to the worshipper.) If women's prayer within the home was superior to their prayer in mosques, did this mean that no merit accrued to the woman from mosque attendance, or simply that prayer at home yielded even greater merit? Did women enjoy the other forms of merit accruing to worshippers from mosque attendance, such as the reward for walking to the mosque? If so, would this ever outbalance the merits of their praying at home? Ibn Daqīq al-ʿĪd addresses the question of merit briefly, but powerfully. "As for the attribute of maleness (*waṣf al-rujūlīya*), when it is permissible for a woman to go out to the mosque she should be equal to a man [in terms of merit], because the attribute of maleness is of no legal significance with regard to the rewards of actions."[141]

Ibn Daqīq al-ʿĪd's comments on women's mosque access were highly influential among later Shafiʿī ḥadīth specialists, who often reproduced them extensively. However, these later scholars were often reluctant to accept the full implications of his arguments, which suggested that women of all ages were permitted to attend mosques if they adhered to proper standards of comportment and that they earned an equal reward from God when they did so. One scholar who drew on his comments was ʿAlī ibn Ibrāhīm ibn al-ʿAṭṭār (d. 724/1324), a Damascene scholar best known as the most distinguished disciple of al-Nawawī and the transmitter of his works. On the issue of merit, Ibn al-ʿAṭṭār appears more ambivalent than Ibn Daqīq al-ʿĪd. He reproduces the latter's comment on merit and goes so far as to state that a woman's prayer at home is more meritorious *only* if she is forbidden to go to the mosque for other reasons.[142] However, elsewhere he states that it is unconditionally superior for a woman to pray at home.[143] These two statements may be reconciled by the fact that he considered mosque-going forbidden for all—or almost all—women of his own time. Commenting on a ḥadīth referencing women's mosque attendance during the Prophet's lifetime, he states:

> What is appropriate in these times is that [women] be forbidden altogether (*al-manʿ muṭlaqan*), unless they are women who are knowledgeable and act according to their knowledge (*illā an yakunna ʿālimāt ʿāmilāt*), who are not tempted and do not tempt others by their appearance, condition, acts, or speech; and God knows best.[144]

Like Ibn Daqīq al-ʿĪd, Ibn al-ʿAṭṭār emphasizes piety and good comportment as the primary criteria for women's mosque access. By deemphasizing a woman's age in favor of attention to her dress and conduct,[145] he perpetuates the tradition specific to the discipline of ḥadīth. However, Ibn al-ʿAṭṭār goes even further than his predecessors in emphasizing that the woman who should be allowed access to the mosque is the one who is knowledgeable and religiously observant. To the prevalent categories of women (the old or young woman, the desirable or undesirable woman), he adds another important class: the learned and pious woman.[146] Nevertheless, for him such a woman represents an exception to a new general rule that latter-day women should be discouraged from going to the mosque at all.

The line of Shāfiʿī *muḥaddiths* who dealt distinctively with the issue of women's mosque attendance culminates with the towering figure of Ibn Ḥajar al-ʿAsqalānī, who reproduces many of Ibn Daqīq al-ʿĪd's comments in his commentary on the *Ṣaḥīḥ* of Bukhārī. Unlike the latter, however, he emphasizes the idea (which he supports with multiple ḥadīth texts) that it is more meritorious for a woman to pray at home. He continues,

> The reason that it is preferable for her to pray out of sight is that there safety from temptation (*fitna*) is ensured. That becomes even more certain after the emergence of women's innovations of public display and adornment (*al-tabarruj wa'l-zīna*). It is for this reason that ʿĀʾisha said what she did. Some of [the legal scholars] have depended on ʿĀʾisha's statement to argue that women should be prevented [from attending mosques] altogether. This is problematic, because [her statement] does not entail a change in the legal ruling (*al-ḥukm*), because she made it dependent on a condition contrary to fact based on an inference that she drew; thus she said, "If the Prophet had seen, he would have forbidden." It can be argued against this that he did not see and did not forbid, so the legal ruling remained; thus, ʿĀʾisha [herself] did not explicitly state that it was forbidden, even if her statement would lead one to believe that she was of the opinion that it should be forbidden. Furthermore, God Most High knew what [women] would innovate, and He did not reveal to His Prophet that he should forbid them. If the things they have innovated made it necessary to prevent them from going to mosques, *a fortiori* they should be prevented from going to other places, such as markets. Furthermore, the innovation occurred on the part of only some women, not of all of them; if it were obligatory to prevent them, it should apply [only] to [the women] who innovated. The most appropriate thing (*al-awlā*) is to see what things threaten corruption and avoid

> them, since [the Prophet] (peace be upon him!) alluded to that by prohibiting perfume and adornment.[147]

Ibn Ḥajar's arguments on this point clearly originate with Ibn Ḥazm. Of the latter's six arguments against the contention that the ʿĀʾisha report establishes a prohibition of women's mosque attendance, Ibn Ḥajar omits only the one asserting that by committing adultery the women of the Prophet's generation reached a degree of sinful innovation that could not be exceeded by later women.[148] It is not difficult to guess why this point is omitted; the insinuation that the female Companions as a group were no more virtuous than subsequent generations of Muslim women was potentially incendiary in a mainstream Sunni context, where the moral probity of the Companions was a matter of creedal orthodoxy.

Ibn Ḥajar thus reproduces Ibn Ḥazm's arguments to a greater extent than would have been possible for a more conventional thinker, although he apparently did not derive them directly from Ibn Ḥazm; they appear to have been assimilated into the tradition of ḥadīth commentary before his time.[149] Although he did not originate these points or even cite them for the first time, his restatement of them led to their wide dissemination among scholars of ḥadīth and *fiqh*. His choice of these particular arguments from the broad repertoire then available suggests that they spoke to Ibn Ḥajar's own values and perceptions. In presenting them, he seems to adopt a more optimistic attitude than Ibn al-ʿAṭṭār toward the likelihood or prevalence of good behavior by women; whereas Ibn al-ʿAṭṭār's learned and religiously observant woman appears to be an exception among the majority who might best be excluded from mosques, Ibn Ḥajar seems to picture the "innovators" as individual wrongdoers. Common to both of them, and to the other ḥadīth specialists on whose work they drew, is the assumption that strictures on mosque attendance do not apply to women in general or to young women in particular; instead, they apply to unacceptable forms of behavior.

A striking element of this list of arguments is the assertion that the mosque is the most desirable destination for a woman's excursion from the home. Rather than representing a particularly problematic space for women, the mosque is posited as preferable to other public spaces (and perhaps ones more commonly frequented by women). As we have seen, this was a sentiment also expressed by the Mālikī Qāḍī ʿIyāḍ. A similar sentiment is expressed by Ibn Daqīq al-ʿĪd, who critically scrutinizes the widespread argument that the ḥadīth forbidding men to deny their wives the right to go to the mosque implied that his permission was required for her to leave the house for any reason. This line of reasoning, while not completely illogical, had allowed scholars to derive a broad and onerous limit on women's mobility from a prophetic statement that, on its face, was completely affirmative about one instance of women's leaving the home. Ibn Daqīq al-ʿĪd offers another line of approach:

> It would be possible to argue on this point that men's forbidding women from going out is well-known and customary, and they have been confirmed in it (*qurrirū ʿalayhi*).[150] The ruling [that women should not be forbidden] was associated [specifically] with mosques in order to make clear the instance in which [women's going out] was licit, and to except it from the ongoing, well-known prohibition. Thus, all other cases [of women's going out] remain forbidden.[151]

In Ibn Daqīq al-ʿĪd's view, the Prophet's statement that men should not bar women from mosques serves not to establish that a man allows his wife to go out at his own discretion (a rule that he considers to be an immemorial custom tacitly endorsed by the Prophet), but to emphasize that the mosque is a special destination specifically exempted from this general rule. He goes on to suggest that the wording of the Prophet's statement "Do not prevent the maidservants of God from [going to] the mosques of God" indicates a relationship of logical association (*munāsaba*) between the permission for women to go out and its rationale.[152] The women are allowed to go out because (and only because) they are going to act as "maidservants of God" by praying in the mosque. Women's mosque-going again appears as a privileged exception to the overall rule restricting women's departures from the marital home, an instance whose uniquely pious character is reflected in their description as "maidservants of God."

Another Shāfiʿī deeply involved in the discipline of ḥadīth also expresses, with a conviction that is only underlined by the brisk and uncontroversial tone of the comment, the idea that mosques are among the legitimate destinations of women's (ideally limited) public mobility. Commenting on verse 33:33 of the Qur'an, which was widely understood to counsel the Prophet's wives to "remain within your homes," the Damascene Ibn Kathīr (d. 774/1373) elucidates: "That is, keep to your homes, and do not go out without need; among the religiously legitimate needs (*al-ḥawāʾij al-sharʿīya*) is praying in the mosque, subject to [the applicable] conditions." He goes on to elaborate on the preferability of women's private worship within the most secluded parts of their houses, a theme that he also emphasizes in his commentary on verse 24:36.[153] However, in that passage he also goes on to state, "Despite this, [a woman] is permitted to attend men's congregational prayers as long as she does not harm any of the men through the manifestation of adornments or pleasant scents."[154] Like other ḥadīth-oriented Shāfiʿīs of his time, he accepts women's presence in mosques provided that they observe the appropriate conditions.

Why did Shāfiʿī scholars with a primary interest in ḥadīth (or who, like al-Nawawī, combined equal distinction in law and tradition) promote such distinctive—and comparatively positive—attitudes toward women's mosque attendance? Specifically, why did they promote attention to proper standards of dress and behavior, rather than age cohort or simply gender itself, as the proper criterion for women's access to mosques? Why did they, unlike many other scholars, casually, but confidently represent the mosque as a preferred destination for women's public mobility? The most obvious argument would be that the contrasting disciplinary commitments of ḥadīth scholars and jurists led them to different conclusions. In this case, the comparatively (and increasingly) restrictive doctrines of the legal schools contrasted with the permissiveness of the most authoritative ḥadīth text on the subject. It might be expected that ḥadīth specialists—who presumably started out by scrutinizing the content and authenticity of ḥadīth reports, rather than by defending prior commitments to school doctrines—might produce different results simply due to the different nature of their methodology.

To some extent, this may be the case. Although jurists often finessed the apparent problems in reconciling school doctrines with their alleged textual foundations, ḥadīth scholars were professionally inclined to take the textual sources very seriously indeed. Thus, for instance, it could not escape them that the ʿĀ'isha report involved (grammatically as well as conceptually) a condition contrary to fact. This willingness to return to the sources and engage in foundational reflections on their meaning and interrelation brought a Shāfiʿī ḥadīth scholar like Ibn Ḥajar astonishingly close to a Ẓāhirī literalist like Ibn Ḥazm. Similarly, the lack (or weak authentication) of ḥadīth documenting distinctions among different age cohorts could not elude the attention of the *muḥaddithūn*.

However, it is not immediately apparent that the opinions of ḥadīth scholars were directly and unambiguously dictated by the clear meanings of ḥadīth texts any more than were those of the legal scholars. For instance, they usually insisted that women should not attend mosques in nice clothing—based on a process of inference similar to juristic analogy (*qiyās*) rather than any explicit ḥadīth texts to this effect.[155] I am not arguing that either jurists or *muḥaddithūn* necessarily violated the letter or spirit of the Prophet's reported statements, about which both of them made conscientious inferences on the basis of voluminous knowledge. Rather, it seems that both groups made plausible (if often debatable) interpretations that strove to harmonize a rich variety of ḥadīth texts with each other and with their own convictions about the values and objectives of the law.[156]

Because both groups followed methodologies that might yield a wide variety of concrete conclusions even when scrupulously applied to their textual sources, the differences between the doctrines of legal specialists and those of ḥadīth scholars associated with the Shāfiʿī school might best be sought in the sociological rather than the methodological differences between the two groups. Although legal thought theoretically affirmed women's ability to study law and to act as muftīs, and some women were recognized for their legal scholarship, overall the legal profession was overwhelmingly dominated by men (and its institutionalized professional positions were limited to males).[157] In contrast, prominent female ḥadīth scholars taught large numbers of students (sometimes, as we shall see, in mosques and other public venues). In thirteenth- to fifteenth-century CE Damascus and Cairo, where many of the ḥadīth scholars we have discussed lived, studied, and taught, the importance of female ḥadīth scholars was a notable feature of intellectual life.[158] Gloomy as Ibn al-ʿAṭṭār may have been about the general behavior of women, the image of the "learned woman who acts according to her knowledge" was one that ḥadīth scholars of his period knew and cherished on the basis of their own life experience.

The attitudes toward women's mosque attendance promoted by Shāfiʿī ḥadīth scholars did not eclipse the standard doctrines of the school, which continued to appear in Shāfiʿī legal compilations. A straightforward distinction between young and old women (sometimes modulated with references to sexual desirability) was restated by scholars including al-Nawawī himself in his legal compendium *al-Majmūʿ*,[159] Zayn al-Dīn al-ʿIrāqī (d. 806/1403–4),[160] Ibn al-ʿImād al-Aqfahsī (d. 808/1405),[161] Jalāl al-Dīn al-Maḥallī (d. 864/459),[162] and Jalāl al-Dīn al-Suyūṭī (d. 911/1505).[163]

Indeed, from the seventh century of the Islamic calendar (the thirteenth century CE), three different tendencies coexisted and intertwined in Shāfiʿī thought. The first, which represented the school's classical legal doctrine and remained remarkably consistent over time (although it reflected only some aspects of the thinking attributed to the school's eponymous founder), was that mosque attendance was objectionable for young women and permissible for the old. Authors strongly influenced by the discipline of ḥadīth advanced, often parallel to this doctrine, a view in which the traditional emphasis on age gave way to a new focus on the individual woman's dress and comportment. Meanwhile, yet another tendency emerged, emphasizing that due to the deterioration of public morals after the death of the Prophet and in later generations, women's mosque attendance should be discouraged altogether. As we have seen, al-Qaffāl advanced this view as early as the fourth/tenth century. The idea that women should be excluded from mosques due to the decadence of the times was expressed by al-Ghazālī in a paraenetic mode, rather than a strictly legal one, at the turn of the sixth century AH. A similar sentiment (expressed in the context of a discussion of the two festival prayers) was echoed by al-Ṣaydalānī (d. 604/1207), who declared that "it is objectionable for [women] to go out to the gathering place of the Muslims (*majmaʿ al-muslimīn*), because people have changed,"[164] and Ibn al-ʿAṭṭār invoked it in passing in the first half of the eighth/fourteenth century.

The persistence of this line of thought is suggested by the comments of Ibn al-Naẓẓār (sometimes also known as Ibn al-ʿAṭṭār), an otherwise obscure Shāfiʿī scholar[165] who composed a work on the legal rules relating to women in 710/1310.[166] After citing a ḥadīth establishing that it is superior for a woman to pray in a secluded spot within her home, he declares, "It is objectionable for a woman in these times to go forth to mosques and pious gatherings (*majāmiʿ al-khayr*) because of the violations of the divine law and the practice of the Prophet (*al-sharʿ wa'l-sunna)* that have occurred in them." He then cites the ʿĀʾisha report.[167] In another passage, he asserts:

> As for going out to mosques in the darkness before dawn (*al-ghalas*), when there is no danger of harm or temptation (*fitna*), it was permitted in the time of the Prophet and in the era of his Companions; then it was forbidden because of the things women had innovated, such as people being tempted by them, perfume, public display of their charms (*tabarruj*), their tempting men, and other things.[168]

Nevertheless, in an earlier passage Ibn al-Naẓẓār sets out the established school doctrine:

> It is better for a woman to pray in her home than in the congregational mosque, regardless of whether she is married or young [and unmarried]; as for the old woman from whose attendance of congregational prayers no harm ensues, there is no harm in it, and it is better for her to pray in the back rows than in the front rows.[169]

This straightforward affirmation of time-honored school teaching suggests that Ibn al-Naẓẓār's sweeping disapproval of women's public worship is advanced more as an ideal exhortation than as a statement of law.

The most influential opponent of women's public prayer in the later Shāfiʿī tradition is the Damascene Taqī al-Dīn al-Ḥiṣnī (d. 829/1426). In the context of his discussion of the two festival prayers, he writes:

> As for our time, [women] go out for the sake of displaying their charms and do not cast down their glances, and neither do men cast down their

> glances; the harms of their [i.e., women's] going out are confirmed. It has been reliably transmitted from ʿĀʾisha (may God be satisfied with her!) that she said, "If the Messenger of God (peace be upon him!) had seen what women have innovated, he would have forbidden them to go to mosques, just as the women of the Children of Israel were forbidden." This is the legal opinion (*fatwā*) of the Mother of the Believers in the best of generations, so what about this corrupt time of ours? A number of people other than ʿĀʾisha expressed the opinion that women should be forbidden to go to mosques, including ʿUrwa [ibn al-Zubayr] (may God be satisfied with him), al-Qāsim, Yaḥyā al-Anṣārī, Mālik, and Abū Ḥanīfa one time (another time he permitted it); similarly, Abū Yūsuf forbade it. This is in that time; as for this time of ours, no Muslim hesitates to forbid them but an ignoramus with little insight into the secrets of the sharīʿa, who clings to the apparent meaning of a proof text which has been interpreted according to its apparent meaning without understanding its [true] meaning, while neglecting to understand ʿĀʾisha and those who shared her opinion, and while neglecting the Qur'anic verses indicating that it is forbidden [for women] to display physical charms and that it is obligatory to cast down one's glances. The correct thing is to hold that it is definitely forbidden and to give legal opinions accordingly (*wa'l-fatwā bihi*), and God knows best.[170]

Al-Ḥiṣnī states earlier in this passage simply that young or attractive women should not attend festival prayers, a position that—although it conflicts with the explicit content of a prophetic ḥadīth—falls within the mainstream of Shāfiʿī opinion. The remainder of the passage, however, appears to promote the contention that women should be forbidden from attending mosques altogether. As we shall see, this was the spirit in which it was interpreted by later Shāfiʿī authors who cited the passage. To support this position, al-Ḥiṣnī invokes the authority of a number of early Muslim figures, some (such as Mālik) with only dubious justification. It is striking that he does not cite a single authority of the Shāfiʿī school; al-Shāfiʿī himself is tellingly (and necessarily) absent from the list, although al-Ḥiṣnī manages to include the eponymous founders of two other schools. In a strikingly non-*madhhab*-based manner, al-Ḥiṣnī appeals directly to the earliest generations of Muslims and to his own independent reasoning about the underlying rationales of prophetic statements. Unlike textual literalists, however, he is not committed to direct adherence to the letter of ḥadīth or the behavioral example of the Prophet's generation (whose mores and life situation he considers to be fundamentally different from those of his contemporaries). At the end of the passage, he inveighs against those who would insist on adhering to the apparent meaning of relevant ḥadīth texts; here he is probably referring obliquely to the ḥadīth "Do not forbid the maidservants of God from [going to] the mosques of God," which he does not deign to cite explicitly.

Unlike earlier authors (such as al-Ghazālī and Ibn al-Naẓẓār) who had paraenetically urged that women be discouraged from mosque attendance, while also perpetuating traditional school doctrine on the subject, al-Ḥiṣnī appears to be advocating actual legal change. The asperity of his condemnation of those who would cling to the apparent meaning of ḥadīth suggests that he may have encountered some staunch opposition to his innovative stance. However, his opinions also proved influential among later Shāfiʿīs. The prominent scholar ʿAlī ibn ʿAṭīya al-Hītī, known as al-Shaykh ʿAlwān (d. 936/1530), cites al-Ḥiṣnī's arguments at length and with emphatic approval.[171]

Another Damascene Shāfiʿī scholar, al-Ḥiṣnī's younger contemporary Muḥammad ibn ʿAbd Allāh al-Balāṭunusī (d. 863/1459), argues with similar fervor that women should be forbidden from attending mosques. Rather than invoking the changing mores of the times, he constructs a simple (if novel) inference from the textual evidence. Citing ḥadīth texts, he first establishes that it is more meritorious for a woman to pray in her home than in the Prophet's mosque, even if a prayer in the Prophet's mosque is worth a thousand ordinary prayers. "If [praying home] is more meritorious," he concludes, "then what motivates her to leave her home [to pray in a mosque] is either hypocrisy and the desire for good reputation—which is forbidden (*ḥarām*)—or some other vain objective, such as recreation or the like, which negates the sincerity of the action [of going to the mosque]. It is not permissible for anyone to issue a legal opinion (*yuftī*) or give permission for [someone else] to abandon sincerity."[172]

Ibn Ḥajar al-Haytamī (d. 974/1567) cites (without attribution) a much longer passage denouncing women's frequentation of mosques that appears to come from a polemic against religious innovations. Based on its references to the author's school authorities and teachers, its author was apparently a Syrian Shāfiʿī writing in the late ninth or early tenth century AH. (Conceivably it could have originated with al-Balāṭunusī himself, who composed such a work.[173]) The author begins by denouncing the practice of women's sleeping in the mosque during Ramadan, which he believes is manifestly forbidden (*ḥarām*) and should be unacceptable to any self-respecting Muslim husband. After citing several proof-texts for the sinfulness of women's jostling men in public places, he addresses an imaginary interlocutor:

> If you say, "Do you hold that women should be forbidden from going out to mosques and religious lessons (*al-mawāʿīd*) and from visiting graves except for the grave of the Prophet?" I say, "How could I not hold that, when it has become the object of consensus (*ṣāra muttafaqan ʿalayh*) because of the absence of the condition for the permissibility of their going out in [the Prophet's] time, which is piety and chastity?!"

The anonymous authority then cites the opinions of al-Ḥiṣnī and of ʿAlāʾ al-Dīn al-Bukhārī (d. 870/465; a Ḥanafī opponent of women's mosque attendance whose opinions will be discussed later) and declares, "What the two of them mentioned is sufficient for anyone who resists his vain whims!"

He does anticipate an objection to his argument: "Some people have fancied that holding [women's mosque attendance] to be forbidden and claiming consensus that it should be forbidden is in contradiction to the doctrine of the school." However, this is merely a misunderstanding. The valid doctrine in these times is that women should be forbidden to go to mosques, "and no one suspends judgment on that except a simpleton who pursues his vain whims, because legal rulings change with the changing of the people of the times; this is true according to the teachings of the ancient and recent scholars."[174] The wording of the standard manuals of the Shāfiʿī school, which tend to classify women's mosque attendance at most as *makrūh*, must be read either in light of the idea that *makrūh* actually means *ḥarām* or in light of an unspoken reservation that women's attendance becomes *ḥarām* when there is the slightest fear of *fitna*.[175]

In support of his position, he draws on selective samples of the opinions of classical and postclassical scholars who emphasized that it was undesirable for women to go out to mosques in the changed conditions of decadent times. Somewhat paradoxically, he invokes the established authority of these figures to justify a departure from the apparent meaning of the standard texts of the *madhhab*:

> These are the opinions of the scholars, including the independent jurisprudents *(al-mujtahidīn)*, the God-fearing authorities, and the virtuous jurists who are skilled in their art; it is obligatory to follow their opinions, because they are the banner of the community and what they choose for us is better than what we choose for ourselves; whoever opposes them follows his own vain desires.[176]

The passages cited above are preserved in a fatwa by Ibn Ḥajar al-Haytamī (d. 973/1566), probably the lengthiest and most passionate Shāfiʿī legal opinion on women's mosque attendance. Al-Haytamī was an Egyptian who resettled in Mecca; the fatwa appears to have been generated during a heated conflict over restrictions on women's access to the Great Mosque of Mecca in 536/1530, which will be discussed in detail in chapter 3 of this book. In addition to (selectively) surveying the opinions of other authorities, both named and unnamed, al-Haytamī offers original arguments of his own. Although the details of this lengthy opinion will be treated in the context of that controversy, al-Haytamī's major points—which suggest evolving and distinctive attitudes both toward women's mosque attendance and toward the authority of the Shāfiʿī *madhhab*—demand discussion within this survey of the opinions of the school.

The essence of al-Haytamī's lengthy discussion is that it is legally obligatory for the authorities to interdict women's mosque attendance when there is any fear of *fitna*. There is no absolute prohibition on women's mosque attendance; there is no reason to forbid, for instance, an elderly, decrepit, and shabbily dressed woman from attending the mosque.[177] Nevertheless, the overall force of his argument seems to suggest that women as a class now habitually attend mosques unacceptably attired and that it is accordingly legitimate to bar them all. As we shall see in a later section of this study, the fatwa was, in fact, elicited by an initiative to exclude women from the mosque altogether, if only at certain times of the day; al-Haytamī's general intention was clearly to endorse this intervention.

Al-Haytamī cites a number of his most prominent Shāfiʿī predecessors, including al-Ghazālī, al-Nawawī, and Ibn Ḥajar al-ʿAsqalānī. In the case of the latter two authorities, though overtly expressing great deference, he also subtly challenges the permissive implications of their comments. Discussing al-Nawawī's famous passage on the conditions under which a woman may be allowed to attend the mosque, he sharply changes its valence by emphasizing the difficulty of fulfilling all of them and the necessity of detaining the woman at home if she fails to fulfill a single one. Al-Haytamī emphasizes that the conditions include the absence of any fear of harm along the way and the woman's ability to avoid any kind of mixing with men (two factors beyond the control of even the most pious and modest individual woman). He then argues that in case of nonfulfillment of one or more conditions, the interdiction of women's mosque-going is not merely permissible, but obligatory.[178] Al-Haytamī leaves the overall impression that, as ostentatious clothing and perfume (as well as the hazard of temptation along the way) are ubiquitous among the women of his day, women as a group should, in fact, be turned away from mosques by the authorities in any situation where there is a conceivable threat to public order. Although technically compatible with al-Nawawī's statements, this argument notably shifts the duty of enforcement from the male kin of individual women to the public authorities. The fatwa is striking in its dependence on postclassical authorities and on works from genres other than standard *fiqh* manuals. It is in part by focusing on material from genres with a more expansive set of hortatory and normative agendas (rather than on standard references for Shāfiʿī doctrine) that he is able to compose a powerful legal statement in favor of the institutionalized limitation of women's mosque access, while expressing fervent (if somewhat misleading) allegiance to the precedents of his school.

In the context of a legal manual, al-Haytamī adheres more closely to the traditional doctrines of his *madhhab*, stating that "it is objectionable for a woman with a pretty dress, perfume, or adornment, even if she is old, and for a young woman even if she has a shabby dress, to attend [prayers] with a man in a mosque or elsewhere."[179] However, al-Haytamī's conviction that it was incumbent on the authorities of his day to regulate women's mosque access did find a place in his most influential legal manual—and through it in the later Shāfiʿī tradition. In his *Tuḥfat al-muḥtāj*, he remarks that it is repugnant for a woman to attend congregational prayers in the mosque if she is sexually desirable (even if unadorned) and if she is adorned or perfumed (even if she is undesirable); in such a case, "the ruler or his representative is then entitled to prevent her [from attending]."[180] This statement was cited and commented on by his Shāfiʿī successors; ʿAlī al-Shabrāmallisī comments that, "if it were stated that it is obligatory [for the ruler to prevent her] if he considers it to be in the [public] welfare, this would not be implausible, since he is obligated to preserve public welfare (*riʿāyat al-maṣāliḥ al-ʿāmma*)."[181] Thus, al-Haytamī's experiences with the women of Mecca may have introduced a new emphasis on the regulatory role of the political authorities into the Shāfiʿī discussion of women's mosque attendance.[182]

Despite the strong assertions of al-Haytamī and his anonymous source of current consensus on the impermissibility of women's mosque attendance due to the deterioration of public morals, Shāfiʿī legal sources of the tenth/sixteenth century and later continued to reproduce the classical doctrine with very little change. One shift in tone, if not in substance, is that a new rationale was offered for women's exemption from public congregational prayer. As we have seen above, al-Rūyānī links the arguably lesser merit of women's congregational prayer to the Qur'anic statement, "And men have a degree above them" (verse 2:228). The same linkage was drawn by a number of later Shāfiʿī jurists, such as Ibn al-Mulaqqin (d. 804/1401), Jalāl al-Dīn al-Maḥallī (d. 864/1459), Zakarīyā al-Anṣārī (d. 926/1520), and Muḥammad al-Shirbīnī (d. 977/1570).[183] In contrast, Aḥmad al-Burullusī (known as ʿUmayra, d. 957/1550) adds that women are exempted "because of the difficulty and hardship involved in their gathering."[184] Shams al-Dīn al-Ramlī (d. 1004/1596) writes that the preference for congregational prayer is less firm with respect to women than to men, "out of fear of corruption in them, and because of the great difficulty it may pose for them, because [congregational prayer] is usually possible only by going out to mosques."[185] (In response to this point,

ʿAlī al-Shabrāmallisī [d. 1087/1676] remarks briskly that the clear sense of the legal rule is that women are less obligated to engage in congregational prayer even if they can do so easily and without hardship and even if they pose no threat of sexual temptation.[186]) Although it involved no shift in substantive doctrine, the idea that women were exempted from congregational prayer out of consideration for their own needs (rather than as an expression of gender hierarchy) reflected a sensitivity among some scholars that long preceded the apologetics of the modern period.

THE ḤANAFĪS

Abū Ḥanīfa's opinions on women's mosque attendance can be reconstructed only from scattered reports by disciples.[187] Abū Ḥanīfa's student Abū Yūsuf (d. 182/798) transmits from him the report that "the Prophet used to give women a special dispensation (*yurakhkhiṣ*) to go out to the dawn and nighttime prayers (*ṣalāt al-ghadā wa'l-ʿishāʾ al-ākhira*)."[188] It is significant that the wording here (which appears to be a paraphrase of the Prophet's position rather than a direct quotation) suggests a limited exception to a general disapproval of women's participation in public worship.[189] Indeed, a report transmitted by Abū Ḥanīfa's younger disciple Muḥammad ibn al-Ḥasan al-Shaybānī (d. 189/805) suggests that the master regarded the Prophet's permission as a temporary measure no longer valid in his own time. In the somewhat artificial dialogue format of his *Kitāb al-Aṣl*, he inquires of Abū Ḥanīfa:

> I said: Is it your opinion that women are obligated to go out for the [prayers of] the two festivals? He said: They used to be given a dispensation for that;[190] as for today, I consider it objectionable for them to do so. I said: Do you consider it objectionable for [women] to attend Friday and obligatory [i.e., the five daily] prayers in congregation? He said: Yes. I said: Do you give them a dispensation to go to any [prayers at all]? He said: I give a dispensation for a very old woman (*al-ʿajūz al-kabīra*) to attend the nighttime and dawn prayers and the two festival prayers; as for anything else, no.[191]

In these two reports, we see both of the main distinctions familiar from the early Mālikī texts: between daytime prayers and those held in full or partial darkness and between young and old women. It is the age distinction that is given most salience in Ḥanafī discussions, where it takes a more restrictive form than it does among the Mālikīs. The phrase *al-ʿajūz al-kabīra* ("the aged, elderly woman"), which redundantly emphasizes the woman's advanced years, suggests a contrast with the mature, but still vigorous *mutajālla* of the early Mālikīs. Indeed, in Abū Ḥanīfa's hometown of Kufa some authorities opposed any loosening of restrictions for elderly women at all. Abū Ḥanīfa's contemporary Sufyān al-Thawrī (d. 161/778) is reported to have declared that "there is no better place for a woman than her house, even if she is old."[192] Whereas Mālik and a number of other early scholars held that men could publicly greet mature women, even if unrelated, the Kufans are credited with the opinion that women should never exchange greetings with unrelated men.[193] By seeking to restrict their mosque-going to the dawn and nighttime prayers, Abū Ḥanīfa is supposed to have placed limitations even on elderly women, although his disciples Abū Yūsuf and al-Shaybānī are said to have held that the old could attend the mosque at any time of day.[194]

The statements attributed to Abū Ḥanīfa obliquely suggest that doctrine "today" may diverge from literal application of the precedents established by the Prophet. This argument was explicitly elaborated by Aḥmad ibn Muḥammad al-Ṭaḥāwī (d. 321/933), an expert in ḥadīth who sought to demonstrate the compatibility of Ḥanafī doctrine with the statements transmitted from the Prophet. In this case, however, he posits discontinuity with the prophetic precedent, writing of "the rules for women *after [the time of] the Messenger of God (peace be upon him!)* relating to going to mosques (*aḥkām al-nisāʾ baʿd rasūl allāh [ṣallāʾllāhu ʿalayhi wa-sallam] fī ityān al-masājid*)" (emphases mine). Citing ʿĀʾisha's statement that "[i]f the Messenger of God (peace be upon him!) had seen what women innovated after him, he would have forbidden them [to go to] mosques, just as the Israelite women were forbidden," he declares:

> ʿĀʾisha's statement on this subject . . . is what demonstrates that women were allowed latitude to go to mosques during the lifetime of the

> Messenger of God only because of a condition that they were in [at that time]; after [his death] they abandoned it for its opposite, so the latitude that was allowed to them to go there in the way that they did during the Messenger of God's lifetime was negated. If this was how they were in the lifetime of ʿĀʾisha, they were even further from that after her[195] death.[196]

Al-Ṭaḥāwī's overall argument in this passage is that, despite apparent prophetic precedents to the contrary, latter-day Muslim women may not hold pious retreats (*iʿtikāf*) in the mosque. It is unclear whether he favored the opinion that women should not visit mosques even to pray; perhaps significantly, elsewhere he cites a divergent report stating that Abū Ḥanīfa did not countenance women's going out for any prayers other than those of the two festivals.[197]

As was the case in other schools of law, early Ḥanafīs seem to have drawn deep distinctions between women of different age cohorts without making explicit the grounds for these distinctions. They differed on the concrete implications of the categorization, with Abū Ḥanīfa maintaining significant limitations on mosque attendance by old women and his two disciples exempting them from such restrictions altogether. Both the category distinction between old and young women and the different approaches of Abū Ḥanīfa and his students were provided with formal (if speculative) rationales by Abū Bakr al-Sarakhsī (d. ca. 490/1097). Much like Ibn Rushd in the Mālikī school, this fifth-/eleventh-century scholar uses the newly explicit concept of *fitna* as the central criterion structuring his interpretation. Al-Sarakhsī writes,

> Abū Yūsuf and Muḥammad (may God Most High have mercy upon them!) said: "It is permitted for old women to attend all prayers...because old women's going out involves no *fitna* and people rarely desire them; they used to go out to engage in warfare with the Messenger of God to tend to the sick, carry water, and cook." Abū Ḥanīfa (may God be satisfied with him!) said: "At the nighttime prayers, the old woman goes out covered up and the darkness of night protects her from men's glances, unlike the daytime prayers, and [unlike] Friday prayers, which are held in the city—because of the great crowds, she may be buffeted and jostled, and

that would cause *fitna*. Even if a young man would not desire an old woman, an old man like her would desire her; extreme lechery might drive even a young man to desire her and jostle her on purpose. As for festival prayers, they are held in the prayer-ground (*al-jabbāna*), so it is possible for her to withdraw to a place removed from the men so that she will not be jostled."[198]

Al-Sarakhsī's overall discussion reflects his implicit assumptions about the relevance of age to women's movements and activities. To justify women's exclusion from most public prayers, he paraphrases verse 33:33 of the Qur'an (in which the Prophet's wives are, according to one interpretation, commanded to "remain in your homes").[199] However, he applies this rule exclusively to young women, using the criterion of *fitna*—a refinement that has no basis in the text.[200] To justify greater latitude for public prayer by old women, he cites the fact that they played an auxiliary role in warfare in the time of the Prophet Muḥammad. Again, the idea that women performed nursing duties on the battlefield is documented in ḥadīth; the idea that the women who did so were elderly seems to be a later inference.[201]

Although al-Sarakhsī's post hoc rationalizations may or may not accurately reflect the considerations that informed the thought of early authorities like Abū Ḥanīfa and Abū Yūsuf—and his apparent "quotations" surely represent his inferences rather than their own words—he vividly displays the kinds of thinking that had become prevalent by his own time. In his eyes, the blanket acceptance of public prayer by old women attributed to Abū Yūsuf and Mūhammad al-Shaybānī reflects their conviction that elderly women exercise no sexual allure. Abū Ḥanīfa's restrictions on old women's public worship, in contrast, are seen to indicate a belief that even senior women are never safely desexualized. Unappealing as aged women may be, the wayward desires of lecherous old men and oversexed youths guarantee that no public mixing between the sexes is without its perils.

Thus, by the fifth century AH/eleventh century CE a systematic focus on the concept of *fitna* was combined with deep skepticism that a woman was sexually innocuous at any age. Later Ḥanafīs continued to support Abū Ḥanīfa's reported imposition of restrictions on the times when old women could attend public prayers by casting doubt on their asexual status. ʿAlāʾ al-Dīn al-Kāsānī (d. 587/1191) supports this position by noting that some individuals may be tempted by them "or they themselves may fall into temptation, because their desire for men persists even when they are old."[202] ʿAbd Allāh ibn Mahmūd al-Mawṣilī (d. 683/1284) notes disparagingly that "for everything that falls, there is someone to pick it up" (*li-kull sāqiṭa lāqiṭa*)—that is, there is no woman so decrepit but that some man will desire her.[203] Attitudes toward the mosque-going of younger women also hardened. Al-Kāsānī writes that the religious scholars "have reached consensus that there is no dispensation allowing young women to go out for Friday prayers, festival prayers, or any other prayer, because of God's statement 'Remain in your homes' [verse 33:33] . . . and because their going out is without doubt a cause of *fitna*; *fitna* is forbidden, and what leads to something forbidden is [itself] forbidden."[204] This view represents both an affirmation and an extension of al-Sarakhsī's emphasis on the concept of *fitna*; Behnam Sadeghi notes that "[a]l-Kāsānī is the first jurist to speak of prohibition rather than undesirability [of mosque attendance] for younger women."[205]

Among later Ḥanafīs, the opinion gradually prevailed that no women should attend any public prayers. Ṭāhir ibn Aḥmad al-Bukhārī (d. 542/1147), after outlining the difference of opinion between Abū Ḥanīfa and his two disciples on mosque attendance by elderly women, writes that "the preferred opinion in our time (*al-jawāb al-mukhtār fī zamāninā*)" is "that they should not go out [for congregational prayers]; [similarly], an old woman should not travel without a close male relative (*maḥram*), and should not be alone with a man, whether young or old; [however], she may shake hands with old men."[206] Al-Bukhārī's repudiation of mosque attendance even by elderly women, which is related to the conditions of "our time" without further specification, is placed within the context of a more general limitation of the social prerogatives of old women. His use of the term "preferred [opinion]" (*al-mukhtār*) implies that it was a preexisting doctrine that had already met with wide acceptance.[207] This terminology is echoed by ʿAbd Allāh al-Mawṣilī, who states that "the preferred opinion in our time is that none of that is permissible [i.e., women are never permitted to go to mosques], because of the corruption of the times and the open commission of obscene acts (*li-fasād al-zamān wa'l-taẓāhur bi'l-fawāḥish*)."[208] In the Ḥanafī literature, no individual authority is credited with establishing this view; rather, in the sixth century AH/twelfth century CE and later, it appears as an anonymous and yet pervasive view that gradually established itself as the new doctrine of the school.

A more detailed legal rationale for women's categorical exclusion from public prayers is provided by Maḥmūd ibn Aḥmad Ibn Māza, a Transoxianan scholar who died in Bukhara in 616/1219–20. After establishing that women are generally forbidden from leaving the house by verse 33:33 of the Qur'an, he writes:

> They were permitted to go out to congregational prayers in the beginning [of Islam] because of [the Prophet's] statement, "Do not forbid the handmaidens of God from [going to] the mosques of God, and if they go out, let them go out *tafilāt*"—that is, unperfumed. Then they were forbidden (*muniʿna*) after that because of the *fitna* that was involved in their going out; God said, "We know those of you who go forward, and those who hang back" [verse 15:24]. . . . It is said in the *tafsīr* that the verse was revealed about the women; the hypocrites were hanging back [in the rear of the congregation] so that they could get a view of the women's private parts, so [the women] were forbidden [from attending prayers] after that. [The Prophet] said, "It is better for a woman to pray in her courtyard in her mosque, and it is better for her to pray in her house than in her courtyard," and [it is reported about] ʿUmar that he forbade women to go out to mosques, so they complained to ʿĀʾisha, and ʿĀʾisha said, "If the Prophet had known what ʿUmar knows, he would not have given them permission to go out!"[209]

Here, without using the technical term *naskh*, Ibn Māza implies that women's entitlement to attend prayers at the mosque was a temporary dispensation that was abrogated during the Prophet's lifetime. In support of this contention, he cites a Qur'anic verse that had long been associated with an anecdote about women being ogled at prayer (although other interpretations were preferred and in any case there was no implication that the incident resulted in women's exclusion from the mosque).[210] Somewhat contradictorily, he also cites a report stating that it was ʿUmar who barred women from mosques (implicitly without a direct precedent from the Prophet).

Ibn Māza continues to observe that Ḥanafīs (*aṣḥābunā*) consider it impermissible for women to go out to mosques at any time, based on the precedent of ʿUmar, while "al-Shāfiʿī said, 'It is permissible for them to go out,' and cited as evidence [the Prophet's] statement, 'Do not forbid the handmaidens of God from [going to] the mosques of God.'" As we have seen, this is not a completely accurate account of al-Shāfiʿī's position, but it suggests the degree to which blanket rejection of women's mosque attendance was, in this period, a distinctively Ḥanafī stance.[211]

Both before and after this passage, Ibn Māza reproduces school doctrines assuming a sharp distinction between old and young women. It is significant, however, that his own argumentation treats "women" as a single category. The newer Ḥanafi doctrine not only erased the division between younger and older women, but also swept aside the distinctions among different times of day attributed to Abū Ḥanīfa. In the fifth/eleventh century, as we have seen, al-Sarakhsī justified Abū Ḥanīfa's opinion with the reflection that "the old woman goes out well covered and the darkness of night protects her from the gaze of men, unlike the case with daytime prayers."[212] In the sixth/twelfth century, ʿAlī ibn Abī Bakr al-Marghīnānī wrote in his definitive legal manual *al-Hidāya* that "corrupt people spread abroad at noontime, in the afternoon, and on Friday, while at dawn and the time of the *ʿishāʾ* prayer they are sleeping, and at sundown they are busy eating."[213] As Sadeghi has rightly observed, there is an arbitrary and ad hoc quality to this rationalization.[214] Whereas the limitation of women's public prayer to the hours of dusk or darkness had once (at least in some contexts) reflected a familiar form of social propriety, by this time it was a rule in search of a rationale. Although the distinction between daytime and nighttime prayers had once been the more restrictive of the two Ḥanafī doctrines, by Ibn Māza's day it was regarded as a dispensation of bygone times. Abū Bakr Ibn al-Ḥaddād (d. 800/1398) remarks, "The ruling (*al-fatwā*) today is that it is objectionable [for old women to go to public prayers] with respect to all prayers, because of the open appearance of wrongdoing (*al-fisq*) in this age."[215]

The progressive hardening of attitudes applied not only to women's participation in congregational prayer, but also to other activities women pursued in the mosque (although these are mentioned far less often in the legal sources, in contrast to the case in nonnormative genres). Ṭāhir al-Bukhārī, who (as we have seen) preferred that women never attend prayers at the mosque at all, stated merely that, "if [a woman] wishes to go out to a session of religious instruction (*majlis al-ʿilm*) *without her husband's permission*, she is not entitled to do that."[216] The view that women should not venture forth to pray in mosques at all was reiterated by ʿAbd Allāh ibn Aḥmad al-Nasafī (d. 710/1310).[217] However, he went on to assert that it is repugnant for women to frequent mosques for any other reason, declaring that "if [women's] attending prayers in the mosque is deemed undesirable, it is all the more undesirable for them to attend preaching (*waʿẓ*), especially with these ignorant ones who put on the garb of scholars."[218] Sadeghi cogently observes that "the intensity of the sentiment and the digressive character of the comment indicate a genuine reflection on reality rather than a fictional legal construction."[219] Whether the teachers involved actually lacked scholarly credentials or whether al-Nasafī dismissed them as "ignorant" merely out of disapproval for their accommodation of women is unclear. As we shall see, the hierarchy of value that al-Nasafī is attempting to impose (in which prayer is, at least theoretically, a better justification for women's presence in the mosque than preaching) may have been asserted in defiance of social practice.

The chasm that sometimes separated Ḥanafī doctrine from current social practice is suggested by a fatwa attributed to ʿAlāʾ al-Dīn Muḥammad ibn Muḥammad al-Bukhārī (d. 841/1437).[220] This fatwa, which probably originated in Syria, appears to be preserved only in a unique manuscript, but its existence and basic sentiment are confirmed by other sources.[221] Al-Bukhārī's fatwa responds to a lengthy inquiry asserting that women throng to preaching sessions at mosques, often mixing with and outnumbering men or even forming the entirety of the audience of a male preacher. It inquires about the validity of the argument that such sessions are justified by the ḥadīth "Do not prevent the maidservants of God from [going to] the mosques of God." Finally (and clearly anticipating a negative answer to his second question), he asks whether the authorities will be rewarded by God for denouncing and restraining preachers who engage in such behavior. Thus, the questioner's premise is not only that women attend teaching sessions in mosques in large numbers, but also that they are supported by religious specialists who welcome their presence and endorse it with ḥadīth. Significantly, it is this inclusive situation that evokes one of the most fierce and categorical denunciations of women's mosque attendance in the history of Islamic legal writing.

Al-Bukhārī begins by establishing that in verse 33:33 of the Qur'an God has forbidden women of any age from going out of their houses and wantonly displaying their charms to men (*al-tabarruj*), whether their destination is the mosque or any other place. Al-Bukhārī states that the divine prohibition originally applied only to women who engaged in wanton display (*al-mutabarrijāt*), not those who were unadorned (*al-ʿāṭilāt*). In the Prophet's time, both young and old women who were unadorned could go out to the Prophet's mosque because the rationale (*ʿilla*) for forbidding them (the fear of *fitna*) was not present. During the lifetime of the Prophet, women were not given to dalliance, nor did men lack the moral fiber to withstand their charms unless they were flaunted. However, all of this changed after the Prophet's demise; in the lifetime of his widow ʿĀʾisha, women's chastity gave way to seductiveness, and the prohibition on women going out in a state of wanton display was extended to include unadorned women. Although the letter of the divine prohibition applied only to *mutabarrijāt*, from the time of ʿĀʾisha young women were included by implication (*faḥwā al-khiṭāb*) because of the existence of the rationale in them (that is, given the deterioration of moral fiber, a young woman was seductive even if appropriately attired).

Second, al-Bukhārī argues that "ignorant storytellers" who hold regular teaching sessions for women in mosques and other places are committing a forbidden action because the rules of jurisprudence (*uṣūl al-fiqh*) dictate that the causes leading to a given action have the same legal status as the action in question, as a matter of pious precaution (*iḥtiyāṭ*), in matters relating to religious proscriptions (*al-ḥurumāt*) and acts of worship (*al-ʿibādāt*). For instance, those actions that lead to intercourse, such as gazing and kissing, are forbidden when intercourse is forbidden. Because it is women's custom to go out of their homes with the intention to display their beauty, mix with men, and be alone with the preacher (all of which are forbidden), it is forbidden for them to do so. (Here al-Bukhārī appears to be describing his perception of the mosque-going habits of women in his own time and place.) The preacher who occasions these actions is committing a number of sins, even on the assumption that he is aware of the error of his ways. In contrast, if he believes that holding such sessions for women is an act of piety (*min jumlat al-qurubāt*), then he is guilty of disbelief in God (*al-kufr bi-rabb al-arḍ wa'l samawāt*) because by the consensus of the community it is disbelief to worship God by committing an act of disobedience.

Al-Bukhārī's third argument is that the prohibition (apparently in the ḥadīth "Do not prevent the maidservants of God from [going to] the mosques of God") cannot be binding for all time; rather, such a prohibition is permanently valid only in the absence of a countervailing proof. In this case, the countervailing proof is clear; it is ʿĀʾisha's statement that, if the Prophet had seen what women innovated after his death, he would have forbidden them to go out to mosques. Later in the fatwa, he sums up this point by stating that the legal ruling (*ḥukm*) of the ḥadīth has lapsed with the disappearance of its rationale (*ʿilla*). Furthermore, to assert the continuing and unqualified applicability of the prohibition on preventing women from going to mosques would be tantamount to calling ʿĀʾisha a liar. It would also violate the consensus of the community on the undesirability (*karāha*) of women's going out to mosques.

Fourth, al-Bukhārī asserts that it is impermissible for a *muqallid* (that is, a layperson or a legal scholar unqualified to engage in independent legal interpretation) to adhere to a ḥadīth that conflicts with the teaching of his legal school, even if the ḥadīth is itself well authenticated and recorded in the authoritative compilations. That is because the ḥadīth scholars who assembled these compilations simply evaluated whether a given statement had issued from the Prophet; they did not delve into the questions of whether the statement in question was abrogated by a later prophetic statement (*mansūkh*), outweighed by a better-authenticated text (*marjūḥ*), subject to evidence that it should not be interpreted literally, or simply rendered inapplicable by the passing away of its rationale (*ʿilla*). As a result, ḥadīth collections are full of texts that are, in fact, not legally relevant. The only people who are qualified to judge the normative force of a ḥadīth are the legal scholars capable of independent reasoning (*al-mujtahidūn*).

Al-Bukhārī concludes,

> Thus, it is obligatory for the authorities of the time and the rulers of Islam to interdict (*ḥajr*) him [i.e., presumably whoever is arguing that the Prophet's statement prohibits the exclusion of women from mosques], and inflict a discretionary punishment on him so that he will be an example to all the world; then to prevent the storytellers who hold teaching sessions with women and gather together females who flaunt their charms (that is one of the greatest repugnant acts!); then to deter women from going out to the mosques and the storytellers' sessions with the utmost degree of punishment (*siyāsa*). By doing so they would attain goodly praise in this world and copious reward in the next, God willing.

It is notable that al-Bukhārī here places responsibility for the regulation of women's mosque-going behavior on the political authorities, rather than on the male guardians of individual women.

Al-Bukhārī's fatwa deploys new and creative legal rationales for what was by then a well-established Ḥanafī doctrine, albeit one that was clearly ineffective (at least in this context) in deterring women from visiting mosques. It can be seen, at least in part, as an apologia for the religious authority of legal scholars over that of ḥadīth specialists. Al-Bukhārī's argument that only jurists master the rules governing the actual applicability of ḥadīth—and that knowledge of ḥadīth alone is not normatively relevant—represents a strategic blow in a conflict between two competing forms of religious authority. The apparently rigid and static postclassical Ḥanafī doctrine against women's mosque attendance here appears both socially and ideologically embattled.

Alāʾ al-Dīn al-Bukhārī's personal aversion for ḥadīth and its practitioners was severe enough to attract adverse comment.[222] Although the Ḥanafī school had traditionally had little affinity for the discipline of ḥadīth, by this period it had produced serious *muḥaddithūn*. However, even Ḥanafīs deeply learned in the discipline of ḥadīth expressed distinctively negative views of women's mosque attendance. The Ḥanafī ḥadīth scholar Ibn al-Humām (d. 861/1457) draws on arguments and texts common to the discipline of ḥadīth, but to very different effect than his Shāfiʿī traditionist colleagues. Ibn al-Humām argues that, although the Prophet's statements appear to establish a general prohibition on excluding women from the mosque, scholars have limited the scope of this rule by identifying a number of conditions, some of which are explicitly stated in ḥadīth and others extrapolated by analogy. Here he is clearly influenced by the wording and approach of the Shāfiʿī traditionist Ibn Daqīq al-ʿĪd;[223] however, he has a quite different evaluation of the current situation and of its overall implications for women's public worship. In his opinion, the conditions imposed by ḥadīth texts (and their analogical extension) on women's public worship are no longer fulfilled in his time "because [women] adorn themselves to go out more than they do when they are at home," so "they are forbidden [to go out to the mosque] completely."[224]

For Ibn al-Humām, unlike the Mālikī and Shāfiʿī traditionists whose mode of argumentation he has partially adopted, ḥadīth-based restrictions on women's dress and comportment do not simply function as guidelines for individual behavior, but also constitute a criterion by which the women of his time are collectively condemned. Furthermore, he holds that issues of public order preclude women's mosque attendance even when they personally fulfill the relevant conditions. Thus, he boldly argues that "in light of the rationale mentioned [i.e., the prevention of *fitna*], a woman who is not adorned is forbidden as well, because of the prevalence of evil-doers (*al-fussāq*); [women are also prohibited from visiting the mosque] at night, even though the text permits it, because in our time evil-doers mostly spread abroad and accost [women] at night."[225]

Ibn al-Humām anticipates the objection that he is actually abrogating the relevant ḥadīth texts. (All scholars agreed that abrogation, *naskh*, could occur only within the lifetime of the Prophet; rulings that remained in force at the Prophet's death would remain so until the Day of Judgment.) Ibn al-Humām offers two possible rejoinders. One is that the prohibition on latter-day women's mosque attendance simply reflects the general application of the texts prohibiting seductive behavior (*al-taftīn*). The other is that when a rule is dependent on a condition or rationale, it is rendered void by the disappearance of that condition or rationale. Here Ibn al-Humām performs a striking inversion of the argumentation of Ibn Daqīq al-ʿĪd. Ibn Daqīq al-ʿĪd had argued that the piety indicated by "going to the mosque" might be the rationale for God's instructing men to allow their wives to go out; thus, it became null in the absence of that rationale, which was going to the mosque.[226] Ibn al-Humām applies the same principle to demonstrate not that the piety of women's mosque-going is the rationale for their being allowed to go out, but that the impiety of women negates the rationale for women's mosque-going.

At first blush, it might seem that the blanket prohibition on women's mosque attendance promoted by many Ḥanafī scholars from the sixth/twelfth century is simply the logical conclusion of the triumph of *fitna* discourse. This adequately describes, for instance, the arguments of ʿAlāʾ al-Dīn al-Bukhārī. The wording and logic of many later Ḥanafī texts, however, reflect a significant shift in emphasis from the older discourse about *fitna*. It appears that, for a number of later Ḥanafī authorities, what is at stake is no longer the insidious sexual temptation that may assail the most pious Muslim as he encounters women in the street or the mosque, but the potential for public mayhem caused by disruptive elements in society. Even on a purely terminological level, although the word *fitna* certainly continues to appear, as a focal term it is largely eclipsed in later Ḥanafī legal manuals by references to "wrongdoers" (*fussāq*) and "corruption" (*fasād*). The question of the visibility of the women involved (reflected, for instance, in al-Sarakhsī's suggestion that an old woman may go out to the mosque at night because "the darkness of night protects her from men's glances") is gradually replaced with claims about the likelihood of encountering male miscreants at different times of day. Ibn al-Humām's argument that bad elements spread abroad and harass women primarily at night is less about modesty than about public order.[227] Regardless of the sociological accuracy of the specific claims, there seems to be shift of emphasis from subtle seductiveness to blatant delinquency.

To some extent, changes in Ḥanafī terminology could be artifacts of the influence of al-Marghinānī (d. 593/1197), who invokes the personal habits of delinquents in his influential legal manual *al-Hidāya*.[228] However, they seem to be broader than this hypothesis would suggest.

In his commentary on the 'Ā'isha report in the *Ṣaḥīḥ* of Bukhārī, the Cairene Ḥanafī *muḥaddith* Al-ʿAynī offers a lengthy recitation of the "innovations" of contemporary Cairene women. In so doing, he emphasizes actual (and sometimes criminal) wrongdoing over the subtler forms of temptation that might be inherent in the public visibility of women, without once using the word *fitna* in the sense of sexual temptation.[229] He inveighs against their sartorial abuses mainly in terms of sumptuary excess rather than of seductiveness, and focuses at greater length on their licentious behavior (such as singing for mixed audiences and drinking alcohol with men on pleasure boats on the Nile) and their sexual violations (including prostitution and pandering). A number of the activities he mentions are examples of outright criminality, including theft and fraud.[230]

Without contextual information, it is difficult to know whether the apparently growing concern with delinquency reflects actual social or political developments or merely the artificiality of legal argumentation. Sadeghi is surely correct to argue that al-Marghinānī's assertion that the delinquents of his time are busy eating at sundown reflects his eagerness to limit women's mosque-going rather than the actual dining habits of twelfth-century lowlifes. Nevertheless, the fact that he bases limits on women's mobility on the possibility of harassment by rowdies—rather than on the visibility of women's charms at different times of day—suggests a new focus of concern. Walter Andrews and Mehmet Kalpaklı have argued that in the early modern Ottoman Empire, as well as in several regions of contemporary Europe, "[t]he presence of . . . unattached, young, sexually aggressive men made public space uncomfortable, and often quite dangerous, for women."[231] Because the newer Ḥanafī discourse on women's mosque attendance was elaborated over a long period of time by scholars who lived in a number of different locales, it is not possible to draw a simple one-to-one correspondence between the invocation of delinquency as a rationale and the demographics or social problems of a specific time and place. Furthermore, even in modern societies where criminality can be tracked more rigorously, it is difficult to distinguish between actual increases in crime and the rhetorical exploitation of crime as a rationale for greater public control.[232] Nevertheless, many later Ḥanafī authorities give new salience to issues of public order, and the possibility that these concerns were raised by contemporary social conditions—or by the changing agenda of the state and the changing relationship of legal scholars with the state—would be worthy of further investigation.

A growing (and changing) preoccupation with *fitna* was not the only element in evolving Ḥanafī discussions of women's mosque access. Ḥanafīs also displayed a historically long-lasting, if quantitatively marginal, concern with women's conflicting duties within the home. This theme is significant if only because it remained almost unique among premodern legal texts. Discussing groups exempted from the obligation to attend Friday congregational prayers, Muḥammad al-Marwazī (d. 334/995) observes that "a woman is also occupied with serving her husband, and forbidden by the divine law to go out."[233] Al-Marghinānī similarly states that "a slave is occupied with serving his master, and a woman with serving her husband." He reasons that a slave's absence at Friday prayers would inflict harm (*ḍarar*) on his master by interrupting his service; similarly, harm would ensue (presumably to the husband) if a woman were obligated to attend.[234] Ibn Māza presents the same argument.[235] Al-Kāsānī writes that travelers are exempted from Friday prayers because attendance might cause them to fall behind their caravans and the ill are exempted because attendance might be burdensome or even impossible; "as for a woman, it is because she is busy serving her husband and [because she is] forbidden to go out to gatherings of men, because [her] going out is a cause of *fitna*."[236] (In contrast, in passages dealing with daily and festival prayers, al-Kāsānī cites the fear of *fitna* to the exclusion of women's need to serve their husbands.[237])

The idea that a woman is excused from public prayer at least in part because of her domestic obligations is rarely encountered in premodern texts outside of the Ḥanafī school,[238] and even here it is somewhat anomalous. Ḥanafīs, like the majority of other Islamic legal scholars, did not consider domestic labor by the wife to be an intrinsic part of the marital relationship.[239] Indeed, far from assuming that a wife must cook or clean for her husband, scholars debated whether the husband was obligated to pay servants to provide such labor for the wife.[240] However, later Ḥanafīs held that, even though the wife could not be compelled by a judge to perform household tasks such as cooking, she was religiously obligated to do so (*hādhihi'l-aʿmāl wājiba ʿalayhā diyānatan*).[241] The idea that women were exempted from Friday prayer at least in part because of their household duties may reflect a lack of unanimity about women's obligation to perform domestic labor among Ḥanafīs; alternatively, it may reflect the tacit recognition that many households did not, in fact, enjoy the labor of servants.

The argument that women are exempted from the obligation to attend Friday congregational prayers by virtue of their duty to serve their husbands suggests that they are relieved of the obligation to attend congregational prayer by virtue of contingent circumstances rather than of inherent unfitness. Just as any slave might one day be freed, any woman might at some times in her life be free of marital obligations. It is also implied that women, like slaves and the ill, are included among the original addressees of the commandment to attend Friday prayers; they are exempted only because of supervening difficulties, ones that might in some circumstances not apply. However, this argument appears only in discussions of Friday prayers rather than of the broader right or duty to attend the mosque; it seems to have been suggested by the parallel with slaves, who were similarly exempted. Furthermore, it is frequently combined with references to *fitna* or to the general undesirability of a woman's leaving the home.

As we have seen, in the Mālikī and Shāfiʿī schools, a rhetorical insistence on the undesirability of women's mosque attendance tended to coexist with reiterations of standard school doctrine condoning it for the mature and the unadorned. Only in the Ḥanafī school is the apparent shift in scholarly sentiment reflected in a genuine shift in legal doctrine. Later Ḥanafī legal textbooks routinely state that the currently valid ruling (*al-fatwā*) is that women should not participate in public worship at any age or at any time of day.[242] Ibrāhīm al-Ḥalabī (d. 956/1549) declares that "according to the [Ḥanafī] *madhhab*, it is categorically undesirable for [women] to attend congregational prayers"; his commentator Muḥammad al-Ḥaṣkafī (d. 1088/1677) elaborates that it is undesirable for them to attend "even for Friday or festival prayers or for preaching (*waʿẓ*)," "even for an old woman at night," "because of the corruption of the times" (*li-fasād al-zamān*)."[243] Only Zayn al-Dīn Ibn Nujaym (d. 970/1563) acknowledges the objection that this trend is in violation of established school doctrine, a reservation that found little favor with later Ḥanafīs.[244] There was no doubt in the minds of most scholars that school doctrine had changed. In a fatwa on the issue of legal change dating from 1104/1693, the Ḥanafī jurist al-Aydinī notes that the Prophet allowed women of all ages to attend public prayers. "Then our authorities (*aʾimmatunā*) forbade the young women [from going to public prayers], and the [scholars] of later times (*al-mutaʾakhkhirīn*) generalized [the ruling] to include them and old women in all of the prayers, because of the prevalence of corruption at all times [of the day]."[245]

In his analysis of Ḥanafī doctrines relating to women and prayer, Sadeghi argues that the school displayed a "maximal hermeneutical flexibility" that allowed legal scholars to derive a wide range of legal inferences from the textual canon they held to be binding. This flexibility allowed them not only to construct hermeneutic justifications for received Ḥanafī doctrines that apparently contradicted the content of ḥadīth (a methological necessity as the legal authority of ḥadīth became increasingly undisputable over the centuries), but also eventually to exercise similar flexibility with respect to the Ḥanafī doctrines themselves.[246] Our examination of the arguments in other schools suggests that they may not have exercised the same degree of flexibility in this respect; among Mālikīs, for instance, the obvious meaning of both ḥadīth texts and statements attributed to Mālik apparently exerted a stronger gravitational pull—although these two sources exercised different degrees of attraction for different individual scholars. Only among the Ḥanafīs was it unmistakable that school doctrine (rather than pious sentiment) had substantively changed.

Despite the strong consensus of the legal manuals, however, it is not clear that Ḥanafī fatwas consistently condemned mosque attendance by all women even in the Ottoman period. Asked whether women should be prevented from attending Friday congregational prayers, the Ottoman chief muftī Abū'l-Suʿūd (d. 982/1574) replied that they should be if they are young.[247] As we shall see, the overall later Ḥanafī (and Ottoman) negativity toward women's presence in mosques obscured some degree of diversity in opinion and practice.

THE ḤANBALĪS

Ḥanbalī legal sources generally do not attribute their doctrines on women's mosque attendance directly to the eponym of their school, although they make passing references to his opinions. Reports claim that when asked about women's attendance at the prayers for the two festivals, Ibn Ḥanbal responded, "[P]eople will be tempted, unless she is a woman far advanced in age,"[248] or "[A]s for in this time of ours, no, because they are a temptation."[249] Although Ibn Ḥanbal's comments do not apply directly to the issue of women's mosque attendance, if authentic, they reflect a distinctively early and explicit concern with *fitna* and a dark perception of the decadence of his times. It is plausible that Ibn Ḥanbal, who lived a century after Abū Ḥanīfa, already reflects a nascent framing of *fitna* as the rationale for limits on women's public worship.[250]

Nevertheless, even among Ḥanbalīs (as in other schools) *fitna* appears to have been systematically elaborated as the juristic rationale of the rules relating to women's mosque attendance significantly later. Abū Yaʿlā ibn al-Farrāʾ (d. 458/1066) is supposed to have pointed to Ibn Ḥanbal's objection to any but old women going out for festival prayers, as well as the textual prohibition on women's using perfume when going to the mosque, to demonstrate that *fitna* was the underlying *ʿilla* of the rules in this area; like his contemporaries of other schools, he had to elicit this rationale from texts where it was not explicit.[251]

Because Ibn Ḥanbal's *fiqh* rested primarily on the transmission of ḥadīth, his vast ḥadīth compilation, the *Musnad*, is also a useful indicator of his attitudes in this area.[252] It includes a number of different versions of the Prophet's command not to bar women from mosques, including several versions of the anecdote in which a son of ʿAbd Allāh ibn ʿUmar expresses his determination to do so and is severely reprimanded by his father. It also includes ʿĀʾisha's statement that the Prophet himself would have barred women from mosques had he witnessed their innovations after his death. There are multiple reports emphasizing that women should under no circumstances attend the mosque while wearing perfume.[253]

Thus far, Ibn Ḥanbal's traditions parallel those central to argumentation in other schools. However, perhaps the most widely cited and influential ḥadīth on women and mosques transmitted by Ibn Ḥanbal is one in which a woman named Umm Ḥumayd declares to the Prophet, "O Messenger of God, I love to pray with you!" The Prophet replies, "I know that you love to pray with me, but it is better for you to pray in your inner chamber than in your house, and it is better for you to pray in your house than in your courtyard, and it is better for you to pray in your courtyard than in the mosque of your clan, and it is better for you to pray in the mosque of your clan than in my mosque." The report concludes, "so she directed that a prayer room (*masjid*) be built for her in the remotest and darkest corner of her chamber; she prayed there until she met God [i.e., died]."[254]

This report seems to bear some hints of Iraqi provenance; the existence of separate mosques associated with specific clans was typical of the garrison cities of early Islamic Iraq[255] rather than of Medina during the Prophet's lifetime. It suggests that the scale of religious merit in prayer is inverted for women; whereas a man (at least with regard to obligatory prayers) earns greater religious reward for venturing forth to join in prayer with the community, and even more if he walks or travels farther to visit a particularly holy mosque, a woman's prayer is depicted as becoming more religiously valuable the more she remains secluded within concentric circles of privacy. Based on the materials transmitted in the *Musnad*, it would seem that Ibn Ḥanbal disseminated reports that supported women's entitlement to attend mosques, but raised concerns about their seductive potential (as exemplified by the use of perfume) and devalued their attendance in favor of private and secluded worship.

In general, despite the lack of textual precedent, the Ḥanbalī school conformed to the overall consensus distinguishing among different age cohorts of women. Classical Ḥanbalī sources state that it is legally neutral for an old woman to attend congregational prayers, but undesirable for a young woman.[256] Ibn Hubayra (d. 560/1165) states that the scholars of all four schools "are in agreement that it is objectionable for young women to attend the congregational prayers of men (*jamāʿāt al-rijāl*)." However, "they differ with respect to attendance by old women"; Mālik and Aḥmad (ibn Ḥanbal) agree that there is no objection whatsoever to their attendance (*lā yukrah ʿalā al-iṭlāq*), whereas Abū Ḥanīfa and al-Shāfiʿī have some reservations even with respect to older women.[257] In support of the Ḥanbalī position that it is completely unproblematic for old women to attend (which contrasts with Abū Ḥanīfa's placement of restrictions even on older women), the fifth-century AH/eleventh-century CE scholar al-ʿUkbarī remarks that "there is no fear of temptation (*fitna*) from her attending, so she is like a man."[258] In rare cases, scholars suggested that it was positively meritorious for old women to attend; the prominent early Ḥanbalī authority Ibn Ḥāmid (d. 403/1012–13) reportedly deemed it desirable for an old woman to go to *jumʿa*.[259]

Ibn Hubayra himself advanced a strikingly affirmative opinion on women's mosque attendance. After laying out the opinions of the eponymous founders of the four schools, Ibn Hubayra states:

> My own opinion (*wa'l-ladhī arā*) is that it is not objectionable but preferable (*masnūn*) that they should go to congregational prayers, and that they should be in the last rows behind the men, according to what is stated in ḥadīth texts and was practiced in the time of [the Prophet] al-Muṣṭafā [i.e., Muḥammad] and the first generation of Muslims (*al-ṣadr al-awwal*). Whoever justifies regarding that as objectionable by the fear of temptation from [the women], that [argument] is refuted by [the example of] the ḥajj.[260]

Here he briskly dismisses the criterion of *fitna* by appealing to the example of the ḥajj, an occasion when women are mandated to go out for a major religious gathering and forbidden to cover their faces in a conventional way. It is unclear whether Ibn Hubayra is here advocating that all women go to public congregational prayers or merely that elderly women go. In any case, his statements represent a bold and unusual vindication of women's right to attend mosques that deemphasizes school tradition in favor of a direct appeal to the practice of the earliest Muslims. It also appears to reflect a rare instance of overt resistance to the growing centrality of the concept of *fitna*; it did not prevail within the school.

The complexity of Ḥanbalī attitudes toward women's mosque attendance is reflected in the work of Abū'l-Faraj Ibn al-Jawzī (d. 597/1201).

In his work *al-Taḥqīḥ*, which deals with points of disagreement among the schools of law, he cites the ḥadīth "Do not forbid the maidservants of God from [going to] the mosques of God" to support the proposition that "it is not objectionable for an old woman to attend congregational prayers," implicitly excluding those who are not old.[261] Once again, it is implied that all schools of law agree upon the undesirability of mosque attendance by young women, a position that Ibn al-Jawzī is said to have affirmed elsewhere.[262] However, he expresses a much more nuanced position—and one that deemphasizes the issue of age—in *Aḥkām al-nisāʾ* (*Legal rules relating to women*), which is unique in its genre (although it is not the only work to bear this title[263]). It is not simply a thematic handbook appropriate for use by a legal scholar, but also a work of religious exhortation aimed at the spiritual formation of women. It is unclear whether it was intended for use by preachers or was directly addressed to a female audience (perhaps even to a specific female patron).

In the section dealing with prayer, Ibn al-Jawzī states that it is religiously neutral (*mubāḥ*) for a woman to go out to the mosque; however, if she fears that anyone will be tempted by the sight of her, she should pray at home.[264] He observes that women "used to go out and pray with the Messenger of God in congregation, except that it is undesirable (*yukrah*) for a woman who it is feared will be seductive to go out."[265] He grounds the fear of *fitna* in the declining mores of the Muslim community since the Prophet's time:

> We have explained that it is legally neutral (*mubāḥ*) for women to go out [to public prayers in the mosque or the festival prayer grounds], but if there is fear of temptation of them or by them, it is better for them to refrain from going out, because the women of the first generation [of Muslims] behaved differently than the women of this time have come to behave, and the same goes for the men.[266]

Ibn al-Jawzī, like Ibn Ḥanbal before him, presents a series of ḥadīth texts supporting the permissibility of women's going to the mosque and the undesirability of forbidding them. However, his discussion of women's mosque attendance is embedded in a wider context that repetitively emphasizes the inadvisability of a woman's leaving her home and the perils of *fitna*. A chapter titled "Warning women against going out (*Fī taḥdhīr al-nisāʾ min al-khurūj*)" begins with the statement: "A woman should beware of going out whenever she is able [to avoid it]; even if she is unharmed, people will not be unharmed by her."[267] The following chapter is titled "The virtue of [staying in] the house for the woman (*Fī dhikr faḍl al-bayt li'l-mar'a*)" and includes reports emphasizing the superiority of a woman's prayer within her home.[268] Overall, Ibn al-Jawzī's comments seem as likely to dissuade a woman from going out to public worship as to encourage her, although he certainly makes clear that (if she is modest) she is entitled to do so.

Ibn al-Jawzī's discussion manifests, in an unusually vivid form, the complexities latent in Ḥanbalī attitudes toward women's mosque attendance. He is firmly committed to the position that women are permitted to go to mosques, but equally persuaded that there is no pious motivation for them to do so. His apparent faith that a woman may pursue and attain normative piety does not entail a corresponding faith that she can appear in public without peril to herself or others. In accordance with the unique nature of this work, Ibn al-Jawzī confides the duty of determining the likelihood of temptation to the woman herself; there is no mention of the authority of the husband or male guardian. It is also notable that he makes the permissibility of the woman's mosque attendance dependent only on the likelihood of *fitna* rather than on her stage of life.

A generation after Ibn al-Jawzī, Muwaffaq al-Dīn Ibn Qudāma (d. 620/1223) produced a vastly influential compendium of Ḥanbalī and comparative law, *al-Mughnī*. Like Ibn al-Jawzī, he deemphasizes the distinction between old and young women that had dominated earlier statements of the doctrine of the school. Ibn Qudāma states, "It is legally neutral (*mubāḥ*) for them [i.e., women] to attend congregational prayers with the men, because the women used to pray with the Messenger of God."[269] Discussing Friday prayers, he distinguishes between older and younger women, but makes no sharp distinction between their legal statuses; he states that "as for a woman, if she is aged (*musinna*) there is no harm in her attending; if she is young, it is permissible (*jāza*) for her to attend. It is better for both of them to pray in their homes."[270] The subtle distinction between "permissible" and "no harm" perhaps implies that the younger woman's attendance is not ideal, but it is notable that Ibn Qudāma does not use the term *makrūh* (objectionable).

Ibn Qudāma also presents a distinctive position on a husband's right to detain his wife from going out to the mosque. As we have seen, most scholars of other schools construed the Prophet's prohibition on barring women from mosques as a moral exhortation rather than a legal ruling. Although Ibn Qudāma emphasizes that a husband may generally forbid his wife from leaving the home for any nonvital reason, he states that he may not forbid her from going to the mosque.[271] In another work, he tersely summarizes his position by stating "a woman's home is better for her, and if she wants to go to the mosque she should not be forbidden to go (*lam tumnaʿ minhu*)."[272] It is notable this opinion does not appear to have been a long-standing school doctrine; the husband's right to forbid her was affirmed by no lesser authority than Abū Yaʿlā ibn al-Farrāʾ.[273]

The complexity of the Ḥanbalī approach toward women's mosque access reflects the school's thoroughgoing fidelity to the mixed textual heritage reflected in the ḥadīth transmitted by the school. Whether or not the Prophet had actually uttered all of the statements attributed to him on the subject, the received body of ḥadīth established that men could not prohibit their wives from going to the mosque, which implied that their going was (at least) legally neutral. (Had the action of attending the mosque been legally repugnant, it would surely have been licit to forbid it.) However, it also emphasized the superior merit of women's prayer in their homes and the hazards of female coquetry, exemplified by the seductive potential of perfume. Overall, Ḥanbalī scholars were thus, in comparison with many of their peers of other schools, simultaneously more categorical in permitting women's mosque attendance and more insistent in deprecating it.

The distinctiveness of the school's attitude is illustrated in the work of Ibn Taymīya (d. 728/1328), who offers no systematic discussion of the issue, but alludes to it in several places. Citing ḥadīth texts asserting the superior merit of women's prayer within the home, he observes that the Prophet "informed the female believers that it is better for them to pray in their houses than to attend Friday and congregational prayers," with the sole exception of the festival prayers. He argues that *ʿīd* (festival) prayers are an exception from the general rule because they occur only twice a year, because there is no substitute for them (whereas "her noon prayer in her home is her Friday prayer"), and because festival prayers (which involve going forth to the "desert" to contemplate God) are in some ways equivalent to the ḥajj (in which women participate alongside of men).[274]

Unlike some scholars who discouraged women's public prayer on the grounds of deteriorating public morality, Ibn Taymīya emphasizes the continuity of the law and the ongoing relevance of the Prophet's example, regardless of changing mores. Rather than seeing the discouragement of women's mosque attendance as a measure responding to the needs of decadent times, he represents women's presence in mosques as rare and undesirable even in the time of the Prophet. Despite the Prophet's express permission for women to go out to the mosque, Ibn Taymīya asserts that the female Companions (or at least the majority of them) did not, in fact, do so. He argues that, given the Prophet's affirmation that it is more meritorious for a woman to pray at home, one must necessarily assume that the majority of them chose the preferred option; otherwise, this would mean that the best of generations did not model the best behavior.[275] He specifically rejects the idea that it may have been preferable for the Prophet's female Companions to pray in the mosque (if only because they could pray behind the Prophet himself), but better for later Muslim women to pray at home.[276] Rather, he holds that women's participation in the mosque had always been conditioned on the absence of *fitna*. In another fatwa, he refutes the idea that it is possible to infer changes in the law as established by ḥadīth texts by hypothesizing that the Prophet might have responded in a certain way, had he been consulted. He denies, however, that this principle applies to ʿĀʾisha's statement that, if the Prophet had seen what women innovated after his death, he would have forbidden them to go to mosques.

> ʿĀʾisha was too god-fearing to countenance the annulment of the law after [the Prophet's] death. Rather, she meant that . . . [the Prophet's] statement "Do not forbid the maidservants of God from [going to] the mosques of God," even if its wording is general, is specified by [the exclusion] of going out that involves corruption. [This is] as most jurists hold: that young women whose going out involves corruption should be prevented.[277]

Despite his general lack of enthusiasm for women's mosque attendance, but in harmony with his fidelity to the content of ḥadīth, Ibn Taymīya nevertheless affirms a woman's right to go to the mosque if she so chooses. Much like Ibn Qudāma, but more forcefully and unambiguously, Ibn Taymīya denies a husband's right to forbid his wife from going out to the mosque. He observes that an opinion attributed to Aḥmad ibn Ḥanbal indicates that a husband must not give permission for his Christian or Jewish wife to go out to the church or synagogue, "in contrast to giving his permission for the Muslim [wife] to go to the mosque; he is commanded to do that."[278]

Ibn Taymīya's student Ibn Qayyim al-Jawzīya (d. 751/1350), like other authorities of his school, affirms the permissibility of women's going out to mosques. Interestingly, he represents women's privilege of leaving the home and frequenting places of worship to be an immemorial custom that the Prophet Muḥammad merely tacitly endorsed (*taqrīr*) rather than something newly legislated in the Islamic dispensation. Among the preexisting customs that the Prophet tolerated, and thus affirmed in their legality, was "affirming (*taqrīr*) women in going out, walking in the streets, attending places of worship (*al-masājid*), and hearing the addresses (*khuṭab*) that people were summoned to gather for."[279] Like Ibn Qudāma and Ibn Taymīya, he also states that a husband may not deny his wife the right to go to the mosque.[280] However, the presence of women in mixed public assemblies is not something he regards as proper or desirable. He notes:

> The benefit of physical acts of worship (*al-ʿibādāt al-badanīya*) . . . is something in which men and women share; each group has equal need of it, so it is not appropriate to distinguish between them. However, a distinction was made between them on the most appropriate point, which is Friday and congregational prayers; they were made obligatory for men to the exclusion of women, because it is not appropriate for [women] to display themselves in public and mix with men.[281]

In a work of advice to rulers, he states that "it is incumbent upon the ruler to prevent the mixing of men and women in markets, places of recreation, and the gathering places (*majāmiʿ*) of men" (this last being a category in which Friday prayers, at least, are often included).

After emphasizing that a woman wearing perfume should be prevented from attending the nighttime prayer, he observes that enabling women to mix with men is "the source of all affliction and evil; it is one of the primary reasons for the infliction of general punishments [by God], as well as being one of the sources for the corruption of the affairs of the commoners and the elite."[282]

As in other schools of law, among Ḥanbalīs over time age distinctions were deemphasized, ultimately being regarded as a mere proxy for a concern with sexual allure. After listing a number of earlier Ḥanbalī authorities who disapproved of young women going to congregational prayers with men, Ibn Mufliḥ (d. 763/1362) remarks, "What is intended—and God knows best—is the woman who is considered pretty (*al-mustaḥsana*)." Furthermore, "it is known that this rationale (*maʿnā*) is present in an old woman who is considered pretty."[283] Ibn Mufliḥ's opinion that it is undesirable for a pretty woman (*al-mustaḥsana/al-ḥasnāʾ*) to go to congregational prayers with men was reproduced by ʿAlī ibn Sulaymān al-Mardāwī (d. 885/1480), Ibn al-Najjār (d. 972/1564), Manṣūr ibn Yūnus al-Bahūtī (d. 1051/1641), and Aḥmad al-Baʿlī (d. 1189/1775) in widely used Ḥanbalī legal manuals.[284]

Age distinctions were not merely an artifact of the early period, and the growing emphasis on sexual attraction did not completely eclipse considerations of life cycle and social role. Ibn Ḥamdān (d. 695/1296) states that "an old woman and a *barza* may go to the congregations of men."[285] Al-Mardāwī attributes the same opinion to a number of Ḥanbalī manuals.[286] The term *barza*, derived from a root meaning "to come out, be apparent, be prominent," refers to a semantic cluster involving public interaction with men, social respect, and (according to some definitions) mature age. The fourteenth-century CE jurist and lexicographer Aḥmad al-Fayyūmī defines the *barza* as "a chaste woman who goes out among men and speaks with them; she is the woman who has grown old and is no longer obligated to veil (*kharajat ʿan ḥadd al-maḥjūbāt*)."[287] Murtaḍā al-Zabīdī (d. 1205/1791), drawing on a number of earlier sources, describes the *barza* as a woman who displays herself openly and/or speaks forthrightly (*al-mutajāhira*); who is mature (*mutajālla*) or, according to another opinion, middle-aged (*kahla*); and who does not veil or conceal herself as young women do (*lā taḥtajib iḥtijāb al-shawābb*). Another definition suggests that the *barza* is a woman who goes out, with whom people (implicitly males) sit and about whom they speak, and who is chaste and intelligent, and still another suggests that she is a woman in whose opinions and chastity people have confidence.[288] This rich term links public visibility with age, yet does not associate it merely with the loss of beauty, but also with the possession of trustworthiness and social esteem. However, despite scattered appearances, it did not become a widespread focal term in the Ḥanbalī discussion of women's mosque attendance.[289]

Ḥanbalī scholars were not immune to the train of thought arguing that both the permissive practices of the Prophet's lifetime and the doctrines of the classical schools had been superseded by the decadence of the times. Ibn Rajab al-Ḥanbalī, writing in Damascus two generations after Ibn Taymīya, resoundingly affirmed the Prophet's endorsement of women's public prayer. Commenting on a ḥadīth stating that the Prophet kept congregational prayers brief in deference to the needs of women with crying infants, he observes that it proves

> that women used to take part in prayer behind the Messenger of God (peace be upon him!) in the mosque, having their children along with them; and that the Prophet knew that, and was considerate of their situation in his prayers, preferring what was easy for them and avoiding what caused hardship for them. That is proof that it was not undesirable (*makrūh*) for them to attend congregational prayers with him; otherwise, he would have forbidden them from attending prayers with him.

However, Ibn Rajab's confidence that women's mosque attendance was licit in the time of the Prophet is balanced by his conviction that it was inappropriate to the needs of later generations. Commenting on the ʿĀ'isha report, he states that "the Prophet used to allow some of the things that he did because there was no corruption (*fasād*) in his time…; so if he had seen what happened after [his death] he would not have continued to allow it, but would have forbidden it, because he only commanded righteousness and forbade corruption." In support of this point, he cites the fact that slave girls used to go into the markets unveiled in the lifetime of the Prophet and in the caliphates of Abū Bakr and ʿUmar, to the point that ʿUmar would punish slave girls for appearing veiled; "that was because of the prevalence of good character in that time; then that passed away, and corruption appeared and spread, so that which they allowed is no longer permitted." (In other words, the decadent mores of later times demand that even slave girls cover themselves modestly.) Ibn Rajab continues,

> So the scholars have differed about [the permissibility of] women's attending congregational mosques to pray with men. Some of them disapproved of it in all cases, which is the clear senses (*ẓāhir*) of what is transmitted from ʿĀ'isha. She inferred that permission was given to them before they did what they did; it was based on a rationale, and that rationale no longer exists.[290]

The length and vigor of Ibn Rajab's discussion suggest that it may express his own sentiments; however, he goes on to detail the classical doctrines without attempting to assert a blanket prohibition on women's mosque attendance as the valid school norm. Overall, Ḥanbalī scholars continued to affirm that mosque attendance was permissible for women. In his influential manual *Kashshāf al-qināʿ*, al-Bahūtī states straightforwardly that it is *mubāḥ* for women to go to congregational prayers, with the permission of their husbands and without perfume, because women did so in the time of the Prophet.[291]

Starting in the seventh/thirteenth century, the traditional distinction between old and young women was thus downplayed in two contrasting ways: by affirming that it was neutral (*mubāḥ*) for all women to go to the mosque and by shifting attention to the woman's physical appearance. Both approaches tended to reduce to the position that women could go to mosques, but subject to reservations about the possibility of *fitna* and the superior merit of prayer within the home. Ḥanbalīs generally (although not unanimously) affirmed that it was meritorious for women to pray in congregation, but asserted vigorously that it was superior to do so at home. Al-Mardāwī notes that whether it is desirable or merely neutral for women to pray in a group, "it is better for her to pray in her home in all cases, without dispute."[292]

As we have seen, in the other Sunnī schools the opinion spread, starting around the seventh/thirteenth century, that it was undesirable for latter-day women to attend the mosque at all. Among Ḥanbalīs, in contrast, the argument that changing times had rendered women's mosque attendance altogether impermissible seems to have had little influence. The opinion that "to forbid them from going out [to mosques] in this time is more beneficial to [women] and to men, in more than one regard" is cited in passing in two of the most comprehensive compendia of Ḥanbalī law, but does not seem to have been prevalent.[293] Certainly there appears to be no equivalent to the emotive and extreme arguments of ʿAlāʾ al-Dīn al-Bukhārī or Taqī al-Dīn al-Ḥiṣnī. The Ḥanbalīs' resistance to this trend may be rooted in their ideological commitment to direct application of ḥadīth, which militated against bold assertions of the current inapplicability of the Prophet's statement that women should not be barred from mosques. It may also be related, as we shall see in a later chapter of this book, to the prominent and respected role of women in the Ḥanbalī culture of religious scholarship (particularly in Damascus, where many of the relevant Ḥanbalī scholars resided). In this respect, it is with right that Melchert observes that "Ḥanbalī writers usually defend the right of women to go to the mosque" and categorizes the Ḥanbalī *madhhab* as the "most permissive" school on the issue of women's mosque attendance.[294]

CONCLUSION

This longitudinal survey of legal opinions on women's mosque access demonstrates a high degree of negotiability in the terms and substance of a legal question of general religious relevance. Not only the concrete content of the legal norms asserted by scholars, but also the basic models of gender underlying them changed significantly over the centuries. Although one of the most important shifts occurred around the fifth century AH/eleventh century CE, when scholars reframed the raw materials of the early *madhhab* traditions into what would prove to be the basic outlines of their school doctrines' "classical" form, serious renegotiation of terminology and norms continued far beyond that period. Thus, this case provides one more example of the occurrence of substantive legal change in the postclassical period, a subject of extensive academic discussion in recent decades.[295] This change included both unprecedented repudiations of women's right to attend the mosque and newly vigorous affirmations of its legitimacy, belying both older stereotypes about the rigidity of Islamic law and somewhat newer assumptions about its progressive and uniform marginalization of women's interests over time. Neither, however, can the scholars involved be characterized as a group (on this particular point) as benevolently invested in the perceived aspirations of Muslim women;[296] prejudicial assumptions about women's nature, rights, and roles were far from monolithic, but they were widespread. More importantly, however, such assumptions were highly variable; they were actively contested by scholars within a given time and school and shifted substantially from one period to another. Indeed, the terminology and underlying assumptions of the debate are in many cases far more revealing than the (sometimes modest) distinctions among the concrete rules advocated by the different scholars.

Perhaps the most central issue in the juristic discussion of women's mosque access is the distinction between older and younger women. Although ḥadīth texts offer scant support for such a distinction, it is attributed to the eponymous founders of each of the four Sunnī schools; disapproval of attendance by young women was repeatedly described as the object of an interschool consensus, and all schools had a much more positive attitude toward mosque-going by elderly women. By the fifth/eleventh century this distinction was often interpreted in terms of sexual allure, rather than of life-cycle. In later centuries the differentiation between old and young women was contested, both by those (including Ḥanbalīs and ḥadīth-oriented Shāfiʿīs) who countenanced mosque attendance by women of all ages, if with many caveats, and by those (including many later Ḥanafīs and some Shāfiʿīs) who wished to discourage mosque attendance by any women at all. The debate over mosque attendance by women of different age cohorts formed part of a wider dialogue over gender, age, and the nature and rationale of the limits placed on the activities of women.

It may be inferred that the early distinction between young and old women was rooted in actual social practice, even though it was subject to critique on textual or normative grounds. The Iraqi litterateur al-Jāḥiẓ (d. 255/869) observed that "a woman who has become too old to marry (*al-marʾa al-muʿannasa*) goes out among men (*tabruz liʾl-rijāl*) and is not ashamed to do so." He himself regards this distinction as being without normative foundation: "If it were forbidden when she was young (*shābba*), it would not become permissible when she became old (*ʿunnisat*); rather, this is a matter that has been exaggerated by people who surpass the bounds of jealousy (*al-ghayra*) to the point of ill-nature and narrow-mindedness."[297] Although his terminology overlaps only in part with that of the early legal sources on women's mosque attendance, it reinforces the impression that the most stringent forms of seclusion were limited to nubile young women who were eligible for marriage. As a matter of custom, a woman considered too old to marry was free to appear in public in mixed company, although the normative basis for this distinction was unclear.[298]

The idea that standards of modesty could be relaxed for older women is one for which scholars found some warrant in the Qur'an. Verse 24:60 states, "As for elderly women (*al-qawāʿid min al-nisāʾ*) who have no hope of marriage, there is no blame upon them if they lay aside their (outer) garments, if they do not flaunt their charms." Interestingly, there seem to have been some efforts to link the terminology of verse 24:60 to the precedent for women's mosque attendance set in the Prophet's lifetime. Al-Ṭabarānī (d. 360/971) records three different versions of a report in which a woman recounts, "I saw the elderly women (*al-nisāʾ al-qawāʿid*) praying in the mosque with the Prophet."[299] The effort to project age distinctions onto the lifetime of the Prophet apparently evoked some resistance; Aḥmad ibn ʿAmr al-Bazzār (d. 292/905) reports an anecdote in which the Prophet's Companion Anas—who survived long after the Prophet's death and thus became an authority on his practice—"was asked about the old women; did they use to go to prayers with the Messenger of God?" He replies with some asperity, "Yes, and the young ones!"[300] In general, as we have seen, efforts to ground an age limitation for women's mosque access in the sunna were fairly minimal and ultimately unsuccessful.

As in the debate over women's mosque attendance, later scholars commenting on verse 24:60 seem to have become increasingly uncomfortable with the idea of a potentially lengthy period of maturity when a woman who was still physically vigorous (and perhaps sexually attractive) would enjoy the freedoms of seniority. The term *qawāʿid* comes from a verbal root indicating either "to cease, desist" or "to sit down"; specifically with respect to a woman, it generally refers to the cessation of menstrual periods and, consequently, of childbearing. The majority of early exegetes seem to have defined the "elderly" women of verse 24:60 straightforwardly as those who were postmenopausal.[301] In contrast, there is a clear trend away from the consensus defining *al-qawāʿid* as postmenopausal women by the sixth/twelfth century. The majority of later exegetes reject this definition apparently less onlexical or textual grounds than because they find its practical implications unacceptable; a postreproductive woman might yet have some allure. For instance, Ibn al-Jawzī emphasizes that *qawāʿid* cannot mean postmenopausal women because such a woman may desire marriage. Rather, it designates a woman who sits a lot because she is too enfeebled by age to move around.[302] Not all Qur'an commentators of the classical and postclassical periods define *qawāʿid* as the very elderly.[303] Nevertheless, there is a clear trend over time to shift the more lenient standards of dress and behavior from active maturity to disability and decrepitude, from the matron to the hag.

Just as later commentaries on verse 24:60 emphasized the potential sexual allure of postmenopausal women (and thus limited the privileges of maturity to the very old), over time the juristic discussion of women's mosque attendance reflected a concern with *fitna* that increasingly extended to the final stages of the life cycle. This trend is discernible in the taxonomy constructed by Ibn Rushd, which limits mosque attendance by the *mutajālla* and posits a new and more senior category, the *ʿajūz*, who alone is entitled to worship publicly as freely as a man.[304] Much later, the Ḥanafī jurist Ibn al-Humām grudgingly allowed an exception only for "old women with a foot in the grave, not including old women who adorn themselves or those who still have a breath of life in them."[305] The redefinition of the "old woman" (*ʿajūz*) as one who stands at death's door was necessary only for those jurists who continued to affirm that some women could attend prayers at the mosque; for those later scholars who discouraged mosque attendance by women of all ages, the word *ʿajūz* could retain a broader meaning. The tenth/sixteenth-century Ḥanafī scholar Shaykh-Zādeh, who asserts that "in our times" no women should go out to the mosque, states simply that "[t]he *shābba* is from fifteen to twenty-nine [years of age], and the *ʿajūz* is from fifty to the end of life."[306]

Over time, in the *fiqh* literature there seems to be a trend away from a deeply held (and largely unexamined) assumption of changing social roles over the female life cycle and toward an increasing tendency to see all women as fundamentally defined by the enduring potential for sexual temptation. Ultimately, this trend was carried to its logical conclusion by scholars who posited that all women to the brink of the grave were latent sources of sexual disorder. Scholars who disputed the distinction between old and young women tended to see sexual allure as inseparable from existence in a female body. At best, they absolved women of the suspicion of *fitna* at the threshold of mortality, limiting the privileges of maturity to the decrepit crone rather than extending it to the entire postreproductive stage of life.

Why did attitudes toward the older woman change so markedly over time? One possible explanation has to do with the evolution of the concept of *fitna*. This term, which occurs thirty-four times in the Qur'an, does not there have specifically erotic or gendered overtones. In general, it designates a test, trial, or temptation; both well-being and adversity are tests, offering both the opportunity for fidelity and the occasion for sin. Within the corpus of ḥadīth, the term *fitna* is still not yet primarily associated with women, with eroticism, or with the mixing of the sexes; it far more often appears with connotations of religious or political dissidence.[307] However, compilations such as those of Bukhārī and Muslim contain the report that most famously and definitively established the association between women and *fitna*: "I have left no temptation after me that is more harmful to men than women."[308] An association between the concept of *fitna* and women and sexuality had thus emerged by at least by the first half of the third/ninth century (and possibly in the time of the Prophet himself), although it was not yet the predominant connotation of the term.[309] At this time, the Iraqi litterateur al-Jāḥiẓ is aware of the sexual meaning of the term (although he applies it only to the erotic wiles of sexually available slave women; he does not use it in his analysis of social and visual contact between free women and men, although this may be because his polemical point is to deny the impropriety of such contact).[310] As we have seen, *fitna* in the sense of disruptive sexual appeal is also said to have been invoked in the same period by Ibn Ḥanbal.

All of this is not to say that the Qur'an and ḥadīth display no concern with sexual temptation, with female modesty, or with the possible bad consequences of the mixing of the sexes. Nevertheless, these concerns (which do appear in various contexts and to various extents) have not yet coalesced around the term *fitna*. Arguably, they have also not yet assumed the centrality or the form that they would assume in later legal discussions. The trajectory of the development of the concept of *fitna* remains to be fully researched, but in the debate over women's public worship it appears to have been current among ḥadīth scholars in the third/ninth century and established as the central category of legal analysis by the fifth/eleventh century. This development is reflected in the work of the Mālikī Ibn Rushd, the Ḥanafī al-Sarakhsī, and the Shāfiʿīs al-Māwardī and Abū Isḥāq al-Shirāzī, all of whom retrospectively construct *fitna* as the global rationale for restrictions on women's participation in public worship. The emphasis on *fitna* in turn raised the concern (addressed explicitly by Ibn Rushd and al-Shirāzī) that elderly women might yet exercise some allure. In a sentiment attributed to al-Ghazālī by his commentator al-Nawawī, "sexual desire cannot be pinned down (*al-shahwa lā tanḍabiṭ*)"; that is, it cannot be stipulated to cease when the woman reaches a specific age.[311]

The division of women into age groups at least potentially subject to significantly different behavioral norms suggests that, particularly in the first to second century, "woman" was not a homogeneous or monolithic category in Islamic legal discourses. The class of "woman" was crosscut not only by age cohorts, but also by a deep division between the norms relating to slave and free women. The distinction between slave and free women did not feature in the overall debate over women's mosque attendance, perhaps because slave women were in any case not at liberty to choose their own destinations and activities.

Like the distinctions in modesty and seclusion practices between younger and older women, those between free women and slaves had little textual basis. However, like the distinctions among age cohorts, they were deeply ingrained in the early period; as we have seen, Ibn Rajab al-Ḥanbalī cited the example of the caliph ʿUmar, who is said to have beaten slave girls who dared to venture forth veiled in imitation of free women. As in the case of distinctions among women of different age cohorts, however, this distinction between slave and free women became increasingly problematic for many thinkers as the concept of *fitna* became more central to their thinking; as a preoccupation with physical attraction displaced the concern for social roles, the physical exposure of the slave girl (or earlier scholars' endorsement of that exposure) increasingly became a problem.[312] Ibn Rajab is not the only thinker who draws an explicit parallel in this regard with the issue of women's mosque attendance. The Qur'an commentator al-Qurṭubī argues that "now" all women, slave and free, must cover themselves and veil their faces (*yajib al-satr wa'l-taqannuʿ*):

> This is similar to [the fact that] the Companions of the Messenger of God forbade women to go to mosques after the death of the Messenger of God, despite the fact that he said "Do not forbid the maidservants of God from [going to] the mosques of God," so that ʿĀʾisha said, "If the Messenger of God had lived until this time of ours, he would have forbidden them from going out to the mosques."[313]

Thus, at least by the seventh/thirteenth century—in a broad development that seems to have crossed boundaries of *madhhab* and geography—women were well established in *fiqh* discourse as a much more monolithic group pervasively associated with the fear of sexual chaos.[314]

Paradoxically, however, the rise of *fitna* as the supreme criterion in analyzing legal rules relating to women sometimes served to undermine, rather than reinforce, the monolithic nature of the category of "woman." Even as a protean and expansive view of sexual desire extended strict standards of modesty to postmenopausal women and to women in bondage, scholars also came to ponder the sexual desirability (always, of course, to men) of some males. The issue of the sultry youth (*al-amrad*)—the adolescent whose beard has just begun to sprout—seems to have loomed large in juristic discussions of modesty and forbidden gazing only after the fifth/eleventh century (although there were relevant reports about the Prophet and early Muslim authorities). One factor that may have brought it into relief was the (at least perceived) homoeroticism of ṣūfī groups.[315] In later Shāfiʿī sources, the beardless youth is introduced to the discussion over mosque attendance. In his commentary on *al-Irshād*, Ibn Ḥajar al-Haytamī states that the beardless young man (*al-amrad*) from whom *fitna* is to be feared is like a woman in this regard.[316] This was a subject that received intermittent and ambivalent treatment from his successors in the school.[317] The Ottoman Ḥanafī muftī Kemalpaşazadeh (d. 940/1534) argued that a teenaged boy could, like a woman, be excluded from the front rows of prayer "if the youth is carnally desirable (*müşteha*)"—the same word that was used to distinguish the nubile women who were to be discouraged from attending the mosque.[318] Thus, as scholarly preoccupation with the issue of *fitna* grew more pervasive, for at least some scholars the binary distinction between males and females was once again fractured (this time perhaps by a hairline crack rather than the gulf that had once separated old women from young women). It was the criterion of *fitna* that allowed Ibn Rushd to declare that the crone was "like a man" with respect to mosque attendance and Ibn Ḥajar al-Haytamī to say that the adolescent boy was "like a woman."

Of course, the decline of the consensus distinguishing between old and young woman with respect to mosque attendance does not indicate the disappearance of social distinctions among women of different age cohorts. Indeed, patterns of female modesty or seclusion continue to be tied to specific stages of the life cycle in some Islamic societies today.[319] Considerations of age and social role continued to be socially relevant in the time period of many of the legal texts deemphasizing issues of age in favor of a broad concept of *fitna*. Writing about Anatolia in the early Ottoman period, Peirce has demonstrated that court documents

> employed a variety of words to denote female and male. . . . Perhaps the most striking feature of this multiple vocabulary was its careful attention to stages in the individual's life cycle. Gender identity continually transformed itself over the course of one's lifespan by associating different normative behaviors with each phase in the life cycle.[320]

However, the Turkish age terminology of the court documents contrasts sharply with that of the Arabic legal texts. Peirce notes that "the scaffolding of social controls around the female began with marriage rather than with the achievement of physical maturation" and that unmarried adolescent girls moved with some freedom;[321] this conflicts with the model posited by Islamic legal discourses, where a girl becomes subject to modesty strictures at puberty and marriage has no impact on the behavioral norms to which she is theoretically subject. Similarly, the Turkish terminology reflects no distinction among adult, married women of different ages, suggesting "that changes in status natural to this period in one's life—aging and widowhood, for example—were less significant than its essential continuity."[322] The contrast with the *fiqh* texts' emphasis on the postsexual status of the aged woman need hardly be emphasized.

The disparity between the Arabic legal terminology and the Turkish vocabulary of Ottoman court records (as well as, presumably, the colloquial terminology used by Ottoman subjects in their own lives) suggests that there is no one-to-one correspondence between the life-cycle rubrics or temporal conventions of the normative legal discourse and the operational categories of local societies over time. Indeed, given the wide geographical dissemination of individual Islamic legal manuals and their terminological conservatism, this would be impossible; the legal texts do not display the kind of diversity or changeability that would reflect immediate responsiveness to current local categories and customs.

As we have seen, however, juristic terminology was not static; new categories sometimes did emerge or gain new salience, presumably in response to newer social developments. An example of a new designation, emerging by the seventh/thirteenth century, is the term *mukhaddara* (which does not appear in early *fiqh* works). For postclassical jurists, the *mukhaddara* is the woman who secludes herself as a sign of high social status. She is defined variously as a woman who is not seen by nonrelated males or who does not go out frequently to perform errands. The status of *mukhaddara* could be ascribed on the basis of the rank or customs of the woman's husband or family, or it could be earned on the basis of personal practice (although, like the repentance of a sinner, it might then be recognized only after a waiting period).[323] Over time, the *mukhaddara* supplanted the "woman who does not go out during the daytime" in discussions of the conditions under which a secluded woman could be summoned from her home to give an oath, although not without some tension between the two conventions.[324]

Although mosque-going was not a central concern in the definition of this term, in his *Tuḥfat al-muḥtāj* Ibn Ḥajar al-Haytamī remarks that a *mukhaddara* may go out for condolence calls, visits, or expeditions to the public baths because such an excursion "does not degrade her, unlike [going to] a mosque or the like."[325]

Despite some evolution in juristic terminology, however, we cannot take it as an unproblematic mirror of social realities. Rather, in the overt content and underlying assumptions of juristic debates like the discussion of women's mosque access we can discern the evolution of potent symbolic constructs. As we shall see in chapter 3, although legal categories neither dictated behavior nor unproblematically reflected it, they were very much available for active deployment when real behavior was at stake. This study posits that the construction and negotiation of gender ideals in the legal discourse are significant not because such constructs were unilaterally efficacious, but because they were actively asserted and contested and because they were of independent cultural significance.

Indeed, the symbolic and ideological importance of legal categories and norms should not be underestimated. Although scholars promoted various evaluations of the permissibility or desirability of women's mosque attendance, in other contexts they often simply assumed that public prayer was a distinctively male activity—one that demonstrated the religious and human superiority of men. Karen Bauer has noted that participation in congregational and Friday prayers is one of the factors cited by exegetes in the interpretation of verse 2:228 of the Qur'an, which refers to a "degree" (of privilege or superiority) enjoyed by men over women. Although this interpretation is attributed to at least one early authority, it becomes prevalent only starting in the fifth/eleventh century (the period, as we have seen, when *fitna* discourse contributed to a broader doctrinal consensus excluding most women from public prayer).[326]

In some cases, the presumed exclusion of women from public worship even shaped scholars' visualization of the rewards that awaited male and female believers in the afterlife. Based on ḥadīth texts suggesting that the blessed in Paradise enjoy the vision of God on occasions corresponding to their acts of worship in this world, Ibn Taymīya argues that, because men commune with God in congregational prayer every Friday, in the afterlife they will attend a corresponding weekly gathering to gaze upon Him. Women will not participate (although Ibn Taymīya affirms that they will enjoy the beatific vision on other occasions) because, even in the afterlife, sexual jealousy (*ghayra*) dictates that they worship within their heavenly homes.[327] Citing traditions stating that in the afterlife people's proximity to God will be based on the order of their arrival at Friday prayers, al-Suyūṭī argues that, because women are not obligated to attend Friday prayers at all, it is not improbable that they would be denied any share in the beatific vision.[328]

Thus, ideas about women's participation or nonparticipation in public prayer deeply informed at least some scholars' religious imaginations and their vision of gender roles in ways that far exceeded the purview of practical social behavior. In the next chapter, we shall examine how legal doctrines on women's mosque attendance may or may not have shaped concrete, this-worldly behavior.

two

RECONSTRUCTING PRACTICE

Whereas the last chapter focused on the contours and development of the legal debate over women's mosque access, this one will examine the evidence for women's de facto presence in mosques. Because premodern authors were generally not motivated by a desire to document women's usage of mosque space for its own sake, however, such information usually emerges from the interstices of works driven by other concerns. Rather than representing a straightforward shift from prescriptive to descriptive sources, this chapter thus reflects a number of normative agendas, which will be acknowledged as we survey the evidence. The sources examined in the first and second chapters overlap at times; thus, for instance, fatwas often contain both contextually specific descriptions of concrete behavior (particularly, although not exclusively, in the sometimes lengthy questions posed to the muftī) and formal analysis of the appropriate legal response. Accordingly, the legal argumentation of some important fatwas has been discussed in the first chapter, and the passages addressing existing practice will be discussed in chapter 2. Nevertheless, it should be remembered that both aspects are components of the same normative enterprise; even the inquiries that evoke fatwas, although frequently rich in circumstantial detail, are often artfully crafted to promote specific agendas and to elicit particular responses. Similarly, works focused on the identification and denunciation of religious innovations (*bidaʿ*) often provide incomparably rich descriptions of practices diverging from the norms set out in legal sources; however, they are also fundamentally shaped by their authors' polemical concerns. Travelers' reports are less overtly normative, but also pervasively reflect the assumptions and agendas of their authors.

Because the evidence of women's actual presence and activities in mosques (or of their absence or preference for other religious venues) is sparse and uneven, this chapter is necessarily shaped by the existence of useful sources. The nature and focus of the data thus vary from case to case, based on the genre and emphases of the available material. The differential focus of the sources is presumably not completely arbitrary, however, but may to some extent reflect substantive differences in regional practices and assumptions. Rather than offering a comprehensive chronological survey of each geographical area studied, each section will focus on the specific period or periods for which the available sources are particularly rich and on the specific issues most salient in those sources. The sections are organized roughly according to their primary chronological cencentration. The first, on Iraq, focuses on the first two centuries after the Muslim conquest and examines the emergence of resistance to women's presence in mosques in relation to contemporary practice. The second section, which focuses on the building and renovation of several of the great mosques of Muslim Spain and North Africa in the eighth to fourteenth centuries CE, examines the construction of architecturally distinct women's prayer spaces and the legal questions it raised. The third section, which centers on Cairo in the fourteenth century CE, examines the range of religious and profane activities women pursued in mosques and compares the appeal of mosques with that of graveyards. The fourth section, on Syria, focuses primarily on mosque-based ḥadīth transmission and preaching in the fourteenth to seventeenth centuries CE. The last section, which takes up the issue of outsider reports of women's mosque access, centers on women's presence in mosques in Ottoman Istanbul in the sixteenth to nineteenth centuries CE.

IRAQ

As we have seen in the section on Ḥanafī doctrine in chapter 1, some early Iraqi (and particularly Kufan) authorities manifested a hostility toward women's public worship that contrasted with the attitudes of their Ḥijāzī colleagues, as well as with the apparent presence of women in the mosque in the lifetime of the Prophet. A number of different reports suggest that the prominent Companion of the Prophet Ibn Masʿūd (d. 32 AH/652–53 CE), a figure who personified the religious heritage of Kufa, vigorously combated women's attendance at Friday prayers; according to some versions, he even pelted them with stones to encourage them to go home.[1] Ibn Masʿūd is similarly reported to have declared that "it is better for a woman to pray in her home than in any other place," with the exception of an old woman who shuffles in her boots or who "is beyond hope of marriage." He is also said to have stated that "when a woman goes out, Satan gazes down upon her," even if she proposes to go out for a pious purpose such as attending a funeral or praying in a mosque.[2] These well-known narratives support the widespread assumption (expressed by some classical Islamic scholars, as well as in modern works) that in the context of the Muslim communities that grew outside of the Arabian Peninsula as a result of the conquests, women's mosque attendance was suppressed relatively soon after the Prophet's passing.

If opposition to women's mosque attendance originated primarily in the conquered territories, it seems to have been especially characteristic of Iraq—and particularly of the garrison city of Kufa. Christopher Melchert argues that "the cluster of hadith allowing women to go to the mosque originated in opposition to a Kufan custom of forbidding women to attend most prayers in the mosque."[3] Examining evidence about early Islamic funerary practices, Leor Halevi concludes that "Muslim pietists from eighth-century Kūfa displayed a novel and unprecedented concern with the segregation of the sexes," including a negative attitude toward women's participation in public worship.[4]

However, despite ideological opposition to women's attendance at public worship, the evidence does not suggest that Iraqi women ceased to frequent mosques during the lifetime of the Prophet's Companions. Indeed, in other reports Ibn Masʿūd himself seeks to regulate women's prayer in mosques rather than prohibiting it. In one, he counsels, "If you [feminine plural] pray in your homes [on Friday], pray four [cycles], and if you pray in the mosque, pray two."[5] He is also said to have placed elderly women in the first rows of women and young women all the way in the back.[6] Regardless of the historicity of any given report about Ibn Mas'ūd, early Iraqi sources did not find it plausible to represent him as finding (or even as leaving) the mosques empty of women.

One gets the impression from other reports as well that religious opposition to women's mosque attendance in Iraqi cities in this period was expressed in the face of women's actual presence in mosques. The prominent Kufan legal authority Ibrāhīm al-Nakhaʿī (d. 96/914) is said to have forbidden his three wives to attend Friday and congregational prayers[7]—apparently a stricture unusual enough to arouse comment—but he is also said to have led congregational prayers under the governorship of the tyrannical al-Ḥajjāj (when fear apparently thinned the ranks of the worshippers) with only a woman behind him.[8] The historian al-Ṭabarī (d. 310/923) recounts that during the uprising of al-Mukhtār in Kufa in 66/685, when men were taken captive and imprisoned in the palace, a woman "would go out as if she was heading to the Great Mosque to pray, or as if she was going to her family or visiting a relative of hers" when she was actually going to the palace to smuggle in food.[9] Here the mosque appears to be an ordinary destination assumed to arouse as little suspicion as a woman's visit to her kin.

Although the data are sparse, the situation would seem to have been little different in Basra; evidence suggests both the presence of women in mosques and the existence of sentiment against it. An anecdote about the Companion of the Prophet Abū Barza, who settled in Basra and died in the sixties of the first century AH, recounts that one day he returned home to find that his concubine (*umm walad*) was not there. Told that she was at the mosque, he greeted her on her return by yelling, "God has forbidden women to go out, and commanded them to remain in their homes, and not to follow a funeral procession, or go to a mosque, or attend Friday prayers!"[10]

The turbulent events of the mid-first century AH also involved dramatic appearances in mosques by women of a group that was not religiously typical, but that was nevertheless deeply rooted in the Iraqi milieu, the Khārijites. In 40 AH, the assassination of ʿAlī ibn Abī Ṭālib is said to have been instigated and orchestrated by a beautiful (and thus likely young) Khārijite woman, Qaṭām ibnat al-Shijna, who was at the time performing a religious retreat (*muʿtakifa*) in the Great Mosque of Kufa.[11] A generation later, during the governorship of al-Ḥajjāj, the Khārijite rebel Shabīb ibn Yazīd entered Kufa with his wife Ghazāla. According to Khalīfa ibn Khayyāṭ (d. 240/854), the latter "entered the mosque of Kufa and recited her litany (*wird*) in the mosque, and ascended the pulpit; she had vowed to do that."[12] According to a report transmitted by al-Ṭabarī, she "had made a vow to pray two prostration cycles (*rakʿatayn*) in the mosque of Kufa in which she would recite [the unusually lengthy Qur'anic chapters of] al-Baqara and Āl ʿImrān—and she did so."[13] The implication of this anecdote seems to be that Ghazāla had vowed to perform these acts in the mosque as a form of thanksgiving, presumably if the rebels managed to enter Kufa. Shabīb is also supposed to have left Ghazāla as his successor after his defeat, in which context she is stated by a much later source to have ascended the pulpit and given the Friday sermon.[14]

Ghazāla's actual delivery of a sermon would have represented the revolutionary egalitarianism of the Khārijite insurgents more than the everyday religious mores of contemporary Iraq. However, Qaṭām's religious retreat and Ghazāla's vow to pray in the mosque apparently fell within the mainstream of women's behavior. A very early source recounts an incident that occurred in Basra. The judge Shurayḥ (who served as judge there during the governorship of Ziyād ibn Abīhi, between 45 and 53 AH) was presented with an issue relating to women's mosque retreats. A woman had vowed to spend the month of Rajab in *iʿtikāf* at the mosque; however, Ziyād had recently heard bad rumors and forbidden the women to spend Rajab in the mosque that year. Shurayḥ reportedly exercised his legal insight by suggesting that the woman could expiate her vow by fasting the whole month and feeding poor people every night when she broke her fast.[15] The fact that Ziyād is said to have forbidden "the women" to spend the month in religious retreat in the mosque on a specific occasion as a result of rumors (presumably of bad behavior) suggests that it was otherwise customary practice. About a half a century later, al-Ḥasan al-Baṣrī (d. 110/728) is said to have been asked about a woman who vowed to pray two *rakʿas* in every congregational mosque in Basra if her husband was released from prison. Al-Ḥasan is supposed to have replied, "She should pray in the mosque of her clan (*masjid qawmihā*); she isn't capable of that! If ʿUmar ibn al-Khaṭṭāb were around to see her, he would beat her over the head (*la-awjaʿa raʾsahā*)."[16] Here al-Ḥasan's skepticism seems to be directed at the ambition and scope of the woman's vow rather than at the fact of her committing to pray in a mosque; to pray in her neighborhood mosque was both more feasible and perhaps (based on the reference to the redoubtable ʿUmar) also more modest.

Scruples about women's mosque attendance, and sporadic efforts at control by both scholarly and political authorities, appear to have coexisted with the apparent reality of women's presence in the mosques of Basra and Kufa at least for the duration of the first century AH. In terms of reconstructing women's mosque-related behavior and objectives, it is interesting to note the importance of vows and retreats, which seem to be mentioned more often than ordinary Friday or congregational prayers and which may reflect the distinctive patterns of early Iraqi Muslim women's mosque-based religiosity. It may be that the episodic nature of vows and retreats—and their adaptability to hopes and needs such as the release of a husband from prison—made them particularly attractive to women. (Of course, it is also possible that the routine nature of congregational prayer offered less occasion for conflict or comment.) Given the state of the sources, the historicity of any individual report is difficult to determine. What is more assured is the set of assumptions and patterns underlying the individual anecdotes. Even more significant than the literal veracity of an incident recounted from the first century AH may be the fact that it was plausible to an Iraqi author of the third or fourth century such as Ibn Abī Shayba (d. 235/849) or al-Ṭabarī (d. 310/923).

Reports about the second century AH similarly reflect the ongoing assumption of Iraqi women's presence in mosques. Some deal with historical figures whose actions may very well be accurately reported; even those that are purely literary or outright jokes, however, reflect the cultural worlds of their authors. The historian Ibn Saʿd (d. 230/845) recounts that the Kufan ḥadīth transmitter Misʿar ibn Kidām (d. ca. 152–55/769–72) had a mother of pietist leanings (*umm ʿābida*); Misʿar, who taught only in the congregational mosque, used to walk with her to the mosque, carrying her felt prayer mat. When they entered, he would spread the mat for her; she would stand and pray (apparently in the rear), while he went to the front of the mosque to teach his disciples.[17] The *Kitāb al-Aghānī* of Abū'l-Faraj al-Isfāhānī (d. 356/967) recounts a humorous anecdote in which a woman approaches the Basran poet al-Farazdaq (d. ca. 110–12/728–30) in the mosque to ask him a question.[18] Another story recounts that Abū Ḥanīfa's own mother avidly followed the preaching of a storyteller (*qāṣṣ*) in the mosque, to the point that she preferred the latter's legal opinion to that of her distinguished son.[19] A much later Iraqi source includes a humorous anecdote in which the Kufan traditionist al-Aʿmash (d. 148/765) is accosted on his way to the mosque with his wife.[20] In a discussion of Basran women devotees, Ibn al-Jawzī (d. 597/1201) cites Abū Khalda (d. 152/769) as reporting that he had never witnessed any man or woman with greater stamina for standing in prayer than Umm Ḥayyān al-Salmīya; "she would stand [in prayer] in the neighborhood mosque (*masjid al-ḥayy*) as if she were a palm tree blown to left and right by the wind."[21] Although these later sources do not necessarily accurately record the events of the second century, they may be rooted in earlier sources and certainly reflect an image of women's presence in mosques that persisted among later Iraqi authors.

In the third century AH, the Basran littérateur al-Jāḥiẓ (d. 255/869) recounts a comic tale, set in his hometown, in which a dog strays into an empty house during Ramadan.[22] The house is empty because the men are off tending their plantations and the women are off praying in the mosque (presumably the *tarāwīḥ* prayers, which take place at night during that month). Interestingly, although in one place the text states that the women are praying "in their [masculine plural] mosque," in another it states that they are "in their [feminine plural] mosque"—offering a tantalizing suggestion of a separate women's place of prayer. In any case, al-Jāḥiẓ's antic tale suggests that prayer in the mosque was a plausible narrative pretext for women's absence from home. In another source of the third century AH, Ibn Ḥanbal's son ʿAbd Allāh transmits a story in which the first-century female mystic Maʿādha al-ʿAdawīya is confronted in her tribal mosque in Basra (*masjid Banī ʿAdī*) by a man who complains, "One of you women comes to the mosque, puts down her head and lifts up her rear end!" She retorts, "Why do you look, then? Put dust in your eyes and don't look!" He protests, "I can't help but look!" Upon this, she explains, "When I am at home the children distract me, and when I am in the mosque it makes me more energetic [for prayer]."[23]

It also appears that early Iraqi judges held court in mosques, where women appeared as litigants and witnesses (although a recent study concludes that, particularly from the third AH/ninth century CE on, elite women were kept away by status-related ideals of seclusion).[24] One of the factors that recommended the main mosque as the site of judicial practice was its accessibility to the general public, including women. An anecdote attributed to Hilāl ibn al-ʿAlāʾ al-Raqqī (d. 280/894) recounts that the early-second-century Basran judge Iyās ibn Muʿāwiya was sitting in the mosque and saw three women entering. He cleverly inferred that one of them was bereaved of a child, the second was pregnant, and the third was menstruating (the last based on her turning away from the door in respect). Even though the anecdote itself may be apocryphal (and exists in several different versions, not all of them explicitly placed in the mosque), it reflects the assumption that women frequented the mosque long before the ripe old age envisioned by many Iraqi legal scholars; at least two of the women envisioned in this vignette are still in their childbearing years.[25]

Although sparse and anecdotal, the evidence clearly suggests that the opposition attributed to authoritative figures such as Ibn Masʿūd did not actually result in the discontinuation of Iraqi women's mosque attendance after the generation of the Prophet's Companions. It seems quite clear that at least some Iraqi women frequented mosques for various purposes, including regular prayers, pious retreats, and Ramadan devotions, well after the first generation of Muslims had died out and new cohorts of native-born Iraqi Muslims had arisen to take their place.

It has been argued that the limitations on women's mobility, visibility, and public participation that emerged in the first three centuries of the Muslim era reflected the new community's assimilation to the patriarchal mores of the new locales and established religious traditions amidst which early Muslims elaborated their faith after the conquests. In one very influential formulation, whereas the early Muslim women of Arabia "mingled freely with men" during the Prophet's lifetime, "Arab mores . . . changed as the Arabs adopted the ways of the conquered peoples."[26] Conversely, some authors have seen later restrictions on the public mobility and participation of Middle Eastern Jewish women (for instance) as resulting from Islamic influence.[27] Because of the paucity of relevant evidence, both arguments appear largely to reflect the preconceptions of the scholars involved.

With respect to the specific issue of women's attendance at public worship, there seems to be little evidence to suggest that disapproving attitudes among early Iraqi Muslim scholars were conditioned by the mores of the subject peoples. Legal debates in both the Palestinian and the Babylonian Talmud appear implicitly to assume the presence of women at synagogue worship.[28] The individual opinions on these issues are attributed to much earlier rabbinic authorities, but they were canonized in the two centuries preceding the rise of Islam and may reflect ongoing assumptions about ritual practice. An Iraqi Christian source of the Islamic period refers to women's customary presence on the western side of church naves.[29] Much like their opposition to women's participation in funerals, early Kufan Muslim authorities' objections to women's public worship seem most likely to have arisen from their own evolving internal religious, social, and political concerns.[30] They appear to have reflected neither the preexisting customs of local populations nor the ongoing de facto practice of Muslim women. Nor did they reflect a monolithic "Islamic" ethic, but rather competed with other pious values, including women's desire to partake of the auspicious and holy aura of the mosque.

SPAIN AND NORTH AFRICA

Unlike in most other areas of the Arabo-Islamic world, accounts of the construction and renovation of major early mosques in North Africa and Andalusia (areas historically dominated from an early period by the Mālikī *madhhab*[31]) often mention spaces explicitly designated for women's prayer. The construction of physically distinct women's prayer space is not a practice with obvious precedents in the sunna. Ḥadīth reports do not describe any architecturally distinct prayer space for women in the Prophet's mosque in Medina, but imply that women simply prayed in rows behind the men.[32] However, a report transmitted from the early Medinian historian Ibn Zabāla (a student of Mālik ibn Anas) describing the expansion of the mosque ordered by the caliph al-Mahdī in 161/777–78, refers to "the women's arcades" (*saqāʾif al-nisāʾ*), which appear to have been at the back of the enclosed courtyard of the mosque.[33]

Not much later, the same arrangement seems to have been reproduced in al-Andalus. The Spanish Umayyad caliph Hishām I (reigned 172–80/788–96) is reported to have built roofed arcades at the back of the Great Mosque of Cordoba specifically as a space for women's prayer (*banā bi-ākhar al-masjid saqāʾif li-ṣalāt al-nisāʾ*).[34] The mosque was further enlarged by ʿAbd al-Raḥmān ibn al-Ḥakam (reigned 206–38/822–52), who broadened the mosque by adding two additional bays (*bahw*) on each side. Each of these two additional bays opened into a gallery (*saqīfa*), supported by nineteen columns, with doors opening onto the already existing women's galleries at the back of the old mosque.[35] (These statements have been taken by some modern scholars as a reference to raised balconies; it is possible that the columns supported the floors of the galleries rather than their roofs, although this is not the most obvious meaning of the word *saqāʾif*, which simply designates an area that is roofed over.[36]) In addition to the two side galleries, one was constructed at the back of the courtyard. Thus, galleries for women (whether elevated or at ground level) surrounded the mosque's courtyard on three sides.[37] The construction of ʿAbd al-Raḥmān's galleries is supposed to have "added thirty prayer spaces for women when they attended the congregational mosque (*istawsaʿa bihinna thalāthīna makān muṣallā li'l-nisāʾ idhā ḥaḍarna al-masjid al-jāmiʿ*)"[38]—which sounds extraordinarily conservative even if the galleries were quite narrow, if each "space" accommodated a single woman.

In later sources, the women's sections are described as "enclosures (*maqāṣīr*, sing. *maqṣūra*)," which suggests that they involved physical and visual barriers rather than simply being demarcated by the pillars of the arcade.[39] The *maqṣūra* in general was understood as an innovation of the early Islamic period, introduced by Ummayad rulers to protect themselves from hostile subjects.[40] It is not clear from the references to the women's *maqāṣīr* in Cordoba whether they were identical with the galleries, enclosed only part of the galleries, or opened out from them. The mosque also had doors specially designated for women, although fewer than were allocated to men. Describing the mosque as enlarged during the reign of Hishām ibn al-Ḥakam (reigned 366–99/976–1009), Ibn Bashukwāl states that on its west side there were nine doors, including a large one reserved for women and leading into their enclosures (*maqāṣīr*); there was a similar arrangement on the east side, and on the north side there were two large doors for men and one for women leading into the *maqāṣīr*.[41] Al-Ḥakam al-Mustanṣir (reigned 350–66/961–76) is said to have demolished the old ablutions fountain that was in the courtyard of the mosque and replaced it with four fountains, on each side a large one for men and a small one for women.[42]

All of this information, fragmentary as it is, suggests that accommodations for women in the Great Mosque of Cordoba were a significant and ongoing concern in successive renovations of the mosque, although the numbers of women were expected to be significantly smaller than those of men, and that efforts to separate male and female worshippers may have increased over time. Despite the measures to demarcate separate space for women, however, the sexes do not seem to have been strictly divided on occasions such as Friday prayers. Aḥmad ibn ʿAbd Allāh ibn ʿAbd al-Raʾūf al-Qurṭubī (d. 424/1032–33), who was in charge of the *maẓālim* courts in Cordoba and wrote a manual for the morals inspector (*muḥtasib*), writes in his advice for keeping order in the mosque on Friday that the *muḥtasib* ought to prevent male beggars from walking between the rows of women in the congregational mosque or its courtyards unless the specific beggar in question is too elderly and enfeebled to feel or excite sexual desire; similarly, he should prevent a young female beggar (*shābba*) from passing between the rows of men in the mosque or its courtyards, but could permit a female beggar who is elderly (*mutajālla*) and enfeebled. He should also prevent men and women from mixing at times of congregational prayer or on festivals.[43]

Women's attendance at Friday congregational prayers in Andalusian cities such as Cordoba was a phenomenon that clearly persisted in later centuries, and despite normative emphasis on the perils presented by younger women, it apparently was not limited to women of advanced age. The judge Ibn al-Munāṣif (d. 620/1223), who served in several Andalusian cities and settled in Cordoba,[44] complains bitterly of the presence of young and nubile women in the Friday mosques. As one of the "objectionable practices that are customary in places of prayer," he mentions "the attendance of some women who are cause for concern such as young and full-figured women (*al-shābbāt al-mumtaliʾāt laḥman*), from whom temptation (*fitna*) can be expected, at the Friday mosques; there is much harm in that."[45] Ibn al-Munāṣif himself advocates that women (whether merely young and buxom ones or all women he does not clarify) should be denied access to the mosque if their presence causes harm, and argues that ʿĀʾisha herself had banned them in a time much less corrupt and fraught with innovations than his own. As in so many other cases, his argument that women should be barred from the mosque stands in stark contrast with his depiction of the actual state of affairs.

Despite efforts at separating men and women, mosques such as the Great Mosque of Cordoba were probably among the few public places where a high-status young woman might tarry and encounter the opposite sex, a fact that seems to have freighted interactions there with some peril of damage to a woman's reputation. Outside of times of communal prayer such as Friday noon, the mosque was the site of teaching and socialization that were not always of a purely religious character. In one anecdote, the littérateur Abū ʿĀmir Ibn Shuhayd (d. 426/1035) is sitting in the Great Mosque of Cordoba with a group of his companions on the night of the twenty-seventh of Ramadan (Laylat al-Qadr). However, Abū ʿĀmir and his friends are engaged not in pious exercises, but in lighthearted banter when a young woman from a prominent Cordoban family comes by accompanied by slave women, "looking for a spot to engage in intimate colloquy with her Lord and seeking a place to ask forgiveness for her sins." She is described as "veiled, fearful and watchful of those who observed her"; with her is a young son described as being "like a myrtle bough, or a gazelle." When she catches sight of Abū ʿĀmir, she quickly turns around and withdraws in alarm, for fear that he will flirt with her or shame her by revealing her name; indeed, when he sees her, he immediately does so.[46] This anecdote, whether or not it records an actual incident, reflects the issues of social propriety and reputation that were involved when young and high-status women ventured into public space to pray.

Evidence from Mālikī North Africa as well suggests that as of the fifth/eleventh century, the use of *maqṣūras* to separate women from men in congregational prayer was still neither uniform nor completely uncontroversial. In an exchange preserved in the collections of al-Burzulī (d. 841/1438) and al-Wansharīsī (d. 914/1508), the Qayrawānī jurists al-Lakhmī (d. 478/1085) and ʿAbd al-Ḥamīd (d. 486/1093) are asked about several problems that had emerged in the congregational mosque (*al-jāmiʿ*).[47] Presumably the mosque in question is the Great Mosque of Qayrawān, particularly because the first question in the series has to do with the cistern located in the courtyard; Qayrawān was known for its dependence on rainwater gathered in cisterns, and the ancient cistern in the courtyard of the Great Mosque (to which others were later added) was also well known.[48]

One query states:

> The women have a custom (*li'l-nisāʾ ʿāda*) of praying in the mosque and in its arcades. On Friday there are many people, and sometimes the rows of men are continuous with the rows of women, and sometimes some of the women mix with the men. The judge and some of the *shuyūkh* were agreed in the opinion that an enclosure (*maqṣūra*) should be erected in one of the [mosque's] arcades (*fī baʿḍ al-saqāʾif minhu*) for the women, and in order to provide a screen it should be secured with bricks,[49] and the women would pray in it at prayer times. A *muḥtasib*[50] from among the students arose and said, "Nothing should be innovated in the mosque that did not exist in the early days until the scholars are consulted."[51]

Al-Lakhmī's reply to this question is curt: "If men are in need of the space where the women pray, such that men would pray there if the women did not get there first, nothing should be built there and the women should be forbidden from coming; the men are more entitled to it. If the men are not crowded and do not need that space, it is good to build a screen and barrier between [the men and the women]."[52] ʿAbd al-Ḥamīd replies simply: "If the construction conceals the women and no harm to the mosque or to the worshipers results from it, that should be done. It is a matter of discretion (*huwa ʿalā qadr al-ijtihād*)."[53]

It is notable that, according to the wording of the inquiry, women would have been restricted to the *maqṣūra* only at prayer times. It would appear that the divider was actually constructed, as the contemporary Abū ʿUbayd al-Bakrī (d. 487/1094) states that "the mosque has ten doors and a *maqṣūra* for women . . . between which and the mosque there is another wall that is perforated (*mukharram*) and skillfully fashioned (*muḥkam al-ʿamal*)."[54]

Other North African mosques offered women's space that appears to have been architecturally more separate from the main prayer space. Women were allocated separate space in the two main mosques of Fez, the Qarawīyīn and al-Andalus mosques. At least as of the eighth/fourteenth century, the Qarawīyīn had a women's prayer room (*bayt al-nisāʾ*) at the back of the courtyard (*bi-muʾakhkhar al-ṣaḥn*) with its own exterior door; the mosque had two small doors reserved exclusively for the use of women, as compared to fifteen larger ones for men.[55] A modern source claims that the judge al-Maghīlī, who oversaw the renovations made on the mosque in the reign of the amīr Abū Yaʿqūb Yūsuf (reigned 685–706/1286–1307), created an upper-story colonnade (*riwāq*) for women above the mosque depository (*mustawdaʿ*), a space from which women could follow the teaching sessions going on below.[56] This would be consistent with modern data about the layout of the mosque. A plan of the mosque from the 1920s shows a "women's mosque," apparently elevated and accessed by a stairway, at the northwest corner of the mosque (and thus at one of the back corners of the courtyard);[57] a Western traveler's account from 1918 refers to "the *mestonda*, or raised hall above the court, where women come to pray"[58]—perhaps a misheard reference to the *mustawdaʿ*, or depository. Lucien Golvin remarks of this space that its small size implies that at the time women were no longer attending congregational prayers in large numbers.[59] However, pending further evidence it is difficult to determine precisely when, or for what purposes, women might have been limited to this space.

The other great congregational mosque of Fez, al-Andalus, also had dedicated space for women; al-Jaznāʾī refers to the construction, at the beginning of the seventh/thirteenth century, of a separate door to the "women's prayer room" (*bayt ṣalāt al-nisāʾ*). This space appears to have been on the ground level, as a chamber for the imams of the mosque was constructed above it.[60] The use of the expression "room (*bayt*)" suggests some degree of enclosure. Again, however, there is no way of knowing whether women were limited to the spaces explicitly reserved for them or what activities they may or may not have been able to pursue in the main body of the mosque.

Women's attendance at Moroccan mosques in the late medieval period was apparently not limited to urban contexts or to the great metropolitan mosques. The Maghribī jurist Abū'l-Qāsim ibn Khajjū (d. 811/1408),[61] in a query probably relating to the hinterland of Fez,

> was asked about a village (*qarya*) in which the Friday congregational prayers were held; the women wanted to perform the Friday prayers, but the mosque could not accommodate them because of the large number of people. Are they permitted to pray in the residential area [of the village] (*al-muʿammara*), or are they permitted to pray only behind the men? And may they pray behind the mosque, near to it, or one or two body-lengths away from it?
>
> He replied: I do not consider it permissible to perform the Friday prayers in the residential area; it is performed only in the mosque and in the plaza around it (*riḥābihi*) and the paths adjacent to it, and it is not permitted to perform it in a privately owned place, even for the owner. [The women] may pray in any of the mosque's paths that are adjacent to it and in the plaza surrounding it (*fī riḥābihi*), even if there is a barrier [*ḥāʾil*, presumably between them and the next row of worshipers or between them and the imam]; indeed, that is preferable.[62]

It is not clear from this fatwa whether the women are already participating in the Friday congregational prayers or whether they simply desire to do so. In any case, they are clearly taking active steps to secure their right to attend. There appears to be no dedicated space for women in the mosque, and the questioner apparently hopes that they can validly follow the prayers from their adjacent homes.[63] Ibn Khajjū replies essentially by applying the general rules for the validity of Friday prayer, which must be performed within the mosque or in continuous rows spreading outside of it—although he would prefer that there be some kind of barrier concealing the women, even if only as a happy side effect of the lack of space within the walls of the mosque. It is significant that Ibn Khajjū does not in any way suggest that the women in question ought to be discouraged from coming, despite the difficulty of accommodating them within the mosque.

The existence of dedicated women's space in major North African and Andalusian mosques, and the terms in which it is discussed in surviving sources, suggests women's participation in congregational prayer. The sources also afford occasional glimpses of a far wider set of activities that women pursued in the mosques of this region. It is clear that to some extent women visited mosques to seek out the expertise of religious authorities. The distinguished scholar Ibn al-Fakhkhār al-Judhāmī (d. 723/1323) is said to have spent his afternoons in the mosque in Málaga, leaning against an arch and teaching; women would approach from behind to ask him for fatwas (presumably to avoid visual contact with an unrelated male).[64] In some cases, women could reside in religious retreat in a mosque; the ascetic ʿĀʾisha bint ʿAbd Allāh ibn ʿĀṣim, who lived in the seventh to eighth century AH, apparently resided in a chamber atop the mosque in Algeciras.[65] For some women, access to the great mosques seems to have opened the doors to substantial religious learning and social prestige. The mother of Shaykh Aḥmad Zarrūq, who was born in 846/1442, "used to attend the study sessions of one of Fes's pre-eminent jurists, ʿAbdallah al-ʿAbdūsī, along with her sister and another scholarly woman, with little Ahmad at their side." It is quite likely that al-ʿAbdūsī, a preacher at al-Qarawīyīn, held his sessions at the mosque.[66] Mosques were also the site of more informal and even more heterodox activities. Abū'l-Qāsim Ibn Khajjū, the same jurist who directed the village women to pray in the plaza and paths adjacent to the mosque, received a query about a *faqīh* who remained constantly in the mosque (*mulāzim li'l-masjid*); women would come to him "with their adornments exposed (*bādiyāt al-zīna*)," and "he would sit with them and perform divination for them (*yukahhinu lahunna*)."[67] In the seventh/thirteenth century, Rāshid al-Walīdī alludes to women gathering along with men to perform ṣūfī *dhikr*, apparently on Thursday evenings.[68]

Overall, there does seem to be significant correspondence between the content of Mālikī legal texts and the evidence for women's presence in mosques in this sampling of locations historically dominated by Mālikīs. The provision of dedicated prayer space for women implies the recognition (and acceptance) of the fact that women may participate in public prayer in mosques; the comparatively small size of women's accommodations (including prayer space, doors, and ablutions fountains) compared to men's suggests the expectation that they will do so in relatively limited numbers. This is exactly what Mālikī doctrine, which endorses women's mosque attendance, but advocates that it be infrequent for all but elderly women, would lead us to expect. However, the foundational Mālikī legal texts would not have led us to anticipate the early and growing emphasis on spatial and visual separation of women's prayer space.

One can catch a fleeting glimpse of more popular attitudes toward women's presence in mosques in this region from a source of another genre, that of *adab* (belles lettres). The story in question, which deals with an elderly habituée of the Great Mosque of Qayrawān, is recorded in a text of the sixteenth century CE (which in turn credits it to a so far unidentifiable earlier source). The story is set in the Aghlabid period (in the third/ninth century), although its provenance is presumably well later, and it is intended to illustrate the devious wiles of old women (*al-ʿajāʾiz*). It begins when a man falls in love with a young girl (*ṣabīya*) who is married to a merchant and lives close to the Friday mosque. He enlists the help of one of the old ladies who regularly frequent the mosque (*min muwāẓibāt al-jāmiʿ*), who promises to get the better of the damsel's virtue. One day the old lady knocks at the young woman's door. She says that she has come early to the mosque for Friday prayers and has canceled her *wuḍūʾ*, and she asks for water to renew her ablutions. Making the same request each week, she gradually wins the young woman's confidence. She then borrows the young wife's jewels on false pretenses and demands that she meet her outside of the home to get them back. The young woman virtuously insists that her husband has taken an oath of threefold divorce if she leaves the house. She informs her husband, who comforts her and sets out to seek redress from the ruler, Ibrāhīm ibn Aḥmad (ruled 261–89/875–902). The ruler directs his mother to invite "the old women of the mosque" (*ʿajāʾiz al-jāmiʿ*) to a banquet. There he begins to winnow and select the suspects, choosing first forty, then ten, and then finally narrowing the field to the one culprit, from whom he succeeds in recovering the jewels. The story ends with the ruler sternly admonishing his mother to have nothing more to do with the old ladies of the mosque.[69]

Although certainly fictional, this entertaining story illustrates certain assumptions about women's mosque attendance and about the relevance of life cycle, social status, and religious prestige. The old lady's habit of regular Friday mosque attendance is represented as unremarkable, and the story assumes that the "old ladies of the mosque" number at least in the scores. The women's mosque attendance is clearly related to their advanced stage of life. Conversely, the young merchant woman's confinement to the home seems to be associated with her tender age and high status and (as represented by this particular story) yields her a much higher degree of perceived virtue than the public religiosity of the old ladies in the mosque. As suggested by the remarks of Ibn al-Munāṣif, women who attended congregational prayers were not always elderly. Nevertheless, it would seem that both Mālikī legal distinctions among women of different age cohorts and the relative Mālikī tolerance for women's attendance at Friday and congregational prayers had some correspondence with ground-level values and practices.

EGYPT: CAIRO

Scattered references suggest the presence of women in Egyptian mosques from the earliest centuries, particularly in the context of study and preaching. At the turn of the third/ninth century, the sister of the prominent scholar al-Muzanī is said to have attended the study circle of al-Shāfiʿī, which was held in the main mosque of Fusṭāt.[70] Two centuries later, the Ismāʿīlī Shīʿī missionaries in the service of the Fāṭimid state held instructional sessions for women in the Azhar mosque.[71] Women's presence in mosques in this period was not limited to the Shīʿī context; the prominent preacher Umm al-Khayr al-Ḥijāzīya, for instance, appears to have been active in the Friday mosque.[72] However, only in the Mamlūk period is there sufficient evidence to reconstruct the range and nature of women's activities in Egyptian mosques.

The work of Ibn al-Ḥājj (d. 737/1336), which represents the richest source of information about religious practice in Mamlūk Cairo, suggests a vibrant and multifarious female presence in mosques. Because Ibn al-Ḥājj seeks to denounce practices he considers religiously deviant, rather than to give a balanced account of contemporary lifeways, he emphasizes women's more vivid or objectionable activities over their more sober and routine participation in religious life. Ibn al-Ḥājj's own austere piety did not represent the mainstream of contemporary Egyptian religiosity, and many of the practices he denounces were stoutly defended—or simply taken for granted—by other prominent members of the religious establishment. His scandalized rejection of a given practice need not suggest that it was regarded as deviant or unorthodox by most contemporary Egyptians, and in many cases the women who engaged in them would not only have assumed their legitimacy but also would have been supported in this view by male relatives and religious professionals.

Ibn al-Ḥājj most strongly emphasizes women's mass attendance at mosques on the occasion of major religious festivals, both canonical and noncanonical. All of the Sunnī schools except the Shāfiʿīs preferred (on the basis of ḥadīth) that the prayers for the two canonical festivals, ʿĪd al-Aḍḥā and ʿĪd al-Fiṭr, be performed on outdoor prayer grounds on the outskirts of the city. However, Ibn al-Ḥājj's discussion indicates that this was not (or at least not always) the current practice in Cairo, a fact that may be related to practical considerations or to the predominance of the Shāfiʿī school. He writes about the festival prayers, "Women ought to be far removed from the men, unlike what they do today, because they usually mix with the men; one usually finds the mosque on the day of the festival filled with women." He complains that men and women mix within the mosque and while entering and exiting through its doors.[73] He goes on to observe that the women go out to the festival prayers "in the way that is known, and has been discussed more than once" in his work—that is, ostentatiously dressed, perfumed, and adorned (even more than was customary on other occasions).

Ibn al-Ḥājj concludes,

> It would be better if [women] were prevented from going out [to the festival prayers]; indeed, that is what is obligatory (*al-mutaʿayyin*) in

> this time. It is [also] obligatory for him [i.e., the ruler?] to approach the preachers (*al-wuʿʿāẓ*) who are working in the mosque and forbid them to speak. It has already been stated that it should be forbidden with respect to the men; *a fortiori*, it should be forbidden with respect to the women, because their corruption exceeds that of the men.[74]

Here, as in several other places in his work, Ibn al-Ḥājj's assertion that contemporary Muslim women should be excluded from mosques altogether (the sentiment to which his comments are sometimes reduced[75]) is clearly a polemical response to a very different reality. Although his wording is somewhat vague, it is quite possible that he is referring to women who engage in public preaching in the mosque on the occasion of the festivals rather than women who simply listen to preachers. If so, it would seem that their public role on such days was very prominent indeed.

Even more vivid was women's presence at mosques for religious observances not explicitly mandated by the sharīʿa. Even though many of these occasions have been treated in the secondary literature as examples of "popular Islam" and Ibn al-Ḥājj himself denounces them as innovations (*bidaʿ*), it is important to remember that little evidence suggests either that they were limited to the unlettered masses or that the religious establishment regarded them as illegitimate. Indeed, in most cases they took place in major mosques where they could not have occurred without the knowledge and cooperation of male religious authorities. One of the holidays whose observance distressed Ibn al-Ḥājj was the day of ʿĀshūrāʾ, a day of mourning for Shīʿīs that in this period was widely observed with festivity and merriment by Sunnīs.[76] Ibn al-Ḥājj describes how on this day the Mosque of ʿAmr ibn al-ʿĀṣ[77] in Cairo is reserved exclusively for women. He complains that they take the opportunity to adorn themselves with finery and revealing clothing—a practice that he associates with the vain display of their charms to men (*al-tabarruj li'l-rijāl*), rather unconvincingly given the sex-segregated setting (unless the unseemly display took place on the way to the mosque rather than within it). "They remain in [the mosque] from the beginning of the day until sunset, to the exclusion of men (*lā yushārikuhunna fīhi al-rijāl*); they rub themselves against the volumes of the Qur'an,[78] the pulpit, and the walls and under the Green Tablet."[79]

Women's exclusive access to one of the most important mosques of Cairo on one of the most holy days of the religious calendar must have been condoned and facilitated by the religious authorities. It is notable that their behavior on this occasion, at least as described by Ibn al-Ḥājj (whose polemical motives are frankly displayed), savors more of shrine visitation than of conventional mosque-based worship. There is no suggestion that congregational prayer featured in their gathering. Instead, the women's aspirations seem to have centered on the reaping of *baraka*, the blessings to be garnered from physical contact with sacred places and objects on a particularly auspicious day in the religious year. However, it is significant that the sanctity of the place arises not from the tomb of a holy figure, but from its very status as a mosque; devotion is centered on the architectural feature that most centrally qualifies it as a Friday mosque (the pulpit), on the walls of the edifice itself, and on the volumes of the Qur'an that represent the most vital and orthodox functions of a mosque, the recitation of the Qur'an and the dissemination of its teachings.[80] In this context, the widespread distinction between *mosque* and *shrine* proves to be of little utility.

Other noncanonical festivals, according to Ibn al-Ḥājj, involved large-scale and indiscriminate mingling of men and women in mosques. On the first Thursday night[81] of the month of Rajab, people gathered in mosques large and small to perform the *Raghāʾib* (Wishes) prayer amidst festive illuminations. In addition to the prayer's problematic status as an innovation (it was not performed by the Prophet and indeed was known to be of relatively recent vintage), it was widely criticized for the mixing of men and women that took place on the occasion.[82] Not only did women go out, according to Ibn al-Ḥājj's familiar plaint, with festive clothing and adornment, but the crowds that gathered in the Friday mosque (*al-jāmiʿ al-aʿẓam*) were so dense that people urinated in the back of the mosque rather than making their way outside. Women in particular, he claims, were embarrassed to go out to relieve themselves and paid a fee to use a vessel that was carried around the mosque.[83] Ibn al-Ḥājj makes a similar complaint about the night of Niṣf Shaʿbān,[84] when crowds of men, women, and small children gathered in the mosque; the presence of small children led to the soiling of the mosque and to even greater hubbub and frivolity (*al-laghaṭ wa'l-lahw*) than on the twenty-seventh of Rajab (celebrated as the anniversary of the Miʿrāj).[85]

Indeed, the nocturnal gatherings that took place on the great annual religious festivals were not new in Ibn al-Ḥājj's time; for at least two centuries, they been notorious for the mixing of men and women in the major mosques of a number of areas in the Islamic world. The Baghdādī Ḥanbalī Ibn ʿAqīl (d. 513/1119) wrote with horror about the "masses of men and women" who gathered at mosques and cemeteries on the nights of the great festivals, which were marred (in his eyes) by the wasteful and ostentatious illumination of the mosques and by the frivolity and liveliness of the gathering.[86] (Ibn Mufliḥ, who cited his comments three centuries later, noted that "in Syria, Iraq, Egypt and other Muslim countries," things had only gotten worse.[87]) Abū Bakr al-Ṭurṭūshī (d. 520/1126–27), an Andalusian scholar who studied in several areas of the Islamic East (but whose polemic in this area is devoted largely to Qayrawān), writes with horror of the misbehavior that allegedly occurred in the dense crowds on the night when the recitation of the Qur'an was completed during Ramadan. Not only did men and women press against each other willy-nilly in the disorder, but "a woman came to us to complain, saying, 'I went to hear the preacher in the Friday mosque, and a man embraced me from behind and took his pleasure with me (*iltadhdha bī*) in the crowd, with nothing to prevent him [from actual intercourse] but [our] clothes; so I vowed never to go again.'"[88] Al-Ṭurṭūshī responds to these phenomena with a barrage of reports advocating the exclusion of women from mosques.[89] Reproducing this passage from al-Ṭurṭūshī a century and a half later, the Syrian Shāfiʿī Abū Shāma (d. 665/1267) remarks that anyone who has attended the festivities for Niṣf Shaʿbān in Damascus and its vicinity knows that the sinful uproar there is even worse than described by al-Ṭurṭūshī;[90] he similarly musters textual evidence in favor of excluding women from mosques.[91] As is so often the case, this seems to have been a form of scholarly protest against a practice that nevertheless persisted; Abū Isḥāq al-Shāṭibī (d. 790/1388) also complains of the gathering together of men and women as one of the offenses committed on the night of Laylat al-Qadr.[92]

In Cairo as well, women clearly continued to attend mosques in droves at particularly holy times of the year, despite occasional efforts at interdiction. Zayn al-Dīn Ibn Shāhīn writes of Ramadan of the year 893/1488 that "in it a proclamation was made that women should not go out to the Mosque of ʿAmr because of the corruption that they were causing during the month of Ramadan . . . ; nevertheless, they were not deterred, and on some of the Fridays of this month in the mosque there was an indescribable uproar and selling of toys and other things."[93]

In Cairo in the time of Ibn al-Ḥājj, women's presence in mosques was by no means limited to such carnivalistic festivals; however, his references to more ordinary cases are more casual and less extensive. For instance, he argues that small children should not be brought to the mosque by men because they might cry when people are praying and distract the worshipers. It is all right for them to attend with their mothers, however, because "it is ordinarily the case that the women's space (*mawḍiʿ al-nisāʾ*) is far enough away [from the lines of male worshipers] that [the babies' crying] will not disturb the men" (and also, he argues, because babies cry less when they are with their mothers than when they are with their fathers). Ibn al-Ḥājj immediately qualifies this observation with the remark that "this is if necessity demanded that the woman pray in congregation in the mosque; it is better for her to pray at home," and he briefly reiterates his legal arguments against women's mosque attendance.[94] However, the incidental quality of his reference in itself suggests the quotidian and familiar nature of women's presence in mosques. It also implies that there was space customarily allocated to women in a mosque and that its location was sufficiently well known that he could unproblematically refer to where it was "ordinarily" found.

Ibn al-Ḥājj also refers, disapprovingly but without hysteria, to women's attendance at Friday prayers. Again, his normative argument that women should not attend mosques stands in clear contrast to his observation that they (at least sometimes) do. He states,

> Women should be forbidden from what they have innovated, and which they have tacitly been allowed to do (*sukita lahunna ʿanhu*), in going in to [participate in] the Friday prayer in the back of the mosque. Even if they have a designated enclosure (*maqṣūra maʿlūma*), it is all the same whether it exists or not, because it does not conceal them; and they usually go out dressed and adorned as is known. [Women pray in the

> mosque] despite the fact that there is no necessity for that, because their space in the addition (*al-ziyāda*)[95] makes it superfluous for them to enter the mosque and be close to the men; it is more befitting for them, as long as they do not mix with the men. There is no difference with respect to this between the Friday prayers, the five[96] [daily prayers], funeral prayers, and others.

He goes on, as usual, to argue that it is better for women to pray individually at home—unless a woman living adjacent to the mosque is able to pray with the congregation from the privacy of her house.[97]

Ibn al-Ḥājj's remarks suggest that enough women attended Friday prayers that they had been assigned space in the "addition" (*ziyāda*), a liminal space attached to the mosque, but outside of its original walls, that existed in more than one major mosque in Cairo.[98] They also suggest that at least some women eschewed this space and ventured to enter the mosque proper, placing themselves in the back of the congregation—sometimes behind a physical barrier (*maqṣūra*) and sometimes not.[99] Ibn al-Ḥājj's comment that the barrier in any case does not conceal the women suggests that, when it existed, such an enclosure was less than a solid wall; it may have been an openwork screen. Despite the apparent provision of dedicated women's prayer space, the authorities are implied not to have advocated women's attendance, but to have failed to address it; attendance at Friday prayers is represented as occurring on the women's own initiative. It is unclear whether this reflects the actual dynamics of women's presence at congregational prayer or Ibn al-Ḥājj's determination to accuse the women of religious innovation and deemphasize the legitimation of their presence by the authorities. It is also unclear whether the modest scope of Ibn al-Ḥājj's references to women's participation in regular congregational prayer reflects the relatively small number of women involved or simply the fact that, as a canonical and decorous ritual, ordinary mosque prayer failed to elicit the detailed and vivid polemics through which Ibn al-Ḥājj revealed so much about the more controversial festivals.

Ibn al-Ḥājj also notes (and objects to) women's attendance at study sessions in the mosques. He observes that it is the practice among some people in his time to gather in the mosque to hear books read aloud; the men and women sit in separate groups facing one another—and apparently without a barrier to conceal them from each other's view. What is worse, female listeners may sometimes be overcome by ecstatic states in which they stand up, scream, and expose parts of their bodies—something that would be impermissible within their own homes, but that is far worse in a mosque in the presence of men.[100] The precise nature of the sessions Ibn al-Ḥājj has in mind remains unclear; the intense emotional reaction that he describes suggest mystical reading-matter or at least impassioned preaching, but again he is presumably emphasizing the most lurid possible scenario.

Women's presence at sessions of preaching and teaching is also mentioned in other sources. In the thirteenth century CE, the satirical work of al-Jawbarī describes a corrupt preacher performing for a large and gullible audience of men and women in an Egyptian mosque in 623 AH.[101] Although the specific story may not be factually based, the assumption that a throng of mixed sexes could gather to hear preaching in a mosque probably was. In a manual for officials charged with keeping the public order (*muḥtasib*s), Ibn al-Ḥājj's Egyptian contemporary Ibn al-Ukhuwwa (d. 729/1329) laments that in his day "people do not assemble about [the preacher] to hear admonition or for edification, but it has become a kind of amusement or sport or social gathering; and in the assembly there takes place that which is improper, men gathering together with women so that they see each other, and there are other things also not proper to be mentioned." He reiterates the admonition of al-Ghazālī (d. 505/1111) that men and women should be separated by a screen during preaching sessions and that women should be discouraged from going to mosques at all, yet clearly these rules do not reflect current realities.[102]

Less frequently mentioned is preaching specifically addressed to women and their religious needs. ʿAbd al-Wahhāb al-Shaʿrānī states that the ṣūfī and jurist Aḥmad [ibn Muḥammad] ibn Sulaymān al-Zāhid (d. 819/1415) "used to preach to women in the mosques, devoting himself to them to the exclusion of men, and teach them the rules of their religion and the marital and neighborly duties that were incumbent upon them."[103] However, an earlier report by al-Sakhāwī states that al-Zāhid was in the habit of seeking out abandoned mosques, sometimes using the ruins of one to rebuild another; finally, he founded his own mosque in al-Maqs,[104] where he preached especially to women.[105]

This account suggests that perhaps al-Zāhid pursued his woman-centered activities largely in mosques that were under his personal control and/or otherwise unused, although this may well relate to the distinctiveness of al-Zāhid's religious style rather than to any difficulty in gathering women in better-established mosques. That his focus on women was somewhat unusual is suggested by the remark attributed to him that "these women do not attend the lessons of the religious scholars, and none of their husbands instructs them!"[106] It is notable that al-Zāhid's homilies, as represented by al-Shaʿrānī (who claims to have the written texts in his possession), focused on inculcating knowledge of women's obligations toward God, their husbands, and their neighbors.

Women of Mamlūk Cairo also sometimes appeared in mosques in their capacity as religious authorities. As has been noted by Jonathan Berkey, "Zaynab, the daughter of Dāwūd Abū 'l-Jawad (d. 1459), apparently succeeded her father as shaykh of the Sufis at the mosque of ʿAlam Dār near the Bāb al-Barqiyya in Cairo."[107] A number of women preachers are known to have flourished in Cairo in the Mamlūk period; although the biographical literature is often vague about the venues of their activities, it seems likely that women sometimes appeared in mosques as religious instructors as well as in the audiences for their sermons.[108] Muhammad Akram Nadwi notes that Ibn al-Ḥājj's contemporary Sitt al-Wuzarāʾ bint ʿUmar ibn al-Munajjā (d. 716/1316) "was popular in Damascus for teaching al-Bukhārī's *Ṣaḥīḥ*, then invited to Cairo where she taught in the great mosque and other venues, her lessons being attended by notable men of the city, including its scholars."[109]

Women were also present in mosques for more profane activities. Some would bring the thread they had spun to the mosque and sit awaiting offers, which led to negotiations and sales (as well as to the soiling of the mosque by the small children that accompanied some of them). Their presence, according to Ibn al-Ḥājj, attracted unsavory characters. Women also came in pursuit of court cases, waiting within the mosque as the judge presided outside (perhaps in the *ziyāda*). The frequentation of the mosque by female litigants, their legal representatives (*al-wukalāʾ*), and their husbands sometimes led to loud disputes.[110]

Other references also support Ibn al-Ḥājj's description of the major Cairo mosques as lively public spaces frequented by both sexes for purposes both sacred and profane. A thirteenth-century Maghribī traveler expressed his dismay at the scene in in the mosque of ʿAmr ibn al-ʿĀṣ, which men and women passed through casually to shorten their way from place to place and in which they ate cakes and nuts sold by itinerant vendors.[111] In 844/1440–41, efforts to renovate and reform the Mosque of al-Ḥākim included directives to the doorkeepers to prevent women and children from entering, sitting in, or passing through the mosque. People of any sex or age were discouraged from passing through the mosque's courtyard in their sandals.[112] Such efforts of reform, however, were usually of short duration.

No other source provides a concentration of synchronic data about Egyptian women's religious practices comparable to the work of Ibn al-Ḥājj; however, scattered references suggest that these practices were sustained in subsequent centuries. In a passing comment that is the more convincing for its casual and offhand nature, the Egyptian scholar Ibn Ḥajar al-ʿAsqalānī (d. 852/1449) refers to "the continuous practice based on the permissibility of women's going out to mosques, markets and journeys when they are veiled so that men cannot see them (*istimrār al-ʿamal ʿalā jawāz khurūj al-nisāʾ ilā al-masājid wa'l-aswāq wa'l-asfār mutanaqqibāt li-allā yarāhunna al-rijāl*)."[113] The Egyptian Shāfiʿī scholar ʿImād al-Dīn al-Aqfahsī (d. 808/1405) writes in his manual on rules relating to mosques that "it is desirable for the prayer leader and the superintendent (*nāẓir*) of the mosque to designate a door of the mosque for the women so that no man enters or exits with them"—a comment that betrays his assumption that women will be present in most mosques.[114]

In this period, the narratives of European travelers begin to offer another source—fragmentary and biased, but sometimes revealing—for the activities of Egyptian women. The Dominican friar Félix Fabri produced a detailed narrative of his sojourn in Cairo in the course of his pilgrimage to Jerusalem in 1483. He reports that the women of the "Saracens" pray in separate sections in their "churches" (in context, clearly mosques) and must do so unadorned. For these "pagans" it is both deplorable and ridiculous for men and women to attend a house of worship together in their worldly finery—an opinion with which

Fabri appears heartily to agree.[115] It would seem, based on this passage, that the impression transmitted to a non-Muslim visitor to Egypt in the late fifteenth century was that women could attend mosques, albeit in modest clothing and in a place apart from the men.

In contrast to this evidence from the Mamlūk period, European visitors to Egypt in the Ottoman period often stated summarily that women did not go to mosques. It is unclear whether this reflects an overall change in Egyptian women's habits, the distinctive practices of the women of the predominantly Ḥanafī Ottoman elite (a sector of the population that loomed large in the eyes of European visitors), or simply the misconceptions of ill-informed outsiders. Jean Palerne, who visited Cairo in 1581, reports that women "do not go to the mosques at all."[116] He states that a woman simply cannot enter a mosque unless she is the wife of a pasha or other dignitary who is privileged to visit by virtue of her status; in this case, however, she goes "out of curiosity" and presumably not to pray.[117] It is difficult to determine the source of Palerne's information, which is associated with some degree of fanciful misinformation.[118] Johann Wild, who lived in Egypt as a slave between 1606 and 1610, similarly reports that "women do not go to church [*sic*] . . . , but are supposed to perform their ablutions, pray and perform their religious duties at home in their houses."[119] Wild, too, refers to "Turkish" women, although it is difficult to know how specifically he intends this term.

Antonius Gonzales, a Franciscan who served as chaplain to the French consul in Cairo in 1665–66, provides a more detailed (and perhaps more convincing) account of Egyptian women's mosque-going habits. He states that the women of Cairo venture out into the streets only rarely, to go to the public bath or to "church" (here, like other travelers, he appears to use the word as a blanket term for places of worship).[120] Respectable women and girls never frequent places where men gather, and on the street one never sees a man address women or girls; what is more, "they perform their devotions after the men depart, or in places separate from them."[121] In another passage he states, "In the mosques, the women have special, separate spaces where they cannot be seen by men. When they enter and exit they are covered up so well that no one can recognize them. It is rarely allowed that the two sexes gather at the same time in a church [i.e., mosque]; rather, [the women] usually come when the men are not present. They are also not obliged to go to church every Friday, as the men are obliged to do."[122]

These passages of Gonzales's account are free of polemic and even somewhat complimentary (he describes the public deportment of Cairene women as "very quiet and modest"[123]). Although it is difficult to determine how much access or exposure to mosques Gonzales may have had, the length of his stay in Egypt and the sensitivity of his attitude may well have allowed him some degree of insight into Cairene life. His reference to women praying in the mosque after the men had left, or using it at alternative times, suggests that women's mosque usage followed independent patterns that were perhaps not dominated by participation in male-led congregational prayer—although separate space was designated for this purpose.

The predominance of the evidence thus suggests that in the Mamlūk period, women could be found in Cairene mosques in many different capacities. Because no other currently available source appears to supply a description of women's presence and activities in mosques comparable to that of Ibn al-Ḥājj, it is difficult to judge whether the magnitude and scope of women's use of mosques declined significantly thereafter or simply becomes harder to document. Even with respect to the Mamlūk period, however, the fact that women played a role in the life of mosques does not tell us what role mosques played in the lives of women. It is impossible to determine the numbers in which women attended Friday prayers, slipped into the mosque to worship individually, or sat in its shade to sell their wares. Women's mosque visitation on major religious festivals seems to have been a mass phenomenon, although it occurred only intermittently in the yearly calendar. The strong possibility remains that, even though women had a significant presence in mosques, most women's religious life may not have been primarily mosque-centered.

Indeed, both the voluminous testimony of Ibn al-Ḥājj and the remarks of Western travelers suggest that women's visitation of graves and shrines was a larger-scale and more pervasive phenomenon (although both "graves" and "shrines" might in some cases also be mosques). Ibn al-Ḥājj complains that women have "innovated for themselves" a rotation assigning specific days to individual holy sites. According to his (possibly hyperbolic) account, Mondays were assigned to the Mosque of al-Ḥusayn in Cairo, Saturdays to al-Sayyida Nafīsa,[124] and Thursdays and Fridays to the great Qarāfa cemeteries on the outskirts of the city.[125] Both al-Ḥusayn and al-Sayyida Nafīsa were mosques in the full sense of the word, but were also notable for the remains of important early members of the Prophet's family. The phenomenon of women's grave visitation, particularly in the Qarāfa on Fridays, appears to have been sufficiently large and problematic to inspire repeated (and clearly vain) efforts to suppress it. In Ibn al-Ḥājj's own era, "Emir ʿAlāʾ al-Dīn Ṭaybars, the Castellan (*wālī bāb al-qalʿa*), barred women from outings to the Qarāfa on special days (*mawsim*)." This was only one of the repeated (and apparently ineffective) bans on women's visitation of the cemeteries in the thirteenth to fifteenth centuries CE.[126] Although considerations of religious orthodoxy may have played some role in these efforts at suppression, the authorities were more likely motivated by concerns for public order inspired by the apparently vast scale of women's grave visitation practices. Rare efforts were made to suppress grave visitation in the Qarāfa altogether,[127] and men were clearly also enthusiastic participants, but the central role of women is clear both from descriptions of visitation practices and from efforts at their regulation.

The scale and visibility of women's grave visitation practices are confirmed by the accounts of Western travelers, who rarely fail to remark upon it. Jean Thenaud, who visited Cairo in the early sixteenth century, writes of the Qarāfa that "every Friday, the women go to visit the graves of their dead, upon which they cast large quantities of [sweet-smelling plants and] perfumes, such as jasmine, basil, roses, and scented oils and waters. They say that on that day, the souls of the departed indulge in scents."[128] Palerne writes—with an eyewitness vividness notably absent from his remarks on women's mosque attendance—that

> every Friday [women] usually go to weep on the graves of their relatives. After having a good weep and wail, they have some chapters of the Qur'an recited by a preacher for the soul of the dead. They give alms to the poor, and eat with them. They bring various kinds of flowers, which they spread on [the grave] and plant there, so that passers-by will remember the dead when they take those flowers. This is so much

> so that on that day, one sees their cemeteries full of women making a marvelous holiday with their weeping, cries, and wailing.[129]

In 1599, Muṣṭafā ʿĀlī, an internal traveler within the Ottoman Empire, described how "every Friday, starting at the time of the morning prayer a countless multitude of people, walking or riding, appearing in the direction of the cemeteries, take the road toward Karafa." The crowds visit first the tombs of al-Shāfiʿī and Abū'l-Layth and then that of Sayyida Nafīsa. "When the women go to the graves of their relatives they always take some green plants and flowers along with them, they visit the tombs of the dead with fragrant herbs."[130] This account emphasizes that large numbers of people of both sexes made the weekly pilgrimage to the cemeteries, including Ṣūfī shaykhs who played a leadership role. In the early eighteenth century, Benoît de Maillet writes that women go to visit their dead at the Qarāfa at least twice a week, weeping and casting *rayḥān* (basil) onto the graves.[131] In the early nineteenth century, Richard Pococke notes that "the time when the women go out is mostly on Fridays, to the burial places, to adorn with flowers and boughs the sepulchres of their relations, to hang a lamp over them, and pour water on their graves, and they place water in vases near."[132]

There is no doubt that women's grave visitation was a practice of enormous popularity and great durability, even in the face of persistent efforts at eradication. It is true that several factors may have contributed to its overrepresentation in our sources, as compared with less flamboyant practices such as women's participation in congregational prayer. For Ibn al-Ḥājj, women's grave visitation was worthy of sustained polemic (and thus of detailed description) both because he considered it religiously illegitimate in itself and because the length of the journey and the lax behavior of the crowds led to a distressing degree of contact and mixing between the sexes.[133] For Western travelers, activities in the cemeteries were presumably far more visible and accessible than those in mosques (from which they were, in most cases, barred until the nineteenth century). Even Muṣṭafā ʿĀlī seems to have found the goings-on in the Qarāfa rather exotic and picturesque. However, even accounting for a certain degree of reporting bias, it seems likely that far more women made frequent Friday visits to the cemeteries than participated in Friday prayers. (It should be noted that the weekly participation of throngs of women in grave visitation at the Qarāfa does not necessarily mean that *ziyāra* was a regular weekly practice for most individual women; as usual, the lack of firsthand testimony by female participants leaves us with an outsider view of undifferentiated female masses.)

The fact that so many women were able to make excursions to the Qarāfa, and particularly on Friday,[134] suggests that the normative legal account of the constraints on women's mosque visitation corresponds poorly to the actual dynamics of women's ritual activities. According to the *fiqh* texts, the primary limiting factor on women's participation in congregational prayer is the strong presumption against their leaving the home in general and their appearing in mixed settings in particular. Visiting the Qarāfa, however, inevitably involved a longer absence from the home and a higher degree of public visibility than the comparatively brief journey to a mosque located within the woman's urban quarter, where she could expect to pray in a location sheltered from the male gaze. Women absenting themselves from public congregational prayer, only to spend their Fridays flamboyantly lamenting in the Qarāfa, were clearly not responding to the ideal of public invisibility promoted by many religious scholars. Although legal authorities generally considered it religiously undesirable for women to attend public congregational prayers (at least if they were young), in most cases they considered it reprehensible for women of any age to engage in grave visitation. Only the Mālikīs argued that grave visitation might be meritorious for sexually unattractive old women, as it was for men;[135] however, the Mālikī Ibn al-Ḥājj gave short shrift to this opinion.

One explanation for women's deviation from the prescriptions of the religious scholars in these cases would be that their exclusion from or marginalization in mosques drove them to the less orthodox consolations of the graveyard and the shrine. One problem with this argument is that, as we have seen, women were not categorically barred from mosques; some women could and did attend congregational prayers, although it is unclear how many of them chose to do so (or what other barriers, familial or reputational, may have discouraged them from trying). Of course, it remains true that scholarly opinion largely discouraged women's mosque attendance, which may have deterred many women. This explanation, however, raises the question of why women were willing to defy scholarly opinion with respect to grave visitation if they submitted to it with respect to mosque attendance.

Women's apparent preference for graveyards could be explained by the assumption that, whereas male authorities exercised effective authority in the context of the mosque, the liminal space of the graveyards evaded effective regulation. The argument that the mixing of the sexes in the Qarāfa was a result of a relative vacuum of normative control has been made in detail by Christopher Taylor in his fascinating study of Egyptian grave visitation.[136] However, Taylor's study and others also demonstrate that the Qarāfa was full of mosques and *khānaqās*, often staffed with full complements of religious personnel;[137] given this fact, it is unclear why it should have eluded official or scholarly regulation. By this period, the Qarāfa was not an unsettled wasteland, but a teeming urban area.[138]

Furthermore, if women's mass public activities were a sign of lack of normative control, Ibn al-Ḥājj's complaints suggest that normative control was also often lacking within the city proper, even at religiously important sites such as major mosques. The Mosque of al-Ḥusayn, arguably the most important religious site within the heart of Cairo, was an important focus of women's weekly visitation; yet al-Ḥusayn could scarcely be characterized as spatially or organizationally outside the purview of normative religious control. As already noted, women's annual takeover of the important Mosque of ʿAmr ibn al-ʿĀṣ either was facilitated by the religious establishment or defied its regulatory authority. Even in more routine contexts, the use of mosques by unruly female litigants and haggling female vendors suggests that far from representing opposite poles in the spectrum of socioreligious regulation, the great mosques and the great cemeteries to a certain extent shared the quality of vibrant public spaces where social intercourse (like religious performance) followed its own dynamics.

Rather than understanding women's grave visitation as a solution to which they resorted as a result either of physical exclusion from mosques or of normative discouragement from mosque-based worship, it is more plausible to regard women's overwhelming presence in the cemeteries—and their clear, but apparently more modest presence at congregational prayers in the mosques—as an expression of the women's own religious priorities. This interpretation is strongly suggested by the testimony of Ibn al-Ḥājj, who disparages the capitulation of ostensibly pious men to their wives' peremptory demands to go to the Qarāfa. He claims that women threaten their husbands with sexual strike or divorce if forbidden to visit the graveyards.[139] His account is clearly intended to motivate his male audience to intervene in their wives' religious activities by representing their acquiescence as a form of henpecked capitulation. Nevertheless, it is significant that Ibn al-Ḥājj represents both mosque attendance and grave visitation as expressions of women's own initiative—albeit two forms that apparently attracted unequal numbers of women. His emphasis on the marital negotiation confirms one aspect of the normative legal model, which is that the most effective locus of control on women's public religious activities would have been at the door of the marital residence. The evidence suggests that once outside of the home, a woman would not have been turned away from either the mosque or the graveyard; however, it was primarily at the graveyard that mass female participation attracted the wonder of travelers and the frustrated attention of the religious and political authorities. On those occasions when comparably vast numbers of women demanded access to urban mosques—for instance, on the nights of the popular festivals and on the day of ʿĀshūrāʾ—the authorities seem to have been just as impotent (or as unwilling) to interdict their activities there as they were in the Qarāfa.

Women's apparent preference for public religious activity in graveyards was not unique to Egypt. In later times, travelers to North Africa also commented on local women's propensity to frequent cemeteries rather than mosques on the day of congregational prayer. Pidou de Saint-Olon, who served as ambassador to Morocco in 1693, writes that "their Women do not enter into the *Mosques* . . . yet they say their Prayers at home; and, on *Fridays*, resort to the Burying-places, to pray and weep over the Graves of their dead Relations."[140] In an independent and somewhat earlier seventeenth-century account, Lancelot Addison (who worked as a chaplain for seven years in Tangier) states that on Friday men don their best garments to go to the Great Mosque; "the women likewise on this day visit the Sepulchres and strew the graves of their deceased Friends with green Boughs and Herbs."[141] Although de Saint-Olon may or may not have been correct in his belief that women simply could not attend the mosque, women's grave visitation is likely to have been openly visible.

Why might some medieval Cairene women—and some women in other times and places—have preferred the graveyard over the mosque? Because their views on this subject have not been directly preserved for us, we can only speculate. In addition to being the occasion for a refreshing outing, grave visitation potentially enabled the cultivation of family networks through the shared care of the dead. In this way, it may have addressed the personal needs of women more directly than congregational prayer in the mosque. Bereavement must have been a pervasive experience for women as well as men, and the maintenance of kinship ties—not only with the deceased but also with the other relatives who cared for the same graves—must have been central to women's emotional and social welfare. When the sultan banned women from the streets of Cairo in 841/1437 (as a gesture of piety intended to end an attack of plague), a woman whose son had died in the plague reacted to her inability to follow the funeral procession to the grave by jumping to her death from the roof of her house.[142] The reaping of *baraka* through the visitation of the graves of the pious and the distribution of food to the poor may have addressed both women's hopes for this-worldly welfare, which could be enhanced by the blessings of auspicious places and activities, and their hopes for otherworldly salvation. Overall, there seems to be little obvious correlation between the distribution of women's public religious activities and the normative doctrines of contemporary *fiqh*; it is more likely to be primarily a reflection of the women's own needs and agendas.

SYRIA

Scattered references suggest that women's presence in Syrian mosques was considerable in the first century AH. However, most of the relevant anecdotes are drawn from sources of a significantly later date. Although this time lapse makes it difficult to confirm the mosque-based activities of specific first-century women, for the purposes of this study—which examines women's presence in mosques over the longer term—what is significant is the lasting and pervasive assumption that women were present in Syrian mosques. Indeed, from this point of view the late date of the relevant material may support the inference that, rather than declining into insignificance after the early period, women's mosque-based activities continued to be accepted and even celebrated among much later generations of Syrians.

One of the early figures most vividly associated with Syrian mosques is Umm al-Dardāʾ the Younger (al-Ṣughrā).[143] She is supposed to have been raised in the household of the Companion of the Prophet Abū al-Dardāʾ, who settled in Damascus after the conquest and remained there for the rest of his life. One report recounts that, as an orphan in his care, she "used to go with Abū al-Dardāʾ dressed in a hooded cloak (*burnus*)[144] to pray in the rows of men and sit in the study circles of the reciters to learn[145] the Qur'an, until [one day] Abū al-Dardāʾ said to her, 'Go to join the rows of women!'"[146] This report suggests that her activities in the mosque were in part a violation (or bending) of gender segregation that was enabled by her young age. Abū al-Dardāʾ finally brings an end to her circumvention of the gender rules by directing her to join the other women.[147] Although Umm al-Dardā's activities may have been anomalous in some ways, there are assumed to be regular "women's rows" within the mosque.

In her later life, Umm al-Dardāʾ is associated with both Damascus and Jerusalem; according to one report, she was in the habit of spending six months of the year in each place.[148] Ibn Kathīr states that "the men used to recite and study law under her direction at the northern wall in the Friday mosque of Damascus; ʿAbd al-Malik ibn Marwān used to sit in her circle with the students of law and study under her direction when he was caliph, may God be pleased with her!"[149] This statement represents Umm al-Dardāʾ in the later stages of her life; ʿAbd al-Malik ruled from 65 to 86 AH, and her last known act was to make the pilgrimage to Mecca in 81 AH.[150] Other anecdotes linking her with ʿAbd al-Malik are set in Jerusalem. One recounts that ʿAbd al-Malik and Umm al-Dardāʾ were sitting together in the Dome of the Rock; when the call to the *maghrib* prayer sounded, they arose, and Umm al-Dardāʾ leaned on him until they entered the mosque (i.e., presumably al-Aqṣā). She sat down with the women, and ʿAbd al-Malik went to the front to lead the people in prayer.[151] As suggested by her physically leaning on the caliph's arm, at the end of her life she may well have been enjoying the privileges of seniority, just as she had enjoyed the privileges of youth in her days as an orphan. Nevertheless, the anecdote also casually assumes the general presence of women in the mosque, just as Ibn Kathīr's scenario suggests that a woman—at least an aged one—could publicly teach (although apparently to an audience of men) in the most important mosque in Damascus.

Women's presence in Syrian mosques in the early period is not presented as being limited to the sacred precincts of Jerusalem or to the metropolis of Damascus. An anecdote in Ibn al-Jawzī's *Ṣifat al-ṣafwa* tells of the female client (*mawlāt*) of Abū Umāma (presumably Abū Umāma al-Bāhilī, a Companion of the Prophet who settled in Ḥimṣ and died in the eighties of the first Islamic century[152]). The narrator of the story, ʿAbd al-Raḥmān ibn Yazīd ibn Jābir, states that he saw her in the mosque of Ḥimṣ teaching the women the Qur'an, the normative practices of the Prophet (*al-sunan*), and their religious duties (*al-farāʾiḍ*).[153] As ʿAbd al-Raḥmān ibn Yazīd ibn Jābir is supposed to have died in 153–54 AH,[154] this story is probably set in the first half of the second century.

In addition to teaching, some early Syrian Muslim women were associated with an extreme and ascetic devotion to worship. These women existed in other areas of the early Islamic world as well; as Umaima Abou-Bakr has noted, their activities were often—although not exclusively—pursued in mosques.[155] Ibn ʿAsākir recounts a report that Umm al-Dardāʾ[156] had a following of women who stood in prayer all night until their feet swelled.[157] This may well have taken place in her home, but other women pursued such activities in the mosque. A Companion of the Prophet, Kathīr ibn Murra, who settled in Ḥimṣ, recounted that "I dreamt that I entered [the branches of] a lofty tree in heaven, and I began to wander in it and marvel at it. In one part I suddenly beheld some of the women of the mosque (*nisāʾ min nisāʾ al-masjid*), and I went and greeted them. Then I asked, 'How did you achieve [this degree of reward]?' They said, 'By [performing] prostrations [in prayer] and [eating] little morsels [of bread] (*bi-sajadāt wa-kusayrāt*).' "[158] This report suggests not only the existence of women engaged in pious exercises (and perhaps in religious retreat, *iʿtikāf*) in the mosque but also the esteem in which they were held.

The assumption that even small-town mosques were accessible to Syrian women persisted in later centuries, as far as the fragmentary evidence allows one to conclude. The poet Abū'l-ʿAlāʾ al-Maʿarrī (d. 449/1058), a lifelong resident of the northern Syrian town of Maʿarrat al-Nuʿmān, refers to women's frequentation of mosques in one of his poems:

Even worse for a woman than her [going to the] public bath
Is for you to give her free rein
And for her to walk [the street] shaking her sleeve
So that the fragrance of her perfume wafts before her
Visiting the mosque in passing,
Praying behind a leader—and there is misfortune
in her praying behind
A falcon who does not restrain himself from [hunting] her [like a] dove;
The Creator grant her refuge from her imam![159]

Although al-Maʿarrī clearly disapproves of women's being given the freedom to visit the mosque, it is presented as a real, if lamentable, phenomenon, similar to the undoubtedly genuine practice of women's visiting the public baths. The implied scenario seems to be a spontaneous individual visit to the mosque, including prayer behind an imam (either a professional religious functionary or simply a male fellow-worshiper) if one is available. It may be that a woman's appearance at Friday prayers was a less routine occurrence. Al-Maʿarrī describes a dramatic incident in 417/1026–27, when a pregnant woman entered the main mosque of Maʿarrat al-Nuʿmān during the Friday prayers to appeal to the community against a tavern keeper who had molested her.[160] It is unclear whether her very presence (in addition to the sensational nature of her public complaint) is anomalous or not.

There is evidence that, at a somewhat later date, women routinely attended Friday prayers in at least some of the towns and villages of Palestine. Significantly, these seem to have been locales where Ḥanbalism was predominant. In a famous passage of his *Aḥkām al-qurʾān,* the Andalusian jurist Abū Bakr ibn al-ʿArabī (d. 543/1148) admiringly describes the behavior of the women of Nablus, whom he observed during a stay of several months in the town. "I never saw a woman on a street during the day except on Friday, when they went out into [the streets] until the mosque was full of them; when the prayer was finished, they returned to their homes, and my eye did not fall on one of them until the next Friday." Ibn al-ʿArabī clearly does not regard the retiring behavior of the women of Nablus as typical; whether the women of other localities attend Friday prayers he does not state.[161] In a unique text studied by Daniella Talmon-Heller, the Syrian scholar Muḥammad ibn ʿAbd al-Wāḥid al-Maqdisī (d. 643/1245) presents an anecdote in which a man goes to attend Friday prayers in the village mosque of Salamīya (near Nablus) with his mother. In the story, the wonder-working local shaykh multiplies a small amount of food to feed everyone present; "then the food was taken up to the women (*rufiʿa ilā al-nisāʾ*)."[162] It is unclear how localized or unusual the practice of women's attendance at Friday prayers in the Nablus area may have been. It may have reflected the distinctive religious culture of the Ḥanbalī community, which predominated in this area. Again, it suggests that women's mosque attendance in Greater Syria was not limited to the great mosques of the metropolis of Damascus or the pilgrimage center of Jerusalem, but extended to at least some village mosques.

More salient than references to women's attendance at Friday prayer, however, are allusions to their presence in mosques at sessions of teaching and preaching. This was clearly not a phenomenon limited to Syria; indeed, the presence of women (and the resulting issue of visually or physically separating the sexes) is a recurrent theme in discussions of preaching. As we have seen, the issue of mixed gatherings of men and women listening to preachers is addressed by Abū Ḥāmid al-Ghazālī (d. 505/1111) in his *Iḥyāʾ ʿulūm al-dīn*, a work composed at the end of his life when he lived in Damascus and in Ṭūs (and thus may reflect, at least in part, his experiences in Syria).[163] There al-Ghazālī complains that young and attractively dressed preachers behave seductively in sessions attended by women. Significantly, he notes that the ill effects of women and men sitting within view of each other are attested by customary experience.[164]

The wide occurrence and long persistence of the habits denounced by al-Ghazālī are suggested by the fact that his remarks are reproduced by later authors of manuals of *ḥisba*, treatises providing guidelines for authorities entrusted with the preservation of public order, as well as in polemics against religious innovations. Portions of al-Ghazālī's comments are reproduced in one of the most famous preaching manuals of the medieval period, the *Kitāb al-Quṣṣāṣ wa'l-mudhakkirīn* of the Baghdādī Ibn al-Jawzī (d. 597/1201),[165] who observes that "these assemblies are never lacking in attractive women."[166] The relevant passage from al-Ghazālī is reproduced verbatim in the early fourteenth century CE by the Egyptian Ibn al-Ukhuwwa and in the seventeenth century by Muḥammad ibn Ṣāliḥ al-Dajjānī.[167] Thus, the spatial and visual separation of men and women at preaching sessions continued to be treated as a relevant concern in texts that claimed to address pragmatic current issues.

A literary anecdote of the thirteenth century, although certainly fictional in its details, similarly assumes the presence of women as well as men at mosque preaching sessions. The *Masnavī* of Jalāl al-Dīn Rūmī (d. 672/1273) was composed in Konya in central Anatolia. It is there that Rūmī spent most of his life and where his sense of social practice must have been formed, although he also visited the Syrian cities of Damascus and Aleppo.[168] In one of the many apparently profane tales that the spiritual master puts to unexpected mystical use, the legendary trickster Jūḥī (Juḥā) disguises himself as a woman for a mixed preaching session:

There once was a preacher of great eloquence
Who gathered men and women beneath the pulpit.
Jūḥī put on a cloak and face-veil
And went among the women unrecognized.

When a questioner asks the preacher how long the pubic hair may grow before it affects the validity of prayer, Juḥā seizes the opportunity to invite a neighboring woman to check the length of "hers" by feeling it with her hand. When the woman feels Juḥā's genitals she screams, leading the preacher to exclaim, "What I have said has struck her heart!"[169]

Although this cheerfully bawdy incident surely never took place, the anecdote reflects a milieu in which men and women attended preaching sessions together, although apparently seated in separate groups and with the women thoroughly veiled. The preacher is ready to address the listeners' most mundane practical questions about ritual practice. Eloquent preaching was valued and apparently sometimes elicited cries of ecstasy from women as well as men (although in this case spiritual transport is clearly not involved).

The fact that mosque preaching sessions were particularly potent attractions for female audiences in various parts of the Islamic world is suggested by a striking account by Ibn Baṭṭūṭa, who traveled through Iran around 726/1326. He states that the people of Shiraz are characterized by virtue, religiosity, and chastity—"particularly its women; they wear boots (*khifāf*) and go out enveloped [in cloaks] and wearing face veils (*multaḥifāt mutabarqiʿāt*) so that no part of them is visible." He praises the women's charitable activities and observes in wonder that "an astonishing circumstance about them (*min gharīb ḥālihinna*) is that they gather to hear the preacher (*al-wāʿiẓ*) every Monday, Thursday and Friday in the Great Mosque; sometimes one or two thousand of them gather, holding fans that they use to fan themselves because of the intense heat." Ibn Baṭṭūṭa concludes by remarking that he has never seen women gather in such numbers in any other town.[170] It is noteworthy that Ibn Baṭṭūṭa is astonished by the magnitude (and perhaps the regularity) of the Shirazi women's gatherings, but apparently not by their presence in the mosque. It is also significant that, like the women of Nablus in the description of Ibn al-ʿArabī, the women of Shiraz here seem to combine a high degree of visibility in the mosque with an otherwise striking devotion to the ideal of female modesty and concealment.

Although it is always difficult to gauge the comparative magnitude of women's participation in different mosque-based activities, the evidence seems to suggest that preaching sessions held a particular appeal and were widely frequently by women in various parts of the Islamic world. In a polemic exchange about ṣūfī audition (*samāʿ*) with Muwaffaq al-Dīn Ibn Qudāma (d. 620/1223), whom he succeeded as the head of the Ḥanbalī school in Damascus, Nāṣiḥ al-Dīn Ibn al-Ḥanbalī (d. 634/1236) argues that the gathering of men and women for pious purposes such as congregational and Friday prayers, preaching sessions, or judicial sittings is not religiously objectionable; indeed, "it is the current practice (*al-ʿāda al-jāriya*) on holy occasions (*al-mawāsim*) with this scholar and jurisprudent and his followers (*ʿinda hādhā'l-faqīh al-muftī wa-jamāʿatihi*), and in sessions of preaching (lit., "reminding") in all Muslim lands (*majālis al-tadhkīr fī sāʾir bilād al-islām*)."[171] It is interesting that women's participation along with men at special times in the religious calendar is here presented as a distinctive practice of the Damascene Ḥanbalī establishment, whereas women's attendance at preaching sessions is posited as a ubiquitous Islamic custom.

If women's presence at mosque preaching sessions was a widespread phenomenon, however, it seems to have been particularly salient in Damascus and other parts of Syria. In the sixth/twelfth century, the Syrian al-Shayzarī writes about preaching sessions in his manual for *muḥtasibs* in a passage dealing with the gathering places of women (emphasizing, as was by now routine, that they should be separated from men by a screen).[172] Women could participate in such sessions not only as members of the audience but also as preachers in their own right. Ibn ʿAsākir (d. 571/1176) observes of his Damascene contemporary Fāṭima (Sitt al-ʿAjam) bint Sahl that "she used to preach to women in some of the mosques."[173] A century and a half later, Fāṭima bint ʿAbbās ibn Abī'l-Fatḥ (d. 714/1315), whose activities as a religious teacher began in Damascus and continued in Egypt after she moved there sometime after 700 AH, was particularly known for the fact that "she used to ascend the pulpit and preach to the women." The circumstance of her preaching from the *minbar* was particularly disturbing to Ibn Taymīya until he had a dream in which the Prophet Muḥammad himself assured him of her virtue.[174]

The enthralling preacher Sibṭ Ibn al-Jawzī (d. 654/1256) attracted crowds of men and women alike to his preaching sessions in the Umayyad Mosque of Damascus and the Jāmiʿ al-Jabal (also known as the Jāmiʿ al-Muẓaffarī or Jāmiʿ al-Ḥanābila, the Mosque of the Ḥanbalīs). His contemporary Abū Shāma recounts that the gatherings at these mosques were crowded with innumerable men and women, with "the women separated from the men (*bi-maʿzal ʿan al-rijāl*)." Interestingly, his description of Sibṭ Ibn al-Jawzī's preaching forms an admiring mirror image of the very qualities and practices that were denounced by al-Ghazālī a century and a half earlier. Sibṭ Ibn al-Jawzī's physical charm and pleasant voice, his dress, and his movements all contributed, according to Abū Shāma, to make his preaching sessions "one of the adornments and pleasures of this world (*min maḥāsin al-dunyā wa-ladhdhātihā*)."[175] Abū Shāma's description is almost defiantly worldly, positioning al-Jawzī's preaching as a gratification in this life (*al-dunyā*) rather than a reminder of the next (*al-ākhira*). Despite Abū Shāma's unabashedly appreciative attitude, his description confirms pious complaints that preaching sometimes constituted a form of mass entertainment.[176]

One of the richest sources for another form of publicly accessible religious instruction is the collection of Damascene *samāʿāt*, records of formal readings of individual works (ḥadīth collections, legal treatises, and the like), compiled by Stefan Leder, Yāsīn al-Sawwās, and Maʾmūn al-Ṣāgharjī. These documents, dating from 550/1155 to 750/1349, record the dates on which the works were read and the names of those who performed the reading, presided over it, and attended it. In most cases, they also state the location of the reading, sometimes only in general terms (for instance, "Damascus"), but more often identifying a specific mosque, madrasa, *dār al-ḥadīth*, or private home. The *samāʿāt* in the collection were compiled as a representative sample from a flourishing period in Syrian intellectual life. Even though the incomplete nature of the record—both of the surviving *samāʿāt* in general and of the compiled selections in particular—precludes absolute or quantitative conclusions about the locales of women's formal learning activities, these documents do provide a unique window into thousands of concrete incidents of religious learning. The *samāʿāt* in this collection make it clear that women participated actively in educational gatherings in mosques, as well as in all of the other venues where such readings occurred. However, they also suggest that women's participation was proportionately quite limited as compared to that of men.[177]

For instance, based on the index of the collection, four of the *samāʿāt* record sessions that occurred in mosques were presided over by women (in three out of the four cases, alongside men).[178] Of these, two took place in the Jāmiʿ al-Muẓaffarī on Mount Qāsiyūn, one in the Masjid al-Bayāṭira of Damascus, and the last (exceptionally) at the Prophet's Mosque in Medina rather than in Damascus. At least thirty-five of the *samāʿāt* record female auditors at readings that took place in mosques.[179] Of these, strikingly, eighteen are recorded to have occurred in a single mosque, the Jāmiᶜ al-Muẓaffarī. Of the remaining sessions, five took place at the Umayyad Mosque, two at the Masjid al-Bayāṭira, and three at the Ḥanbalī mosque in the town of Baᶜlabakk. The rest took place at a scattering of other mosques. The incidence of women's participation appears to reflect different patterns for individual mosques; for instance, women appear to have been present at a small fraction of the many sessions recorded for the Umayyad Mosque, but at a relatively high proportion of the smaller numbers recorded for the Jāmiᶜ al-Muẓaffarī and for the Ḥanbalī mosque of Baᶜlabakk.[180] It is significant that both of these mosques were associated specifically with the Ḥanbalī *madhhab*; the Jāmiᶜ al-Muẓaffarī (also known as the Jāmiᶜ al-Ḥanābila) served the important Ḥanbalī community on Mount Qasyūn.

In his study of the Jāmiᶜ al-Muẓaffarī, Muḥammad Muṭīᶜ al-Ḥāfiẓ identifies seven *samāᶜāt* documenting sessions of ḥadīth transmission at that mosque presided over by one or more female authorities.[181] He observes that it was a distinctive practice at that particular mosque for ḥadīth sessions to be held under the auspices of a group of people authorized to transmit the text rather than of an individual; such sessions were unusually likely to include female scholars (who otherwise might prefer to hold sessions in their homes).[182] One session held in 707/1307 was presided over by fourteen shaykhs, including six women.[183]

Overall, the evidence of these Damascene *samāᶜāt* suggests that mosques (particularly certain individual mosques) were accessible to women who wished to attend readings of scholarly works. Nevertheless, mosques were not the main venue where they did so, and their numbers were comparatively small. Konrad Hirschler notes that in the Damascus *samāᶜāt,* "the relatively low importance of mosques as venues for readings under female authorized teachers contrasts with the overall figure . . . where 29 percent of all readings were held in mosques." However, it would be difficult to draw sharp categorical distinctions between (for instance) madrasas and mosques, which tended to be multifunctional spaces; madrasas in this period were places of regular congregational prayer and often housed pulpits for the Friday sermon, and mosques routinely functioned as places of both formal and informal group instruction. The two terms were sometimes used interchangeably for the same institution.[184]

There is reason to think that at least some women preferentially participated in sessions held in private homes (and perhaps, in some cases, in madrasas). For instance, the prominent ḥadīth authority Zaynab bint al-Kamāl is recorded to have co-led at least three sessions in the Jāmiᶜ al-Muẓaffarī.[185] However, of the thirty-four sessions that she is recorded to have led or attended in the *samāᶜāt* collected by Leder, al-Sawwās, and al-Ṣāghirjī, only one is explicitly stated to have been held in a mosque, as compared to thirteen in her home and eight in madrasas.[186] Zaynab bint ᶜAbd Allāh ibn ᶜAbd al-Raḥmān presided over four readings of one specific text between 706 and 718, all of them in her own home, but apparently did not participate in readings of the same work in 705 or 708 at the Umayyad Mosque.[187] Several other women listed in the index show similar patterns of selectively attending readings in private homes.[188] Of course, without further information (which is unavailable for many of the women listed in the *samāᶜāt*) it is impossible to isolate many of the factors that might have kept some women away from readings held in mosques. As Asma Sayeed has observed,[189] Zaynab bint al-Kamāl was very elderly at the dates of all of the *samāᶜāt* recorded in the collection; it may be that the privileges of age allowed her greater public activity than would have been possible in her youth or that her prestige as a transmitter rose with the death of others who had heard ḥadīth from the same authorities. Not all of the women who presided over ḥadīth sessions in mosques were in their dotage; Ḥabība bint Ibrāhīm al-Maqdisīya is reported to have been born in 654 AH, which would have made her fifty-three lunar years old at the time of the session she co-led in the Jāmiᶜ al-Muẓaffarī in 707 (she lived another thirty-eight years, until 745/1344–45).[190] Fāṭima al-Maqdisīya, who participated in the same session and died in 734 at "over eighty," was probably in her mid-fifties.[191] These women may have enjoyed the privileges of maturity, but they were not crones, and their role cannot be attributed to their outliving other transmitters.

It is probably not coincidental that a number of scholars who affirmed women's entitlement to visit the mosque were linked with the Syrian Ḥanbalī milieu and with the Jāmiᶜ al-Muẓaffarī of Damascus in particular. Muwaffaq al-Dīn Ibn Qudāma came from the Jerusalem area (where, as we shall see, there was a history of women's attendance at Friday prayers) and moved with his family to the Ṣāliḥīya quarter of Damascus, where he served at times as imam and khaṭīb of the Jāmiʿ al-Muẓaffarī.[192] The Ḥanbalī ḥadīth network of al-Ṣāliḥīya also influenced traditionists of other origins and schools. Ibn Ḥajar al-ʿAsqalānī spent time there and studied extensively with at least one female scholar, as well as spending time in the Jāmiʿ al-Muẓaffarī; it seems likely that he encountered women traditionists within the mosque.[193]

The fragmentary but fascinating evidence of the Damascene *samāʿāt* suggests both that a number of women functioned (often with great distinction) in the public arena of formal textual transmission and that it was quite possible for them to do so in at least some mosques (particularly within the Ḥanbalī community). The relatively small proportion of women reflected in the published selection of *samāʿāt* also suggests, however, that this form of educational participation may have been limited to a relatively small sector of the female population as compared to attendance at preaching and teaching sessions where believers listened without playing a part in the formal process of textual transmission. (It also involved a relatively small proportion of the overall male population, of course, although male participants far outnumbered women.) Women (like men) identified in *samāʿ* documents represented a wide socioeconomic range, from craftsmen's daughters to members of the ruling house;[194] however, those with the training to preside over sessions enjoyed some degree of social and religious prestige. A taboo against women's presence within mosques would not unilaterally explain the relative paucity of women at sessions of formal transmission or the most famous female transmitters' apparent preference for other venues. It may be that the relatively high social status and distinctive piety of women who distinguished themselves as ḥadīth transmitters, rather than any categorical difficulty in venturing into mosques, contributed to the overrepresentation of female-led sessions in other locations.

The widespread, but (to some scholars) sometimes disturbing presence of women at preaching sessions is addressed in a fatwa by ʿAlāʾ al-Dīn Muḥammad ibn Muḥammad al-Bukhārī (d. 841/1437), whose legal reasoning has already been discussed in the first chapter of this study.[195] Al-Bukhārī spent the later years of his life in Syria, and this fatwa is preserved in manuscript in Jerusalem, leading to a strong inference that it was composed in the Syrian period of al-Bukhārī's life (although it is possible that he received the question from farther afield). As is the case with many inquiries directed to legal scholars, this one is carefully crafted to elicit a specific response through an alarming description of the existing reality. The beginning of the question (*istiftāʾ*) reads as follows:

> What do their honors the religious scholars . . . say about some of the preacher-storytellers (*quṣṣāṣ*) who sit in the mosques while throngs of women gather around them so that the gathering is packed with [women]; [the preacher] is sitting on a seat (*kursī*) and they [feminine plural] are sitting in front of him, to his right, and to his left; sometimes [the women] are by themselves, no man being with them, and sometimes there are men in the gathering sitting in it with [the women]—is this right, or is it one of the objectionable matters (*al-umūr al-munkara*) that the rulers are obligated to denounce and change, and to prevent the preachers from [holding] them and prevent the women from attending them?[196]

Al-Bukhārī responds to this anguished inquiry as if he is personally well aware of the phenomenon in question; rather than expressing incredulity or surprise, he implies that it is both perfectly familiar and personally distressing. In his answer, he refers to "those ignorant *quṣṣāṣ* holding the *mīʿād* for women in mosques and other locations."[197] Al-Bukhārī's remark suggests two things. First, by stating that the preachers "hold" or "convene" (*ʿaqd*) such sessions "for women," he implies that women were not simply present at spontaneous instances of storytelling and preaching that occurred informally within the mosques. The word *mīʿād* (literally, "appointment") inherently designates a regularly scheduled session, and according to al-Bukhārī some preachers were holding such sessions specifically "for women." Writing about contemporary Cairo, Berkey has observed that the word *mīʿād* came to designate a regular (often weekly) lesson intended to disseminate general religious knowledge to a broader public.[198] Relatively accessible religious texts, particularly ḥadīth, seem to have predominated. Although these sessions were "popular" in the sense of being directed broadly and inclusively at the Muslim public, one must not conflate broad accessibility with "popular" or "folk" Islam; as Berkey observes, "becoming a *shaykh al-mīʿād* [the officially designated teacher of such a session] required considerable training, as did any other educational post."[199] Similar caution is in order in interpreting "preacher-storyteller" (*qāṣṣ*, pl. *quṣṣāṣ*), as used by the questioner in his inquiry. Even though the term can evoke an uneducated purveyor of wild tales (and is probably selected by al-Bukhārī and his disapproving questioner for precisely this reason), preaching and storytelling in mosques were also legitimate religious functions that were exercised by many individuals of genuine learning and unquestionable orthodoxy.[200] The accusation that such sessions were convened by "ignorant *quṣṣāṣ*" is probably polemical, although we cannot know the precise nature of the knowledge these unnamed individuals purveyed.

Regardless of the precise content of the preaching or teaching involved, al-Bukhārī's fatwa manifestly reflects a situation where large audiences composed partially or completely of women routinely attended sessions in many mosques. Both the questioner and al-Bukhārī himself seem to regard this as an existing social reality, although they are far from being resigned to it on religious terms; as we have seen in chapter 1, the prevalence of women's presence in mosques spurred al-Bukhārī to an unprecedented level of normative condemnation of women's mosque attendance. Other evidence similarly suggests that women's presence in the mosques of Damascus in the Mamlūk period was widespread, but sometimes controversial. The diarist Ibn Ṭawq writes of Shawwāl of 889 (October–November 1484):

> It occurred that women attended the congregational mosque (*ḥadatha ḥuḍūr al-nisāʾ fī'l-jāmiʿ*) in the aforementioned month every night; al-Najmī emboldened them (*qawwāhunna*) to do that. When the day that the completion of the reading of the [Prophet's] life story (*yawm khatmat al-sīra*) came, their numbers increased greatly—may God not increase his [al-Najmī's] or their likes!—and they mixed (*ikhtalaṭna*) with the men. There is no might and no power except in God! The same thing happened in Jāmiʿ al-Manjak and Masjid al-Aqṣāb, [the women] mixing with the men. Shameless things increased in quantity and magnitude; there is no power except with God! We ask God for that to pass away, and that He not hold us accountable for our bad actions.[201]

These sincerely appalled remarks, recorded in a personal diary rather than in a scholarly polemic, suggest that women's unsegregated presence in Syrian mosques at night was sufficiently unusual to evoke shock and wonderment from a contemporary observer. It is also notable that Ibn Ṭawq names an individual who has apparently actively encouraged the women's attendance, suggesting that it was not completely routine.[202] However, it was also clearly not unique, as the same thing was occurring in at least two other mosques in Damascus. It is unclear whether Ibn Ṭawq would have been equally offended if the women had attended the mosque without "mixing" with men.

In any case, the mass presence of women and children on such occasions was far from unique. Around the beginning of the same century, the Damascene Ibn al-Naḥḥās (d. 814/1411) had complained—echoing concerns expressed by predecessors such as Ibn al-Ḥājj, but quite clearly describing the sordid details of practice in his own time—of the excesses that occurred at al-Aqṣā and other mosques (*al-jawāmiʿ wa'l-masājid*) on the night of the Miʿrāj (celebrated on the twenty-seventh of Rajab) and on Niṣf Shaʿbān, when richly illuminated mosques were thronged with riotous crowds of men, women, and children. He describes in particular detail the sanitary problems caused when women and children spent the night in the mosque and soiled its carpets.[203]

As in other parts of the Islamic world, in Syria the mosque was also the site for activities other than worship and religious teaching. As recorded in Ibn Ṭawq's diary, marriages were often concluded in mosques, although the bride would not necessarily have been present on such an occasion. Nevertheless, women sometimes attended; in one case, Ibn Ṭawq states that the female matchmaker (*khāṭiba*) was present at a marriage solemnized in a mosque.[204] Despite the disapproval of the prevalent Shāfiʿī school, judicial sessions continued to be held in mosques in medieval Syria. Al-Shayzarī's manual for *muḥtasibs* states that those officials ought to "frequent the sessions of the judges and arbiters and forbid them from sitting in the Friday prayer mosques and ordinary mosques to judge between the people" because menstruating women and other ritually impure people often must appear before them; furthermore, loud altercations disturb the peace of the mosque.[205] Although al-Shayzarī states that these things are forbidden (*ḥarām*), he also clearly assumes that they occur.

In the early sixteenth century, a prominent Shāfiʿī scholar from the northern Syrian city of Hama wrote a series of works touching on the issue of women's presence in mosques. ʿAlī ibn ʿAṭīya al-Ḥamawī, known as al-Shaykh ʿAlwān (d. 936/1530), was a legal scholar and celebrated ṣūfī who was also well known for his preaching.[206] His critique of the conduct of his contemporaries in Syrian mosques suggests that Muslims of both genders continued to flock to hear popular preachers. He writes in one work,

> As for the praise-chanter (*maddāḥ*) of [our] time, if he is a preacher (*wāʿiẓ*) his main concern is to make an ostentatious show of his voice, to attract the regard of women and men and have them crowd around him . . . so that a woman will tell her [female] friend that "So-and-so the preacher has a voice that would bring the birds down from the trees" and she will have a yen to see him and hear his voice, and will go out without her husband's permission, disobeying God and His Prophet. If [the preacher] sees that his gathering (*majlis*) is packed with women he becomes conceited about his voice when he chants.[207]

Furthermore, the sight of the handsomely turned-out preacher may inspire envy and discontent in women with less well-dressed and attractive spouses.[208] He concludes,

> What is obligatory is for every Muslim who believes in God and the Last Day to abandon this person's gathering—it is a satanic (*shayṭānī*) gathering, not a godly (*raḥmānī*) one—and to restrain his wife and prevent her from attending it. If he does not do so, he is cheating her and not discharging God's obligation with respect to her. God Most High said, "O you who believe, protect yourselves and your wives from [hellfire]" [Qur'an 66:6] and "Men are in authority over women" [4:34], and [the Prophet] said, "Each of you is a shepherd, and each of you is responsible for his flock." Similarly, he should forbid her from attending any gathering where men and women mix without a barrier (*ḥijāb*) [between them]. . . . If [the Prophet] knew what women have innovated he would have forbidden them [to visit] the mosques; they go out scented and perfumed, wearing a wrapper, with an [attractive] appearance and with [showy] attire (*fī izār wa-hay'a wa-bi-zayy*), so that they corrupt the

> religion of the religious devotee, not to mention anyone else. Similarly, delinquent youths (*shubbān min ahl al-fasād*) and wine-drinkers attend the gathering only for the sake of looking at [the women], and the gathering is made a means for this; there is no might and no power except with God, the Exalted, the Glorious![209]

Shaykh ʿAlwān goes on to complain of the preacher whose pretentious comportment discourages ordinary listeners from inquiring about things that they do not understand, while eliciting their admiration for his erudition. He also caters to his audience's lower tastes by playing on their emotions, so that "women and men come from the lesson (*al-mīʿād*) deluded and dazzled by its attractiveness because of the corrupt gratifications their lower souls enjoyed from it, saying, 'Today the *faqīh* made the men and women cry until the gathering was in a clamor.'"[210] He also criticizes the preacher's recitation of erotic and mystical verses. In response to an anticipated objection that the Companions are reported to have recited poetry in the mosque in the presence of the Prophet himself (who sometimes smiled in response), he asks rhetorically, "See if they had with them in their gathering women who surrounded them, displaying their charms (or adornments: *zīna*) to them, and the men too displaying their charms to [the women], neither of the two groups casting down its eyes from the other?!"[211]

Shaykh ʿAlwān's discussion of this problem insistently observes that it affects both men and women, who may be left without the knowledge correctly to discharge such basic religious duties as ablution and prayer.[212] He exhorts preachers to remedy this situation by lecturing on the elementary knowledge that believers need in order to fulfill their religious obligations. False modesty should not prevent them from explaining necessary (if embarrassing) matters such as the rules of menstrual purity.[213]

In a work of the "mirrors for princes" genre, Shaykh ʿAlwān counsels that the doors of mosques should be kept locked except at prayer time and that "seductive women (*al-nisāʾ al-muftināt*) should be prevented from entering them when there is fear of insult [to the mosque] or of corruption." It is also necessary to "prevent preachers and traditionists (*al-muḥaddithīn*) from bringing together women and men without a barrier (*ḥijāb*) [between them]."[214] Nevertheless, this does not seem to have been the practice in reality. In another work, Shaykh ʿAlwān complains of what is done by "some of those who claim to be scholars and sit in the neighborhood or Friday mosque (*al-masjid wa'l-jāmiʿ*) on the preacher's seat (*kursī*) to recite the ḥadīth of the Prophet." He describes how "a group of men and women gathers around him without a barrier [separating them] or any shame; he recites to them things that will ingratiate him to them and for which they will praise him, such as special dispensations (*al-rukhaṣ*) and ḥadīths related to hope [of God's mercy]," as if he were trying to lure them into sin. All of this, he declares, is motivated by the preacher's desire to win money from the poor (presumably by attracting donations from a maximally large audience).[215] In support of his objection to this practice, Shaykh ʿAlwān then presents lengthy verbatim citations of the relevant opinions of al-Ghazālī and Taqī al-Dīn al-Ḥiṣnī, who both (as we have seen in chapter 1) emphasize the alleged statement of ʿĀʾisha as grounds for the position that latter-day women should not attend mosques at all.[216] Resuming his discussion of contemporary ḥadīth scholars and preachers, Shaykh ʿAlwān exclaims,

> How remarkable for someone who knows this [i.e., the authoritative doctrine of al-Ghazālī and al-Ḥiṣnī], has affirmed it, memorized it, and taught it—how he sits with women in the worst of generations [i.e., the present one] in the houses of God—glorious and exalted is He!—without a curtain or barrier, [the women] being mingled with young men, single men, and the like, and sees them commit various kinds of objectionable actions with respect to their wrappers, the "cockscomb" caps[217] that they wear on their heads, and the like, including thin clothes, fragrant scents, noise, the crying of children and their urinating on the carpets, [the women's] omitting to perform the dawn prayer, and other things. Sometimes a woman among them enters the congregational mosque (*al-jāmiʿ*) when she is in a state of pollution from menstruation or sexual intercourse because of her ignorance; and not one of them asks her husband's permission [to go out].[218]

One of the mixed-gender practices that Shaykh ʿAlwān singles out for censure is the completion of a full recitation (*khatm*) of the ḥadīth compilation of al-Bukhārī, which was not only an authoritative source for the statements and actions of the Prophet Muḥammad but also a work of enormous sanctity whose ritualized recitation was considered highly auspicious.[219] Writing about the reforms that were introduced to his own mosque by his ṣūfī master ʿAlī ibn Maymūn, a North African well versed in Mālikī law, Shaykh ʿAlwān states,

> Our mosque used to be prepared to receive guests and for people to eat food in it at weddings and condolence gatherings (*al-ʿazāʾ*); this continued until God facilitated [its abolition] and protected [the mosque] from the refuse of food, bones, and dogs entering. Many innovations were eliminated from it, including [the fact] that we used to recite [the *Ṣaḥīḥ* of] al-Bukhārī and men would mingle with women without a barrier [between them], which is a sin. He [i.e., ʿAlī ibn Maymūn] allowed us to recite it only with a barrier erected between us and the women.[220]

In another passage, Shaykh ʿAlwān expresses his remorse for his own past participation in this practice and again complains of the innovations (*bidaʿ*) associated with it, particularly the mixing of men and women.[221] It is perhaps significant that both references to mixed-sex audiences at readings of the *Ṣaḥīḥ* of al-Bukhārī occur in immediate conjunction with critiques of practices associated with weddings; it is possible that such ceremonies were used to generate religious merit on the auspicious occasion of a marriage, although Shaykh ʿAlwān does not state so explicitly. The presiding reader was paid by the sponsor of the ceremony (*ṣāḥib al-qirāʾa*) and was apparently showered with costly items on the occasion of the reading, which were then returned when the sponsor paid the cash that was owed. The reading seems to have culminated with the scholar leading a celebratory procession of both sexes, the women ululating festively.[222]

Shaykh ʿAlwān describes the mosque as a lively community space where people gather to celebrate, to mourn, and to partake of religiously edifying entertainment. What emerges most vividly from his frequent and passionate remarks about the presence of women in mosques is the sharp tension between his religious conviction that women should not be present (or at least visible to men) in mosques and his factual recognition that they are. Although his description of women's dress and behavior in the mosque is fundamentally shaped by stereotyped language drawn from the normative sources of the Qur'an and ḥadīth (and by the polemics produced by his ṣūfī master), his rueful recognition of women's high visibility in mosques is clearly an acknowledgment of social realities in contemporary Syria and in his own local mosque. He writes,

> [Women] go out to mosques, [religious] gatherings, graveyards, public baths, and visits of congratulation and condolence in a seductive way and with an objectionable appearance, flaunting their adornments [c.f. Qur'an 24:60], "swaying and sashaying, their heads like the humps of lean camels"[223] with fillets, "cockscomb" headdresses (*al-ʿaṣāʾib wa'l-muqanzaʿāt*) and the like. The curse of God is upon them, so they are accursed, and they will not smell the scent of Paradise or enter it, as is authoritatively transmitted in many reports. And they are not rebuked for this (*lā yunkar dhālika ʿalayhinna*); rather, in [religious] gatherings and Friday mosques (*al-majāmiʿ wa'l-jawāmiʿ*) they are mixed with the men, and surrounded by forbidden gazing.[224]

A few pages later in the same work, he laments the "afflictions and calamities observed in our land," averring that "I am honest and not lying in what I report!" He continues,

> How little and insignificant is the manly honor (*murūʾa*) of someone who enables his daughter to be present at these corruptions! The valid legal ruling (*al-fatwā*) in this time of ours, according to those possessing religious knowledge and piety, is that [women] should be forbidden from going to mosques—nay, ʿĀʾisha (may God be satisfied with her!) [already] gave a legal opinion to this effect in her own generation, the best of generations, so what do you think of the corrupt tenth century [of the hijra]? You should not imagine that she was the only one who held this opinion; rather, a vast number of earlier and later religious scholars held it.[225]

The tension between normative condemnation of women's mosque attendance—at least on the part of a vocal minority of religious scholars—and its apparent de facto prevalence is also reflected in the work of Shaykh ʿAlwān's religious mentor, the Maghribī ṣūfī master

Abū'l-Ḥasan ʿAlī ibn Maymūn (d. 917/1511).[226] Ibn Maymūn came from North Africa and settled for a time in the Ṣāliḥīya neighborhood of Damascus, where in 910/1504–5 he wrote a polemic condemning what he considered to be the religiously deviant practices of religious scholars and ṣūfīs in the Islamic East (*al-mashriq*)—practices that (he states in the introduction to the work) he had not observed in North Africa.[227] Embarking on his polemic against preachers, he begins by inveighing against

> their satanic practices (*aḥwālihim al-shayṭānīya*) in Damascus and other [localities] in its province (*ʿamal*) of bringing together men and women without a barrier [separating them] in neighborhood and Friday mosques (*al-masājid wa'l-jawāmiʿ*), the women trailing their finery of jewelry and robes, mincing, perfumed, seductive, swaying and sashaying, with [headdresses] on their heads "like the humps of lean camels." This misguided and misguiding, rebellious sinner mounts the preacher's seat above them in the garments of his worldly adornment.[228]

Although the preacher cites verses of the Qur'an and ḥadīth texts, Ibn Maymūn continues, he himself is condemned and cursed by them. In particular, he is acting in contravention of verse 33:53 (which instructs the Believers that, if they must ask the wives of the Prophet for something, they should do so "from behind a curtain" or barrier, *ḥijāb*) and verse 33:33 (which instructs the wives of the Prophet to "remain in your homes" and not to flaunt their beauty, as was done in the pre-Islamic Time of Ignorance).[229] He characterizes those who gather men and women together without a barrier in the houses of God as causing more corruption to Islam than tavern keepers or fornicators; everyone recognizes that the latter are sinning, and thus no one emulates them.[230] Not only the preachers but also their audiences are condemned by their participation in mixed preaching gatherings. Ibn Maymūn's lurid description of the men's and women's mutual gazing culminates with the assertion that they are effectively committing adultery (*zinā*) with their eyes and leave accursed by God and His angels.[231]

Significantly, Ibn Maymūn's comments make it clear that he considers mixed preaching gatherings to be distinctively a feature of religious life in Damascus and its environs. Certainly it would appear that, whatever the presence of women in North African mosques in his time, Syrian women's high level of visibility in such gatherings struck him as noteworthy and offensive. It is also significant that Shaykh ʿAlwān appears to have been a full and unquestioning participant in mixed-sex readings of al-Bukhārī before becoming the disciple of ʿAlī ibn Maymūn; only retrospectively does he regard his own participation in this custom as cause for repentance and remorse. On this issue as well as others of the same kind, Shaykh ʿAlwān would appear to have had an unusually censorious attitude toward the social and religious practices prevalent in his environment.[232] As we have seen, evidence from North Africa suggests that in that region there was a long tradition of architecturally and visually distinct women's space in mosques. It is possible that the crowded gatherings of Syrian preachers, where women often seem to have sat in full view of men, would have been genuinely novel to a Maghribī observer. Of course, disapproval of women's activities in Syrian mosques was not a completely new or alien phenomenon; objections had already been expressed by Syrians such as al-Ḥiṣnī. The glaring discrepancy between Shaykh ʿAlwān's normative sentiments on women's mosque attendance and the realities of contemporary Syrian religious practice probably reflects both a systemic dissonance between religious discourses and local practice and this particular scholar's exposure to influences rooted in another region of the Islamic world.

JERUSALEM: AL-AQṢĀ

The case of the Aqṣā Mosque of Jerusalem is sufficiently distinctive to warrant separate attention. Anecdotal evidence suggests that a small but lively subculture of female ascetics lived in pious retreat there in the early period. Again, the available evidence dates from a later period and may reflect a lasting awareness of women's presence in the mosque in Jerusalem more than the concrete circumstances of women in the historical period when the anecdotes are set. Omaima Abou-Bakr has noted that such references are particularly plentiful in the *Ṣifat al-ṣafwa* of Abū'l-Faraj Ibn al-Jawzī (d. 597/1200).[233]

Ibn al-Jawzī's hagiographical accounts of often anonymous early figures show little interest in historical specificity; however, overall the anecdotes suggest that extended or permanent retreats in the mosque (*iʿtikāf*) were a particularly prominent feature of the pious practice of some women in Jerusalem. In one, a visitor reports, "I saw many women wearing chemises of wool and veils (*khumur*), dwelling in retreat in the mosque (*muʿtakifāt fi'l-masjid*), not speaking during the day."[234] In another, a group of men encounters a young woman (*jāriya*) in the mosque wearing a hair chemise and a woolen veil.[235] In both of these cases, the women's attire clearly signifies asceticism and self-mortification. Another anecdote speaks of a group of about ten female devotees who have brought their spindles to the mosque "and leave it only for a polluting bodily function (*ḥadath*) or a necessary errand (*ḥāja*)."[236] Although historically unspecific, based on their (admittedly rather casual) attribution these anecdotes would appear to be set in the late first or the second century AH. However, the culture of female devotees resident in the Aqṣā Mosque seems to have survived for centuries. In the first half of the twelfth century, Ibn al-ʿArabī (d. 543/1148) reports, "I saw in the Aqṣā Mosque chaste women who did not go out of their place of religious retreat (*muʿtakafihinna*) until they died as martyrs there."[237]

Descriptions of the Aqṣā Mosque also suggest that it had several enclosures (*maqāṣīr*) reserved specifically for women. Writing at the turn of the tenth century CE, Ibn al-Faqīh notes that "within the mosque are three enclosures for women, the length of each enclosure being seventy cubits (*dhirāʿ*)."[238] Early in the same century, Ibn ʿAbd Rabbih writes that "in the mosque there are three enclosures for women, each of which is eighty cubits long by fifty cubits in width."[239] It is ambiguous, however, whether such descriptions of the "mosque of Jerusalem" refer exclusively to al-Aqṣā or to the entirety of the Ḥaram—that is, the enclosed complex of holy sites also known as the Temple Mount. In the context of the sanctuary at Jerusalem, the term *masjid* was used in both ways.[240] The large reported size of the women's enclosures suggests that they may not have been within the mosque proper. If the women's enclosures were indeed in the plaza surrounding the Aqṣā Mosque and the Dome of the Rock, this suggests extensive female attendance at the large communal prayers—on

Fridays and festivals—when the plaza itself would have been one large place of worship, with rows of both male and female worshipers filling the pavement. This would leave open the nature of women's accommodations within the mosque building.

In later centuries, one of the buildings contiguous to the Aqṣā Mosque came to be known as the Women's Mosque (*Jāmiʿ al-Nisāʾ*). It seems natural to assume that this name originated with the use of the structure as a women's prayer space; however, available sources do not appear to provide further information about such use. In the first half of the fourteenth century CE, Ibn Faḍl Allāh al-ʿUmarī points out that the Women's Mosque, like the Mosque of the Moroccans, is colloquially known by the term designating Friday mosques (*jāmiʿ*) despite the fact that it does not have a Friday sermon; each of them simply has an imam who leads the five daily prayers.[241] He says nothing about an exclusively female congregation, perhaps implying that by his time "Women's Mosque" was a traditional label rather than a current functional description. Nevertheless, his other remarks reflect the existence of facilities for women's prayer activities in the Ḥaram complex in his own time. Describing one part of the complex, he mentions an arcaded space nineteen and one-half cubits long and nine cubits wide, "where some women now perform the five prayers behind the imams."[242] Al-ʿUmarī also indicates the existence of separate sanitary facilities for women, which also suggests the significant presence of female worshipers.[243] In any case, even if special accommodations were provided for women's group prayer at times of communal worship, women clearly also used space within the main body of the mosque. Mujīr al-Dīn refers in passing to "the place where the women sit near Biʾr al-Waraqa," a location within the Aqṣā Mosque.[244]

In the late fifteenth century, Félix Fabri provided a rather detailed (and frankly admiring) description of women's presence in the Aqṣā Mosque. Whatever separate or external spaces might have been reserved for women at times of particular crowding, he makes it clear that they also have space (apparently unenclosed) within the mosque proper: "Women have a door of their own, through which they enter both the temple and the courtyard thereof, and their own aisle in the temple, wherein they pray apart from the men."[245] Comparing the cleanliness and reverent atmosphere of the mosques of Jerusalem favorably with the disorder and disrepair of Christian churches (in Jerusalem and elsewhere), Fabri writes with some pathos:

> O human brother, would that thou couldst see at Jerusalem how reverend is the appearance of this temple of the execrable Mahomet . . . how bright and neat everything is kept, how devoutly the worshippers enter therein, how gravely they bear themselves in praying, how modestly the women show themselves there, with their faces always veiled, and how the men pray in silence apart from them! Couldst thou see this, thou wouldst be deeply shocked and grievously wroth with the neglect and irreverence shown by the faithful in our own churches.[246]

Again, it sounds as if women pray at a modest remove from the men, but not in an architecturally separate space. It is unclear what kind of prayers (daily or Friday) Fabri is claiming to have witnessed.

Greater separation of men and women may have been asserted somewhat later; toward the end of the seventeenth century, ʿAbd al-Ghanī al-Nābulusī describes how "to the left of someone entering the Masjid al-Aqṣā . . . there is an enclosed space (*makān maḥūṭ*) that has only a door opening in the direction of the *qibla*, which is provided for the women to pray in on Fridays and festivals."[247] At the beginning of the nineteenth century, the traveler Ali Bey observed that "the three naves to the left on entering the temple, are inclosed by a wall about seven feet high; this is the place destined for the women."[248] Because the ceiling is elevated far more than seven feet, the enclosure would have been open at the top, allowing women to hear prayers and sermons.

Al-Nābulusī's remark suggests both that women's participation in Friday and festival prayers at al-Aqṣā was a routine occurrence and that they may not have been confined to that specific area of the mosque outside of special occasions of communal prayer. Despite the existence of an enclosed section reserved for women's congregational prayer, it seems that in his time women participated in other ritual activities in the main space of the mosque. Writing of a ceremony in commemoration of the Prophet's birthday (the *mawlid al-nabawī*) held in the Aqṣā Mosque after the nighttime prayer, he describes how "the people gathered according to their ranks, the lords (*mawālī*) and grandees, the religious scholars and learned men, the prayer leaders and preachers, the elite and common men—even women (*dhawāt al-ḥijāl*), gathered in one area (*nāḥiya*) of the mosque, and with them the small boys and girls."[249] Here the women are modestly separated from the men, but apparently visible to them.

In any case, the magnitude of women's participation in congregational prayer in the Aqṣā Mosque appears consistently to have impressed visiting observers, both Muslim and European. Taqī al-Dīn al-Ḥiṣnī (d. 829/1426) argued that women should be forbidden from attending Friday prayers in his own decadent time because of the corruption and mixing with men that could result from their participation, as had actually come to pass, particularly in pilgrimage sites such as Jerusalem.[250] Eugène Roger, a Franciscan who traveled in Egypt and Syria and made a pilgrimage to Palestine in 1634, states that "women never go to the mosque at all, but on Fridays [the women] of Jerusalem go to the Temple [i.e., the Aqṣā Mosque], and every day in Ramadan."[251]

In a polemic of the first half of the seventeenth century against objectionable practices current in the Aqṣā Mosque, one of the abuses listed is "the mixing of women with men on Friday without a barrier (*ḥāʾil*) between them; indeed, some of [the women] remove the horsehair veils[252] from their faces, despite their beauty, adornment, and perfume—and what temptation (*fitna*) could be greater than that?! By God, [the women] sit in various [study] circles among the men, as if the men were close relatives (*maḥārim*) of theirs, or they were in their homes." Male food vendors noisily hawk their wares; to the author's horror they wander among the women and even sit down among them.[253] The author of this work, Muḥammad ibn Ṣāliḥ al-Dajjānī (d. 1071/1661), appears to be concerned less with women's attendance at Friday prayers than with their participation in study circles and their presence in the audience of preachers (*al-wāʿiẓ*) without any barrier between the sexes.[254] Significantly, he does not represent the presence of mixed audiences at preaching sessions as a phenomenon specific to al-Aqṣā; it appears in a list of "innovations" that are practiced in neighborhood and congregational mosques (*al-masājid wa'l-jawāmiʿ*). He also describes mosques as the sites of celebrations (*ḍiyāfa*) for weddings and circumcisions and of judicial transactions such as the documentation of bridal payments and *khulʿ* divorces.[255]

Much like Ibn al-Ḥājj several centuries before, al-Dajjānī describes major noncanonical festivals as occasions for carnivalistic behavior in mixed crowds. On the eighth of the month of Shawwāl, a holiday celebrated in honor of the Virgin Mary, "you see, O my brother, men and women, throng upon throng, troop upon troop; lads hop and shriek in it [i.e., the mosque]," while "vendors sell sweets, pan-pipes (*zamāmīr*), spinning-tops, drums, tambourines, pictures, and other things." Even worse is a festival known as the "days of visitors," when the mosque turns into a fair full of vendors' booths; "everyone who has wares guards a spot and puts his things there to sell them, and among them are women."[256] Al-Dajjānī also complains of mingling among men and women on more conventional religious occasions, such as the night of Niṣf Shaʿbān, when the mosque was illuminated with thousands of lamps.[257]

It is striking that on a normative level al-Dajjānī seems to be advocating women's almost complete exclusion from the mosque, largely by citing the comments of al-Ghazālī. Elsewhere, when listing undesirable elements and practices that should be excluded from the mosque, he states (in between references to dirty sandals and noisy children) that "women should not be allowed to enter it."[258] It is unclear whether al-Dajjānī makes such statements in a legal or a hortatory mode. In any case, the sharp contrast between al-Dajjānī's stated ideal (a mosque with a minimal female presence) and his depiction of reality (mosques with a significant and lively female presence) again suggests the degree to which normative statements on the subject of women's mosque attendance often wistfully respond to social practice rather than imperiously dictating it.

OTTOMAN ISTANBUL

Although this study focuses on the Arabic sources, another interesting perspective on women's mosque attendance before the twentieth century is provided by European travelers' accounts. In the foregoing sections, we have encountered the occasional testimony of a Western traveler. Starting in the fifteenth century CE and expanding significantly in the sixteenth, there is a relative wealth of reports issuing from Western sojourners in the Muslim Middle East. Many of them address a geographical area not otherwise covered here, Istanbul and Turkey. The prevalence of the Ḥanafī legal school in this region (and its institutionalization by the Ottoman state) makes it a useful component of our examination of the relationship between social practice and the normative doctrines of the *madhāhib*.

Because of the unique questions raised by the interpretive bias and factual accuracy of such outsider sources, this section will begin with an analysis of the changing polemical valence of European travelers' depiction of women's presence in (or exclusion from) mosques over the centuries. Despite the problematic nature of these "outsider" sources, however, in other ways they provide a useful point of comparison for the quite different biases and agendas of the "insider" sources used in the rest of the study. They are certainly not more accurate (and indeed they are sometimes blatantly distorted or simply ill-informed), but the addition of an alternative perspective helps us to triangulate somewhat closer to the patterns of women's mosque usage before the twentieth century.

Although (as discussed in the introduction) the Ottoman archives are unlikely to yield comprehensive data on women's mosque attendance for the simple reason that women's routine presence in mosques would rarely have generated documentation in the first place, Ottoman Turkish sources of many genres will certainly contribute a much more complete picture of women's activities than is reconstructed here. This particular sampling of sources provides only a fragmentary and provisional picture of women's usage of mosques in Ottoman Istanbul, but it should suffice to suggest broad patterns that can usefully be contrasted with the other locations and periods surveyed in this book.

The purported exclusion of women from mosques (or their physical separation from men while worshipping there) was a trope of orientalist literature, although its content and significance shifted over time. Particularly in earlier writings, the segregation of women was regarded not as a negative peculiarity of Muslims or of "Eastern" peoples, but as a manifestation of pious propriety that might well be emulated by Christians. (It is also notable that these sources refer to the separation of the sexes, not to the exclusion of women from mosques.) Ramon Lull, a Spaniard who was granted royal permission to preach to captive audiences in mosques and synagogues in 1299, makes one of his alter egos in an imaginary theological dialogue argue that men and women should be segregated in church as they were in "the temples of the Saracens and the Jews."[259] In the early fourteenth century, the Italian jurist Giovanni d'Andrea similarly "remarked . . . with favor" on the separation of men and women in mosques.[260] In the fifteenth century, Félix Fabri (whose admiration for the separation of the sexes in mosques we have already encountered) described the Egyptian women's practice of praying in a separate and secluded part of the mosque, "all frivolous and worldly elegance left at home," as being in conformity with biblical commandments.[261]

A European traveler before the sixteenth century would have been unlikely to find gender segregation and veiling completely alien, nor would they have appeared as distinctive attributes of "oriental" societies. The gendering of public space in some regions of contemporary Europe shared some features with that in the Ottoman Empire. Elite or young women sometimes avoided excessive exposure in public spaces, and in some locales (for instance, Venice) complete veiling was the norm.[262] The gendering of sacred space was different in Europe; for instance, in conservative Venice the churches were among the few public places congenial to women.[263] However, neither the segregation of the sexes for worship and preaching nor concerns about the visibility of women were completely unfamiliar to European Christians of this period (although physical and visual separation may have been less stringent than in mosques). Margaret Aston notes that "from long before the Reformation until long after," depictions of Christian sermons show men and women in separate groups, and "the prevailing view of church pundits was that men and women could not be trusted to behave at worship and must be kept apart."[264] Noting the gender segregation of mosques in Istanbul in 1610–11, the Scottish traveler William Lithgow observes that he has encountered a similar separation among Protestants in southern and eastern Europe, "and truly me thought it was a very modest and necessary observation."[265]

By the zenith of Ottoman power in the sixteenth and early seventeenth centuries, however, the sex segregation of mosques elicited more categorically negative reflections from many European visitors to Istanbul. Although the segregation of the sexes continued to prevail in many English as well as European churches after the Reformation,[266] expressions of empathy or admiration for the propriety of Muslim worship arrangements were soon outnumbered by sentiments of disapproval for supposed Muslim misogyny. The idea that women were completely excluded from mosques became commonplace and was conventionally paired with the baseless contention that Islam assigned women no place in paradise.[267] This durable, if easily disprovable, trope seems to have been based on an assumed parallelism between the sacred space of the mosque and the heavenly realm, with women believed to be equally banished from both. This idea is expressed by the French travelers Philippe Du Fresne-Canaye (1573) and Pierre Lescalopier (1574).[268] Stephan Gerlach, who served as the Lutheran chaplain to the Viennese embassy in Istanbul in the 1570s, reports that "the wives of Turks do not come into any mosque, because women are believed to enter into a different [part of] paradise."[269] This opinion was also reproduced by Salomon Schweigger, who served as Protestant chaplain for a Habsburg embassy to Istanbul in the same decade.[270]

If the trope saw its first flowering in the 1570s, it was reiterated with great regularity thereafter. It is reproduced by Jean Thévenot (who visited the Levant in the middle of the seventeenth century),[271] by Germain Moüette (captured by Moroccan pirates in the late seventeenth century),[272] by François Pidou de Saint-Olon (who served as French ambassador to Morocco in 1693),[273] and by Aaron Hill at the beginning of the eighteenth century.[274] Adrianus Reland, an early Dutch orientalist scholar, records (but then refutes with Qur'anic verses) the idea that "as the Mahometans do not suffer Women to be present at publick prayers in the Church; so neither will they be bury'd with them in the same Grave, which is without doubt founded upon this, that they believe they shall not be with them in Paradise, because they shall get younger and fairer Damsels there."[275]

The emergence of stigmatizing pseudoexplanations for women's supposed exclusion from mosques reflects an overall chronological trend in the development of European attitudes toward Muslims in general and toward their Ottoman antagonists in particular. Mohja Kahf writes that "if European culture in the seventeenth century discovered the seraglio or harem and located the Muslim woman in it, the

Enlightenment declared her unhappy there."[276] In this particular case, perceptions of oppression seem to have emerged somewhat earlier. Nevertheless, some European Christians remained ambivalent or positive about sex segregation in prayer. In the late eighteenth century, for instance, Baron de Tott writes that the separation of the sexes in Muslim worship should remind Christians that "nothing ought to be permitted which may lessen the solemnity of Adoration in the Temples consecrated to [God's] Service."[277] Similarly William Hunter, who traveled in Turkey in 1792, wrote that "women are . . . excluded from the moschs, from a fear of their engrossing too much of the attention of the men, which is so frequently the case at our own churches, where a pair of fine eyes is apt to relax the fervor of devotion, and to render us totally forgetful of the moral lessons of the preacher."[278]

The idea that Islamic doctrine denied that women can enter Paradise was a misconception (or a slander) that proved to be remarkably resistant to factual challenge.[279] George Sale labeled the assertion that Islam denies women an afterlife a "vulgar imputation," and Pierre Bayle also refuted it in the first half of the eighteenth century.[280] Nevertheless, it maintained a tenacious hold on the European imagination, as did the idea that women never entered mosques. As late as the 1830s, both Julia Pardoe and Horatio Southgate found it necessary to refute both beliefs in tandem, clearly believing them to remain prevalent among their readers.[281] Southgate notes that women, in fact, do not attend congregational prayers due to concerns about mutual distraction, but also notes that the separation of the sexes at worship "is an Oriental, not a Muhammedan prejudice" prevailing equally among Christians and Muslims.[282]

Although Southgate denies that the separation of the sexes is specifically Islamic, it is now labeled as "Oriental." Presumably this was possible in part because gender segregation in places of worship was no longer prevalent among Western Christians in his time, although the final victory of the "family pew" (where men and women sat together) was still relatively recent.[283] In Southgate's American homeland, by the early nineteenth century the segregation of women in synagogues "violated the gender norms associated with bourgeois American Protestant religious practice." In the view of Christian observers, by this time the spatial separation of Jewish women in American synagogues "highlighted disreputable behavior among women and concretized male domination and female marginality" and was labeled as "Asiatic."[284] Thus, ideals of gender separation that had once seemed familiar (and praiseworthy) to Western Christians were gradually repudiated and exoticized. Southgate's framing of gender segregation in mosques as "Oriental" also reflected the underlying dichotomy of East and West that had become the structuring convention of European travel writing.

As orientalist attitudes hardened in the context of colonial administration, women's putative exclusion from mosques was overtly cited as a symptomatic instance of "eastern despotism." Colonel Sir John Malcolm, who represented the British administration of India at the Persian court at the beginning of the nineteenth century, writes that "women are not allowed to join in the public prayers at the mosques" and observes that "this practice . . . is calculated to confirm that inferiority and seclusion to which the female sex are doomed by the laws of Mahomed."[285] In the context of Malcolm's book, women's lack of access to mosques is explicitly interpreted as a sign of subordination, and the subordination of women in turn is explicitly interpreted as a sign of the inability of Muslim peoples to lead themselves into freedom and progress.

Over the course of the nineteenth century, international travel became accessible to increasing numbers of Europeans. Missionaries and tourists, officials and governesses produced travel narratives and memoirs of the Middle East for an eager reading public, and a recognizable repertoire of tropes emerged within the genre. Unsurprisingly, both religious practice and the lives of women played prominent roles in these tropes. The mosques visited by European and American travelers evoked deep and conflicted emotions, ranging from reverence and longing to condescension and theological critique. Travelers were often sincerely moved by the serenity of mosque space and its accessibility to people from all walks of life who rested in its shelter or busied themselves with their own pursuits without hierarchy or exclusion.[286] However, the presence or absence of women was often grounds for disparaging comment. Florence Nightingale, writing of the mosques of Cairo in 1850, combined both themes when she observed:

> Here is silence, here is space, here is room for thought in these vast colonnades; turn in here, walk up and down among those columns, no one will disturb you but those prostrate men, with their faces to the ground, as silent as yourself. Are you tired of your daily work and the busy city? Here are places where everyone may have rest and thought. . . . Oh! if the poor women had but been there, I could have said, this is the very thing I have often sighed for in London.[287]

Nightingale's experience of Egyptian mosques was very much shaped by her country's increasing power, which ensured her access to these spaces through means that even she found disturbing. "The great drawback is that, as you must have a firman and a Pacha's janissary, and pistols, and whips, and I don't know what besides, to visit them."[288] Consequently, her grasp of the normal usage of an Egyptian mosque must have been very limited. It seems likely that the Alexandrian mosque she visited had "a gallery out of sight, where women are allowed," but she is presumably relying on hearsay in stating that it was accessible "only on the evenings of the feasts, and only [to] old women."[289]

With the rise of organized tourism and the proliferation of religious missions in the Middle East in the nineteenth century, European and American women began to produce accounts of travel and residence in the region that often reflected greater direct access to Muslim women and, in some cases, greater empathy toward them.[290] Pardoe, who had an extended stay in Istanbul in 1835–36, wrote a work that has been described as "the most detailed, most sympathetic description of the Turkish élite before the *Tanzimat*, or reform era."[291] We have already encountered in the introduction her description of the routine presence of women in Istanbul mosques and of the dissonance between this fact and the preconceptions of European visitors.

Even for female observers, however, women's access to mosques and other holy places was often taken as an index of Muslim attitudes toward gender (and, implicitly, of the validity of Islam and the moral level of Muslim polities). Sarah Barclay Johnson (who spent three years in Jerusalem) writes in the 1850s of the Dome of the Rock that it is "an unusual thing for females (who, in Mohammedan estimation, are no better than brutes) to pollute with their presence so holy a place"[292]; of al-Aqṣā, she remarks disapprovingly, "I noticed that the worshipping-place of the men was covered with carpeting, while that of the women was spread with tattered matting!" Once again, women's accommodation in mosque space was taken as an index of their standing in Muslim society. In contrast, Johnson does not assign any symbolic significance to the fact that her own access to at least one holy site in the Ḥaram (the Temple Mount) was impeded by crowds of women.[293]

Western perceptions of women's exclusion from mosques—and the persistently associated belief that Islam denied women's possession of souls—eventually became a factor in some Muslim thinkers' perceptions of their own religious predicament. Muḥammad ʿAbduh lamented that ill-informed Europeans "accuse us of barbarism in the treatment of women" and attribute the perceived mistreatment to Islam.

> A European tourist visited me at al-Azhar, and while we were passing through the mosque the European saw a girl passing through it. He was astonished and said, "What is that? A female entering the mosque!" I said to him, "What is unusual about that?" He said, "We believe that Islam posits that women do not have souls, and are not obligated to pray!" I cleared up his mistake for him and explained some of the Qurʾanic verses about [women] for him.[294]

In light of this history, Western travelers' reports about women's mosque access must be handled with care. Nevertheless, when used with caution, they offer potentially helpful outsider glimpses of practice.

One of the earliest observations about women's mosque attendance in the Ottoman Empire is by a Bavarian, Johann Schiltberger, who was taken prisoner at the Battle of Nicopolis and spent the years from 1396 to 1402 in the service of Sultan Bayezid. He reports that "they do not allow any woman in the temple, so long as they are inside."[295] Although brief and vague, this report interestingly suggests that women are excluded from the mosque specifically at the times of congregational prayer. Konstantin Mihailović, a Serbian who was captured by the Turks in 1455 and served in the Janissary corps, is more categorical in his brief denial that women go to mosques; he states that the Turks "admit no woman to the temple, nor do they go."[296]

The claim that women did not go to mosques (at least at times of congregational prayer) is nuanced by an anonymous German who was taken captive by the Ottomans as a teenager in the 1430s. Over the course of his twenty years in Turkey, he claimed to have mastered Turkish, feigned conversion to Islam, and even pursued some degree of Muslim religious learning.[297] In his memoir, he strongly emphasizes the veiling and seclusion of Turkish women, practices that he depicts in a positive light and compares favorably with the demeanor of Christian women (presumably those at home in Germany). In the "churches [i.e., mosques]," he reports, "they have an enclosed place separated from the men, so that no one can see them or go in to them." Furthermore, not all women can go to the mosque, nor do they frequent it often; only "noble" women can go for a time on Friday afternoon to pray. Otherwise, they are not allowed to go because it is considered unseemly.[298] This information (that only high-status women can go to mosques, but do so seldom, and that women have an enclosed section separate from the men) also appears in the account of Leonhart Rauwolff in the sixteenth century, but the parallel is sufficiently close that it may be dependent on this earlier source.[299]

Another account of Ottoman Turkish women's access to mosques was offered in the mid-sixteenth century by Bartholomej Georgijevic, a Croat who was taken prisoner in the Battle of Mohács (1526) and remained enslaved for thirteen years.[300] He reports that in mosques women never mix with the men, but have "a separate place to sit," where they can be neither seen nor heard by the rest of the congregation. Furthermore, women very rarely go to the mosque, only "at Easter [*sic*]" or on Fridays. He continues in a somewhat different vein, stating that

> they pray in the churches [i.e., mosques] at night from the ninth to the twelfth hour, or midnight. While praying they twist and cry out so piteously, and get into such a piteous (*kläglich*) state, that a few of them faint and often fall powerless onto the floor. If it so happens that one of them feels as if she were pregnant while she prays, she believes that she has conceived by the grace of the Holy Ghost; when [such women] give birth, they call the child *nefes oğlu*, that is, "child of the spirit or the Holy Ghost." This I have heard from one of the female servants and not seen myself, because no man may see their prayer.

He states, however, that he has often seen men pray and gone there (presumably to the mosque) himself.[301]

Despite the incongruous Christian terminology, Georgijevic is clearly speaking of Muslim women; the context of his comments is a passage describing Islamic prayer. What Georgijevic means by "Easter" is unclear, but it is possible that he is referring to Ramadan because this would probably have been the most visible religious season (involving a lengthy period of fasting and a final multiday festival, something like Lent and Holy Week) and is known from later sources to be a time when women particularly frequented mosques. More surprising is Georgijevic's account of ecstatic worship by women in the mosques at night, which sounds like a form of ṣūfī *dhikr*. Assuming that he is indeed referring to Ramadan, this could also be a reference to *tarāwīḥ* prayers. Georgijevic was an outside observer (and a man) whose report depends on hearsay. Nevertheless, it is not impossible that this report offers a tantalizing glimpse of women's activities in sixteenth-century Ottoman mosques.

An Italian named Antonio Menavino, who claimed in his dedicatory letter to the King of France to have been a slave for many years in the household of the Ottoman sultan in the first half of the sixteenth century, provides a detailed, but confusing and somewhat suspect account of the limitations placed on women's mosque attendance. He claims that prostitutes and "women that are not bound in marriage" may not attend mosques, but that "virgins and widows of five months, not having any use of men," are admitted; "there in church [i.e., the mosque] they are covered and aside in such a way that the men are without sight of them so that seeing them does not conceive in their mind some evil thought whence they commit some sin."[302] It is unclear what might distinguish "virgins" from "women that are not bound in marriage," and it seems odd for "virgins" to be identified as exempt from strictures upon women's presence in mosques (unless he is referring to preadolescent girls). His reference to "widows of five months" is also opaque, although it does very roughly correspond to the four months and ten days of seclusion (the *ʿidda*) incumbent on a woman after the death of her husband. The same, somewhat garbled information appears in a work supposedly composed by a Spanish slave around the same time; it is unclear which text has priority, or how much credibility either deserves.[303] In any case, it reinforces the general impression, apparently originating in actual experience of the Ottoman Empire, that limited categories of women did have access to mosques, but that they were spatially separated from the rest of the congregation and concealed from male view.

Although travelers of the fifteenth and sixteenth centuries often suggested that there were social and reputational barriers to women's attendance of mosques, they give no clear or unanimous account of the parameters of these limitations. Hans Dernschwam, who traveled to Istanbul and Asia Minor in 1553–55, states that in Turkey only disreputable women go to "church"; rather, women pray at home, having learned how to do so from their parents and husbands.[304] "If some old woman wants to pray in the church, she must stay in the very back, behind all of the men. Because of the Turks' whoring, the women cannot go to church among the men."[305] Although the mention of elderly women is unsurprising, it is striking that Dernschwam believes that only less respectable women go to the mosque, whereas the anonymous German captive represents mosque attendance as the privilege of a few "noble" women. Another European who sojourned in Istanbul in the early 1550s, the diplomat Nicolas de Nicolay, similarly states that very few women enter mosques "unless they are ladies of great authority and reputation."[306] It is difficult to know whether these inconsistencies should be attributed to the different time periods, social contexts, and locations where the authors got their information or simply to the limitations of their knowledge of local practice. In any case, although the multiple authors who offer more detailed remarks collectively refute the stereotyped claim that Turkish women simply had no access to mosques, they do reinforce the idea that women's attendance was perceived as limited (with the possible exception of the nights of Ramadan).

Two centuries later, a more coherent account of the social pressures limiting women's mosque attendance is offered by Ignatius Mouradgea ḍ'Ohsson (d. 1809), an Armenian Christian life-long resident of Istanbul whose description of Ottoman life was intended for a European audience. D'Ohsson, whose perspective appears to be informed by his extensive contact with the upper reaches of Ottoman society, describes Turkish women as leaving the home rarely—and then only if accompanied by slaves and guarded by eunuchs or domestic servants. It is for this reason, he states, that only older women can go to the mosque (and most women of all social stations pray individually in their homes).[307] Here the primary factor appears to be a preference for women's seclusion, a consideration that presumably would have applied primarily to women of high social status and ample resources.

It is notable that with the exception of Dernschwam (who implies that women simply placed themselves behind the men—perhaps in smaller mosques), travelers' reports that acknowledge women's worshiping in mosques suggest that they were allocated spatially and visually separate spaces in which to do so. The location and nature of these spaces are not always clear. In some cases, women are implied to be outside of the mosque proper. Lescalopier, who visited Istanbul in 1574, writes that there are "porticoes, tombs (*charniers*) and squares" at the front of (*devant*) the mosques where the Turkish women can worship because they are not allowed into the mosques; although difficult to interpret, this remark may suggest that women prayed in the arcades and courtyards that preceded entry into the mosque proper.[308] Writing of a visit to Istanbul in the early 1610s, Sandys states that "the women are not permitted to come into their temples (yet have they secret places to look in thorow [through] grates)."[309] This might conceivably mean that women peeked into mosques from outside of the buildings, but it is more likely that he refers to women's sections that communicated with the main mosque space through gratings. De Tott, who lived in Istanbul and learned Turkish for a number of years in the middle of the eighteenth century, remarks that "the Women, who are also admitted into the Mosques, have a particular Place alotted them."[310] Hill (who lived in Istanbul for three years starting in 1700[311]) states that "women are but rarely suffer'd to appear in *Mosques*, and then are plac'd *all over Veiled*, behind a large and darkn'd Lettice [lattice]."[312]

These descriptions (even though vague) seem to suggest that women's sections were separated by screens, but not necessarily that they were on a separate level from the main prayer space. Because in the twentieth century balconies have become a paradigmatic form of mosque space that is often anachronistically projected into the past, it is worth pausing to examine the historical origin of the "women's balcony." Certainly pre-Ottoman mosque architecture did not routinely include balconies. Across the Muslim Middle East, historically one of the most common arrangements seems to have been for women to pray under the arcades that enclosed the courtyard of the mosque; we have already encountered this arrangement in Medina and in Cordoba (although, as we have seen, even here descriptions are sometimes gratuitously assumed to refer to balconies). Anselme Adorno, a European who traveled to the Holy Land in 1470–71 (visiting Tunis, Cairo, Damascus, and Beirut in the course of his trip), describes the layout of a typical mosque as follows: "Their churches [i.e., mosques] or *djemmas* [i.e., *jāmiʿ*, Friday mosque] are not made like ours. They generally have colonnades or galleries with polished columns all around, in which women are admitted. In the middle there is a great courtyard or atrium, usually as long as it is wide, also paved with polished marble."[313]

There is some pre-Ottoman evidence that has been interpreted to suggest that women were located in balconies, but on closer examination it proves to be ambiguous. As we have seen, Talmon-Heller cites an anecdote from thirteenth-century Syria in which, after all the men in the village mosque eat their fill, "the food was taken up to the women (*rufiʿa ilā al-nisāʾ*)."[314] Talmon-Heller infers from the verb "taken up" that the women "apparently sat in an upper gallery."[315] Although this is a plausible inference, the Arabic verb *rufiʿa* may also simply mean that the food was picked up and taken to the women (wherever the women were located).

More striking is the visual evidence of an illustration of the *Maqāmāt* of al-Ḥarīrī (figure 2.1), dated 634/1237, whose exact geographical provenance is unknown.[316] Here women appear in a row placed high above the men who sit at the foot of the preacher's pulpit. However, unlike other miniatures in the same manuscript,[317] this image does not provide any architectural context for the upper row of figures; the line of women floats high in the composition, without any structural elements indicating a balcony. Thus, it remains unclear whether the women are placed above the men as a literal depiction of their location in a structure on an upper level of the mosque or simply as a visual shorthand for their separation from the men.[318] In contrast, another thirteenth-century illustration of the same *maqāma*[319] unambiguously

FIGURE 2.1 Women listen to a preacher in a miniature from the *Maqāmāt* of al-Ḥarīrī (thirteenth century).

Courtesy of the Bibliothèque Nationale. Paris

depicts an arcaded balcony on the upper level of the mosque, but due to the intentional defacement of the human figures in that manuscript, the gender of the figures located there can only be inferred. Oleg Grabar thus observes that "the upper gallery . . . contains (*presumably* female) figures behind a wooden baluster," whereas in describing the previous miniature, he remarks that the women sit in "what is *presumably* a separate galleried area of the mosque" (emphases mine).[320]

Thus, a pervasive assumption that women are located in balconies—and that, conversely, balconies are intended for women—has informed the reading of the relevant visual evidence rather than being unambiguously dictated by that evidence. Another example is a mid-sixteenth-century Persian miniature, similarly depicting a preaching session with men gathered at the foot of the minbar and veiled women watching from what appears to be a balcony (figure 2.2).[321] Wiebke Walther describes the women as "taking part in a service in a mosque from a position in a gallery of their own."[322] Although this "gallery" may well be a balcony, the artist has depicted the floor of the mosque essentially vertically; the "gallery" is certainly not an entire story above the line marking the end of the floor. In the absence of naturalistic perspective, spatial relations in such miniatures are difficult to interpret; the image may or may not depict a true women's balcony.

The interrelationships among visual representations, physical spaces, and textual evidence are complex, and it is all too easy for ambiguous evidence in one category to support questionable readings of another, leading to a self-reinforcing—if not necessarily invalid—circle of interpretations. For instance, Sheila Blair writes of Iran in the Ilkhanid period (thirteenth to fourteenth centuries CE) that in illustrated manuscripts women are often depicted "peeking out" of upper-story windows. "The depiction of women in second stories may reflect actual practice, for this period was when second-story balconies were introduced into congregational mosques, as at Varamin and Yazd."[323] This is certainly a plausible inference. However, it is also conceivable that the placement of women in an upper register in part represents an artistic convention rather than a literal depiction of the allocation of space.[324] Similarly, the existence of balconies in mosques cannot in itself serve as evidence that they were intended for the use of women.

FIGURE 2.2 Women listen to a preacher in a miniature from Ḥusayn Baiqarā's *Majālis al-ʿushshāq* (sixteenth century).

Courtesy of the Bodleian Libraries, Oxford, UK

The existence of pre-Ottoman women's balconies thus remains unclear pending further evidence. By the Ottoman period, in contrast, it is clear not only that balconies were often present but also that they were at least sometimes used by women. An Ottoman manuscript dated 1600 unmistakably displays veiled women listening to preaching from the second-floor balcony of a mosque.[325] However, it is not automatically to be assumed either that the large balconies of major Ottoman mosques were initially built with women in mind or that the women who did frequent these mosques were consistently located in the balconies.[326] It is well known that, for instance, the balcony of the Byzantine church of Hagia Sophia (after the conquest in 1453 the premier mosque of Istanbul) was known as the *gynaeceum*, or "women's section"; however, it is far from clear that this was the primary function of the church balcony by the time of the Ottoman conquest. It appears that by the fourteenth century the balconies were reserved for the emperor and the nobility (particularly noble women) rather than for women per se.[327] Similarly, after the conquest the balconies of major Ottoman mosques often housed royal loges where members of the dynasty of both sexes could worship in seclusion.[328] Describing the balconies of several major Ottoman mosques, the seventeenth-century Ottoman traveler Evliya Çelebi makes no reference to their use by women. Other than providing extra space on occasions that attracted a particularly large congregation, the balconies seem to have been devoted to providing an enclosed prayer space for the ruler and sometimes space for Qur'an reciters.[329]

However, by the eighteenth century the use of balconies as women's prayer space is mentioned as being standard in at least some Ottoman mosques. A European description, published in the mid-eighteenth century but based on older sources, states that in mosques men pray downstairs, women "in the upper galleries or under the exterior arcades."[330] D'Ohsson states that on those occasions when women do attend the mosque, they pray in galleries elevated over the entrance to the mosque; this arrangement guarantees that they are located at the back of the congregation, as required by the sharīʿa.[331] Antoine-Laurent Castellan, a French painter (d. 1838) who visited the Ottoman Empire at the turn of the nineteenth century, reports that "the women have pews [*sic*] enclosed with lattice-work, and situated above the doors. They are not numerous, because the law permits elderly females only to attend meetings of the other sex."[332]

Nevertheless, even in a much later period it does not appear that balconies were consistently identified as women's space or that women were confined exclusively to balconies in mosques where they were available. In the nineteenth century, Pardoe describes the balcony of Hagia Sophia as having been "devoted originally to the use of the women"; there is no sense that she perceives this as its current use.[333] Interestingly, Southgate describes screened balconies as a Near Eastern Christian, rather than a Muslim, convention.[334] Not all mosques necessarily offered (or required) physically separate accommodations for women even during congregational prayers; James Boulden reports in the mid-nineteenth century that "women are permitted to worship in the mosques, but are compelled to form themselves into a distinct group, somewhat remote from the men."[335] This could be true even when a balcony was present; writing about a visit to the pilgrimage mosque of Eyüp in the early twentieth century, Grace Ellison describes watching from the screened gallery originally reserved for the sultan as both men and women, separated by a partition, perform the prayer on the main floor below.[336]

It is clear that between the hours of formal congregational prayer, women freely frequented the main floors of major mosques. This was true even in an edifice characterized, like Hagia Sophia, by the presence of vast upper galleries. In the eighteenth century, Elizabeth Craven mentions that on a visit to Hagia Sophia "I went and sat some time up stairs, to look down into the body of the temple—I saw several Turks and women kneeling, and seemingly praying with great devotion."[337] As we have seen, in the mid-1830s Pardoe observed some women praying on the main floor.[338] Late in the nineteenth century, Edmondo de Amicis similarly describes looking down from the balcony of Hagia Sophia to see "some veiled women on their knees in solitary corners" on the floor below.[339]

Indeed, Ottoman women seem to have preferentially frequented mosques between prayer times, to the point that from an early date some European observers believed that they visited mosques only when the men were not there. We have seen that Schiltberger implied as much. Schweigger, the German who acted as preacher for a diplomatic delegation to Istanbul in the late 1570s, writes that women do not pray at mosques but at home unless they visit the mosque simply for the sake of sightseeing (*sehens haben*) when no services are being held.[340] Lithgow, who visited Istanbul in 1610–11, writes that in mosques "the men observe their turnes and times, and the women theirs, going alwayes when they goe, either of them alone to their devotion."[341] Southgate writes in the 1830s that "women are not . . . allowed to be present in the mosques at the time of public prayers," but that "in the intervals between the public prayers, Turkish females are allowed to enter the mosques and perform their devotions, if no man is present. They are also permitted to hear the discourses of the preacher, though often of a character unfit for modest ears."[342] Writing about Bosnia in the late nineteenth century, Thomson writes that women "are not allowed to enter the mosque at the same time as the men. There are, however, certain hours allotted to them when they may go there to pray."[343]

In the light of other information, it seems unlikely that women were completely barred from mosques at times of communal prayer, although they may more often have engaged in private devotions between official prayer times. There are scattered suggestions that Ottoman policy may have barred women from mosques at night, although this is also difficult to confirm. Lady Wortley Montagu, visiting the Sultan Selim Mosque in Edirne at the beginning of the eighteenth century, writes of its myriad lamps that "this must look very glorious when they are all lighted; but that being at night, no women are suffered to enter."[344] Pardoe states that entrance to mosques "is forbidden to them [i.e., women] only during the midnight [*sic*] prayer."[345]

In the nineteenth century, the profusion of relatively well-informed accounts by European and American travelers and residents in Istanbul—and their greater access to mosques, although it remained limited—provides a composite picture of women's usage of mosque space. At least in major mosques, women do seem to have been present during congregational worship, but apparently they attended in relatively small numbers; Lucy Garnett writes that "the few elderly women and children who may be present" are "concealed in a latticed gallery approached by a separate entrance."[346]

As in other periods and geographical areas, the opportunity to hear preaching seems to have been one of the main reasons for women to visit mosques. As we have seen, Southgate identifies preaching as an activity to which women were admitted. Writing later in the nineteenth century about a visit to Hagia Sophia, Annie Jane Harvey describes watching from the balcony as the congregation performs Friday prayers. At the end of the formal service, "those who wished retired. The remainder approached nearer a small pulpit into which another Imaun [*sic*] mounted, who, seated cross-legged on a cushion, commenced an exposition of some portion of the Koran. No women had hitherto been present during the service, but a few now entered and seated themselves behind the men."[347]

Although some women may have attended mosque preaching sessions in various contexts, a number of sources agree that they attended in particularly large numbers during the fasting month of Ramadan. The author William Makepeace Thackeray visited Istanbul during Ramadan in 1844 and describes the following scene at the Mosque of Sultan Ahmet:

> Any infidels may enter the court without molestation, and, looking through the barred windows of the mosque, have a view of its airy and spacious interior. A small audience of women was collected there when I looked in, squatted on the mats, and listening to a preacher, who was walking among them, and speaking with great energy. My dragoman interpreted to me the sense of a few words of his sermon: he was warning them of the danger of gadding about to public places, and of the immorality of too much talking.[348]

It sounds somewhat odd for the preacher to be "walking among" the women, but the scene otherwise sounds highly plausible. It is interesting that, if Thackeray's interpreter was to be believed, the women's foray into public space was apparently being used to dissuade them from "gadding about in public places." If accurate, this is another example of the paradoxical ways in which access to mosque space could be used to expose women to religious norms that potentially constrained them.

The prevalence, or even dominance, of women at some major mosques during Ramadan is also vividly described by a Turkish author,

Halidé Edib, whose memoirs describe events of her childhood in the Istanbul of the 1890s. Visiting the Suleimaniye Mosque with her wet nurse on the first day of Ramadan, she describes how men chanted the Qur'an and swayed before the *miḥrāb* while preachers held forth from multiple pulpits on the floor of the mosque. She notes that "there were more groups of women than men around the preachers."[349] The party returns to the mosque at night for the *tarāwīḥ* prayers; on this occasion "the women prayed in the gallery above."[350] Here the segregation of men and women (and the location of women in the balcony) appears to be specific to the performance of congregational prayers. The fact that women in nineteenth-century Istanbul frequented mosques particularly in Ramadan is corroborated by Fanny Blunt, the wife of Britain's consul general to Constantinople, who is credited with "one of the most reliable accounts of everyday life" in Turkey.[351] In her book, published in 1878, she states that "in most mosques women are admitted to a retired part of the edifice; but it is only elderly ladies who go. In some mosques at Stamboul, where the women's department is partitioned off, the attendance is larger, especially during Ramazan."[352]

Hester Donaldson Jenkins, writing in the early twentieth century, sums up her experience with the religious practices of Turkish women as follows: "A girl has . . . nothing corresponding to our Sunday schools, nor does she often attend services in the mosques. . . . There is an occasional mosque reserved for women, and in some others, arrangements are made by which a congregation of women and girls may be accommodated behind curtains, where they may hear the chanting of the *Imams*, but cannot be seen by the male worshippers. I know Turkish women who have never been inside a mosque."[353] Jenkins believes that women could benefit from the "sensible, practical" sermons that men hear at the mosque and that very few women do. In contrast, she speaks with admiration of the magnificent sights that can be enjoyed by women who attend the nighttime prayers in the gallery of Hagia Sophia during Ramadan.[354]

Overall, the evidence suggests that women were not strictly barred from mosques, but that in most cases their presence was perceived as being minimal. There are several possible explanations for this pattern. As we have seen, D'Ohsson relates women's relative absence from mosques to overall limitations on their mobility and visibility outside the home (a consideration that may have been particularly relevant in the elite circles that he frequented). However, other (somewhat later) observers cast doubt on this interpretation.[355] Southgate recounts of the festival prayers on the Greater Bairam (ʿĪd al-Aḍḥā) in Istanbul in 1839 that "so much of the ample space of the Atmeidan as was not occupied by the worshippers, was filled with throngs of Turkish maids and matrons, on foot and in arabas [carriages], idle spectators of a ceremony of their religion in which they could not participate."[356] In this case, it was clearly not women's seclusion within the home that prevented them from taking part. Rather, the anecdote suggests adherence to a widespread position in Ḥanafī jurisprudence that affirmed women should swell the crowds at festival prayers, but denied they should take part in the congregational prayers.[357] In the later nineteenth century, the women of the royal household rode in open carriages in the procession to Friday prayers with the sultan; however, upon arrival at the mosque they remained waiting in their carriages until the congregational prayers were concluded.[358] Again, the issue appears to be more one of doctrine (the undesirability of the women's participation in mixed prayers at the mosque) than of female invisibility or seclusion. To the extent that this is the case, however, it reflects a divorce between received Ḥanafī rules and their formal rationales, which based disapproval for women's mosque attendance largely on the undesirability of their venturing out of the home.[359]

Indeed, the relative absence of women appears to have applied more to the specific ritual activity of congregational prayer than to mosque space per se. Not only did women flock to major mosques during Ramadan, but also outside of organized prayer times mosque space seems to have played a role in the everyday lives of many (although certainly not all) women. As we have already seen, travelers often noted the presence of women tarrying or praying in mosques outside the times of organized worship. Edmondo de Amicis, who spent time in Istanbul in 1874, charmingly evokes the outdoor activities of local women as follows: "It is amusing to follow one of them from a distance to see how she manages to eke out and refine the pleasures of gadding about. She enters the nearest mosque to say a prayer, and then stays for a quarter of an hour under the portico chatting with a friend; then she's off to the bazaar."[360]

Indeed, nineteenth-century travelers' accounts of Ottoman Egypt similarly suggest that, if women rarely attended congregational prayers, they nevertheless freely used major mosques at other times. Edward William Lane, who resided in Cairo for extended periods between 1825 and 1835 (and who conformed to Muslim practices in order to facilitate his integration into local society), had extensive exposure to life in Cairene mosques. He writes categorically that "in Cairo . . . neither females nor young boys are allowed to pray with the congregation in the mosque, or even to be present in the mosque at any time of prayer."[361] Nevertheless, outside of the formal "time of prayer" women's presence was routinely noted. At the beginning of the nineteenth century, Ulrich Seetzen describes visiting the Mosque of ʿAmr ibn al-ʿĀṣ in Cairo and encountering women who showed him the sacred sights of the edifice.[362] James Augustus St. John, who also traveled in Egypt at the beginning of the 1830s, reported of the mosque of al-Azhar that "contrary to the ideas commonly prevailing in Europe, a large portion of the votaries consisted of ladies, who were walking to and fro without the slightest restraints, conversing with each other, and mingling freely among the men."[363] In a travel narrative published in 1850, the Reverend J. A. Spencer describes a visit to the mosque of Aḥmad ibn Ṭūlūn in Cairo: "At this hour, being about the middle of the forenoon, there were very few persons present; one old man, doubtless a mendicant, from his looks, lay stretched out at full length, asleep on the matting, not far from the pulpit: a number of children were running about, and playing very noisily; and several women seemed to be lounging around, more to gratify their curiosity than anything else."[364]

A quarter century later, Charles Dudley Warner wrote of the myriad mosques of Cairo:

> At all hours you will see men praying there or reading the Koran, unconscious of any observers. Women I have seen in there occasionally, but rarely, at prayer; still it is not uncommon to see a group of poor women resting in a quiet corner, perhaps sewing or talking in low voices. The outward steps and open courts are refuges for the poor, the friendless, the lazy, and the tired. Especially the old and decaying mosques, do the poor frequent. There about the fountains, the children play, and under the stately colonnades the men sleep and the women knit and sew.[365]

Like other writers of this period, Warner sees the mosque—particularly between times of congregational prayer—as a haven for the Muslim populace at large, and the presence of women is an integral part of the mosque's inclusive embrace.

Whereas in Istanbul women's mosque attendance appears to have peaked in the month of Ramadan, Lane describes women's mass participation in the observation of a round of festivals reminiscent of those denounced by Ibn al-Ḥājj. He provides a lengthy and vivid description of the Mosque of al-Ḥusayn on the occasion of ʿĀshūrāʾ, when the mosque "was crowded with visitors, mostly women, of the middle and lower orders, with many children."[366] According to Lane, the normal etiquette of mosque visitation was suspended for this festival because the density of the throngs and the dirt they tracked into the mosque made it impossible to prostrate and pray in the normal manner.[367]

Overall, this sampling of evidence about women's mosque attendance in Ottoman Istanbul (which will surely be supplemented and emended in the future by Ottoman Turkish sources) suggests that it may have been quite limited. Even largely discounting the validity of repeated outsider reports that women simply did not go, which often bear clear marks of bias and misinformation, there seems to be a clear consensus even among better-informed observers that congregational prayers were attended by very small numbers of women—and often only at an advanced age.[368] Nevertheless, the patterns indicated by these sources suggest not primarily the gendering of space, but the gendering of activities. Although women's participation in congregational prayer appears to have been very limited, there seems to have been no consistent taboo on women's presence in mosques. If the specific occasions differed from those familiar in Egypt, it was similarly the case that women flocked to mosques on those occasions when their presence was customary, and for at least some women mosques were among the urban spaces that might be visited casually over the course of a day.

To a certain extent, this is what might have been anticipated on the basis of Ḥanafī doctrine, which (as we have seen) assigns no special value to congregational prayer by women and by the Ottoman period usually discouraged women's participation in public worship altogether. However, on the basis of such normative texts the widespread presence of designated women's sections could not have been anticipated; neither could the mass presence of women in major mosques during Ramadan. Both of these things suggest that practice was, again, shaped by the desires and lived practices of women, as well as by the teachings of the legal scholars. Legal doctrine appears to have substantially informed or constrained women's behavior, but clearly did not unilaterally dictate it.

CONCLUSION

In the mid-sixteenth century CE, a Mālikī scholar whom we shall encounter in greater depth in the next chapter observed of the categorical disapproval of women's mosque attendance expressed by many postclassical Islamic jurists, "This is an opinion that was not accompanied by practice, because in all ages the women of the Islamic domains have continued to attend mosques."[369] As we have seen, a century earlier Ibn Ḥajar al-ʿAsqalānī referred to "the continuous practice based on the permissibility of women's going out to mosques and markets."[370] The evidence collected in this chapter, fragmentary though it may be, demonstrates the overall accuracy of these two scholars' observations as regards the Middle East and North Africa. Legal scholars rarely actively encouraged women's mosque attendance and often vigorously deprecated it; however, sources of many dates and genres demonstrate that women often had a significant presence in mosques in most regions of the premodern Arab Islamic world. They frequented mosques to participate in congregational prayer, to celebrate the great nocturnal festivals of the medieval Islamic calendar, to hear preaching, to teach, to socialize, and to rest.

To say that women had access to mosques, however, does not imply that they frequented mosques to the same degree, at the same times, or for the same reasons as men. To categorize mosques (or at least the great mosques of the major metropolises) as "male space" would be to ignore the fluidity of mosque space and the multiple uses to which it was put. Neither, however, were mosques used identically by men and women. The divergence between women's and men's practices reflects not merely women's ignorance or defiance of the norms established by elite male scholars but also their own distinctive goals and priorities, which sometimes favored other religious venues and activities. The scholarly religious establishment could not exercise unilateral control over the behavior of the broader public, male or female, even within formal religious venues such as mosques. Nor was its agenda monolithic; ritual practices denounced by some religious scholars might be tolerated, endorsed, or even presided over by others. Few activities were exclusive to either men or women; however, their differential distribution must have yielded quite different overall patterns. For instance, although in many times and places both men and women thronged to mosques on nights like the Prophet's birthday and Niṣf Shaʿbān, such occasions must have loomed larger in the mosque experience of those women who did not regularly attend Friday prayers.

Furthermore, the distribution of activities was not uniform across different regions, although the patterns are difficult to reconstruct with any specificity. The relative prevalence of references to designated space for women's congregational prayer and to women's presence at Friday prayers in Spain and North Africa suggests that this may have been a more salient activity for women in those regions than in some areas further to the east—or perhaps that there was greater attention to gender segregation, at least in the context of congregational prayer, than there was in Egypt or Syria. In contrast, the wealth of references to women's presence at preaching sessions in Syria suggests that it may have been a predominant focus of women's mosque activities there. The ingrained nature of such regional patterns is suggested by the shock of the North African ʿAlī ibn Maymūn when he encountered mixed preaching sessions after his move to Syria; it may also be reflected in the more frequent (and sometimes positive) allusions of later Egyptian Mālikīs to women's participation in sessions of teaching, preaching, and *dhikr*.

The relationship between social practice and normative discourse seems to have been complex. Overall, there is a broad correspondence between the teachings of the various *madhhab*s and the evidence of women's behavior in regions where they prevailed. The Mālikīs' comparative receptivity to women's participation in congregational prayers corresponds to the relative frequency of references to women's presence at Friday prayers (and the construction of designated spaces to accommodate them) in North Africa and Spain. The Ḥanbalī jurists' broad affirmation of the permissibility of women's mosque attendance is well reflected in the Syrian milieux in which they were most strongly represented (including both in Ḥanbalī villages and in the scholarly circles of al-Ṣāliḥīya in Damascus). At the other end of the spectrum, the restrictive teachings of the later Ḥanafīs find expression in the apparent sparseness of women's presence at congregational prayers in Ottoman Istanbul. To the extent that Shāfiʿīs were strongly represented (both numerically and politically) in Mamlūk Egypt and Syria, the abundance of evidence for women's presence in mosques (with a particular preponderance of references to their participation in sessions of preaching and teaching) may reflect both the school's fair degree of legal receptivity to women's presence in mosques and its lack of specific emphasis on the merit of women's participation in congregational prayer with men. (The Shāfiʿī case is the most difficult to interpret, both because of the lack of a uniformly Shāfiʿī milieu within our sample and because of the wide variation of opinions on this issue expressed within the school.[371])

Nevertheless, within these broad parameters women's patterns of mosque usage show a diversity and vitality that could not be anticipated on the basis of the legal texts. Many of the activities for which they flocked to mosques in the greatest numbers (for instance, to celebrate on the nights of the great noncanonical festivals) are neither mentioned nor condoned in the standard legal compilations, and their appeal can be explained only with reference to the women's own preferences and agendas.

Furthermore, if the evidence suggests that legal doctrine influenced or constrained women's mosque-going behavior, it also suggests that women's behavior had an impact on the thinking of legal scholars. As we have seen, the relative ubiquity of women in Syrian mosques in the Mamlūk and early Ottoman periods is well documented in our sources. It is probably no coincidence that Damascene scholars of the Mamlūk period produced some of the most accommodating positions on women's mosque attendance in the history of the debate on that subject. Syrian Shāfiʿī ḥadīth scholars (as well as some of their Egyptian colleagues) reframed the issue of women's mosque access as a question of the pious and decorous deportment of individuals rather than of blanket assumptions about the seductive potential of premenopausal women. It is also likely that the affirmation of women's right to attend mosques by Syrian Ḥanbalīs from the seventh/thirteenth century (which is arguably greater than could have been anticipated based on the doctrinal history of the school) reflected, as well as enabling, the striking presence of Syrian Ḥanbalī women in mosques.

However, the substantial presence of women in mosques did not always elicit affirmative reactions from scholars; it also stimulated unusually vigorous resistance and condemnation. Indeed, the extent and visibility of women's presence in mosques in Mamlūk Syria and Egypt seem to have elicited some of the most vigorous legal argumentation on both sides of the debate, including vehement denunciations from scholars such as al-Ḥiṣnī and ʿAlāʾ al-Dīn al-Bukhārī. The writings of scholars such as Ibn al-Ḥājj, al-Bukhārī, Shaykh ʿAlwān, and al-Dajjānī, who both passionately deplore women's presence in mosques and vividly describe it, suggest that some of the most categorical prohibitions of women's mosque attendance may have been evoked precisely by the magnitude of women's presence in mosques.

Mamlūk and early Ottoman Syria and Egypt are not unique in this regard. The evidence suggests that Ibn Rushd, whose single-minded focus on the problem of *fitna* and postponement of unrestricted female mosque attendance to the final stage of life formed a turning point in the Mālikī treatment of this issue, would have witnessed extensive women's mosque attendance in Cordoba.[372] This trend is also exemplified by Ibn al-Munāṣif, whose assertion that women should be discouraged from going to mosques altogether is overtly elicited by the presence of young and nubile women at Friday prayers.

Overall, the evidence collected here suggests that legal doctrine had a discernible impact in defining basic parameters for women's presence in mosques, particularly in terms of its overall magnitude. However, legal texts do not allow us to predict the nature of the concrete activities that women chose to pursue; juxtaposition of legal and nonlegal sources suggests that jurists did not succeed in setting the ritual agenda for most women. Furthermore, to the extent that there is a clear connection between the sentiments of legal scholars and the behavior of women, the jurists' role was often reactive; in many cases, scholars were left to bemoan activities that they were unable effectively to control.

three

DEBATING WOMEN'S MOSQUE ACCESS IN SIXTEENTH-CENTURY MECCA

What is probably the most extensive and explicit legal and political debate over women's mosque access in premodern Islamic history was stimulated by an incident in 937 AH/1530 CE, when the authorities in Mecca decided to exclude women from the Sacred Mosque during the nighttime hours. As we shall see, this episode is reflected in two long-published works by the prominent Shāfiʿī jurist Ibn Ḥajar al-Haytamī (d. 974/1567), who sketches the sequence of events in one work and analyzes the legal issues involved in a lengthy fatwa.[1] However, al-Haytamī does not fully clarify the nature of the exclusionary policy or its historical and political context. These are elucidated by a unique manuscript preserved in Cairo, a work by Aḥmad ibn ʿAbd al-Ghaffār. This remarkable document is an extraordinarily lengthy (121-folio) personal account, legal polemic, and fatwa collection documenting the decision to exclude women from the mosque during the nighttime, the reactions of the legal scholars, and the author's passionate efforts to reverse the ban. In terms of genre, it is sui generis; at many points, it abandons conventional forms of legal writing in order to address a current issue with copious firsthand testimony and circumstantial detail.

THE MANUSCRIPT AND ITS CONTEXT

The manuscript itself is undated. However, the final page contains a marginal notation that the text has been checked against the original and provided with emendations (*iṣlāḥāt*) "in the handwriting of its author, may God Most High preserve him, grant blessings to his life, and perpetuate his benefit and that of his knowledge."[2] It would thus seem that the copy was produced in the lifetime of its author and under his supervision. Ibn ʿAbd al-Ghaffār's precise death date is unknown;[3] however, he apparently died before 966/1558–59, the date of al-Jazīrī's *ʿUmdat al-ṣafwa*, which refers to him as deceased.[4]

The earliest available biographical entry on Ibn ʿAbd al-Ghaffār was produced by Badr al-Dīn al-Qarāfī (d. ca. 1008/1600). It gives his full name as Aḥmad ibn Mūsā Sharaf al-Dīn[5] ibn ʿAbd al-Ghaffār. He is stated to have been born in Egypt and to have settled in Medina, where he devoted himself to acts of piety (*ʿakafa ʿalā al-ṭāʿa*) and made frequent trips to visit the Meccan sanctuary.[6] The entry describes him as a scholar of high caliber who distinguished himself among his contemporaries for his achievements in multiple fields (*nādirat al-zamān fī'l-funūn*). After settling in the Ḥijāz, he gave instruction in several (unspecified) disciplines and became the leading authority to whom the people of the region resorted (*aqraʾa al-ʿulūm wa-ṣāra al-marjaʿ fī tilka al-amākin al-muṭahhara*). He numbered among his students the prominent jurist Muḥammad al-Ḥaṭṭāb (d. 954/1547), whose commentary on the classic manual *Mukhtaṣar Khalīl* became a standard work in Mālikī law.

As listed by al-Qarāfī, Ibn ʿAbd al-Ghaffār's works suggest that his main focus was on mathematics and its application in Islamic law; for instance, he produced a work on the calculation of inheritance shares in cases where one or more heirs die before the division of the original estate (*al-munāsakha*), a difficult problem in the already complex system of fractional shares established by the Qur'an.[7] The nature of Ibn ʿAbd al-Ghaffār's interests is also suggested by a passing reference in a biographical notice on Khalīl al-Ḥalabī, which states that the latter traveled to Cairo in the year 924/1517 "and there devoted himself to the study of inheritance shares, arithmetic, the calculation of prayer times, geometry, music, and medicine under the supervision of Shaykh Aḥmad ibn ʿAbd al-Ghaffār."[8] However, the fact that Ibn ʿAbd al-Ghaffār is known as a teacher of al-Ḥaṭṭāb suggests a legal dimension to his teaching, and indeed the latter cites Ibn ʿAbd al-Ghaffār's legal opinions several times in his work.[9]

Another source suggests that Ibn ʿAbd al-Ghaffār had a lively interest in the social and legal controversies of Mecca in his time. He was the author of a circumstantial account and polemical analysis of a controversy over the legality of coffee in Mecca in 917/1511.[10] This work, whose original title appears to be unknown, was abridged and revised by his contemporary ʿAbd al-Qādir ibn Muḥammad al-Jazīrī in his well-known work *ʿUmdat al-ṣafwa fī ḥall al-qahwa*. In the introduction to his own book al-Jazīrī praises Ibn ʿAbd al-Ghaffār's work in defense of the permissibility of coffee, but observes that he "was so expansive in expressing his refutation of the opponent . . . and exposed so many copious and choice proofs that, because of the extensiveness and prolixity of the statements he presented, it makes tedium and boredom on the part of those who peruse it almost inevitable."[11] Although some elements of the resulting work clearly originate with al-Jazīrī, both his introduction and the many occasions in the body of the text where he explicitly resumes his citation of Ibn ʿAbd al-Ghaffār's text suggest that it substantially reproduces the original composition.

The basic elements of this work, although unusual in terms of the ordinary genres of Islamic legal (or historical) writing, are very much reminiscent of the work on women's access to the Great Mosque of Mecca that interests us here. It combines a detailed narrative of the origins of the controversy and its political context, transcripts of key documents (including the official "minutes," *maḥḍar*, of a council of scholars convened by the authorities, as well as partial transcriptions of fatwas solicited by both sides), and original legal argumentation characterized both by a spirited and sometimes satirical authorial voice and by a keen insistence on empirical corroboration of the factual assumptions underlying legal claims. In some ways, the substance of his arguments in the two works is also parallel. In both cases, he argues that the behavioral excesses that sometimes accompany the activity in question (coffee drinking in one case, women's presence in the mosque at night in the other) do not affect the legal status of the activity itself, that only the actual infractions (rather than potential harms) can be interdicted by the authorities, and that the harms claimed to accompany the practice are either altogether illusory or outweighed by the benefits it yields. In both cases, he focuses on the value of the activity in question as an aid to individual spiritual development; the consumption of coffee can keep the aspiring devotee awake and alert for nighttime vigils, and women's presence in the mosque at night may be conducive to meritorious actions and positive spiritual states. In both cases, he asserts that the formal legal arguments of his opponents are placed in question by the social pressures and political intrigues that tacitly informed them. At a broader level, each work can be read as a critique of the intervention of the political authorities in the hermeneutic process of Islamic law.

Interestingly, although it must have been a substantial work and was clearly admired in some circles, Ibn ʿAbd al-Ghaffār's monograph on the permissibility of coffee is not mentioned by the bio-bibliographical sources. His work on women's access to the Great Mosque at Mecca fared only somewhat better. Al-Qarāfī notes that Ibn ʿAbd al-Ghaffār has a work on "refraining from forbidding women to go to the evening (*ʿishāʾ*) prayer" and cites al-Ḥaṭṭāb as stating "I believe he called it (*aẓunnuhu sammāhu*) *Kashf al-ghishā fī ʿadam manʿ al-nisā min ṣalāt al-ʿishā*." The fact that al-Qarāfī reports the title secondhand from al-Ḥaṭṭāb—who himself seems to be unsure about it—suggests that the book was not directly familiar to him. Indeed, unless part of the title has been dropped by a later copyist, either al-Ḥaṭṭāb or al-Qarāfī was sufficiently imprecise in reproducing it that the actual subject of the work was obscured. Its inaccuracy suggests that one or both of them were ill-informed not only about the title of Ibn ʿAbd al-Ghaffār's polemic but also about the issue that gave rise to it. Later biographical compilations neither correct the title nor provide any additional information about Ibn ʿAbd al-Ghaffār.[12]

Furthermore, it does not appear that the content of *Izālat al-ghishāʾ* is cited or alluded to in later treatments of the problem of women's mosque access, although much of the argumentation would have been relevant (if only for purposes of refutation) to the discussions of subsequent scholars. All of this suggests that *Izālat al-ghishāʾ* was essentially a piece of ephemera. Despite the substantive (and sometimes brilliant) legal analysis it contained, it addressed a concrete problem that appears to have been resolved relatively swiftly. After the reversal of the policy of excluding women from the Meccan mosque at night, the specific issue at stake lost its currency. The work was produced in the living context of an open controversy, and although it may have circulated briefly thereafter, it largely passed into obscurity after that controversy was resolved. Only the physical survival of Ibn ʿAbd al-Ghaffār's passionate intervention in the debate has preserved this fleeting moment for posterity.

THE BAN

At the time of the events discussed by ʿAbd al-Ghaffār, the power structure in Mecca had several major components. The Meccan religious establishment reflected the diversity of a population constantly augmented by newcomers from all parts of the Islamic world. By the period in question, there were four chief judges representing the four major Sunnī schools of law, as well as four prayer leaders presiding over the daily congregational prayers in the Sacred Mosque. Because the predominant school of the local population was Shāfiʿī, a Shāfiʿī served as chief judge (*qāḍī al-quḍāt*).[13] Politically, Mecca had long been governed by a lineage claiming descent from the Prophet Muḥammad (the Sharīfs). This dynasty in turn acknowledged the suzerainty of regional powers—until the beginning of the tenth century AH/sixteenth century CE, the Mamlūks of Cairo.

The interaction of the various components of this authority structure is suggested by the earlier controversy chronicled by Ibn ʿAbd al-Ghaffār, the coffee debate of 917/1511. At this time, coffee was a beverage relatively newly introduced to the Arabian Peninsula. According to the official account of this event (recounted in the *maḥḍar* reproduced by Ibn ʿAbd al-Ghaffār), the controversy was initiated by the Mamlūk pasha Khāʾir Beg, who was at that time the *muḥtasib* of Mecca (a position that combined the duties of a market inspector and an enforcer of public morality). His intervention was ostensibly based on an encounter with a furtive group of coffee drinkers in the Great Mosque of Mecca during a night in the month of the Prophet's birthday.

Although they claimed to be celebrating the *mawlid*, Khāʾir Beg was sufficiently suspicious of the nature of their gathering (and the reports of coffee drinking in locales "like taverns") that he decided to convene a council of the leading Meccan legal scholars. It seems that Ibn ʿAbd al-Ghaffār contested this version of events, alleging that Khāʾir Beg's intervention was instigated by morally dubious private individuals with alleged medical training.[14] Representatives of the Shāfiʿī, Mālikī, and Ḥanafī schools of law were convened and expressed a mixed consensus. On the one hand, they held that the gatherings at which coffee was consumed were illicit and should be interdicted; on the other, they denied that coffee was in itself a prohibited substance. However, on the basis of medical testimony obtained by Khāʾir Beg, they ultimately held that coffee was forbidden. This ruling was promulgated in Mecca and dispatched to the political authorities in Cairo. Despite the arrival of an official decree of prohibition from Cairo, however, the ban proved ineffective in suppressing the sale and consumption of coffee.[15]

These events suggest the interdependence of the Meccan religious establishment with the multilayered political context within which it functioned. The *muḥtasib*, a representative of the Mamlūk administration but also (at least on an ideological level) of Islamic ethical standards, was clearly in need of the moral imprimatur of the religious scholars. They in turn, however, were sufficiently vulnerable to the temporal authorities that the disinterestedness of their legal interpretations was subject to dispute. According to Ibn ʿAbd al-Ghaffār, the intervention of the Mamlūk *muḥtasib* was itself instigated by the lobbying of private individuals of questionable motivations.

The Great Mosque of Mecca, the site where the licitness of coffee at least ostensibly first presented itself as a social problem, appears in this narrative as an important locus of Meccan sociability. Whether the gathering had a religious purpose (as the participants claimed) or whether it was politically or socially subversive (as Khāʾir Beg clearly suspected), the mosque was a rare site where Meccans could assemble in ways that were both public and autonomous. Until the rise of coffeehouses, a development just beginning when these events transpired, the mosque was almost unique in this regard; it was a space where concerns about social propriety, religious rectitude, and political order converged.

The incident of 937 occurred after the downfall of the Mamlūks and the advent of an Ottoman administration in the Ḥijāz. Following his military victory over the Mamlūk Sultan al-Ghawrī's forces at Marj Dābiq in 922/1516, the Ottoman Sultan Selim agreed to send a document of investiture (*tawqīʿ*) to the Sharīf Barakāt of Mecca, as al-Ghawrī had done before him, and confirmed Barakāt's young son Abū Numayy as his coregent.[16] The administration of the Sacred Mosque was one area where the Ottomans swiftly demonstrated their concern—perhaps significantly, particularly with respect to the maintenance of order during the nighttime hours. Ibn Fahd records that already in Dhū'l-ḥijja of 923/1517, the Ottoman amīr Muṣliḥ al-Din summoned the judges of the four schools of law and the gatekeepers (*bawwābūn*) of the mosque and objected to the doors of the mosque being left open at night, allowing dogs to enter. He ordered them to lock (*qafl*) the doors at night.[17] He also inquired into the practice of paying deputies (*nuwwāb*) to guard the doors, an intervention that led to an altercation that threatened to become physically violent.[18] It appears that initiatives to enhance the order and cleanliness of the mosque were less problematic than interventions in the financial and professional arrangements of the guards. The Ottoman administration also took measures to enhance the role of the Ḥanafī prayer leader in the Meccan sanctuary, who represented the preferred *madhhab* of the Ottoman state (but not of the majority of the local population).[19]

The political authorities could also become involved with issues of ritual propriety and public authority on the initiative of religious scholars. One of the most vigorously contested (but also the most entrenched and cherished) of Meccan religious practices was the observance of the Prophet's birthday festival, or *mawlid*. In the tenth/sixteenth century, this holiday was commemorated in Mecca with an elaborate public ceremony that began in the Sacred Mosque after the *maghrib* prayer. The Shāfiʿī chief judge would lead the dignitaries and people of Mecca in a procession from the mosque to the Prophet's birthplace, where a special sermon was delivered. The procession then returned to the Great Mosque, where the ceremony ended with the performance of the *ʿishāʾ* prayer.[20] Ibn Ḥajar al-Haytamī, who settled permanently in Mecca in 940/1533, describes "the mixing of men and women in the mosque" as one of the most offensive aspects of the observance of the *mawlid*, particularly in Mecca. Women also participated in the procession from the mosque to the Prophet's birthplace. Al-Haytamī describes the women as turning out for this occasion adorned with their best jewelry and clothing and wearing their finest perfume; he claims that their mixing with men has led to improprieties too dreadful to mention. According to al-Haytamī, a certain judge became aware of the situation and forbade the women to go out for the *mawlid*; however, the women "vanquished" or "overpowered" him (*ghalabnahu*) time after time. He finally forbade people from going out to the Prophet's birthplace on the *mawlid* festival altogether. However, the festival was restored, only to be banned again, and so on (*hākadhā*).[21]

Early in the year 937 AH (which began in August 1530 CE), one of the temporal rulers (*baʿḍ umarāʾ al-shawka*) instructed the custodians of the Sacred Mosque to regulate women's behavior in the mosque. Ibn ʿAbd al-Ghaffār never identifies this amīr by name; even though the sharīf Abū Numayy would appear to be an obvious candidate, one also might assume that he would be qualified as "*the* amīr" rather than merely "*one of* the amīrs." Nevertheless, Ibn ʿAbd al-Ghaffār's pious disinclination to assign blame to identifiable individuals may have given him reason for ambiguity, as may reluctance to insult a powerful reigning ruler. It is perhaps more likely that the amīr in question was a *muḥtasib*; among other things, this would fit well with Ibn ʿAbd al-Ghaffār's extensive analysis of the legal duty of "commanding right and forbidding wrong," which was often seen as the basis for this office in the sharīʿa. It is also conceivable that the reference is to some other figure, such as the Ottoman governor of Jeddah or the *amīr al-ḥajj* (although the latter's presence throughout the period discussed would seem unlikely).[22] In any case, Ibn ʿAbd al-Ghaffār states that that the amīr in question undertook his initiative without consulting any of the religious scholars.[23]

This initial directive was that woman were forbidden to "sit in the middle of the mosque" after the last of the five daily prayers (the *ʿishāʾ*, which occurs after complete darkness has fallen); however, they were still permitted to circumambulate the Kaʿba throughout the night. Based on this, about an hour after the Ḥanbalī imam had completed the *ʿishāʾ* prayer the guards would make women who were sitting in the mosque get up; some women would then leave, and others would go to make *ṭawāf* without interference from the custodians. However, the mosque guards appear to have exceeded their mandate; when about a fourth to a third of the night had passed, they would begin harassing the women until finally all of them were cleared out of the mosque. Then they would shut the doors of the mosque and go away. Thus, for the remainder of the night the area around the Kaʿba was empty of worshiping women, whereas before that there were almost always some present.[24] One interesting aspect of this account is that it implies that women were the only worshipers left making circumambulation in the middle of the night, so that when they departed, the custodians of the mosque could take the rest of the night off. It is unclear whether this is what is intended, although (as we shall see) Ibn ʿAbd al-Ghaffār does state elsewhere that women often dominated the mosque during the nighttime hours. It is also conceivable that the remaining (male) worshipers were locked inside the mosque.

Ibn ʿAbd al-Ghaffār recounts that he disapproved intensely of these measures, which deprived women of the opportunity to circumambulate at a particularly holy time of night. He found them especially inappropriate because most of the women present at that time were elderly and shabbily dressed and manifestly had no objective for their presence in the mosque but worship. He recounts that one night he witnessed one of the guards speaking roughly to a shabbily dressed woman, wanting her to leave so that he could depart himself because she was the only person left in the circumambulation area (*maṭāf*). He insisted that she had completed her set of seven circuits, although she swore to God that she had not. Ibn ʿAbd al-Ghaffār tried to intervene, saying "Even if she has finished, let her circumambulate the House as much as she wants; it is God's House, and no one is entitled to deny anyone else access to it, whether by night or day." The guard was unimpressed, retorting "Tell it to the amīr!"—followed by something that Ibn ʿAbd al-Ghaffār found too inappropriate to repeat. However, he allowed the woman to complete her seven circuits before forcibly ejecting her.[25]

This incident disturbed Ibn ʿAbd al-Ghaffār so much that he consulted a religious scholar (presumably one more prominent and influential than himself). The latter agreed that the strictures on women's access to the Holy Mosque were impermissible and promised to speak to the amīr, but for some reason failed to do so. Then, on Saturday the seventeenth of Jumādā al-ūlā of the same year (January 6, 1531) the amīr convened a council of the noteworthy figures and religious scholars of Mecca. The amīr consulted the gathered notables about the possibility of creating a barrier between the men and women in the Sacred Mosque, either by building an enclosed section (*maqṣūra*) for the women or by hanging curtains or the like, for fear of the corruption resulting from the mixing (*ikhtilāṭ*) of men and women. Interestingly, the council participants did not agree to the construction of a *maqṣūra* or the equivalent. However, they agreed that women should be forbidden from attending the mosque inappropriately adorned (*mutabarrijāt*; c.f. Qur'an 33:33) and should be commanded to go there attired only in the manner stipulated by the sharīʿa and without mixing with men. Furthermore, they agreed that the women should be expelled from the mosque after the *ʿishāʾ* prayer and not allowed to return until just before the dawn prayer and also that they should be prohibited from attending altogether on specific nights (i.e., those of major nocturnal festivals).[26]

The amīr then issued a memorandum (*maḥḍar*) stating that he had become aware of the mixing of men and women and describing how he had consulted with certain figures and they had come to an agreement on measures to prevent this. In addition to the provisions already mentioned, the decree stated that women should not be located in front of men during prayers. All of this was justified by "the fear of temptation and corruption (*khawf al-fitna wa'l-fasād*)." The contents of the decree were to be publicly proclaimed, with stern warnings against infractions. When it was finished and signed, the guards of the sanctuary were ordered to prevent women from entering the area of the Kaʿba after the *ʿishāʾ* prayer. After they made the women leave, they circulated through the mosque with lanterns, searching every corner for women who might be hiding.[27]

Ibn ʿAbd al-Ghaffār reports with displeasure that the guards carried out the ban zealously, not exempting women who were manifestly innocent of any seductive display, even hunchbacked crones and indigents in threadbare clothes. In contrast, they were willing to make exceptions for women with social prestige and economic resources—even, ironically, if the women in question were the female relatives of the very men who had issued the decree. This became clear on the night of the twenty-seventh of Rajab, when there were large crowds of men and women circumambulating the Kaʿba as part of the minor pilgrimage (*ʿumra*) that was customary in Mecca on that date. Some women who wanted to circumambulate during the forbidden time succeeded in doing so by identifying their powerful male relatives (the authors of the ban) to the guards.[28] As Ibn ʿAbd al-Ghaffār remarks elsewhere with withering contempt, "I do not know by what [verse of the Holy] Book or by what precedent of the Prophet (*sunna*) the Farewell Circumambulation has become inaccessible except by means of high rank (*jāh*)!"[29] Furthermore, he argues, the guards' practice of allowing only individual women of status to circumambulate at the forbidden times frustrates the intent of the ban. Whereas women circumambulating amidst crowds enjoyed a certain degree of anonymity and concealment, the exceptional presence of individual women on the *maṭāf* at night led people to speculate about their identity and to specify that a given woman was so-and-so, the wife of so-and-so, or the daughter of so-and-so.[30]

What is worse, the guards ejected women in a coarse and demeaning way, verbally abusing them and then (if that failed) dragging them off by their clothes. Their removal from the mosque, Ibn ʿAbd al-Ghaffār claims, became a pretext for harassment and even physical mistreatment. On some nights, this led to panic and disorder among the women hastening to exit the mosque; in the confusion, women lost prayer rugs and other personal effects, and it was particularly difficult for children, pregnant women, and the physically infirm. Ironically, disreputable men could take advantage of the disordered crowd of women as they were herded out of the mosque.[31] Ibn ʿAbd al-Ghaffār emphasizes that he witnessed these abuses himself. He recounts that one night he saw three or four women who had slipped into the area around the Kaʿba after the curfew when the guards were not paying attention; they circumambulated as fast as they could, hoping to finish a set of seven circuits before they were caught. One of them was holding a baby. When the guards caught up with the women, the one with the baby explained that it was forty days old and she wanted to do *ṭawāf* with him for the sake of the resulting blessings, according to the custom of the people of Mecca. They told her to come back when the mosque reopened; she and the other women explained that they lived too far away, but the guards would not relent. The guards told the women that they should be ashamed for the sake of their honor, although the author thought it was the guards who should be ashamed.[32] (Elsewhere, the author notes that women were so intent upon circumambulating with their forty-day-old infants that they sometimes bribed the guards with food or money to ignore them as they hid in a corner awaiting their chance.[33])

In addition to the poor conduct of the guards, Ibn ʿAbd al-Ghaffār complains of the discrepancy between the application of the ban and the rationales cited in its support. He points out that outside of the forbidden times, the guards do not confront women no matter what their level of perfume or adornment. Even the creators and zealous enforcers of the ban allow their womenfolk to go out to the mosque scented and adorned. Whenever men and women are present in the mosque at the same time, they are not prevented from mixing. In short, the guards ignore everything else mentioned in the decree and make the time of day the one relevant factor in allowing or excluding women.[34]

The inconsistency of application of the ban was exemplified for Ibn ʿAbd al-Ghaffār by the fact that the prince who had forcibly imposed it was willing to relax it for his own (religiously dubious) purposes. After his recovery from a severe illness, he held a ritual in commemoration of the birth of the Prophet (a *mawlid*) in thanks to God. He invited everyone, or perhaps everyone who was anyone (*jamīʿ al-nās*), and summoned all of the professional *mawlid* reciters in town; the mosque was illuminated with lamps and torches. On that occasion, women were not made to leave the mosque at the usual time; they attended the *mawlid* and lifted their voices in ululation. Sweets (or possibly sugar syrup: *sukkar*) were circulated among women and men alike. Many of the dignitaries who were responsible for the ban attended this ceremony without raising the slightest objection. Then, "when the *mawlid* was over, the lights were extinguished, and the time of the descent of the Lord into the lowest heaven[35] and the time when hearts are fully receptive to prayer arrived, *then* the women were expelled from the mosque and prevented from circumambulating. There is no power and no might but with God, the Supreme, the Great; we take refuge with God from the reversal of things (*inʿikās al-aḥwāl*)!"[36] Ibn ʿAbd al-Ghaffār was clearly aghast that the ban was suspended for the sake of a ceremony that he regarded as ostentatious and religiously baseless (he remarks skeptically that the prince held the *mawlid* "in thanks to God, as he alleged"), whereas it prevented the inconspicuous performance of religious acts of undisputed merit.

Ibn ʿAbd al-Ghaffār did not abandon his efforts to challenge the ban. First, he consulted with the religious authorities who had signed the decree, seeking to clarify their justifications for it. He states that they failed to provide sound legal reasoning in support of their position and summarily dismissed his appeal to the ḥadīth forbidding Muslims to "forbid the maidservants of God from [going to] the mosques of God." He composed a piece courteously explaining the grounds for objection to the ban, but it was not well received.[37] After his efforts to persuade the local authorities through religious debate proved fruitless, he strove to mobilize religious opinion internationally by sending a legal inquiry (*istiftāʾ*) to scholars in Medina, Egypt, Yemen, and other places. (As we shall see, like most such questioners he phrased his inquiry in such a way as to elicit reactions favorable to his cause.) Although (perhaps as a result of his carefully framed inquiry) he was able to claim that all the scholars "who are to be taken seriously" agreed on the illegitimacy of the decree, this still did not convince the Meccan establishment. The composition of his work *Izālat al-ghishāʾ* was itself a part of his vigorous and sustained effort to stimulate opposition to the ban, one on which he embarked only after long reflection and in the face of grave reservations about casting aspersions on other scholars. After the failure of his other efforts to sway elite opinion, he performed the prayer of *istikhāra* seeking God's guidance on the matter and decided to write the book.[38]

Whether Ibn ʿAbd al-Ghaffār's reluctance reflects genuine personal scruples or simply a conventional stance of deference and humility, the religious etiquette of scholarly debate places certain limits on his discussion despite the generally spirited (and in many places devastating) tone of his polemic. Most importantly, although he routinely expresses an incredulous disdain at the arguments of his opponents, he preserves the proprieties by leaving them anonymous. Not one of his antagonists, from the prince who initiated the ban through the notables and scholars who supported it, is identified by name. This makes historical reconstruction of the debate over the ban more difficult, although the overall sequence of events suggests that the major scholars in Mecca at the time must have supported it.[39] In general, the opposite side of the debate can be reconstructed only from the discussion of Ibn ʿAbd al-Ghaffār, who cannot be assumed to be representing it favorably. The only prominent legal thinker whose fatwa in support of the ban appears to be identifiable and preserved is Ibn Ḥajar al-Haytamī.

In another work, a devotional piece about the birth of the Prophet Muḥammad, al-Haytamī provides a much shorter—yet still revealing—alternative account of the genesis and fate of the ban. He writes,

> It occurred soon before our settlement in Mecca that many of the scholars of the four schools of law in the Noble Mecca advocated and promoted with all possible vigor (*qāmū ashadd al-qiyām wa'ntaṣarū ashadd al-intiṣār*) that women be forbidden from leaving their homes to go to the Sacred Mosque altogether because of the shameful acts (*qabāʾiḥ*) that were well-known, nay, incontrovertibly reported (*ishtahara bal-tawātara*) to be committed by them even in the mosque [itself]. Others opposed them so that fatwas proliferated, and each party composed works in refutation of the other; each party sent enquiries to the scholars of Egypt based on their own agendas (*bi-ḥasb gharaḍihim*), and [the scholars of Egypt] responded to each enquiry as was appropriate to it. So much correspondence, error, and abuse transpired between them that it became an occasion of temptation for sinful people (*al-fasaqa*) and those with deviance and vain desires in their hearts to defend the wrong and allow those shameful acts to continue as they were. So [the shameful acts] increased, overflowed, spread and became general.[40]

Although al-Haytamī did not settle permanently in Mecca until 940/1533, he sojourned there for a year following his second pilgrimage in 937/1531—that is, in the year of the events in question and presumably while the ban was still in effect. Thus, although not an eyewitness to the initiation of the ban, he must have been personally well acquainted with the controversy that surrounded it.

One interesting feature of al-Haytamī's account is that, unlike Ibn ʿAbd al-Ghaffār, he represents the ban as having been initiated by the religious scholars. It seems likely that Ibn ʿAbd al-Ghaffār's more detailed account provides a fuller picture of the multiple constituencies (mosque personnel, political authorities, notables, judges) whose intersecting agendas informed the ban. Al-Haytamī's narrative, however, reflects the extent to which scholarly argumentation could be isolated from its social context. Because legal interventions formally emerged from the intersection of legally problematic actions with abstract hermeneutic processes, the role of intersecting social and political processes—the events and interventions through which given behaviors were raised as an issue and framed as a legal problem requiring solution—could easily be elided. Because of Ibn ʿAbd al-Ghaffār's eagerness to represent opposing legal scholars as victims of the abrupt and independent measures of actors without religious authority, he is distinctively motivated to reveal the extraneous factors that suddenly isolated women's activities as problematic and presented them as a subject for legal interpretation. In contrast, al-Haytamī wishes to represent the Meccan scholarly establishment's support for the ban as a legitimate expression of scholarly reflection, and thus he depicts it as an independent exercise of hermeneutic reasoning applied directly to a pressing social problem.

Al-Haytamī's account also raises another issue, namely, how the fashioning of a legal inquiry (*istiftāʾ*) could predetermine the legal analysis of a question by framing it in a specific way. By stating that the parties to the conflict produced inquiries "based on their own agendas" and that the responses were "appropriate" to the inquiries presented, he implies that skillful questioners (in this case, themselves scholars) had the ability to elicit legal reasoning to support either side of a disputed question. Ibn ʿAbd al-Ghaffār was clearly aware of the accusation that he had predetermined the responses to his inquiry by misstating the facts.[41] Because a muftī is not responsible for inquiring into questions of fact, by its very nature a fatwa addresses the fact pattern presented by the questioner rather than the actual state of affairs on the ground. In this case, it is quite clear that the initial framing of the question substantially contributed to the shaping of the answers. Ibn ʿAbd al-Ghaffār provides the verbatim text of the inquiry that he sent to scholars in Egypt (although elsewhere he suggests that it is merely a summary of a more comprehensive—and, it is implied, more balanced—presentation of the question).[42] The question reads as follows:

> What is your opinion (may God be satisfied with you!) about what occurred in Noble Mecca, that is, the banning from the Kaʿba after the *ʿishāʾ* prayer until soon before the dawn prayer of all women without exception, and their being prevented from circumambulating then, without distinction between a virtuous and a depraved woman, an old woman and a young one, an adorned woman and one dressed in workaday clothes, a woman who is perfumed and one who is not perfumed, such that that [ban] is applied as well to women visiting from abroad (*al-āfāqiyāt*) and women who are performing the minor pilgrimage and to someone who wishes to perform the Farewell Circumambulation and has performed part of her series of seven circuits before the *ʿishāʾ* but *ʿishāʾ* came before she could complete it—she is prevented from completing it after *ʿishāʾ*. The person who banned [the women from circumambulating after *ʿishāʾ*] has claimed that there are harms in their mixing with men in the middle of the night and that it is difficult to distinguish between a woman who is committing harmful acts and others, so that he considered it more appropriate—indeed, imperative—to ban them generally. Is [he] correct in that or mistaken and sinful, because the harm [of women's presence] is speculative (*ghayr muḥaqqaqa*)? Give us a legal opinion, and may God reward you with paradise by His grace and favor![43]

The inquiry that elicited al-Haytamī's fatwa is very different in emphasis. It reads:

> In these times, it has become a frequent occurrence that women go out to the markets and the mosques to hear preaching, and to circumambulate the Kaʿba, etc., in the mosque of Mecca, presenting themselves in unaccustomed ways that will definitely have a seductive effect. Specifically, they adorn themselves when going out for any of these purposes with the best adornments, jewelry and garments at their disposal, such

> as ankle rings, bracelets, and gold that is visible on their hands, and large amounts of incense and perfume. In addition, they expose large portions of their bodies, such as their faces, hands, and other parts, and sashay as they walk in a way that is noticeable to anyone who looks at them, whether intentionally or unintentionally. Is it incumbent on the imam or on other holders of authority and power to exclude them from these places, even from the mosques, and even from the mosque of Mecca, despite the fact that they cannot perform the circumambulation [of the Kaʿba] outside of it, unlike prayer? Or should the two [activities—i.e., circumambulation of the Kaʿba and prayer] be distinguished on that basis?[44]

Although both of these inquiries are ultimately about the legal status of the actions of the authorities who banned women from the mosque at night, rather than of the women themselves, each one of them elicits a specific reaction by depicting the women in a distinctive and emotionally evocative way. In Ibn ʿAbd al-Ghaffār's inquiry, the women are vividly depicted as victims of an unjust deprivation of access to the Kaʿba. By presenting the detailed scenario of the woman who is prevented from completing her seven-circuit circumambulation in the context of a pilgrimage, he highlights the most distressing (and ritually problematic) potential effects of the ban. In contrast, al-Haytamī's questioner focuses on the role of women as provocative actors in their own right. It is also striking that Ibn ʿAbd al-Ghaffār treats the ban as a fait accompli whose (baneful) effects are subject to evaluation, whereas the question addressed by al-Haytamī posits the women's bad behavior as an ongoing problem that could prospectively be solved by barring women from the mosque (and indeed from other public places). It is possible that this difference simply reflects time sequence; that is, the inquiry could have been presented to al-Haytamī before the imposition of the ban. However, Ibn ʿAbd al-Ghaffār's narrative suggests that the solicitation of fatwas followed the ban rather than preceding it. It seems possible, or indeed likely, that the question addressed by al-Haytamī is fashioned as it is to present the ban as an attractive solution rather than a problematic and disputed reality.

MECCAN WOMEN'S USAGE OF THE SACRED MOSQUE

According to Ibn ʿAbd al-Ghaffār, his opponents base their defense of the ban less on the strength of the legal arguments they can offer than on the enormity of the misbehavior they claim the women to be committing. In response to legal critique, one of them will reply, "You are excused, because you aren't aware of the dreadful offenses that women are committing at that time, which are not approved by God, His Prophet, or any of the Muslims; if you knew that, you wouldn't doubt the necessity and obligatoriness of this ban." Ibn ʿAbd al-Ghaffār humorously describes how the opponent then shakes his head in wonderment and horror.[45] Thus, the claims of the ban's supporters can be refuted only by clarifying what it is that women are actually doing in the mosque at night.[46] As a result, many of his comments are devoted to describing the nature of women's presence in the mosque. These provide an unusual glimpse of women's activities in a major (if atypical) mosque from an author who is not polemicizing against them. Indeed, in juxtaposing his opponents' flamboyant claims about women's misbehavior with what he asserts to be a more sober account of their actual activities, he helps to give some insight into the kinds of exaggeration and distortion generated by many scholars' preoccupation with issues of *fitna*. Although he himself is undoubtedly biased, his willing admission that Meccan women violate many ideal standards of Islamic propriety—combined with his generally temperate and plausible account of their behavior—suggests that his discussion is not merely a counterpolemic.

Ibn ʿAbd al-Ghaffār states of women's habits of frequenting the mosque,

> As for what is manifest of their behavior and observable to all, both elites and commoners, it is merely that [the women] become numerous in the mosque and the *maṭāf* from soon before the sunset prayer (*maghrib*) to the beginning of the period of *ʿishāʾ*; at that point their numbers reach their fullest extent. Some of them are busy circumambulating [the Kaʿba], and some of them are sitting in the place that is

> ordinarily reserved for them (*al-makān al-muʿadd lahunna ghāliban*), which is near to the Ṣafā Gate, without any manifest suspicious conduct or palpable misbehavior. Then, after the *ʿishāʾ* prayer, their numbers decline gradually for some time into the night (*ilā jānib min al-layl*). Then [in the morning] they become numerous after that again on the *maṭāf* until the sun becomes very high and its heat is felt, and then their numbers decrease. They may also be present in large numbers during the day, to the extent that it is possible [for them], as on women's days (*ayyām al-nisāʾ*). The *maṭāf* is rarely empty of [women] during the night or day, just as it is rarely empty of men; what is more, for an hour or so after the Ḥanbalī [imam] completes the *ʿishāʾ* prayer and from the time when the sun rises until its heat is felt, they [i.e., women] are usually far more numerous than men, because at those two times there are few men, and the women take advantage of it because of the benefits they reap from it . . . , including kissing the [Black] Stone, touching [the stone and the corner of the Kaʿba], and other things.[47]

Based on Ibn ʿAbd al-Ghaffār's description, the most popular time for local Meccan women to attend the mosque was in the evenings between the *maghrib* (sunset) and *ʿishāʾ* (nighttime) prayers (followed by the early morning hours). He states elsewhere that at this time there were large crowds of men and women in the mosque and it was difficult for men to find a break in the continuous ranks of women to get to the *maṭāf*.[48] Although most women clearly departed for home after the *ʿishāʾ* prayer, many also cultivated the pious practice of spending the entire night in circumambulation. For many women, according to Ibn ʿAbd al-Ghaffār, the period between the sunset and nighttime prayers might be the only appropriate occasion to visit the mosque. Some women, particularly if they were young and nubile (*shābba*), did not go out during the daytime (presumably as a form of modest seclusion) and could now visit only in the early evening hours or immediately before daybreak—times when the area around the Kaʿba was crowded with men.[49] Other women were occupied with their livelihoods (*maʿāsh*) during the daytime hours.[50] Indeed, a source from a somewhat earlier period suggests that a certain informal deference seems to have been paid to Meccan women's desire to circumambulate discretely during the hours of darkness. Around the end of the seventh/thirteenth century, a pious Egyptian Sufi who circumambulated at all hours of the day and night offended public opinion in Mecca by his obliviousness toward this custom. During the nighttime hours, he would find himself circumambulating with both secluded and unsecluded women (*nisāʾ mukhaddarāt wa-ghayr mukhaddarāt*), and in violation of local norms he took the opportunity to greet and converse with them. It was found particularly offensive that he addressed the women by name, thus revealing their identities to everyone in the vicinity.[51]

Ibn ʿAbd al-Ghaffār states that of the evenings of the week, the most popular visitation times for Meccan women were Monday and Friday eves (i.e., Sunday and Thursday nights).[52] It is notable that this description correlates well with other accounts of the mosque-going habits of Ḥijāzī women. In the second half of the fifteenth century, the Shāfiʿī scholar al-Samhūdī noted of the Prophet's Mosque in Medina that on major festivals[53] and indeed "on most Friday nights" (Thursday nights in English parlance, as the new day was taken to start at sundown),

> women gather in large numbers between the sundown and nighttime prayers in the direction of the Noble Face [i.e., the head end of the Prophet's tomb], [the women] being adorned and perfumed with various kinds of aromatic fragrances in a way that is forbidden when they go out. Then a large number of men who seek corruption join them and speak to them at that time; as for virtuous people and anyone who has any shame, they avoid visiting [the Prophet's grave] at that time.

Interestingly, al-Samhūdī suggests as a remedy for the scandalous behavior rumored to occur on these occasions that the period between the *maghrib* and *ʿishāʾ* prayers be reserved for women's visitation; men would be able to enter only before *maghrib* or after *ʿishāʾ*. He claims that this solution was, in fact, attempted by the servants of the sanctuary during the sojourn of an unnamed "virtuous person" in Medina; however, the effort was unsuccessful "due to the obstinacy of the spreaders of corruption."[54] He states that the only way to achieve this reform would be for the ruler of the city to impose it personally until it became an established custom.[55] Ḥijāzī women's long-standing preference for attending the mosque in the evening hours is also reflected in the comment of al-Muḥibb al-Ṭabarī (seventh/thirteenth century) that "today" the women of the Two Sanctuaries (Mecca and Medina) most often attend the nighttime (*ʿishāʾ*) prayer.[56]

Not only did women prefer to frequent the mosque during the evening hours, but the social and religious function and tone of their evening visits to the mosque also differed significantly from those of their visits during the daytime. Ibn ʿAbd al-Ghaffār reports more than once that during the daytime respectable women would go out to visit the mosque (and, apparently, to other locations) only dressed in conformity with the best standards of modesty. They did not wear perfume or adorn themselves ostentatiously, nor did they wear jewelry whose tinkling would be audible to men. To do so during the day would have been universally recognized as unbecoming; indeed, such behavior occurred during the day only rarely, on the part of women who were notoriously ill-reputed. During the evening hours, in contrast, the same women who dressed and comported themselves so decorously during the daytime would venture out to the mosque only if splendidly turned out in all of the ways forbidden by the sharīʿa, with perfume, jewelry, and other adornments. Indeed, the Meccan custom of affluent women's perfuming and adorning themselves to attend the mosque in the evening was so entrenched that, if a woman was unable to do so, she would simply refrain from going there.[57] After the *ʿishāʾ* prayers, most of the richly adorned women would depart the mosque. Those who remained into the night were primarily elderly and poor or intermediate in wealth.[58]

Ibn ʿAbd al-Ghaffār's account of the habits of Meccan women suggests that their conventions of modesty and self-presentation intersected with (and were partially informed by) the norms formally articulated by Islamic scholars, but were not fully congruent with them. Their modesty and concealment during the daylight hours and preference for frequenting the mosque in the gloom of evening or early morning reflected textual norms. As articulated by male scholars, however, constraints on women's public display were not time-bound; it was never appropriate for a woman to enhance her attractions with fine clothes, perfume, or the like when exposed to the gaze of unrelated men. It is not sufficient to assume, as is sometimes implied by the comments of male scholars, that Meccan women simply flouted recognized norms out of frivolity, self-indulgence, or ignorance. Had this been the case, they would have been equally oblivious or indifferent to normative standards at all times of the day. Instead, proper self-presentation—in this case, the use of fine clothes and adornment when appearing in public in the evening hours—was itself an alternative norm observed by at least some Meccan women. Ibn ʿAbd al-Ghaffār's reference to "affluent" women (*mūsarāt*) suggests that one function of the women's behavior was the display of economic resources, which presumably contributed to the establishment and maintenance of social status.[59] As such, it formed part of a culture of female sociability that we can infer, but not completely reconstruct. It is also very possible that for Meccan women, self-beautification and perfuming for nighttime visits to the mosque represented a way of honoring the sanctity of the place and time, very much as men were encouraged to honor the sanctity of the Friday prayers by beautifying and perfuming themselves.

Indeed, Meccan women's reputation for copious use of scent even (or perhaps especially) when visiting the Sacred Mosque had been commented on for centuries. Ibn Baṭṭūṭa recounted in the fourteenth century,

> The women of Mecca are exceedingly pretty, surpassing in beauty, possessed of virtue and chastity. They use a great deal of perfume, to the point that one of them will go to bed hungry and buy perfume with her foodstuffs. They go to perform the circumambulation of the House [i.e., the Kaʿba] every Friday night [i.e., Friday eve, or Thursday night]. They come in the prettiest clothes, and the scent of their perfume pervades the sanctuary; one of them departs and the trace of her perfume remains redolent after her departure. The people of Mecca have good customs and a jealousy (*ghayra*) that we shall mention, God willing.[60]

It is notable that Ibn Baṭṭūṭa's description contains no hint of censure; the Meccan women are virtuous, chaste, and heavily perfumed. Similarly, al-Sakhāwī describes a daughter of the amīr of Mecca in the early ninth/fifteenth century as going to extremes in her application of scent, a fact that did not prevent him from describing her as "modest."[61] In contrast, the Shāfiʿī jurist ʿIzz al-Dīn Ibn Jamāʿa (d. 767/1366) complains that the Meccan women's wafting fragrances within the mosque distract people and attract their glances; he considers it an abuse worthy of intervention by the authorities.[62] Nevertheless, the custom persisted; in the seventeenth century, the Ottoman traveler Evliya Çelebi would observe of the Meccans that "if a woman passes by a man of God his brain is suffused with the perfumes of musk and ambergris and civet."[63]

A certain degree of informal gender separation prevailed within the mosque, even in the context of circumambulation of the Kaʿba. Ibn ʿAbd al-Ghaffār states that it is the women's custom to perform *ṭawāf* exactly as is prescribed by the sharīʿa, in rows behind those of the men (i.e., presumably in circles concentrically surrounding them) and not mixing with the men.[64] If it happened that a woman jostled in among the men to kiss the Black Stone or to touch the *rukn*, people would rebuke her severely; indeed, some ignorant devotees and uncouth commoners would take it as an excuse to indulge in vulgar abuse.[65] Despite the accusations of his adversaries, Ibn ʿAbd al-Ghaffār insists that women adhered to the custom of circumambulating separately from the men even on major nocturnal festivals.[66]

However, gender separation within the mosque was not strictly observed in other contexts. Ibn ʿAbd al-Ghaffār speaks of men sitting near to, or even among, women at *mawlids* "and the like."[67] He also makes it clear that the mosque custodians did not intervene to impose gender segregation during daylight hours and implies that mixing was both possible and routine. He notes that between the sunset and nighttime prayers, the women still sit in their usual place near the Ṣafā gate of the mosque, just as they used to before the ban; men walk past them and sit between, in front of, and behind them, and no one objects.[68] This suggests that there was a recognized area where women gathered, particularly in the evening hours that they favored for mosque visitation. However, the area where women were concentrated was not physically or visually separated from the rest of the mosque, and men could pass through it—or even sit down among the women—at will.

Because Ibn ʿAbd al-Ghaffār is interested in the timing and spatial location of women's activities in the mosque, rather than in their content, he does not specify precisely what women did during their evening visits to the mosque. His references to women who went to great lengths to bring their infants to the mosque forty days after birth suggests that drawing on the auspicious power of the sacred sanctuary at the end of the period of seclusion after childbirth was an important women's ritual. Bringing an infant to evening prayers and having a mosque custodian hold it close to the Kaʿba (or the Prophet's grave) is a women's ritual that is also documented for later centuries in both Mecca and Medina. A description of the Prophet's Mosque in Medina from 1303/1885 states that "on every Friday night, and sometimes on Monday night, [women] crowd to bring babies on the fortieth day after their birth into the [Prophet's grave] chamber after the *maghrib* [prayer]; [the child] is placed under the curtain for about two or three minutes, and then the eunuch who put him in brings him out, the face of the child being illuminated, and gives him to his mother."[69]

A similar description is provided by the contemporary Medinian Jaʿfar al-Barzanjī, who notes that it is done "for the sake of blessings (*tabarrukan*) and in the hopes that they will be granted protection, soundness from defects and illnesses, long life, and other things."[70] Also in the late nineteenth century, Snouck Hurgronje recounts that after observing the forty-day period of seclusion after childbirth, a new mother in Mecca would invite her friends to a party.

> In the afternoon the ladies eat and drink together. Towards sunset they go with the young mother into the mosque, and take the child wrapped in the most costly clothes on a small silken mattress shining with gold and silver. This they hand over to a mosque eunuch (*âgha*) who at once understands that this is the fortieth day after birth and lays the child on the raised threshold five feet high of the Kaabah. . . . Ten minutes the child lies there: then the eunuch gives it back to the mother, and receives a gift for his trouble. The women then with the congregation perform the sunset prayer.[71]

It thus appears that this postchildbirth rite was an important practice of women in the Ḥijāzī sanctuaries over a period of centuries.

Women also flocked to the mosque in particularly large numbers during the evening hours at holy times in the religious calendar. Meccan women were accustomed to making the minor pilgrimage (*ʿumra*)—which involved circumambulating the Kaʿba and making seven circuits back and forth between the adjacent hills of Ṣafā and Marwa—frequently from the month of Rajab through the end of Ramadan.[72] During this three-month period of enhanced religious activity, a woman who wanted to make *ʿumra* would ordinarily leave for the mosque sometime after the midafternoon (*ʿaṣr*) prayer and try to arrive in time to pray *ʿishāʾ* with the congregation; if she had to walk a long distance, she might come earlier to give herself time to rest. After the *ʿishāʾ*, she would circumambulate the Kaʿba and then go out to perform the *saʿy* between Ṣafā and Marwa.[73]

The crowds of women were particularly dense on the twenty-seventh of Rajab and during the last ten nights of Ramadan, two of the holiest times of the Islamic calendar.[74] The supporters of the ban complained that on those nights the raised voices of the masses of women and the provocative tinkling of their ornaments made the mosque noisier than a marketplace; the women appeared with their faces uncovered and mixed with men, their charms exposed in the glare of the lamps and candles that illuminated the mosque. Furthermore, because the women circumambulating the Kaʿba on those occasions outnumbered virtuous men by a factor of ten to one, it was almost impossible for a man who sincerely wished to focus on his devotions to pray or circle the Kaʿba. (Because it is unknown what proportion of the men were regarded by the anonymous complainant as "virtuous," it is unclear whether women vastly outnumbered men overall or simply the minority of sincere worshipers.) Women were so numerous that it was impossible for a man to avert his eyes; rather, he had to look carefully to find a path between them on his way to pray or circumambulate, exposing him to the danger that his glances might become lustful and that his state of ritual purity could be canceled.[75] Furthermore, on such occasions women would often spend the night in the mosque, bringing bedding, eating and drinking there, and sullying the sanctuary by washing their hands and engaging in other questionable activities.[76] Again, the patterns of behavior described (and the objections raised against them) are reflected in other sources. The Meccan Ḥanafī jurist Ibn al-Ḍiyāʾ (d. 854/1450) complains of "the women of Mecca's going out to the mosque and to the noble place of circumambulation (*al-maṭāf*) and their gathering there on Friday [i.e., Thursday] night and the nights of the festivals (*al-aʿyād*) and of the sacred nights (*al-layālī al-fāḍila*) of the year. On those occasions they engage in much frolic and raise their voices, which is an occasion for temptation/misbehavior (*fitna*) between women and men."[77]

Ibn ʿAbd al-Ghaffār disputes the factual accuracy of much in his opponents' description of women's behavior during nighttime festivals. He denies that the women have their faces uncovered on such occasions, or that they have audibly tinkling ornaments, or that they mix with men during circumambulation. (To the extent that they do commit such acts, he fully agrees that they should be prevented.[78]) He also denies that women bring actual bedding to the mosque; at most, they bring prayer carpets. They do not bring full meals and spread out tablecloths; rather, at most they eat sweets. During the nights of Ramadan, men do this and more—indeed, they are in the habit of spending the nighttime hours in the mosque for purely social reasons.[79] As for the final nights of Ramadan, in Ibn ʿAbd al-Ghaffār's opinion the problem is not the presence of women, but the practice of illegitimate religious innovations, including the illumination of the mosque with lamps and candles and the erection of pulpits from which the prayer leaders give sermons. These customs do lead to the mixing of men, women, and attractive adolescent boys, problematic bodily contact, and the raising of voices in the mosque, and they have been denounced by scholars in the past.[80] The solution is not to exclude women, but to abolish these innovations.

Interestingly, most of the problematic behavior by women in the mosque—whether routine appearances with inappropriate dress and perfume or special practices associated with holy nights of the Muslim calendar—seems to have been distinctively associated with local Meccan women. The conduct of female pilgrims and of foreign women dwelling in Mecca as a form of pious retreat (*mujāwirāt*) was perceived as far less problematic. Ibn ʿAbd al-Ghaffār states on numerous occasions that it is only the Meccan women who are accused of bad behavior.[81] This may in part have been because female pilgrims and visitors were religiously on their best behavior, inhabiting a liminal state where displays of status and wealth would have been inappropriate. Indeed, persons in the state of ritual preclusion required for the pilgrimage (*iḥrām*) were explicitly forbidden from anointing themselves with perfume. However, the contested behavior of Meccan women probably did not simply originate in a religious laxity bred of greater familiarity with an easily accessible sanctuary. Rather, for local women the mosque was much more complexly integrated into their social and religious lives; it was the locus for customary forms of sociability and piety that were embedded in local concepts and practices of status and value, ones that sometimes diverged from the formal norms articulated by cosmopolitan male scholars.

THE LEGAL ANALYSIS

Ibn ʿAbd al-Ghaffār's legal discussion is lengthy, detailed, and often repetitive. However, his main arguments can be condensed to a small set of central points. His opponents argue in support of the ban that women's comportment in the mosque at night gives rise to social and sexual corruption that can be prevented only by forbidding women's presence in the mosque. Because of the severity of the sins involved, it is imperative that they be forestalled by interdicting the smaller infractions that lead to them. Although not all women are guilty of bad behavior, identification of individual transgressors would require unacceptably intrusive examination of individual women. Thus, the only solution is a blanket prohibition on attendance by women as a group.

Ibn ʿAbd al-Ghaffār responds to these contentions on several different levels. First, he disputes the factual accuracy of claims that corrupt activities are rampant in the mosque, arguing that behavioral infractions are both less frequent and less severe than claimed by his opponents. Second, he argues that the definite religious benefits of women's worship (in particular, circumambulation of the Kaʿba) that are lost as a result of the ban outweigh the speculative benefits (i.e., the prevention of anticipated misbehavior) accruing from its imposition. Third, he argues that it is impermissible to penalize all women for the infractions of individuals. He uses a wide variety of legal arguments and hypothetical examples to argue that it is invalid to generalize (*taʿmīm*) to all women accusations about the wrongdoing of a few. Fourth, he argues that it is not permissible for the authorities to interdict behavior that is merely disapproved, rather than forbidden, or that may be conscientiously regarded as permissible (even if undesirable) by the individuals who are engaging it. Finally, he argues that his opponents' position is a legal innovation (*bidʿa*) involving an impermissible degree of original argumentation diverging from the established doctrines of the four schools of law. He bases his arguments firmly on the authority of the legal tradition, representing his interlocutors as rash and unqualified in their construction of legal responses to what they claim are newly emerging social needs.

One of the most striking and atypical qualities of Ibn ʿAbd al-Ghaffār's legal analysis is the extent to which it problematizes the categorization of all women as a homogeneous class and the treatment of this class in a way significantly different from—and less advantageous than—that of men. In this sense, one could characterize his arguments as a critique of his opponents' gender discourse. One of his most characteristic and effective rhetorical techniques is to equate his opponents' arguments about the legal implications of women's alleged bad behavior with parallel cases of infractions committed by men. Denuded of the sexualized overtones of the discussion about women, such examples often sound tellingly absurd.

In a motif that he repeats often throughout his discussion, Ibn ʿAbd al-Ghaffār raises the example of eating garlic or other pungent foodstuffs in (or before going to) the mosque.[82] It is accepted by all schools of law that it is at best undesirable, and at worst forbidden, to enter the mosque after eating garlic, onions, or leeks, based on several explicit prophetic statements to this effect.[83] In this sense, it parallel's women's entering the mosque while wearing perfume; in each case, the presence of a person emanating a scent (good or bad) that may be disturbing to other worshipers is regarded as legally repugnant. However, no one was in the habit of forcibly excluding men who had eaten garlic from mosques. Thus, the formal parallelism of the two cases pointed up the differential spirit in which they were treated. In his most striking use of this parallel, which he repeats twice, Ibn ʿAbd al-Ghaffār evokes the hypothetical case of a person who becomes aware of a race (*jins*) of people (for instance, Indians) who have become accustomed to eating onions and other noxious things in the mosque between the noon and midafternoon prayers. He then forbids all people of that race—or indeed all men—from sitting in the mosque during that period of time, even if they have not eaten onions, and allows them to sit there at other times, even if they have eaten onions. Furthermore, he attempts to establish this as an element of the sharīʿa that will remain in force for future generations.[84]

Ibn ʿAbd al-Ghaffār is well aware that this example will strike his readers as absurd, and it is clearly intended to shock them into reflecting on the fact that they do not find such a legal intervention absurd when it is applied to women. It is worth noting that in an introductory passage of his discussion, he states that his disputation against his opponents is in the mode of dialectical argumentation (*al-abḥāth al-jadalīya*), where the objective is to refute the arguments of the other side rather than to establish the position that is correct in itself.[85] Thus, many of his comments must be taken simply as thought experiments to demonstrate the inconsistency or (when extended to their logical conclusions) the absurdity of his opponents' stance. Nevertheless, this is as close as an otherwise conventional legal thinker of Ibn ʿAbd al-Ghaffār's time could come, with the available analytic vocabulary, to accusing his opponents of sexual discrimination.

In contrast, al-Haytamī comments in his legal manual *Tuḥfat al-muḥtāj* that "the ruler or his representative is entitled to prevent" women from going to mosques if they are physically attractive, perfumed, or adorned, "just as he is entitled to prevent someone who has eaten something smelly from entering the mosque."[86] It is conceivable that this novel analogy reflects al-Haytamī's response to the arguments made by Ibn ʿAbd al-Ghaffār or like-minded participants in this very controversy; it seems calculated to demonstrate that the exclusion of women is not capricious or unfair rather than to identify its traditional legal basis (which was the fear of *fitna*). If so, this would represent a case in which the polemics surrounding a specific controversy generated arguments that were canonized in an influential work of substantive law.[87]

In another passage, Ibn ʿAbd al-Ghaffār provides a broader and less fanciful account of the ways in which the sins of men and women are being differentially treated by his opponents. Every man knows by personal observation that there is scarcely a time when the mosque is empty of groups of men sitting together to amuse themselves with various kinds of malicious gossip (*ghība*, which is considered *ḥarām* by the consensus of the scholars), up to and including unsupported accusations of adultery (*qadhf*, which is universally acknowledged to be a mortal sin, *min al-kabāʾir*). Ibn ʿAbd al-Ghaffār gives examples of scholarly complaints against such behavior to illustrate its gravity, pointing out that the Mālikī authority al-Qurṭubī actually advocated expelling men who were known for vain speech and lying in the mosque, just as one might (hypothetically) be expelled for eating onions or garlic.[88] Furthermore, rumors attest to the gathering of adolescent boys (assumed to be the object of erotic interest for older men) in the mosque and the bad behavior to which it gives rise. There is no doubt, he concludes, that tolerating all of these infractions leads to corruption more flagrant and repugnant than that which is attributed to women. Furthermore, it is more difficult to distinguish the individual culprits (gossips and the like) than it is to identify individual women who are perfumed or mix with men. Thus, on analogy (*qiyās*) with his opponents' arguments, it would be obligatory to expel all of the men from the mosque and forbid them to circumambulate the Kaʿba; yet they do not advocate this. Ibn ʿAbd al-Ghaffār asks sarcastically what their rationale for this might be, "unless it be that they distinguish between men and women in that respect, and infer that men are forgiven for committing sins that are not forgiven to women because of the lowliness of [women's] rank and the deficiency of their intellects and religion!"[89]

Ibn ʿAbd al-Ghaffār also cites a ḥadīth adduced by his opponents, in which God tells the Prophet to instruct the people that no one should enter a house of worship except with a sound heart, a truthful tongue, clean hands, and pure (i.e., chaste) genitals.[90] He notes that—even were the ḥadīth to be authentic—no caliph, judge, or scholar in Islamic history is known to have expelled anyone from a mosque for lacking a sound heart. Even assuming that people could be held accountable for such qualities, "What is the rationale for applying it to women to the exclusion of men? . . . And how do they know that men always have sound hearts, truthful tongues, and the rest of the qualities, and do not deserve to be excluded during the night or day? And if the men's genitals are always pure, how do the women's genitals come to be impure—does it suffice for [women] to be doing it among themselves?"[91]

In another passage, Ibn ʿAbd al-Ghaffār asks rhetorically "why it is more appropriate to prevent women from circumambulating for the benefit of men, rather than vice versa." Invoking the example of early Muslim authorities who forbade men from circumambulating with women, he suggests that men should be barred at times when women are more numerous, and vice versa. Referring to his opponents' arguments that on some festival nights women outnumber pious men around the Kaʿba by a factor of ten to one, he asks why they have chosen to prioritize the interests of men. Implicitly likening the Meccan sanctuary to a pious foundation (*waqf*) established by God, he asks sarcastically, "Did they find in the conditions of the donor that men should be given precedence over women?!"[92]

Ibn ʿAbd al-Ghaffār sees the issue not simply as one of technical legal argumentation but also as one of gender bias. He believes that the internal inconsistency in his opponents' thinking and their palpably unequal treatment of the sins of men and women are ultimately manifestations of a visceral sense of disrespect for women that is subject to misrecognition as religious zeal. He argues that his opponents acted "in conformity with the natural disposition (*wāziʿ*), which is innate for many people, to go to excesses in condemning women and disdaining them." Such people do not believe that women have any dignity or sanctity (*ḥurma*) at all. This natural tendency becomes conflated for them with the motivation of adherence to the law (*yaltabis ʿalayhim hādhā al-wāziʿ al-ṭabīʿī bi'l-wāziʿ al-sharʿī*), and they falsely fancy that it is an example of the zeal (*ghayra*) that is considered praiseworthy in religion rather than one of the vestiges of the pre-Islamic Time of Ignorance.[93] Although this is a sentiment that might be endorsed by many modern Muslims encountering premodern juristic discussions of issues such as women's mosque access, it is rare indeed for a premodern jurist to suggest that the formally neutral hermeneutic processes of his peers reflect a visceral bias against women that they conveniently mistake for fidelity to pious ideals.

Unlike his opponents, who (at least in his depiction) implicitly regard every woman as laboring under the suspicion of moral turpitude or seductive intent, Ibn ʿAbd al-Ghaffār emphasizes the likelihood of a given woman's innocence and indeed the possibility of her sanctity. In the case where a man uses abusive means to deprive an innocent woman of an opportunity for worship, it is he, not she, who is the transgressor. Such a man, he writes, runs the risk of falling under the divine warnings "Why should God not punish them when they are barring [people] from the Sacred Mosque?" (Qur'an 8:34) and "Those who abuse believing men and women undeservedly, bear a calumny and a glaring sin" (Qur'an 33:58). What is more, such a person is in peril of falling under an extra-Qur'anic divine warning, "Whoever bears enmity towards an intimate (*walī*) of mine, I have declared war upon him"[94]—for God's intimates, both male and female, are numerous and their identity is unknown.[95]

Ibn ʿAbd al-Ghaffār is no advocate of strict gender equality, at least with regard to ritual duties. He does not perceive women's rights to mosque access as rigorously symmetrical to men's, but rather concedes that men have "greater entitlement (*aḥaqqīya*)" to the mosque than women with respect to prayer. However, in his view the imbalance falls far short of justifying women's actual expulsion from a mosque, just as it would not make it permissible to expel male slaves or travelers from the mosque on Friday due to their exemption from the duty to attend.[96] Based both on the relevant ḥadīth texts and on the consensus of the legal scholars, Ibn ʿAbd al-Ghaffār affirms that it is preferable for a woman to worship in her home. This does not apply, of course, to circumambulation of the Kaʿba; yet some scholars affirm that prayer (*ṣalāt*) is superior even to *ṭawāf*. However, he does not believe that this fact invalidates the motives of women who prefer to go to the mosque to circumambulate or pray.

> No one is entitled to stand in judgment over anyone else with respect to worship, forbid him from performing a less meritorious (*mafḍūla*) act of worship and compel him to perform a more meritorious act of worship. Rather, the legally responsible person (*mukallaf*) is his own master in that respect. He performs whatever acts of worship God has facilitated for him and opened his heart to perform, regardless of whether they are the most meritorious or less meritorious, without being interdicted from doing so. It may be that he feels enthusiasm for one act of worship that he does not feel for others, even if they are more meritorious. The first proof for the impermissibility of interdicting him with respect to that is . . . [the report that] the Messenger of God (peace be upon him!)

> said, "Do not forbid your women from [going to] the mosques, and their homes are better for them." Despite his explicit statement that it is better for [women] to pray at home, [the Prophet] forbade people to prevent them from going to mosques, which is less meritorious.[97]

Based on this logic, Ibn ʿAbd al-Ghaffār rejects al-Balāṭunusī's inference that a woman who chooses to go to the mosque to pray (rather than performing a more meritorious prayer at home) must have ulterior or sinful motivations.[98] Overall, his arguments reflect a willingness to accept women as autonomous legal and spiritual agents who can and should select their acts of worship based on their individual religious needs.

Although Ibn ʿAbd al-Ghaffār staunchly defends the human dignity and the religious agency of women, he is certainly not a feminist *avant la lettre*. He is perfectly willing to acknowledge gender asymmetry—and indeed gender hierarchy—when he believes that it is textually well grounded and authorized by legal precedent. He makes a sharp distinction between husbands and male guardians, who may legitimately detain women at home, and public authorities who bar them from the mosque. He has no objection to the idea that a woman's own guardian may choose to prevent her from going to the mosque. Both the protection (*ṣawn*) of the woman and sexual jealousy (*ghayra*) are entitlements (*ḥaqq*) of the guardian, particularly of the husband; the legal scholars have established that the husband's permission is one of the conditions for the permissibility of her going. Ibn ʿAbd al-Ghaffār declares, "If it should happen that the mosque were altogether empty of women because their guardians had forbidden them [to go] in a [legally] permissible way, even if they were perfectly attired according to the norms of the sharīʿa, we would not oppose [the guardians] in that, because a stranger [i.e., a nonrelative] has nothing to say about it."[99]

Ibn ʿAbd al-Ghaffār does not contend that women are to be equated with men (although neither are women to be mistreated simply as a result of their sex); rather, he rejects the idea that all women are to be equated with each other, regardless of behavior, age, or appearance. Indeed, Ibn ʿAbd al-Ghaffār likens his opponents to an unjust judge who not only beats both of the opposing litigants but also goes on to beat everyone else present simply because they were found in the same house or mosque—or because they share with them the qualities of maleness or femaleness.[100] For Ibn ʿAbd al-Ghaffār, this is an example of "generalization" (*taʿmīm*), an unusual coinage that he uses to label (and condemn) the extension of a ruling applying to a specific offender to all members of a larger class—in this case, specifically women.[101] The theme of *taʿmīm* is also reflected in the inquiry that he sent to the scholars of Egypt, where his central objection to the ban is that it applies to "all women without exception . . . without distinction between a virtuous and a depraved woman, an old woman and a young one, an adorned woman and one dressed in workaday clothes, a woman who is perfumed and one who is not perfumed."[102] It is a recurring motif of his argument that, although he does not condone religiously sinful and legally questionable actions such as women's attendance at the mosque while perfumed or adorned, he likewise does not condone the imposition of a sanction on other individuals who are innocent.

Again turning to parallel infractions committed by men, Ibn ʿAbd al-Ghaffār argues that, if the smell of alcohol or of garlic was wafting from a group of people, it would presumably not be legitimate to inflict the *ḥadd* penalty for wine drinking on all of them in the first case or expel them all from the mosque in the second.[103] He also rejects the idea that a whole group of people could be held presumptively guilty of a given infraction simply because it had become customary among them as a group. For instance, even if one knew that swearing on pain of divorce and then breaking one's oath had become ubiquitous in society, it would not be permissible presumptively to separate any couple without knowing whether the husband had actually violated an oath of divorce.[104]

The argument that all women cannot be barred from the mosque (even if only at specific times of day) for the infractions of a few is rendered more forceful by Ibn ʿAbd al-Ghaffār's choice of framing exclusion from the mosque as a punishment (*taʿzīr*). This pointed definition of the legal problem brings it into the purview of an area of Islamic law subject to evidentiary and procedural standards. For Ibn ʿAbd al-Ghaffār, such discretionary punishments (that is, sanctions not textually established by Qur'anic decree) fall under the more general rubric of the Qur'anic obligation to "command right and forbid wrong."[105] Significantly, he does not overtly argue the point that exclusion from the mosque is a punitive sanction (as opposed to, say, an administrative measure necessary for public order). It is one that his opponents would almost certainly have disputed; the legal tradition on women's mosque attendance dismisses it tacitly by declining to discuss it at all. This is acknowledged to be the case by Ibn ʿAbd al-Ghaffār; however, he sees it simply as a shortcoming in the arguments of his opponents, who have failed to address the stipulated conditions of this area of the law.[106]

The duty of "commanding right and forbidding wrong," Ibn ʿAbd al-Ghaffār argues, is subject to several significant limitations. First, the rules of "forbidding wrong" do not allow proactive and invasive investigation of suspected wrongdoing. According to the scholars of the Mālikī *madhhab* (as well as others), the wrong in question must be publicly manifest; one cannot seek it out by intrusive inspection (*taftīsh*) or, for instance, by sniffing someone or searching for things concealed under his garments. Although this limitation may make it difficult to confirm precisely who (if anyone) is guilty of suspected wrongdoing, one may not proceed if it is not possible to identify the individual culprits.[107] Second, one must always put the best possible construction on the acts of one's fellow Muslims, even in cases where an innocent explanation would be far-fetched. Third, one may not sanction others for engaging in behavior that is legally objectionable (*makrūh*) but not actually forbidden (*ḥarām*). If the legal status of the act in question is disputed, one may not rebuke or sanction another person who is doing something that he or she does not personally believe to be forbidden.[108]

Of course, the supporters of the ban were not, in fact, conducting or condoning searches of women. They rejected out of hand the notion (clearly absurd to everyone involved) that women might be inspected at the gate of the mosque for their clothing, age, and comportment before being allowed to enter at night—an obvious violation of prevalent ideas of modesty.[109] Rather, they argued that due to the difficulty of distinguishing individual women who were guilty of infractions in the mosque, it was necessary to exclude all women as a class during the most problematic hours of the day. Admittedly this involved barring some women who were innocent of any intent but sincere worship, but the only alternative was to condone the bad behavior occurring in the mosque.[110]

Ibn ʿAbd al-Ghaffār questions both the substantive accuracy and the legal cogency of his opponents' position. First, he disputes that it is prohibitively difficult to distinguish women who are blameless from women who pose a threat to public order. He points out that many women are observably innocent; they are visibly old, shabbily dressed, and otherwise innocuous. Second, his opponents have arbitrarily established the time of day, rather than the dress or comportment of the woman, as the sole criterion; during the day, they do not bar any woman from entry, even assuming that she is visibly adorned and redolent of perfume.[111] In response to the argument that perfume may be palpably present in a group, but difficult to trace to an individual, he argues (somewhat impractically) that it is perfectly possible to distinguish a strongly perfumed woman from a group by asking them to stand far apart from each other, thus isolating the source of the scent.[112]

However, Ibn ʿAbd al-Ghaffār does not appear to be seriously advancing the position that individual women should be more rigorously scrutinized for admission to the mosque. In a different passage of the work, he advocates that the ruler appoint an upstanding inspector (*muḥtasib*) for the mosque, aided by similarly trustworthy assistants. These people should circulate through the mosque, particularly checking secluded corners. If they catch men or women engaging in blameworthy behavior, they should castigate the culprits to the exclusion of anyone else.[113] Individual men who pursue women, in the mosque and elsewhere, are known in the community and would be familiar to the mosque inspector within the space of a month. Fear of the embarrassment and gossip caused by individual expulsion from the mosque would be a sufficient deterrent for both male and female offenders.[114]

The position of the supporters of the ban is that, even if sinful behavior is not manifest, to perpetuate the current situation is to enable and condone unacceptable acts. Even if one cannot see sexual misbehavior being committed openly, one knows that it is happening and bears the responsibility for preventing it. Ibn ʿAbd al-Ghaffār responds to this logic with the bold contention that, in fact, the sharīʿa imposes no obligation to investigate or prevent wrongdoing that is not publicly manifest. It is only openly observable offenses that are legally significant and subject to sanctions; discreetly committed sins impose no obligations on the religious or temporal authorities.

> We have not been made responsible for what occurs *de facto* (*lam nukallaf bi-mā fī nafs al-amr*); rather, it is forbidden for us to pursue it. Sins of every kind have always occurred *de facto* in every town and in every age, even in the days of the prophets (God's blessings upon all of them!), and [the prophets] were not commanded to eliminate them so that they could be assured of their non-existence. Similarly, we are certain that very many repugnant acts are [now] occurring *de facto* in God's Holy City [of Mecca], the City of His Prophet [Medina], and other towns, including *zinā*, the drinking of wine, the taking of interest, and other mortal sins, because there are many times as many incontrovertibly transmitted reports (*li-tawātur al-akhbār*) about the occurrence of that as there are about the women [allegedly misbehaving in the mosque].[115]

As we have seen, Ibn ʿAbd al-Ghaffār also holds that it is not permissible to interdict behavior whose impermissibility is disputed, and one may not object if a member of another school of law performs an action that is permitted in that school (even if it is forbidden by one's own school).[116] With respect to this requirement, he states that most scholars hold that the presence of adorned and perfumed women in the mosque is merely *makrūh* (undesirable). More specifically, he observes that most Meccan women are Shāfiʿīs, so they would consider it *makrūh* rather than *ḥarām* (forbidden).[117] Therefore, he contends that their behavior in this respect should not be interdicted. His argument here depends on a rigorous distinction between the categories of *makrūh* and *ḥarām* that his opponents might have disputed; in some contexts, scholars understood *karāha* to be tantamount to *taḥrīm*. In any case, Ibn ʿAbd al-Ghaffār does not find it necessary to argue that anyone considers the presence of perfumed and adorned women in the mosque legally neutral (let alone desirable), and it would have been impossible for him to do so; rather, he treats *makrūh* actions as ones that, although perhaps suboptimal, are not forbidden and are therefore at the discretion of the individual.

Ibn ʿAbd al-Ghaffār invokes the authority of al-Qarāfī for the principle that in commanding acts that are merely recommended and forbidding acts that are merely disapproved, one should engage in counsel (*irshād*) rather than rebuke (*tawbīkh*).[118] Citing a ḥadīth in which the Prophet, upon seeing a woman decked out in her finery entering the mosque, instructs the people to forbid their wives to adorn and flaunt themselves in the mosque, Ibn ʿAbd al-Ghaffār points out that—far from expelling all women from the mosque—in this report the Prophet does not even eject the culprit herself. From this he infers that the order to forbid women to display themselves in the mosque must express a recommendation rather than an obligation (*amr nadb lā wujūb*).[119] (This argument cleverly parallels the more traditional contention that the Prophet's negative command "Do not forbid the maidservants of God from [going to] the mosques of God" establishes a recommendation rather than a prohibition, but to the opposite effect.) Thus, Ibn ʿAbd al-Ghaffār is able to reinterpret apparent precedents for the limitation of women's presence in mosques as instances of respectful exhortation. Although some women in the Prophet's time are reported to have left the mosque swiftly after prayers, he notes that they did so by their own choice (*bi'khtiyārihinna*).[120] Overall, Ibn ʿAbd al-Ghaffār strongly emphasizes the distinction between courteous exhortation that leads to voluntary action and acts of coercion (*kurh*).

Related to Ibn ʿAbd al-Ghaffār's argument that it is not permissible to interdict actions that are not themselves legally forbidden is his analysis of the concept of *manʿ* (forbidding). He argues that there are two distinct meanings of the term that are conflated by his opponents. One of them refers to the legal status of the act in question and the other to the issue of enforcement. In the first sense, it refers to the act's being prohibited, as a matter either of *taḥrīm* or simply of *karāha*. It is this kind of abstract, theoretical prohibitedness that is the purview of scholars engaging in legal reasoning (*ijtihād*). The results of their analysis are not binding on any specific individual.[121] In the second sense, *manʿ* refers to actual prevention of someone's performing a given act. This function is performed by the public authorities with respect to the general population and also by husbands with respect to wives (and masters with respect to slaves). It applies to specific individuals and does not establish abstract general rules. *Manʿ* in the second sense (i.e., that of actual interdiction) is legitimate only if *manʿ* in the first sense (i.e., that of abstract legal prohibitedness) is present.[122]

It is notable that in his fatwa on women's mosque access, Ibn Ḥajar al-Haytamī offers support for the opposite view on this particular point.[123] He notes approvingly the view that the public exposure of a woman's face is permissible with respect to the woman herself, but that it is nevertheless permissible or even obligatory for the authorities to interdict it for fear of its seductive effect on other people. By this logic, al-Haytamī argues, it is incumbent upon the authorities to prevent women from appearing in public at all if they engage in any behavior (such as attending the mosque adorned and perfumed) that is likely to have a seductive effect—presumably, regardless of whether such behavior is actually forbidden from the viewpoint of the women themselves.[124] Once again, Ibn ʿAbd al-Ghaffār emphasizes the moral subjectivity and choice of the individual woman, whereas his opponents prioritize considerations of public order.

Ibn ʿAbd al-Ghaffār concedes that some of the more dire offenses that are alleged to be associated with women's presence in the mosque at night, which include actual sexual misbehavior, are absolutely forbidden. However, he emphasizes that even in this case, the authorities can intervene to interdict and punish only if they know through legally valid channels that offenses have occurred. In fact, the evidence is merely baseless gossip. It is rumored that, beginning with the fall of darkness and continuing into the night, many reprobate men mix among the women, immoral women steal off to be alone with them in the corners of the mosque and plan future sexual assignations, and people even manage to kiss or fondle each other within the mosque itself. Some youths claim that actual fornication has occurred within the mosque. Ibn ʿAbd al-Ghaffār emphasizes, however, that such reports are rarely heard from reliable informants. Some scholars claim to have heard such things from the culprits themselves, and this is the only likely way that one could learn of them; one does not plan future fornication in a voice that is audible to others, and one steals kisses only discreetly. Nevertheless, someone who does report such things of himself may merely be bragging.

In any case, these rumors do not deal with things that happen every night or even every few nights. Usually they are based on old stories that have been in circulation for years and are set in the reigns of bygone rulers. Overall, Ibn ʿAbd al-Ghaffār characterizes the accusations of actual sexual misconduct in the mosque as mere rumors (*ishāʿāt*), as well as "exaggerations and speculations" (*al-mubālaghāt wa'l-mujāzafāt*).[125] The doubt that he casts on reports of sexual misconduct serves two purposes. One is to remove much of the urgency from the argument that exclusion of women is necessary to prevent greater harms. It also serves to show that women are being sanctioned for crimes that have not been proven and may, in fact, never have occurred.

Ibn ʿAbd al-Ghaffār's discussion of the role of rumor in the construction of an illusory image of female wrongdoing in the mosque is supported by a tragic incident recounted by his Meccan contemporary Ibn Fahd. Despite its sanctity, the Sacred Mosque of Mecca was also a public place where a woman could experience an otherwise rare degree of exposure to the attentions of unrelated men. This may have been particularly true for Meccan women, who visited the mosque not in the liminal state of a pilgrim temporarily removed from her ordinary social context, but in the course of their daily lives and normal social relations. Ibn Fahd records in his account of the year 927/1521 that the unnamed daughter of a man whose name is omitted in the manuscript (there is a blank in its place) went out after the *ʿishāʾ* prayer to the mosque, where she encountered a man (identified by name) who was drunk. He accosted her and snatched her outer wrapper (*izār*). An indignant passerby struck him with his dagger (*janbīya*) and wounded him. Perhaps because the incident involved actual physical injury, it became widely known. The woman's father, returning from a trip to Egypt, was taunted with a reference to the gossip—and promptly killed his daughter. He was said to have confessed to killing her because of her bad character (*fisq*). Such an act was clearly not normal or routine, as it led to public outrage and legal intervention. However, inquiries by a local judge and by the Ottoman governor (*nāʾib*) of Jeddah were frustrated when the father bribed the medical witnesses to state that his daughter died of natural causes. Ibn Fahd finishes the anecdote with the mournful exclamation, "The command belongs to God, before and after; there is no might and no power but in God!"[126]

Although surely rare and shocking (as witnessed by Ibn Fahd's indignant narration and anguished final comments), the story of this anonymous young woman suggests the vulnerability that could result from a woman's presence in what was probably the only public place accessible to a respectable (and apparently unaccompanied) female. She chose a time, after nightfall, that was preferred by Meccan women for their excursions to the mosque. However, the cover of darkness apparently did not prevent her from being recognized; the rumor spread, and soon reached her father. This appears to be a very rare case of a documented premodern "honor killing," and it is significant that it appears to have been anomalous and offensive in the eyes of many contemporary Meccan men—whether because they considered honor killing generally unacceptable or simply because they considered this particular woman innocent is unclear. Although there is no indication that gossip about this tragic incident contributed to the exclusion of the women from the mosque at night that occurred a decade later, it supports Ibn ʿAbd al-Ghaffār's contention that rumors about rare incidents of alleged impropriety involving women in the mosque could become magnified beyond all proportion with the actual events.

Unsurprisingly, given his outspoken support for the ban, al-Haytamī has a very different view of the reliability and significance of reports about sexual impropriety in the mosque. As we have seen, he states that the ban was imposed "because of the shameful acts (*qabāʾiḥ*) that were well-known, nay, incontrovertibly reported (*ishtahara bal-tawātara*) to be committed by [the women] even in the mosque [itself]." Here he uses terminology derived from the discipline of ḥadīth to suggest that the reports of women's misdeeds were so numerous as to preclude error or collusion (*tawātur*). Some of "precursors of *zinā*" were committed in the mosque—and on the very occasion of kissing the Black Stone.

> One of the religious students (*ṭalabat al-ʿilm*)—may God have mercy upon him!—related to me that while he was kissing the Black Stone, a woman jostled him; he left the circumambulation area (*maṭāf*), and she followed him to its margin. He fell victim to her temptations (*iftatana bihā*) and went with her to her house; [however], God protected him from committing fornication (*al-fāḥisha*) with her, because she found

> he had no money with him (*lam tara maʿahu shayʾan*). I was [also] informed by someone who attended my classes . . . that when he was kissing the Black Stone a woman jostled him to kiss the Black Stone and he kissed her [instead]; so God afflicted him with a condition that made him completely give up [seeking] knowledge, then it made him a laughingstock and an object of ridicule to everyone who saw him. . . . May God give us refuge from His anger, testing, trials, and tribulations by His favor and grace, amen![127]

Al-Haytamī's comments support Ibn ʿAbd al-Ghaffār's contention that shocking stories about sexual indiscretions in the sanctuary (and the possibility of their leading to actual *zinā*) played a potent role in evoking support for the ban. The first anecdote obliquely suggests that the woman in question was a prostitute: after taking home her helpless prey, she refuses to have sex only when he proves unable to pay. In the second anecdote, in contrast, it is not apparent that the woman is guilty of anything worse than an excess of religious fervor. The fleeting (if intimate) nature of the inadvertent physical contact is counterbalanced by the gravity and permanence of its purported effects; a promising religious scholar is transformed into a distraught social outcast. (Al-Haytamī continues with a description that, from a modern secular point of view, suggests mental illness.) It is clear that al-Haytamī invests contact between the sexes—whether flagrantly immoral (as in the first case) or apparently innocent (as in the second)—with an awesome potency that completely confounds the logic of Ibn ʿAbd al-Ghaffār's sober and pragmatic approach to the possibility of sexual misconduct.

In addition to allegations of bias against women and denial that actual interdiction is legally permissible, Ibn ʿAbd al-Ghaffār engages with his opponents on the level of legal theory. He writes that their principal mode of argumentation "is the method of the people of independent reasoning (*ahl al-ijtihād*): basing the legal ruling on the rationale (*ʿilla*) and deriving it from the legal proofs of the Qur'an, the *sunna*, the practice of earlier generations (*ʿamal man maḍā*), and juristic principles (*al-qawāʿid al-uṣūlīya*), such as the principle of 'blocking the paths' (*sadd al-dharāʾiʿ*) and the principle that legal rulings change with the changing of [social] conditions, and the like." Only secondarily do they invoke school precedents on the basis of *taqlīd*.[128] Ibn ʿAbd al-Ghaffār is himself passionately opposed to this form of argumentation. He devotes a significant portion of his legal analysis to demonstrating that even the most famously brilliant and independent legal scholars of the past were, in fact, highly deferential to the established doctrines of their schools.[129] Thus, his first mode of refutation of the opposition's arguments is simply to assert their lack of qualifications (*ahlīya*) to perform independent legal reasoning. Accordingly, he declares analysis of their original reasoning to be "a useless waste of time"—although, of course, he proceeds to engage with it in great detail. In his view, even those qualified to engage in independent legal reasoning based on the methodology of the founder of a specific school (*al-mujtahid al-muqayyad*) are nonexistent in his own time. The only valid line of argumentation is to adduce an applicable precedent from within a school.[130]

After adducing an impressive series of examples intended to demonstrate that even the most distinguished muftīs of the Mālikī and Shāfiʿī *madhhabs* refused to diverge from the preferred (*mashhūr*)[131] doctrines of their schools, Ibn ʿAbd al-Ghaffār concludes with great fervor that "for the likes of us," it is impermissible to construct new legal rulings based on independent proofs (*al-adilla al-ijtihādīya*):

> With respect to us, that is a forbidden action (*min al-muḥarramāt*); nay, it is a mortal sin (*min al-kabāʾir*); nay, it is one of the worst of them, because it is the greatest means to calamities and the principle path to mortal sins. There is no comparison between it and the "path" (*dharīʿa*) of corruption of which women are accused, or even to the ultimate corruption to which that path leads, because its utmost extent is the occurrence of adultery (*zinā*), which always occurs frequently and which harms no one except those who commit it (because they are the ones who bear the sin and they alone experience its evil consequences), while this "path" threatens to destroy the pillars of the sharīʿa, or rather, to efface its traces altogether. It is [the "path" of engaging in independent legal reasoning] that we must go to extremes in blocking, because it is the *fitna* whose fire cannot be extinguished.[132]

In this passage, which is difficult to render in English because of its multifaceted and playful use of terminology, Ibn ʿAbd al-Ghaffār cleverly equates the violation of religious law that he believes his opponents are committing with the violation that they are attributing to women in justification of the ban. Whereas the behavioral infractions cited by opponents of the ban may ultimately lead to adultery, he argues that the illegitimate exercise of legal authority in which they are themselves engaged may ultimately lead to the complete destruction of the divine law. His remarks culminate in labeling their unauthorized exercise of *ijtihād* as a *fitna*, thus appropriating a central trope of his opponents' arguments and (in a typical rhetorical move) applying it to the nonsexual transgressions of men.

This passage evokes the major legal argument of the supporters of the ban. At least as represented by Ibn ʿAbd al-Ghaffār, they regarded the prohibition of women's attendance at the Sacred Mosque during the nighttime as an example of the juristic principle of *sadd al-dharāʾiʿ*, or the "blocking of the paths." This principle, applied most extensively in the Mālikī school, posits that an otherwise permissible action may be prohibited if it leads to a forbidden action.[133] In this case, although it is not inherently *ḥarām* for a woman to be present in the mosque at night, it would be rendered so by the likelihood that it would lead to actions that are themselves textually forbidden. In response, Ibn ʿAbd al-Ghaffār argues that *sadd al-dharāʾiʿ* is not, in fact, a comprehensive legal principle that can be applied systematically to all areas of the law; latter-day scholars cannot discern the subtle considerations that led Mālik to apply it in some cases but not in others, and can only follow his precedent.[134]

Ibn ʿAbd al-Ghaffār also argues that his opponents do not actually sustain the implications of their argument, because the principle of *sadd al-dharāʾiʿ* dictates that the action in question actually becomes forbidden as a result of its likelihood of leading to prohibited actions. For instance, it is actually forbidden to engage in trade when the call to prayer summons worshipers to Friday prayers (due to the likelihood that it will lead one to omit the prayers themselves). In contrast, even the supporters of the ban do not argue that women's presence in the mosque or performance of circumambulation during the hours of the ban has actually become *ḥarām*, such that any woman who did so would be committing a sin.[135] They merely argue that it is permissible for the authorities to forbid her. In fact, it is less a question of declaring otherwise permissible actions (women's nighttime attendance and circumambulation) forbidden than of declaring otherwise forbidden actions (punishing innocent women and preventing believers from engaging in acts of worship) permitted. This is the converse of the legal principle in question; Ibn ʿAbd al-Ghaffār facetiously argues that it should be called "opening the paths (*fatḥ al-dharāʾiʿ*)" rather than "closing the paths."[136]

In response to the argument that one must act to prevent even suspected harms, Ibn ʿAbd al-Ghaffār contends that the public interest in preventing harms must be balanced against the goods that are lost as a consequence.[137] Interestingly, he concedes that the benefits in a woman's attending congregational prayers and helping to populate (*iḥyāʾ*) the mosques are outweighed by the benefit of protecting (*ṣawn*) the woman by keeping her at home.[138] However, the same does not apply to her performance of circumambulation, which yields great merit.[139] Furthermore, most vital human activities—such as trade—involve the potential that grave sins will be committed. Preventing sins by excluding women from the mosque makes no more sense than preventing wrongdoing by closing the markets.[140] Once again, Ibn ʿAbd al-Ghaffār implicitly places in question the unique urgency attributed to issues of female visibility and sexual morality.

Unlike Ibn ʿAbd al-Ghaffār, who posits that the harms that may be prevented by a legal intervention must be balanced against the benefits that may be lost, in his defense of the ban al-Haytamī posits a general principle that "the prevention of harms has precedence over the acquisition of benefits."[141] Furthermore, he argues that no woman will be prevented from performing an obligatory circumambulation of the Kaʿba altogether. For al-Haytamī, the only unacceptable harm would be a woman's inability to fulfill the obligatory rites of the pilgrimage; for Ibn ʿAbd al-Ghaffār, women's deprivation of voluntary acts of piety is harm enough.

According to Ibn ʿAbd al-Ghaffār, the second theoretical principle on which his opponents depend in their defense of the ban is that of "the changing of legal rulings with the changing of the circumstances" (*taghayyur al-aḥkām bi-taghayyur al-aḥwāl*).[142] Indeed, al-Haytamī's fatwa cites an anonymous source forcefully arguing that the valid ruling in the present day is that women should be prevented from going out to mosques "and no one would hesitate in [affirming] that except a fool who follows his fancies, because legal rulings change with the changing of the people of the times."[143] Al-Haytamī also cites the precept (which he attributes to the Imam Mālik and asserts to have been accepted by the founders of all of the schools) that "New legal opinions arise for the people in proportion to the corruption that they innovate (*yaḥduth li'l-nās fatāwā bi-qadr mā aḥdathū min al-fujūr*)."[144]

In contrast, Ibn ʿAbd al-Ghaffār emphasizes that even in cases of apparent social need, the great scholars of the past applied the established doctrines of their schools and did not resort to the (supposed) principle that rulings change with the changing of the times; indeed, this would have been permissible only for an absolute *mujtahid* not constrained by affiliation to a *madhhab*.[145] He presses his point by citing instances where the greatest authorities of the past declined to resort to new legal remedies even in the face of dire social consequences—for instance, when it seemed that theft or wine drinking could be deterred only by enhanced punishments.[146] If it were permissible to invent new legal solutions for emerging social needs, Ibn ʿAbd al-Ghaffār asserts, this would swiftly erode the foundations of the law. For instance, someone might observe that illegitimate sexual intercourse (*zinā*) and sodomy had become ubiquitous and propose relaxing the impossibly stringent evidentiary requirements, thus fundamentally revising a clear provision of the sharīʿa.[147]

Another argument that Ibn ʿAbd al-Ghaffār is at pains to refute is the contention that women's misbehavior in the mosque is a new problem. He argues that this premise is indispensable to his opponents' application of the principle of *sadd al-dharāʾiʿ*, presumably because no new means of "blocking the paths" are necessary if no fresh problems have emerged.[148] He points out that women's "innovation" of going to the mosque adorned and perfumed has been the object of continuous comment and condemnation from the time of ʿĀʾisha onward.[149] He demonstrates that, far from being a novel phenomenon, this is a durable trope of the literature on the pilgrimage to Mecca and of polemics about legal innovations.[150] There is similarly no evidence to support the idea that misconduct palpably increased in the period immediately preceding the ban. In fact, he states that far worse rumors of women's scandalous conduct in the Meccan sanctuary were circulating when he lived in Egypt in the time of Qāʾiṭ Bāy, whose reign had ended thirty years earlier.[151] Furthermore, earlier scholars who complained about improper contact between men and women in mosques did not advocate barring women, but simply eliminating the innovative religious practices (such as the illumination of the mosques on noncanonical nighttime festivals) that gave occasion for provocative behavior.[152]

By inventing a new legal response to an old situation that had already been addressed by the scholarly authorities of the past, Ibn ʿAbd al-Ghaffār argues, his opponents are guilty of a religious innovation (*bidʿa*). In the opening passage of his work, he characterizes the ban as "an extremely repugnant innovation, the likes of which has never been heard of in the Islamic era or, indeed, in the Age of Ignorance [before Islam]."[153] This is one of the book's most pervasive and devastating rhetorical devices. Like his characterization of their legal reasoning as a *fitna*, from the point of view of his opponents this would have been a paradoxical—and perhaps willfully perverse—accusation; after all, it was precisely of "innovation" that women were accused (in the famous statement of ʿĀʾisha and elsewhere). However, Ibn ʿAbd al-Ghaffār argues that by stipulating the parameters and timing of women's worship in the Sacred Mosque, they are in effect legislating on acts of worship. By "preventing women . . . from worshiping at one time and commanding that they do so at another, and by determining each of those times . . . without this being stipulated by the [divine] Legislator," they are applying their own common sense or intellectual standards (*raʾy*, *ʿaql*) or indeed their vain fancies (*wahm*) in place of the legal indicator (*dalīl sharʿī*) that is alone the proper basis for establishing ritual practice.[154]

The response of Ibn ʿAbd al-Ghaffār's opponents to the objection that women's misbehavior in the mosque was far from a new phenomenon seems to have been, quite reasonably, that they had never intended to imply that it was chronologically recent. In fact, *bidʿa* is a normative rather than a temporal category; they could quite appropriately argue that it was innovative (that is, alien) with respect to the religion without having been newly manifested in the period preceding the ban. The fact that an abuse has prevailed over a long period of time does not make it less forbidden as a matter of law, as is the case with illegal taxes (*al-maks*), which have been notoriously ubiquitous despite their religious prohibition. Ibn ʿAbd al-Ghaffār retorts in response that this is not an analogous case; far from being a long-tolerated abuse, women's circumambulation of the Kaʿba at night is an act of piety that prevailed from the lifetime of the Prophet until the year of the ban. It is the ban itself that is an objectionable innovation that has been newly introduced into the religion. Indeed, he goes so far as to compare the ban to an illegal tax on the Kaʿba, one that reaches as high as 25 percent because it bars "more than one half of the *umma* (Muslim community)" almost half of the time.[155]

The fact that there was no textual basis for the newly introduced time contraints on women's ritual activities in the mosque was probably one of the most effective arguments against the ban. Perhaps precisely because of this fact, it seems that the response of supporters was largely to ignore it. It is striking that both in his brief narrative of the imposition of the ban and in his fatwa supporting it, al-Haytamī completely omits to mention that women were being excluded only at specific times of day. Indeed, reading his treatment of the issue in isolation one would assume that women were excluded from the Great Mosque altogether—however, because this would have prevented them from performing the pilgrimage, such a blanket ban would surely have attracted widespread condemnation. (The timing of the ban is obliquely acknowledged only when al-Haytamī states that an unmarried young woman may wait to perform circumambulation when the *maṭāf* is sparsely populated in the heat of noonday—an inversion of the traditional convention that she should do so under cover of darkness.[156])

In pointing to the arbitrary and innovative character of the ban, Ibn ʿAbd al-Ghaffār repeatedly emphasizes that a temporally limited exclusion of women only from the mosque itself (and only between specific hours) does not achieve the stated objective of the ban, the prevention of sexual mixing and impropriety. He points out that with the exception of the mosque itself during the hours of the ban, women go wherever they want, wearing whatever they want.[157] The stated objective of protecting women from *fitna* would be achieved only by preventing them from leaving their homes, which is far from the case.

Indeed, upon being expelled from the mosque at night a woman can go anywhere she pleases.[158]

Although Ibn ʿAbd al-Ghaffār presents extensive original analysis in rebuttal of his opponents' legal reasoning, he fundamentally denies the validity of such analysis for non-*mujtahids*. Although he engages dialectically with the supporters of the ban, in his own view its legal status can be determined only with reference to the transmitted doctrines of the four schools. In surveying the history of legal doctrine on this subject, he emphasizes one fundamental point throughout: whereas scholars of various schools have expressed varying degrees of disapproval for mosque attendance by women of different categories, they have never actually declared it to be forbidden. He argues that he knows of not a single scholar from any school who argues that going to mosques is categorically *ḥarām* for women, such that any woman (even if elderly and unadorned) who entered a mosque and performed a single prayer would be committing a forbidden action.[159]

Within the framework that Ibn ʿAbd al-Ghaffār has constructed, which defines the interdiction of women's mosque attendance either as a punishment or as an instance of "forbidding wrong," it suffices to show that it is not *ḥarām* in the strict legal sense and that its status is subject to disagreement. To support his view, Ibn ʿAbd al-Ghaffār must resort to some subtle reintepretation. When Ibn Rushd declares of his youngest category of women that "the preferred option is that she not go out at all," Ibn ʿAbd al-Ghaffār explains that "the most that can be understood from this expression is that her going out is sub-optimal (*khilāf al-awlā*) or extremely undesirable; if [such women] wanted to go out, it would not be obligatory to prevent them."[160]

Ibn ʿAbd al-Ghaffār also addresses the opinions of more recent Mālikī scholars who suggest that due to the corruption of the times, latter-day women should be forbidden from going to mosques altogether. Once again, he places his emphasis largely on the enduring authority of the foundational texts of the school. He points out that the later authorities cited by his opponents do not state that forbidding women to go to mosques is the *madhhab*, but first cite the established doctrine and then add comments about their own preferences. In his view, they wish to encourage women's guardians to keep them at home (which is in any case their prerogative) rather than to establish a new prohibition to be enforced by the authorities. Their own opinions, rather than constituting legal norms per se, are expressions of pious caution (*min bāb al-waraʿ*).[161]

Ibn ʿAbd al-Ghaffār's arguments in this section of his work, where he surveys the opinions on women's mosque attendance in the standard manuals of the four schools of law, can be described as an example of "virtuoso *taqlīd*." His overt approach is to reproduce and scrutinize the relevant statements transmitted in the legal sources of the past, all the while emphatically reasserting their authority. The results of this approach, however, are far from the static repetition of a sterile set of authority statements; rather, they constitute a thorough reinterpretation of the law. By framing the issue in terms of the (arguable) requirements of "forbidding wrong," which limit interdiction to cases of actual legal prohibition (*taḥrīm*), he is able to extract a radical affirmation of women's right to frequent mosques from a set of texts that often express reservations or disapproval toward this activity.

As we have seen in an earlier chapter of this study, it was often a delicate and ambiguous process to map the range of formulations used in legal texts onto a dichotomy between "permitted" and "forbidden." For instance, the Prophet's command not to prevent women from visiting mosques could be interpreted either as a legally binding prohibition or as an optional moral exhortation. Similarly, the term *makrūh* could be interpreted as indicating either that the action in question was forbidden or that it was merely suboptimal (*karāhat al-taḥrīm* versus *karāhat al-tanzīh*).[162] Often, this terminological flexibility was used to limit the prerogatives of women and maximize those of men. In this case, in contrast, the semantic openness of such terminology is consistently exploited for the opposite objective: to maximize the area of discretion where women (or their individual male guardians) voluntarily choose among a range of alternatives in light of their own circumstances and needs.

Ibn ʿAbd al-Ghaffār's resourceful assertion of the liberatory potential of (creative) adherence to established school doctrine in the face of (reactionary) claims of original legal reasoning inverts the accepted wisdom about the comparative social impact of *ijtihād* and *taqlīd*. It once again demonstrates that, as Sherman Jackson has observed, "the tendency to associate such categories as 'liberal' or 'progressive' with *ijtihād* and 'conservative' or even 'patriarchal' with *taqlīd* is not only unwarranted but dangerously misleading."[163] However, in another respect the controversy over women's access to the Great Mosque of Mecca diverges from the pattern analyzed by Jackson. He argues that virtuoso displays of legal argumentation were by this period (the tenth/sixteenth century) framed in terms of fresh legal analysis of authoritative school sources, rather than of the primary sources of the Qur'an and ḥadīth, because by that point the institutionalization of the Sunnī *madhhab*s had established a "regime of *taqlīd*." In the controversy at issue here, however, it seems to have been quite possible for scholars to introduce overt elements of *ijtihād* into their legal arguments. To the extent that we can trust Ibn ʿAbd al-Ghaffār's representation of the case of his opponents, they seem to have emphasized original legal reasoning far more than any attempt to assert a restrictive interpretation of the relevant language in the legal manuals of their schools. Although al-Haytamī does make some (problematic) effort to represent his opinion as continuous with those of prominent Shāfiʿī authorities, he clearly sees no necessity to cite or interpret the relevant language from the school's standard works of *furūʿ*. In this case, the "regime of *taqlīd*" is not a given constraining all of the participants in the debate, but an ideal that Ibn ʿAbd al-Ghaffār must explicitly strive to assert.

In our analysis of the historical development of the legal argumentation on the issue of women's mosque attendance in chapter 1 of this study, we identified several different stages. The first, which may be termed *preclassical*, distinguishes as a matter of course among different stages in the female life cycle. Although explicit rationales are not offered by the earliest texts, there seems to be a tacit assumption that women's social roles change as they move through different stages of life. At a secondary (*classical*) stage, from approximately the fifth/eleventh century, this differentiation among different age cohorts is systematically rationalized with reference to *fitna*, the sexual temptation or disorder that may result from women's mixing with men. Finally, in a *postclassical* stage beginning approximately in the seventh/thirteenth century, there is a growing trend to regard all women (to the threshold of senescence and death) as possible sources of *fitna*, effacing the traditional division of women into age cohorts. Each stage did not decisively and irreversibly replace the one preceding it, however; they remained as alternatives and as superimposed elements within a growing repertoire of interpretive alternatives.

In his critique of the ban, Ibn ʿAbd al-Ghaffār repeatedly emphasizes distinctions among different groups of women.[164] He consistently differentiates among young and old women and also frequently invokes distinctions among those who are well dressed and those who are shabbily attired, those who are perfumed and those who are not. Indeed, in his inquiry to the scholars of Egypt and other international centers, it is the ban's failure to distinguish among different categories of women that he centrally invokes as evidence of its illegitimacy. He even coins the distinctive term *taʿmīm* (generalization) to refer to the illegitimate extension of strictures applying to some women to all women without distinction. In contrast, although al-Haytamī occasionally acknowledges distinctions among women, his conclusion is categorically that the authorities ought to prevent "women" from going out to mosques if abuses occur. In part, the two scholars' different views may reflect the greater conservatism of the Mālikī school on this point, at least on a legal (rather than a rhetorical) level.

However, ultimately Ibn ʿAbd al-Ghaffār is advocating not the reaffirmation of distinctions between different categories of women, but the entitlement of individual women to worship unmolested unless they are personally guilty of infractions. His arguments focus on concrete actions (inappropriate dress, perfuming, mixing with men, or even sexual misbehavior) and the requirement that they be proven against specific offenders. In this respect, his approach echoes that of ḥadīth specialists such as al-Nawawī and Ibn Ḥajar al-ʿAsqalānī, who similarly (as we have seen in chapter 2) emphasized the comportment of individual women. However, Ibn ʿAbd al-Ghaffār mounts a far more direct assault against the gendered logic of postclassical limitations on women's mosque access. By emphasizing tangible actions rather than the diffuse concept of *fitna*, he circumvents what by that time had become the term's global and essentialistic association with the presence and visibility of women. He tacitly refuses to deal with the legal status of the atmosphere of, or potential for, sexual temptation amorphously associated with women; rather, he focuses rigorously on the overt actions of morally responsible individuals.

Indeed, it is largely Ibn ʿAbd al-Ghaffār's focus on issues of individual moral desert that determines the outcome of his arguments. *Fitna* does not necessarily require an agent; a woman does not have to "commit" it for it to exist, nor does she have to be at fault for it to require intervention. By framing the exclusion of women from the mosque as a "punishment," Ibn ʿAbd al-Ghaffār is able to argue that it is unjust (and unjustifiable) in the absence of individual culpability. It is this prior choice of legal categories ("punishment" and "forbidding wrong"), which precedes and conditions his explicit argumentation, that dictates the outcome of his discussion. It should be noted that, even given this choice, his premises are not unassailable. His own authority al-Qarāfī, although he did advocate tolerance in cases of legal disagreement, states that neither punishment nor the duty of "forbidding wrong" is necessarily contingent on the moral culpability of the individual involved. Rather, these interventions may seek to secure benefits or avoid harms.[165] Ibn ʿAbd al-Ghaffār's emphasis on the moral agency of individual women is thus an affirmative choice, one that also informs his repeated distinction between moral exhortation (which he hopes will motivate poorly comported women to change their behavior voluntarily) and actual coercion.

THE FATWAS

The fatwas presented by Ibn ʿAbd al-Ghaffār demonstrate that he was able to elicit supportive responses from prominent jurists of all four schools of law. There are some discernible differences among the opinions originating from different *madhhab*s. For instance, the Ḥanafī chief judge of Egypt Shams al-Dīn al-Samdīsī, whom Ibn ʿAbd al-Ghaffār identifies as "the sultan's imam," states that it is not permissible to prevent women from circumambulating the Kaʿba at any time of day, but continues, "As for their praying in the mosque, he stated in *al-Kāfī*: The valid opinion today is that it is undesirable [for women to attend mosques] for all of the prayers."[166] This is the most restrictive opinion in the set of fatwas, although (perhaps significantly) the other two Ḥanafī fatwas express no such sentiments. Mālikī authorities seem distinctively concerned with identifying and upholding the established doctrine of their school, which they hold to allow women's mosque attendance. For instance, Nāṣir al-Dīn al-Laqānī[167] notes Khalīl's remark in *al-Tawḍīḥ* that "in our time" women should be forbidden to go to mosques, but concludes, "He mentioned this in the mode of personal speculation (*ʿalā wajh al-baḥth*), but what he mentioned first is the transmitted doctrine (*al-manqūl*) on the issue."[168] Sharaf al-Dīn Yaḥyā al-Damīrī brings up the same remark of Khalīl's, but firmly asserts, "Personal speculations (*al-abḥāth*) do not refute transmitted doctrines or render them void, and neither does reasoning on the basis of ʿĀʾisha's statement [that the Prophet would have forbidden women to go to mosques if he had seen what they have innovated] put an end to the principle of the school."[169]

Overall, the content of the fatwas suggests that the pointed nature of the inquiry (and perhaps the selectivity of the compiler) sufficed to ensure a fairly high degree of unanimity among the responses. However, the fatwas vary widely in tone and emphasis. On one end of the spectrum, the Ḥanbalī scholar Shihāb al-Dīn al-Shuwaykī[170] questions whether the alleged corruption is happening during actual circumambulation or even within the mosque, declaring that only "one who believes in God and the Last Day" will seek out the mosque for prayer and circumambulation. Furthermore, women should not be excluded for the alleged infractions of others: "How can this one be held accountable for the sin of that one, when God Most High says, 'No soul will bear another's burden'?!"[171] In contrast, the Medinian Shāfiʿī Sirāj al-Dīn ʿUmar ibn ʿAbd al-Raḥīm emphasizes the danger of bad behavior and the consequent legitimacy of interdiction. In cases of infraction, the ruler (*walī al-amr*) may "prevent and threaten" the woman in question. If she obstinately goes out in violation of the conditions or intentionally mixes with men around the Kaʿba, then she is a sinner, not a virtuous worshiper. However, the good must be distinguished from the corrupt based on manifest signs, not by spying and baseless speculation.[172]

Most of the fatwas collected by Ibn ʿAbd al-Ghaffār seem like relatively perfunctory and predictable responses to a biased formulation of the legal problem. Two of them, however, are of a magnitude and substance that suggest significant personal investment on the part of their authors. One of these is by Aḥmad ibn ʿAbd al-Ḥaqq al-Sunbāṭī, a Shāfiʿī jurist and a popular and influential preacher (*wāʿiẓ*) at the Azhar Mosque in Cairo who sojourned in Mecca in the early 930s.[173] Ibn ʿAbd al-Ghaffār presents only excerpts from al-Sunbāṭī's fatwa, which he describes as both extensive and excellent.[174] The vehemence of al-Sunbāṭī's denunciation of the ban rivals that of Ibn ʿAbd al-Ghaffār's; indeed, their arguments appear to be so closely entwined that at least at one point the voices of the two authors become indistinguishable.[175] Al-Sunbāṭī begins his fatwa with the resounding affirmation that "someone who prevents women from circumambulating in the way described errs in doing so and is a wrongdoer who transgresses the limits (*ḥudūd*) of God Most High."[176] Although it is unknown how al-Sunbāṭī disseminated his fatwa or what the response may have been, his intervention in the contemporary controversy over the licitness of coffee suggests the possible impact of his opinion. His fatwa against coffee is supposed to have inspired rioting in the streets of Cairo, as well as a new round of fatwas on the legal status of the beverage.[177]

Another lengthy opinion suggests a more institutionalized mechanism to endow a fatwa with force and effectiveness. This is the fatwa of Aḥmad ibn al-Ṭayyib al-Ṭanbadāwī, the leading Shāfiʿī legal authority of the Yemeni town of Zabīd.[178] Al-Ṭanbadāwī's opinion covers much familiar ground, including the citation of school doctrine that it is preferable for a young or noble woman to delay her circumambulation until she can be concealed by darkness, the assertion that the ban violates ḥadīth texts forbidding prevention of anyone from circumambulating and women from visiting mosques, and the insistence that individual women can be sanctioned only if they are observably perfumed or ill-behaved.[179] Al-Ṭanbadāwī notes that, although it is more meritorious for women to pray in congregation at home, manuals of *ḥisba* do not state that women should be excluded from mosques but instead instruct that men and women should be separated by a barrier when listening to a preacher. Because listening to preachers in mosques is at best a pious action on the part of old women and those without attractive appearances, then *a fortiori* women should not be excluded from the mosque if they intend to perform a ritual that is religiously required. Significantly, Ibn ʿAbd al-Ghaffār notes that al-Ṭanbadāwī's fatwa was endorsed by "other scholars of Zabid," who added signed notes of approval below his opinion.[180] Thus, not only was the fatwa a lengthy and detailed legal argument produced by the leading authority of the legal school that overwhelmingly predominated in Zabid, but the solicitation of supporting signatures rendered it a group opinion by the local establishment. Fatwas like those of al-Sunbāṭī and al-Ṭanbadāwī suggest that, despite the dearth of legal opinions on this controversy preserved outside of Ibn ʿAbd al-Ghaffār's collection, it was a cause célèbre in its own time. Although the ban itself was very vulnerable to legal critique and a wide range of scholars opposed it, their agreement on this one point disguised the diversity of their sentiments about the propriety of women's presence in the mosque and the legitimacy of regulatory efforts by the authorities.

CONCLUSION

Although it is often possible to juxtapose legal arguments about the desirability or undesirability of women's mosque attendance with descriptions of women's mosque-based behavior originating from the same general time and place, usually the connection between the two is fairly loose and conjectural. The documentation generated by the events of 937/1530–31 provides a unique opportunity to examine the dynamics connecting social practice, governmental regulation, and legal discourse in a concrete case where different agendas collided in the most sacred mosque of the Islamic world.

Ibn ʿAbd al-Ghaffār's account illustrates that the very issues that had been debated on a theoretical level over the centuries—specifically, the division of women into separate categories by age cohort and comportment and the distinction between daytime and nighttime—were disputed on the ground as well as in the more rarified arena of textual exegesis. As we have seen, the early doctrines of the four schools posited different behavioral parameters for women of different age cohorts, whereas criteria developed within the tradition of ḥadīth commentary proposed that women's access be regulated on the basis of dress and behavior. Within the latter tradition, scholars like Ibn Ḥajar al-ʿAsqalānī had raised the question of whether alleged "innovations" in women's self-presentation entailed sweeping changes in the law or merely restrictions on individual offenders. At a very basic level, the debate recorded by Ibn ʿAbd al-Ghaffār is over the question of whether "women" represent a monolithic category whose behavior can be regulated without regard to individual age or conduct. More obliquely, but in a way that is eloquent by its omissions, he disputes whether *fitna*—as a presumptive capacity for sexual allure that can be associated with women, regardless of their individual behavior or moral deserts—can function as a rationale for categorical limitations on all women.

The distinction between night and day—one that, as we have seen, was both well established and disputed in the legal literature—also had immediate relevance for the ban of 1530. In the course of these events, a deeply seated local belief that the hours of dusk or darkness were the most appropriate times for women's public worship collided with a newer (or imported) attitude that it was perilous and disreputable for women to be out at night. The colorful accounts of the seventeenth-century Ottoman traveler Evliya Çelebi suggest that conventions regarding women's mobility at different times of day varied in different regions of the Ottoman Empire, accommodating both the idea that respectable women should venture out only under cover of darkness (which prevailed, for instance, in Cairo) and the opposite assumption that it was safe or proper to do so only during the day. As Robert Dankoff observes, "Evliya assumes that his readers—elite Ottomans like himself, with Istanbul as the reference point—will agree that gallivanting at night is not something women should do."[181] Indeed, there is some evidence that in later times excluding women from mosques at night was an Ottoman policy.[182] However, more evidence would be required to establish whether the incidents at Mecca in 937 AH reflected a wider Ottoman policy. Furthermore, without knowing the identity of the amīr who initiated the ban, it is impossible to determine whether it can be seen as an intervention by the Ottoman authorities at all.

Ibn ʿAbd al-Ghaffār's unusual account reflects the multiple constituencies and agendas involved in the identification, framing, disputation, and resolution of a significant legal question. Not only the temporal rulers (who sought to preserve public order and perhaps to assert the primacy of their preferred school of law) but also the mosque guards (who sought to minimize their own labor by limiting the mosque's accessibility and hours) seem to have played central roles. Although Ibn ʿAbd al-Ghaffār represents the ʿulamāʾ as having been compelled to respond hastily to an issue they did not raise,[183] he also sees their authority and prestige as vital to the ban. He urges them to speak to the amīr if they do not genuinely support it, as their *maḥḍar* is his only basis for the initiative; as for the mosque guards, they display it to anyone who objects and declare, "This is by order of the ʿulamāʾ, not our order or that of the amīr."[184] At the bottom of the pyramid are ordinary individuals who take it upon themselves to discipline and exhort their fellow Believers. Ibn ʿAbd al-Ghaffār depicts these people as self-aggrandizing hypocrites who use the religious duty of "commanding good and forbidding wrong" to justify harassing and abusing women, and he argues that they are emboldened by the scholars' justifications for barring women from the mosque.[185] Although the influence of such freelance "commanders of right" is difficult to gauge, it is quite possible that such moral pressure from below may have influenced the holders of more overt religious authority. Thus, the ʿulamāʾ and their legal argumentation stood at the intersection of the agendas and influence of multiple groups; although their authority sustained the ban, Ibn ʿAbd al-Ghaffār's exhaustive picture suggests that they were by no means autonomous in producing it.

Ibn ʿAbd al-Ghaffār presents no account of the suspension of the ban, whether it was officially reversed or gradually and tacitly fell into desuetude. Furthermore, no contemporary chronicles seem to cover these events; that of Ibn Fahd, which would be the most likely source, has a lacuna covering the key period in question. By the time Ibn ʿAbd al-Ghaffār completed his work (or perhaps when he later corrected or revised it), the ban was already lifted, a fact to which he refers in passing.[186] (Based on his own account and on the tone of the book, it would seem that the initial composition of the work must have occurred when it was still in force or at least still enjoying substantial juristic support.) Unless further sources come to light, it is thus impossible to know whether the restoration of women's access to the mosque at night reflected the successful resistance of the women of Mecca (as in the case of their continued participation in the public celebration of the Prophet's birthday), the influence of their powerful male kin, or the scholarly success of a legal critique representing the ban as an unfounded innovation. It seems likely that all of these factors may have played a role.

Overall, Ibn ʿAbd al-Ghaffār's account—which depicts legal scholars as relatively passive recruits to a plan initiated by others—tends to represent legal reasoning as a dependent variable, wielded ex post facto by scholars with different preexisting investments in the local Meccan political order and the functioning of the mosque. His own response seems to be grounded in a visceral and preanalytic reaction to the injustice of seeing innocent women harshly ejected from the site of their religious devotion; only secondarily is it elaborated in the form of a legal treatise. However, the passion with which he pursues both the fashioning of his legal arguments and the solicitation of opinions from others attests to the efficacy that he attributes to sharʿī discourse. If he depicts his adversaries' initial responses as superficial and self-interested, he clearly maintains the faith that a shared commitment to the authority of the law can be activated to vindicate the rights of Believers, both male and female.

four
MODERN DEVELOPMENTS

Whereas for the premodern period we have an abundance of normative sources and a paucity of information about de facto ritual practice, for more recent times the situation is reversed. Particularly for the later part of the twentieth century and the opening of the twenty-first, growing numbers of ethnographic and social-scientific studies illuminate women's growing presence in mosques and the religious, political, and gender dynamics surrounding it. Rather than attempting to add to that literature, which goes beyond the textual source-base and methodology of this study, this chapter will bring our discussion full circle by returning to the analysis of the underlying construction of gender in modern legal discussions of women's mosque access.

ISLAMIC REFORM FROM THE TURN OF THE TWENTIETH CENTURY

The turn of the twentieth century saw the emergence of newly positive attitudes toward women's mosque attendance by reformist Islamic thinkers. However, the agenda of these authors was not simply to grant women access to mosques but also to ensure that mosques served as loci for the dissemination of religiously sound practices and doctrines to women. Their receptivity to women's public prayer and enthusiasm for women's religious education was balanced by their disdain for many of the mosque-based practices that women had traditionally pursued.

For instance, the Syrian modernist Jamāl al-Dīn al-Qāsimī (d. 1914) complains bitterly about women's visitation of sacred sites within mosques. He notes that it is a women's custom to visit and circumambulate the shrine of John the Baptist in the Umayyad Mosque of Damascus on Saturday mornings; one of their "superstitions," al-Qāsimī observes with disdain, is the belief that doing so for forty Saturdays will ensure the fulfillment of any wish.[1] However, it was precisely in mosques that women were to be disabused of their unorthodox religious ideas and instilled with sound knowledge. "How much women today need a preacher (*wāʿiẓ*)," he lamented, "particularly since innovations, objectionable practices, deviant beliefs, disobedience of husbands, and uncountable forbidden things have become prevalent among them." His proposed solution was that the public authorities designate a mosque where women would receive instruction on a specific day, at which time guards should be posted to prevent the entry of men. It is the religious scholars' misplaced zeal in excluding women from mosques that has contributed to women's ignorance, al-Qāsimī concludes—and all of this is the inauspicious result of defying the Prophet's guidance, which clearly prohibits men from excluding women from mosques. As for the report of ʿĀʾisha, by saying that, if the Prophet had seen what women innovated he would have forbidden "them" from going to mosques, she must have meant "the ones who wear perfume." "For this reason a woman is instructed to refrain from wearing perfume and displaying herself immodestly; otherwise, closing the door [of the mosque] against them completely means opening it to endless ignorance. For they are commanded to acquire knowledge and learn, because it is an obligation of every male and female Muslim."[2]

Much like al-Qāsimī, Egyptian reformers sometimes expressed concern about the unorthodox or "superstitious" ways in which women traditionally accessed the sacred space of mosques. Muḥammad ʿAbduh advocated intervention by the state against women's mosque and shrine visitation practices that had been noted as early as the fourteenth century in the work of Ibn al-Ḥājj. In 1297 AH/1880 CE, he wrote in the official government journal *al-Waqāʾiʿ al-miṣrīya* that the authorities should forbid the crowded gatherings that took place in the "famous mosques" on specific days of the week, such as those in the Mosque of Sayyida Zaynab on Sundays and Wednesdays and in the Mosque of al-Ḥusayn on Saturdays and Tuesdays (as well as on the festival of ʿAshūrāʾ). On these occasions, he writes, "women and men mix in a way that is forbidden by both the sacred law and [human] nature (*al-sharʿ wa'l-ṭabʿ*)." Aside from the repugnant acts that are committed, he claims, these boisterous gatherings make it impossible for worshipers to pray undisturbed.[3]

In 1904, ʿAbduh's student Rashīd Riḍā (d. 1935) published a fatwa in response to an inquiry from a village in the province of Damietta that provides a rare glimpse of women's activities in a mosque outside of the metropolis. It describes how some women furtively brought a sick child to the mosque and sat under the pulpit during the Friday sermon, hoping that this would bring about healing. The discovery of the group led to their expulsion by the imam (exclaiming, "These are innovations, and [women][4] are not allowed to enter the mosques of God in this way!") and vigorous defense by the congregation. Riḍā responded briskly that "the imam was correct to forbid women and children from sitting beneath the pulpit to seek healing."[5]

In contrast, Riḍā wished to promote women's participation in congregational prayer. In a fatwa published in 1905, he affirms that women prayed with men in the Prophet's time without a barrier, "so their praying in the mosque is an established and long-observed sunna whose authenticity has not been disputed by any Muslim." Ḥadīth texts stating that it is preferable for women to pray at home should be interpreted as applying to prayers that are not performed in congregation. As for the ʿĀʾisha report, "it is on that opinion that the later jurists based the prohibition of women's going to mosques; [but] it is a legal inference (*ijtihād*) that cannot abrogate an explicit and definitively-established text and make forbidden what God and His Prophet have made permissible." He acknowledges the conditions for women's dress and comportment stipulated by ḥadīth, but holds that it is necessary to exclude only individual women who seem likely to behave seductively.[6]

In 1911, a few years after Riḍā's and al-Qāsimī's contributions to the debate over women's mosque access, the Egyptian feminist Malak Ḥifnī Nāṣif presented the First Egyptian Congress with a list of ten points relating to women's rights. The "First Proposition" stated: "Women should, in cities, as well as in the villages, be allowed to enter the Mosques for prayer, and for hearing preaching, as was their practice in the days of Islamic Renaissance." Her manifesto points to the seclusion of women as a source of Muslim decline, particularly in comparison to Jews and Christians, who make their places of worship available to both sexes. Interestingly, her call for women's inclusion is paired with advocacy for their segregation: "Should the Congress approve of this proposition, then there should be established in each Mosque a special entrance for Women, and inside, raised platforms where they might pray and hear the preaching of the Sheiks, without mixing with men." She even proposes that "women should enter and leave the Mosques half an hour before the men" to avoid any occasion for any "evil passion" (with the proviso that "the reason I stipulate these precautions is to give no excuse to the old-fashioned or jealous people").[7]

Nāṣif also advocates that elementary education be made mandatory for girls as well as boys, that Islamic religious instruction be provided in public and private schools, that more women be trained as nurses to treat other women, that institutes be founded to teach women home economics, and that every school employ "a wise and educated lady whose work would be to watch over the girl's [*sic*] conduct and the performance of their religious duties." Her final proposal was that women be prohibited from participating in funeral processions.[8] None of her proposed reforms were enacted. As Valerie Hoffman observes, Nāṣif's demands "do not defy traditional norms, they uphold them" by emphasizing the inculcation of correct religious beliefs and of gender norms of modesty and domesticity.[9] Although from the vantage point of a later age Nāṣif's program of reform may seem reactionary, it actually involved values that were to a large extent substantively new. The mosque was to become one of the sites for the formation of a new woman who combined knowledge of a newly reformed "correct" Islam with scientifically advanced modern home economics and the technical skills to train and treat other women in an (ideally) segregated society. Only by educating previously "ignorant" mothers, as

Nāṣif argued in other writings, would it be possible to raise a healthier and more disciplined generation of Egyptians.[10]

This new view of the role of mosques in crafting Islamically and socially correct femininity came to be normative in the Egyptian religious establishment, even as it emphasized continuity with the doctrines of the classical *madhhabs*. A fatwa composed by Shaykh ʿAbd al-Majīd Salīm (d. 1946) and issued by Dār al-Iftāʾ in 1940 surveys the opinions of the four schools and concludes that the most appropriate opinion is the Ḥanbalī doctrine that women's mosque attendance is permissible, due to its conformity to the content of many ḥadīth texts (and subject to the condition that it not be accompanied by harmful things like the wearing of perfume). He remarks in closing,

> The superiority of [women's] praying at home over their praying in the mosque is interpreted to apply to the case that prayer in the mosque is not accompanied by hearing preaching or the like that is not available to women in their homes. As for if their attending is for the sake of prayer and to hear things that will instruct them about their religion, the raising of their children, and the fulfillment of their husbands' rights, the most likely interpretation is that their attendance in this case is superior.[11]

Here again attendance at the mosque forms part of a larger program of inculcating correct religious and social attitudes, including proper gender roles and a modern sense of domesticity.[12]

If the mosque could be promoted as an arena for the communication of normative messages about women's role within the family and the home, the growing elaboration of this role also came to be a rationale for the limitation of women's presence within the mosque. The Syrian Shāfiʿī scholar Muḥammad Saʿīd Ramaḍān al-Būṭī (1929–2013) responds to a question about the legal status of women's going out to the mosque at night by stating that she may do so under several conditions, including the proviso that her going does not result in "her neglecting a more important Islamic duty, such as taking care of her children or her husband, or the like."[13] Al-Būṭī's list of conditions roughly parallels that of the ḥadīth tradition (particularly al-Nawawī), but it also modifies it significantly by reducing the fear of *fitna* to the threat of "exposure to harm" and by giving new emphasis to the woman's familial duties, thus desexualizing and domesticating the observant Muslim woman. This emphasis contrasts sharply with the fact that, as noted by Asma Sayeed, "the various [classical] jurists . . . focus resolutely on the disorder that may result from women's attendance at mosques and pay little or no attention to domestic duties that may prevent a woman from joining congregational prayers."[14]

By the mid-twentieth century, scholars also recognized that women were publicly active in, and intellectually and politically engaged with, many activities and trends that competed with Islamic piety for their allegiance. In this context, mosque attendance was an alternative not merely to isolation and ignorance within the home but also to activity in other, secular arenas. ʿAbd al-Ḥalīm Maḥmūd (1910–78), who served as rector of al-Azhar, wrote in this vein: "Since in this age women have penetrated into many of the affairs of life, entered many fields, and have begun to be present in most public places—even if [these activities] divert them from religion, such as the cinema and the like—their going to the mosque for Friday prayers reinforces their faith, strengthens their religion, and increases their [pious] works."[15] In another fatwa, he declared that "if it was a necessary thing for women to pray in mosques and hear lessons in bygone times, it is even more necessary in this time; perhaps the atmosphere of the mosque and the sermons, Qur'anic verses and prophetic ḥadīth they hear in it will guide them towards virtue and repentance."[16]

In statements emanating from the Egyptian religious establishment in the last decades of the twentieth century, affirmation of the benefits of women's mosque attendance coexisted with vigorous reaffirmations of the preference for women to pray at home. A 1977 fatwa from Dār al-Iftāʾ cited the Umm Ḥumayd ḥadīth to demonstrate that it is more meritorious for a woman to pray at home and reasserts the husband's right to forbid her going in part on the grounds that it is not religiously optimal for her to pray in the mosque.[17] In a 1985 fatwa, the muftī of Egypt ʿAbd al-Laṭīf Ḥamza reiterated that it was preferable for a woman to pray at home, although vigorously affirming the legitimacy of women's instruction in the mosque by a male shaykh (who could inform them not only about "their religion" but also about "the good treatment of their husbands").[18] In the 1980s and 1990s, Shaykh ʿAṭiya

Ṣaqr (at that time head of the Fatwa Committee of Majmaᶜ al-Buḥūth al-Islāmīya at al-Azhar) strongly emphasized reports in which the Prophet encouraged women to pray at home, although he affirmed that it was permissible for a woman to frequent the mosque to acquire religious knowledge—particularly "if it was not possible for her learn at home through reading or through hearing or watching religious lectures in audio or visual broadcasts."[19]

However, these views have not gone unchallenged even within the establishment of al-Azhar. In a 1986 study, Suᶜād Ṣāliḥ, a female professor at al-Azhar, reviewed the doctrines of the classical schools only to conclude summarily: "Whoever consults the proof-texts available in the purified *sunna* will see that it is desirable for women to attend congregational prayers with men." The contention that the merit of attending congregational prayer in the mosque is limited to men, she notes, contradicts the explicit sense of well-authenticated ḥadīth texts.[20] By the turn of the twenty-first century, a fatwa issued by a telephone advice line based at al-Azhar stated straightforwardly that it is more meritorious for a young woman to pray in the mosque than at home, citing texts that had traditionally been applied only to men.[21]

Legal opinions issued by official Egyptian bodies associated with al-Azhar often are based on the opinions of the four Sunnī schools of law, even when they substantively diverge from traditional doctrines; this is also true of scholars such as al-Būṭī. Other major trends in twentieth-century Islamic thought did not simply review, reframe, and modulate the legal frameworks of the classical *madhhabs*, but advocated fresh approaches altogether. Although the diversity of modern Sunnī legal thought cannot easily be reduced to a small number of labeled categories, two of the most influential trends among Sunnīs in the Arab Middle East can roughly be identified with the Muslim Brotherhood (historically rooted in Egypt) and Salafism, including its Wahhābī form developed in Saudi Arabia.

THE MUSLIM BROTHERHOOD

The Muslim Brotherhood (al-Ikhwān al-Muslimūn) originated in British-ruled Egypt in the 1920s and has long been active—although often not officially tolerated—in other countries in the Middle East. Even beyond its formal organizational presence, the Ikhwān (and the style of thinking that it promotes) has had a broad influence. Its approach, sometimes labeled "Ikhwānī" (although not everyone who fits this category belongs to the organization), represents one significant element in the spectrum of contemporary Islamic attitudes in the Middle East. The Brotherhood emphasizes the reform of society and government through the training of Islamically committed cadres that are able to exercise influence in the educational, professional, cultural, and political spheres. Where allowed, the Ikhwān participate in electoral politics; individuals associated with the Ikhwān are often also active (and sometimes dominant) participants in student government and in professional associations.

The movement's founder, Ḥasan al-Bannā (d. 1949), did not envision a major public role for women within his social and political program. He did emphasize that women are the half of society that most affects the life of a people because they are "the first school" that shapes the rising generation. Girls must be taught reading, writing, arithmetic, religion, and the stories of the exemplary early Muslims, both male and female, in addition to home economics, health, and the principles of child rearing. More than this, al-Bannā cautions, is vain and unnecessary. He further emphasizes the powerful attraction that naturally prevails between men and women, the hazard of *fitna*, and the consequent imperative of avoiding mixing (*ikhtilāṭ*) between the sexes. According to al-Bannā, Islam requires gender segregation. It requires the wearing of modest clothing, forbids unrelated men and women from being alone together, and demands that men and women avert their eyes from each other's charms; it is one of its distinctive rites (*shaʿīra min shaʿāʾirihi*) that a woman remain within her home even to pray.[22] Although women are permitted to attend festival and congregational prayers, as well as to go out to battle in case of dire necessity, these are exceptions.[23]

For al-Bannā, the ḥadīth-based preference for women's prayer within the home illustrates a general preference for women to remain within the domestic sphere. Islam prohibits a woman from exposing her body or being alone with an unrelated man, and it encourages her to pray in her home; "can it be said after this," al-Bannā asks rhetorically, "that

Islam does not explicitly prohibit a woman from working in public?"[24] He concludes that Islam considers home and children to be the natural and fundamental mission of a woman, which will scarcely leave her time to pursue other tasks; she may work outside of the home only if compelled by necessity.[25] In al-Bannā's discourse, although he does allude to the permissibility of women's participation in festival and congregational prayers, a strong preference for their praying at home is emblematic of a more general emphasis on their proper absorption with family matters.

In this respect, al-Bannā's position contrasted sharply with that of his much older contemporary Rashīd Riḍā. In a piece on women's rights in Islam, Riḍā connected women's participation in public worship with their involvement in social and political life, characterizing congregational, Friday, and festival prayers as "social acts of worship (*al-ʿibādāt al-ijtimāʿīya*)" attended by women as well as men.[26] In contrast, al-Bannā saw women's prayer within the home as a corollary of (and a central piece of evidence for) their general exclusion from public roles in society. However, in many ways Riḍā's view rather than al-Bannā's presaged the later program of the Ikhwān. As the gender ideology of the Ikhwān evolved over time, the issue of women's mosque access was gradually reevaluated.

In 1953, the Ikhwān published a short book written by al-Bahī al-Khūlī and titled *Women Between the Home and Society* (*al-Marʾa bayna al-bayt wa'l-mujtamaʿ*). In its introduction, the leader of the Ikhwān, Ḥasan al-Huḍaybī, recounted that he had commissioned it to address the concerns of members of the Ikhwān who faced uncertainty about proper Islamic conduct regarding the women of their households; for instance, should they go out in public with their wives, and should they send their daughters to university?[27] In treating the issue of women's activities outside of the home, the book expresses acute awareness of the negative perceptions arising from religious argumentation premised on the inherent sexual volatility of women. Al-Khūlī notes that some people have the impression that opponents of the Western model of women's rights believe that "a woman is inherently a satanic creature, lustfully awaiting any opportunity [for sexual misbehavior], so that she is entitled only to be treated with suspicion and prevented from seeing the light outside of the home." This is incorrect; rather, Islamic writers acknowledge women's full intellectual and ethical capacities, but oppose calls for "licentiousness and libertinism" in a social situation fraught with means of sexual temptation and seduction. It is significant that in this passage the word *fitna* is associated consistently with the social atmosphere rather than with women themselves.[28]

Nevertheless, the book emphasizes repeatedly that "the home is the natural arena for the mission of women,"[29] and to some extent the danger of neglecting domestic duties takes the place of *fitna* in limiting women's activities outside of the home. Al-Khūlī states that a woman "is entitled to go out to prayers—[although] it is better to perform them at home," and emphasizes that she may go to lectures and the like to improve her mind and learn about her religion.[30] Although this work is at pains to repudiate the image of woman as seductress, it is uninterested in promoting women's engagement with mosques. However, this would change over time.

One figure whose trajectory parallels and exemplifies that of the Ikhwān as a whole (although he ultimately ended his formal affiliation with the organization) is the Egyptian scholar Muḥammad al-Ghazālī (1917–96). Al-Ghazālī was a personal associate of Ḥasan al-Bannā and wrote for Ikhwān publications; he was jailed along with other members of the organization in 1948–49 and broke his official tie to the organization in 1952. In his book *Min hunā naʿlam*, published in the early 1950s, he expresses positions quite similar to those of al-Khūlī: a woman's essential duties are in the home; she is entitled to pray in the mosque, but it is more meritorious not to.[31] "Islam also realized that woman's occupation at home, the nature of her role in the life of society, and her relation to her children make it hard, if not impossible, for her to go to the mosque for prayer five times a day. In true appreciation of her position, Islam declared woman's prayer at home more worthy than her prayer in the mosque, and yet reserved for her the right to go to the mosque as often as she could."[32]

By the 1980s, al-Ghazālī's arguments had shifted significantly in favor of a public role for women, including participation in public worship. He returned to the issue at some length in an influential but controversial work on ḥadīth, which cast doubt on the authenticity of a number of widely cited and legally relevant statements attributed to the Prophet. Turning to the subject of congregational prayer, he emphasizes that from the rise of Islam, mosques have been pivotal sites of community activity and solidarity, as well as of piety and contemplation. In addition to raising people's spiritual level, "repeated meetings preserve private and public relationships, and let the *umma* face today and tomorrow in a state of mutual recognition, not of mutual ignorance." The mosque also provides a pure and spiritual atmosphere that removes people from the materialism and self-interestedness of the surrounding society.[33]

Al-Ghazālī cites the Prophet's reported designation of one of the doors of the mosque for women, his assignment of the rear rows to the women, and his reprimands of men and women who approached the rows of the other sex as evidence of his accommodation of women's attendance at public prayers. However, women's status soon declined to the point that ḥadīth were forged that denied women the right to attend congregational prayers and even asserted that a woman should pray in the gloomiest and most remote corner of her house. Al-Ghazālī declares of the latter report, "The person who transmits this ḥadīth casts behind his back incontrovertibly transmitted practical sunnas (*al-sunan al-ʿamalīya al-mutawātira*) from the Prophet (*ṣāḥib al-risāla*). He regards a praying woman as if she were an impurity (*adhan*) that must be contained in the furthest and most restricted area."[34]

It is notable that the very ḥadīth that al-Ghazālī so fervently disavows was highly praised by Ḥasan al-Bannā, who cited it in support of his argument that Islam consecrates the woman to the domestic sphere. In contrast, al-Ghazālī finds the content of the ḥadīth inherently preposterous and expects his reader to do so as well. He argues that in addition to demeaning women, it is incompatible with the fact that the Prophet allowed women to attend prayers at all hours of the day: "Why did he not counsel them to stay in their houses instead of [making] this vain effort?" Al-Ghazālī's argument here is clearly inspired by that of Ibn Ḥazm, whom he later cites explicitly. However, he again qualifies his arguments for the importance of congregational prayer in light of women's domestic duties:

> A well-authenticated *sunna* establishes that a woman is a shepherd in her home, and is responsible for her flock. There is no doubt that the needs of children, particularly infants, and the preparation of the home

> to receive the man when he returns home from his work, all of that impedes a woman from regular attendance at the five daily congregational prayers. For that reason, we are of the opinion that she must attend congregational prayers [only] after she finishes her household tasks. If she has performed her duties, her man is not permitted to prevent her from going to the mosque.[35]

In other works as well, al-Ghazālī combines an affirmation that women's congregational prayer in mosques is equally as meritorious as men's with the qualification that its desirability is conditional on her fulfillment of her duties as a wife and mother. He asserts (unlike many classical scholars) that the ḥadīth stating that congregational prayer is "twenty-seven degrees" more meritorious than individual prayer applies to both sexes, but continues:

> I do not agree with Ibn Ḥazm that both men and women are equal in the *sunna* of congregational prayer. My opinion is that the woman is a shepherd in her husband's house and she is responsible for her flock. If the man and the children need food to be prepared or relaxation to be provided, the woman must remain in her home and she is not permitted to go to the mosque and leave the home neglected and bereft; she will [still] receive the reward for congregational prayer. As for if she has fulfilled all of her household duties, then it is better for her to go to the mosque and participate in congregational prayers.[36]

He observes in a somewhat later work, "There is no doubt that [a woman's] refraining from going to the mosque for the sake of her responsibilities in the home makes her deserving before God of the reward for congregational prayers, even if she did not attend them."[37]

For al-Ghazālī, the legitimacy and merit of women's attendance at mosques were not merely a theoretical issue; he saw the exclusion of women from mosques as a genuine problem that both disadvantaged observant Muslim women in comparison with their secular sisters and disadvantaged Islam in the world marketplace of religions. A conversation with a friend whose Christian maid had asked for time off to attend church evoked the wistful response that at home, "neither ladies nor maids desire to go to the mosque, because extremists have poured it into their ears that going to the mosque is forbidden."[38] Whereas women of every other faith could participate in public worship, he lamented that "there are tens, nay hundreds of thousands of mosques where the shadow (*shabaḥ*) of a woman cannot be glimpsed in the villages and cities."[39] He reported sympathetically the plight of a group of women who had attempted to pray in the back of a mosque (whose location he does not specify), only to be upbraided by the imam, who cited Qur'anic verses to "prove" that women are forbidden to attend mosques.[40]

By the late twentieth century, the Ikhwān's strong emphasis on the training and deployment of highly qualified individuals committed to their religious program was explicitly framed to include women. Although it continued to emphasize the primary and unique role of women as wives and mothers, it did not envision this role as precluding significant involvement in other spheres of activity. The Ikhwān argued that mothers, as the primary moral, religious, and intellectual influence on their children in the formative years of their lives, must have a sound religious education and an informed grasp of the contemporary world in order to raise a generation of Muslims prepared to undertake the reform of society. Furthermore, most women could be expected to fulfill the task of childbearing and early childhood care by the time they reached middle age, at which point they might choose to take on a larger role in public life.[41] For authors associated with or influenced by the Ikhwān, the mosque is one of the venues of Islamic consciousness-raising and training where the mobilization of women for the Islamic reform of society should occur.

One of the most influential Islamic scholars emerging from Egyptian Ikhwān circles is Yūsuf al-Qaraḍāwī. An Azhar-trained *ʿālim* who nevertheless has adopted the more fluid role of the contemporary *dāʿī*,[42] he has attained international prominence as the featured scholar of a regular show on the al-Jazeera satellite channel, as the founder and supervisor of the popular Islamic website IslamOnline, and as the chair of the European Council for Fatwa and Research.[43] Al-Qaraḍāwī writes at length about women's presence in the mosque during the lifetime of the Prophet in a fatwa responding to an inquiry about the issue of *ikhtilāṭ*, the mixing of unrelated men and women. Al-Qaraḍāwī asserts that this term is alien to the authentic vocabulary of Islamic law and that exaggerated emphasis of this human concept has deprived women of their rightful role in the life of the Muslim community, up to and including participation in warfare (which they partook of in the early days). Here mosque-going is associated with the acquisition of knowledge and with active participation in the life of the *umma*.[44]

Al-Qaraḍāwī's interest in women's mosque-going is not exclusively focused on its capacity to foster social and religious engagement; neither is his approval unconditional. His most concrete comments on women's mosque access occur in a fatwa on women's attendance at the special nighttime prayers (*tarāwīḥ*) held during the month of Ramadan. After affirming the meritorious (although not obligatory) character of *tarāwīḥ* prayers, he continues:

> This includes both men and women, except that it is better for a woman to pray in her home than in the mosque, as long as there is no other benefit resulting from her going to the mosque other than prayer alone, such as hearing a religious exhortation or a lesson in [religious] knowledge, or hearing the Qur'an from a reverent and excellent reciter. Going to the mosque for this purpose is more meritorious and more appropriate, particularly since most men in our time do not instruct their women in the religion.

Furthermore, many women would not "find the desire or resolve that helps them to perform the *tarawīḥ* prayers alone, unlike in the mosque and in congregation." Al-Qaraḍāwī affirms that a wife must seek her husband's permission to go out of the house, "even to the mosque," because of his general authority over the affairs of the house. Nevertheless, he may not forbid her without a valid reason, such as "if the husband is sick and needs her to remain by his side to serve him and take care of his needs, or if she has small children who will be harmed by being left alone in the house for the time required for prayer and there is no one to watch them." In closing, al-Qaraḍāwī points out that it is irrational to exclude women from mosques when they have access to all other arenas of contemporary life: "Modern life has opened doors to the woman; she has gone out of her house to the school, the university, the market, etc., and [yet] has remained deprived of the best spot and the most superior place, which is the mosque."[45]

In this fatwa, the importance of women's mosque attendance lies in its potential for the acquisition of religious knowledge, as well as in its capacity to evoke pious feeling and motivate acts of worship. Indeed, al-Qaraḍāwī's emphasis on the benefits to the woman's spiritual and devotional life (as opposed to simply her acquisition of knowledge, particularly of gendered norms of behavior) is distinctive and striking.[46] However, he subordinates these considerations to the woman's fulfillment of her familial role, subject to the lawfully exercised authority of her husband.

More overt thematic development of the political importance of women's mosque access is present in the work of other Egyptian scholars who moved in the same circles. ʿAbd al-Ḥalīm Abū Shuqqa (1924–95), who was a personal associate of Ḥasan al-Bannā and involved with the Ikhwān (among a diverse set of scholarly and religious contacts and influences), embarked in the 1950s on a project focusing on the role of Muslim women during the lifetime of the Prophet. This resulted two decades later in an influential multivolume compilation titled *The Liberation of Women in the Era of the Prophet's Mission* (*Taḥrīr al-marʾa fī ʿaṣr al-risāla*), with prefaces by Muḥammad al-Ghazālī and Yūsuf al-Qaraḍāwī.

Abū Shuqqa places his extensive treatment of women's presence in mosques in a section titled "The Muslim Woman's Participation in Social Life and Her Meeting with Men," where the multipurpose site of the mosque features prominently among the "public arenas" where the earliest Muslim women took part in communal life.[47] Although he emphasizes that a woman's primary and paramount role revolves around the home and family,[48] he depicts her presence in the Prophet's mosque as enabling a broad engagement with society:

> The mosque is the first institution in Muslim society; firstly, the center of worship; secondly, the center of knowledge; and thirdly, the center of social and political action. Additionally, it is the hall for public meetings and the athletic field when necessary. Due to all of these factors together, the woman was given free scope in the prophetic period to visit the mosque whenever she was able. Her occasional visiting of the

> mosque gave her a direct connection to the public life of the Muslims. In addition to her participation in worship and hearing the Qur'an recited in prayer, she hears lessons on religious knowledge and words of public guidance. She knows something of the social and political news of the Muslims.

For this reason, he asserts, it is not permissible for anyone to deprive a woman of her right to visit the mosque or to force her to pray at home on the pretext that it is more meritorious.[49]

A much younger Egyptian female scholar, Hiba Raʾūf (b. 1965), has put women's mosque access into an even more explicitly politicized context. A political scientist by training, she has independent views and has sometimes been critical of the Muslim Brotherhood; yet her views have clear elements in common with the trend established by thinkers of the Ikhwān.

> The study of the rules of the sharīʿa makes clear that the intent of the Lawgiver was to raise the consciousness of the Muslim community through the acts of worship. The objective of connecting political and social activity with the mosque as an arena of worship was to ensure the continuation of political participation and the development of political consciousness for the Muslim individual. . . . This is something that makes it extremely difficult to falsify his consciousness, divert (*taḥyīd*) his role or marginalize his opinion in the political process, as long as the mosque plays its role.[50]

Raʾūf observes that some studies have examined the way in which, over the course of early Islamic history, various functions originally performed by the mosque branched off and developed as independent institutions. However, "there is a school that holds that the principle is that the [various] cultural functions should remain connected to the mosque, so they do not lose their religious spirit and complementarity continues between that which is religious and that which is social and political in the framework of *tawḥīd* [the unicity of God and of society]."[51]

Raʾūf argues that, even though women suffer no permanent or intrinsic deficits of intellect or competence, a woman may be affected by a temporary deficit in knowledge of public affairs when she is near-confined to the home by pregnancy or breast-feeding. In addition to the role of modern mass media, she emphasizes that in this case the religious duties of a Muslim woman—including public worship—will provide her with at least the minimum degree of awareness of public events requisite for political participation.[52] She stresses that it is obligatory for all women to attend the two yearly festival prayers (a position that is well founded in ḥadīth texts, although not held by most classical scholars). At the festival prayers, "the affairs of the *umma* are discussed," thus ensuring "the minimum degree of consciousness necessary for all women who may be prevented by family responsibilities from attending gatherings like the Friday and congregational prayers." She continues, "As for women who enjoy special competency (*ahlīya*) and a higher degree of consciousness, and whose circumstances permit them to attend Friday and congregational prayers, the prophetic guidance has guaranteed that to them and commanded the man not to prevent them from going."[53]

Because these discussions take place outside of the framework of the *madhhab* system, many of the timeworn tropes of the premodern debate over women's mosque attendance simply disappear. The distinction between old and young women is not mentioned in these texts even to be critiqued. Although it may occasionally be acknowledged that only in middle age will most women enjoy leisure from domestic duties, it is not suggested that younger women are barred from participation by anything but the practical demands of childbearing and housework. Perhaps the most fundamental shift in these thinkers' construction of gender is that femininity is now defined in terms of domesticity and nurture rather than in terms of sexual allure and social danger. Even when Muḥammad al-Ghazālī admonishes that women should go to the mosque modestly dressed because "they have not gone out to a beauty contest or a fashion show,"[54] his concern seems to be more with the religious seriousness of the women than with their potential for sexual volatility. Indeed, the word *fitna*—for centuries the focal point of analyses of the legal status of women's public worship—is largely conspicuous for its absence. Whereas Ḥasan al-Bannā did emphasize this traditional theme, his successors in the later twentieth century elide it (at least in this particular context) in favor of evocations of women's maternal and conjugal duties. The paradigmatic woman is now a desexualized mother and wife; even in her marital role, she is represented less as a source of sexual satisfaction (the key issue in many premodern discussions of limitations of the wife's right to leave the marital home) than of domestic labor and of restful solace from the husband's strivings in the outside world.

In part, this reframing of the issue of women's mosque access may be apologetic. Whereas in classical discussions women's public religious participation was subordinated to concerns about public propriety, in these modern discussions it is often subordinated to concerns about the multiple demands on the Muslim homemaker. Given that these authors are acutely aware both of the gaze of non-Muslims and of the scrutiny of informed and vocal Muslim women, this reinterpretation may seem strategic rather than substantive; fear of women as a sexual threat is replaced by solicitude for them as harried wives and mothers, but in both cases women's participation at the mosque is subordinated to other values. However, the reframing of the problem is more than cosmetic. By the 1980s, these scholars were affirming that women's attendance at mosques was positively desirable—a position that had been affirmed by some (and not all) classical scholars only in the case of elderly women and usually not for all prayers.

Furthermore, all of these thinkers place the value of women's mosque attendance at least partially in the opportunities for education and personal development that it affords. Whereas an eagerness to attend preaching, acquire religious knowledge, and engage in religiously sanctioned sociability is clearly discernible in descriptive accounts of women's activity in premodern mosques, these considerations played little role in juristic works' treatment of the issue of women's mosque attendance. In these modern discussions, the value of the mosque as a venue for women's acquisition of religious, social, and political awareness looms far larger than in any premodern analysis. In part, this may reflect these contemporary scholars' livelier and more direct responsiveness to the actual demands and concerns of female Muslims; unconstrained by the conventions of traditional legal genres and functioning in contexts where women have easier access to learned and popular media, they address women's aspirations more immediately than did their premodern predecessors. Their affirmation of the mosque as an arena for women's participation also reflects their desire to maximize the mobilization of a religiously committed sector of the community that often appeared marginalized by other trends within elite society and their recognition of women as a relatively untapped social and political resource.

Because of shifts in women's social roles in the surrounding society, the significance of the theme of domesticity in the discussion of women's mosque access shifted appreciably from the early to the late twentieth century. At the beginning of the century, reformers such as Rashīd Riḍā, Jamāl al-Dīn al-Qāsimī, and Malāk Ḥifnī Nāṣif saw women's isolation within the home as a source of religious "superstition" and deviance, as well as of ignorance and backwardness. In part, their encouragement of women's religious and educational participation in the public sphere sought to penetrate and control the autonomy of women's religious life by bringing them more firmly within the purview of official Islam. By the end of the century, scholars tended to base the desirability of women's mosque attendance less on the need to stamp out deviant folk practices than on the need to make Islamic guidance and inspiration equally as accessible as other educational, political, and social activities available to women.

SALAFISM

Another major current of twentieth- and twenty-first-century Islam is Salafism, a modern movement that seeks a return to the pristine Islam of the earliest generations of Muslims (the *salaf*). This movement denies the authoritativeness of the classical schools (*madhāhib*), advocates direct consultation of the revelational texts of the Qur'an and ḥadīth, and rejects the complex hermeneutics of the medieval jurisprudential tradition in favor of the assertion that these texts are fundamentally transparent. The reformism of modernists inspired by the work of Rashīd Riḍā can also be seen as a form of Salafism, but in contemporary practice the term is applied to groups that combine direct reference to the primary sources in the field of law with a theological stance rooted in the thought of early figures such as Aḥmad ibn Ḥanbal.[55]

The rise in Saudi oil wealth in the final quarter of the twentieth century, combined with the prestige of presiding over the Islamic holy places of the Ḥijāz, enabled the international dissemination of the form of Salafism rooted in the thinking of the eighteenth-century reformer Muḥammad ibn ʿAbd al-Wahhāb. Ibn ʿAbd al-Wahhāb himself wrote primarily about doctrinal and theological matters; to the extent that he dealt with issues of normative behavior, he focused primarily on devotional acts (such as shrine visitation and the wearing of amulets) whose theological implications he believed to conflict with the central Islamic tenet of *tawḥīd* (the unicity of God). Formally, the legal thinking of the Saudi religious establishment that claims his legacy is based both on direct reference to the Qur'an and ḥadīth and on an underlying continuity with Ḥanbalī doctrine.

To the extent that the early Wahhābī movement manifested distinctive attitudes toward women's mosque attendance, these seem to have been mixed. Women are recorded to have been present at Friday prayers in some early communities within the movement, and in the nineteenth century Richard Burton could identify the "two principal tenets" of Wahhābīs as "public prayer for men daily, for women on Fridays, and rejection of the Prophet's mediation."[56] Nevertheless, as time passed Wahhābīs were also known for their severity in limiting women's presence in mosques; describing Mecca in 1925, just after the Saudi conquest, Eldon Rutter writes that "the Wahhâbîs discourage the presence of women in the Mosque, even at prayer time. They do not obstruct female hâjjis, but in the months when Mekka was empty of hâjjis, I have seen the Aghas, and also special guards from the Sharta, or City police, drive Mekkan women from the Haram with blows of their sticks."[57]

Nevertheless, Saudi scholars do not appear to have produced formal arguments for the exclusion of women from the mosque. In a fatwa dated 1374/1955, the powerful Muftī of Saudi Arabia, Muḥammad ibn Ibrāhīm Āl al-Shaykh, wrote that "women are not to be prevented from going to mosques with their children during Ramadan; the sunna indicates that women went to the mosque with their children during the time of the Prophet (peace be upon him!)...." It is significant that the issue raised by the questioner was specifically the presence of small children accompanying the women and that the one reservation expressed by the muftī was that women should take care that their youngsters did not soil the mosque. The specific reference to Ramadan probably reflects local practice, as there is nothing in the textual evidence or argumentation of the fatwa that is specific to Ramadan.[58]

Probably the most influential Saudi scholar of the second half of the twentieth century was ʿAbd al-ʿAzīz Ibn Bāz (1909–99), who served as Grand Muftī of Saudi Arabia (appointed in 1992), head of the Council of Senior Scholars, and president of the Permanent Council for Research and Fatwas in addition to a number of other important posts. In a widely circulated fatwa, he is asked by a female questioner, "Is it permissible for a woman to pray in the mosque if she is [fully] covered and modest, has not applied perfume, and does not engage in vain display and she does so only out of devotion to God, except that her husband is not pleased with her [doing so]?" Ibn Bāz replies, "A woman is entitled to pray in the mosque if she is [fully] covered and does not wear perfume; her husband is not entitled to prevent her from doing so if she adheres to proper comportment as defined by the sharīʿa, because the Prophet said, 'Do not forbid the maidservants of God from [going to] the mosques of God.'" He continues to emphasize that this applies "even if her husband is not happy." Nevertheless, "if she prays in her home and does not go out in order to please her husband and avoid causes of *fitna*, it is better, because the Prophet said, 'Do not forbid the maidservants of God from [going to] the mosques of God, and their homes are better for them.'"[59]

Other fatwas issued by the Saudi religious establishment express the same basic position: it is permissible for a woman to attend prayers in the mosque as long as she adheres to sharʿī standards of modesty and gender segregation; her husband may not forbid her from doing so, provided that she fulfills these conditions; nevertheless, it is more meritorious for her to pray at home. This stance corresponds closely to classical Ḥanbalī doctrine, as expressed by such scholars as Ibn Qudāma, Ibn Taymīya, and Ibn Qayyim al-Jawzīya. The Saudi Permanent Council for Fatwas consistently supports women's right to attend mosques, even when it conflicts with established custom or with traditional legal doctrines. For instance, one fatwa responds to a query from a recent convert to Islam in an unnamed location who attempted to attend Friday prayers with his (also newly converted) wife, only to have her turned away by an imam who claimed that women were forbidden to attend mosques. The fatwa resoundingly affirms that a properly attired woman may not be forbidden from attending the mosque.[60] In another case, the council responds to a questioner who states that "in our country" (one published version of the fatwa specifies Tanzania) a controversy has arisen over the claim that women may not enter mosques because they are ritually impure, a position that the council briskly refutes.[61] Yet another fatwa summarily dismisses a query whether women are entitled to pray in the mosque "in this time," a clear allusion to the postclassical doctrine (dominant among Ḥanafīs and, to a lesser extent, among other schools) that women should no longer be admitted to mosques in the decadent conditions of latter-day Muslim societies.[62]

Nevertheless, these Saudi fatwas are distinguished both by their insistence on the superior merit of women's worship within the home and by their more general concern about women's public visibility. The fatwa responding to the new convert, although affirming his wife's right to attend the mosque, states severely that "if she is exposed so that some part of her body that unrelated men are forbidden to look at is visible, or she is wearing perfume, in this case it is not permissible for her to leave her home, let alone to go out to the mosque and pray there, because of the *fitna* that this involves."[63] It is notable that, whereas contemporary fatwas issued by scholars associated with al-Azhar or with the Muslim Brotherhood tend to deemphasize the issue of *fitna* and instead focus on women's domestic duties, official Saudi fatwas continue to invoke women's sexual allure as the rationale for the limitation of their access to mosques—and indeed of any mobility in public. Like most classical scholars, these Saudi scholars emphasize the inherently superior merit of women's prayer within the home (rather than alluding to the likelihood that they will be busy with their obligations as wives and mothers). The emphasis on the educational and spiritual benefits of mosque attendance is also notable by its absence. To a leading question about whether it is better for a woman to pray during the nights of Ramadan at home or in the mosque, "particularly if there are sermons and admonitions in [the mosque]," Ibn ʿUthaymīn responds briskly that it is always superior for a woman to pray at home because of the ḥadith to this effect and because of the fear of *fitna*; as for sermons and other instruction, she can listen to tapes.[64] The contrast with al-Qaraḍāwī's fatwa on the same subject could not be more acute.

The influential Ibn ʿUthaymīn summarizes his views on women's mosque attendance in a commentary on a widely studied Ḥanbalī legal manual, where he states that, although (based on the relevant ḥadīth) a man may not forbid wife to go to the mosque, he nevertheless should *dissuade* her from doing so, due to the corruption of the times. He may actually forbid her from going to the mosque for purposes other than prayer (for instance, for sightseeing or to attend a lecture), and he *must* forbid her if she is perfumed or the like. Ibn ʿUthaymīn hermeneutically resolves the tension between the Prophet's command not to bar women from mosques and his preference for women's prayer within the home by positing that they are directed to different addressees: the command not to forbid women is addressed to men, and the statement that "your homes are better for you" is directed to women.[65]

The opinions of Saudi establishment scholars are characterized by their direct references to the relevant ḥadīth texts,[66] by a clear continuity with Ḥanbalī doctrine, and by a lively concern with the issue of *fitna* and the hazards of women's public mobility and visibility. As Khaled Abou El Fadl has analyzed in great detail, overall the concept of *fitna* plays a pivotal role in Saudi scholars' legal reasoning on issues relating to women.[67] Indeed, within Saudi Arabia the official scholars' overt affirmation of women's right to attend the mosque seems to have had less practical impact than their emphasis on the relative undesirability of women's public worship and the perils of their visibility to men.[68] Nevertheless, their consistent and emphatic assertion of women's entitlement to pray in mosques contrasted with customary practice and received doctrine in many parts of the broader Islamic world in which their fatwas have been consumed.

Another of the scholars most influential among late-twentieth-century Salafīs globally was Nāṣir al-Dīn al-Albānī (1914–99), an Albanian whose family migrated to Damascus when he was a child. A self-taught ḥadīth expert, al-Albānī taught in Saudi Arabia in the early 1960s, but he was expelled from the country in 1963 as a result of his insistence that face veils were not mandatory for women, and ultimately settled in Jordan. He also objected to the lingering Ḥanbalī loyalties of the Wahhābī scholars.[69] His reevaluations of the authenticity of ḥadīth, though sometimes controversial,[70] have become an almost universal point of reference among Salafīs[71] and are influential even outside of their circles. His followers have made large numbers of his legal opinions available on the Internet, largely in the form of audio clips of Arabic question-and-answer sessions with groups of his followers.

Women's mosque access is one of the many areas where al-Albānī's opinions are both distinctive and influential. Al-Albānī notes that there is an apparent discrepancy between the ḥadīth texts establishing that it is more meritorious for a woman to pray at home and the fact that women in the Prophet's lifetime zealously attended the mosque. The seeming contradiction is resolved by the fact that worshipping in the mosque provided them with an opportunity to acquire knowledge about religious obligations (*farāʾiḍ*) that they could not obtain in their homes.[72] Asked whether it is preferable for a woman to pray at home or in a mosque, al-Albānī replies that it is preferable for her to pray at home unless there is a lesson or preaching at the mosque from which she will learn; in this case, the legal ruling is reversed, and it becomes more meritorious for her to pray in the mosque. If all she is going to do in the mosque is pray in congregation, on the other hand, it is better for her to stay at home.[73] (Elsewhere he elaborates that "it is better for a woman to pray in her home, indeed, in her own private room; the more she is removed from sight, the better it is for her."[74])

Like Ibn Bāz, al-Albānī takes the textually literalist position that a man is actually forbidden to prevent his wife from going to the mosque—a question that he dispatches with the citation of the relevant ḥadīth and the curt observation, "The text is explicit about that."[75] However, elsewhere he affirms that a man can (and presumably should) forbid his wife from visiting the mosque if there is fear of *fitna* (for instance, if she has perfumed herself with incense). He argues that this does not conflict with the prohibition on preventing women from going to the mosque; what is actually prohibited in that ḥadīth is "the jealousy (*ghayra*) that issues from arrogance, rather than the fear of *fitna*."[76]

To this point, al-Albānī would appear to be promoting a view rather similar to that of the Ikhwān. The emphasis is on the educational value of a woman's presence in the mosque, which can outweigh other considerations. However, al-Albānī ultimately has a far more restricted concept of women's public Islamic activities, including those pursued in the mosque. Al-Albānī does acknowledge that some women can (and should) obtain a degree of religious knowledge that will allow them to advise and instruct other women; indeed, he notes that many women are hesitant to consult male scholars about their private affairs. Nevertheless, he has significant reservations about the nature and location of their religious activities. (Indeed, he alludes with some bitterness to "Islamic groups [*jamāʿāt*]" that organize women to engage in religious activity or activism [*nashāṭ*].)[77]

Asked about female preachers (*dāʿiyāt*) who visit other women in their homes to give them religious instruction, he first objects to the label and role of the "preacher" (*dāʿī*) as a contemporary innovation.[78] He asserts, based on verse 33:33 of the Qur'an, that women are to "remain in their houses" and that it is not legitimate for a woman to travel about as if she were a man, which he considers an instance of gender-inappropriate behavior (*tashabbuh*) forbidden by the sunna.[79] Instead, women should visit such a female authority in her home. (This appears to be preferable because it involves individual forays outside of the home by a number of women rather than constant professional mobility by a single woman.) It is different, in his view, for an individual woman to visit the mosque in order to acquire knowledge (which he affirms to be legitimate) than for a woman to hold lessons in the mosque or to mimic male behavior by traveling about as a religious teacher. Al-Albānī laments, "Things have gotten to the point in our country [presumably Jordan] and perhaps in other countries that [the female preacher] ascends the pulpit in the mosques and delivers lessons to women; there may be men in the courtyard of the mosque, and when the time comes for them to pray in congregation, they come in and pray! There is no doubt, and I do not hesitate to say, that this is an innovation!"[80] On another tape, he mournfully recounts an anecdote in which he and a group of men are refused entrance to a mosque because it is full of women listening to a female preacher. He declares it to be "an innovation without basis in the sunna" for a woman to teach in a mosque.[81]

In yet other respects, however, al-Albānī took positions on women's usage of mosques that were strikingly liberal. For example, he firmly rejects the classical position that menstruating women should not tarry in mosques (or, according to other scholars, that they should not even enter). He argues this point on the basis of two proofs, one negative and the other positive. The negative proof is the juristic axiom that the default setting for all acts is permissibility; prohibition requires textual evidence. Al-Albānī argues that, although there are several widely cited ḥadīth prohibiting both menstruating women and persons in a state of *janāba* (major impurity occurring after sexual intercourse or emission) from entering the mosque, none of them are authentic according to rigorous standards of ḥadīth criticism. Thus, the relevant ḥadīth do not have sufficient evidentiary value to override the original presumption of permissibility. The positive proof is an anecdote in which the Prophet is on the ḥajj and tells his wife ʿĀʾisha, who has gotten her period, that she can do everything except circumambulate the Kaʿba and pray. Al-Albānī infers from this statement that a menstruating woman can do anything else a pilgrim might do in the Great Mosque and that, if the Prophet had intended to bar her from the mosque altogether, he would have said so explicitly. Al-Albānī also cites a ḥadīth in which the Prophet asks ʿĀʾisha to fetch something for him from the mosque; when she objects that she is menstruating, he declares that "your menstruation is not in your hand."[82] Al-Albānī is not unique in his approach to this question; the influential Egyptian Salafī Muṣṭafā al-ʿAdawī, the author of a popular manual on women's ritual practice, similarly argues that a menstruating woman may spend time within the mosque.[83]

The extent to which the elimination (or at least the questioning) of menstrual purity concerns might transform women's mosque access should not be overemphasized because (as we have seen in the first chapter of this study) ritual purity was not an issue that played a central role in the discussion of women's mosque attendance in classical legal works. The assumption of some modern studies that women's mosque access has historically been limited primarily by purity strictures is thus unfounded, at least on the level of formal legal discourse.[84] However, it does appear that in some regions of the Islamic world the possibility of menstrual pollution has been used as a rationale for the general exclusion of women from mosques or for the exclusion of premenopausal women.[85] Furthermore, even in contexts where the issue of menstrual pollution is not raised as a bar to the access of women in general, it could present challenges for individual women (particularly in the case of regular classes located in the mosque). As one of Richard Gauvain's female Salafī informants in Cairo observed, because a woman has her period every month, "I just don't see the good in stopping her studies every time. I mean, *haram*! (smiling) It's enough that we have to leave our prayers. It's ok for some of the sisters to say that we can just study at home, but what if the classes take place in the mosques...?"[86] Nevertheless, the question remained controversial even within this network of Salafī women. Continuous attendance at mosque lessons inevitably revealed that a woman was not avoiding the mosque during menstruation (particularly when she abstained from prayer), giving rise to comment and debate. As another woman observed, "There will always be someone whispering something about her [i.e., the woman assumed to be menstruating]. Actually, sometimes it's not whispering. Many of us aren't shy!"[87]

In addition to his distinctive views on ritual purity, al-Albānī passionately opposed the relegation of women to separate and enclosed prayer spaces from which they could not see or (often) even hear the imam. Rather, he emphasized that women in the time of the Prophet had prayed in rows behind the men without a physical barrier and that this is the preferable arrangement if the mosque can accommodate it. Although it is permissible for women to pray on another level by hearing rather than seeing the imam, this is a suboptimal arrangement to which they should resort only if no space is available on the same floor where the male worshippers are located.[88] Separate women's prayer rooms, al-Albānī argues, are a religious innovation (*bid*ʿ*a*)—a devastating accusation to be made by a Salafī in a ritual context. Al-Albānī's position here is one of textual literalism, although the emotional tenor of his response—he speaks repeatedly of the "confinement (*ighlāq*)" or "imprisonment (*ḥabs*)" of women in enclosed women's sections—suggests a genuine personal distress at the exclusion of women from the main prayer space. He vigorously rejects the argument that new arrangements have been necessitated by the corruption of society. It is true that women are now entering mosques improperly dressed, in short *jilbābs* (overdresses) or transparent stockings, which motivates people to remove them from men's view by enclosing them in separate prayer rooms. However, the correct approach is to restore society to its proper Islamic character—and women to their proper Islamic dress—rather than to introduce innovations that may invalidate women's prayer. Defying a long history of legal argumentation that we have encountered in previous chapters of this study, he asserts that it is impermissible to create new legal rulings deviating from the sunna as a remedy for problems created by the decadence of society; the solution is to reform society, not to exclude women from the main space of the mosque.[89] As long as women are properly covered, there is no need to conceal them from unrelated men—and thus no reason to erect a barrier in the mosque.[90]

Overall, in his affirmation that it is meritorious for a woman to go to the mosque if it affords her religious instruction, his denial of her husband's entitlement to detain her from the mosque without cause, his dismissal of the purity concerns surrounding menstruation, and his firm rejection of women's relegation to separate and isolated prayer spaces, al-Albānī presents a strikingly positive attitude toward women's usage of mosques. His views are both clearly grounded in ḥadīth (as one would expect based on his methodological approach) and occasionally outspoken in their distaste for exaggerated limitations on women's religious practice. However, his sunna-based inclusiveness toward women is significantly tempered by his broader view of gender roles, which posits that women's activities are fundamentally defined by a primary commitment to house and home. As he states in another fatwa, "The basic principle . . . is that a woman should know that she was created to remain in her home, serve her husband, and bring up her children if she has children."[91] However, his ultimate concern is not with public versus private space, but with issues of gender and authority; he repeatedly emphasizes that a woman can go to the mosque to learn, but denies that she can do so to teach. Although the theme of *fitna* is not completely absent from his arguments, he is much less preoccupied with the potential sexual volatility of women's presence in mosques than with the maintenance of proper role distinctions between men and women. It is characteristic that in his work denying any obligation for women to cover their faces, he cites the superior merit of women's prayer within the home in the context of the rule that women must avoid any resemblance (*tashabbuh*) with men in their dress and comportment.[92] In al-Albānī's view, women's concealment from the male gaze is not merely an issue of physical allure but also inextricably intwined with proper femininity as mandated by the Qur'an and sunna.

The practical impact of al-Albānī's teachings in the circles where his scholarship is revered can be determined only by further research. It seems possible that his affirmation of women's right to presence (and even visibility) in the main space of the mosque could be wielded advantageously by Salafī women. However, in other cases his reservations about women's public teaching may have helped to diminish the existing magnitude and variety of women's mosque-based activities. Anne Sofie Roald reports that in 1991 she attended women's lessons in a mosque in Jordan, but "[w]hen I returned to Jordan in the beginning of 1992 I discovered that these lessons had been moved to private homes. It was explained to me that al-Albānī had proclaimed a *fatwa* that women should not have meetings in the mosques."[93] The fatwa in question was presumably the one discussed above that suggests that women preachers should hold sessions privately in their homes.

Al-Albānī is somewhat unusual for explicitly scrutinizing and critiquing the very existence (as well as the nature) of separate women's prayer space within mosques. The legal legitimacy and parameters of enclosed women's prayer space are not a subject that is extensively discussed in the classical *fiqh* literature. As we have seen in chapter 2, it is clear that over time there were various forms of accommodation for women within mosques that involved different degrees of spatial and architectural separation (including *maqāṣīr* enclosed by openwork screens and eventually upstairs balconies). As emerges from the North African fatwas discussed there, the construction of such barriers could evoke both approval and critique; even though they served a widely accepted purpose (concealing women from the view of unrelated men), they could also be questioned as a potential *bidʿa* (innovation).

The history of different forms of architecturally separate women's prayer space in mosques (particularly outside of Andalusia and North Africa) remains to be written, and their development may be difficult to reconstruct. However, it appears that in many cases separate women's accommodations were introduced quite late. For instance, in the Prophet's mosque in Medina it was only in the mid-nineteenth century that an enclosed women's prayer space was constructed.[94] The enclosure for women's prayer is referred to in nineteenth-century sources as a "cage (*qafaṣ*)" made of wood, probably openwork (one source describes it as a "lattice," *shabaka*).[95] It is notable that contemporary Arabic sources refer to the women's enclosure as something that was "newly created" or "innovated" (*uḥditha*), an expression that ordinarily has negative connotations in the context of Islamic ritual practice (although clearly none are intended in this case).[96]

The lengthy inquiry that elicited the fatwa on women's mosque attendance from the Egyptian Dār al-Iftāʿ in 1940 suggests the degree to which the legitimacy of separate women's prayer rooms within the mosque remained debatable at the time. It carefully specifies that the walls of the proposed women's room, adjacent to the main body of the mosque, would stop two meters below the roof, allowing the women to hear preaching and participate in prayer. The resulting fatwa applies the criteria for valid prayer leadership from classical sources, which in some cases allow someone to follow an imam from a separate building or across a visual barrier.[97] By the late twentieth century, muftīs rarely bothered to address the legitimacy of separate women's accommodations and often stated that designated women's space is desirable without specifying the nature of its visual and aural access to the imam.[98]

In accordance with their general allegiance to the patterns mandated by ḥadīth, establishment Saudi muftīs sometimes allude to women's prayer in rows behind the men without a barrier as a valid, or indeed normative, option.[99] However, other fatwas affirm that the introduction of enclosed women's sections has rendered obsolete the ḥadīth instructing women to seek out the back rows of the congregation by removing its rationale; women who are completely separated and concealed from men should seek out the front, rather than the back, row.[100] Indeed, anecdotal evidence about arrangements in Saudi mosques suggests that (outside of the anomalous, if symbolically potent, context of Mecca) in contemporary Saudi mosques, complete architectural separation of women's sections is the norm, including (at least in some cases) such innovative measures as the installation of one-way glass.[101] Thus, the norms applied within Saudi Arabia do not appear to correspond to the textually literalist model promoted in some of the opinions of its most august fatwa-issuing body. Overall, it is surprising how little formal legal discourse has addressed the location and quality of women's prayer space and the visual and aural accessibility of the imam. For instance, the rise and spread of the "women's balcony" as a norm for large and official mosques in the twentieth century is architecturally unmistakable, but textually near-invisible in the legal sources.[102] Given the concerns that are being raised by some Muslim women, this issue is likely to generate more legal debate in the future.

CONCLUSION

The proliferation of legal opinions supporting women's mosque access, beginning in the early twentieth century and reaching full flower in the 1980s, has certainly been accompanied by substantial increases in women's mosque attendance in many parts of the Middle East. However, causality is difficult to gauge. Did the development of normative justifications for women's mosque attendance by influential thinkers embolden women to attend mosques (and motivate mosque administrators to accommodate them), or did many women's increasingly successful assertion of their desire to be present in mosques ultimately lead to acknowledgment by religious thinkers? Although it is likely that there was a complex interrelationship between the two, only fieldwork-based case studies can elucidate the process in specific contexts. The following remarks, which place the legal developments analyzed above in the context of documented developments in concrete practice, can only be general and provisional.

In many cases, access to mosque space is clearly a demand raised by women wielding contemporary forms of religious legitimation. Soraya Duval quotes a female member of the Ikhwān as declaring, "During the time of the Prophet women attended the prayers from dawn to sunset. No man has the right to deprive a woman from her Islamic mission." Another Egyptian woman interviewed by Duval, this one a Salafī, "expressed her anger at a man who didn't want her to attend to her lesson with a group of children in the main part of the mosque—usually the men's domain." The woman reported, "I thought to myself,

I am wearing the Islamic dress, and am totally respectable in every way, so I just gave him my back and ignored him totally."[103] The claim that proper dress and comportment entitle a woman to her place in the mosque, already articulated by some medieval scholars, is here asserted with new vigor and assurance.

However, historical examples suggest that the encouragement of women's mosque attendance does not always spring from the wishes and advocacy of women—or even from a simple recognition of women's human equality or pious aspirations. Rather, in some cases religious activists and authorities have sought to encourage women's mosque participation when the role of Islam in society is disputed, making it strategically important to maximize the mobilization of observant Muslims. This appears to have been the case, for instance, in some Muslim regions in the early decades of the Soviet Union.[104] (Conversely, authorities seeking to limit political and religious mobilization overall may discourage women from going to mosques.[105]) The same has been true of some politically activist Shīʿīs in the late twentieth century. Classical Imāmī Shīʿī jurisprudence emphasized the desirability of women's worship within the home,[106] but Ayatollah Khomeini asserted that, if women could shield themselves from the view of men, it was better for them to pray in the mosque.[107] Similarly, the Lebanese Ayatollah Muḥammad Ḥusayn Faḍl Allāh (who is widely revered in Ḥizb Allāh circles and strongly supports women's Islamic mobilization) writes that "there is no distinction in terms of the desirability of prayer in the mosque between men and women."[108] Certainly these developments have been promoted and welcomed by many women; however, others have had reservations about the use of the mosque to promote political and governmental agendas, including the definition of gender roles.[109]

Thus, modern advocates of women's mosque attendance have sometimes sought to co-opt women, as well as to liberate them—although both projects can and do coexist and women are by no means passive objects of these enterprises. Advocates may seek to assimilate women into their normative frameworks, as well as to mobilize them for their sociopolitical programs. Heba El-Kholy, examining the mosque participation of lower-income women in Cairo in the late 1990s, emphasizes the salience in Friday sermons and women's mosque classes of "the articulation of appropriate roles for women," including such themes as "the need for women to demonstrate modesty, *hishma*, and to fulfill their obligations to their husband and children."[110] Studies of other locations have reached similar conclusions.[111] However, other work has demonstrated both that women's engagement in mosque instruction leads to opportunities for active appropriation and reinterpretation of religious gender norms and that women's mastery of religious knowledge and techniques of pious self-cultivation may be empowering even in the absence of overt challenges to established norms.[112] Ultimately, women's ability to master such norms empowers as well as constrains them.

Despite the widely attested expansion of women's mosque attendance in many places in recent decades, developments in women's relationship to mosque space should not be described simply in terms of a unidirectional progress toward greater affirmation and inclusion. For instance, even within the Middle Eastern and North African region examined in this study, the expansion of women's access often does not apply to village mosques or to small neighborhood mosques.[113] To the extent that women have come to participate more extensively and in greater numbers in mosques shared with men, it can be argued that women's mosque usage has been reconfigured and restructured rather than that women have simply gained mosque access where they had earlier lacked it. Writing of her fieldwork in Cairo in the 1970s, Evelyn Early describes how working-class women use the mosque: "while baladi men tend to gather at the coffeehouses, baladi women's one acceptable meeting place is in the mosques, where they not only pray but also sit in the quiet coolness, a welcome respite from the dusty streets outside." Furthermore, although these women prayed in specially demarcated areas during congregational worship, "at other times they move[d] freely throughout the mosque."[114] This fluid pattern of use of mosque space resembles that documented for earlier centuries.

As we have seen in earlier chapters of this study, before the "Islamic revival" of the 1970s and 1980s in many cases women did use mosque space, but often at different times and for different social and ritual activities than men; strict spatial separation of the sexes was often limited to the specific context of congregational prayer. The developments of the late twentieth century, in contrast, have tended to draw more women into the mosque at the same times, and for the same activities, as men.[115] Thus, for instance, attendance at Friday prayers has become a more salient feature of many women's religious lives. As the temporal patterning of women's mosque usage has shifted toward greater parallelism with men's (although in most places they are still by no means identical), in some cases the spatial patterning of mosque space has tended to become more rigid. Renata Holod and Hasan-Uddin Khan remark that the rise of the women's balcony as a quasi-standard feature of major mosques in the second half of the twentieth century has had

> a paradoxical impact on the place of women in the mosque. Insistence on a clearly defined physical separation for them, unlike the more flexible arrangements adopted in the past, has in practice limited the actual and potential use of the space by women. On the other hand, by making the provision of some space for them nearly obligatory in a new mosque, the programming has ensured the inclusion of facilities for women in instances where they had previously been denied access.[116]

In her moving memoir *A Border Passage*, Leila Ahmed reflects on Islam as she received it from the women of her family and contrasts it with some aspects of the Islamic literary heritage. She argues that this "women's Islam" was sustained in the past in part by women's limited ability to read works of religious scholarship and in part by the fact that "mosque going was not part of the tradition for women at any class level. . . . Women therefore did not hear the sermons that men heard. And they did not get the official (male, of course) orthodox interpretations of religion that men (or some men) got every Friday." Nevertheless, "visiting mosques privately and informally to offer personal prayers" was something "which women have always done."[117]

Of course, historically women have not always been excluded from the formal and learned Islam propagated in mosques, nor have they always found it inimical to their interests. Furthermore, as we have seen in earlier chapters, mosques have by no means been sites for the practice and dissemination of a monolithic "orthodox" Islam. To the discomfiture of many scholars, both preaching and ritual practice have been responsive to the demands of their audiences, which often (at least in the times and places we have examined) included women as well as men. In some cases, modern mosques are subject to more extensive bureaucratic control by the state, limiting the pluralism of the messages communicated there. Furthermore, major modern mosques are often not the vital and populist multipurpose spaces that they sometimes were in centuries past. Only by appreciating the long and varied history of women's usage of mosque space can we recognize the ways in which mosques have historically functioned as women's space as well as men's, and the complex issues of inclusion and autonomy raised by recent developments.

NOTES

INTRODUCTION

1. Julia Pardoe, *City of the Sultan; and Domestic Manners of the Turks, in 1836* (London: Henry Colburn, 1837), 2:51, 2:53.
2. Leila Ahmed, *Women and Gender in Islam: Historical Roots of a Modern Debate* (New Haven, CT: Yale University Press, 1992), 60–61, 79.
3. Ibid., 101, see also 184, 228.
4. See, for instance, *The Oxford Encyclopedia of the Modern Islamic World*, ed. John L. Esposito (New York: Oxford University Press, 1995), s.v. "Women and Islam: Women's Religious Observances" (by Valerie J. Hoffman-Ladd); *Encyclopedia of Women and Islamic Cultures*, ed. Suad Joseph, vol. 4, *Economics, Education, Mobility and Space* (Leiden: Brill, 2007), s.v. "Space: Mosques, Arab States (excepting the Gulf and North Africa)" (by Asma Sayeed); Asma Sayeed, "Early Sunni Discourse on Women's Mosque Attendance," *ISIM Newsletter* 7 (2001): 10; Hilary Kalmbach, "Social and Religious Change in Damascus: One Case of Female Religious Authority," *British Journal of Middle Eastern Studies* 35 (2008): 38. On the expansion of women's presence and religious authority in mosques in the contemporary Arab world, see also Saba Mahmood, *Politics of Piety* (Princeton, NJ: Princeton University Press, 2005); Annabelle Böttcher, "Islamic Teaching Among Sunni Women in Syria," in *Everyday Life in the Muslim Middle East*, ed. Donna Lee Bowen and Evelyn A. Early (Bloomington: Indiana University Press, 2002), 290–99; Masooda Bano and Hilary Kalmbach, eds., *Women, Leadership, and Mosques: Changes in Contemporary Islamic Authority* (Leiden: Brill, 2012).

5. *Encyclopaedia of Islam*, 2nd ed., s.v. "Masdjid, I. In the Central Islamic Lands" (by J. Pedersen); Christopher Melchert, "Whether to Keep Women Out of the Mosque: A Survey of Medieval Islamic Law," in *Authority, Privacy and Public Order in Islam, Proceedings of the 22nd Congress of L'Union Européenne des Arabisants et Islamisants*, ed. B. Michalak-Pikulska and A. Pikulski (Leuven: Uitgeverij Peeters, 2006), 59–69; Behnam Sadeghi, *The Logic of Law-Making in Islam: Women and Prayer in the Legal Tradition* (Cambridge: Cambridge University Press, 2012).
6. See, for instance, Wiebke Walther, *Women in Islam* (Princeton, NJ: Markus Wiener, 1993), 53 and fig. 12; Huda Lutfi, "Manners and Customs of Fourteenth-Century Cairene Women: Female Anarchy Versus Male Sharʿi Order in Muslim Prescriptive Treatises," in *Women in Middle Eastern History: Shifting Boundaries in Sex and Gender*, ed. Nikki R. Keddie and Beth Baron (New Haven, CT: Yale University Press, 1991), 106, 107. For observations on the diversity in the magnitude of women's presence in the mosque before the revival of the 1970s and 1980s, see Robert W. Fernea and Elizabeth W. Fernea, "Variation in Religious Observance Among Islamic Women," in *Scholars, Saints, and Sufis*, ed. Nikki R. Keddie (Berkeley: University of California Press, 1972), 385–89.
7. Sayeed, "Space: Mosques," 549.
8. It seems likely that this pattern reflects both the de facto distribution of women's ritual activities in many places and the biases of a scholarly approach that often assumes "orthodoxy" to be exclusive of (and inimical to) women. An early, but characteristic example of this trend is Lois Beck's 1980 article "The Religious Lives of Muslim Women," which contains sections devoted to "saints and saintly lineages," "tombs and shrines," "prayer and religious gatherings" (excluding canonical *ṣalāt* prayers), "religious orders," "spirits," "curing and spirit possession cults," "evil eye," "spells," and "vows"—but no separate discussion devoted to canonical *ṣalāt* prayers, Ramadan fasting, or pilgrimage to Mecca. Lois Beck, "The Religious Lives of Muslim Women," in *Women in Contemporary Muslim Societies*, ed. Jane I. Smith (Lewisburg, PA: Bucknell University Press, 1980), 28–60.
9. For one plausible example of this inference, see Anne H. Betteridge, "Muslim Women and Shrines in Shiraz," in *Mormons and Muslims*, ed. Spencer J. Palmer (Provo, UT: Religious Studies Center, Brigham Young University, 1983), 129–30; Beck also concludes that "since women are often encouraged not to attend the mosque, they find other places of sanctity and worship, such as tombs and shrines." Beck, "Religious Lives," 50, see also 44–45.
10. ʿAbd al-Raḥmān ibn ʿAlī Ibn al-Jawzī, *Kitāb Aḥkām al-nisāʾ* (Ṣaydā/Beirut: al-Maktaba al-ʿAṣrīya, 1424/2003), 96.
11. Ibid., 149.

12. Cited in Lutfi, "Manners and Customs," 101; Ibn al-Ḥājj al-ʿAbdarī, *Kitāb al-Madkhal* (Beirut: Dār al-Kutub al-ʿIlmīya, 1415/1995), 3:220.
13. As has been widely noted, he does affirm that, if a woman's husband is unable or unwilling to provide her with necessary religious knowledge, she may go out without his permission to inquire about it. However, he seems to regard this as a measure of last resort to provide the knowledge necessary for the woman to fulfill her basic religious duties rather than an open-ended justification for her pursuit of religious education in mosques and madrasas. Ibn al-Ḥājj, *Madkhal*, 1:197–200, 2:388.
14. Shampa Mazumdar and Sanjoy Mazumdar, "In Mosques and Shrines: Women's Agency in Public Sacred Space," *Journal of Ritual Studies* 16 (2002): 167.
15. Ibn al-Ḥājj, *Madkhal*, 2:383–87, 2:393–401; see also Aḥmad ibn ʿAlī al-Maqrīzī, *al-Mawāʿiẓ wa'l-iʿtibār bi-dhikr al-khiṭaṭ wa'l-āthār* (Cairo: Maktabat al-Madbūlī, 1998), 2:9. On the legally disputed practice of holding court in mosques, see Emile Tyan, *Histoire de l'organisation judiciaire* (Leiden: Brill, 1960), 111, 115, 223, 276–79; Daniella Talmon-Heller, *Islamic Piety in Medieval Syria: Mosques, Cemeteries and Sermons Under the Zangids and Ayyūbids (1146–1260)* (Leiden: Brill, 2007), 51–52; Christian Lange, *Justice, Punishment, and the Medieval Muslim Imagination* (Cambridge: Cambridge University Press, 2008), 46 and n125 there. It was Ottoman policy to establish separate law courts. However, even in Ottoman Egypt, some adjudication continued to occur in mosques; see Evliya Çelebi, *Siyāḥatnāmeh-ye Miṣr*, translated into Arabic by Muḥammad ʿAlī ʿAwnī (Cairo: Maṭbaʿat Dār al-Kutub wa'l-Wathāʾiq al-Qawmīya bi'l-Qāhira, 1424/2003), 273. On the also disputed, but also prevalent practice of scholars and indigents dwelling in the mosque, see George Makdisi, *The Rise of Colleges: Institutions of Learning in Islam and the West* (Edinburgh: Edinburgh University Press, 1981), 22–23; Talmon-Heller, *Mosques, Cemeteries and Sermons*, 52, 54.
16. See the examples from the *Arabian Nights* (fictional, but reflective of cultural assumptions) discussed by Muhsin al-Musawi, who notes that in one tale the mosque is the place where an unrelated woman and man are able to meet and confer. Muhsin J. al-Musawi, *The Islamic Context of* The Thousand and One Nights (New York: Columbia University Press, 2009), 88–89.
17. For instance, see M. de Chabrol, "Essai sur les moeurs des habitans modernes de l'Égypte," in *Description de l'Égypte, ou Recueil des Observations et des Recherches qui ont étés faites en Égypte pendant l'expédition de l'armée française* (Paris: Imprimerie Royale, 1822), l'État Moderne, vol. 2, pt. 2, 379 (Biodiversity Heritage Library e-book): "The mosques present a monstrous collection of individuals engaged in things most contrary to the majesty of the place, and sometimes in disgusting activities. One

can see mixed indiscriminately devotees at prayer, unfortunates destroying their vermin, idlers sleeping, and artisans engaged in their professions; these abuses are tolerated, and Egypt is not the only Muslim region where they are consecrated by custom." Translation mine.

18. Ibn al-Ḥājj, *Madkhal*, 1:32–38, 1:44.
19. See, for instance, Ibn Duqmāq, *al-Intiṣār li-wāsiṭat ʿiqd al-amṣār* (Beirut: al-Maktaba al-Tijārīya li'l-Ṭibāʿa wa'l-Nashr wa'l-Tawzīʿ, n.d.), 1:74–75.
20. See, for instance, Mālik ibn Anas [Saḥnūn ibn Saʿīd al-Tanūkhī], al-*Mudawwana al-kubrā* (Beirut: Dār Ṣādir, facsimile of Cairo, n.d.), 5:199 (oaths are to be administered in the locations in mosques that are most awe-inspiring), 5:201 (Jews and Christians should be made to give oaths in locations they venerate, thus in their own places of worship). This work will be cited henceforth as Saḥnūn, *Mudawwana*.
21. Robert C. Davis, "The Geography of Gender in the Renaissance," in *Gender and Society in Renaissance Italy*, ed. Judith C. Brown and Robert C. Davis (London: Longman, 1998), 20.
22. Fadwa El Guindi, *Veil: Modesty, Privacy and Resistance* (Oxford, UK: Berg, 1999), 81.
23. For a recent survey of the academic debate over the authenticity of ḥadīth, see Jonathan A. C. Brown, *Hadith: Muhammad's Legacy in the Medieval and Modern World* (Oxford, UK: Oneworld, 2009), 197–239.
24. See, for instance, Howayda al-Harithy, "Female Patronage of Mamluk Architecture in Cairo," in *Beyond the Exotic: Women's Histories in Islamic Societies*, ed. Amira El-Azhary Sonbol (Cairo: American University in Cairo Press, 2006), 321–35; Lucienne Thys-Şenocak, *Ottoman Women Builders: The Architectural Patronage of Hadice Turhan Sultan* (Aldershot, Hampshire, UK: Ashgate, 2006).
25. The connection between women's patronage of mosque construction and their physical presence in mosques is complex and sometimes difficult to reconstruct. Writing of Ottoman royal women, Gülru Necipoğlu observes that "if Sinan's female patrons did not frequent the Friday mosques they founded . . ., their patronage of this building type takes on a special significance." Gülru Necipoğlu, *The Age of Sinan: Architectural Culture in the Ottoman Empire* (London: Reaktion Books, 2005), 69; see also Thys-Şenocak, *Ottoman Women Builders*, 220, 230, which suggests how Hadice Turhan Sultan may have physically and visually accessed the mosque she built. Conversely, it has been noted that, despite the increase in women's mosque attendance in many regions in the twentieth century, women were almost absent as patrons when compared with the premodern record. See Renata Holod and Hasan-Uddin Khan, *The Contemporary Mosque: Architects, Clients and Designs since the 1950s* (New York: Rizzoli, 1997), 20.
26. On this issue, see Ahmed Elewa and Laury Silvers, "I *Am* One of the People: A Survey and Analysis of Legal Arguments on Women-Led Prayer

in Islam," *Journal of Law and Religion* 26 (2010–11): 141–71; Simonetta Calderini, "Contextualizing Arguments About Female Ritual Leadership (Women Imāms) in Classical Islamic Sources," *Comparative Islamic Studies* 5 (2009): 5–32.

27. For a critique of this practice, see Melchert, "Whether to Keep Women Out of the Mosque," 67–68.
28. See Talal Asad, *The Idea of an Anthropology of Islam* (Washington, DC: Center for Contemporary Arab Studies, Georgetown University, 1986), 15–16; Marion Holmes Katz, *The Birth of the Prophet Muḥammad: Devotional Piety in Sunni Islam* (London: Routledge, 2007).
29. Lutfi, "Manners and Customs," 99–121.
30. It should not be assumed that scholars' reactions to women's piety were always condemnatory, however. For examples of often sympathetic scholarly reception of noncanonical ritual practices, see Raquel Ukeles, "Innovation or Deviation: Exploring the Boundaries of Islamic Devotional Law" (PhD diss., Harvard University, 2006).
31. See, for instance, Ibn al-Ḥājj, *Madkhal*, 2:300. On the cultivation of pious desires, see Mahmood, *Politics of Piety*, 123.
32. On this genre, see Maribel Fierro, "The Treatises Against Innovations (*kutub al-bidaʿ*)," *Der Islam* 69 (1992): 204–46.
33. For the use of records of women's pew rentals, see Margaret Aston, "Segregation in Church," in *Women in the Church: Papers Read at the 1989 Summer Meeting and the 1990 Winter Meeting of the Ecclesiastical History Society*, ed. W. J. Sheils and Diana Wood (Cambridge, MA: Basil Blackwell, 1990), 264–65, 266–67; Katherine L. French, *The Good Women of the Parish: Gender and Religion After the Black Death* (Philadelphia: University of Pennsylvania Press, 2008), 100–15; Karla Goldman, *Beyond the Synagogue Gallery: Finding a Place for Women in American Judaism* (Cambridge, MA: Harvard University Press, 2000), 54.
34. For examples of women being disciplined for nonattendance at church, see Patricia Crawford, *Women and Religion in England 1500–1720* (London: Routledge, 1993), 58–59; Jeffrey R. Watt, "Women and the Consistory in Calvin's Geneva," *Sixteenth Century Journal* 24 (1993): 429–39.
35. See, for instance, Necipoğlu, *Age of Sinan*, 69–70.
36. Abū Shāma al-Maqdisī, *Tarājim rijāl al-qarnayn al-sādis wa'l-sābiʿ*, ed. Muḥammad Zāhid al-Kawtharī (Cairo, 1366/1947), 221–22.

1. WOMEN'S MOSQUE ATTENDANCE AS A LEGAL PROBLEM

1. Mālik, *Muwaṭṭaʾ*, *Kitāb al-Qibla*, *Bāb Mā jāʾa fī khurūj al-nisāʾ ilā al-masājid*. This is a remarkably well attested and widely distributed ḥadīth; it is transmitted in the *Ṣaḥīḥ*s of Bukhārī (d. 256/870), Muslim (d.

261/875), and Ibn Khuzayma (d. 311/923); the *Sunan* of Abū Dāwūd (d. 275/889); the *Musnads* of Aḥmad ibn Ḥanbal (d. 241/855), al-Ḥumaydī (d. 219/834), and Abū ʿAwāna (d. 316/928); and the *Muṣannaf* of Ibn Abī Shayba (d. 235/849), among other important ḥadīth compilations. Some versions of the ḥadīth conclude with a reservation—either "and let them go out unperfumed" or "and their homes are better for them" (see, for instance, Abū Dāwūd, *Sunan, Kitāb al-Ṣalāt, Bāb Mā jāʾa fī khurūj al-nisāʾ ilā al-masājid*). For references, see Muḥammad al-Saʿīd Basyūnī Zaghlūl, *Mawsūʿat aṭrāf al-ḥadīth al-nabawī al-sharīf* (Beirut: Dār al-Kutub al-ʿIlmīya, n.d.), 7:218–19. As we will see below, the ḥadīth was also cited by al-Shāfiʿī (d. 204/820). As discussed in the introduction, this study will not address the issue of the authenticity of ḥadīth texts; however, it is worth noting that no parties to the juristic debate over women's mosque attendance disputed the authenticity of this report, even when they were strongly opposed to women's public prayer.

2. This report is also transmitted (with variations) in the *Musnad* of Ibn Ḥanbal, the *Ṣaḥīḥ* of Muslim, and the *Sunan* of al-Nasāʾī (d. 303/915–16).
3. Versions of this anecdote are transmitted in the *Ṣaḥīḥ* of Bukhārī, the *Musnad* of Ibn Ḥanbal, and the *Muṣannaf* of Ibn Abī Shayba, as well as in Ibn Saʿd, *Kitāb al-Ṭabaqāt al-kubrā* (Beirut: Dār Ṣādir/Dār Bayrūt, 1377/1958), 8:267; and Ibn Qutayba al-Dīnawarī, *ʿUyūn al-akhbār* (Cairo: Maṭbaʿat Dār al-Kutub al-Miṣrīya, 1349/1930), 4:115. For a discussion of some of the different versions of this anecdote, see Marion Holmes Katz, *Prayer in Islamic Thought and Practice* (New York: Cambridge University Press, 2013), 191–92.
4. This report is transmitted in the *Ṣaḥīhs* of Bukhārī, Muslim, and Ibn Khuzayma; the *Sunan* of Abū Dāwūd; the *Musnads* of Aḥmad ibn Ḥanbal and Isḥāq ibn Rāhawayh (d. 238/853); and the *Muṣannaf* of Ibn Abī Shayba.
5. For a representative selection of relevant ḥadīth texts from the *Ṣaḥīḥ*s of Bukhārī and Muslim, see ʿAbd al-Ḥalīm Muḥammad Abū Shuqqa, *Tahrīr al-marʾa fī ʿaṣr al-risāla* (Kuwait: Dār al-Qalam li'l-Nashr wa'l-Tawzīʿ, 1430/2009), 2:179–94.
6. On the authenticity and dating of the *Mudawwana*, see Norman Calder, *Studies in Early Muslim Jurisprudence* (Oxford, UK: Clarendon Press, 1993), 1–19; and the critique of his arguments in Jonathan Brockopp, *Early Mālikī Law: Ibn ʿAbd al-Ḥakam and His Major Compendium of Jurisprudence* (Leiden: Brill, 2000), particularly 94–100.
7. Mālik ibn Anas [Saḥnūn ibn Saʿīd al-Tanūkhī], *al-Mudawwana al-kubrā* (Beirut: Dār Ṣādir, n.d.), 1:106. (This work will henceforth be referenced as Saḥnūn, *Mudawwana*.)
8. Ibid., 2:464. It is perhaps indicative of the waning role of mosques in women's lives (or the growing resistance of legal thinkers to women's presence there) that in later centuries that subsequent Mālikī works tend

to omit the right of mosque attendance when discussing the mobility of the divorced woman in her waiting period.

9. Ibid., 1:106.
10. The *Mudawwana* states that Mālik used the same terminology in discussing the special prayers performed on the occasion of an eclipse (*ṣalāt al-khusūf*): "Mālik said: 'I consider it appropriate for a woman to perform the *ṣalāt al-khusūf* in her house'; he [also] said, 'And I do not see any harm in women who are mature (*al-mutajāllāt min al-nisāʾ*) going out for the prayer for a solar eclipse (*khusūf al-shams*).'" Saḥnūn, *Mudawwana*, 1:164.
11. Abū'l-Walīd Ibn Rushd, *al-Bayān wa'l-taḥṣīl wa'l-sharḥ wa'l-tawjīh wa'l-taʿlīl fī masāʾil al-Mustakhraja*, ed. Muḥammad Ḥajjī (Beirut: Dār al-Gharb al-Islāmī, 1404/1984), 1:420; compare Ibn Abī Zayd al-Qayrawānī, *al-Nawādir wa'l-ziyādāt ʿalā mā fī'l-Mudawwana min ghayrihā min al-ummahāt*, ed. ʿAbd al-Fattāḥ Muḥammad Ḥilw (Beirut: Dār al-Gharb al-Islāmī, 1999), 1:536.
12. As we shall see, an awkward emendation of this word in the text of the *Ṭabaqāt al-kubrā* of Ibn Saʿd suggests that it was unfamiliar to later transmitters or scribes. The modern handbook *Mawsūʿat al-fiqh al-mālikī* renders this phrase as "*kull imraʾa mutajalbiba*" (every woman wearing a *jilbāb*, an overdress). Khālid ibn ʿAbd al-Raḥmān al-ʿAkk, *Mawsūʿat al-fiqh al-mālikī* (Damascus: Dār al-Ḥikma, 1993), 3:160. Even within the Mālikī commentarial tradition, the term caused some confusion; the sixth-century AH author Muḥammad ibn Manṣūr al-Maghrāwī defines the *mutajālla* as a woman "who displays her face because of her advanced age" and insouciantly derives it from the root j-l-y rather than j-l-l. Muḥammad ibn Manṣūr al-Maghrāwī, *Ghurar al-maqāla fī sharḥ gharīb al-Risāla*, published with Ibn Abī Zayd al-Qayrawānī, *al-Risāla al-fiqhīya*, ed. al-Hādī Ḥammū and Muḥammad Abū'l-Ajfān (Beirut: Dār al-Gharb al-Islāmī, 1406/1986), 262.
13. Ibn Manẓūr, *Lisān al-ʿarab* (Beirut: Dār Ṣādir, 1990/1410), art. "j-l-l."
14. Ibn Saʿd, *Kitāb al-Ṭabaqāt al-kubrā*, ed. Carl Brockelmann (Leiden: Brill, 1904), 8:317; Ibn Saʿd, *Kitāb al-Ṭabaqāt al-kubrā* (Beirut: Dār Ṣādir/Dār Bayrūt, 1377/1958), 8:296. Both of these editions have "*takhālalnā*" rather than "*tajālalnā*"; however, this does not make sense. Furthermore, the lexicographer Ibn Manẓūr discusses the report under the root j-l-l and understands it to mean "had become mature/elderly."
15. ʿUmar is reported to have whipped a slave woman whom he saw veiled, crying, "Cast off your veil, bondswoman! Are you trying to look like a free woman?!" See Ibn Abī Shayba, *Muṣannaf Ibn Abī Shayba fī'l-aḥādīth wa'l-āthār*, ed. Saʿīd al-Laḥḥām (Beirut: Dār al-Fikr, 1428–29/2008), 2:135 (parallels on 2:134–35).
16. Ibn Rushd, *al-Bayān*, 9:335; Ibn Abī Zayd al-Qayrawānī, *Kitāb al-Jāmiʿ fī'l-sunan wa'l-ādāb wa'l-ḥikam wa'l-maghāzī wa'l-tārīkh wa-ghayr dhālika*, ed.

ʿAbd al-Majīd Turkī (Beirut: Dār al-Gharb al-Islāmī, 1990), 243; Aḥmad al-Qabbāb al-Fāsī, *Mukhtaṣar kitāb al-Naẓar fī aḥkām al-naẓar bi-ḥāssat al-baṣar li-Ibn al-Qaṭṭān* (Riyadh: Maktabat al-Tawba, 1418/1997), 229; Ibn Qayyim al-Jawzīya, *al-Ṭuruq al-ḥukmīya fī'l-siyāsa al-sharʿīya aw al-firāsa al-murḍiya fī aḥkām al-siyāsa al-sharʿīya* (Cairo: Dār al-Ḥadīth, 1423/2002), 239.

17. Qayrawānī, *Jāmiʿ,* 283 (but compare al-Qayrawānī, *Nawādir,* 2:361, where there is no distinction by age).
18. Qayrawānī, *Jāmiʿ,* 243.
19. Saḥnūn, *Mudawwana,* 5:144; Abū'l-Walīd al-Bājī, *al-Muntaqā sharḥ Muwaṭṭaʾ al-Imām Mālik* (Beirut: Dār al-Kitāb al-ʿArabī, 1404/1984), 5:184. Mālik reportedly counseled that the judge should hold sessions in the outer courtyard of the mosque (*riḥābihi al-khārija*) so that non-Muslims and menstruating women would have access.
20. Saḥnūn, *Mudawwana,* 5:134–35.
21. Ibid., 5:136.
22. Qayrawānī, *Nawādir,* 8:157.
23. Abd al-Razzāq al-Ṣanʿānī, *al-Muṣannaf,* ed. Ḥabīb Allāh al-Aʿẓamī (Beirut: al-Majlis al-ʿIlmī, n.d.), 3:146–47. Ibn Jurayj's concern is presumably that verse 62:9 of the Qur'an ("O believers! When the call to prayer is given on Friday, go earnestly to the Remembrance of God") apparently applies to women as well as men.
24. Al-Jāḥiẓ, *al-Ḥayawān,* ed. ʿAbd al-Salām Muḥammad Hārūn (Cairo: Maktabat Muṣṭafā al-Bābī al-Ḥalabī wa-Awlādihi, 1356/1938), 1:303. Interestingly, leaving the home only at night also appears to be a practice cultivated by elite Christian women in pre-Islamic Arabia. See Eleanor A. Doumato, "Hearing Other Voices: Christian Women and the Coming of Islam," *International Journal of Middle East Studies* 23 (1991): 184.
25. Bukhārī, *Ṣaḥīḥ, Kitāb Mawāqīt al-ṣalāt, Bāb Waqt al-fajr.*
26. See Ibn Qutayba, *ʿUyūn al-akhbār,* 4:115.
27. Bukhārī, *Ṣaḥīḥ, Kitāb al-Jumʿa, Bāb* 13 (*Ḥaddathanā Ibn ʿUmar*).
28. Bukhārī, *Ṣaḥīḥ, Kitāb al-Adhān, Bāb Khurūj al-nisāʾ ilā 'l-masājid bi'l-layl wa'l-ghalas*; Muslim, *Ṣaḥīḥ, Kitāb al-Ṣalāt, Bāb Khurūj al-nisāʾ ilā 'l-masājid idhā lam yatarattab ʿalahi fitna wa-annahā lā takhruj mutaṭayyiba.*
29. ʿĀʾisha bint Saʿd ibn Abī Waqqāṣ, who is said to have met Mālik, is reported to have been seen wearing clothes dyed with saffron at the nighttime (*ʿatama*) prayers on several occasions. Another anecdote describes her coming out of the mosque in Medina with a group of women, holding a lighted torch (*ḍawʾ nār*)—again, presumably in the hours of darkness. Ibn Saʿd, *al-Ṭabaqāt al-kubrā* (Beirut: Dār Ṣādir/Dār Bayrūt, 1377/1958), 8:468.
30. Printed with Aḥmand ibn Ghunaym al-Nafrāwī, *al-Fawākih al-dawānī ʿalā Risālat Ibn Abī Zayd al-Qayrawānī* (Beirut: Dār al-Kutub al-ʿIlmīya, 1418/1997), 1:408.

31. Ibid., 1:450, 1:505–6.
32. Ibn ʿAbd al-Barr, *al-Istidhkār al-jāmiʿ li-madhāhib fuqahāʾ al-amṣār wa-ʿulamāʾ al-aqṭār fīmā taḍammanahu al-Muwaṭṭaʾ min maʿānī al-raʾy wa'l-āthār wa-sharḥ dhālika bi'l-ījāz wa'l-ikhtiṣār*, ed. Sālim Muḥammad ʿAṭāʾ and Muḥammad ʿAlī Muʿawwaḍ (Beirut: Dār al-Kutub al-ʿIlmīya, 1423/2002), 2:468.
33. Cited from *al-Ṭirāz* in al-Ḥaṭṭāb al-Ruʿaynī, *Mawāhib al-jalīl li-sharḥ Mukhtaṣar Khalīl* (Beirut: Dār al-Kutub al-ʿIlmīya, 1416/1995), 2:451; also in Shihāb al-Dīn Aḥmad ibn ʿAbd al-Ghaffār al-Mālikī, *Izālat al-ghishāʾ ʿan ḥukm ṭawāf al-nisāʾ baʿd al-ʿishāʾ*, Cairo ms., Dār al-Kutub, 109 Fiqh Mālik, microfilm 1965, 98b–99a. *Al-Ṭirāz* is the title of a massive unfinished commentary on the *Mudawwana* by Sind ibn ʿInān that was used extensively by al-Ḥaṭṭāb. See Muḥammad Ibrāhīm, ʿAlī, *Iṣṭilāḥ al-madhhab ʿinda al-mālikīya* (Dubai: Dār al-Buḥūth li'l-Dirāsāt al-Islāmīya wa-Iḥyāʾ al-Turāth, 1421/2000), 330.
34. Ibn Rushd, *Bayān*, 1:421.
35. This word was used to refer to a woman's embonpoint; see Murtaḍā al-Zabīdī, *Tāj al-ʿarūs*, s.v. "th-kh-n." Ibn Rushd regarded a woman's fleshiness to be an alluring quality demanding greater concealment from public view; see *Bayān*, 2:222, where he states that a magnificently fat woman should not go out at all. Compare the references to the "corpulent woman" (*al-jasīma*) cited in Ḥaṭṭāb, *Mawāhib*, 3:486. On the cultivation of fatness in a somewhat later period in Cairo, see Ibn al-Ḥājj, *Madkhal*, 1:273–77.
36. Ibn Rushd, *Bayān*, 1:422.
37. It appears, with slight variations in wording, in the *Ṣaḥīḥs* of Bukhārī and Muslim, the *Muṣannaf* of Ibn Abī Shayba, the *Musnad* of Ibn Ḥanbal, and other sources; for references, see Zaghlūl, *Mawsūʿa*, 8:96–97.
38. See Saḥnūn, *Mudawwana*, 1:83, 1:337, 1:377, 2:12, 2:49, 5:254 (civil unrest); 1:174, 1:175 (torment of the grave).
39. Of about thirty uses of the term *fitna* in *al-Umm*, I have located only one that associates it specifically with the theme of women and sexual temptation; see Muḥammad ibn Idrīs al-Shāfiʿī, *al-Umm* (Beirut: Dār al-Maʿrifa, n.d.), 5:144 (which relates the rationale for marriage to "the sexual desire and fear of *fitna* that was created in [women]").
40. ʿAlī ibn Khalaf Ibn Baṭṭāl, *Sharḥ Ibn Baṭṭāl ʿalā Ṣaḥīḥ al-Bukhārī*, ed. Muṣṭafā ʿAbd al-Qādir ʿAṭā (Beirut: Dār al-Kutub al-ʿIlmīya, 1424/2003), 2:543.
41. Cited in Ibn Rushd, *Bayān*, 1:421. For the general Mālikī doctrine relating to conditions added to marriage contracts, see Wahba al-Zuḥaylī, *al-Fiqh al-islāmī wa-adillatuhu* (Damascus: Dār al-Fikr, 1425/2005), 9:6541–43.
42. Ibn Rushd, *Bayān*, 4:377.
43. See, for instance, Ibn ʿArafa al-Warghamī, *al-Mukhtaṣar al-fiqhī*, ed. Saʿīd Sālim Fāndī (Beirut: Dār al-Madār al-Islāmī, 2003), 1:301.

44. Cited from *al-Ṭirāz* in Ḥaṭṭāb, *Mawāhib*, 2:451; also in Ibn ʿAbd al-Ghaffār, *Izāla*, 98b-99a.
45. Ibn Rushd, *Bayān*, 4:377–78.
46. See also ibid., 17:629–30.
47. Ibid., 1:421.
48. Cited in Muḥammad ibn Khalīfa al-Washtānī al-Ubbī, *Ikmāl Ikmāl al-muʿlim*, printed with Muslim ibn Ḥajjāj al-Qushayrī al-Naysābūrī, *Ṣaḥīḥ Muslim* (Beirut: Dār al-Kutub al-ʿIlmīya, 1415/1994), 2:332–33.
49. Ibn ʿAbd al-Ghaffār, *Izāla*, 100b–101a.
50. Ibid., 97b, 101a (reference to ʿIyāḍ's *Tanbīhāt*).
51. Ubbī, *Ikmāl*, 2:333.
52. Cited in Ibn ʿArḍūn, *Muqniʿ al-muḥtāj fī ādāb al-zawāj*, ed. ʿAbd al-Salām al-Zayyānī (Beirut: Dār Ibn Ḥazm, 1430/2010), 2:763–64.
53. Ibn ʿAbd al-Barr, *Fatḥ al-barr fī'l-tartīb al-fiqhī li-Tamhīd Ibn ʿAbd al-Barr*, arranged by Muḥammad ibn ʿAbd al-Raḥmān al-Maghrāwī (Riyadh: Majmūʿat al-Tuḥaf al-Nafāʾis al-Dawlīya, 1416/1996), 5:44. Ibn ʿAbd al-Barr did not consider this restriction to be absolute or unquestionable, however; see *Fatḥ*, 5:26–27. On additions to ḥadīth, see Ibn al-Ṣalāḥ, *ʿUlūm al-ḥadīth* (Damascus: Dār al-Fikr, 1406/1986), 85–87.
54. Ibn Baṭṭāl, *Sharḥ*, 2:543; also see 2:545.
55. Bājī, *Muntaqā*, 1:342.
56. ʿAlī ibn Aḥmad al-ʿAdawī, *Ḥāshiyat al-shaykh ʿAlī ibn Aḥmad al-ʿAdawī*, published with Muḥammad ibn ʿAbd Allāh al-Khurashī, *Ḥāshiyat al-Khurashī ʿalā Mukhtaṣar sayyidī Khalīl*, ed. Zararīyā ʿUmayrāt (Beirut: Dār al-Kutub al-ʿIlmīya, 1417/1997), 2:168.
57. Published with Haṭṭāb, *Mawāhib*, 2:449–50.
58. Ibid., 2:547, 2:549. One ambiguity in this formulation is whether, in the statement "her husband is not legally compelled," the pronoun refers to the "young woman" of the previous phrase or to women in general. This led some later scholars to ponder whether an older woman did, in fact, have a legally enforceable right to go to the mosque. ʿAbd al-Bāqī ibn Yūsuf al-Zurqānī, *Sharḥ al-Zurqānī ʿalā Mukhtaṣar sayyidī Khalīl* (Beirut: Dār al-Kutub al-ʿIlmīya, 1422/2002), 2:33–34.
59. Khalīl ibn Isḥāq al-Jundī, *al-Tawḍīḥ fī sharḥ al-Mukhtaṣar al-farʿī li-Ibn al-Ḥājib*, ed. Aḥmad ibn ʿAbd al-Karīm Najīb (Cairo: Markaz Najībawayh, 1429/2008), 2:477.
60. Ibid., 1:476. Cited in Ibn ʿAbd al-Ghaffār, *Izāla*, 103b; ʿAdawī, *Ḥāshiya*, 2:168.
61. See ʿAbd Allāh Ibn Abī Jamra, *Bahjat al-nufūs wa-taḥallīhā bi-maʿrifat mā lahā wa-ʿalayhā*, ed. Bakrī Shaykh Amīn (Beirut: Dār al-ʿIlm li'l-Malāyīn, 1997), 1:339 (compare also 1:301).
62. The editor of *Bahjat al-nufūs* observes that the admiring comments of Ibn al-Ḥājj in his *Madkhal* are the major source of biographical information about Ibn Abī Jamra. See editor's preface, dāl—hāʾ.

63. Ibn al-Ḥājj al-ʿAbdarī, *Kitāb al-Madkhal* (Beirut: Dār al-Kutub al-ʿIlmīya, 1415/1995), 2:399.
64. Cited in Ibn ʿAbd al-Ghaffār, *Izāla*, 103b.
65. Cited in ibid., 103b. Al-Aqfahsī was a student of Khalīl's and served as a judge in Cairo.
66. Ibn ʿAbd al-Ghaffār speculates that he may have been referring to the depredations of government troops (*ʿaskar al-sulṭān*) who seized women from public baths and raped them; this inference clearly reflects his desire to relate al-Aqfahsī's disapproval of women's mosque attendance to extraordinary circumstances rather than to the routine bad behavior of women. *Izāla*, 105a.
67. *Nisāʾ mujtahidāt*. This phrase may refer to women qualified to engage in independent legal reasoning, who certainly existed. In context, however, it seems more likely to refer to women who are zealous in their ritual practices (*al-mujtahidāt fī'l-ʿibāda*); for this usage in a near-contemporary Maghribī text, see Ibn Baṭṭūṭa, *Riḥlat Ibn Baṭṭūṭa* (Ṣaydā/Beirut: al-Maktaba al-ʿAṣrīya, 1425/2005), 1:41.
68. Reading *ʿalāma* rather than *ʿalāqa*, as it appears in the printed text.
69. Aḥmad ibn Yaḥyā al-Wansharīsī, *Al-Miʿyar al-muʿrib wa'l-jāmiʿ al-mughrib ʿan fatāwā ahl ifrīqīya wa'l-andalus wa'l-maghrib*, ed. Muḥammad Ḥajjī (Rabat: Wizārat al-Awqāf wa'l-Shuʾūn al-Islāmīya li'l-Mamlaka al-Maghribīya, 1401/1981), 11:227–28. For al-Walīdī, see Aḥmad Bābā al-Tunbuktī, *Kitāb Nayl al-ibtihāj bi-taṭrīz al-Dībāj* (Fez: al-Maṭbaʿ al-Jadīda, n.d.), 101.
70. Al-Fāsī/Ibn al-Qaṭṭān, *Mukhtaṣar Kitāb al-naẓar*, 230.
71. Ubbī, *Ikmāl*, 2:333.
72. Muḥammad ibn Ibrāhīm ibn Khalīl al-Tatāʾī, *Jawāhir al-durar fī ḥall alfāẓ al-Mukhtaṣar*, ms. Rabat, al-Khizāna al-Ḥasanīya, #11225 (I), 62a; see also al-Khurashī, *Ḥāshiya*, 2:270.
73. Zurqānī, *Sharḥ*, 2:33.
74. Aḥmad ibn Ghunaym al-Nafrawī, *al-Fawākih al-dawānī ʿalā Risālat Ibn Abī Zayd al-Qayrawānī* (Beirut: Dār al-Kutub al-ʿIlmīya, 1418/1997), 408.
75. Khurashī, *Ḥāshiya*, 2:168. Al-Khurashī shares al-Tatāʾī's opinion about young women going to Friday prayers, however. *Ḥāshiya*, 2:270.
76. Aḥmad ibn Muḥammad al-Ṣāwī, *Bulghat al-sālik li-aqrab al-masālik ilā madhhab al-imām Mālik* (Cairo: ʿĪsā al-Bābī al-Ḥalabī, 1978), 1:336.
77. Khurashī, *Ḥāshiya*, 2:168.
78. Ibrāhīm ibn Marʿī al-Shabrakhītī, *Sharḥ ʿalā Mukhtaṣar Khalīl* ([Morocco], [1900?]), 1:334. As is noted in a correction in the margin of the printed text, there is a "*lā*" missing; however, the end of the sentence ("even if she is far away . . .") clearly implies the negation, and it is cited this way by al-ʿAdawī.
79. Printed with Khurashī, *Ḥāshiya*, 2:168.

80. Muḥammad ibn Aḥmad al-Dasūqī, *Ḥāshiyat al-Dasūqī ʿalā al-Sharḥ al-kabīr* (Cairo: ʿĪsā al-Bābī al-Ḥalabī, n.d.), 1:335–36. It seems probable that this version of Ibn Rushd's discussion is a secondary development. The itemized lists of permissible activities are likely to have originated as explanatory glosses that were later understood as an integral part of the text. Some of the discrepancies presumably reflect scribal errors; for instance, *al-farṭ* ("rare occasions") can easily be mistaken for *al-farḍ* ("obligatory" prayers) in written Arabic, and *najāba* ("nobility") is graphically very similar to *thakāna* ("portliness"). In both cases, the version in the edition of Ibn Rushd's *Bayān wa'l-tabyīn* is the *lectio difficilior* and thus more likely to reflect the author's original wording. A thirteenth-century rendition of Ibn Rushd's opinion replaces *al-farṭ* with *al-nudra*, which confirms the meaning and suggests that some people sought to replace it with a more common term. Aḥmad ibn Idrīs al-Qarāfī, *al-Dhakhīra*, ed. Saʿīd Aʿrāb (Beirut: Dār al-Gharb al-Islāmī, 1994), 2:230.
81. Ṣāwī, *Bulghat al-sālik*, 1:336.
82. Bājī, *Muntaqā*, 1:342.
83. Cited in Ḥaṭṭāb, *Mawāhib*, 2:451.
84. Abū Bakr Ibn al-ʿArabī, *al-Qabas fī sharḥ Muwaṭṭaʾ Ibn Anas* (Beirut: Dār al-Kutub al-ʿIlmīya, 1419/1998), 1:255.
85. Ubbī, *Ikmāl*, 2:332.
86. Ibn al-Ḥājj, *Madkhal*, 2:400.
87. Ibn Abī Jamra, *Bahja*, 1:339.
88. *Encyclopaedia of Islam*, 2nd ed., ed. H.A.R. Gibb (Leiden: Brill, 1954–2002), s.v. "Ibn Ḥazm, Abū Muḥammad ʿAlī b. Aḥmad b. Saʿīd" (by R. Arnaldez).
89. See ibid.
90. For discussions of some of the gendered issues and themes in the writings of Ibn Ḥazm, see Abdel Magid Turki, "Femmes privilégiées et privilèges féminins dans le système théologique et juridique d'Ibn Ḥazm," *Studia Islamica* 47 (1978): 25–82; Camilla Adang, "Women's Access to Public Space According to *al-Muḥallā bi-l-Āthār*," in Manuela Marín and Randi Deguilhem, eds., *Writing the Feminine: Women in Arab Sources* (London: I. B. Tauris, 2002), 75–94.
91. ʿAlī ibn Aḥmad Ibn Ḥazm al-Andalusī, *al-Muḥallā bi'l-āthār*, ed. ʿAbd al-Ghaffār Sulaymān al-Bundārī (Beirut: Dār al-Kutub al-ʿIlmīya, 1425/2003), 2:174; see Adang, "Women's Access," 85.
92. Ibn Ḥazm, *Muḥallā*, 2:167. For another summary of Ibn Ḥazm's arguments on this point, see Adang, "Women's Access," 82–86; see also Asma Sayeed, "Early Sunni Discourse on Women's Mosque Attendance," *ISIM Newsletter* 7 (2001): 10.
93. Ibn Ḥazm, *Muḥallā*, 2:170.
94. Ibid., 2:169, 2:170.

95. Ibid., 2:172.
96. Ibid., 2:176.
97. Ibid., 2:173–74.
98. On the rare occasions when Ibn Ḥazm uses the term *fitna* in *al-Muḥallā*, it tends to be in its meaning of "civil strife" or "punishment" (for instance, in the grave). On some occasions, he uses it in the sense of "sexual temptation/disorder caused by the presence of a woman among men," but this tends to be within citations from the legal opinions of other authorities; for instance, see *al-Muḥallā*, 3:361.
99. Adang notes that "Ibn Ḥazm imposes no special restrictions on young women nor does he makes [sic] special allowances for older women for, in his view, they are equal." "Women's Access," 82.
100. See Ignaz Goldziher, *The Ẓāhirīs: Their Doctrine and Their History*, trans. Wolfgang Behn (Leiden: Brill, 1971), 169–71. Aron Zysow has questioned whether Ibn ʿArabī can rightly be termed a Ẓāhirī on the basis of his legal theory. See Aron Zysow, "The Economy of Certainty: An Introduction to the Typology of Islamic Legal Theory" (PhD diss., Harvard University, 1984), 495–96.
101. Muḥyī al-Dīn Ibn ʿArabī, *al-Futūḥāt al-makkīya*, facsimile ed. (Beirut: Dār Ṣādir, n.d.), 1:741. Compare Ibn Ḥazm, *Muḥallā*, 2:177, where he argues that there is no sin in a man's not liking his wife to go to the mosque, even if it is permitted by God, because "There is no blame (*ḥaraj*) in a person's liking something forbidden, and he is not capable of turning away his heart from it; all that matters is whether he forbears or does it."
102. Shāfiʿī, *Umm*, vol. 5 (final, unnumbered volume printed with *Mukhtaṣar al-Muzanī*), 513–15. For a skeptical view of the attribution and dating of *al-Umm*, see Calder, *Studies*, 67–85. For a more recent discussion, see Christopher Melchert, "The Meaning of *Qāla 'l-Shāfiʿī* in Ninth Century Sources," in *ʿAbbasid Studies: Occasional Papers of The School of ʿAbbasid Studies* (Leuven: Uitgeverij Peeters, 2004), 277–301.
103. The distinction between general (*ʿāmm*) and specific or particular (*khāṣṣ*) statements is an important feature of al-Shāfiʿī's jurisprudence; see Muḥammad ibn Idrīs al-Shāfiʿī, *al-Risāla*, ed. Aḥmad Muḥammad Shākir (n.p., n.d.), 53–62, 226–28; Joseph E. Lowry, *Early Islamic Legal Theory: The* Risāla *of Muḥammad ibn Idrīs al-Shāfiʿī* (Leiden: Brill, 2007), 69–87.
104. Shāfiʿī, *Umm*, 5:513.
105. See Lowry, *Early Islamic Legal Theory*, 327–30.
106. Shāfiʿī, *Umm*, 5:514–15. Here al-Shāfiʿī seems to be obliquely alluding to the belief that women could go to public prayers during the hours of darkness.
107. Saḥnūn, *Mudawwana*, 1:152. Interestingly, in the *Mudawwana* this report is immediately followed by another one (whose *isnād* also bypasses Mālik), stating that they did not do so for the Friday prayers. This could

mean either that they entered the mosque itself for Friday prayers or that they did not pray *jumʿa.*

108. Sayeed states that al-Shāfiʿī's position "is perhaps the most elaborate rationalization of the view that women can indeed be prevented from attending mosques." Sayeed, "Early Sunni Discourse," 10.
109. This is a significant point because the Friday noon prayer ordinarily comprises four sets of prostrations, while the Friday congregational prayer includes only two sets in addition to the two sermons. If the prayer performed at the mosque did not "count" as a *jumʿa* prayer, one would have performed an invalid two-set prayer at a time when one was under an obligation to perform a four-set noon prayer.
110. Shāfiʿī, *Umm*, 1:24.
111. Ibid., 1:189.
112. Ibid., 1:246 (information on location of prayer in 1:245). Interestingly, al-Shāfiʿī holds that, if a group of women performs this prayer together, "it is not appropriate for women to give a [formal] sermon (*al-khuṭba*), but it is good if one of them "reminds" them [that is, exhorts them religiously]." Ibid., 1:246.
113. Ibid., 1:197.
114. Yaḥyā ibn Sharaf al-Nawawī, *al-Majmūʿ sharḥ al-Muhadhdhab*, ed. ʿAdil Aḥmad ʿAbd al-Mawjūd et al. (Beirut: Dār al-Kutub al-ʿIlmīya, 1423/2002), 6:63.
115. Sulaymān ibn Muḥammad ibn ʿUmar, *Ḥāshiyat al-Bujayrimī* (Beirut: Dār al-Kutub al-ʿIlmīya, 1420/2000), 1:554.
116. See Louise Marlow, *Hierarchy and Egalitarianism in Islamic Thought* (Cambridge: Cambridge University Press, 1997), 27–28. Al-Ṭaḥāwī (d. 321/933) defines "*dhawī al-hayʾāt*" in this context as referring to people of integrity (*ṣalāḥ*) and good character (*murūʾa*). See Aḥmad ibn Muḥammad al-Ṭaḥāwī, *Sharḥ mushkil al-āthār*, ed. Shuʿayb al-Arnaʾūṭ (Beirut: Muʾassasat al-Risāla, 1415/1994), 6:150, 6:153.
117. ʿAlī ibn Muḥammad al-Māwardī, *al-Ḥāwī al-kabīr fī fiqh madhhab al-imām al-Shāfiʿī raḍiya Allāh ʿanhu wa-huwa sharḥ Mukhtaṣar al-Muzanī* (Beirut: Dār al-Kutub al-ʿIlmīya, 1414/1994), 2:455.
118. See al-Ḥusayn ibn Masʿūd al-Baghawī, *al-Tahdhīb fī fiqh al-imām al-Shāfiʿī*, ed. ʿĀdil Aḥmad ʿAbd al-Mawjūd and ʿAlī Muḥammad Muʿawwaḍ (Beirut: Dār al-Kutub al-ʿIlmīya, 1418/1997), 2:255.
119. Al-Shāfiʿī's statements supporting the desirability of elderly women's attendance at mosque prayers are cited in ʿAbd al-Wāḥid ibn Ismāʿīl al-Rūyānī, *Baḥr al-madhhab fī furūʿ madhhab al-imām al-Shāfiʿī* (Beirut: Dār Iḥyāʾ al-Turāth al-ʿArabī, 1423/2002), 3:16, 3:231. See also Muḥammad ibn Bahādur al-Zarkashī, *Iʿlām al-sājid bi-aḥkām al-masājid* (Cairo, 1384), 360. Shāfiʿī sources that simply affirm the neutral or legally unproblematic nature of elderly women's attendance include al-Ghazālī,

al-Wasīṭ fi'l-madhhab, ed. ʿAlī Muḥyī al-Dīn al-Qaradāghī (Cairo: Dār al-Naṣr li'l-Ṭibāʿa al-Islāmīya, 1404/1984), 2:700; al-Ghazālī, *al-Wajīz*, in ʿAbd al-Karīm ibn Muḥammad al-Rāfiʿī, *al-ʿAzīz sharḥ al-Wajīz*, ed. ʿAlī Muḥammad Muʿawwaḍ and ʿĀdil Aḥmad ʿAbd al-Mawjūd (Beirut: Dār al-Kutub al-ʿIlmīya, 1417/1997), 2:314; Yaḥyā ibn Abī'l-Khayr al-ʿImrānī, *al-Bayān fī fiqh al-imām al-Shāfiʿī*, ed. Aḥmad Ḥijāzī Aḥmad al-Saqqā' (Beirut: Dār al-Kutub al-ʿIlmīya, 1423/2002), 2:359; al-Rāfiʿī, *ʿAzīz*, 2:142; and Nawawī, *Majmūʿ*, 5:253.

120. Abū Isḥāq al-Shīrāzī, *al-Muhadhdhab fī fiqh al-imām al-Shāfiʿī* (Damascus: Dār al-Qalam/Beirut: al-Dār al-Shāmīya, 1412/1992), 1:310. Al-Ghazālī makes a similar statement in *Iḥyā'*, 2:25. It is clear from other passages that al-Ghazālī does, in fact, make a distinction between old and young women (see discussion below in this chapter); however, it is also clear that the only decisive criterion is physical attractiveness (rather than, say, social role), so it is possible for him to elide the distinction.

121. See Aḥmad ibn al-Ḥusayn al-Bayhaqī, *al-Sunan al-kubrā* (Beirut: Dār al-Maʿrifa, n.d.), 3:131; ʿImrānī, *Bayān*, 2:359; Yaḥyā ibn Sharaf al-Nawawī, *Khulāṣat al-aḥkām*, ed. Ḥusayn Ismāʿīl al-Jamal (Beirut: Mu'assasat al-Risāla, 1418/1997), 2:680–81; Zarkashī, *Iʿlām*, 360; Zayn al-Dīn al-ʿIrāqī, *Ṭarḥ al-tathrīb fī sharḥ al-Taqrīb* (Beirut: Dār Iḥyā' al-Turāth al-ʿArabī, n.d.), 2:317; Ibn Ḥajar al-ʿAsqalānī, *Talkhīṣ al-ḥabīr bi-takhrīj aḥādīth al-Rāfiʿī al-kabīr* (n.p.: Mu'assasat Qurṭuba, 1416/1995), 2:58. The exact significance of an old woman's going out "in her boots" (*manqalayhā*) is unclear; al-ʿImrānī explains that *manqal* means boot (*khuff*) and that "He [i.e., the Prophet] did not intend that [wearing] boots is a condition of the dispensation (*rukhṣa*) [for old women to attend mosques]; he merely mentioned it because old women usually wear boots." It is possible that boots (because they are less open than sandals) were considered a more modest form of footwear. In the eighth/fourteenth century, the traveler Ibn Baṭṭūṭa admiringly describes the women of Shiraz as going out to the mosque completely concealed by veiling and wearing boots; boots also seem to have formed part of the modest outerwear of the Mamlūk-era woman. See Ibn Baṭṭūṭa, *Riḥla*, 1:183; Yedida Kalfon Stillman, *Arab Dress: A Short History from the Dawn of Islam to Modern Times* (Leiden: Brill, 2003), 21, 82.

122. It is also possible that the "al-Qaffāl" to whom this passage is attributed is Muḥammad ibn ʿAlī ibn Ismāʿīl al-Qaffāl al-Shāshī (d. 365/976), the father of al-Qāsim; the two of them were leading Shāfiʿī authorities of the period preceding al-Rūyānī, who cites the passage. However, it seems most likely that it is drawn from al-Qāsim's *Taqrīb*, which was an authoritative source for Shāfiʿī legal doctrine.

123. The context is a discussion of women's attendance at festival prayers.

124. Rūyānī, *Baḥr*, 3:231–32.

125. Ibid., 3:231.
126. Abū Ḥāmid al-Ghazālī, *Kīmyā-ye saʿādat*, ed. Ḥusayn Khedīvjam (Tehran: Markaz-e Intishārāt-e ʿElmī ve-Farhangī, 1983), 521.
127. Abū Ḥāmid al-Ghazālī, *Iḥyāʾ ʿulūm al-dīn* (Beirut: Dār al-Fikr, 1994/1414), 2:365.
128. Ibid., 2:53.
129. Ghazālī, *al-Wasīṭ*, 2:700; Ghazālī, *Wajīz*, in Rāfiʿī, *ʿAzīz*, 2:314, 2:354.
130. Yaḥyā ibn Sharaf al-Nawawī, *Rawḍat al-ṭālibīn* (Beirut: Dār al-Kutub al-ʿIlmīya, 1412/1992), 1:444; Nawawī, *Majmūʿ*, 5:253–34; Nawawī, *Kitāb al-Taḥqīq*, ed. ʿĀdil ʿAbd al-Mawjūd and ʿAlī Muʿawwaḍ (Beirut: Dār al-Jīl, 1413/1992), 258.
131. The status of *karāhat al-tanzīh* means that it is commendable to refrain from the action in question, but the action is not strictly forbidden.
132. al-Nawawī, *Ṣaḥīḥ Muslim bi-sharḥ al-imām Muḥyī al-Dīn al-Nawawī al-musammā al-Minhāj sharḥ Ṣaḥīḥ Muslim ibn al-Ḥajjāj* (Beirut: Dār al-Maʿrifa, 1414/1994), 3:382–83.
133. Nawawī, *Majmūʿ*, 5:622–23.
134. See Tāj al-Dīn al-Subkī, *Ṭabaqāt al-shāfiʿīya al-kubrā*, ed. Maḥmūd Muḥammad al-Ṭanāḥī and ʿAbd al-Fattāḥ Muḥammad al-Ḥilw (Cairo: Hajar, 1413/1992), 9:207, 9:208, 9:231, 9:240.
135. Muḥammad ibn ʿAlī Ibn Daqīq al-ʿĪd, *Iḥkām al-aḥkām sharḥ ʿUmdat al-aḥkām* (Beirut: Dār al-Kutub al-ʿIlmīya, n.d.), 1:168–69.
136. Ibid., 1:133–34.
137. Ibn Ḥajar al-ʿAsqalānī, *Fatḥ al-bārī bi-sharḥ Ṣaḥīḥ al-Bukhārī* (Cairo: Maktabat al-Kullīyāt al-Azharīya, 1398/1978), 4:283. See also ʿAsqalānī, *Talkhīṣ*, 2:58, where he questions the attribution to the Prophet of the statement that no woman should go to the mosque except "an old woman in her boots."
138. See, for instance, Baghawī, *Tahdhīb*, 2:254; Nawawī, *Rawḍa*, 1:444.
139. Rūyānī, *Baḥr*, 3:14.
140. Abū Bakr Muḥammad ibn Aḥmad al-Shāshī al-Qaffāl, *Ḥilyat al-ʿulamāʾ fī maʿrifat madhāhib al-fuqahāʾ*, ed. Yāsīn Aḥmad Ibrāhīm Darādikah (Beirut: Muʾassasat al-Risāla; Amman: Dār al-Arqam, 1400/1980), 2:156; Shīrāzī, *Muhadhdhab*, 1:310; Rāfiʿī, *ʿAzīz*, 2:142; Nawawī, *Rawḍa*, 1:444.
141. Ibn Daqīq al-ʿĪd, *Iḥkām al-aḥkām*, 1:162.
142. ʿAlī ibn [Ibrāhīm ibn] Dāwūd Ibn al-ʿAṭṭār, *al-ʿUdda sharḥ al-ʿUmda* (Beirut: Dār al-Bashāʾir al-Islāmīya, 1427/2006), 1:347. For Ibn al-ʿAṭṭār's identity and works, see Carl Brockelmann, *Geschichte der arabischen Litteratur* (Leiden: Brill, 1943), Grundband II, 85.
143. Ibn al- ʿAṭṭār, *ʿUdda* 1:290.
144. Ibid.
145. Like Ibn Daqīq al-ʿĪd (but unlike al-Nawawī), Ibn al-ʿAṭṭār omits any mention of age in his enumeration of conditions for a man to allow his

wife or ward to go out to the mosque. He reproduces the latter's comment that the ʿĀʾisha ḥadīth says nothing about age. Ibid., 1:289. Elsewhere he states of women's attendance at festival prayers that "a well-attired young woman (*al-shābba dhāt al-hayʾa*) does not go out, and one who is not well-attired (*ghayr dhāt al-hayʾa*) goes out to attend." Ibid., 2:710. Again, the traditional age distinction is discarded in favor of an emphasis on modest self-presentation.

146. Ibn al-ʿAṭṭār's points are reiterated by ʿUmar ibn ʿAlī ibn Aḥmad al-Anṣārī al-Shāfiʿī (d. 804/1401), *al-Iʿlām bi-fawāʾid ʿUmdat al-aḥkām*, ed. ʿAbd al-ʿAzīz ibn Aḥmad al-Mushayqiḥ (Riyadh: Dār al-ʿĀṣima, 1417/1997), 2:240–241.
147. Ibid., 3:284.
148. See Ibn Ḥazm, *Muḥallā*, 2:173–74.
149. See Badr al-Dīn al-ʿAynī, *ʿUmdat al-qāriʾ sharḥ Ṣaḥīḥ al-Bukhārī* (Beirut: Muḥammad Amīn Damj, 1971), 6:159, where these arguments are attributed to Muḥammad ibn Yūsuf al-Kirmānī (d. 786/1384). The printed edition of al-Kirmānī's commentary on Bukhārī contains only a fraction of the passage; however, Kirmānī composed multiple commentaries on Bukhārī of varying lengths, and al-ʿAynī's citation may well provide a more complete rendition of Kirmānī's arguments. [al-Kirmānī], *Ṣaḥīḥ al-Bukhārī bi-sharḥ al-Kirmānī* (Cairo: Muʾassasat al-Maṭbūʿāt al-Islāmīya, n.d.), 5:208–9.
150. Ibn Daqīq al-ʿĪd is suggesting that men's preexisting habit of detaining women within the home was tacitly endorsed by the Prophet Muḥammad. The Prophet's sunna, or normative example, was understood to be established not only by his reported statements and actions, but also by instances where he is known to have witnessed a given practice and refrained from criticizing it (*al-iqrār*, a verbal noun closely related to Ibn Daqīq al-ʿĪd's verb *qurrirū*). On this point, see Bernard G. Weiss, *The Search for God's Law* (Salt Lake City: University of Utah Press, 1992), 178–79.
151. Ibn Daqīq al-ʿĪd, *Iḥkām*, 1:169.
152. For a discussion of *munāsaba* or "suitability" as a means of "ascertaining the occasioning factor behind a rule," see Weiss, *Search*, 607–11.
153. ʿImād al-Dīn Ibn Kathīr, *Tafsīr al-qurʾān al-ʿaẓīm* (Giza: Muʾassasat Qurṭuba/Maktabat Awlād al-Shaykh li'l-Turāth, 1421/2000), 11:150.
154. Ibid., 10:250–51.
155. There is a ḥadīth in which the Prophet tells the congregation, "O people, forbid your women to wear adornment and display themselves vainly in the mosque," but it is rarely cited and poorly attested; see Zaghlūl, *Mawsūʿa*, 11:94.
156. For a more probing (and more skeptical) view of relationships among source texts, interpretive methodology, and the outcomes of legal reasoning, see Behnam Sadeghi, *The Logic of Law-Making in Islam: Women and*

Prayer in the Legal Tradition (Cambridge: Cambridge University Press, 2012).

157. See, for instance, Jonathan Berkey, *The Transmission of Knowledge in Medieval Cairo* (Princeton, NJ: Princeton University Press, 1992), 165–66.
158. See ibid., 175–81; Asma Sayeed, "Women and Ḥadīth Transmission: Two Cases from Mamlūk Damascus," *Studia Islamica* 95 (2004): 71–94; Mohammad Akram Nadwi, *al-Muhaddithat: The Women Scholars in Islam* (Oxford, UK: Interface Publications, 2007).
159. Al-Nawawī, *Majmūʿ*, 5:253–54 (although he is clearly citing the doctrine of the school and not necessarily his own opinion). For a later rendition of a similar view, see Zarkashī, *Iʿlām*, 359.
160. ʿIrāqī, *Ṭarḥ al-tathrīb*, 2:317.
161. Ibn al-ʿImād al-Aqfahsī, *Tashīl al-maqāṣid li-zuwwār al-masājid*, Cairo ms., Dār al-Kutub, Fiqh Shāfiʿī 1440, 242a–b; see also 245b. He also states that it is desirable (*mustaḥabb*), but not obligatory, for the husband to allow her to go to the mosque if she is old and unattractive and there is no fear of harm (*mafsada*). Ibid., 243a.
162. Jalāl al-Dīn Muḥammad ibn Aḥmad al-Maḥallī, *Kanz al-rāghibīn sharḥ Minhāj al-ṭālibīn*, printed with *Ḥāshiyat Shihāb al-Dīn Aḥmad ibn Salāma al-Qalyūbī . . . wa-Shihāb al-Dīn Aḥmad al-Burullisī al-mulaqqab bi-ʿUmayra . . . ʿalā Kanz al-rāghibīn* (Beirut: Dār al-Kutub al-ʿIlmīya, 1417/1997), 1:328.
163. Jalāl al-Dīn al-Suyūṭī, *al-Ashbāh wa'l-naẓā'ir*, ed. Muḥammad al-Muʿtaṣim bi'llāh al-Baghdādī (Beirut: Dār al-Kitāb al-ʿArabī, 1407/1987), 411.
164. Cited in Rāfiʿī, *ʿAzīz*, 2:154.
165. A work by an Ibn al-Naẓẓār or Ibn al-ʿAṭṭār under the title *Aḥkām al-nisā'* is not mentioned in *Kashf al-ẓunūn*; Ismāʿīl Bāshā al-Baghdādī notes that it is attributed to an Ibn al-Naẓẓār, but is clearly in doubt. Al-Baghdādī, *Īḍāḥ al-maknūn* (Istanbul: Milli Eğitim Basımevi, 1945), 1:37. Ibn Ḥajar al-Haytamī cites the same text as the work of an Ibn al-ʿAṭṭār. Al-Haytamī, al-*Fatāwā al-kubrā al-fiqhīya* (Beirut: Dār al-Kutub al-ʿIlmīya, 1417/1997), 1:287. The content of the discussion on our subject does not seem to be compatible with the doctrines of al-Nawawī's student ʿAlā al-Dīn ʿAlī ibn Ibrāhīm Ibn al-ʿAṭṭār.
166. Ibn al-Naẓẓār, *Kitāb Aḥkām al-nisā'*, Cairo ms., Dār al-Kutub, Fiqh Shāfiʿī mīm, microfilm 2742 (the date of the author's completion of the work is given on 118a).
167. Ibid., 6b.
168. Ibid., 17b; Haytamī, *Fatāwā*, 1:287.
169. Ibn al-Naẓẓār, *Aḥkām*, 10a.
170. Taqī al-Dīn Abū Bakr ibn Muḥammad al-Ḥiṣnī, *Kifāyat al-akhyār fī ḥall Ghāyat al-ikhtiṣār*, ed. Muḥammad ʿAwaḍ Haykal (Cairo: Dār al-Salām, 1426/2005), 204–5.

171. ʿAlī ibn ʿAṭīya al-Hītī, *ʿArāʾis al-ghurar wa-gharāʾis al-fikar fī aḥkām al-naẓar*, ed. Muḥammad Faḍl ʿAbd al-ʿAzīz al-Murād (Damascus: Dār al-Qalam; Beirut: al-Dār al-Shāmīya, 1410/1990), 144.
172. Cited in Ibn ʿAbd al-Ghaffār, *Izāla*, 84a–b; see also Haytamī, *Fatāwā*, 1:286.
173. Al-Balāṭunusī's work was titled *Al-Bāʿith ʿalā mā tajaddada min al-ḥawādith*; see ʿUmar Riḍā Kaḥḥāla, *Muʿjam al-muʾallifīn* (Beirut: Mu'assasat al-Risāla, 1414/1993), 3:438.
174. Haytamī, *Fatāwā*, 1:287.
175. Ibid., 1:288.
176. Ibid., 1:288.
177. Ibid., 1:286.
178. Ibid., 1:284–85. It is notable that al-Nawawī states in the relevant passage that it is actually forbidden for anyone other than a husband or guardian (*walī*) to prevent a woman from going to the mosque if she fulfills the conditions. Both from the content of the fatwa and from the historical context of its composition, it is clear that al-Haytamī was supporting an initiative in which the public authorities limited access to the mosque by *all* women due to the alleged prevalence of bad behavior.
179. Ibn Ḥajar al-Haytamī, *Fatḥ al-jawād bi-sharḥ al-Irshād* (Beirut: Dār al-Kutub al-ʿIlmīya, 1426/2005), 1:253.
180. al-Haytamī, *Tuḥfat al-muḥtāj*, printed in margin of ʿAbd al-Ḥamīd al-Shirwānī and Aḥmad ibn Qāsim al-ʿAbbādī, *Ḥawāshī al-Shirwānī wa-Ibn Qāsim al-ʿAbbādī* (Beirut: Dār Ṣādir, 1972), 2:252.
181. ʿAlī ibn ʿAlī al-Shabrāmallisī, *Ḥāshiya*, published with Shihāb al-Dīn al-Ramlī, *Nihāyat al-muḥtāj ilā sharḥ al-Minhāj* (Cairo: Muṣṭafā al-Bābī al-Ḥalabī wa-Awlāduhu, 1386/1967), 2:140. See also al-Ramlī, *Nihāya*, 2:140; ʿAbd al-Ḥamīd al-Shirwānī, *Ḥāshiya*, in *Ḥawāshī al-Shirwānī wa-Ibn Qāsim al-ʿAbbādī*, 2:252.
182. On the process by which concrete issues evoked fatwas, which were then incorporated into legal manuals, see Wael B. Hallaq, *Authority, Continuity and Change in Islamic Law* (Cambridge: Cambridge University Press, 2001), 174–83.
183. See Ibn al-Mulaqqin, *ʿUjālat al-muḥtāj ilā tawjīh al-Minhāj*, ed. Hishām ibn ʿAbd al-Karīm al-Badrānī (Irbid, Jordan: Dār al-Kitāb, 1421/2001), 1:295; Jalāl al-Dīn al-Maḥallī, *Kanz al-rāghibīn sharḥ Minhāj al-ṭālibīn*, printed in Qalyūbī and ʿUmayra, *Ḥāshiya*, 1:327; Muḥammad ibn Aḥmad al-Shirbīnī, *Mughnī al-muḥtāj ilā maʿrifat maʿānī alfāẓ al-Minhāj* (Beirut: Dār al-Kutub al-ʿIlmīya, 2006), 1:321.
184. In Qalyūbī and ʿUmayra, *Ḥāshiyatā Qalyūbī wa-ʿUmayra* (Beirut: Dār al-Kutub al-ʿIlmīya, 2001), 1:327.
185. Ramlī, *Nihāyat al-muḥtāj*, 2:138; see also Qalyūbī and ʿUmayra, *Ḥāshiyatā Qalyūbī wa-ʿUmayra* (Beirut: Dār al-Kutub al-ʿIlmīya, 1417/1997), 1:327.

186. Shabrāmallisī, *Ḥāshiya*, printed in the margin of Ramlī, *Nihāyat al-muḥtāj*, 2:138.
187. See Sadeghi, *Logic of Law-Making*, 110. Chapter 5 of Sadeghi's study provides the only thorough examination of legal discourse on women's mosque attendance for any school of law, and readers are urged to consult it. Sadeghi's central (and compelling) argument is that Ḥanafī legal scholars' opinions did not arise naturally or inevitably from their textual sources, but reflect the ex post facto exercise of hermeneutic ingenuity in the service of certain desired outcomes (in this case, the imposition of strict limits on women's mosque attendance).
188. Abū Yūsuf Yaʿqūb ibn Ibrāhīm al-Anṣārī, *Kitāb al-Āthār* (Beirut: Dār al-Kutub al-ʿIlmīya, n.d.), 56.
189. See Sadeghi, *Logic of Law-Making*, 107.
190. This would appear to be an allusion to the widely circulated report stating that the Prophet instructed all women (including those who were young and secluded) to go out to the prayers for the two festivals. See Muslim, *Ṣaḥīḥ*, *Kitāb Ṣalāt al-ʿīdayn*, *Bāb Dhikr ibāḥat khurūj al-nisāʾ fi'l-ʿīdayn*, 1:347.
191. Muḥammad ibn al-Ḥasan al-Shaybānī, *Kitāb al-Aṣl al-maʿrūf bi'l-Mabsūṭ* (Beirut: ʿĀlam al-Kutub, 1410/1990), 1:343–44. See also Muḥammad ibn al-Ḥasan al-Shaybānī, *Kitāb al-Ḥujja ʿalā ahl al-madīna* (Beirut: ʿĀlam al-Kutub, 1983), 1:306. On the nature and attribution of al-Shaybānī's works, see Calder, *Studies*, 39–66; and Sadeghi, *Logic of Law-Making*, 177–88.
192. Aḥmad ibn Muḥammad al-Ṭaḥāwī, *Mukhtaṣar Ikhtilāf al-fuqahāʾ*, abridged by Abū Bakr Aḥmad ibn ʿAlī al-Jaṣṣās, ed. ʿAbd Allāh Nadhīr Aḥmad (Beirut: Dār al-Bashāʾir al-Islāmīya, 1416/1995), 1:231.
193. Muḥammad ibn Aḥmad al-Qurṭubī, *Tafsīr al-Qurṭubī (al-Jāmiʿ li-aḥkām al-qurʾān)*, ed. Sālim Muṣṭafā al-Badrī (Beirut: Dār al-Kutub al-ʿIlmīya, 1424/2004), 5:195.
194. Ṭaḥāwī, *Mukhtaṣar*, 1:231. Many Ḥanafīs held that a *mujtahid* was free to choose between the opinion of Abū Ḥanīfa and a dissenting one shared by both Abū Yūsuf and al-Shaybānī. Thus, both positions were perpetuated and interpreted by scholars within the school. See Hallaq, *Authority, Continuity and Change*, 26n5.
195. The printed text reads "his"; I have emended it for the sense.
196. Aḥmad ibn Muḥammad al-Ṭaḥāwī, *Sharḥ mushkil al-āthār*, ed. Shuʿayb al-Arnaʾūṭ (Beirut: Muʾassasat al-Risāla, 1415/1994), 12:142.
197. Taḥāwī, *Mukhtaṣar*, 1:231. In the same passage, however, he also transmits a report that Abū Ḥanīfa permitted old women to attend the dawn and nighttime prayers.
198. Muḥammad ibn Aḥmad al-Sarakhsī, *Kitāb al-Mabsūṭ*, ed. Muḥammad Ḥasan Ismāʿīl al-Shāfiʿī (Beirut: Dār al-Kutub al-ʿIlmīya, 1421/2001), 2:63.

199. See Aḥmad ibn ʿAlī al-Jaṣṣāṣ, *Aḥkām al-qurʾān*, ed. ʿAbd al-Salām Shāhīn (Beirut: Dār al-Kutub al-ʿIlmīya, 1428/2007), 3:471.
200. Sarakhsī, *Mabsūṭ*, 2:63.
201. See Muḥammad ibn Aḥmad al-Sarakhsī, *Kitāb al-Siyar al-kabīr*, ed. Ṣalāḥ al-Dīn al-Munajjid (Cairo: Maʿhad al-Makhṭūṭāt bi-Jāmiʿat al-Duwal al-ʿArabīya, 1971), 1:185, where the reservation that the woman must be elderly (*al-ʿajūz al-kabīra*) seems to originate with al-Shaybānī (and the invocation of *fitna* belongs to al-Sarakhsī).
202. ʿAlāʾ al-Dīn al-Kāsānī, *Badāʾiʿ al-ṣanāʾiʿ* (Cairo: Zakarīyā ʿAlī Yūsuf, n.d.), 2:697.
203. ʿAbd Allāh ibn Mahmūd al-Mawṣilī, *al-Ikhtiyār li-taʿlīl al-mukhtār* (Amman: Dār al-Fikr, 1420/1999), 1:122; see also Abū Bakr Ibn al-Ḥaddād, *al-Jawhara al-nayyira sharḥ Mukhtaṣar al-Qudūrī*, ed. Ilyās Qablān (Beirut: Dār al-Kutub al-ʿIlmīya, 1427/2006), 1:164. The proverb was generally understood to refer to careless remarks, which would inevitably be heard and reported by someone. See Aḥmad ibn Muḥammad al-Naysābūrī al-Maydānī, *Majmaʿ al-amthāl* (Beirut: Dār al-Kutub al-ʿIlmīya, 1408/1988), 2:229. *Lāqiṭa* is feminine, and probably refers to receptive ears; here the reference is clearly to men.
204. Kāsānī, *Badāʾiʿ al-ṣanāʾiʿ*, 2:697.
205. Sadeghi, *Logic of Law-Making*, 115.
206. Ṭāhir ibn ʿAbd al-Rashīd al-Bukhārī, *Khulāṣat al-fatāwā* (Lahore: Amjad Akīdīmī, 1397/[1977?]), 1:214.
207. See Hallaq, *Authority, Continuity and Change*, 162.
208. Mawṣilī, *Ikhtiyār*, 1:122; Sadeghi, *Logic of Law-Making*, 115–16. As the title of al-Mawṣilī's book suggests, his objective was to establish the most accepted doctrines of the Ḥanafī school.
209. Maḥmūd ibn Aḥmad Ibn Māza, *al-Muḥīṭ al-burhānī* (Beirut: Dār Iḥyāʾ al-Turāth al-ʿArabī, 1424/2003), 2:217. The report that ʿUmar barred women from mosques cited at the end of this passage does not appear to be transmitted in any of the major collections of ḥadīth or *āthār*.
210. See Sadeghi, *Logic of Law-Making*, 117n27 (discussing al-Bābartī, who reproduces Ibn Māza's argument).
211. Ibn Māza, *Muḥīṭ*, 2:217. It is conceivable that the text here is corrupt, as it immediately proceeds to an unacknowledged reproduction of al-Sarakhsī's discussion of the rules relating to older women (which do allow them to attend some or all prayers).
212. Sarakhsī, *Mabsūṭ*, 2:63.
213. ʿAlī ibn Abī Bakr al-Maghīnānī, *al-Hidāya sharḥ Bidāyat al-mubtadiʾ*, ed. Muḥammad Muḥammad Tāmir and Ḥāfiẓ Āshūr Ḥāfiẓ (Cairo: Dār al-Salām, 1420/2000), 1:149.
214. See Sadeghi, *Logic of Law-Making*, 114 ("al-Marghīnānī . . . contrives an entirely different and colorful explanation in terms of [the presumably

regular and synchronized] sleeping and eating schedules of those who harrassed women").

215. Ibn al-Ḥaddād, *Jawhara*, 1:164.
216. Al-Bukhārī, *Khulāṣa*, 2:53. Emphasis mine.
217. Sadeghi, *Logic of Law-Making*, 116.
218. Ibid.
219. Ibid.
220. Muḥammad ibn Muḥammad ibn Muḥammad al-Bukhārī, "*Suʾāl wa-jawāb bi-shaʾn al-quṣṣāṣ, yajlisūna fi'l-masājid wa-tajtamiʿ ʿalayhim al-niswa*," Jerusalem ms., Isḥāq al-Ḥusaynī, 1/28, 6; listed in *al-Fihris al-shāmil li'l-turāth al-ʿarabī al-islāmī al-makhṭūṭ, al-Fiqh wa-uṣūlihi* (Amman: Muʾassasat Āl al-Bayt li'l-Fikr al-Islāmī, 1421), 4:693, #299. For biographical notices on al-Bukhārī, see Ibn Ḥajar al-ʿAsqalānī, *Inbāʾ al-ghumr bi-anbāʾ al-ʿumr* (Beirut: Dār al-Kutub al-ʿIlmīya, 1406/1986), 9:23–24; Muḥammad ibn ʿAbd al-Raḥmān al-Sakhāwī, *al-Ḍawʾ al-lāmiʿ* (Beirut: Manshūrāt Dār Maktabat al-Ḥayāt, n.d.), 9:291–95.
221. Haytamī, *Fatāwā al-kubrā*, 1:287. Both printed versions of the text give the name as ʿAlāʾ al-Dīn Muḥammad ibn Muḥammad ibn Muḥammad al-Najjārī, which must be amended to al-Bukhārī (a change that involves shifting only one dot). A brief citation of "al-ʿAlāʾ al-Bukhārī" in Ibn ʿAbd al-Ghaffār, *Izāla*, 72b, does not appear in the text of the preserved fatwa, although it is very consistent with the sentiments expressed there.
222. Cited from al-Maqrīzī's *ʿUqūd* in Sakhāwī, *Ḍawʾ*, 9:294.
223. For instance, each states that perfume is forbidden because it "arouses the sexual desire" of men (*taḥrīk al-dāʿiya / dāʿiyat al-rijāl*). See Ibn al-Humām, *Sharḥ Fatḥ al-qadīr* (Cairo: Muṣṭafā al-Bābī al-Ḥalabī bi-Miṣr, 1389/1970), 1:365; Ibn Daqīq al-ʿId, *Iḥkām al-aḥkām*, 1:167. See also the commentary by Ibn al-Humām's teacher Abū Zurʿa and his father Zayn al-Dīn ibn al-ʿIrāqī, *Ṭarḥ al-tathrīb fī sharḥ al-Taqrīb* ([Beirut?]: [Dār Iḥyāʾ al-Turāth al-ʿArabī?], n.d.), 2:316.
224. Ibn al-Humām, *Fatḥ*, 1:365.
225. Ibid., 1:366.
226. Ibn Daqīq al-ʿĪd, *Iḥkām*, 1:169; Ibn al-ʿIrāqī, *Ṭarḥ al-tathrīb*, 2:316.
227. Ibn al-Humām, *Fatḥ*, 1:366; Sirāj al-Dīn Ibn Nujaym similarly claims that in his time delinquents are abroad at all hours of the day, cited in Muḥammad Amīn Ibn ʿĀbidīn, *Ḥāshiyat Radd al-muḥtār* (Cairo: Muḥammad Maḥmūd al-Ḥalabī wa-Shurakāh, 1386/1966), 1:566.
228. Marghīnānī, *Hidāya*, 1:149.
229. He does use the plural, *fitan*, to refer to the conflicts that may occur between husband and wife if the woman seeks out another partner.
230. ʿAynī, *ʿUmda*, 6:158–59.
231. Walter G. Andrews and Mehmet Kalpaklı, *The Age of Beloveds: Love and the Beloved in Early-Modern Ottoman and European Culture and Society*

(Durham, NC: Duke University Press, 2005), 52. For a comparative case, see Robert C. Davis, "The Geography of Gender in the Renaissance," in *Gender and Society in Renaissance Italy*, ed. Judith C. Brown and Robert C. Davis (London: Longman, 1998), 19–38. On the excess of bachelors in one early Ottoman context, see Leslie Peirce, *Morality Tales: Law and Gender in the Ottoman Court of Aintab* (Berkeley: University of California Press, 2003), 369, 376.

232. For example, Leslie Peirce has argued that the Ottoman regime's increasing efforts to "regulate the sociosexual behavior of its subjects" was in part a function of a political context in which they accused their Safavid rivals "of practicing heresy that was shot through with sexual license." Peirce, *Morality Tales*, 384–85.
233. Muḥammad ibn Muḥammad al-Marwazī, *al-Mukhtaṣar*, printed in al-Sarakhsī, *al-Mabsūṭ*, 2:36–37.
234. Marghīnānī, *Hidāya*, 1:206–7. For a discussion of the structural connections between early jurists' models of marriage and slavery, see Kecia Ali, *Marriage and Slavery in Islam* (Cambridge, MA: Harvard University Press, 2010), passim, esp. chap. 5.
235. Ibn Māza, *Muḥīṭ*, 2:198.
236. Kāsānī, *Badāʾiʿ al-ṣanāʾiʿ*, 2:659–60.
237. Ibid., 2:697–98. The idea that women are relieved from the duty to attend Friday prayers in part because of their need to serve their husbands is also mentioned by Abū Bakr Ibn al-Ḥaddād (d. 800/1398). *Jawhara*, 1:227.
238. A rare early allusion to a possible conflict between women's attendance at public prayers and their domestic duties occurs when Mālik is asked whether, given their lack of legal obligation to attend the festival prayers, women and slaves could leave before the Friday sermon "to hasten after the needs of their masters and the affairs of their homes"; he replies that they must remain until the prayer leader departs. Saḥnūn, *Mudawwana*, 1:168.
239. For Ḥanafī opinions on the wife's domestic labor, see ʿAbd al-Karīm Zaydān, *al-Mufaṣṣal fī aḥkām al-marʾa wa'l-bayt al-muslim fī'l-sharīʿa al-islāmīya* (Beirut: Muʾassasat al-Risāla, 1420/2000), 7:302–3.
240. Zayn al-Dīn Ibn Nujaym, *al-Baḥr al-rāʾiq sharḥ Kanz al-daqāʾiq* (Beirut: Dār al-Kutub al-ʿIlmīya, 1997), 4:310.
241. See, for instance, Ibn al-Humām, *Fatḥ*, 4:412; Ibn Nujaym, *al-Baḥr al-rāʾiq*, 4:311.
242. See, for instance, ʿAbd al-Raḥmān ibn Mūḥammad, known as Shaykhzādeh, *Majmaʿ al-anhur fī sharḥ Multaqā al-abḥur* (Beirut: Dār Iḥyāʾ al-Turāth al-ʿArabī, n.d.), 1:109.
243. Printed with Ibn ʿĀbidīn, *Ḥāshiyat Radd al-muḥtār*, 1:566.
244. Zayn al-Dīn Ibn Nujaym, *al-Baḥr al-rāʾiq sharḥ Kanz al-daqāʾiq* (Beirut: Dār al-Kutub al-ʿIlmīya, 1418/1997), 1:628. His son Sirāj al-Dīn Ibn

Nujaym (d. 1005/1596) responded in his commentary *al-Naḥr al-fāʾiq sharḥ Kanz al-daqāʾiq* that this objection was unfounded because the later fatwa was based on the principle of the Imām (i.e., Abū Ḥanīfa) that even older women should not go to the mosque at times when miscreants are abroad—which is now always the case. See Ibn ʿĀbidīn, *Minḥat al-khāliq ʿalā al-Baḥr al-rāʾiq*, printed in lower margin of Ibn Nujaym, *Baḥr*, 1:628; also cited in Ibn ʿĀbidīn, *Ḥāshiyat Radd al-muḥtār*, 1:566.

245. A. Kevin Reinhart, "When Women Went to Mosques: al-Aydini on the Duration of Assessments," in *Islamic Legal Interpretation: Muftis and Their Fatwas*, ed. Muhammad Khalid Masud, Brinkley Messick, and David S. Powers (Cambridge, MA: Harvard University Press, 1996), 123.
246. See Sadeghi, *Logic of Law-Making*, 30, 125.
247. See Peirce, "Seniority, Sexuality, and Social Order: The Vocabulary of Gender in Early Modern Ottoman Society," in *Women in the Ottoman Empire: Middle Eastern Women in the Early Modern Era*, ed. Madeline C. Zilfi (Leiden: Brill, 1997), 170.
248. Muḥammad ibn Mufliḥ, *Kitāb al-Furūʿ* (Beirut: ʿĀlam al-Kutub, 1404/1984), 1:578.
249. Aḥmad ibn Ḥanbal (attributed), *Aḥkām al-nisāʾ*, ed. ʿAbd al-Qādir Aḥmad ʿAṭāʾ (Beirut: Dār al-Kutub al-ʿIlmīya, 1406/1986), 46. This work, excerpted from a collection of Aḥmad's *masāʾil* transmitted from Abū Bakr al-Marwadhī and Abū Bakr al-Khallāl, provides two versions of this report and another in which Aḥmad states, "Women used to sit with men at teaching sessions (*al-majālis*); as for now, a single finger of a woman is a temptation."
250. The relevant chapter heading in the Ṣaḥīḥ of Ibn Ḥanbal's younger contemporary and student Muslim ibn al-Ḥajjāj (*Bāb Khurūj al-nisāʾ ilā al-masājid idhā lam yatarattab ʿalayhi fitna wa-annahā lā takhruj mutaṭayyiba*) invokes the concept of *fitna*; however, the chapter headings are not an integral component of the text, and do not appear in the earliest manuscripts.
251. Ibn Mufliḥ, *Furūʿ*, 1:578.
252. Ibn Ḥanbal "intended [the *Musnad*] to be a reference for students of Islamic law"; see Jonathan A. C. Brown, *Hadith: Muhammad's Legacy in the Medieval and Modern World* (Oxford, UK: Oneworld, 2009), 30.
253. See Aḥmad ʿAbd al-Raḥmān al-Bannā, *al-Fatḥ al-rabbānī l-tartīb Musnad al-imām Aḥmad Ibn Ḥanbal al-Shaybānī* (Beirut: Dār Iḥyāʾ al-Turāth al-ʿArabī, 1976), 5:193–202.
254. Aḥmad ibn Ḥanbal, *Musnad al-imām Aḥmad ibn Ḥanbal*, ed. Shuʿayb Arnaʾūṭ and ʿĀdil Murshid (Beirut: Muʾassasat al-Risāla, 1421/2001), 45:37; Zaghlūl, *Mawsūʿa*, 5:675. This report is also transmitted in the ḥadīth collections of Ibn Khuzayma, and Ibn Ḥibbān (d. 354/965). A related statement is also attributed to the Shīʿī Imām Jaʿfar al-Ṣādiq.

Muḥammad ibn ʿAlī Ibn Bābawayh al-Qummī (known as al-Ṣadūq), *Man lā yaḥḍuruhu al-faqīh* (Beirut: Dār Ṣaʿb/Dār al-Taʿāruf, 1401/1981), 1:259. It is not completely clear what is intended by each of the terms in the series referring to different parts of the house, and the precise wording varies among versions of the report; here I am following an understanding of the report prevalent among later commentators.

255. Najam Haider notes that in Kufa "at the turn of the 1st/7th century, most Muslims frequented their local clan mosques except on special occasions (e.g., the Friday prayer) when they would venture to the cathedral mosque in the geographic center of the city." Najam Haider, *The Origins of the Shīʿa: Identity, Ritual, and Sacred Space in Eighth-Century Kufa* (Cambridge: Cambridge University Press, 2011), 232.
256. Abū Yaʿlā Ibn al-Farrāʾ, *al-Jāmiʿ al-ṣaghīr fī'l-fiqh ʿalā madhhab al-imām Aḥmad ibn Ḥanbal* (Riyadh: Dār Aṭlas li'l-Nashr wa'l-Tawzīʿ, 1421/2000), 51; Ibn Mufliḥ, *Furūʿ*, 1:578; Ibrāhīm ibn Muḥammad ibn Mufliḥ, *al-Mubdiʿ sharḥ al-Muqniʿ* (Beirut: al-Maktab al-Islāmī, n.d.), 2:57.
257. Yaḥyā ibn Muḥammad ibn Hubayra, *al-Ifṣāḥ ʿan maʿānī al-ṣiḥāḥ* (Beirut: Dār al-Kutub al-ʿIlmīya, 1417/1996), 1:103–4.
258. Al-Ḥusayn ibn Muḥammad al-ʿUkbarī, *Ruʾūs al-masāʾil al-khilāfīya bayna jumhūr al-fuqahāʾ* (Riyadh: Dār Ishbīlīyā, 1421/2001), 1:282.
259. Muḥammad ibn ʿAbd Allāh Ibn Sunayna, *al-Mustawʿib*, ed. Musāʿid ibn Qāsim al-Fāliḥ (Riyadh: Maktabat al-Maʿārif, 1413/1993), 3:78.
260. Ibn Hubayra, *Ifṣāḥ*, 1:104. See also Ibn Mufliḥ, *Furūʿ*, 1:578.
261. Abū'l-Faraj ʿAbd al-Raḥmān ibn ʿAlī ibn al-Jawzī, *al-Taḥqīq* (Cairo: al-Fārūq al-Ḥadītha li'l-Ṭibāʿa wa'l-Nashr, 1422/2001), 4:15–16.
262. See ʿAlī ibn Sulaymān al-Mardāwī, *al-Inṣāf fī maʿrifat al-rājiḥ min al-khilāf ʿalā madhhab al-imām al-mubajjal Aḥmad ibn Ḥanbal*, ed. Muḥammad Ḥāmid al-Faqqī, 2nd printing (Beirut: Dār Iḥyāʾ al-Turāth al-ʿArabī, 1406/1986), 2:212.
263. In addition to the later Shāfiʿī work by Ibn al-Naẓẓār that has already been cited, Ibn Baṭṭa al-ʿUkbarī (d. 387/997) produced a work titled *Aḥkām al-nisāʾ* that is not preserved, although citations survive in later sources. See Kaḥḥāla, *Muʿjam*, 2:354.
264. ʿAbd al-Raḥmān ibn ʿAlī Ibn al-Jawzī, *Kitāb Aḥkām al-nisāʾ* (Ṣaydā/Beirut: al-Maktaba al-ʿAṣrīya, 1424/2003), 141 (see also 140).
265. Ibid., 133.
266. Ibid., 145.
267. Ibid., 146.
268. Ibid., 147–49.
269. Muwaffaq al-Dīn Ibn Qudāma, *al-Mughnī* (Beirut: Dar al-Kutub al-ʿIlmiya, n.d.), 2:35.
270. Ibid., 2:196.
271. Ibid., 8:129.

272. Muwaffaq al-Dīn Ibn Qudāma, *al-Kāfī fī fiqh al-imām Aḥmad ibn Ḥanbal*, ed. Muḥammad Fāris and Musʿad ʿAbd al-Ḥamīd al-Saʿdanī (Beirut: Dār al-Kutub al-ʿIlmīya, 1414/1994), 1:287–88. Compare the opinion of al-Kalwadhānī (d. 510/1116): "It is repugnant (*yukrah*) to forbid a woman from [going to] the mosque, and her home is better [for her]." ʿAbd al-Muʾmin ibn ʿAbd al-Ḥajj al-Qaṭīʿī, *Idrāk al-ghāya fī ikhtiṣār al-Hidāya*, ed. Nāsir ibn Saʿūd al-Salāma (Riyadh: Maktabat al-Rushd, 1428/2007), 30.
273. See sources cited in Ibn Mufliḥ, *Furūʿ*, 1:601; Mardāwī, *Inṣāf*, 2:242–3; Christopher Melchert, "Whether to Keep Women Out of the Mosque: A Survey of Medieval Islamic Law," in *Authority, Privacy and Public Order in Islam, Proceedings of the 22nd Congress of L'Union Européenne des Arabisants et Islamisants,* ed. B. Michalak-Pikulska and A. Pikulski (Leuven: Uitgeverij Peeters, 2006), 63.
274. Taqī al-Dīn Ibn Taymīya, *Majmūʿ al-fatāwā*, ed. Muṣṭafā ʿAbd al-Qādir ʿAṭāʾ (Beirut: Dār al-Kutub al-ʿIlmīya, 1421/2000), 6:231.
275. Ibid., 6:230.
276. Ibid., 6:231.
277. Ibid., 29:135. See also ibid., 22:63–65, where he argues that, since a woman may expose parts of her body in prayer that she must conceal when in public, this indicates that "she prays at home" (and that women in the early Islamic period did so).
278. Ibn Taymīya, *Kitāb al-Ikhtiyārāt al-ʿilmīya*, compiled by ʿAlī ibn Muḥammad al-Baʿlī, in Ibn Taymīya, *al-Fatāwā al-kubrā* (Cairo: Dār al-Kutub al-Ḥadītha, 1966), 4:561.
279. Ibn Qayyim al-Jawzīya, *Iʿlām al-muwaqqiʿīn ʿan rabb al-ʿālamīn* (Beirut: Dār al-Kutub al-ʿIlmīya, 1417/1996), 2:280.
280. Ibn Qayyim al-Jawzīya, *Aḥkām ahl al-dhimma*, ed. Ṣubḥī Ṣāliḥ (Beirut: Dār al-ʿIlm li'l-Malāyīn, 1381/1961), 1:438.
281. Ibn Qayyim al-Jawzīya, *Iʿlām*, 2:114.
282. Ibn Qayyim al-Jawzīya, *al-Ṭuruq al-ḥukmīya*, 241.
283. Ibn Mufliḥ, *Furūʿ*, 1:578.
284. ʿAlī ibn Sulaymān al-Mardāwī, *al-Tanqīḥ al-mushbiʿ fī taḥrīr aḥkām al-Muqniʿ* (n.p.: al-Maṭbaʿa al-Salafīya, n.d.), 56; Muḥammad ibn Aḥmad al-Futūḥī al-Ḥanbalī, known as Ibn al-Najjār, *Muntahā al-irādāt fī jamʿ al-Muqniʿ maʿa al-Tanqīḥ wa-Ziyādāt* (n.p.: ʿĀlam al-Kutub, n.d.), 1:106; Ibn al-Najjār, *Maʿūnat ūlī al-nuhā sharḥ al-Muntahā*, 3rd printing (Beirut: Dār Khiḍr, 1419/1998), 1:328; Manṣūr ibn Yūnus al-Bahūtī, *al-Rawḍ al-murbiʿ sharḥ Zād al-mustanqiʿ* (Beirut: Dār al-Arqam ibn al-Arqam, n.d.), 1:105; Muḥammad ibn ʿAbd Allāh ibn Aḥmad al-Baʿlī, *al-Rawḍ al-nadī sharḥ Kāfī al-mubtadī* (n.p.: al-Maktaba al-Salafīya, n.d.), 97. See also ʿUthmān ibn ʿAbd Allāh ibn Jāmiʿ al-Ḥanbalī, *al-Fawāʾid*

al-muntakhabāt f ī sharḥ Akhṣar al-mukhtaṣarāt, ed. ʿAbd al-Salām ibn Barjas Āl ʿAbd al-Karīm (Beirut: Maktabat al-Risāla, 1424/2003).

285. Aḥmad Ibn Ḥamdān, *al-Riʿāya al-ṣughrā fī'l-fiqh ʿalā madhhab al-imām Aḥmad ibn Muḥammad ibn Ḥanbal*, ed. Nāṣir ibn Suʿūd ibn ʿAbd ʿAllāh al-Salāma (Riyadh: Dār Ishbīlīyā, 1423/2002), 1:105; see also Mardāwī, *Inṣāf*, 2:212.
286. Mardāwī, *Inṣāf*, 2:212.
287. Aḥmad ibn Muḥammad ibn ʿAlī al-Maqqarī al-Fayyūmī, *al-Miṣbāḥ al-munīr fī gharīb al-Sharḥ al-kabīr li'l-Rāfiʿī* (Beirut: Dār al-Kutub al-ʿIlmīya, 1398/1978), 1:56–57.
288. Murtaḍā al-Zabīdī, *Tāj al-ʿarūs*, s.v. "b-r-z"; Muḥammad ibn Yaʿqūb al-Fayrūzābādī, *al-Qāmūs al-muḥīṭ* (n.p.: [al-Mu'assasa al-ʿArabīya li'l-Ṭibāʿa wa'l-Nashr], n.d.), 2:171; *al-Mawsūʿa al-fiqhīya* (Kuwait: Wizārat al-Awqāf wa'l-Shuʾūn al-Islāmīya, 1406/1986), 8:74–75.
289. It appeared primarily in the context of a judge's prerogative to summon a nonsecluded woman to give testimony. See *Mawsūʿa al-fiqhīya*, 8:74–75. For a reference to the *barza* in a Ḥanafī discussion of women's witnessing, see Mohammad Fadel, "Two Women, One Man: Knowledge, Power, and Gender in Medieval Sunni Legal Thought," *International Journal of Middle East Studies* 29 (1997): 195.
290. Ibn Rajab al-Ḥanbalī, *Fatḥ al-bārī sharḥ Ṣaḥīḥ al-Bukhārī*, ed. Maḥmūd Shaʿbān ibn ʿAbd al-Maqṣūd et al. (Madina: Maktabat al-Ghurabā' al-Atharīya, 1417/1996), 8:40–42.
291. Manṣūr ibn Yūnus al-Bahūtī, *Kashshāf al-qināʿ ʿan matn al-Iqnāʿ* (Riyadh: Maktabat al-Naṣr al-Ḥadītha, [1968?]), 1:456.
292. Mardāwī, *Inṣāf*, 2:213.
293. See Ibn Mufliḥ, *Furūʿ*, 1:601.
294. Melchert, "Whether to Keep Women Out of the Mosque," 63, 64.
295. See, for instance, Hallaq, *Authority, Continuity and Change*; David S. Powers, *Law, Society, and Culture in the Maghrib, 1300–1500* (Cambridge: Cambridge University Press, 2002).
296. Compare on this point, for instance, Judith E. Tucker, *In the House of the Law* (Berkeley: University of California Press, 1998); and Wael Hallaq, *Sharīʿa: Theory, Practice, Transformations* (Cambridge: Cambridge University Press, 2009), esp. 184–96. Both of these, however, focus more centrally on issues of adjudication than on legal discourse or matters of ritual.
297. For the use of similar terminology in a much later source, see Ibn Qudāma, *Mughnī* (citing al-Qāḍī [Abū Yaʿlā, d. 458/1066], 4:518, who states that an unmarried woman gains control of her own financial assets "when she becomes to old to marry and goes out among men (*idhā ʿanasat wa-barazat ilā al-rijāl*)—that is, when she gets old (*kaburat*)." Lexicographers define the *ʿānis* (unmarried/unmarriageable virgin) as being of middle

age; see Edward William Lane, *An Arabic-English Lexicon* (Beirut: Libraire du Liban, 1980), 5:2173.

298. In a humorous anecdote from a fifth-/eleventh-century source, set in the time of the ʿAbbāsid caliph al-Maʾmūn (reigned 198–218/813–833), a man suggests that his wife should take their marriageable daughters to Friday prayers to survey the available bachelors themselves, since reports that virgins (*al-abkār*) should not attend Friday services conflict with commands in the Qur'an and the sunna for all believers to do so. Ghars al-Niʿma Abū'l-Ḥasan Muḥammad ibn Hilāl al-Ṣābiʾ, *al-Hafawāt al-nādira*, ed. Ṣāliḥ al-Ashtar (Damascus: Maṭbūʿāt Majmaʿ al-Lugha al-ʿArabīya, 1387/1967), 289. It is probably not the wife's ability to go to Friday prayers, but the idea of her taking her nubile daughters (in the story's words, the attendance of "virgins") that is implied to be ridiculous.

299. ʿAlī ibn Abī Bakr al-Haythamī, *Bughyat al-rāʾid fī taḥqīq Majmaʿ al-zawāʾid wa-manbaʿ al-fawāʾid*, ed. ʿAbd Allāh Muḥammad Darwīsh (Beirut: Dār al-Fikr, 1412/1991), 2:155–56. In a later effort to link the juristic rule on women's mosque attendance with Qur'anic terminology, the Imāmī Shīʿite authority al-Shaykh al-Mufīd (d. 413/1032) writes that there is no harm in elderly women (*al-qawāʿid min al-nisāʾ*, whom he defines as "old women who are no longer fit for marriage") attending Friday and festival prayers. Al-Shaykh al-Mufīd, *Aḥkām al-nisāʾ*, vol. 9 of *Muṣannafāt al-Shaykh al-Mufīd* (n.p.: al-Muʾtamar al-ʿĀlamī li-Alfīyat al-Shaykh al-Mufīd, 1413), 58.

300. Ibn Ḥajar al-ʿAsqalānī, *Mukhtaṣar zawāʾid Musnad al-Bazzār ʿalā al-kutub al-sitta wa-Musnad Aḥmad*, ed. Ṣabrī ibn ʿAbd al-Khāliq Abū Dharr (Beirut: Muʾassasat al-Kutub al-Thaqāfīya, 1412/1992), 1:223.

301. See Muqātil ibn Sulaymān, *Tafsīr Muqātil ibn Sulaymān*, ed. Aḥmad Farīd (Beirut: Dār al-Kutub al-ʿIlmīya, 1424/2003), 2:426; Abū Jaʿfar Muḥammad ibn Jarīr al-Ṭabarī, *Jāmiʿ al-bayān ʿan taʾwīl āy al-qurʾān* (Beirut: Dār al-Fikr, 1408/1988), 17:165; authorities cited in Ibn Kathīr, *Tafsīr*, 10:272.

302. Abū'l-Faraj ʿAbd al-Raḥmān ibn ʿAlī Ibn al-Jawzī, *Zād al-masīr fī ʿilm al-tafsīr* (Beirut: al-Maktab al-Islāmī, 1404/1984), 6:62; see also al-Qurṭubī, *Tafsīr*, 12:203; al-Fakhr al-Rāzī, *al-Tafsīr al-kabīr*, 3rd printing (Beirut: Dār Iḥyāʾ al-Turāth al-ʿArabī, n.d.), 24:33.

303. See, for instance, ʿAlī ibn Muḥammad al-Māwardī, *al-Nukat wa'l-ʿuyūn: tafsīr al-Māwardī* (Beirut: Dār al-Kutub al-ʿIlmīya, 1412/1992), 4:121; al-Ḥasan ibn Muḥammad al-Qummī al-Naysābūrī, *Gharāʾib al-qurʾān wa-raghāʾib al-furqān*, ed. Ibrāhīm ʿAṭwa ʿAwaḍ (Cairo: Muṣṭafā al-Bābī al-Ḥalabī, 1386/1967), 18:113.

304. Ibn Rushd, *Bayān*, 1:420.

305. Ibn al-Humām, *Sharḥ fatḥ al-qadīr*, 1:366 (translation from Sadeghi, *Logic of Law-Making*, 120).

306. Shaykh-Zādeh, *Majmaʿ al-anhur*, 1:109.
307. Given the overwhelming preponderance of nonsexual usages of the root f-t-n in the Qur'an and ḥadīth, it is not surprising that scholarly work on the early development of the concept of *fitna* often completely neglects any gendered or sexual connotations. See Jean-Claude Vadet, "Quelques remarques sur la racine ftn dans le coran et la plus ancienne littérature musulmane," *Revue des Études islamiques* 37 (1969), 81–101; *Encyclopaedia of Islam*, 2nd ed., s.v. "Fitna" (by L. Gardet). See also Widād Qāḍī, "Mafhūm al-fitna wa-ṣuwaruhā fī adab ʿAbd al-Ḥamīd al-Kātib," *Fuṣūl adabīya wa-tārīkhīya li-majmūʿa min al-ʿulamāʾ wa'l-udabāʾ muhdāt ilā Nāṣir al-Dīn al-Asad*, ed. Ḥusayn ʿAṭwān (Beirut: Dār al-Jīl, 1993), 337–61.
308. This ḥadīth is transmitted in the *Ṣaḥīḥs* of al-Bukhārī and Muslim, the *Sunan* of al-Tirmidhī, the *Musnad* of Aḥmad ibn Ḥanbal, and a number of later collections; it thus must have been in circulation by the first half of the third/ninth century. For references, see Zaghlūl, *Mawsūʿa*, 8:96–97.
309. See A. H. Wensinck and J. P. Mensing, *Concordance et indices de la tradition musulmane* (Leiden: Brill, 1965), 5:59–64. Because the dating and authenticity of ḥadīth remain highly contested issues that are unlikely to be definitively resolved in the foreseeable future, it must remain an open question whether the small minority of ḥadīth reports associating *fitna* with women and sex represent an authentic prophetic kernel that grew in prominence through later interpretation or a secondary back-projection from later times.
310. Al-Jāḥiẓ, *Rasāʾil al-Jāḥiẓ*, ed. ʿAbd A. Muhannā (Beirut: Dār al-Ḥadātha, [1988?]), 2:96–104, 2:113, 2:115–16.
311. Nawawī, *Rawḍat al-ṭālibīn*, 5:370.
312. I examine this development in a work in progress.
313. Qurṭubī, *Tafsīr*, 14:157.
314. Nevertheless, al-Qurṭubī emphasizes that a woman "may not be forbidden . . . from praying in mosques as long as no *fitna* is feared for her." It is signficant that here the *fitna* is feared "for" her (*ʿalayhā*) rather than "from" her. Qurṭubī, *Tafsīr*, 2:54 (commentary on verse 2:114).
315. See, for instance, Abū'l-Faraj ʿAbd al-Raḥmān Ibn al-Jawzī al-Baghdādī, *Naqd al-ʿilm wa'l-ʿulamāʾ aw Talbīs Iblīs* ([Cairo?]: Idārat al-Ṭibāʿa al-Munīrīya, [1966?]), 256–61. The figure of the beardless or downy-cheeked youth as the object of the erotic attention of adult men is discussed exhaustively in Khaled El-Rouayheb, *Before Homosexuality in the Arab-Islamic World, 1500–1800* (Chicago: University of Chicago Press, 2005).
316. Haytamī, *Fatḥ al-jawād*, 1:253.
317. See Ramlī, *Nihāyat al-muḥtāj*, 2:140; Shabrāmallisī, *Ḥāshiya*, in the margins of al-Ramlī, *Nihāyat al-muḥtāj*, 2:140.

318. Peirce, "Seniority, Sexuality, and Social Order," 178.
319. See, for instance, Balaraba B. M. Sule and Priscilla E. Starratt, "Islamic Leadership Positions for Women in Contemporary Kano Society," in *Hausa Women in the Twentieth Century*, ed. Catherine Coles and Beverly Mack (Madison: University of Wisconsin Press, 1991), 46 ("In recent history it has been the custom for women of child bearing age to avoid being seen in public in daylight hours"). Engseng Ho writes that in Hadramaut, Yemen, girls undergo "a period of relative confinement . . . from the age of ten or eleven until marriage, which may be as early as fourteen." Engseng Ho, *The Graves of Tarim: Genealogy and Mobility Across the Indian Ocean* (Berkeley: University of California Press, 2006), 72.
320. Peirce, "Seniority, Sexuality, and Social Order," 169.
321. Ibid., 181.
322. Ibid., 182.
323. Ibn al-Humām, *Fatḥ al-qadīr*, 7:509; Haytamī, *Tuḥfat al-muḥtāj*, printed with *Ḥawāshī al-Shirwānī wa-Ibn Qāsim al-ʿAbbādī*, 10:193; Sulaymān ibn ʿUmar, known as al-Jamal, *Ḥāshiyat al-Jamal ʿalā Sharḥ al-Minhāj* (Beirut: Dār al-Kutub al-ʿIlmīya, 1417/1996), 8:415; Leslie Peirce, "'The Law Shall Not Languish': Social Class and Public Conduct in Sixteenth-Century Ottoman Legal Discourse," in *Hermeneutics and Honor: Negotiating Female "Public" Space in Islamic/ate Societies*, ed. Asma Afsaruddin (Cambridge, MA: Harvard University Press, 1999), 140–44.
324. For instance, the Egyptian Ḥanafī jurist Qāriʾ al-Hidāya (d. 879/1426) briskly denies that a woman can be deemed *mukhaddara* on the basis of the local custom that secluded women did not go out in the daytime. Sirāj al-Dīn ʿUmar ibn ʿAlī al-Ḥanafī, *Kitāb Fatāwā Qāriʾ al-Hidāya*, ed. Muḥammad al-Raḥīl Gharāyaba and Muḥammad ʿAlī al-Zughūl (Amman: Dār al-Furqān, 1420/1999), 104–5. For two tenth-/sixteenth-century Shāfiʿī fatwas expressing the opposite opinion (i.e., that a *mukhaddara* stays home specifically in the daytime), see Ibn ʿAbd al-Ghaffār, *Izāla*, 114b–115a.
325. Haytamī, *Tuḥfat al-muḥtāj*, printed with *Ḥawāshī al-Shirwānī wa-Ibn Qāsim al-ʿAbbādī*, 10:193.
326. Karen Bauer, "Room for Interpretation: Qurʾānic Exegesis and Gender" (PhD diss., Princeton University, 2008), 17, 127–29, 131. Bauer identifies al-Thaʿlabī (d. 427/1035) as the first author to present this argument in a preserved commentary and finds that it figures in approximately one-fourth of the commentaries she consulted for the fifth/eleventh to eighth/fourteenth centuries.
327. See Ibn Taymīya, *Majmūʿ al-fatāwā*, 6:205, 6:210, 6:214–15, 6:229–30.
328. Jalāl al-Dīn al-Suyūṭī, *Isbāl al-kisāʾ ʿalā al-nisāʾ* (Beirut: Dār al-Kutub al-ʿIlmīya, n.d.), 24.

2. RECONSTRUCTING PRACTICE

1. Ibn Abī Shayba, *Muṣannaf Ibn Abī Shayba fī'l-aḥādīth wa'l-āthār*, ed. Saʿīd al-Laḥḥām (Beirut: Dār al-Fikr, 1428–29/2008), 2:277; Sulaymān ibn Aḥmad al-Ṭabarānī, *al-Muʿjam al-kabīr*, ed. Ḥamdī ʿAbd al-Majīd al-Silafī (Beirut: Dār Iḥyāʾ al-Turāth al-ʿArabī, 1422/2002), 9:294.
2. Ṭabarānī, *Muʿjam*, 9:293–95. Ibn Abī Shayba, *Muṣannaf*, 2:276–77; ʿAbd al-Razzāq, *Muṣannaf*, ed. Ḥabīb Allāh al-Aʿẓamī (Beirut: al-Majlis al-ʿIlmī, n.d.), 3:150, #5116; Muḥammad ibn Isḥāq ibn Khuzayma, *Ṣaḥīḥ Ibn Khuzayma* (Beirut: al-Maktab al-Islāmī, 1395/1975), 3:93, see also 3:95. In another report from an Iraqi source, the caliph ʿUmar ibn ʿAbd al-ʿAzīz writes to his governor of Kūfa, ʿAbd al-Ḥamīd ibn ʿAbd al-Raḥmān, "Look to the women who are with you and do not allow them to attend congregational prayers or funerals; they are not entitled to attend Friday prayers or funerals." Ibn Abī Shayba, *Muṣannaf*, 2:19.
3. Christopher Melchert, "Whether to Keep Women Out of the Mosque: A Survey of Medieval Islamic Law," in *Authority, Privacy and Public Order in Islam, Proceedings of the 22nd Congress of L'Union Européenne des Arabisants et Islamisants*, ed. B. Michalak-Pikulska and A. Pikulski (Leuven: Uitgeverij Peeters, 2006), 61.
4. Leor Halevi, *Muhammad's Grave: Death Rites and the Making of Islamic Society* (New York: Columbia University Press, 2007), 140. Behnam Sadeghi argues that women were prohibited from going to the mosque in first-century Medina and Kufa despite the prophetic precedent to the contrary, whereas "Mecca and Basra . . . preserved the status quo." Behnam Sadeghi, *The Logic of Law-Making in Islam: Women and Prayer in the Legal Tradition* (Cambridge: Cambridge University Press, 2012), 105. His evidence will be presented in a forthcoming publication.
5. Ibn Abī Shayba, *Muṣannaf*, 2:19; Mālik ibn Anas, *al-Mudawwana al-kubrā*, transmitted by Saḥnūn ibn Saʿīd al-Tanūkhī from ʿAbd al-Raḥmān ibn al-Qāsim (Beirut: Dār al-Kutub al-ʿIlmīya, 1426/2005), 1:238.
6. Ibn Abī Shayba, *Muṣannaf*, 2:278.
7. ʿAbd al-Razzāq, *Muṣannaf*, 3:150–51; Ibn Abī Shayba, *Muṣannaf*, 2:277.
8. Muḥammad ibn Naṣr al-Marwazī, *Qiyām al-Layl wa-Qiyām Ramaḍān wa-Kitāb al-Witr*, abridged by Aḥmad ibn ʿAlī al-Maqrīzī (Sangla Hill, Pakistan: al-Maktaba al-Atharīya, 1389/1969), 162.
9. Muḥammad ibn Jarīr al-Ṭabarī, *Taʾrīkh al-umam wa'l-mulūk*, ed. Muḥammad Abū'l-Faḍl Ibrāhīm (Beirut: Dār al-Turāth, n.d.), 6:105.
10. Jalāl al-Dīn al-Suyūṭī, *al-Durr al-manthūr fī'l-tafsīr bi'l-maʾthūr* (Beirut: Dār al-Maʿrifa, n.d.), 5:196 (citing Ibn Abī Ḥātim).
11. Ṭabarī, *Taʾrīkh*, 5:144–45.

12. Khalīfa ibn Khayyāṭ al-ʿUṣfurī, *Ta'rīkh Khalīfa ibn Khayyāṭ*, ed. Akram Ḍiyāʾ al-ʿUmarī (Beirut: Mu'assasat al-Risāla, 1397/1977), 274. He also cites a piece of Khārijī poetry lauding Ghazāla and her vow.
13. Ṭabarī, *Taʾrīkh*, 6:273. There was some confusion about whether Ghazāla was Shabīb's wife or his mother; see Joseph van Ess, *Theologie und Gesellschaft im 2. und 3. Jahrhundert Hidschra* (Berlin: Walter de Gruyter, 1992), 2:461.
14. ʿAbd al-Qāhir al-Baghdādī, *al-Farq bayna al-firaq*, ed. Muḥammad ʿUthmān al-Khisht (Cairo: Maktabat Ibn Sīnā, [1988/1408–9]), 101, 102. It is unclear whether the vague reference to "ascending the pulpit" in the much earlier account of Khalīfa ibn Khayyāṭ refers to the delivery of a sermon or simply to a physical ascent.
15. Muḥammad ibn Khalaf Wakīʿ, *Akhbār al-quḍāt*, ed. ʿAbd al-ʿAzīz Muṣṭafā al-Marāghī (Cairo: al-Maktaba al-Tijārīya, 1366/1947), 2:360.
16. Ibn Abī Shayba, *Muṣannaf*, 2:157.
17. Cited from Ibn Saʿd in Abū'l-Faraj Ibn al-Jawzī, *Ṣifat al-ṣafwa* (Beirut: Dār al-Kutub al-ʿIlmīya, 1409/1989), 3:124–25.
18. Abū'l-Faraj al-Iṣfahānī, *Kitāb al-Aghānī* (Cairo: al-Hayʾa al-Miṣrīya al-ʿĀmma li'l-Kitāb, 1993), 21:365–66.
19. Ibn al-Jawzī, *Kitāb al-Quṣṣāṣ wa'l-mudhakkirīn*, trans. Merlin L. Swartz (Beirut: Dār al-Mashriq, 1971), para. #235 (Arabic text, 108; English translation, 192).
20. Ibn Khallikān, *Wafayāt al-aʿyān*, ed. Iḥsān ʿAbbās (Beirut: Dār al-Thaqāfa, n.d.), 2:401.
21. Ibn al-Jawzī, *Ṣifat al-ṣafwa*, 4:32.
22. Abū ʿUthmān ʿAmr ibn Baḥr al-Jāḥiẓ, *al-Ḥayawān*, ed. ʿAbd al-Salām Muḥammad Hārūn (Cairo: Maktabat Muṣṭafā al-Bābī al-Ḥalabī wa-Awlādihi, 1356/1938), 2:231–33.
23. Aḥmad ibn Ḥanbal, *Kitāb al-zuhd* (Beirut: Dār al-Kutub al-ʿIlmīya, n.d.), 318; also in Abū Nuʿaym al-Iṣfahānī, *Ḥulyat al-awliyāʾ wa-ṭabaqāt al-aṣfiyāʾ* (Beirut: Dār al-Kitāb al-ʿArabī, 1387/1967), 2:251. See also Melchert, "Whether to Keep Women Out of the Mosque," 61.
24. See Mathieu Tillier, "Women Before the Qāḍī Under the Abbasids," *Islamic Law and Society* 16 (2009): 280–301, esp. 292–93, 295, 297, 299–301.
25. Abū'l-Ḥajjāj Yūsuf al-Mizzī, *Tahdhīb al-Kamāl fī asmāʾ al-rijāl*, ed. Bashshār ʿAwwād Maʿrūf (Beirut: Muʾassasat al-Risāla, 1403/1983), 3:428.
26. Leila Ahmed, *Women and Gender in Islam: Historical Roots of a Modern Debate* (New Haven, CT: Yale University Press, 1992), 68. Also see Halevi, *Muhammad's Grave*, 139 and references 103–7 on 301. Zoroastrians were numerically a relatively small proportion of the Iraqi population. According to a Zoroastrian ritual manual of the early Islamic period, "a woman could worship at fire temples" or even "perform basic rites at the sacred

fires when men were unavailable." Jamsheed K. Choksy, *Evil, Good, and Gender: Facets of the Feminine in Zoroastrian Religious History* (New York: Peter Lang, 2002), 91.

27. For instance, Mordechai Friedman argues that, although the Geniza documents manifest Jewish men's sentiment that "their wives should not be allowed to move about freely outdoors," this is primarily "a reflection of prevailing Islamic mores." Mordechai A. Friedman, "The Ethics of Medieval Jewish Marriage," in *Religion in a Religious Age*, ed. S. D. Goitein (Cambridge, MA: Association for Jewish Studies, 1974), 88–91.
28. Discussing the ritual status of food prepared by non-Jews, the Babylonian Talmud states that "a woman puts her food pots upon the stove, leaving her non-Jewish servants alone and home, until she comes from the bathhouse or the synagogue, and is not concerned." Whereas a jealous husband may forbid his wife to be alone with one man, he may not forbid her to gather with many men in the synagogue. Women were expected to say "amen" after the priests pronounced the blessing over the congregation. See Hannah Safrai, "Women and the Ancient Synagogue," in *Daughters of the King*, ed. Susan Grossman and Rivka Haut (Philadelphia: Jewish Publication Society, 1992), 40.
29. George, Bishop of Mosul and Arbel (attributed), *A Commentary on the Mass*, trans. from Syriac by R. H. Connolly, ed. F. Robert Matheus (Vadavathoor, Kottayam, India: Pontifical Oriental Institute of Religious Studies, 2000), 4; see also J. M. Fiey, *Mossoul Chrétienne* (Beirut: Imprimerie Catholique, 1959), 78.
30. See Halevi, *Muhammad's Grave*, 140.
31. See Alfonso Carmona, "The Introduction of Mālik's Teachings in al-Andalus," in *The Islamic School of Law: Evolution, Devolution, and Progress*, ed. Peri Bearman, Rudolph Peters, and Frank E. Vogel (Cambridge, MA: Islamic Legal Studies Program, Harvard Law School, 2005), 41–56; Maribel Fierro, "Proto-Malikis, Malikis, and Reformed Malikis in al-Andalus," in Bearman, Peters, and Vogel, eds., *The Islamic School of Law*, 57–76.
32. See, for instance, ʿAbd al-Ḥalīm Muḥammad Abū Shuqqa, *Taḥrīr al-marʾa fī ʿaṣr al-risāla* (Kuwait: Dār al-Qalam li'l-Nashr wa'l-Tawzīʿ, 1430/2009), 2:195, 2:197.
33. ʿAlī ibn Aḥmad al-Samhūdī, *Wafāʾ al-wafā bi-akhbār dār al-Muṣṭafā*, ed. Muḥammad Muḥyī al-Dīn ʿAbd al-Ḥamīd (Cairo: Maṭbaʿat Dār al-Saʿāda, n.d.), 2:537; see also Ibn Rusteh, *Les Atours Précieux*, ed. Gaston Wiet (Cairo: Publications de la Société d'Égypte, 1955), 78. The report implies that the *saqāʾif al-nisāʾ* predated al-Mahdī's enlargement of the mosque. It is unclear when these arcades began to be used specifically to accommodate women or how long this use remained customary; later descriptions of the mosque do not mention special spaces for women, and by the

time al-Samhūdī reproduced Ibn Zabāla's report in the ninth/fifteenth century, even the term "women's arcades" required explanation.

34. Ibn al-ʿIdhārī al-Marrākushī, *al-Bayān al-mughrib*, ed. G. S. Colin and É. Lévi-Provençal (Beirut: Dār al-Thaqāfa, n.d.), 2:230. (The source is Aḥmad al-Rāzī, who died in the middle of the tenth century AH.)
35. É. Lévi-Provençal, "Documents et Notules: Les Citations du *Muqtabis* d'Ibn Ḥayyān Relatives aux Agrandissements de la Grande-Mosquée de Cordoue au IXe Siècle," *Arabica* 1 (1954): 91 (the source is Ibn al-Naẓẓām, who wrote in the tenth century AH); *Dhikr bilād al-andalus li-muʾallif majhūl*, ed. and trans. Luis Molina (Madrid: Consejo Superior de Investigaciones Científicas Instituto "Miguel Asín," 1983), 37.
36. See Elie Lambert, "L'histoire de la Grande Mosquée de Cordoue aux VIIIe et IXe siècles d'après des textes inédits," *Annales de l'Institut d'Études Orientales* 2 (1936): 172. Lucien Golvin observes that, although examples of elevated galleries exist, they date from a much later period. Lucien Golvin, *Essai sur l'architecture religieuse musulman*, vol. 4, *L'Art hispano-musulman* (Paris: Éditions Klincksieck, 1979), 31.
37. See Lambert, "L'histoire," 175.
38. Lévi-Provençal, "Documents," 92.
39. See Aḥmad ibn Muḥammad al-Maqqarī al-Tilimsānī, *Nafḥ al-ṭīb min ghuṣn al-Andalus al-raṭīb*, ed. Iḥsān ʿAbbās (Beirut: Dār Ṣādir, 1388/1968), 1:547, 1:550; Muḥammad ibn ʿAbd Allāh al-Ḥimyarī, *Ṣifat jazīrat al-andalus muntakhaba min kitāb al-Rawḍ al-miʿṭār fī khabar al-aqṭār*, ed. É. Lévy-Provençal (Cairo, 1937), 157.
40. See Jāḥiẓ, *Ḥayawān*, 2:161; Ṭabarī, *Taʾrīkh*, 5:215, 5:236. Ibn Taymīya writes that "the great authorities of Islamic law (*al-aʾimma*) have disapproved of the erection of enclosures (*maqāṣīr*) in the mosque, because they were innovated by one of the kings." Taqī al-Dīn Ibn Taymīya, *al-Fatāwā al-kubrā* (Cairo: Dār al-Kutub al-Ḥadītha, 1966), 22:104. Indeed, the Great Mosque of Qayrawān also had a royal *maqṣūra*. See Abū ʿUbayd al-Bakrī, *al-Mughrib fī dhikr bilād ifrīqīya wa'l-maghrib, wa-huwa juzʾ min kitāb al-Masālik wa'l-mamālik*, ed. William MacGuckin de Slane (Baghdad: Maktabat al-Muthannā, n.d.), 24.
41. Maqqarī, *Nafḥ al-ṭīb*, 1:550, also see 1:547; al-Ḥimyarī, *Ṣifat jazīrat al-andalus*, 157; *Dhikr bilād al-andalus*, 1:39.
42. Maqqarī, *Nafḥ al-ṭīb*, 1:555.
43. Aḥmad ibn ʿAbd Allāh ibn ʿAbd al-Raʾūf al-Qurṭubī, *Ādāb al-ḥisba wa'l-muḥtasib*, ed. Fāṭima al-Idrīsī (Beirut: Dār Ibn Ḥazm, 1425/2005), 37–38.
44. See ʿUmar Riḍā Kaḥḥāla, *Muʿjam al-muʾallifīn* (Beirut: Mu'assasat al-Risāla, 1414/1993), 3:575.
45. Muḥammad ibn ʿĪsā Ibn al-Munāṣif, *Tanbīh al-ḥukkām ʿalā maʾākhidh al-aḥkām*, ed. ʿAbd al-Ḥafīẓ Manṣūr (Tunis: Dār al-Turkī li'l-Nashr, 1988), 334.

46. Maqqarī, *Nafḥ al-ṭīb*, 1:622, second version of anecdote 3:262–63; cited in Manuela Marín, *Mujeres en al-Ándalus* (Madrid: Consejo Superior de Investigaciones Científicas, 2000), 231–32. Interestingly, in the second version of the anecdote the woman is represented as frightened largely on behalf of her son, who she fears will be the object of the (apparently erotic) attentions of the group of men. For Abū ʿĀmir, see Kaḥḥāla, *Muʿjam*, 1:187.
47. For these two figures, see Ibn Farḥūn, *al-Dībāj al-mudhhab fī maʿrifat aʿyān ʿulamāʾ al-madhhab*, ed. Maʾmūn ibn Muḥyī'l-Dīn al-Jannān (Beirut: Dār al-Kutub al-ʿIlmīya, 1417/1996), 260 (ʿAbd al-Ḥamīd ibn Muḥammad al-Harawī), 298 (Abū'l-Ḥasan ibn Muḥammad al-Lakhmī).
48. See al-Muqaddasī, *Aḥsan al-taqāsīm fī maʿrifat al-aqālīm* (Leiden: Brill, 1906), 225; Bakrī, *Mughrib*, 23.
49. *Wa-tuthbat li'l-satr bi'l-ājurr*; abridged by al-Wansharīsī as "that enclosures for women should be built of bricks in the arcades of the mosque to conceal the women." Aḥmad ibn Yaḥyā al-Wansharīsī, *Al-Miʿyar al-muʿrib wa'l-jāmiʿ al-mughrib ʿan fatāwā ahl ifrīqīya wa'l-andalus wa'l-maghrib*, ed. Muḥammad Ḥajjī (Rabat: Wizārat al-Awqāf wa'l-Shuʾūn al-Islāmīya li'l-Mamlaka al-Maghribīya, 1401/1981), 8:441.
50. In this context, "*muḥtasib*" presumably simply means someone (here probably a private individual) who is engaging in the religious duty of "commanding the right and forbidding the wrong." On this concept, see Michael Cook, *Commanding Right and Forbidding Wrong in Islamic Thought* (Cambridge: Cambridge University Press, 2000).
51. Abū'l-Qāsim ibn Aḥmad al-Balawī, known as al-Burzulī, *Fatāwā al-Burzulī: Jāmiʿ masāʾil al-aḥkām li-mā nazala min al-qaḍāyā bi'l-muftīn wa'l-ḥukkām*, ed. Muḥammad al-Ḥabīb al-Hīla (Beirut: Dār al-Gharb al-Islāmī, 2002), 1:391; compare a shorter rendition in al-Wansharīsī, *Miʿyār*, 8:441 (translated in Vincent Lagardère, *Histoire et Société en Occident Musulman au Moyen Âge: Analyse du* Miʿyār *d'al-Wanšarīsī* (Madrid: Consejo Superior de Investigaciones Científicas, 1995), 311.
52. Burzulī, *Fatāwā*, 1:392.
53. Ibid., 1:393; a somewhat abbreviated version appears in Wansharīsī, *Miʿyār*, 8:442 (translated in Lagardère, *Histoire*, 312).
54. Bakrī, *Mughrib*, 24. This statement appears immediately after a description of the expansion of the mosque under Ibrāhīm ibn Aḥmad ibn al-Aghlab (reigned 261–89/875–902), but is expressed in the present tense and thus appears to describe the state of the mosque in al-Bakrī's time.
55. Abū'l-Ḥasan ʿAlī al-Jaznāʾī, *Kitāb zahrat al-ās fī bināʾ madīnat Fās*, ed. and trans. Alfred Bel (Algiers: Jules Carbonel, 1923), 152 and n4 of translation (70–71 of Arabic text); Ibn Abī Zarʿ, *Rawḍ al-Qirṭās*, trans. and annotated by Ambrosio Huici Miranda (Valencia, 1964), 127, 133. The Rabat edition of *Zahrat al-ās* (al-Maṭbaʿa al-Malikīya, 1411/1991) has "*bāb bayt al-nisāʾ*

al-aṣghar," which could be read as "the door of the smaller women's [prayer] room"; the Algiers edition has "*al-aṣfar,*" which Bel translates as "the yellow door" ("*la porte jaune*"), which seems less likely. If the word is actually *aṣghar*, this could imply that there was another (and larger) prayer room for women.

56. ʿAbd al-Hādī al-Tāzī, *Jāmiʿ al-Qarawīyīn: al-masjid wa'l-jāmiʿa bi-madīnat Fās, mawsūʿa li-taʾrīkhihā al-miʿmārī wa'l-fikrī* (Beirut: Dār al-Kitāb al-Lubnānī, 1973), 2:319–20. I have been unable to trace this information in the primary sources, although it is compatible with the information found there; for al-Maghīlī's role in the renovation of the mosque, see al-Jaznāʾī, *Zahra*, 143.
57. "Communications: Le plan de l'Université de Qarawiyin à Fès," *Hespéris* 3 (1923): 515; also see plans in *Encyclopaedia of Islam*, 2nd ed., s.v. "al-Ḳarawiyyīn" (which also labels the adjoining back arcade up to the "Bab el Ouard" as the "mosquée des femmes"), and in Georges Marçais, *L'Architecture Musulmane d'Occident* (Paris: Arts et Métiers Graphiques, 1954), 199.
58. Edith Wharton, *In Morocco* (New York: Charles Scribner's Sons, 1919; Hopewell, NJ: Ecco Press, 1996), 99. Another Western work of the first half of the twentieth century states that "in every [Moroccan] mosque of any significance (*un peu importante*), there is a small room without a ceiling reserved for women so that they can hear the voices of the preacher and the imām and follow the prayer with the men, without being mixed with them." O. Pesle, *La Femme Musulmane dans le Droit la Religion et les Mœurs* (Rabat: Les éditions de la porte, 1946), 177.
59. Golvin, *Essai*, 4:204.
60. Al-Jaznāʾī, *Zahra*, 172 of French translation (83 of Arabic text).
61. For Ibn Khajjū, see Kaḥḥāla, *Muʿjam*, 2:645 (note error in Gregorian death date).
62. Abū ʿĪsā Sayyidī al-Mahdī al-Wazzānī, *al-Nawāzil al-jadīda al-kubrā fīmā li-ahl Fās wa ghayrihim min al-badū wa'l-qurā* ([Rabat?]: al-Mamlaka al-Maghribīya, Wizārat al-Awqāf wa'l-Shuʾūn al-Islāmīya, 1417/1996), 1:517–18.
63. In a later historical period, the Moroccan scholar and Sufi Muḥammad ibn ʿAbd al-Salām al-Nāṣirī (d. 1239/1823–24) alludes to this possibility when he argues that the function of the *muballigh* (who repeats and amplifies the recitation of the prayer leader from the roof of the mosque) is to afford the merit of congregational prayer to latter-day women who are no longer allowed to go out to the mosque. Muḥammad ibn ʿAbd al-Salām al-Nāṣirī, *al-Mazāyā fi-mā uḥditha min al-bidaʿ fī umm al-zawāyā*, ed. ʿAbd al-Majīd al-Khayālī (Beirut: Dār al-Kutub al-ʿIlmīya, 1424/2003), 142–3.
64. Lisān al-Dīn Ibn al-Khaṭīb, *al-Iḥāṭa fī akhbār gharnāṭa* (Cairo: Maktabat al-Khānjī, n.d.), 3:92. For Ibn al-Fakhkhār, see Ibn Farḥūn, *Dībāj*, 395–36;

Ibn Ḥajar al-ʿAsqalānī, *al-Durar al-kāmina fī aʿyān al-miʾa al-thāmina* (Beirut: Dār al-Kutub al-ʿIlmīya, 1418/1997), 4:51. I thank Professor Nadia Lachiri for drawing my attention to Ibn al-Fakhkhār.

65. "*Kānat muqīma bi-ghurfa lahā bi-aʿlā al-jāmiʿ al-muʿallaq bi'l-jazīra al-khaḍrā bi'l-andalus.*" Ibn Ḥajar al-ʿAsqalānī, *al-Durar al-kāmina,* 2:144.
66. Scott Kugle, *Rebel Between Spirit and Law: Ahmad Zarruq, Sainthood, and Authority in Islam* (Bloomington: Indiana University Press, 2006), 47, 48. I thank Professor Kugle for his thoughtful reply to my query on this subject.
67. Laḥsan al-Yūbī, *al-Fatāwā al-fiqhīya fī ahamm al-qaḍāyā min ʿahd al-Saʿdīyīn ilā mā qabla al-ḥimāya* ([Rabat?]: al-Mamlaka al-Maghribīya, Wizārat al-Awqāf wa'l-Shuʾūn al-Islāmīya, 1419/1998), 266 (reference to *Nawāzil* of al-Tusūlī).
68. Wansharīsī, *Miʿyār*, 11:228.
69. Ibn ʿArḍūn, *Muqniʿ al-muḥtāj fī ādāb al-zawāj*, ed. ʿAbd al-Salām al-Zayyānī (Beirut: Dār Ibn Ḥazm, 1430/2010), 2:774–76.
70. Ahmed El Shamsy, "From Tradition to Law: The Origins and Early Development of the Shāfiʿī School of Law in Ninth-Century Egypt" (PhD diss., Harvard University, 2009), 109–10 (citing Jalāl al-Dīn al-Suyūṭī, *Ḥusn al-muḥāḍara*, ed. Muḥammad Abū al-Faḍl Ibrāhīm [Cairo: ʿĪsā al-Bābī al-Ḥalabī, 1967–68], 1:399).
71. Aḥmad ibn ʿAlī al-Maqrīzī, *al-Mawāʿiẓ wa'l-iʿtibār bi-dhikr al-khiṭaṭ wa'l-āthār, al-maʿrūf bi'l-Khiṭaṭ al-maqrīzīya*, ed. Muḥammad Zaynhum and Madīḥa al-Sharqāwī (Cairo: Maktabat al-Madbūlī, 1998), 2:122; Narīmān ʿAbd al-Karīm Aḥmad, *al-Marʾa fī miṣr fī al-ʿaṣr al-mamlūkī* (Cairo: al-Hayʾa al-Miṣrīya al-ʿĀmma li'l-Kitāb, 1993), 85–86; Delia Cortese and Simonetta Calderini, *Women and the Fatimids in the World of Islam* (Edinburgh: Edinburgh University Press, 2006), 33.
72. See Maqrīzī, *Khiṭaṭ*, 3:663, for an anecdote describing Umm al-Khayr on her way out of the mosque accompanied by her "grandchildren and maidservants (*fī ḥafadatihā wa-jawārīhā*)." Perhaps her great fame was acquired through preaching in the mosque, although she also appears to have had a *ribāṭ*. A statement in wide circulation in modern sources holds that she used to hold study sessions for women in the Mosque of ʿAmr ibn al-ʿĀṣ, according to some versions around the year 415/1024. See, for instance, Aḥmad, *al-Marʾa al-fī miṣr*, 86n51; Cortese and Calderini, *Women and the Fatimids*, 33. Although this may well be correct, I have been unable to locate a primary source documenting it; it may possibly reflect an educated guess based on al-Maqrīzī's anecdote.
73. See Ibn al-Ḥājj al-ʿAbdarī, *Kitāb al-Madkhal* (Beirut: Dār al-Kutub al-ʿIlmīya, 1415/1995), 2:435–36, 2:440; Huda Lutfi, "Manners and Customs of Fourteenth-Century Cairene Women: Female Anarchy Versus Male Shar'i Order in Muslim Prescriptive Treatises," in *Women in Middle*

Eastern History: Shifting Boundaries in Sex and Gender, ed. Nikki R. Keddie and Beth Baron (New Haven, CT: Yale University Press, 1991), 115. On the location of *ʿīd* prayers, see Wahba al-Zuḥaylī, *al-Fiqh al-islāmī wa-adillatuhu* (Damascus: Dār al-Fikr, 1425/2005), 2:1394.

74. Ibn al-Ḥājj, *Madkhal*, 2:440.
75. See *Encyclopaedia of Islam*, 2nd ed., s.v. "Masdjid. I. In the Central Islamic Lands" (by J. Pedersen), which states that "Ibn al-Ḥādjdj would prefer to exclude [women from mosques] altogether and gives ʿĀʾisha as his authority for this."
76. See *Encyclopaedia of Islam*, 2nd ed., s.v. "ʿĀshūrāʾ" (by A. J. Wensinck and P. Marçais); Marion Katz, *The Birth of the Prophet Muḥammad* (London: Routledge, 2007), 114–17.
77. The Jāmiʿ al-ʿAtīq, also known as Tāj al-Jawāmiʿ (Crown of Mosques) or the Mosque of ʿAmr ibn al-ʿĀṣ, was the original Friday mosque founded in the city of Fusṭāṭ at the time of the Muslim conquest. By Mamlūk times, it had long ceased to be the only Friday mosque of Cairo, but it remained very important. See al-Maqrīzī, *Khiṭaṭ*, 3:144–70; Ibn Duqmāq, *al-Intiṣār li-wāsiṭat ʿaqd al-amṣār* (Beirut: al-Maktab al-Tijārī li'l-Ṭibāʿa wa'l-Nashr wa'l-Taʾlīf, n.d.), 1:59–75.
78. The Jāmiʿ al-ʿAtīq possessed a number of precious volumes of the Qurʾan, including a copy of the Qur'an claimed (controversially) to have been the one ʿUthmān was reading at the time of his assassination. Maqrīzī, *Khiṭaṭ*, 3:156; Ibn Duqmāq, *Intiṣār*, 1:72–74.
79. On the "Green Tablet (*al-lawḥ al-akhḍar*)," see Maqrīzī, *Khiṭaṭ*, 3:154, 3:155. The religious significance of the tablet is unclear; however, Ibn Duqmāq lists "opposite the Green Tablet" as one of the "places known for *baraka* and for the answering of prayers" in the Jāmiʿ al-ʿAtīq. Ibn Duqmāq, *Intiṣār*, 1:74–75.
80. In the *Encyclopaedia of Islam* article "Masdjid," it is noted that in general "in the house of God, the *miḥrāb* and the *minbar* enjoyed particular sanctity."
81. That is, Friday night (*laylat al-jumʿa*) according to the convention that the day begins at nightfall.
82. The prayer is said to have been performed first in Jerusalem in the eleventh century CE. For a discussion of the legal debate surrounding the legitimacy of the *Raghāʾib* prayer, see Raquel Margalit Ukeles, "Innovation or Deviation: Exploring the Boundaries of Islamic Devotional Law" (PhD diss., Harvard University, 2006), 239–97; see also Katz, *Birth*, 150–51.
83. Ibn al-Ḥājj, *Madkhal*, 1:211, 1:214.
84. The eve of the fifteenth day of the month of Shaʿbān.
85. Ibn al-Ḥājj, *Madkhal*, 1:221.

86. Cited in Ibn Mufliḥ, *al-Ādāb al-sharʿīya*, ed. Shuʿayba Arnaʾūṭ and ʿUmar al-Qayyām (Beirut: Mu'assasat al-Risāla, 1416/1996), 2:309–10, 3:381–82.
87. Ibid., 3:382.
88. Abū Bakr Muḥammad ibn al-Walīd al-Ṭurṭūshī, *al-Ḥawādith wa'l-bidaʿ*, ed. Muḥammad Ḥasan Ismāʿīl (Beirut: Dār al-Kutub al-ʿIlmīya, 1424/2003), 30, see also 52.
89. Ibid., 28–29.
90. Abū Shāma, *al-Bāʿith ʿalā inkār al-bidaʿ wa'l-ḥawādith* (Cairo: Maktabat Majd al-Islām, 2007), 127.
91. Ibid., 176–77.
92. Wansharīsī, *Miʿyār*, 11:114.
93. Ibn Shāhīn, *Nayl al-amal fī dhayl al-duwal*, ed. ʿUmar ʿAbd al-Salām Tadmurī (Ṣaydā: al-Maktaba al-ʿAṣrīya, 1422/2002), vol. 2, pt. 8, 121. I thank Guy Burak for this reference.
94. Ibn al-Ḥājj, *Madkhal*, 2:399.
95. The Dār al-Kutub al-ʿIlmīya edition has "*ziyāra*"; it is emended to *ziyāda* for the sense and based on the reading in another edition: Ibn al-Ḥājj, *al-Madkhal* (Cairo: Muṣṭafā al-Bābī al-Ḥalabī, 1380/1960), 2:239.
96. Reading "*khams*" instead of "*khamīs*."
97. Ibn al-Ḥājj, *Madkhal*, 2:399–400.
98. By the time of Ibn al-Ḥājj, Friday prayers were being held in many mosques throughout Cairo, although Ibn al-Ḥājj is here very likely envisioning one of the major sites; see al-Maqrīzī, *Khiṭaṭ*, 3:131. K. A. C. Creswell documents the existence of *ziyādas* on the mosques of ʿAmr and Ibn Ṭūlūn in Cairo; he also speculates that the Jāmiʿ al-Azhar once had a *ziyāda* that was eliminated by the construction of a madrasa. K. A. C. Creswell, *The Muslim Architecture of Egypt* (Oxford, UK: Clarendon Press, 1952; New York: Hacker Art Books, 1978), I:60. Discussing the mosque of Ibn Ṭūlūn, he writes that the *ziyāda* "serves to shelter the mosque proper from immediate contact with the secular buildings of the town"; in general, *ziyādas* often "contained latrines, ablution places, and other subsidiary buildings." Ibid., II:239, II:240. Despite Creswell's reference to latrines, however, the *ziyādas* of the Mosque of ʿAmr are described by Ibn Duqmāq as roofed additions that housed important religious functions such as religious courts and were equipped with prayer niches; at least in this case, the *ziyāda* should be imagined not as unclean or profane, but as an important annex to the mosque. See Ibn Duqmāq, *Intiṣār*, 1:61.
99. Enclosures (*maqāṣīr*) served a number of different purposes in Egyptian mosques by the time of Ibn al-Ḥājj and were sometimes denounced as nuisances and usurpations of space to which all worshippers were in principle entitled. Al-Maqrīzī, for instance, describes a case where *maqāṣīr*

were removed from the Azhar mosque as a reform measure. Al-Maqrīzī, *Khiṭaṭ*, 3:219.

100. Ibn al-Ḥājj, *Madkhal*, 2:388; also cited in Jonathan Berkey, *The Transmission of Knowledge in Medieval Cairo* (Princeton, NJ: Princeton University Press, 1992), 171–72.
101. Manuela Höglmeier, *al-Ǧawbarī und sein Kašf al-asrār—ein Sittenbild des Gauners im arabisch-islamischen Mittelalter (7./13. Jahrhundert): Einführung, Edition und Kommentar* (Berlin: Klaus Schwarz Verlag, 2006), 124–25.
102. Ibn al-Ukhuwwa (d. 729/1329), *The* Maʿālim al-Qurba fī aḥkām al-ḥisba *of Ḍiyāʾ al-Dīn Muḥammad ibn Muḥammad al-Qurashī al-Shāfiʿī known as Ibn al-Ukhuwwa*, ed. and trans. Reuben Levy, E. J. W. Gibb Memorial Series, New Series 12 (London: Cambridge University Press, 1938), 66–67.
103. ʿAbd al-Wahhāb al-Shaʿrānī, *al-Ṭabaqāt al-kubrā li'l-Shaʿrānī* (Cairo: Maktabat wa-Maṭbaʿat Muḥammad ʿAlī Ṣabīḥ wa-Awlādihi, n.d.), 1:75.
104. For the location of al-Maqs, see Boaz Shoshan, *Popular Culture in Medieval Cairo* (Cambridge: Cambridge University Press, 1993), 2, map 1.
105. Muḥammad ibn ʿAbd al-Raḥmān al-Sakhāwī, *al-Ḍawʾ al-lāmiʿ* (Beirut: Manshūrāt Dār Maktabat al-Ḥayāt, n.d.), 2:112; see Shoshan, *Popular Culture*, 12, 13, 89n37 (and references there).
106. Shaʿrānī, *Ṭabaqāt*, 1:75.
107. Berkey, *Transmission*, 175n50 (with reference to al-Sakhāwī).
108. For a representative sampling of names, see Aḥmad ʿAbd al-Razzāq, *al-Marʾa fī Miṣr al-mamlūkīya* (Cairo: al-Hayʾa al-Miṣrīya al-ʿĀmma li'l-Kitāb, 1999), 35.
109. Mohammad Akram Nadwi, *Al-Muhaddithat: The Women Scholars in Islam* (Oxford, UK: Interface Publications, 2007), 152.
110. Ibn al-Ḥājj, *Madkhal*, 2:394; Lutfi, "Manners and Customs," 106, 107.
111. Maqrīzī, *Khiṭaṭ*, 2:9; discussed in Melchert, "Whether to Keep Women Out of the Mosque," 68. It seems possible that North African mosques were more decorous in this regard; the Mālikī school emphasized, for instance, that one should eat or sleep in a mosque only under limited conditions.
112. Aḥmad ibn ʿAlī al-Maqrīzī, *Kitāb al-sulūk li-maʿrifat duwal al-mulūk*, ed. Saʿīd ʿAbd al-Fattāḥ ʿĀshūr ([Cairo?]: Dār al-Kutub, 1973), vol. 4, pt. 3, 1223. The exclusion of women from the Mosque of al-Ḥākim appears to have been part of a larger (and unsuccessful) campaign to limit women's public circulation; see Maqrīzī, *Sulūk*, vol. 4, pt. 3, 1209.
113. Ibn Ḥajar al-ʿAsqalānī, *Fatḥ al-bārī* (Cairo: Maktabat al-Kullīyāt al-Azharīya), 19:401. Despite his geographical *nisba* to ʿAsqalān, Ibn Ḥajar was born, bred, and died in Egypt; see Kaḥḥāla, *Muʿjam*, 1:210.

114. Ibn al-ʿImād al-Aqfahsī, *Tashīl al-maqāṣid li-zuwwār al-masājid*, Cairo ms., Dār al-Kutub Fiqh Shāfiʿī 1440, 247a.
115. Félix Fabri, *Voyage en Egypte (1483)*, translated from Latin and annotated by R. P. Jacques Masson, S.J. (Cairo: L'Institut Français d'Archéologie Orientale du Caire, 1975), 2:578–79. Based on the terminology Fabri uses elsewhere in his narrative, he does not refer to Egyptian Christians as "Saracens" or "pagans"; conversely, he routinely uses the word *church* to refer to places of worship of all religious types. See ibid., 2:556–58, esp. 2:558.
116. Jean Palerne, *Voyage en Égypte de Jean Palerne, Forésien 1581*, ed. Serge Sauneron (Cairo: L'Institut Français d'Archéologie Orientale du Caire, 1971), 56.
117. Ibid., 77.
118. He relates Egyptian women's exclusion from mosques to the fact of their being uncircumcised (an idea without basis in Islamic sources) and contrasts them with Persian women, who he says are circumcised and may enter mosques ("churches"). His statement that local women were uncircumcised is odd, given the historical prevalence of the practice of female genital cutting in Egypt, although the context suggests that he may be referring specifically to the "Turkish" women of the Ottoman elite.
119. Johann Wild, *Voyages en Égypte*, trans. and annotated by Oleg V. Volkoff (Cairo: Institut Français d'Archéologie Orientale, 1973), 102.
120. *Le Voyage en Égypte du Père Antonius Gonzales, 1665–1666*, translated from the Dutch, edited, and annotated by Charles Libois, S.J. (Cairo: Institut Français d'Archéologie Orientale du Caire, 1977), 1:197.
121. Ibid., 1:200.
122. Ibid., 1:221.
123. Ibid., 1:197.
124. On the mosque and tomb of al-Sayyida Nafīsa, see *Encyclopaedia of Islam*, 2nd ed., s.v. "Nafīsa" (by R. Strothmann); on the piety surrounding the shrine, and also on the activities of modern Cairene women at the shrine, see Nadia Abu-Zahra, *The Pure and Powerful: Studies in Contemporary Muslim Society* (Reading, UK: Ithaca Press, 1997), 85–170.
125. Ibn al-Ḥājj, *al-Madkhal*, 1:194.
126. Shoshan, *Popular Culture*, 69; Ohtoshi Tetsuya, "Cairene Cemeteries as Public Loci and Mamluk Egypt," *Mamlūk Studies Review* 10 (2006): 113.
127. Shoshan, *Popular Culture*, 69.
128. "Le voyage et itineraire de Frere Jehan Thenaud," in Jean Thenaud, *Le voyage d'outremer* (Paris, 1884; Geneva: Slatkine Reprints, 1971), 51. Also quoted in Adam Sabra, *Poverty and Charity in Medieval Islam: Mamluk Egypt, 1250–1517* (Cambridge: Cambridge University Press, 2000), 97.
129. Palerne, *Voyage*, 83.

130. Andreas Tietze, *Muṣṭafā ʿĀlī's Description of Cairo of 1599: Text, Translation, Notes* (Vienna: Verlag der Österreichischen Akademie der Wissenschaften, 1975), 33.
131. [Benoît] de Maillet and M. L'Abbé Le Mascrier, *Description de L'Égypte* (Paris, 1735), 91* (there are two series of pagination in one volume, the second of which has an asterisk).
132. Richard Pococke, "Travels in Egypt," in *A General Collection of the Best and Most Interesting Voyages and Travels in All Parts of the World; Many of Which Are Now First Translated into English*, ed. John Pinkerton (London: Longman, Hurst, Rees, Orme, and Brown, 1814), 324–25.
133. Ibn al-Ḥājj, *Madkhal*, 1:193–94.
134. Louis Massignon describes Cairene women's Friday grave visitation while the men attend the mosque as a means by which the separation of the sexes is maintained, although he also describes it as a "violation of seclusion" (*rupture de clôture*) and notes that the practice sometimes led to improper sexual mixing. Louis Massignon, "La Cité des Morts au Caire," *Bulletin de l'Institut Français de l'Archéologie Orientale* 57 (1958): 29–30.
135. For an overview of the Sunnī schools' positions on grave visitation, see Zuḥaylī, *Fiqh*, 2:1570.
136. Christopher S. Taylor, *In the Vicinity of the Righteous:* Ziyāra *and the Veneration of Muslim Saints in Late Medieval Egypt* (Leiden: Brill, 1999). Taylor writes that "Al-Qarāfa had the quality of being a marginal zone, enticingly beyond the reach of the ʿulamāʾ, the traditional guardians of routine social conformity" (ibid., 57–58) and that it was "a place physically and spiritually beyond the control of these watchful guardians of the holy Law of Islam" (ibid., 61). His conclusions are substantially based on the testimony of Ibn al-Ḥājj.
137. See Sabra, *Poverty*, 97–99, 101; Shaun Marmon, *Eunuchs and Sacred Boundaries* (New York: Oxford University Press, 1995), 18–19, 24–25). Interestingly, Marmon reasons that "the sheer numbers of such Qur'an readers, as well as affiliated students and faculty, Sufis, orphan boys, teachers, imams, and muezzins, along with janitors, cooks, water carriers, and doorkeepers contributed to the possibilities of disorder" (ibid., 25). With the possible exception of the orphan boys, however, it is unclear why these personnel should have been sources of disorder rather than order. The Friday grave visitation itself was subject to a certain degree of official oversight; see Massignon, "La Cité des Morts," 43.
138. See Taylor, *Vicinity*, 20 (based on Maqrīzī); Tetsuya, "Cairene Cemeteries," 83–115, esp. 89–90, 97–103.
139. Ibn al-Ḥājj, *Madkhal*, 1:194.
140. François Pidou de Saint-Olon, *The Present State of the Empire of Morocco, with a Faithful Account of the Manners, Religion, and Government of That People, by Monsieur de St. Olon, Ambassador There in the Year 1693* (London,

1695), 52–53. An almost identical statement is made by Germain Moüette in an account of his eleven years as a captive in Morocco, published a few years after the work of de Saint-Olon; it is unclear which account has priority, although one must be dependent on the other. Germain Moüette, *The Travels of the Sieur Mouette, in the Kingdoms of Fez and Morocco, During His Eleven Years Captivity in Those Parts* (London, 1710), 96. E-book.

141. Lancelot Addison, *West Barbary, or, a Short Narrative of the Revolutions of the Kingdoms of Fez and Morocco. With an Account of the Present Customs, Sacred, Civil, and Domestick* (Oxford, 1671), 164, see also 206. E-book. Addison represents these as his own observations (ibid., 165). He claims that women "are denyed admission into the Assembly" at the mosque, but that they are provided with religious education on Fridays by the imām's wife in his home (ibid., 158–59).

142. ʿAlī ibn Dāwūd al-Ṣayrafī, *Nuzhat al-nufūs wa'l-abdān fī tawārīkh al-zamān*, ed. Ḥasan Ḥabashī ([Cairo]: Maṭbaʿat Dār al-Kutub, 1983), 3:409.

143. Umm al-Dardāʾ's name was Hujayma (or Juhayna) bint Ḥuyayy al-Awṣābīya. For biographical notices on her, see Ibn Ḥibbān al-Bustī, *Kitāb al-Thiqāt* (Hyderabad: Dāʾirat al-Maʿārif al-ʿUthmānīya, 1399/1979), 5:517; ʿAlī ibn al-Ḥasan Ibn ʿAsākir, *Taʾrīkh madīnat dimashq* (Damascus: Dār al-Fikr, 1419/1998), 70:146–64; Muḥammad ibn Aḥmad al-Dhahabī, *Siyar aʿlām al-nubalāʾ*, ed. Shuʿayb Arnaʾūṭ and Maʾmūn al-Ṣāghirji (Beirut: Muʾassasat al-Risāla, 1981/1401), 4:277–79; Ibn Kathīr, *al-Bidāya wa'l-nihāya* (Beirut: Dār al-Fikr, 1398/1978), 9:47; Ibn Ḥajar al-ʿAsqalānī, *Tahdhīb al-Tahdhīb* (Hyderabad, 1327; Beirut: Dār Ṣādir, n.d.), 12:465–67.

144. Ibn Manẓūr, *Lisān al-ʿarab*, s.v. "b-r-n-s," cites a report from al-Jawharī that a *burnus* is a "long hood (*qalansūwa*); ascetics (*al-nussāk*) used to wear it in the early Islamic period (*ṣadr al-islām*)." It is thus possible that the depiction of Umm al-Dardāʾ in a *burnus* is intended to suggest ascetic tendencies rather than merely modesty.

145. Or possibly "to teach" if the verb is voweled *tuʿallimu* (the editor of al-Dhahabī has made it passive). Umm al-Dardāʾ seems to be young in this anecdote, although she already may have been an authority giving instruction to others.

146. Ibn ʿAsākir, *Taʾrīkh madīnat dimashq*, 70:151; Dhahabī, *Siyar*, 4:278; Ibn Ḥajar al-ʿAsqalānī, *Tahdhīb*, 12:466.

147. Umm al-Dardāʾ al-Ṣughrā is also reported to have used men's postures in some aspects of the canonical prayer. See Ibn ʿAsākir, *Taʾrīkh madīnat dimashq*, 70:156.

148. Ibn Ḥibbān, *Thiqāt*, 5:517.

149. Ibn Kathīr, *Bidāya*, 9:47.

150. See Ibn ʿAsākir, *Taʾrīkh madīnat dimashq*, 70:164; Ibn Ḥajar al-ʿAsqalānī, *Tahdhīb*, 12:466–47.

151. Ibn ʿAsākir, *Taʾrīkh madīnat dimashq*, 70:164.

152. See Ibn Saʿd, *al-Ṭabaqāt al-kubrā* (Beirut: Dār Ṣādir/Dār Bayrūt, 1377/1958), 7:411–12; Dhahabī, *Siyar*, 3:359–63.
153. Ibn al-Jawzī, *Ṣifat al-ṣafwa*, 4:253. *Al-farāʾiḍ* could also refer to the apportionment of the estate according to the Qur'anic rules of inheritance. In this case, it would imply that she possessed (and was imparting to other women) some degree of expertise in a sought-after area of the law.
154. See Dhahabī, *Siyar*, 7:177.
155. Omaima Abou-Bakr, "*Qirāʾa fī taʾrīkh ʿābidāt al-islām*," in *Zaman al-nisāʾ wa'l-dhākira al-badīla: Majmūʿat abḥāth*, ed. Hudā al-Ṣadda, Sumayya Ramaḍān, and Omaima Abou-Bakr (Cairo: Taḥrīr, 1998), 151.
156. It is not clear whether the woman in question is Abū'l-Dardāʾ's first or second wife.
157. Ibn ʿAsākir, *Taʾrīkh madīnat dimashq*, 70:284.
158. Ibid., 50:60.
159. Abū'l-ʿAlāʾ al-Maʿarrī, *Dīwān Luzūm mā lā yalzam*, ed. Kamāl al-Yāzijī (Beirut: Dār al-Jīl, 1992), 2:363; see Nadia Lachiri, "Abū'l-ʿAlāʾ al-Maʿarrī wa'l-marʾa," in *Nadwat Abī'l-ʿAlāʾ al-Maʿarrī (al-juzʾ al-thānī), Maʿarrat al-Nuʿmān, 24–7 Rajab 1418 A.H./November 24–27 1997* [n.p., n.d.], 2:787–88. I thank Dr. Lachiri for referring me to this very useful article.
160. See the discussion of this event in *Encyclopaedia of Islam*, 2nd ed., s.v. "al-Maʿarrī, Abu 'l-ʿAlāʾ Aḥmad b. ʿAbd Allāh b. Sulaymān" (by P. Smoor).
161. Abū Bakr Ibn al-ʿArabī, *Aḥkām al-qurʾān*, ed. Muḥammad Bakr Ismāʿīl (Cairo: Dār al-Manār, 1422/2002), 3:544. This passage is discussed by Daniella Talmon-Heller in "*The Cited Tales of the Wondrous Doings of the Shaykhs of the Holy Land* by Ḍiyāʾ al-Dīn Abū ʿAbd Allāh Muḥammad b. ʿAbd al-Wāḥid al-Maqdisī (569/1173–643/1245): Text, Translation and Commentary," *Crusades* 1 (2002): 146 n131, and in *Islamic Piety in Medieval Syria: Mosques, Cemeteries and Sermons Under the Zangids and Ayyūbids (1146–1260)* (Leiden: Brill, 2007), 59.
162. Talmon-Heller, "*Cited Tales*," 146.
163. For a discussion of the chronology of al-Ghazālī's residence in different locations, see *Encyclopaedia of Islam*, 2nd ed., s.v. "al-G͟Hazālī, Abū Ḥāmid Muḥammad b. Muḥammad al-Ṭūsī" (by W. Montgomery Watt).
164. Abū Ḥāmid al-Ghazālī, *Iḥyāʾ ʿulūm al-dīn* (Beirut: Dār al-Fikr, 1994/1414), 2:365.
165. Swartz, *Ibn al-Jawzī's* Kitāb, 174, 226.
166. Ibid., 200. Although he does not specify the location of such assemblies, his references to the pulpit (*minbar*) in his directions for their appropriate conduct strongly suggest a mosque setting. Ibid., 220–21.
167. Ibn al-Ukhuwwa, *The* Maʿālim al-Qurba, 66–67; Moshe Perlmann, "A Seventeenth Century Exhortation Concerning Al-Aqṣā," *Israel Oriental Studies* 3 (1973): 263, 279.

168. See *Encyclopaedia of Islam,* 2nd ed., s.v. "Djalāl al-Dīn Rūmī" (by H. Ritter).

169. Jalāl al-Dīn Muḥammad-i Balkhī-ye Rūmī, known as Mawlawī, *Masnavi-ye maʿnawī,* ed. Qiwām al-Dīn Khurramshāshī (Tehran: Intishārāt-i Nāhīd, 1375/[1955–56]), 773; translation, Reynold A. Nicholson, *The Mathnawí of Jalálu'ddín Rúmí* (London: Cambridge University Press for the Trustrees of the E. J. W. Gibb Memorial, 1934), 6:200. Because of the smutty nature of the anecdote, Nicholson translates most of it into Latin.

170. Ibn Baṭṭūṭa, *Riḥlat Ibn Baṭṭūṭa al-musammā Tuḥfat al-nuẓẓār fī gharāʾib al-amṣār wa-ʿajāʾib al-asfār* (Ṣaydā: al-Maktaba al-ʿAṣrīya, 1425/2005), 1:183.

171. Ibn Rajab al-Ḥanbalī, *Dhayl Ṭabaqāt al-ḥanābila* (Beirut: Dār al-Maʿrifa, n.d.), 2:195–96. Daniella Talmon-Heller notes this passage in *Islamic Piety,* 60.

172. *The Book of the Islamic Market Inspector:* Nihāyat al-Rutba fī Ṭalab al-Ḥisba *(The Utmost Authority in the Pursuit of Ḥisba) by ʿAbd al-Raḥmān b. Naṣr al-Shayzarī,* trans. R. P. Buckley (Oxford: Oxford University Press, 1999), 127. Buckley infers, based on the content of the book, that "the manual was written in Syria, or at least that al-Shayzarī drew on his personal knowledge of that country for much of his information," although "in one or two places in the text al-Shayzarī clearly has an Egyptian audience in mind." Ibid., 14. It is conceivable that al-Shayzarī's remarks are inspired by al-Ghazālī's, but the parallel is not close enough to allow a firm conclusion.

173. Ibn ʿAsākir, *Taʾrīkh madīnat dimashq,* 70:25; see also Melchert, "Whether to Keep Women Out of the Mosque," 68. That she was a contemporary of Ibn ʿAsākir is indicated by his remark that "I met her, but did not transmit anything from her."

174. Ṣalāḥ al-Dīn Khalīl ibn Aybak al-Ṣafadī, *Aʿyān al-ʿaṣr wa-aʿwān al-naṣr,* ed. ʿAlī Abū Zayd et al. (Beirut: Dār al-Fikr al-Muʿāṣir/Damascus: Dār al-Fikr, 1418/1998), 4:28–29; see also Ibn Ḥajar, *al-Durar al-kāmina,* 3:226, where she is listed as Fāṭima bint ʿAyyāsh (and alphabetized accordingly). Fāṭima's mosque-based activities were brought to my attention by Irfana Hashmi and by Saadia Yacoob in "Women and Law in the Pre-Modern Middle East: Reconstructing the Lives of Female Jurists (faqihat)" (paper presented at the Middle East Studies Association annual conference, Washington DC, November 24, 2008).

175. Abū Shāma al-Maqdisī, *Tarājim rijāl al-qarnayn al-sādis wa'l-sābiʿ* (Cairo, 1366/1947), 49; also cited in Louis Pouzet, *Damas au VIIe/XIIIe s.: Vie et structures religieuses dans une métropole islamique* (Beirut: Dar El-Machreq Sarl Éditeurs, 1988), 398; Talmon-Heller, *Islamic Piety,* 129.

176. Another description of the mass appeal of his preaching states that people would spend the night in the mosque to secure a good spot to hear

his sermons. Quṭb al-Dīn Mūsā ibn Muḥammad al-Yūnīnī, *Dhayl Mirʾāt al-zamān* (Hyderabad: Dāʾirat al-Maʿārif al-ʿUthmānīya, 1374/1954), 1:40.

177. Stefan Leder, Yāsīn Muḥammad al-Sawwās, and Maʾmūn al-Ṣāgharjī, *Muʿjam al-samāʿāt al-dimashqīya: Les certificates d'audition à Damas, 550–750 h./1155–1349* (Damascus: L'Institut Français d'Études Arabes de Damas, 1996).
178. Ibid., 955:9, *samāʿ* 17 (p. 32); 1088:3, *samāʿ* 24 (p. 48); 1139:1, *samāʿ* 48 (p. 64); 3757:10, *samāʿ* 11 (p. 89).
179. In order to identify sessions that took place in mosques that had female participants, I looked at the entry for each woman listed in the index and cross-checked each of the *samāʿāt* for the location of the session. Because of the painstaking nature of this process (as well as the possibility of some errors in the index), the tally should be taken as an approximation.
180. It should be noted that these patterns result not from the consistent participation in mosque sessions of a few individual women, but from the sporadic participation of a relatively large number of women. However, in most cases only two to four women were present at a given reading, and in many cases there was only one.
181. Muḥammad Muṭīʿ al-Ḥāfiẓ, *Jāmiʿ al-Ḥanābila "al-Muẓaffarī" bi-Ṣāliḥīyat jabal Qāsiyūn* (Beirut: Dār al-Bashāʾir al-Islāmīya, 1423/2002), 597–607.
182. Ibid., 439.
183. Ibid., 443. However, all of the auditors listed appear to be men; see 444–45.
184. Konrad Hirschler, *The Written Word in the Medieval Arabic Lands: A Social and Cultural History of Reading Practices*. (Edinburgh: Edinburgh University Press, 2013), 46. Hirschler attributes the underrepresentation of mosques to legal scholars' disapproval of women's participation in congregational prayer; however, as we have seen, this disapproval was largely based on concerns about women's mobility and mixing with men that would have applied to madrasas as well. For a discussion of the multifunctionality of madrasas and mosques in the context of contemporary Cairo, see Berkey, *Transmission*, 48–50.
185. Asma Sayeed, "Women and Ḥadîth Transmission: Two Case Studies from Mamluk Damascus," *Studia Islamica* 95 (2002): 81; Leder, *Muʿjam al-samāʿāt*, 3757:10, *samāʿ* 11 (p. 89); al-Ḥāfiẓ, *Jāmiʿ al-ḥanābila*, 606.
186. See Hirschler, 46. The mosque session took place at the Jāmiʿ al-Muẓaffarī; Zaynab bint al-Kamāl co-presided with a group of other authorities over a gathering of over a hundred auditors. See Sayeed, "Women and Ḥadîth Transmission," 81.
187. Leder, *Muʿjam al-samāʿāt*, 94–96, 313.
188. See ibid., 319 (Sitt al-Fuqahāʾ); 320 (Sitt al-Munā); 345 (Ḍayfa bt. ʿAbd al-Ḥalīm); 463 (Fāṭima bt. Al-Malik al-Muḥassan); 465 (Fāṭima bt. [Zayn al-Dīn] ʿAbd al-Raḥmān).

189. Sayeed, "Women and Ḥadîth Transmission," 81.
190. Ḥāfiẓ, *Jāmiʿ al-ḥanābila,* 443 (*samāʿ*), 606–7 (biography of Ḥabība bint Ibrāhīm).
191. Ibid., 603.
192. Ibid., 84.
193. Ibid., 594, 607.
194. See Hirschler, *Written Word,* 44, 46.
195. Muḥammad ibn Muḥammad ibn Muḥammad al-Bukhārī, "*Suʾāl wa-jawāb bi-shaʾn al-quṣṣāṣ, yajlisūna fi'l-masājid wa-tajtamiʿ ʿalayhim al-niswa,*" Jerusalem ms., Isḥāq al-Ḥusaynī, 1/28, 6; listed in *al-Fihris al-shāmil li'l-turāth al-ʿarabī al-islāmī al-makhṭūṭ, al-Fiqh wa-uṣūlihi* (Amman: Muʾassasat Āl al-Bayt li'l-Fikr al-Islāmī, 1421), 4:693, #299.
196. al-Bukhārī, "*Suʾāl,*" 151b. (NB The numbering is partially or completely cut off of most of the images of the manuscript pages that were available to me, so it is possible that this numbering is off by one.)
197. Ibid., 154b.
198. Berkey, *Transmission,* 207.
199. Ibid., 209.
200. For an overview of the issues of authority and orthodoxy raised by preaching and storytelling in this period, see Jonathan Berkey, *Popular Preaching and Religious Authority in the Medieval Islamic Near East* (Seattle: University of Washington Press, 2001).
201. Aḥmad Ibn Ṭawq, *al-Taʿlīq,* ed. Jaʿfar al-Muhājir (Damascus: L'Institut Français de Damas, 2000), 1:395. For Ibn Ṭawq, see Najm al-Dīn al-Ghazzī, *al-Kawākib al-sāʾira bi-aʿyān al-miʾa al-ʿāshira,* ed. Jibrāʾīl Sulaymān Jabbūr (Beirut: Jāmiʿat Bayrūt al-Amīrkīya, 1945), 1:126.
202. Unfortunately, I have been unable to identify al-Najmī.
203. Aḥmad ibn Ibrāhīm al-Dimashqī, known as Ibn al-Naḥḥās, *Tanbīh al-ghāfilīn ʿan aʿmāl al-jāhilīn wa-taḥdhīr al-sālikīn min aʿmāl al-hālikīn* (Ṣaydā / Beirut: al-Maktaba al-ʿAṣrīya, 1424/2003), 330. For a later Ottoman instance, see Uriel Heyd, *Ottoman Documents on Palestine, 1552–1615: A Study of the Firman According to the* Mühimme Defteri (Oxford: Clarendon Press, 1960), 152–53. I am grateful to Professor Leslie Peirce for this reference.
204. Ibn Ṭawq, *al-Taʿlīq,* 4:1702.
205. Al-Shayzarī, *Book of the Islamic Market Inspector,* 131.
206. See Ghazzī, *Kawākib,* 2:206–11. Carl Brockelmann states that his followers hailed him as the renewer of the Islamic faith (*mujaddid*), presumably for the tenth century of the Islamic era. Carl Brockelmann, *Geschichte der arabischen Literatur* (Leiden: Brill, 1943), Grundband 2, 333.
207. ʿAlī ibn ʿAṭīya ibn al-Ḥasan ibn Muḥammad al-Hītī, known as al-Shaykh ʿAlwān, *Nasamāt al-asḥār fī manāqib wa-karāmāt al-awliyāʾ al-akhyār,* ed. Aḥmad Farīd al-Mazīdī (Beirut: Dār al-Kutub al-ʿIlmīya, 1421/2001), 338.

208. Ibid., 350.
209. Ibid., 339.
210. Ibid., 41.
211. Ibid., 46.
212. Ibid., 340, 341.
213. Ibid., 342–43.
214. ʿAlī ibn ʿAṭīya al-Hītī al-Ḥamawī, *al-Naṣāʾiḥ al-muhimma li'l-mulūk wa'l-aʾimma*, ed. Nashwa al-ʿAlwānī (Damascus: Dār al-Maktabī, 1420/2000), 179. The passage also refers to madrasas (schools of law) and *rubuṭ* (ṣūfī hostels). However, these specific remarks clearly refer to mosques, which are the only religious institutions that could have been closed outside of prayer times.
215. ʿAlwān ibn ʿAlī ibn ʿAṭīya al-Ḥamawī, *Asnā al-maqāṣid fī taʿẓīm al-masājid* (Beirut: Dār al-Kutub al-ʿIlmīya, 1424/2003), 41. Although this book is published under the name ʿAlwān *ibn* ʿAlī (rather than ʿAlwān ʿAlī), it appears to be a work of the same Shaykh ʿAlwān. See Bağdatlı Ismail Paşa, *Keşf-el-zunun zeyli* (Istanbul: Millî Eğitim Başevi, 1945), 1:82.
216. ʿAlwān, *Asnā al-maqāṣid,* 42–44.
217. Emending the dotting to read *muqanzaʿa* for *muqtariʿa*. The *ʿiṣāba muqanzaʿa* was a tall women's headdress that excited some disapproval on the part of the authorities. An edict of the Mamlūk Sultan Qāʾiṭ Bāy (ruled 872–901/1468–96) forbade women from wearing it in public. See Yedida Kalfon Stillman, *Arab Dress: A Short History from the Dawn of Islam to Modern Times* (Leiden: Brill, 2000), 81–82.
218. ʿAlwān, *Asnā al-maqāsid,* 43.
219. See Jonathan Brown, *The Canonization of al-Bukhārī and Muslim* (Leiden: Brill, 2007), 338.
220. ʿAlwān, *Nasamāt,* 311.
221. Ibid., 349.
222. Ibid., 349–50.
223. This description is taken from a ḥadīth in which the Prophet describes two groups of people who are destined for hell. See, for instance, Muslim, *Ṣaḥīḥ, Kitāb al-Libās wa'l-zīna, Bāb al-Nisāʾ al-kāsiyāt al-ʿāriyāt al-māʾilāt al-mumīlāt.* The phrase *māʾilāt mumīlāt* (which I have translated as "swaying and sashaying") can also be interpreted to mean "deviating [from the truth] and causing others to deviate." Commentators explained that the women's heads were likened to camels' humps because they were enlarged by ostentatious turbans and headdresses.
224. ʿAlī ibn ʿAṭīya ibn al-Ḥasan al-Hītī al-Ḥamawī al-Shāfiʿī, *ʿArāʾis al-ghurar wa-gharāʾis al-fikar fī aḥkām al-naẓar,* ed. Muḥammad Faḍl ʿAbd al-ʿAzīz al-Murād (Damascus: Dār al-Qalam/Beirut: al-Dār al-Shāmīya, 1410/1990), 141.
225. Ibid., 144.

226. On ʿAlī ibn Maymūn al-Maghribī, see Ignaz Goldziher, "ʿAlî b. Mejmûn al-Maġribî und sein Sittenspiegel des östlichen Islam: Ein Beitrag zur Culturgeschichte," *Zeitschrift der Deutschen Morganländischen Gesellschaft* 28 (1874): 293–330. Al-Maghribī's birthplace is unclear and may have been in Morocco or Spain.
227. ʿAlī ibn Maymūn al-Idrīsī, *Risālat Bayān ghurbat al-islām bi-wāsiṭat ṣinfay al-mutafaqqiha wa'l-mutafaqqira min ahl miṣr wa'l-shām wa-mā yalīhā min bilād al-aʿjām*, Princeton ms., Garrett 828H, 4a. Despite the reference to Egypt in the book's title, the author makes it clear that he is resident in Syria at the time of writing and has spent five years in the heart of the Ottoman Empire (including Istanbul and Edirne), but has never been to Egypt; see ibid., 1b, 4b. This manuscript (and its condemnation of mixed-gender audiences for preaching) has been discussed by Berkey, *Popular Preaching*, 30–31.
228. Idrīsī, *Bayān ghurbat al-islām*, 55b.
229. Ibid., 56a.
230. Ibid., 60b.
231. Ibid., 62b.
232. Two centuries later another Syrian authority, ʿAbd al-Ghanī al-Nābulusī, categorized al-Shaykh ʿAlwān as one of several jurists who "had taken to the reprehensible practice of issuing general prohibitions . . . that were not based on sound juridical principles, but merely out of a moralistic conviction that wickedness and depravity were widespread." Khaled El-Rouayheb, *Before Homosexuality in the Arab-Islamic World, 1500–1800* (Chicago: University of Chicago Press, 2005), 114.
233. Abou-Bakr, "Qirāʾa," 151.
234. Ibn al-Jawzī, *Ṣifat al-ṣafwa*, 4:212.
235. Ibid., 4:212.
236. Ibid., 4:211–12.
237. Ibn al-ʿArabī, *Aḥkām al-qurʾān*, 3:544.
238. Aḥmad ibn Muḥammad al-Hamadhānī, known as Ibn al-Faqīh, *Kitāb al-Buldān* (Beirut: ʿĀlam al-Kutub, 1416/1992), 151; Guy Le Strange, *Palestine Under the Moslems*, with a new introduction by Walid Khalidy (Beirut: Khayats, 1965), 161.
239. Ibn ʿAbd Rabbih, *al-ʿIqd al-farīd*, vol. 8, *Ṭabāʾiʿ al-insān wa'l-ḥayawān* (Beirut: Maktabat Dār Ṣādir, n.d.), 104; Le Strange, *Palestine*, 162–63.
240. See Muḥammad ibn ʿAbd al-Wahhāb al-Miknāsī, *Riḥlat al-Miknāsī*, ed. Muḥammad Būkabūl (Beirut: al-Muʾassasa al-ʿArabīya li'l-Dirāsāt wa'l-Nashr, 2003), 313.
241. Ibn Faḍl Allāḥ al-ʿUmarī, *Masālik al-abṣār fī mamālik al-amṣār*, ed. Fuat Sezgin (Frankfurt am Main: Institute for the History of Arabic-Islamic Studies at the Johann Wolfgang Goethe University, 1988), 1:111, see also 1:110. Compare Mujīr al-Dīn al-Ḥanbalī, *al-Uns al-jalīl bi-taʾrīkh*

al-quds wa'l-khalīl (Najaf, Iraq: Manshūrāt al-Maṭbaʿa al-Ḥaydarīya, 1388/1968), 2:13.

242. Al-ʿUmarī, *Masālik*, 1:117.
243. Ibid., 1:120.
244. Mujīr al-Dīn, *Uns*, 2:33.
245. Félix Fabri, *Felix Fabri (circa 1480–1483 A.D.)*, trans. Aubrey Stewart (New York: AMS Press, 1971), 2:249.
246. Ibid., 2:259–60. Fabri implies that he has actually been inside the Aqṣā Mosque. By his own account, nonbelievers were forbidden to enter on pain of death, but many took the risk. See ibid., 2:251. He had certainly been inside of other mosques, although he had not entered the Dome of the Rock. Ibid., 2:245.
247. ʿAbd al-Ghanī al-Nābulusī, *al-Ḥaḍra al-unsīya fī al-riḥla al-qudsīya*, ed. Akram Ḥasan al-ʿUlbī (Beirut: al-Maṣādir, 1990), 144.
248. Ali Bey, *Travels of Ali Bey in Morocco, Tripoli, Cyprus, Egypt, Arabia, Syria, and Turkey, Between the Years 1803 and 1807* (London: Longman, Hurst, Rees, Orme, and Brown, 1816), 217; see also floor plan, plate 71, opposite 2:214. The space in question is labeled with the number 44 (although the map appears to have no key).
249. ʿAbd al-Ghanī ibn Ismāʿīl al-Nābulusī, *al-Ḥaqīqa wa'l-majāz fi'l-riḥla ilā bilād al-shām wa-miṣr wa'l-ḥijāz*, ed. Aḥmad ʿAbd al-Majīd al-Huraydī (Cairo: al-Hayʾa al-Miṣrīya al-ʿĀmma li'l-Kitāb, 1986), 133.
    See also Elizabeth Sirriyeh, *Sufi Visionary of Ottoman Damascus: ʿAbd al-Ghanī al-Nābulusī, 1641–1731* (London: Routledge Curzon, 2005), 100–101.
250. Taqī al-Dīn Abū Bakr ibn Muḥammad al-Ḥiṣnī, *Kifāyat al-akhyār fī ḥall Ghāyat al-ikhtiṣār*, ed. Muḥammad ʿAwaḍ Haykal (Cairo: Dār al-Salām, 1426/2005), 195.
251. Eugène Roger, *La Terre Sainte ou Terre de Promission: Description topographique des Saints Lieux, avec un traité des nations de différantes religions qui l'habitent, leurs moeurs, croyances, cérémonies et police*, ed. Elias Kattar (Kaslik, Lebanon: Université Saint-Esprit, 1992), 265.
252. Perlmann provides the lexicographer Reinhart Dozy's definition of *al-shaʿārī*, a word that refers to small, black horsehair veils that cover only the eyes and are worn with the *niqāb*, a larger veil that covers the face and leaves an opening for the eyes. Perlmann, "Seventeenth Century Exhortation," 286n16.
253. Ibid., 286.
254. Ibid., 281.
255. Ibid., 263, 279.
256. Ibid., 264, 287.
257. Ibid., 289.
258. Ibid., 283.

259. David Abulafia, "The Apostolic Imperative: Religious Conversion in Lull's *Blaquerna*," in *Religion, Text, and Society in Medieval Spain and Northern Europe: Essays in Honor of J .N. Hillgarth*, ed. Thomas E. Burman, J. N. Hillgarth, Mark D. Meyerson, and Leah Shopkow (Toronto, Ontario, Canada: Pontifical Institute of Mediaeval Studies, 2002), 115. However, Abulafia raises doubts that men and women were fully segregated in contemporary Spanish synagogues. Ibid., 115n25. See also Norman Daniel, *Islam and the West: The Making of an Image* (Oxford, UK: Oneworld, 1993), 241.
260. Daniel, *Islam and the West*, 241.
261. Fabri, *Voyage en Egypte*, 2:578–79.
262. Walter G. Andrews and Mehmet Kalpaklı, *The Age of Beloveds: Love and the Beloved in Early-Modern Ottoman and European Culture and Society* (Durham, NC: Duke University Press, 2005), 51–54; Dennis Romano, "Gender and the Urban Geography of Renaissance Venice," *Journal of Social History* 23 (1989): 339–53.
263. See Romano, "Gender and the Urban Geography," 343. Also writing about Renaissance Venice, John Martin describes the parish church as "one of the few public places [women] could visit." John Martin, "Out of the Shadow: Heretical and Catholic Women in Renaissance Venice," *Journal of Family History* 10 (1985): 26.
264. Margaret Aston, "Segregation in Church," in *Women in the Church: Papers Read at the 1989 Summer Meeting and the 1990 Winter Meeting of the Ecclesiastical History Society*, ed. W. J. Sheils and Diana Wood (Cambridge, MA: Basil Blackwell, 1990), 259.
265. William Lithgow, *The Totall Discourse of the Rare Adventures and Painefull Peregrinations of Long Nineteene Yeares Travayles from Scotland to the Most Famous Kingdomes in Europe, Asia and Affrica* (Glasgow: James MacLehose and Sons, 1906), 128.
266. See Aston, "Segregation," 281.
267. See Jane I. Smith, "Old French Travel Accounts of Muslim Beliefs Concerning the Afterlife," in *Christian-Muslim Encounters*, ed. Yvonne Yazbeck Haddad and Wadi Zaidan Haddad (Gainesville: University Press of Florida, 1995), 231; Gülru Necipoğlu, *The Age of Sinan: Architectural Culture in the Ottoman Empire* (London: Reaktion Books, 2005), 69–70.
268. See Smith, "Old French Travel Accounts," 231; E. Cleray, "Le Voyage de Pierre Lescalopier 'Parisien' de Venise a Constantinople, l'an 1574," *Revue d'Histoire Diplomatique* 35 (1921): 40. Lescalopier seeks to explain women's exclusion from both mosques and paradise with reference to the idea that women were uncircumcised—an idea with no basis in Islamic thought. This idea was also expressed by George Sandys in the early seventeenth century. George Sandys, *A Relation of a Journey Begun an. Dom. 1610* (London: Andrew Crooke, 1637), 55.

269. See Necipoğlu, *Age of Sinan*, 70.
270. Salomon Schweigger, *Ein Newe Reyßbeschreibung auß Deutschland nach Constantinopel und Jerusalem* (Nuremberg, 1608; facsimile edition Graz: Akademische Druck- und Verlagsanstalt, 1964), 185.
271. François Billacois, *L'Empire du Grand Turc vu par un sujet de Louis XIV, Jean Thévenot* (Paris: Calmann-Lévy, 1965), 156.
272. Moüette, *Travels*, 96.
273. Pidou de Saint-Olon, *Present State*, 52–53.
274. Aaron Hill, *A Full and Just Account of the Present State of the Ottoman Empire in All Its Branches* (London: John Mayo, 1709), 41–42.
275. Adrianus Reland, "A Short System of Mahometan Theology," in *Four Treatises Concerning the Doctrine, Discipline and Worship of the Mahometans* (London, 1712), 77, Gale Eighteenth Century Collections Online, http://gdc.gale.com.
276. Mohja Kahf, *Western Representations of the Muslim Woman, From Termagant to Odalisque* (Austin: University of Texas Press, 1999), 111.
277. *Memoirs of Baron de Tott, Containing the State of the Turkish Empire and the Crimea, During the Late War with Russia, with Numerous Anecdotes, Facts, and Observations, on the Manners and Customs of the Turks and Tatars*, translated from the French (London: G. G. J. and J. Robinson, 1785; New York: Arno Press, 1973), 1:231.
278. William Hunter, *Travels Through France, Turkey, and Hungary, to Vienna, in 1792* (London: J. White, 1803), 1:278.
279. See Smith, "Old French Travel Accounts," 230–32.
280. E. M. Wherry, *A Comprehensive Commentary on the Qurán: Comprising Sale's Translation and Preliminary Discourse, with Additional Notes and Emendations* (1882; repr., Osnabrück, Germany: Otto Zeller Verlag, 1973), Préliminary Discourse 162–63; Pierre Bayle, *Dictionnaire Historique et Critique par Pierre Bayle, Cinquième édition de 1740 revue, corrigée et augmentée* (1740; repr., Geneva: Slatkine Reprints, 1995), 3:262. See also *Voyages du chevalier Chardin en Perse, et autres lieux de l'orient*, new ed., revised by L. Langlès (Paris: Le Normant, Imprimeur-Libraire, 1811), 6:257.
281. Julia Pardoe, *City of the Sultan; and Domestic Manners of the Turks, in 1836* (London: Henry Colburn, 1837), 2:51–53; Horatio Southgate, *Narrative of a Tour Through Armenia, Kurdistan, Persia and Mesopotamia* (New York: D. Appleton, 1840), 2:205–6. At the end of the nineteenth century, H. C. Thomson still feels obliged to address the "popular fallacy that the Mahommedan religion denies that women have souls, or that they will rise again," which he believes to have arisen partially from the fact that women are barred from mosques (a "fact" that he also emends significantly). H. C. Thomson, *The Outgoing Turk: Impressions of a Journey Through the Western Balkans* (London: William Heinemann, 1897), 72.

282. Southgate, *Narrative*, 2:206.
283. In England, the practice of separating men and women in church fell into desuetude gradually over the sixteenth to eighteenth centuries, and the "family pew" (where men and women sat together) prevailed by the early nineteenth century; see Aston, "Segregation," 283, 286–87, 289–90.
284. Karla Goldman, *Beyond the Synagogue Gallery* (Cambridge, MA: Harvard University Press, 2000), 48, 80.
285. Colonel Sir John Malcolm, *The History of Persia from the Most Early Period to the Present Time* (London: John Murray, 1815), 2:333.
286. See, for instance, Charles Dudley Warner, *My Winter on the Nile* (1876; repr., Boston: Houghton, Mifflin, 1900), 80.
287. Florence Nightingale, *Letters from Egypt: A Journey on the Nile, 1849–1850* (New York: Weidenfeld and Nicholson, 1987), 190.
288. Ibid., 189.
289. Ibid., 26.
290. See Billie Melman, *Women's Orients: English Women and the Middle East, 1718–1918* (Ann Arbor: University of Michigan Press, 1992).
291. Ibid., 50; see ibid., 331, for a thumbnail biography of Pardoe.
292. Sarah Barclay Johnson, *Hadji in Syria: or, Three Years in Jerusalem* (Philadelphia: James Challen & Sons, 1858; New York: Arno Press, 1977), 175.
293. Ibid., 174.
294. Muḥammad ʿAbduh, "*Al-musāwāt bayna al-rijāl wal'l-nisā*ʾ," in Muḥammad ʿImāra, *al-Islām wa'l-marʾa fī raʾy al-imām Muḥammad ʿAbduh* (Cairo: Dār al-Hilāl, 1979), 52.
295. Johann Schiltberger, *The Bondage and Travels of Johann Schiltberger, a Native of Bavaria, in Europe, Asia, and Africa, 1396–1427*, trans. J. Buchan Telfer (London: Hakluyt Society, 1879), 68; see also xxi for his time in Ottoman service.
296. Konstantin Mihailović, *Memoirs of a Janissary*, trans. Benjamin Stolz, historical commentary and notes by Svat Soucek (Ann Arbor: University of Michigan Press, 1975), 13, see also xxi for biographical information.
297. *Chronica und Beschreibung der Türckey*, with an introduction by Carl Göllner ([Nürnberg?], 1530; facsimile edition Köln, Wien: Böhlau Verlag, 1983), xi.
298. Ibid., 41.
299. Leonhart Rauwolff, *Aigentliche Beschreibung der Raiss inn die Margenlaender*, with an introduction by Dietmar Henze (1583; repr., Graz, Austria: Akademische Druck- und Verlagsanstalt, 1971), 51. Karl H. Dannenfeldt points out that Rauwolff apparently did not enter any mosques. Karl H. Dannenfeldt, *Leonhard Rauwolf: Sixteenth-Century Physician, Botanist, and Traveler* (Cambridge, MA: Harvard University Press, 1968), 182, see also 214.
300. Bartholomej Georgijevic, *Türckey Oder Von yetziger Türcken kirchen gepräng... Verdeutsch durch Joannem Herold*, published with *Chronica und*

Beschreibung der Türckey (Basel, 1545; facsimile, Köln, Wien: Böhlau Verlag, 1983), xix. Georgijević ultimately fled to Holland, where he wrote his account of Turkey.

301. Ibid., 171.
302. *I costumi, et la vita de Turchi di Gio. Antonio Menavino Genovese da Vultri: con una Prophetia, & altre cose turchsche/tradotte per m. Lodouico Domenichi* (Fiorenza: Appresso Lorenzo Torrentino, 1551), 19. I thank Jessica Goethals for translating this passage from the Italian.
303. See Necipoğlu, *Age of Sinan*, 69; *Pedro'nun Zorunlu İstanbul Siyahati* (Istanbul: Güncel Yayıncılık, 1995), 80; [Cristóbal Villalón?], *Viaje de Turquía*, ed. Fernando G. Salinero (Madrid: Ediciones Cátedra, 1980), 392.
304. *Hans Dernschwam's Tagebuch einer Reise nach Konstantinopel und Kleinasien (1553/55)*, ed. Franz Babinger (Munich: Verlag von Duncker & Humblot, 1923), 73; see also Necipoğlu, *Age of Sinan*, 69.
305. Dernschwam, *Tagebuch*, 131.
306. Nicolas de Nicolay, *Dans l'empire de Soliman le Magnifique*, ed. Marie-Christine Gomez-Géraud and Stéphane Yérasimos (Mesnil-sur-l'Estrée, France: Presses du CNRS, 1989), 138.
307. Ignatius Mouradgea d'Ohsson, *Tableau Général de l'Empire Othoman* (Paris, 1788), 2:174–75, 4:321.
308. Cleray, "Voyage de Pierre Lescalopier," 40. Gülru Necipoğlu interprets the statement to mean "that women prayed in spaces reserved for them at the back of mosques." Necipoğlu, *Age of Sinan*, 69–70.
309. Sandys, *Relation*, 55.
310. De Tott, *Memoirs of Baron de Tott*, 1:231.
311. Christine Gerrard, *Aaron Hill: The Muses' Projector, 1685/1750* (Oxford, UK: Oxford University Press, 2003), 11.
312. Hill, *A Full and Just Account*, 41.
313. Anselme Adorno, *Itinéraire d'Anselme Adorno en Terre Sainte (1470–1471)*, ed. and trans. Jacques Heers and Georgette de Groer (Paris: Éditions du Centre National de la Recherche Scientifique, 1978), 81 (translation mine, from the French text). Despite identifying where women prayed in a typical mosque, however, Adorno is of the opinion that only very young or old women attend because women in their childbearing years may be menstruating. Ibid., 73. This, of course, is not a rationale mentioned in the Islamic normative sources.
314. Talmon-Heller, "Cited Tales," 146.
315. Talmon-Heller, *Islamic Piety*, 60.
316. *Maqāmāt* of al-Ḥarīrī, Paris, Bibliothèque Nationale, arabe 5847, 58v. The entire manuscript can be viewed online at http://gallica.bnf.fr/ark:/12148/btv1b8422965p/f11.image.r=hariri.langEN (as of January 7, 2014). Its provenance is discussed in Oleg Grabar, *The Illustrations of the Maqāmāt* (Chicago: University of Chicago Press, 1984), 10.

317. For instance, *Maqāmāt* of al-Ḥarīrī, 33r.
318. For instance, in the immediately juxtaposed miniature, illustrating the same *maqāma*, the governor is depicted in an upper register, but is not necessarily intended to be located in a balcony. Ibid., 59r. See Grabar, *Illustrations*, 64.
319. Istanbul ms., Suleymaniye, *Esad Efendi* 2961; see Grabar, *Illustrations*, 12. The miniature can be viewed on the microfiche accompanying the book, image 4E5.
320. Grabar, *Illustrations*, 177. Emphases mine.
321. Ḥusayn Baiqarā, *Maǧālis al-ʿuššāq*, The Bodleian Libraries, Oxford, ms. Ouseley Add. 24, f54a.
322. Wiebke Walther, *Women in Islam* (Princeton, NJ: Markus Wiener, 1993), fig. 12 (reference on 268).
323. Sheila S. Blair, "Islamic Art as a Source for the Study of Women in Premodern Societies," in *Beyond the Exotic*, ed. Amira El-Azhary Sonbol (Syracuse, NY: Syracuse University Press, 2005), 345.
324. I thank Finbarr Barry Flood for this insight.
325. *Jamiʿ al-Siyar*, 1600, Istanbul ms. Topkapı, Hazine 1230, folio 112a. See Nancy Mickelwright, "Musicians and Dancing Girls," in *Women in the Ottoman Empire*, ed. Madeleine Zilfi (Leiden: Brill, 1997), 158n16.
326. The assumption that balconies existed for the accommodation of women—and that women were confined to balconies—is one that has prevailed (and been challenged) in non-Muslim contexts as well. It has been argued that archaeological evidence for the existence of balconies in the ancient synagogue may have been misinterpreted in light of assumptions based on much later Jewish practice; see Bernadette J. Brooten, *Women Leaders in the Ancient Synagogue: Inscriptional Evidence and Background Issues* (Atlanta: Scholars Press, 1982), 104 and *passim*. David Abulafia notes that "a women's gallery in the Trasito synagogue of Samuel Abulafia at Toledo . . . has been identified, but another view is that it was Don Samuel's balcony from which he could view religious services on entering from his palace next door." Abulafia, "Apostolic Imperative," 115n25. In the absence of literary or inscriptional evidence about the usage of space in individual cases, arguments remain speculative. However, for medieval Cairo the use of synagogue balconies as dedicated women's space is documented by Geniza documents. See S. D. Goitein, *A Mediterranean Society*, vol. 2, *The Community* (Berkeley: University of California Press, 1971), 144.
327. Robert F. Taft, "Women at Church in Byzantium: Where, When—and Why?" *Dumbarton Oaks Papers* 52 (1998): 49: "There is no indication whatever that the galleries . . . were assigned to women." Ibid., 55–56, 86–87.
328. For an example of a mosque loge used by both male and female Ottoman royalty, see Lucienne Thys-Şenocak, *Ottoman Women Builders: The*

Architectural Patronage of Hadice Turhan Sultan (Aldershot, Hampshire, UK: Ashgate, 2006), 222, 233.

329. See Evliya [Çelebi] Efendí, *Narrative of Travels in Europe, Asia, and Africa*, trans. Joseph von Hammer (London: Oriental Translation Fund of Great Britain and Ireland, 1834; New York: Johnson Reprint Co., n.d.), 1:76 (describing the Aya Sofia), 1:113 (describing the Sultan Ahmet Mosque), 2:45 (describing a mosque in Trebizond, formerly a church). It may be, however, that other parts of Evliya Çelebi's voluminous travel narrative provide more insights into this matter.
330. M. Guer, *Moeurs et usages des Turcs, leur religion, leur gouvernement civil, militaire et politique, avec un abregé de l'Histoire Ottomane* (Paris: Merigot and Piget, 1747), 264.
331. d'Ohsson, *Tableau Général*, 2:174–75, 4:321.
332. A.-L. Castellan, *Turkey, A Description of the Manners, Customs, Dresses, and Other Peculiarities Characteristic of the Inhabitants of the Turkish Empire; to which is prefixed a sketch of the history of the Turks*, translated from the French (London: R. Ackermann, [1821?]), 5: 124–25.
333. Pardoe, *City of the Sultan*, 2:55.
334. Southgate, *Narrative*, 2:206. Pardoe describes latticed balconies at both a Christian church and a Mevlevi ṣūfī lodge. Pardoe, *City of the Sultan*, 2:2 (also see 2:7), 1:40.
335. James E. P. Boulden, *An American Among the Orientals* (Philadelphia: Lindsay and Blakiston, 1855), 128.
336. Grace Ellison, *An Englishwoman in a Turkish Harem* (London: Methuen, 1915), 164.
337. Elizabeth Craven, *A Journey Through the Crimea to Constantinople* (1789; repr., New York: Arno Press and New York Times, 1970), 286.
338. Pardoe, *City of the Sultan*, 2:51.
339. Edmondo de Amicis, *Constantinople*, trans. Stephen Parkin, with a foreword by Umberto Eco (London: Hesperis Classics, 2005), 129.
340. Schweigger, *Newe Reyßbeschreibung*, 185, see also xv–xvi for information on Schweigger and his journey.
341. Lithgow, *Totall Discourse*, 128.
342. Southgate, *Narrative*, 206–7. Southgate is presumably referring to the comparative frankness with which Islamic scholars have traditionally treated matters such as ritual purity and sexual relations.
343. Thomson, *Outgoing Turk*, 72.
344. Lady Wortley Montagu, *The Letters and Works of Lady Mary Wortley Montagu, Edited by Her Great-Grandson, Lord Wharncliffe*, 3rd ed., ed. W. Moy Thomas (New York: AMS Press, 1970), 1:325.
345. Pardoe, *City of the Sultan*, 2:51–52.

346. Lucy M. J. Garnett, *Turkish Life in Town and Country* (London: George Newnes, [1904?]), 101; see also Lucy M. J. Garnett, *Home Life in Turkey* (New York: Macmillan, 1909), 117.
347. Mrs. Harvey, *Turkish Harems and Circassian Homes* (London: Hurst and Blackett, 1871), 22, 24–25.
348. William Makepeace Thackeray, *Notes of a Journey from Cornhill to Grand Cairo* (New York: Charles Scribner's Sons, 1904), 356.
349. Halidé Edib, *Memoirs of Halidé Edib* (New York: Century, n.d.), 68–69.
350. Ibid., 72.
351. Melman, *Women's Orients*, 321.
352. [Fanny Blunt], *The People of Turkey: Twenty Years' Residence Among Bulgarians, Greeks, Albanians, Turks, and Armenians*, ed. Stanley Lane Poole (London: John Murray, 1878; New York: Elibron Classics, 2005), 2:280.
353. Hester Donaldson Jenkins, *Behind Turkish Lattices: The Story of a Turkish Woman's Life* (London: Chatto and Windus, 1911), 135.
354. Ibid., 135, 136.
355. J. R. Wellsted, who traveled primarily in Iraq in the 1830s, notes that mosques are attended by only a few elderly women. Nevertheless, "whatever is the cause, it cannot be referred to the disinclination of their husbands to permit their appearance in public, for they are allowed to visit each other and the baths as often as they please." J. R. Wellsted, *Travels to the City of the Caliphs, Along the Shores of the Persian Gulf and the Mediterranean* (London: Henry Colburn, 1840), 1:260.
356. Southgate, *Narrative*, 1:116.
357. See, for instance, Badr al-Dīn al-ʿAynī, *al-Bināya sharḥ al-Hidāya* (Beirut: Dār al-Kutub al-ʿIlmīya, 1420/2000), 2:355.
358. Princess Ayşe (1887–1960) writes that "the Princess Mother and the High Hazinedar were required to attend every Friday Mosque Procession, while the princesses and the Imperial Consorts could attend if they wished. . . . When the harem carriages arrived at the courtyard of the mosque their horses were detached and they were lined up according to precedence." *The Concubine, The Princess, and the Teacher: Voices from the Ottoman Harem*, trans. and ed. Douglas Scott Brookes (Austin: University of Texas Press, 2008), 176. See also Karl Braun-Wiesbaden, *Eine türkische Reise* (Stuttgart: Verlag von August Auerbach, 1877), 3:278, 3:280.
359. Women's exclusion from the actual prayers, even if they left the home, might also reflect the disctinctively Ḥanafī concern that men's prayers might be rendered invalid by adjacency to a praying woman. See Sadeghi, *Logic of Law-Making*, pp. 50-75.
360. De Amicis, *Constantinople*, 129; also cited in Pars Tuğlacı, *Women of Istanbul in Ottoman Times* (Istanbul: Cem Yayinevi, 1984), 55. The American

Clara Erskine Clement, who visited at the end of the nineteenth century, similarly observes that "the Turkish ladies go about with a freedom that ought to be sufficient for those of any nation. . . . They make their devotions in the mosques or at the tombs of the Sultans." Cited in Judy Mabro, *Veiled Half-Truths: Western Travellers' Perceptions of Middle Eastern Women* (London: I. B. Tauris, 1991), 198.

361. Edward William Lane, *An Account of the Manners and Customs of the Modern Egyptians* (Cairo: American University in Cairo Press, 2003), 81–82.
362. Fr. Kruse, ed., *Ulrich Jasper Seetzen's Reisen durch Syrien, Palästina, Phönicien, die Transjordan-Länder, Arabia Petraea und Unter-Aegypten* (Berlin: G. Reimer, 1855), 3:389.
363. James Augustus St. John, *Egypt and Mohammed Ali; or, Travels in the Valley of the Nile*, 2 vols. (London: Longman, Rees, Orme, Brown, Green, and Longman, 1834), 2:335; cited in Leila Ahmed, *Women and Gender in Islam*, 114.
364. J. A. Spencer, *The East: Sketches of Travel in Egypt and the Holy Land* (New York: George G. Putnam, 1850), 194.
365. Charles Dudley Warner, *My Winter on the Nile* (1876; repr., Boston: Houghton, Mifflin, 1900), 80. Warner recorded a similar impression (including the presence of women) of the Umayyad Mosque of Damascus. Charles Dudley Warner, *In the Levant* (Boston: James R. Osgood, 1877), 187.
366. Lane, *Manners and Customs*, 430.
367. Ibid., 431.
368. Although outside of the scope of this project, it would be helpful to compare practices in Istanbul with those of other regions of the Ottoman Empire—for instance, the (equally Ḥanafī) Balkans. There is some reason to think that women's attendance at public prayers was historically more routine in this area. See, for instance, Matija Mažuranić, *A Glance into Ottoman Bosnia, or A Short Journey into that Land by a Native in 1839–40*, trans. Branka Magaš (London: SAQI and Bosnian Institute, 2007), 100.
369. Shihāb al-Dīn Aḥmad ibn ʿAbd al-Ghaffār al-Mālikī, *Izālat al-ghishāʾ ʿan ḥukm ṭawāf al-nisāʾ baʿd al-ʿishāʾ*, Cairo ms., Dār al-Kutub, 109 Fiqh Mālik, microfilm 1965, 45b.
370. Ibn Ḥajar al-ʿAsqalānī, *Fatḥ al-bārī*, 19:401.
371. In the formative period (for instance, during the early development of Mālikism in a place like Qayrawān) and at points of transition in school doctrine, the influences between doctrine and practice may have flowed in both directions. At other times, doctrines may have done much to inform and constrain women's behavior.
372. This is not to suggest that Ibn Rushd is generally hostile to women's presence in mosques, but that his intervention was restrictive with respect to received Mālikī doctrine in his time.

3. DEBATING WOMEN'S MOSQUE ACCESS IN SIXTEENTH-CENTURY MECCA

1. Aḥmad ibn Muḥammad Ibn Ḥajar al-Haytamī, *Itmām al-niʿma al-kubrā ʿalā al-ʿālam bi-mawlid sayyid wuld Ādam* (Beirut: Dār al-Kutub al-ʿIlmīya, 1422/2001), 27; Haytamī, *al-Fatāwā al-kubrā al-fiqhīya* (Beirut: Dār al-Kutub al-ʿIlmīya, 1417/1997), 1:283–89. For an analysis of these sources (some aspects of which require revision in light of the new information presented in this chapter), see Marion Holmes Katz, "The 'Corruption of the Times' and the Mutability of the *Shari'a*," *Cardozo Law Review* 28 (2006): 171–85.
2. Shihāb al-Dīn Aḥmad ibn ʿAbd al-Ghaffār al-Mālikī, *Izālat al-ghishāʾ ʿan ḥukm ṭawāf al-nisāʾ baʿd al-ʿishāʾ*, ms. Cairo, Dār al-Kutub, 109 Fiqh Mālik (microfilm 1965), 121a. The title page also follows the author's name with "may God benefit [us] through him," which would typically be used for a living person. The manuscript does indeed contain a large number of corrections, deletions, and insertions. See, for instance, 18b, 21a, 23a, 37a, 38b, 39b, 52a, 70a, 87a, 114b. It is clear that not all of the marginal notations originate with the author. See, for instance, 29a, where a note exclaims, "May God have mercy on this author; how charitably he regards others, and how sound is his scholarship!"
3. Al-Qarāfī closes his biographical entry with "he died in the year…," leaving the date of death blank. Badr al-Dīn al-Qarāfī, *Tawshīḥ al-dībāj wal-ḥilyat al-ibtihāj*, ed. Aḥmad al-Shatyawī (Beirut: Dār al-Gharb al-Islāmī, 1983/1403), 67.
4. For the date of the work, see ʿAbd al-Qādir ibn Muḥammad al-Jazīrī, *ʿUmdat al-ṣafwa fī ḥall al-qahwa*, ed. ʿAbd Allāh ibn Muḥammad al-Ḥibshī (Abu Dhabi: Cultural Foundation Publications, 1996), editor's preface, 29; for invocations implying that Ibn ʿAbd al-Ghaffār is deceased, see 34. The blessings on the departed Ibn ʿAbd al-Ghaffār seem unlikely to have been inserted by a copyist because they are lengthy and thoroughly incorporated into the rhymed prose of the text (which in any case refers to him in the past tense).
5. The manuscript (folio 1a) has Shihāb al-Dīn.
6. Although he did not reside primarily in Mecca, he clearly spent time there in the 930s; Ibn Fahd notes his arrival in Mecca with the Medinian caravan in Shawwāl of 935/1529. Muḥammad ibn ʿAbd al-ʿAzīz Ibn Fahd, *Nayl al-munā bi-dhayl Bulūgh al-qirā li-takmilat Itḥāf al-warā*, ed. Muḥammad al-Ḥabīb al-Hayla ([Riyadh?]: Muʾassasat al-Furqān li'l-Turāth al-Islāmī, 2000), 1:464.
7. ʿAlī ibn Muḥammad al-Jurjānī, *Kitāb al-Taʿrīfāt* (*Le Livre des Définitions*), trans. Maurice Gloton (Beirut: Albouraq, n.d.), 452; also see article

"*munāsakha*" in *al-Mawsūʿa al-fiqhīya* (Kuwait: Wizārat al-Awqāf wa'l-Shuʾūn al-Islāmīya, 1420/2000), 39:63ff.

8. Najm al-Dīn al-Ghazzī, *al-Kawākib al-sāʾira bi-aʿyān al-miʾa al-ʿāshira*, ed. Jibrāʾīl Sulaymān Jabbūr (Beirut: Jāmiʿat Bayrūt al-Amīrkīya, 1945), 3:148.
9. Aḥmad Bābā al-Tunbuktī, *Kifāyat al-muḥtāj li-maʿrifat man laysa fī'l-Dībāj*, ed. Muḥammad Muṭīʿ ([Rabat]: al-Mamlaka al-Maghribīya, Wizārat al-Awqāf wa'l-Shuʾūn al-Islāmīya, 1421/2000), 1:135; Muḥammad ibn Muḥammad Makhlūf, *Shajarat al-nūr al-zakīya fī ṭabaqāt al-mālikīya* (Beirut: Dār al-Kitāb al-ʿArabī, n.d.; offset edition of first edition of 1349), 271; Muḥammad al-Ḥaṭṭāb al-Ruʿaynī, *Mawāhib al-jalīl li-sharḥ Mukhtaṣar Khalīl* (Beirut: Dār al-Kutub al-ʿIlmīya, 1416/1995), 5:348, 7:163, 7:646.
10. See Ralph S. Hattox, *Coffee and Coffeehouses: The Origins of a Social Beverage in the Medieval Near East* (Seattle: University of Washington Press, 1988), 14–15, 30–31. The report about Khalīl al-Ḥalabī suggests that Ibn ʿAbd al-Ghaffār remained in Egypt well into the 920s. Either his account of the coffee controversy of 917 was compiled retrospectively from the reports of others, or he traveled to the Ḥijāz more than once in this period.
11. Jazīrī, *ʿUmdat al-ṣafwa*, 34.
12. Ismāʿīl Pasha al-Baghdādī gives the title correctly, having seen the manuscript in the khedival collection in Cairo. Bağdatlı Ismail Paşa, *Keşf-el-zunun zeyli* (Istanbul: Millî Eğitim Başevi, 1945), 1:65. For other biographical notices, clearly based on that of Badr al-Dīn al-Qarāfī, see al-Tunbuktī, *Kifāyat al-muḥtāj*, 1:135; al-Tunbuktī, *Nayl al-ibtihāj bi-taṭrīz al-Dībāj* (Fez: al-Maṭbaʿa al-Jadīda, n.d.), p. 78; Makhlūf, *Shajara*, 271.
13. See, for instance, Snouck Hurgronje, *Mekka in the Latter Part of the Nineteenth Century*, trans. J. H. Monahan (Leiden: Brill, 2007), 199–200.
14. Jazīrī, *ʿUmdat al-ṣafwa*, 59–64.
15. Hattox, *Coffee*, 32–36.
16. See Muḥammad ibn Aḥmad al-Nahrawālī, *Kitāb al-Iʿlām bi-aʿlām bayt allāh al-ḥarām*, ed. ʿAlī Muḥammad ʿUmar (Cairo: Maktabat al-Thaqāfa al-Dīnīya, 1425/2004), 289–90; Suraiya Faroqhi, *Pilgrims and Sultans: The Hajj Under the Ottomans 1517–1683* (London: I. B. Tauris, 1994), 147–49.
17. Legally, the issue of locking mosques outside of the times of congregational prayer was controversial, particularly among Ḥanafīs; the eighth-/fourteenth-century Ḥanafī scholar al-Bābartī held that it was acceptable to lock a mosque if there was fear for the safety of its contents "because people's conditions vary according to the changing of the times; just as women used to attend congregational prayers and then were prohibited from doing so, and the prohibition was correct, the same applies to locking mosques in our time." Akmal al-Dīn al-Bābartī, *al-ʿInāya*

sharḥ al-Hidāya (Beirut: Dār al-Kutub al-ʿIlmīya, 1428/2007), 1:342. The Ḥanbalī scholar Ibn Rajab (d. 795/1393) argued that it was even more repugnant to lock the Great Mosque of Mecca than an ordinary mosque because people could perform *ṣalāt* elsewhere, but not *ṭawāf*. Ibn Rajab al-Ḥanbalī, *Fatḥ al-bārī sharḥ Ṣaḥīḥ al-Bukhārī* (Medina: Maktabat al-Ghurabāʾ al-Atharīya, 1417/1996), 3:468.

18. Ibn Fahd, *Nayl al-munā*, 1:38–39.
19. Nahrawālī, *Iʿlām*, 295–96; Aḥmad ibn Muḥammad al-Makkī, *Ikhbār al-kirām bi-akhbār al-masjid al-ḥarām*, ed. Al-Ḥāfiẓ Ghulām Muṣṭafā (n.p.: Dār al-Ṣaḥwa, 1405/1985), 197–98.
20. For a historical survey of the sources on the celebration of the Prophet's birthday in Mecca, see Nico Kaptein, "Materials for the History of the Prophet Muhammad's Birthday Celebration in Mecca," *Der Islam* 69 (1992): 193–203.
21. Aḥmad ibn Muḥammad ibn Ḥajar al-Haytamī, *Itmām al-niʿma al-kubrā ʿalā al-ʿālam bi-mawlid sayyid wuld Ādam* (Beirut: Dār al-Kutub al-ʿIlmīya, 1422/2001), 26. For another account of the complex negotiations among different religious and political authorities over the observance of the *mawlid*, see Ibn Fahd, *Nayl al-munā*, 1:315.
22. The *amīr al-ḥajj* in 936 and 937 would have been Yūsuf al-Ḥamzāwī. ʿAbd al-Qādir ibn Muḥammad al-Jazīrī, *al-Durar al-farāʾid al-munaẓẓama fī akhbār al-ḥajj wa-ṭarīq Makka al-mukarrama*, ed. Ḥamad al-Jāsir (Riyādh: Dār al-Yamāma, 1403/1983), 2:825, 2: 827.
23. Ibn ʿAbd al-Ghaffār, *Izāla*, 8b.
24. Ibid., 8b.
25. Ibid., 9a.
26. Ibid., 9a–b.
27. Ibid., 9b.
28. Ibid., 10a.
29. Ibid., 15b.
30. Ibid., 15b.
31. Ibid., 10a–b, 22b (note that two folios are labeled 22 in the manuscript; this is the second).
32. Ibid., 11a.
33. Ibid., 22b.
34. Ibid., 11a–b.
35. This is a reference to a ḥadīth in which the Prophet declares, "Every night our Lord (blessed and exalted is He!) descends to the lower heaven where He stays for the last hird of the night saying, 'Who is calling out to Me so that I can respond; who is asking Me so that I can give to him; who is asking forgiveness so I can forgive him?'" Bukhārī, *Ṣaḥīḥ*, *Kitāb al-Tahajjud, Bāb al-Duʿāʾ wa'l-ṣalāt min ākhar al-layl.*
36. Ibid., 90a–b.

37. Ibid., 2b–3a.
38. Ibid., 3a, 112b.
39. Ibn ʿAbd al-Ghaffār states at one point that his account of his opponents' arguments is an aggregate picture based on both oral and written communication with various people and that, because multiple members of the opposing camp had praised and endorsed each other's arguments, most of the arguments could be attributed to all of them as a group. Ibid., 25b–26a.
40. Haytamī, *Itmām al-niʿma*, 27.
41. See Ibn ʿAbd al-Ghaffār, *Izāla*, 33b.
42. See ibid., 33b.
43. Ibid., 112b.
44. Haytamī, *Fatāwā*, 1:283.
45. Ibn ʿAbd al-Ghaffār, *Izāla*, 27a.
46. Ibid., 26b.
47. Ibid., 27a–b; see also 12a.
48. Ibid., 91b.
49. Ibid., 12a, 13b. The fatwas of the Medinian Shāfiʿīs ʿAfīf al-Dīn al-Samhūdī and Sirāj al-Dīn ʿUmar ibn ʿAbd al-Raḥīm similarly state that a woman who is secluded due to her status (*al-mukhaddara*) may not go to the mosque during the daytime (ibid., 114b–115a).
50. Ibid., 13b.
51. ʿAbd Allāh ibn Muḥammad Ibn Farḥūn, *Naṣīḥat al-mushāwir wa-tasliyat al-mujāwir*, ed. ʿAlī ʿUmar (Cairo: Maktabat al-Thaqāfa al-Dīnīya, 1427/2006), 119–120. This individual's intentional flouting of convention seems to have reflected his Sufi ethic.
52. Ibn ʿAbd al-Ghaffār, *Izāla*, 27b.
53. He mentions the first Friday in the month of Rajab (traditionally the date of the controversial *raghāʾib* prayers), the twenty-seventh of Rajab (i.e., the night of the Miʿrāj), Niṣf Shaʿbān, and the twenty-seventh of Ramadan (one of the traditional dates for Laylat al-Qadr).
54. It is conceivable that al-Samhūdī's reference is to the pilgrimage of ʿAlāʾ al-Dīn al-Bukhārī, who, as we have seen in an earlier chapter of this work, was very much concerned by what he considered to be the improper mixing of women with men in mosques. During his sojourn in Medina in the context of his ḥajj pilgrimage, he reportedly closed the doors to the chamber containing the Prophet's tomb and denied the people access to it. Muḥammad ibn ʿAbd al-Raḥmān al-Sakhāwī, *al-Ḍawʾ al-lāmiʿ li-ahl al-qarn al-tāsiʿ* (Beirut: Manshūrāt Dār Maktabat al-Ḥayāt, n.d.), 9:294. Al-Bukhārī's pilgrimage would have been in the first half of the ninth/fifteenth century, which fits chronologically; although the report simply states that he closed people out of the tomb chamber, it is conceivable that this was a generalization based on the exclusion of men during certain hours.

55. ʿAlī ibn ʿAbd Allāh al-Ḥasanī al-Samhūdī, "*al-Wafā bi-mā yajib li-ḥaḍrat al-Muṣṭafā*," in *Rasāʾil fī taʾrīkh al-madīna*, ed. Ḥamad al-Jāsir (Riyadh: Manshūrāt Dār al-Yamāma, [1972?]), 162.
56. Muḥibb al-Dīn Aḥmad ibn ʿAbd Allāh al-Ṭabarī, *Ghāyat al-iḥkām fī aḥādīth al-aḥkām*, ed. Ḥamza Aḥmad al-Zayn (Beirut: Dār al-Kutub al-ʿIlmīya, 1424/2004), 2:771.
57. Ibn ʿAbd al-Ghaffār, *Izāla*, 23a–b, 28a.
58. Ibid., 31a.
59. For a parallel, roughly contemporary example from Britain, see Katherine L. French, *The Good Women of the Parish: Gender and Religion After the Black Death* (Philadelphia: University of Pennsylvania Press, 2008), 91, 93. French observes that, even though Christian "prescriptive literature has a long tradition of condemning women's love of finery, and their use of the mass as an occasion to display it," for women "church attendance was an opportunity for expressing concern and care for family, which included the promotion and protection of a family's reputation through the wearing of nice clothing and the assertion of status." In Renaissance Venice, elite women's "rituals of competitive self-display" were manifested notably in church, which was one of the few legitimate public venues where they could appear. See Robert C. Davis, "The Geography of Gender in the Renaissance," in *Gender and Society in Renaissance Italy*, ed. Judith C. Brown and Robert C. Davis (London: Longman, 1998), 36.
60. Ibn Baṭṭūṭa, *Riḥlat Ibn Baṭṭūṭa al-musammā Tuḥfat al-nuẓẓār fī gharāʾib al-amṣār wa-ʿajāʾib al-asfār* (Ṣaydā and Beirut: al-Maktaba al-ʿAṣrīya, 1425/2005), 128. See also Ibn al-Mujāwir, *A Traveller in Thirteenth-Century Arabia: Ibn al-Mujāwir's* Tārīkh al-Mustabṣir, trans. G. Smith (Aldershot, UK: Ashgate, 2007), 37.
61. Sakhāwī, *Ḍawʾ*, 12:69.
62. Ibn Jamāʿa, *Hidāyat al-sālik ilā al-madhāhib al-arbaʿa fīʾl-manāsik* (Beirut: Dār al-Bashāʾir al-Islāmīya, 1414/1994), 2:868; cited in Haytamī, *Fatāwā*, 1:286; Muḥammad ibn Aḥmad ibn Ḍiyāʾ al-Makkī, *al-Baḥr al-ʿamīq fī manāsik al-muʿtamir wa'l-ḥājj ilā bayt allāh al-ʿatīq*, ed. ʿAbd Allāh Nadhīr Aḥmad ʿAbd al-Raḥmān Mizzī (Beirut: Mu'assasat al-Rayyān, 1427/2006), 2:1250–51.
63. I thank Professor Robert Dankoff for kindly supplying and translating this passage (Evliya IX 358a).
64. Compare the description of Joseph Pitts, a British sailor who was taken captive by Algerian pirates and visited Mecca as a slave in the late seventeenth century. He wrote that when circumambulating "the women walk outside the men, and the men nearest to the *beat* [i.e., *bayt Allāh*, the Kaʿba]." Because of the crowds, not everyone gets the opportunity to touch and kiss the Black Stone; however, "when there are but few men at *towoaf*, then the women get opportunity to kiss the said stone, and when

they have gotten it, they close in with it as they come round and walk round as quick as they can to come to it again and so keep possession of it for a considerable time. . . . When the women are at the stone, then it's esteemed a very rude and abominable thing to go near them, respecting the time and place." "Joseph Pitts, A True and Faithful Account of the Religion and Manners of the Mohammetans, with an Account of the Author's Being Taken Captive (1704)," in *Piracy, Slavery, and Redemption*, selected and edited by Daniel J. Vitkus and introduced by Nabil Matar (New York: Columbia University Press, 2001), 277.

65. Ibn ʿAbd al-Ghaffār, *Izāla*, 27b.
66. Ibid., 90b.
67. Ibid., 27b.
68. Ibid., 11a–b. Ibn ʿAbd al-Ghaffār also alludes to women's presence at Bāb al-Ṣafā. Ibid., 22a, 27a, 65a.
69. al-Afandī ʿAlī ibn Mūsā, "*Waṣf al-Madīna al-munawwara fī 1303 h./1885 m.*," in *Rasāʾil fī taʾrīkh al-Madīna*, ed. Ḥamad al-Jāsir (Riyadh: Manshūrāt Dār al-Yamāma li'l-Baḥth wa'l-Tarjama wa'l-Nashr, n.d.), 65. The verb "they crowd" is in the masculine plural in the printed version, but the context clearly indicates that the custom is performed by women. This inference is confirmed by al-Barzanjī's contemporary testimony; although the information contained in the two passages is almost identical, the wording is sufficiently different that they seem to be independent accounts.
70. Jaʿfar ibn Ismāʿīl al-Barzanjī, *Hādhā al-taʾrīkh al-musammā Nuzhat al-nāẓirīn fī masjid sayyid al-awwalīn wa'l-ākharīn* ([Cairo]: Maṭbaʿat al-Jamālīya, 1332/1914), 112.
71. Hurgronje, *Mekka*, 112–13.
72. Rajab is the seventh month of the Islamic calendar, Shaʿbān is the eighth, and Ramadan is the ninth.
73. Ibn ʿAbd al-Ghaffār, *Izāla*, 14a.
74. The twenty-seventh of Rajab is the traditional date of the Miʿrāj. It is on one of the odd-numbered nights of the last ten days of Ramadan that the "Night of Power" (*Laylat al-Qadr*)—the night when the Qur'an was first revealed and on which the rewards for acts of piety are vastly magnified (c.f. Qur'an chap. 97)—is said to fall. The exact date of *Laylat al-Qadr* is not specified, but its occurrence is said to be discernible to those who experience it with sufficient spiritual awareness.
75. Ibn ʿAbd al-Ghaffār, *Izāla*, 87b, 88a. The anonymous interlocutor explains that, if the man in question were a Shāfiʿī, his *wuḍūʾ* (minor ablution) would be canceled by mere physical contact with a woman; other schools were less stringent. For a discussion of these rules, see Marion Holmes Katz, *Body of Text: The Emergence of the Sunni Law of Ritual Purity* (Albany, NY: SUNY Press, 2007), 153–54.

76. Ibn ʿAbd al-Ghaffār, *Izāla*, 28a, 87b.
77. Abū'l-Baqāʾ Aḥmad Ibn al-Ḍiyāʾ al-Qurashī, "*Mukhtaṣar Tanzīh al-masjid al-ḥarām ʿan bidaʿ al-jahala wa'l-ʿawāmm*," ed. Niẓām Muḥammad Ṣāliḥ Yaʿqūbī, published as #4 in volume 1 of *Liqāʾ al-ʿashar al-awākhir bi'l-masjid al-ḥarām* (Beirut: Dār al-Bashāʾir al-Islāmīya, 1420/1999), 1:18. Interestingly, this pattern is reported as late as the twentieth century; Eldon Rutter, who visited Mecca in the 1920s, stated that "Mekkan women very seldom pray in the Haram, save on Thursday evening. On that day a number of them usually enter the Mosque just before sunset, and having performed the towâf, they congregate near Bâb Ali in order to join in the sunset prayer. After the prayer, those who were too late to perform the towâf before sunset accomplish that act of devotion. Then they leave the Mosque without tarrying." Eldon Rutter, *The Holy Cities of Arabia* (London: G. P. Putman's Sons, 1930), 1:268.
78. Ibn ʿAbd al-Ghaffār, *Izāla*, 93b.
79. Ibid., 94a.
80. Ibid., 88b.
81. Ibid., 31a, 55b, 56a, 58b. Significantly, on 31a he suggests that the foreign women resident in Mecca ordinarily far outnumbered the native Meccan women in the mosque.
82. See, for instance, ibid., 32b, 56b.
83. Ḥanafīs and Mālikīs have traditionally held that it is positively forbidden. See Wahba al-Zuḥaylī, *al-Fiqh al-islāmī wa-adillatuhu* (Damascus: Dār al-Fikr, 1425/2005), 1:548.
84. Ibn ʿAbd al-Ghaffār, *Izāla*, 19b, 56b–57a.
85. Ibid., 26a.
86. Ibn Ḥajar al-Haytamī, *Tuḥfat al-muḥtāj bi-sharḥ al-Minhāj*, printed in margins of *Ḥawāshī ʿAbd al-Ḥamīd al-Shirwānī wa-Aḥmad ibn Qāsim al-ʿAbbādī* (Beirut: Dār Ṣādir, 1972), 2:252.
87. On the process by which fatwas responding to real situations were incorporated into *furūʿ* works, see Wael B. Hallaq, *Authority, Continuity and Change in Islamic Law* (Cambridge: Cambridge University Press, 2001), 166–235.
88. Ibn ʿAbd al-Ghaffār, *Izāla*, 61b–62a.
89. Ibid., 62a–b. The idea that women are "deficient in intellect and religion" is drawn from a ḥadīth. See al-Bukhārī, *Ṣaḥīḥ*, *Kitāb al-Ḥayḍ*, *Bāb Tark al-ḥāʾiḍ al-ṣawm*.
90. Ibn ʿAbd al-Ghaffār, *Izāla*, 74a. For the ḥadīth, see, for instance, Aḥmad ibn Muḥammad al-Thaʿlabī, *al-Kashf wa'l-bayān fī tafsīr al-qurʾān* (Beirut: Dār al-Kutub al-ʿIlmīya, 1425/2004), 1:190 (commentary on verse 2:125).
91. Ibn ʿAbd al-Ghaffār, *Izāla*, 74a–75a.
92. Ibid., 93a.
93. Ibid., 6a; see also 22a, where the author makes a passing reference to "the aforementioned natural disposition (*wāziʿ ṭabīʿī*)."

94. For references for two versions of this ḥadīth, see Muḥammad al-Saʿīd Basyūnī Zaghlūl, *Mawsūʿat aṭrāf al-ḥadīth al-nabawī al-sharīf* (Beirut: Dār al-Kutub al-ʿIlmīya, n.d.), 9:5.
95. Ibn ʿAbd al-Ghaffār, *Izāla*, 22b–23a and marginal note on 23a. The note seems to be in the voice of the original author; it may either be the restoration of a passage that was dropped by the copyist or a later amplification.
96. Ibid., 93b.
97. Ibid., 14a–b.
98. Ibid., 85b.
99. Ibid., 31b–32a.
100. Ibid., 65a–b.
101. Ibid., 44b, 47b, 60a, 76b.
102. Ibid., 112b.
103. Ibid., 64a–b.
104. Ibid., 43a. On the problems raised by such oaths, see Yossef Rapaport, *Marriage, Money and Divorce in Medieval Islamic Society* (Cambridge: Cambridge University Press, 2005), 89–110.
105. C.f. Qur'an 3:110, 3:114; 9:71, 9:112; 22:41; 31:27.It is far from obvious that *taʿzīr* is a subcategory of *amr bi'l-maʿrūf*; the two subjects are not conventionally treated together in classical Islamic works. See Michael Cook, *Commanding Right and Forbidding Wrong in Islamic Thought* (Cambridge: Cambridge University Press, 2000), 309 and n14.
106. Ibn ʿAbd al-Ghaffār, *Izāla*, 56b–57a.
107. Ibid., 57b.
108. Ibid., 57b–59a. On these limitations in the wider legal literature, see Cook, *Commanding Right*, 100, 438.
109. See Ibn ʿAbd al-Ghaffār, *Izāla*, 64a, where an opponent is made to protest that surely Ibn ʿAbd al-Ghaffār does not wish the authorities to seize the wives of the Believers and sniff them one by one!
110. Ibid., 23b, see also 61a.
111. Ibid., 33a.
112. Ibid., 64b.
113. Ibid., 110b–111a.
114. Ibid., 111b.
115. Ibid., 62b.
116. For a summary of al-Ghazālī's discussion on this point, see Cook, *Commanding Right*, 436–37.
117. Ibn ʿAbd al-Ghaffār, *Izāla*, 56a, see also 58b–60a.
118. Ibid., 55a; (see also 58b); see Aḥmad ibn Idrīs al-Qarāfī, *Kitāb al-Furūq* (*Anwār al-burūq fī anwāʾ al-furūq*), ed. Muḥammad Aḥmad Sarrāj and ʿAlī Jumʿa Muḥammad (Cairo: Dār al-Salām, 1421/2001), 4:1400.
119. Ibn ʿAbd al-Ghaffār, *Izāla*, 75b–76a.
120. Ibid., 84b.

121. Ibid., 45a.
122. Ibid., 46a–b.
123. Haytamī, *Fatāwā*, 1:283.
124. Contrast the argument of an anonymous source cited by al-Haytamī, who asks rhetorically, "How can it be said that it is obligatory to prevent her [from going to the mosque] if it is permissible for her to go? That does not exist in the divine law (*al-sharʿ*)!" Haytamī, *Fatāwā*, 1:287.
125. Ibn ʿAbd al-Ghaffār, *Izāla*, 28a–29a.
126. Ibn Fahd, *Nayl al-munā*, 1:343.
127. Haytamī, *Itmām al-niʿima*, 27–28.
128. Ibn ʿAbd al-Ghaffār, *Izāla*, 23a.
129. Ibid., 35a–37b.
130. Ibid., 33b–34a.
131. On the concept of *al-mashhūr*, see Hallaq, *Authority, Continuity, and Change*, 147–52.
132. Ibn ʿAbd al-Ghaffār, *Izāla*, 38b.
133. See Mohammad Hashim Kamali, *Principles of Islamic Jurisprudence* (Cambridge, UK: Islamic Texts Society, 1991), 310–20.
134. Ibn ʿAbd al-Ghaffār, *Izāla*, 51b–52a.
135. Ibid., 46b–47a.
136. Ibid., 65b–66b.
137. Ibid., 63b–64a.
138. Ibid., 70a.
139. Ibid., 33a.
140. Ibid., 107a, 109a.
141. Haytamī, *Fatāwā*, 1:284. For this principle (*qāʿida*), see Muḥammad Ṣadīq ibn Aḥmad al-Būrnū, *Mawsūʿat al-qawāʿid al-fiqhīya* (Beirut: Muʾassasat al-Risāla, 1424/2003), 5:315–16.
142. Ibn ʿAbd al-Ghaffār, *Izāla*, 25b.
143. Haytamī, *Fatāwā*, 1:287, also see 1:288.
144. Ibid., 1:285.
145. Ibn ʿAbd al-Ghaffār, *Izāla*, 36a.
146. Ibid., 38b–39a.
147. Ibid., 39a.
148. Ibid., 48a.
149. Ibid., 31a, 42b.
150. Ibid., 48a–49b.
151. Ibid., 48b.
152. Ibid., 48b–49a.
153. Ibid., 2a.
154. Ibid., 19a.
155. Ibid., 49b–50a; compare ibid., 21b, where Ibn ʿAbd al-Ghaffār also refers to women as "more than half of the community."

156. Haytamī, *Fatāwā*, 1:284.
157. Ibn ʿAbd al-Ghaffār, *Izāla*, 32a.
158. Ibid., 70b.
159. Ibid., 95b.
160. Ibid., 98b.
161. Ibid., 104a–b.
162. For this distinction, see Kamali, *Principles*, 331–33.
163. Sherman A. Jackson, "*Kramer Versus Kramer* in a Tenth/Sixteenth Century Egyptian Court: Post-Formative Jurisprudence Between Exigency and Law," *Islamic Law and Society* 8 (2001): 50.
164. For instance, with respect to the report that the Prophet's Companion Ibn ʿAbbās discouraged women from the festival prayers, Ibn ʿAbd al-Ghaffār points out that Ibn ʿAbbās barred only young women (*shawābb*), whereas his own opponents have extended the ban to include old women (*ʿajāʾiz*) and those who are no longer the object of male desire (*al-mutajāllāt al-lātī inqataʿa minhunna arab al-rijāl*). Ibn ʿAbd al-Ghaffār, *Izāla*, 81b.
165. Qarāfī, *Furūq*, 1:357; 4:1399–1400. I thank Mohammad Fadel for drawing my attention to al-Qarāfī's argument on this point.
166. Ibn ʿAbd al-Ghaffār, *Izāla*, 118b–119a. Interestingly, however, the following fatwa from the Ḥanafī chief judge of Medina makes no mention of the purported undesirability of mosque-going for latter-day women and indeed notes that a woman can be barred from the mosque only if she is menstruating. Ibid., 119a.
167. This scholar died in Cairo in 957/1551; see Kaḥḥāla, *Muʿjām*, 3:226.
168. Ibn ʿAbd al-Ghaffār, *Izāla*, 117a.
169. Ibid., 118a.
170. On this figure, see Ghazzī, *Kawākib*, 2:99.
171. C.f. Qur'an 6:164, 17:15, 35:18, 39:7, 53:38. Ibn ʿAbd al-Ghaffār, *Izāla*, 120a–b. Al-Shuwaykī argues that it is the duty of a woman's guardian to prevent her from leaving the house if she is likely to cause *fitna*; if he is unable to do so, then he should refer the matter to the ruler.
172. Ibid., 115a.
173. See Ghazzī, *Kawākib*, 2:111–12; Ibn al-ʿImād, *Shadharāt*, 8:332–33; Jazīrī, *ʿUmdat al-ṣafwa*, 53.
174. Ibn ʿAbd al-Ghaffār, *Izāla*, 113a.
175. It is clear that Ibn ʿAbd al-Ghaffār inserts his own comments as well as abridging al-Sunbāṭī's words, because the text includes a cross-reference to an earlier passage of Ibn ʿAbd al-Ghaffār's work; see ibid., 113b. Ibn ʿAbd al-Ghaffār states at the end of his summary that "most of" it is in al-Sunbāṭī's words.
176. Ibid., 113a.
177. Jazīrī, *ʿUmdat al-ṣafwa*, 53–54.

178. For this figure, who also participated in the coffee controversy (on the side of permissibility), see ʿAbd al-Qādir ibn Shaykh al-ʿAydarūsī, *Taʾrīkh al-Nūr al-sāfir ʿan akhbār al-qarn al-ʿāshir* ([Egypt?], n.d.), 228–32.
179. Ibn ʿAbd al-Ghaffār, *Izāla*, 115a–116b.
180. Ibid., 116b.
181. Robert Dankoff, "*Ayıp değil!* (No Disgrace!)," *Journal of Turkish Literature* 5 (2008): 77. See also ibid., 78, regarding Evliya's observation that the women of Cairo venture out only at night.
182. Lady Wortley Montagu, *The Letters and Works of Lady Mary Wortley Montagu*, 3rd ed., ed. W. Moy Thomas (New York: AMS Press, 1970), 1:325; Julia Pardoe, *City of the Sultan; and Domestic Manners of the Turks, in 1836* (London: Henry Colburn, 1837), 2:51–52. As far as Mecca is concerned, however, our sequence of events does not seem to have displaced the long-term tradition of women (including pilgrims) favoring the less-crowded nighttime hours to perform *ṭawāf*. See, for instance, al-Jazīrī, *al-Durar al-farāʾid*, 3:1915.
183. Ibn ʿAbd al-Ghaffār, *Izāla*, 6a.
184. Ibid., 11a.
185. Ibid., 22a.
186. Ibid., 21a.

4. MODERN DEVELOPMENTS

1. Al-Qāsimī, *Iṣlāḥ al-masājid*, 210, cited in Khayr al-Dīn Wānilī, *al-Masjid fi'l-islām: risālatuhu, niẓām bināʾihi, aḥkāmuhu, ādābuhu, bidaʿuhu* (n.p., n.d.), 300. On al-Qāsimī's views regarding women, see David Dean Commins, *Islamic Reform: Politics and Social Change in Late Ottoman Syria* (New York: Oxford University Press, 1990), 82–84.
2. Al-Qāsimī, *Iṣlāḥ*, 224–25, cited in Wānilī, *Masjid*, 122.
3. Muḥammad Rashīd Riḍā, *Tārīkh al-ustādh al-imām al-shaykh Muḥammad ʿAbduh* (Cairo: Maṭbaʿat al-Manār, 1344/[1925–26]), 2:135.
4. Literally, "they" (feminine plural).
5. *Fatāwā al-imām Muḥammad Rashīd Riḍā*, collected and edited by Ṣalāḥ al-Dīn al-Munajjid and Yūsuf Q. Khūrī (Beirut: Dār al-Kitāb al-Jadīd, 1390/1970), 1:212–13.
6. Ibid., 2:436–37.
7. *Minutes of the Proceedings of the First Egyptian Congress Assembled at Heliopolis (Near Cairo) from Saturday 30 Rabi-al-Thani 1329 (29 April 1911) to Wednesday 5 Gamad-ul-Awwal 1329 (4 May 1911)* (Alexandria, 1329/1911), 114.
8. Ibid., 114–18.
9. Valerie J. Hoffman-Ladd, "The Religious Life of Muslim Women in Contemporary Egypt" (PhD diss., University of Chicago, 1986), 277.

10. On Malak Hifnī Nāṣif's contribution to the new discourse of motherhood and domestic science, see Omnia Shakry, "Schooled Mothers and Structured Play: Child Rearing in Turn-of-the-Century Egypt," in *Remaking Women: Feminism and Modernity in the Middle East*, ed. Lila Abu-Lughod (Princeton, NJ: Princeton University Press, 1998), 145–48.
11. Muḥammad ʿAbduh et al., *al-Fatāwā al-islāmīya min Dār al-Iftāʾ al-Miṣrīya* (Cairo: Wizārat al-Awqāf, al-Majlis al-Aʿlā li'l-Shuʾūn al-Islāmīya, 1400/1980), 1:76.
12. This tendency is epitomized by the program for the international development of mosques presented by the Muslim World League in 1975, which mandated that mosques provide both separate doors for men and women and facilities for women's instruction in home economics. Cleo Cantone, *Making and Remaking Mosques in Senegal* (Leiden: Brill, 2012), 260.
13. Muḥammad Saʿīd Ramaḍān al-Būṭī, *Maʿa al-nās: Mashwarāt... wa-fatāwā* (Damascus: Dār al-Fikr, 1419/1999), 34–38, see also 18.
14. Asma Sayeed, "Early Sunni Discourse on Women's Mosque Attendance." *ISIM Newsletter* 7 (2001): 10.
15. ʿAbd al-Ḥalīm Maḥmūd, *Fatāwā al-imām ʿAbd al-Ḥalīm Maḥmūd* (Cairo: Dār al-Maʿārif, n.d.), 1:461.
16. Ibid., 1:478.
17. ʿAbduh et al., *al-Fatāwā al-islāmīya*, 5:1720.
18. As of May 1, 2007, this fatwa was available on the official Dār al-Iftāʾ website at http://www.dar-alifta.org/viewfatwa.aspx?ID=4782, but is no longer available there; as of the time of finalization of this manuscript (January 7, 2014, a copy reproduced from the Dār al-Iftāʾ website was available at http://www.manqol.com/topic/print.aspx?t=19534.
19. ʿAṭīya Ṣaqr, *Mawsūʿat al-usra taḥta riʿāyat al-islām* ([Cairo]: al-Dār al-Miṣrīya li'l-Kitāb, 1410/1990), 2:189–91, 2:198; ʿAṭīya Ṣaqr, *Mawsūʿat Aḥsan al-kalām fī al-fatāwā wa'l-aḥkām* (Cairo: Maktabat Wahba, 1432/2011), 3:228.
20. Suʿād Ṣāliḥ, *Aḥkām ʿibādat al-marʾa fī al-sharīʿa al-islāmīya* (Cairo: Dār al-Ḍiyāʾ, 1406/1986), 236, 237.
21. Khālid al-Jundī, ed., *Fa'sʾalū ahl al-dhikr* (Beirut: Dār al-Maʿrifa, 1423/2003), 122.
22. Ḥasan al-Bannā, *al-Marʾa al-muslima*, ed. Muḥammad Nāṣir al-Dīn al-Albānī (Cairo: Dār al-Kutub al-Salafīya, 1404/1983), 16.
23. Ibid., 15.
24. Ibid., 23–25.
25. Ibid., 25–26.
26. Muḥammad Rashīd Riḍā, *Ḥuqūq al-nisāʾ fī'l-islām (Nidāʾ ilā al-jins al-laṭīf)* (Beirut: al-Maktab al-Islāmī, 1395/1975), 11.

27. Al-Bahī al-Khūlī, *al-Marʾa bayna al-bayt wa'l-mujtamaʿ* (Cairo: Min Rasāʾil al-Ikhwān al-Muslimīn, [1953?]), 3, 5.
28. Ibid., 115.
29. Ibid., 116, 118.
30. Ibid., 119.
31. Muhammad al-Ghazzāli, *Our Beginning in Wisdom*, trans. Isma'il R. el Faruqi (New York: Octagon Books, 1975), 104. See also Haifaa Khalafallah, "Public Authority, Scriptures, and 'Islamic Law,'" in *Beyond the Exotic: Women's Histories in Islamic Societies*, ed. Amira El-Azhary Sonbol (Syracuse, NY: Syracuse University Press, 2005), 40.
32. al-Ghazzāli, *Our Beginning in Wisdom*, 113.
33. Muḥammad al-Ghazālī, *al-Sunna al-nabawīya bayna ahl al-fiqh...wa-ahl al-ḥadīth* (Beirut: Dār al-Shurūq, 1409/1989), 52–53.
34. Ibid., 53, 54.
35. Ibid., 54.
36. Muḥammad al-Ghazālī, *al-Islām wa'l-ṭāqāt al-muʿaṭṭala*, 143, cited in Suhayla al-Ḥusaynī, *al-Marʾa fī manhaj al-imām al-Ghazālī* (Cairo: Dār al-Rashād, 1419/1998), 30–31.
37. Muḥammad al-Ghazālī, *Qaḍāyā al-marʾa bayna al-taqālīd al-rākida wa'l-wāfida* (Cairo: Dār al-Shurūq, 1411/1990), 199.
38. Al-Ghazālī, *al-Islām wa'l-ṭāqāt al-muʿaṭṭala*, cited in Ḥusaynī, *Marʾa*, 38.
39. Cited in ibid., 39.
40. Cited in ibid., 36–37. The passage in question is 24:36–37, which speaks of "houses" where God's name is glorified "by men whom neither trade nor merchandise can divert from the remembrance of God." The classical exegete al-Qurṭubī had taken this reference to indicate that "women have no share in mosques," although this appears to be an isolated interpretation; Muḥammad al-Ghazālī dismisses it out of hand. See Muḥammad ibn Aḥmad al-Qurṭubī, *al-Jāmiʿ li-aḥkām al-qurʾān*, ed. Muṣṭafā al-Badrī (Beirut: Dār al-Kutub al-ʿIlmīya, 1424/2004), 12:184.
41. See "The Role of Muslim Women in an Islamic Society," official translation at http://www.jannah.org/sisters/ikhwom.html, accessed April 6, 2010. For a general overview of the Ikhwān's attitudes toward women, see Richard P. Mitchell, *The Society of the Muslim Brothers* (London: Oxford University Press, 1969), 254–59.
42. Jakob Skovgaard-Petersen defines *dāʿiya* (sing. *dāʿī*) as "the new Islamic media preachers," "who command huge audiences, in particular the middle-class audiences so attractive to the commercial TV stations." See Jakob Skovgaard-Petersen, "In Defense of Muḥammad: ʿUlamaʾ, Daʿiya and the New Islamic Internationalism," in *Guardians of Faith in Modern Times: ʿUlamaʾ in the Middle East*, ed. Meir Hatina (Leiden: Brill, 2009), 291.

43. For the role of al-Qaraḍāwī, see Bettina Gräf and Jakob Skovgaard-Petersen, eds., *Global Mufti: The Phenomenon of Yusuf al-Qaradawi* (New York: Columbia University Press, 2009), particularly the article "Yūsuf al-Qaraḍāwī and the Muslim Brothers: The Nature of a Special Relationship" by Husam Tammam, 55–83.
44. Yūsuf al-Qaraḍāwī, *Fatāwā al-marʾa al-muslima* (Beirut: Mu'assasat al-Risāla, 1422/2001), 38–43.
45. Yūsuf al-Qaraḍāwī, *Hudā al-islām: Fatāwā muʿāṣira* (Cairo: Dār Āfāq al-Ghadd, 1401/1981), 280–81.
46. A similar point is made by the contemporary Egyptian Salafī Abū Isḥāq al-Ḥuwaynī, who argues that a woman should be allowed to go to the mosque for Friday prayers "to re-charge her heart with faith" and to renew her religion by listening to preaching, although he combines it with the argument that, if women stay home, they will busy themselves with malicious gossip. http://www.alheweny.org/aws/play.php?catsmktba=9104, accessed February 10, 2013.
47. ʿAbd al-Ḥalīm Muḥammad Abū Shuqqa, *Tahrīr al-marʾa fī ʿaṣr al-risāla* (Kuwait and Cairo: Dār al-Qalam li'l-Nashr wa'l-Tawzīʿ, 1430/2009), 2:15–16.
48. Ibid., 2:19.
49. Ibid., 2:178.
50. Hiba Raʾūf ʿIzzat, *Al-Marʾa wa'l-ʿamal al-siyāsī: ruʾya islāmīya* (Herndon, VA: al-Maʿhad al-ʿĀlamī li'l-Fikr al-Islāmī, 1416/1995), 112.
51. Ibid., 112.
52. Ibid., 102.
53. Ibid., 107–8.
54. Al-Ghazālī, *Qaḍāyā*, 197. This remark comes in the context of a passage denying that women's bad behavior could lead to a legal prohibition on their attending mosques.
55. On the nature and doctrines of the Salafī movement see Roel Meijer, ed., *Global Salafism: Islam's New Religious Movement* (New York: Columbia University Press, 2009).
56. Cited in Eleanor Abdella Doumato, *Getting God's Ear: Women, Islam, and Healing in Saudi Arabia and the Gulf* (New York: Columbia University Press, 2000), 101–4.
57. Eldon Rutter, *The Holy Cities of Arabia* (London: G. P. Putman's Sons, 1930), 1:268–69. One highly idealized account of the lifestyle of Bedouin Ikhwān settled in Saudi *ḥujar* appears to suggest that women attended noon prayers every day. Muḥammad Mughayribī al-Madanī, *Firqat al-ikhwān al-islāmīya bi-najd aw wahhābīyat al-yawm* (n.p., n.d.), 40, referenced in Doumato, *Getting God's Ear*, 108. I thank Justin Stearns for making this text available to me.

58. Muḥammad ibn Ibrāhīm Āl al-Shaykh, *Fatāwā wa-rasāʾil samāḥat al-shaykh Muḥammad ibn Ibrāhīm ibn ʿAbd al-Laṭīf Āl al-Shaykh*, arranged and edited by Muḥammad ibn ʿAbd al-Raḥmān ibn Qāsim (Mecca: Maṭbaʿat al-Ḥukūma, 1399/[1978–79]), 4:149.
59. ʿAbd al-ʿAzīz ibn ʿAbd Allāh Ibn Bāz, *Majmūʿ fatāwā wa-maqālāt mutanawwiʿa taʾlīf al-faqīr ilā ʿafw rabbihi ʿAbd al-ʿAzīz ibn ʿAbd Allāh ibn ʿAbd al-Raḥmān ibn Bāz*, collected and arranged by Muḥammad ibn Saʿd Shuwayʿir (Riyadh: Dār Aṣdāʾ al-Mujtamaʿ, 1421/[2000–2001]), 12:79–80, see also 12:80–81.
60. *al-Fatāwā al-jāmiʿa li'l-marʾa al-muslima*, collected and arranged by Amīn ibn Yaḥyā al-Wazzān (Riyadh: Dār al-Qāsim li'l-Nashr, 1419/[1998–99]), 1:201–3.
61. Ibid., 1:212–13; *Fatāwā al-Lajna al-Dāʾima li'l-Buḥūth al-ʿIlmīya wa'l-Iftāʾ*, collected and arranged by Aḥmad ibn ʿAbd al-Razzāq al-Duwaysh (Riyadh: Dār al-ʿĀṣima, 1416/1996), 7:334.
62. *al-Fatāwā al-jāmiʿa,* 1:203.
63. Ibid., 1:202.
64. Ibid., 1:208.
65. Muḥammad ibn Ṣāliḥ al-ʿUthaymīn, *al-Sharḥ al-mumtiʿ ʿalā Zād al-mustanqiʿ* (al-Dammām: Dār Ibn al-Jawzī, 1423), 4:202–3.
66. Like their premodern Ḥanbalī predecessors, the Saudi scholars centrally focus on the application of ḥadīth to legal problems. However, one cannot uncritically assume that they are more "literal" in their application of ḥadīth than other scholars (including those who take more liberal approaches on issues of gender). In this case, they emphasize texts asserting the superior merit of womenʾs prayer within the home over other, sometimes better authenticated, texts that emphasize the merit of prayer in congregation and in mosques (sometimes in gender-neutral terms).
67. Khaled Abou El Fadl, *Speaking in Godʾs Name: Islamic Law, Authority and Women* (Oxford, UK: Oneworld, 2001), 232–47.
68. See Jeffrey Lang, *Even Angels Ask: A Journey to Islam in America* (Beltsville, MD: Amana Publications, 1418/1997), 111; Jamillah Karim, "Voices of Faith, Faces of Beauty: Connecting American Muslim Women Through *Azizah*," in *Muslim Networks from Hajj to Hip Hop*, ed. Miriam Cooke and Bruce B. Lawrence (Chapel Hill: University of North Carolina Press, 2005), 173.
69. On al-Albānī, see Stéphane Lacroix, "Between Revolution and Apoliticism: Nasir al-Din al-Albani and His Impact on the Shaping of Contemporary Salafism," in *Global Salafism: Islam's New Religious Movement*, ed. Roel Meijer (New York: Columbia University Press, 2009), 58–80.
70. See Jonathan A. C. Brown, *The Canonization of al-Bukhārī and Muslim* (Leiden: Brill, 2007), 325–31.

71. See Richard Gauvain, *Salafi Ritual Purity: In the Presence of God* (London: Routledge, 2013), 101–2.
72. Ibid., 422–23, see also 559.
73. See Nāṣir al-Dīn al-Albānī, *al-Masāʾil al-ʿilmīya waʾl-fatāwā al-sharʿīya, fatāwā al-shaykh Muḥammad Nāṣir al-Dīn al-Albānī fi'l-Madīna waʾl-Imārāt*, collected, organized, and commented on by ʿUmar ʿAbd al-Munʿim Salīm (Tanta, Egypt: Dār al-Ḍiyāʾ, 2006), 440. This is the thirteenth fatwa from the fourth audiotape of the series *al-Hudā wa'l-Nūr*; the entire series (along with a searchable content index) is available at http://www.alalbany.net/albany_tapes_huda_noor.php, accessed January 18, 2013.
74. Albānī, *al-Masāʾil al-ʿilmīya*, 423.
75. Nāṣir al-Dīn al-Albānī, *al-Hudā wa'l-Nūr*, tape 15.
76. Muḥammad Nāṣir al-Dīn al-Albānī, *al-Taʿlīqāt al-raḍīya ʿalā al-Rawḍa al-nadīya li'l-ʿallāma Ṣiddīq Ḥasan Khān*, ed. ʿAlī bn Ḥasan al-Ḥalabī (Cairo: Dār Ibn ʿAffān, 1420/1999), 1:327.
77. Albānī, *al-Masāʾil al-ʿilmīya*, 272–73.
78. For a discussion of the emergence of the modern Islamic concept of *daʿwa* and the role of the *dāʿiya*, see Saba Mahmood, *Politics of Piety* (Princeton, NJ: Princeton University Press, 2005), 61–72.
79. For several versions of a ḥadīth in which the Prophet curses "women who make themselves resemble men" and "men who make themselves resemble women," see Muḥammad Zaghlūl, *Mawsūʿat aṭrāf al-ḥadīth al-nabawī al-sharīf* (Beirut: Dār al-Kutub al-ʿIlmīya, n.d.), 6:597, 6:603, 6:604.
80. Albānī, *al-Masāʾil al-ʿilmīya*, 558.
81. Albānī, *al-Hudā wa'l-Nūr*, tape 24.
82. See Albānī, *al-Masāʾil al-ʿilmīya*, 232–34; Nāṣir al-Dīn al-Albānī, *al-Thamr al-mustaṭāb fī fiqh al-sunna wa'l-kitāb* (Kuwait: Ghirās, 1422/[2001–2002]), 2:738–55.
83. Gauvain, *Salafi Ritual Purity*, 219–20.
84. A particularly striking (and problematic) example of this line of argumentation is Julie Marcus, *A World of Difference: Islam and Gender Hierarchy in Turkey* (London: Zed, 1992), especially chap. 5.
85. See Pieternella van Doorn-Harder, *Women Shaping Islam: Reading the Qur'an in Indonesia* (Urbana: University of Illinois Press, 2006), 79; Cantone, *Making and Remaking Mosques*, 318, 331.
86. Gauvain, *Salafi Ritual Purity*, 223.
87. Ibid., 222.
88. On tape 24 of the *Hudā wa'l-Nūr* series, al-Albānī raises questions about whether a women's prayer room in the basement of a mosque can be considered legally a part of the mosque—and thus about the validity of the women's prayer behind the imam. See also Cantone, *Making and Remaking Mosques*, 349–50.
89. Albānī, *al-Hudā wa'l-Nūr*, tape 329.

90. Ibid., tape 484.
91. Albānī, *al-Masāʾil al-ʿilmīya*, 469.
92. Nāṣir al-Dīn al-Albānī, *Jilbāb al-mar'a al-muslima fi'l-kitāb wa'l-sunna* (n.p.: Dār al-Salām, [2002?]), 155. This passage is based on a fatwa of Ibn Taymīya.
93. Anne Sofie Roald, *Women in Islam: The Western Experience* (London: Routledge, 2001), 51–52.
94. The origins of the women's prayer section reportedly went back to a visit to Medina by the wife of the Ottoman Sultan Maḥmūd II (ruled 1808–39); a "small enclosure" was built to accommodate her. This original royal enclosure was enlarged and modified in the reign of Sultan ʿAbd al-Majīd to become a space generally dedicated to women's prayer and again enlarged in 1863–64. Muḥammad Labīb al-Batanūnī, *al-Riḥla al-ḥijāzīya li-walī al-niʿam al-ḥājj ʿAbbās Ḥilmī al-thānī Khedīw Miṣr*, 2nd printing (Cairo, 1329/[1911–12]), 240; Jaʿfar ibn Ismāʿīl al-Barzanjī, *Hādhā al-taʾrīkh al-musammā Nuzhat al-nāẓirīn fī masjid sayyid al-awwalīn wa'l-ākharīn* ([Cairo]: Maṭbaʿat al-Jamālīya, 1332/1914), 35; Ibrāhīm Rifʿat Bāshā, *Mirʾāt al-ḥaramayn* (Cairo: Dār al-Kutub al-Miṣrīya, 1344/1925), 1:450, 1:467; Muḥammad Hazzāʿ al-Shahrī, *al-Masjid al-nabawī al-sharīf fi'l-ʿaṣr al-ʿuthmānī, 923–1344, dirāsa miʿmārīya ḥaḍārīya* (Cairo: Dār al-Qāhira li'l-Kitāb, 2003), 139 (with references to relevant Ottoman archival documents). Ibrāhīm Rifʿat Bāshā's text appears to be dependent on Barzanjī's.
95. al-Afandī ʿAlī ibn Mūsā, "Waṣf al-Madīna al-munawwara fī 1303 h./1885 m," in *Rasāʾil fī taʾrīkh al-Madīna*, ed. Ḥamad al-Jāsir (Riyadh: Manshūrāt Dār al-Yamāma li'l-Baḥth wa'l-Tarjama wa'l-Nashr, n.d.), 65; al-Batanūnī, *Riḥla*, 240. Maʾmūn Maḥmūd Yāsīn, who visited Medina in 1359/1940 (but also apparently drew on al-Batanūnī), describes the women's section as being "screened by a wooden lattice (*mastūr bi-shabaka khashabīya*)." Maʾmūn Maḥmūd Yāsīn, *al-Riḥla ilā al-Madīna al-munawwara* (n.p., 1407/1987), 123.
96. Barzanjī, *Nuzha*, 35; Ibrāhīm Rifʿat Bāshā, *Mirʾāt*, 467. Barzanjī is explicitly laudatory about the extension of the women's section to avoid mixing of women with men outside of the enclosure, citing it as an example of good Islamic etiquette (*adab*).
97. ʿAbduh et al., *al-Fatāwā al-islāmīya*, 1:74–76.
98. The prominent Egyptian preacher ʿAbd al-Ḥamīd Kishk (d. 1996) lists the designation of a space for women's prayer as one of the "requirements of the modern mosque." ʿAbd al-Ḥamīd Kishk, *Dawr al-masjid fi'l-mujtamaʿ al-muʿāṣir* (Cairo: al-Mukhtār al-Islāmī, n.d.), 45; see also al-Jundī, *Fa'sʾalū ahl al-dhikr*, 122.
99. *Al-Fatāwā al-jāmiʿa*, 1:213. See *Fatāwā al-Lajna al-Dāʾima*, 6:333, 6:336.
100. See the three fatwas by ʿAbd Allāh ibn Jabrīn and Ṣāliḥ al-Fawzān in *al-Fatāwā al-jāmiʿa*, 1:209–11.

101. For instance, the American convert Jeffrey Lang describes his family's experience in the 1990s in a mosque in Khobar, Saudi Arabia: "When we reached the mosque, my wife and three daughters entered the ladies' section—a very small, dark room, with a dark plexiglas window that looked out upon the area of the mosque where the men prayed." Jeffery Lang, *Struggling to Surrender: Some Impressions of an American Convert to Islam* (Beltsville, MD: Amana Publications, 1415/1994), 111.
102. On the issue of the relative lack of constructive thought on the placement of women's space in twentieth-century mosques, see Renata Holod and Hasan-Uddin Khan, *The Contemporary Mosque: Architects, Clients and Designs since the 1950s* (New York: Rizzoli, 1997), 21.
103. Soraya Duval, "New Veils and New Voices," in *Women and Islamization: Contemporary Dimensions of Discourse on Gender Relations*, ed. Karin Ask and Marit Tjomsland (Oxford, UK: Berg, 1998), 62–63.
104. See Shoshana Keller, "The Struggle Against Islam in Uzbekistan, 1921–1941: Policy, Bureaucracy, and Reality" (PhD diss. Indiana University, 1995), 373; Yaacov Ro'i, *Islam in the Soviet Union* (New York: Columbia University Press, 2000), 223n196.
105. Ro'i, *Islam in the Soviet Union*, 213 (Dagestan in the 1950s–1960s). In a much more recent case, in 2004 the Tajik Council of Ulema issued a fatwa prohibiting women from attending Friday congregational prayers in Tajikistan. This was seen in the context of a general program of control of Tajik society.
106. See, for instance, al-Shahīd al-Awwal, *al-Lumʿa al-dimashqīya* (Qum: Mu'assasat Ismāʿīlīyān, 1416/[1995–96]), 1:93–94; al-Shahīd al-Thānī, *al-Fawāʾid al-Malīya li-sharḥ al-Risāla al-naflīya* (Qum: Markaz Intishārāt-i Daftar-i Tablīghāt-i Islāmī, 1420/[1999–2000]), 108.
107. Ayatollah Sayyed Ruhollah Mousavi Khomeini, *A Clarification of Questions, An Unabridged Translation of* Rasaleh Towzih al-Masael, trans. J. Borujerdi (Boulder, CO: Westview Press, 1984), 123; see also L'Ayatollah Ali Khamenei, *Les principales fatwas*, trans. from the Arabic and annotated by Fouad Noun (Beirut: Dar Albouraq, 1427/2006), 132.
108. Muḥammad Ḥusayn Faḍl Allāh, *Fiqh al-sharīʿa* (Beirut: Dār al-Malāk, 1420/1999), 1:274–75.
109. See Azam Torab, *Performing Islam: Gender and Ritual in Iran* (Leiden: Brill, 2007), 52–53, 57.
110. Heba Aziz El-Kholy, *Defiance and Compliance: Negotiating Gender in Low-Income Cairo* (New York: Berghahn Books, 2002), 181–82.
111. See, for instance, Diane D'Souza, "Women's Presence in the Mosque: A Viewpoints [*sic*]," in *Islam, Women and Gender Justice*, ed. Asghar Ali Engineer (New Delhi: Gyan, 2001), 208.
112. See Mahmood, *Politics of Piety*.

113. See, for instance, Judy Brink, "Lost Rituals: Sunni Muslim Women in Rural Egypt," in *Mixed Blessings: Gender and Religious Fundamentalism Cross Culturally*, ed. Judy Brink and Joan Mencher (London: Routledge, 1997), 201.
114. Evelyn A. Early, *Baladi Women of Cairo: Playing with an Egg and a Stone* (Boulder, CO: Lynne Rienner, 1993), 93.
115. The creation of separate mosques for women (as opposed to prayer rooms, *muṣallayāt*, that offer space for worship without the personnel or organized prayer and study activities of a fully developed mosque) does not seem to have been a popular option in the Arab Middle East. In 1957, the muftī Muḥammad Ḥasanayn Makhlūf responded to a query about a plan for a women's mosque in Cairo in which women would perform as imām, give the sermon, and pronounce the call to prayer. Makhlūf briskly replied that this was a *bidʿa* (innovation). *Majallat al-Azhar* (Ramadan 1376/[April 1957?]), 861, 864. In contrast, separate women's mosques proliferated in Central China from the early twentieth century and were founded by Indonesian women activists in the 1930s. See Maria Jaschok and Shui Jingjun, *The History of Women's Mosques in Chinese Islam* (Richmond, Surrey, UK: Curzon Press, 2000); van Doorn-Harder, *Women Shaping Islam*, 79.
116. Holod and Khan, *The Contemporary Mosque*, 20.
117. Leila Ahmed, *A Border Passage: From Cairo to America—A Woman's Journey* (New York: Farrar, Straus and Giroux, 1999), 123–24.

BIBLIOGRAPHY

PRIMARY SOURCES

ʿAbd al-Ghanī al-Nābulusī. *al-Ḥaḍra al-unsīya fī al-riḥla al-qudsīya*, edited by Akram Ḥasan al-ʿUlbī. Beirut: al-Maṣādir, 1990.

——. *al-Ḥaqīqa wa'l-majāz fial-riḥla ilā bilād al-shām wa-miṣr wa'l-ḥijāz*, edited by Aḥmad ʿAbd al-Majīd al-Huraydī. Cairo: al-Hayʾa al-Miṣrīya al-ʿĀmma li'l-Kitāb, 1986.

ʿAbd al-Qāhir al-Baghdādī. *al-Farq bayna al-firaq*, edited by Muḥammad ʿUthmān al-Khisht. Cairo: Maktabat Ibn Sīnā, [1988].

ʿAbduh, Muḥammad, et al. *al-Fatāwā al-islāmīya min Dār al-Iftāʾ al-Miṣrīya*. 11 vols. Cairo: Wizārat al-Awqāf, al-Majlis al-Aʿlā li'l-Shuʾūn al-Islāmīya, 1400/1980.

Abū Dāwūd, Sulaymān ibn al-Ashʿath. *Sunan Abī Dāwūd*. 2 vols. Vaduz, Liechtenstein: Thesaurus Islamicus Foundation, 2000.

Abū Isḥāq al-Shīrāzī. *al-Muhadhdhab fī fiqh al-imām al-Shāfiʿī*. 6 vols. Damascus: Dār al-Qalam/Beirut: al-Dār al-Shāmīya, 1412/1992.

Abū'l-Baqāʾ al-Makkī al-Ḥanafī, Muḥammad ibn Aḥmad ibn Muḥammad ibn Ḍiyāʾ. *al-Baḥr al-ʿamīq fī manāsik al-muʿtamir wa'l-ḥājj ilā bayt allāh al-ʿatīq*, edited by ʿAbd Allāh Nadhīr Aḥmad ʿAbd al-Raḥmān Mizzī. 5 vols. Beirut: Muʾassasat al-Rayyān, 1427/2006.

Abū'l-Faraj al-Iṣfahānī. *Kitāb al-Aghānī*. 23 vols. Cairo: al-Hayʾa al-Miṣrīya al-ʿĀmma li'l-Kitāb, 1993.

Abū Nuʿaym al-Iṣfahānī. *Ḥulyat al-awliyāʾ wa-ṭabaqāt al-aṣfiyāʾ*. 10 vols. Beirut: Dār al-Kitāb al-ʿArabī, 1387/1967.

Abū Shāma, ʿAbd al-Raḥmān ibn Ismāʿīl al-Maqdisī. *al-Bāʿith ʿalā inkār al-bidaʿ wa'l-ḥawādith*. Cairo: Maktabat Majd al-Islām, 2007.

——. *Tarājim rijāl al-qarnayn al-sādis wa'l-sābiʿ*. Cairo, 1366/1947.

Abū Shuqqa, ʿAbd al-Ḥalīm Muḥammad. *Taḥrīr al-marʾa fī ʿaṣr al-risāla*. 6 vols. in 3. Kuwait and Cairo: Dār al-Qalam li'l-Nashr wa'l-Tawzīʿ, 1430/2009.

Abū Yaʿlā Ibn al-Farrāʾ. *al-Jāmiʿ al-ṣaghīr fī'l-fiqh ʿalā madhhab al-imām Aḥmad ibn Ḥanbal*. Riyadh: Dār Aṭlas li'l-Nashr wa'l-Tawzīʿ, 1421/2000.

Abū Yūsuf Yaʿqūb ibn Ibrāhīm al-Anṣārī. *Kitāb al-Āthār*. Beirut: Dār al-Kutub al-ʿIlmīya, n.d.

al-ʿAdawī, ʿAlī ibn Aḥmad. *Ḥāshiyat al-shaykh ʿAlī ibn Aḥmad al-ʿAdawī*. Published with Muḥammad ibn ʿAbd Allāh al-Khurashī. *Ḥāshiyat al-Khurashī ʿalā Mukhtaṣar sayyidī Khalīl*, edited by Zakarīyā ʿUmayrāt. 8 vols. Beirut: Dār al-Kutub al-ʿIlmīya, 1417/1997.

Addison, Lancelot. *West Barbary, or, a Short Narrative of the Revolutions of the Kingdoms of Fez and Morocco. With an Account of the Present Customs, Sacred, Civil, and Domestick*. Oxford, 1671. E-book.

Adorno, Anselme. *Itinéraire d'Anselme Adorno en Terre Sainte (1470–1471)*, edited and translated by Jacques Heers and Georgette de Groer. Paris: Éditions du Centre National de la Recherche Scientifique, 1978.

Aḥmad Ibn Ṭawq. *Al-Taʿlīq*, edited by Jaʿfar al-Muhājir. 4 vols. Damascus: Institut Français de Damas, 2000.

Ahmed, Leila. *A Border Passage: From Cairo to America—A Woman's Journey*. New York: Farrar, Straus and Giroux, 1999.

al-ʿAkk, Khālid ibn ʿAbd al-Raḥmān. *Mawsūʿat al-fiqh al-mālikī*. 6 vols. Damascus: Dār al-Ḥikma, 1993.

al-Albānī, Muḥammad Nāṣir al-Dīn. *al-Masāʾil al-ʿilmīya wa al-fatāwā al-sharʿīya, fatāwā al-shaykh Muḥammad Nāṣir al-Dīn al-Albānī fīʾl-Madīna waʾl-Imārāt*, collected, organized, and commented on by ʿUmar ʿAbd al-Munʿim Salīm. Tanta, Egypt: Dār al-Ḍiyāʾ, 2006.

——. *al-Hudā wa'l-nūr*. Available online at http://www.alalbany.net/albany_tapes_huda_noor.php, accessed January 18, 2013. Audiotape series.

——. *al-Taʿlīqāt al-raḍīya ʿalā al-Rawḍa al-nadīya li'l-ʿallāma Ṣiddīq Ḥasan Khān*, edited by ʿAlī bn Ḥasan al-Ḥalabī. 3 vols. Cairo: Dār Ibn ʿAffān, 1420/1999.

——. *al-Thamr al-mustaṭāb fī fiqh al-sunna wa'l-kitāb*. 2 vols. Kuwait: Ghirās, 1422.

Ali Bey. *Travels of Ali Bey in Morocco, Tripoli, Cyprus, Egypt, Arabia, Syria, and Turkey, Between the Years 1803 and 1807*. 2 vols. London: Longman, Hurst, Rees, Orme, and Brown, 1816.

ʿAlī ibn Mūsā, al-Afandī. "Waṣf al-Madīna al-munawwara fī 1303 h./1885 m." In *Rasāʾil fī taʾrīkh al-Madīna*, edited by Ḥamad al-Jāsir, 3–81. Riyadh: Manshūrāt Dār al-Yamāma li'l-Baḥth wa'l-Tarjama wa'l-Nashr, n.d.

al-Anṣārī al-Shāfiʿī, ʿUmar ibn ʿAlī ibn Aḥmad. *al-Iʿlām bi-fawāʾid ʿUmdat al-aḥkām*, edited by ʿAbd al-ʿAzīz ibn Aḥmad al-Mushayqiḥ. 11 vols. Riyadh: Dār al-ʿĀṣima, 1417/1997.

al-Aqfahsī, Ibn al-ʿImād. *Tashīl al-maqāṣid li-zuwwār al-masājid*. Cairo ms., Dār al-Kutub, Fiqh Shāfiʿī 1440.

al-ʿAydarūsī, ʿAbd al-Qādir ibn Shaykh. *Taʾrīkh al-Nūr al-sāfir ʿan akhbār al-qarn al-ʿāshir.* [Egypt], n.d.

al-ʿAynī, Badr al-Dīn. *al-Bināya sharḥ al-Hidāya*. 13 vols. Beirut: Dār al-Kutub al-ʿIlmīya, 1420/2000.

——. *ʿUmdat al-qāriʾ sharḥ Ṣaḥīḥ al-Bukhārī*. 25 vols. in 12. Beirut: Muḥammad Amīn Damj, 1971.

al-Bābartī, Akmal al-Dīn. *al-ʿInāya sharḥ al-Hidāya*. 6 vols. Beirut: Dār al-Kutub al-ʿIlmīya, 1428/2007.

al-Baghawī, al-Ḥusayn ibn Masʿūd. *al-Tahdhīb fī fiqh al-imām al-Shāfiʿī*, edited by ʿĀdil Aḥmad ʿAbd al-Mawjūd and ʿAlī Muḥammad Muʿawwaḍ. 8 vols. Beirut: Dār al-Kutub al-ʿIlmīya, 1418/1997.

al-Baghdādī, Ismāʿīl Bāshā. *Īḍāḥ al-maknūn*. 2 vols. Istanbul: Milli Eğitim Basımevi, 1945.

al-Bahūtī, Manṣūr ibn Yūnus. *Kashshāf al-qināʿ ʿan matn al-Iqnāʿ*. 6 vols. Riyadh: Maktabat al-Naṣr al-Ḥadītha, [1968].

——. *al-Rawḍ al-murbiʿ sharḥ Zād al-mustanqiʿ*. 2 vols. in 1. Beirut: Dār al-Arqam ibn al-Arqam, n.d.

Baiqarā, Ḥusayn. *Maǧālis al-ʿuššāq*. Bodleian Library, Oxford, ms. Ouseley Add. 24.

al-Bājī, Abū'l-Walīd. *al-Muntaqā sharḥ Muwaṭṭaʾ al-Imām Mālik*. 7 vols. in 4. Beirut: Dār al-Kitāb al-ʿArabī, 1404/1984.

al-Bakrī, Abū ʿUbayd. *al-Mughrib fī dhikr bilād ifrīqīya wa'l-maghrib, wa-huwa juzʾ min kitāb al-Masālik wa'l-mamālik*, edited by William MacGuckin de Slane. Baghdad: Maktabat al-Muthannā, n.d.

al-Baʿlī, Muḥammad ibn ʿAbd Allāh ibn Aḥmad. *al-Rawḍ al-nadī sharḥ Kāfī al-mubtadī*. N.p.: al-Maktaba al-Salafīya, n.d.

al-Bannā, Aḥmad ʿAbd al-Raḥmān. *al-Fatḥ al-rabbānī l-tartīb Musnad al-imām Aḥmad Ibn Ḥanbal al-Shaybānī.* 24 vols. in 12. Beirut: Dār Iḥyāʾ al-Turāth al-ʿArabī, 1976.

al-Bannā, Ḥasan. *al-Marʾa al-muslima*, edited by Muḥammad Nāṣir al-Dīn al-Albānī. Cairo: Dār al-Kutub al-Salafīya, 1404/1983.

al-Barzanjī, Jaʿfar ibn Ismāʿīl. *Hādhā al-taʾrīkh al-musammā Nuzhat al-nāẓirīn fī masjid sayyid al-awwalīn wa'l-ākharīn.* Cairo: Maṭbaʿat al-Jamālīya, 1332/1914.

al-Batanūnī, Muḥammad Labīb. *al-Riḥla al-ḥijāzīya li-walī al-niʿam al-ḥājj ʿAbbās Ḥilmī al-thānī Khedīw Miṣr*. 2nd printing. Cairo, 1329/[1911-12].

al-Bayhaqī, Aḥmad ibn al-Ḥusayn. *al-Sunan al-kubrā*. 10 vols. Beirut: Dār al-Maʿrifa, n.d.

Billacois, François. *L'Empire du Grand Turc vu par un sujet de Louis XIV, Jean Thévenot*. Paris: Calmann-Lévy, 1965.

[Blunt, Fanny]. *The People of Turkey: Twenty Years' Residence Among Bulgarians, Greeks, Albanians, Turks, and Armenians*, edited by Stanley Lane-Poole. 2 vols. London: John Murray, 1878; New York: Elibron Classics, 2005.

Boulden, James E. P. *An American Among the Orientals*. Philadelphia: Lindsay and Blakiston, 1855.

Braun-Wiesbaden, Karl. *Eine türkische Reise*. 3 vols. Stuttgart: Verlag von August Auerbach, 1877.

al-Bujayrimī, Sulaymān ibn Muḥammad. *Ḥāshiyat al-Bujayrimī*. 4 vols. Beirut: Dār al-Kutub al-ʿIlmīya, 1420/2000.

al-Bukhārī, Muḥammad ibn Ismāʿīl. *Ṣaḥīḥ al-Bukhārī*. 3 vols. Vaduz, Liechtenstein: Thesaurus Islamicus Foundation, 2000.

al-Bukhārī, Muḥammad ibn Muḥammad ibn Muḥammad. "*Suʾāl wa-jawāb bi-shaʾn al-quṣṣāṣ, yajlisūna fī'l-masājid wa-tajtamiʿ ʿalayhim al-niswa*." Jerusalem ms, Isḥāq al-Ḥusaynī, 1/28.

al-Bukhārī, Ṭāhir ibn ʿAbd al-Rashīd. *Khulāṣat al-fatāwā*. 4 vols. in 2. Lahore: Amjad Akīdīmī, 1397/[1977].

al-Burzulī, Abū'l-Qāsim ibn Aḥmad al-Balawī. *Fatāwā al-Burzulī: Jāmiʿ masāʾil al-aḥkām li-mā nazala min al-qaḍāyā bi'l-muftīn wa'l-ḥukkām*, edited by Muḥammad al-Ḥabīb al-Hīla. 7 vols. Beirut: Dār al-Gharb al-Islāmī, 2002.

al-Būṭī, Muḥammad Saʿīd Ramaḍān. *Maʿa al-nās: Mashwarāt . . . wa-fatāwā*. Damascus: Dār al-Fikr, 1419/1999.

Castellan, A. L. *Turkey, A Description of the Manners, Customs, Dresses, and Other Peculiarities Characteristic of the Inhabitants of the Turkish Empire; to which is prefixed a sketch of the history of the Turks*. 6 vols. London: R. Ackermann, [1821].

[Çelebī], Evliya Efendí. *Narrative of Travels in Europe, Asia, and Africa*, translated by Joseph von Hammer. 2 vols. in 1. London: Oriental Translation Fund of Great Britain and Ireland, 1834; New York: Johnson Reprint Co., 1968.

——. *Siyāḥatnāmeh-ye Miṣr*, translated into Arabic by Muḥammad ʿAlī ʿAwnī. Cairo: Maṭbaʿat Dār al-Kutub wa'l-Wathāʾiq al-Qawmīya bi'l-Qāhira, 1424/2003.

Chabrol, M. de. "Essai sur les moeurs des habitans modernes de l'Égypte." In *Description de l'Égypte, ou Recueil des Observations et des Recherches qui ont étés faites en Égypte pendant l'expédition de l'armée française*, l'État Moderne, vol. 2, pt. 2, 361–524. Paris: Imprimerie Impériale, 1822. Biodiversity Heritage Library E-book.

Chardin, Jean. *Voyages du chevalier Chardin en Perse, et autres lieux de l'orient*, new ed., revised by L. Langlès. 10 vols. Paris: Le Normant, Imprimeur-Libraire, 1811.

Chronica und Beschreibung der Türckey. [Nürnberg], 1530; facsimile edition Köln, Wien: Böhlau Verlag, 1983.

Cleray, E. "Le Voyage de Pierre Lescalopier 'Parisien' de Venise a Constantinople, l'an 1574." *Revue d'Histoire Diplomatique* 35 (1921): 21–55.

Craven, Elizabeth. *A Journey Through the Crimea to Constantinople*. 1789; repr., New York: Arno Press and New York Times, 1970.

al-Dasūqī, Muḥammad ibn Aḥmad. *Ḥāshiyat al-Dasūqī ʿalā al-Sharḥ al-kabīr*. 4 vols. Cairo: ʿĪsā al-Bābī al-Ḥalabī, n.d.

De Amicis, Edmondo. *Constantinople*, translated by Stephen Parkin. London: Hesperis Classics, 2005.

Dernschwam, Hans. *Hans Dernschwam's Tagebuch einer Reise nach Konstantinopel und Kleinasien (1553/55)*, edited by Franz Babinger. Munich: Verlag von Duncker and Humblot, 1923.

al-Dhahabī, Muḥammad ibn Aḥmad. *Siyar aʿlām al-nubalāʾ*, edited by Shuʿayb Arnaʾūṭ and Maʾmūn al-Ṣāghirji. 25 vols. Beirut: Muʾassasat al-Risāla, 1401/1981.

al-Duwaysh, Aḥmad ibn ʿAbd al-Razzāq, arr. *Fatāwā al-Lajna al-Dāʾima li'l-Buḥūth al-ʿIlmīya wa'l-Iftāʾ*. 20 vols. Riyadh: Dār al-ʿĀṣima, 1416/1996.

Edib, Halidé. *Memoirs of Halidé Edib*. New York: Century, n.d.

Ellison, Grace. *An Englishwoman in a Turkish Harem*. London: Methuen, 1915.

Fabri, Félix. *Felix Fabri (circa 1480–1483 A.D.)*, translated by Aubrey Stewart. New York: AMS Press, 1971.

——. *Voyage en Egypte (1483)*, translated from Latin and annotated by R. P. Jacques Masson, S.J. 3 vols. Cairo: L'Institut Français d'Archéologie Orientale du Caire, 1975.

Faḍl Allāh, Muḥammad Ḥasan. *Fiqh al-sharīʿa*. 3 vols. Beirut: Dār al-Malāk, 1420/1999.

al-Fayrūzābādī, Muḥammad ibn Yaʿqūb. *al-Qāmūs al-muḥīṭ*. 4 vols. [al-Mu'assasa al-ʿArabīya li'l-Ṭibāʿa wa'l-Nashr], n.p., n.d.

al-Fayyūmī, Aḥmad ibn Muḥammad. *al-Miṣbāḥ al-munīr fī gharīb al-Sharḥ al-kabīr li'l-Rāfiʿī*. Beirut: Dār al-Kutub al-ʿIlmīya, 1398/1978.

Garnett, Lucy M. J. *Home Life in Turkey*. New York: Macmillan, 1909.

——. *Turkish Life in Town and Country*. London: George Newnes, [1904].

George, Bishop of Mosul and Arbel (attributed). *A Commentary on the Mass*, translated from Syriac by R. H. Connolly and edited by F. Robert Matheus. Vadavathoor, Kottayam, India: Pontifical Oriental Institute of Religious Studies, 2000.

Georgijevic, Bartholomej. *Türckey Oder Von yetziger Türcken kirchen gepräng . . . Verdeutsch durch Joannem Herold*. Basel, 1545; facsimile, Köln, Wien: Böhlau Verlag, 1983.

Ghars al-Niʿma Abū'l-Ḥasan Muḥammad ibn Hilāl al-Ṣābiʾ. *al-Hafawāt al-nādira*, edited by Ṣāliḥ al-Ashtar. Damascus: Maṭbūʿāt Majmaʿ al-Lugha al-ʿArabīya, 1387/1967.

al-Ghazālī, Abū Ḥāmid. *Iḥyāʾ ʿulūm al-dīn*. 5 vols. Beirut: Dār al-Fikr, 1414/1994.

——. *Kīmyā-ye saʿādat*, edited by Ḥusayn Khedīvjam. Tehran: Markaz-e Intishārāt-e ʿElmī ve-Farhangī, 1983.

——. *al-Wajīz*. In ʿAbd al-Karīm ibn Muḥammad al-Rāfiʿī, *al-ʿAzīz sharḥ al-Wajīz*, edited by ʿAlī Muḥammad Muʿawwaḍ and ʿĀdil Aḥmad ʿAbd al-Mawjūd. 13 vols. Beirut: Dār al-Kutub al-ʿIlmīya, 1417/1997.

——. *al-Wasīṭ fī al-madhhab*, edited by ʿAlī Muḥyī al-Dīn al-Qaradāghī. 2 vols. Cairo: Dār al-Naṣr li'l-Ṭibāʿa al-Islāmīya, 1404/1984.

al-Ghazzāli, Muhammad. *Our Beginning in Wisdom*, translated by Isma'il R. el Faruqi. New York: Octagon Books, 1975.

——. *Qaḍāyā al-marʾa bayna al-taqālīd al-rākida wa'l-wāfida*. Cairo: Dār al-Shurūq, 1411/1990.

——. *al-Sunna al-nabawīya bayna ahl al-fiqh . . . wa-ahl al-ḥadīth*. Beirut: Dār al-Shurūq, 1409/1989.

al-Ghazzī, Najm al-Dīn. *al-Kawākib al-sāʾira bi-aʿyān al-miʾa al-ʿāshira*, edited by Jibrāʾīl Sulaymān Jabbūr. 3 vols. Beirut: Jāmiʿat Bayrūt al-Amīrkīya, 1945.

Guer, M. *Moeurs et usages des Turcs, leur religion, leur gouvernement civil, militaire et politique, avec un abregé de l'Histoire Ottomane*. 2 vols. Paris: Merigot and Piget, 1747.

al-Ḥanbalī, Ibn al-ʿImād. *Shadharāt al-dhahab fī akhbār man dhahab*. 9 vols. Beirut: Dār al-Kutub al-ʿIlmīya, 1419/1998.

al-Ḥanbalī, ʿUthmān ibn ʿAbd Allāh ibn Jāmiʿ. *al-Fawāʾid al-muntakhabāt fī sharḥ Akhṣar al-mukhtaṣarāt*, edited by ʿAbd al-Salām ibn Barjas Āl ʿAbd al-Karīm. 4 vols. Beirut: Maktabat al-Risāla, 1424/2003.

al-Ḥarīrī. *Maqāmāt*. Istanbul ms., Suleymaniye, Esad Efendi 2961.

——. *Maqāmāt*. Ms. Paris, Bibliothèque Nationale, arabe 5847.

Harvey, Mrs. [Annie Jane Tennant]. *Turkish Harems and Circassian Homes*. London: Hurst and Blackett, 1871.

al-Ḥaṭṭāb al-Ruʿaynī. *Mawāhib al-jalīl li-sharḥ Mukhtaṣar Khalīl*. 8 vols. Beirut: Dār al-Kutub al-ʿIlmīya, 1416/1995.

al-Haythamī, ʿAlī ibn Abī Bakr. *Bughyat al-rāʾid fī taḥqīq Majmaʿ al-zawāʾid wa-manbaʿ al-fawāʾid*, edited by ʿAbd Allāh Muḥammad Darwīsh. 10 vols. Beirut: Dār al-Fikr, 1412/1991.

Hill, Aaron. *A Full and Just Account of the Present State of the Ottoman Empire in All Its Branches*. London: John Mayo, 1709.

al-Ḥimyarī, Muḥammad ibn ʿAbd Allāh. *Ṣifat jazīrat al-andalus muntakhaba min kitāb al-Rawḍ al-miʿṭār fī khabar al-aqṭār*, edited by E. Lévy-Provençal. Cairo, 1937.

al-Ḥiṣnī, Taqī al-Dīn Abū Bakr ibn Muḥammad. *Kifāyat al-akhyār fī ḥall Ghāyat al-ikhtiṣār*, edited by Muḥammad ʿAwaḍ Haykal. Cairo: Dār al-Salām, 1426/2005.

Hunter, William. *Travels Through France, Turkey, and Hungary, to Vienna, in 1792*. 2 vols. London: J. White, 1803.

Ibn ʿAbd al-Barr. *Fatḥ al-barr fī'l-tartīb al-fiqhī li-Tamhīd Ibn ʿAbd al-Barr*, arranged by Muḥammad ibn ʿAbd al-Raḥmān al-Maghrāwī. 13 vols. Riyadh: Majmūʿ al-Tuḥaf wa'l-Nafāʾis al-Dawlīya, 1416/1996.

——. *al-Istidhkār al-jāmiʿ li-madhāhib fuqahāʾ al-amṣār wa-ʿulamāʾ al-aqṭār fīmā taḍammanahu al-Muwaṭṭaʾ min maʿānī al-raʾy wa'l-āthār wa-sharḥ dhālika bi'l-ījāz wa'l-ikhtiṣār*, edited by Sālim Muḥammad ʿAṭāʾ and Muḥammad ʿAlī Muʿawwaḍ. 9 vols. Beirut: Dār al-Kutub al-ʿIlmīya, 1423/2002.

Ibn ʿAbd al-Ghaffār, Shihāb al-Dīn Aḥmad al-Mālikī. *Izālat al-ghishāʾ ʿan ḥukm ṭawāf al-nisāʾ baʿd al-ʿishāʾ*. Cairo ms., Dār al-Kutub, 109 Fiqh Mālik, microfilm 1965.

Ibn ʿAbd al-Ḥaqq, ʿAbd al-Muʾmin al-Qaṭīʿī. *Idrāk al-ghāya fī ikhtiṣār al-Hidāya*, edited by Nāṣir ibn Saʿūd al-Salāma. Riyadh: Maktabat al-Rushd, 1428/2007.

Ibn ʿAbd Rabbih. *al-ʿIqd al-farīd*. 8 vols. Beirut: Maktabat Dār Ṣādir, n.d.

Ibn ʿĀbidīn, Muḥammad Amīn. *Ḥāshiyat Radd al-muḥtār*. 8 vols. Cairo: Muḥammad Maḥmūd al-Ḥalabī wa-Shurakāh, 1386/1966.

——. *Minḥat al-khāliq ʿalā al-baḥr al-rāʾiq*. Printed in lower margin of Zayn al-Dīn Ibn Nujaym. *al-Baḥr al-rāʾiq sharḥ Kanz al-daqāʾiq*. 9 vols. Beirut: Dār al-Kutub al-ʿIlmīya, 1997.

Ibn Abī Jamra, ʿAbd Allāh. *Bahjat al-nufūs wa-taḥallīhā bi-maʿrifat mā lahā wa-ʿalayhā*, edited by Bakrī Shaykh Amīn. 2 vols. Beirut: Dār al-ʿIlm li'l-Malāyīn, 1997.

Ibn Abī Shayba. *Muṣannaf Ibn Abī Shayba fī'l-aḥādīth wa'l-āthār*, edited by Saʿīd al-Laḥḥām. 9 vols. Beirut: Dār al-Fikr, 1428–29/2008.

Ibn Abī Zarʿ. *Rawḍ al-Qirṭās*, translated and annotated by Ambrosio Huici Miranda. 2 vols. Valencia, 1964.

Ibn Abī Zayd al-Qayrawānī. *al-Nawādir wa'l-ziyādāt ʿalā mā fī'l-Mudawwana min ghayrihā min al-ummahāt*, edited by ʿAbd al-Fattāḥ Muḥammad Ḥilw. 15 vols. Beirut: Dār al-Gharb al-Islāmī, 1999.

——. *Kitāb al-Jāmiʿ fī'l-sunan wa'l-ādāb wa'l-ḥikam wa'l-maghāzī wa'l-tārīkh wa-ghayr dhālika*, edited by ʿAbd al-Majīd Turkī. Beirut: Dār al-Gharb al-Islāmī, 1990.

Ibn al-ʿArabī, Abū Bakr. *Aḥkām al-qurʾān*, edited by Muḥammad Bakr Ismāʿīl. 4 vols. Cairo: Dār al-Manār, 1422/2002.

——. *al-Qabas fī sharḥ Muwaṭṭaʾ Ibn Anas*. 4 vols. Beirut: Dār al-Kutub al-ʿIlmīya, 1419/1998.

Ibn ʿArabī, Muḥyī al-Dīn. *al-Futūḥāt al-makkīya*. 4 vols. Facsimile ed. Beirut: Dār Ṣādir, n.d.

Ibn ʿArafa al-Warghamī. *al-Mukhtaṣar al-fiqhī*, edited by Saʿīd Sālim Fāndī. Beirut: Dār al-Madār al-Islāmī, 2003.

Ibn ʿArdūn. *Muqniʿ al-muḥtāj fī ādāb al-zawāj*, edited by ʿAbd al-Salām al-Zayyānī. 2 vols. Beirut: Dār Ibn Ḥazm, 1430/2010.

Ibn ʿAsākir, ʿAlī ibn al-Ḥasan. *Taʾrīkh madīnat dimashq*, edited by Muḥibb al-Dīn Abī Saʿīd ʿUmar ibn Gharāma al-ʿAmrī. 80 vols. Damascus/Beirut: Dār al-Fikr, 1419/1998.

Ibn al-ʿAṭṭār, ʿAlī ibn [Ibrāhīm ibn] Dāwūd. *al-ʿUdda sharḥ al-ʿUmda*. 3 vols. Beirut: Dār al-Bashāʾir al-Islāmīya, 1427/2006.

Ibn Bābawayh, Muḥammad ibn ʿAlī al-Qummī. *Man lā yaḥḍuruhu al-faqīh*. 4 vols. Beirut: Dār Ṣaʿb/Dār al-Taʿāruf, 1401/1981.

Ibn Baṭṭāl, ʿAlī ibn Khalaf. *Sharḥ Ibn Baṭṭāl ʿalā Ṣaḥīḥ al-Bukhārī*, edited by Muṣṭafā ʿAbd al-Qādir ʿAṭā. 10 vols. Beirut: Dār al-Kutub al-ʿIlmīya, 1424/2003.

Ibn Baṭṭūṭa. *Riḥlat Ibn Baṭṭūṭa*. Ṣaydā/Beirut: al-Maktaba al-ʿAṣrīya, 1425/2005.

Ibn Bāz, ʿAbd al-ʿAzīz ibn ʿAbd Allāh. *Majmūʿ fatāwā wa-maqālāt mutanawwiʿa taʾlīf al-faqīr ilā ʿafw rabbihi ʿAbd al-ʿAzīz ibn ʿAbd Allāh ibn ʿAbd al-Raḥmān ibn Bāz*, collected and arranged by Muḥammad ibn Saʿd Shuwayʿir. 17 vols. Riyadh: Dār Aṣdāʾ al-Mujtamaʿ, 1421.

Ibn Daqīq al-ʿĪd, Muḥammad ibn ʿAlī. *Iḥkām al-aḥkām sharḥ ʿUmdat al-aḥkām*. 4 vols. in 2. Beirut: Dār al-Kutub al-ʿIlmīya, n.d.

Ibn al-Ḍiyāʾ, Abū'l-Baqāʾ Aḥmad al-Qurashī. *Mukhtaṣar Tanzīh al-masjid al-ḥarām ʿan bidaʿ al-jahala wa'l-ʿawāmm*, edited by Niẓām Muḥammad Ṣāliḥ Yaʿqūbī. Published as #4 in volume 1 of *Liqāʾ al-ʿAshar al-Awākhir bi'l-Masjid al-Ḥarām*. Beirut: Dār al-Bashāʾir al-Islāmīya, 1420/1999.

Ibn Duqmāq. *al-Intiṣār li-wāsiṭat ʿiqd al-amṣār*. Beirut: al-Maktaba al-Tijārīya li'l-Ṭibāʿa wa'l-Nashr wa'l-Tawzīʿ, n.d.

Ibn Faḍl Allāh al-ʿUmarī. *Masālik al-abṣār fī mamālik al-amṣār*, edited by Fuat Sezgin. 30 vols. in 27. Frankfurt am Main: Institute for the History of Arabic-Islamic Studies at the Johann Wolfgang Goethe University, 1988–2001.

Ibn Fahd, Muḥammad ibn ʿAbd al-ʿAzīz. *Nayl al-munā bi-dhayl Bulūgh al-qirā li-takmilat Itḥāf al-warā*, edited by Muḥammad al-Ḥabīb al-Hayla. 2 vols. [Riyadh]: Muʾassasat al-Furqān li'l-Turāth al-Islāmī, 2000.

Ibn al-Faqīh, Aḥmad ibn Muḥammad al-Hamadhānī. *Kitāb al-Buldān*. Beirut: ʿĀlam al-Kutub, 1416/1992.

Ibn Farḥūn, ʿAbd Allāh ibn Muḥammad. *Naṣīḥat al-mushāwir wa-tasliyat al-mujāwir*, edited by ʿAlī ʿUmar. Cairo: Maktabat al-Thaqāfa al-Dīnīya, 1427/2006.

Ibn Farḥūn, Ibrāhīm ibn ʿAlī. *al-Dībāj al-mudhhab fī maʿrifat aʿyān ʿulamāʾ al-madhhab*, edited by Maʾmūn ibn Muḥyī'l-Dīn al-Jannān. Beirut: Dār al-Kutub al-ʿIlmīya, 1417/1996.

Ibn al-Ḥaddād, Abū Bakr. *al-Jawhara al-nayyira sharḥ Mukhtaṣar al-Qudūrī*, edited by Ilyās Qablān. 2 vols. Beirut: Dār al-Kutub al-ʿIlmīya, 1427/2006.

Ibn Ḥajar al-ʿAsqalānī. *al-Durar al-kāmina fī aʿyān al-miʾa al-thāmina*. 4 vols. in 2. Beirut: Dār al-Kutub al-ʿIlmīya, 1418/1997.

——. *Fatḥ al-bārī bi-sharḥ Ṣaḥīḥ al-Bukhārī*. 28 vols. in 14. Cairo: Maktabat al-Kullīyāt al-Azharīya, 1398/1978.

——. *Inbāʾ al-ghumr bi-anbāʾ al-ʿumr.* 9 vols. in 5. Beirut: Dār al-Kutub al-ʿIlmīya, 1406/1986.

——. *Mukhtaṣar zawāʾid Musnad al-Bazzār ʿalā al-kutub al-sitta wa-Musnad Aḥmad,* edited by Ṣabrī ibn ʿAbd al-Khāliq Abū Dharr. 2 vols. Beirut: Muʾassasat al-Kutub al-Thaqāfīya, 1412/1992.

——. *Tahdhīb al-tahdhīb.* 12 vols. 1327. Hyderabad, 1327; repr., Beirut: Dār Ṣādir, n.d.

——. *Talkhīṣ al-ḥabīr bi-takhrīj aḥādīth al-Rāfiʿī al-kabīr.* 4 vols. [Cairo]: Muʾassasat Qurṭuba, 1416/1995.

Ibn Ḥajar al-Haytamī. *al-Fatāwā al-kubrā al-fiqhīya.* 4 vols. Beirut: Dār al-Kutub al-ʿIlmīya, 1417/1997.

——. *Fatḥ al-jawād bi-sharḥ al-irshād.* 3 vols. Beirut: Dār al-Kutub al-ʿIlmīya, 1426/2005.

——. *Itmām al-niʿma al-kubrā ʿalā al-ʿālam bi-mawlid sayyid wuld Ādam.* Beirut: Dār al-Kutub al-ʿIlmīya, 1422/2001.

——. *Tuḥfat al-muḥtāj.* Printed in margin of ʿAbd al-Ḥamīd al-Shirwānī and Aḥmad ibn Qāsim al-ʿAbādī. *Ḥawāshī al-Shirwānī wa-Ibn Qāsim al-ʿAbbādī.* 10 vols. Beirut: Dār Ṣādir, 1972.

Ibn al-Ḥājj al-ʿAbdarī. *Kitāb al-Madkhal.* 4 vols. in 2. Beirut: Dār al-Kutub al-ʿIlmīya, 1415/1995.

Ibn Ḥamdān, Aḥmad. *al-Riʿāya al-ṣughrā fī'l-fiqh ʿalā madhhab al-imām Aḥmad ibn Muḥammad ibn Ḥanbal,* edited by Nāṣir ibn Suʿūd ibn ʿAbd ʿAllāh al-Salāma. 2 vols. Riyadh: Dār Ishbīlīyā, 1423/2002.

Ibn Ḥanbal, Aḥmad (attributed). *Aḥkām al-nisāʾ,* edited by ʿAbd al-Qādir Aḥmad ʿAṭāʾ. Beirut: Dār al-Kutub al-ʿIlmīya, 1406/1986.

——. *Musnad al-imām Aḥmad ibn Ḥanbal,* edited by Shuʿayb Arnaʾūṭ et al. 52 vols. Beirut: Muʾassasat al-Risāla, 1421/2001.

——. *Kitāb al-Zuhd.* Beirut: Dār al-Kutub al-ʿIlmīya, n.d.

——. Ibn Ḥazm, ʿAlī ibn Aḥmad al-Andalusī. *al-Muḥallā bi'l-āthār,* edited by ʿAbd al-Ghaffār Sulaymān al-Bundārī. 12 vols. Beirut: Dār al-Kutub al-ʿIlmīya, 1425/2003.

Ibn Ḥibbān al-Bustī. *Kitāb al-Thiqāt.* 9 vols. Hyderabad: Dāʾirat al-Maʿārif al-ʿUthmānīya, 1399/1979.

Ibn Hubayra, Yaḥyā ibn Muḥammad. *al-Ifṣāḥ ʿan maʿānī al-ṣiḥāḥ.* 2 vols. Beirut: Dār al-Kutub al-ʿIlmīya, 1417/1996.

Ibn al-Humām. *Fatḥ al-qadīr.* Cairo: Sharikat wa-Maṭbaʿat Muṣṭafā al-Bābī al-Ḥalabī wa-Awlādihi bi-Miṣr, 1970.

——. *Sharḥ Fatḥ al-qadīr.* 7 vols. Cairo: Muṣṭafā al-Bābī al-Ḥalabī, n.d.

Ibn al-ʿIdhārī al-Marrākushī. *al-Bayān al-mughrib,* edited by G. S. Colin and É. Lévi-Provençal. 4 vols. Beirut: Dār al-Thaqāfa, n.d.

Ibn Jamāʿa. *Hidāyat al-sālik ilā al-madhāhib al-arbaʿa fī'l-manāsik.* 3 vols. Beirut: Dār al-Bashāʾir al-Islāmīya, 1414/1994.

Ibn al-Jawzī, Abū'l-Faraj ʿAbd al-Raḥmān ibn ʿAlī. *Kitāb Aḥkām al-nisāʾ*. Ṣaydā/Beirut: al-Maktaba al-ʿAṣrīya, 1424/2003.

——. *Naqd al-ʿilm wa'l-ʿulamāʾ aw Talbīs Iblīs*. [Cairo]: Idārat al-Ṭibāʿa al-Munīrīya, [1966].

——. *Kitāb al-Quṣṣāṣ wa'l-mudhakkirīn*, translated by Merlin L. Swartz. Beirut: Dār al-Mashriq, 1971.

——. *Ṣifat al-ṣafwa*. 4 vols. in 2. Beirut: Dār al-Kutub al-ʿIlmīya, 1409/1989.

——. *al-Taḥqīq*. 8 vols. Cairo: al-Fārūq al-Ḥadītha li'l-Ṭibāʿa wa'l-Nashr, 1422/2001.

——. *Zād al-masīr fī ʿilm al-tafsīr*. 9 vols. Beirut: al-Maktab al-Islāmī, 1404/1984.

Ibn Juzayy al-Kalbī, Muḥammad ibn Aḥmad. *al-Qawānīn al-fiqhīya*. Tunis: al-Dār al-ʿArabīya li'l-Kitāb, 1982.

Ibn Kathīr, ʿImād al-Dīn. *al-Bidāya wa'l-nihāya*. 14 vols. in 7. Beirut: Dār al-Fikr, 1398/1978.

——. *Tafsīr al-qurʾān al-ʿaẓīm*. 15 vols. Giza: Muʾassasat Qurṭuba, 1421/2000.

Ibn Khallikān. *Wafayāt al-aʿyān*, edited by Iḥsān ʿAbbās. 8 vols. Beirut: Dār al-Thaqāfa, n.d.

Ibn al-Khaṭīb, Lisān al-Dīn. *al-Iḥāṭa fī akhbār Gharnāṭa*. 4 vols. Cairo: Maktabat al-Khānjī, n.d.

Ibn Khuzayma. *Ṣaḥīḥ Ibn Khuzayma*. 4 vols. Beirut: al-Maktab al-Islāmī, 1395/1975.

Ibn Manẓūr. *Lisān al-ʿarab*. 15 vols. Beirut: Dār Ṣādir, 1410/1990.

Ibn Māza, Maḥmūd ibn Aḥmad. *al-Muḥīṭ al-burhānī*. 11 vols. Beirut: Dār Iḥyāʾ al-Turāth al-ʿArabī, 1424/2003.

Ibn Mufliḥ, Ibrāhīm ibn Muḥammad. *al-Mubdiʿ sharḥ al-Muqniʿ*. 10 vols. Beirut and Damascus: al-Maktab al-Islāmī, n.d.

Ibn Mufliḥ, Muḥammad. *al-Ādāb al-sharʿīya*, edited by Shuʿayb Arnaʾūṭ and ʿUmar al-Qayyām. 3 vols. Beirut: Mu'assasat al-Risāla, 1416/1996.

——. *Kitāb al-Furūʿ*. 6 vols. Beirut: ʿĀlam al-Kutub, 1404/1984.

Ibn al-Mujāwir. *A Traveller in Thirteenth-Century Arabia: Ibn al-Mujāwir's* Tārīkh al-Mustabṣir, translated by G. Smith. Aldershot, UK: Ashgate, 2007.

Ibn al-Mulaqqin. *ʿUjālat al-muḥtāj ilā tawjīh al-Minhāj*, edited by Hishām ibn ʿAbd al-Karīm al-Badrānī. 4 vols. Irbid, Jordan: Dār al-Kitāb, 1421/2001.

Ibn al-Munāṣif, Muḥammad ibn ʿĪsā. *Tanbīh al-ḥukkām ʿalā maʾākhidh al-aḥkām*, edited by ʿAbd al-Ḥafīẓ Manṣūr. Tunis: Dār al-Turkī li'l-Nashr, 1988.

Ibn al-Naḥḥās, Aḥmad ibn Ibrāhīm al-Dimashqī. *Tanbīh al-ghāfilīn ʿan aʿmāl al-jāhilīn wa-taḥdhīr al-sālikīn min aʿmāl al-hālikīn*. Ṣaydā/Beirut: al-Maktaba al-ʿAṣrīya, 1424/2003.

Ibn al-Najjār, Muḥammad ibn Aḥmad al-Futūḥī al-Ḥanbalī. *Maʿūnat ūlī al-nuhā sharḥ al-Muntahā*. 12 vols. in 6. 3rd printing. Beirut: Dār Khiḍr, 1419/1998.

——. *Muntahā al-irādāt fī jamʿ al-Muqniʿ maʿa al-Tanqīḥ wa-Ziyādāt*. 2 vols. N.p.: ʿĀlam al-Kutub, n.d.

Ibn al-Naẓẓār. *Kitāb Aḥkām al-Nisāʾ*. Cairo ms., Dār al-Kutub, Fiqh Shāfiʿī mīm, microfilm 2742.

Ibn Nujaym, Zayn al-Dīn. *al-Baḥr al-rāʾiq sharḥ Kanz al-daqāʾiq*. 9 vols. Beirut: Dār al-Kutub al-ʿIlmīya, 1997.

Ibn Qayyim al-Jawzīya. *Aḥkām ahl al-dhimma*, edited by Ṣubḥī Ṣāliḥ. 2 vols. Beirut: Dār al-ʿIlm li'l-Malāyīn, 1381/1961.

——. *Iʿlām al-muwaqqiʿīn ʿan rabb al-ʿālamīn.* 4 vols. Beirut: Dār al-Kutub al-ʿIlmīya, 1417/1996.

——. *al-Ṭuruq al-ḥukmīya fi'l-siyāsa al-sharʿīya aw al-firāsa al-murḍiya fī aḥkām al-siyāsa al-sharʿīya*, edited by Sayyid ʿImrān. Cairo: Dār al-Ḥadīth, 1423/2002.

Ibn Qudāma, Muwaffaq al-Dīn. *al-Kāfī fī fiqh al-imām Aḥmad ibn Ḥanbal*, edited by Muḥammad Fāris and Musʿad ʿAbd al-Ḥamīd al-Saʿdanī. 4 vols. Beirut: Dār al-Kutub al-ʿIlmīya, 1414/1994.

——. *al-Mughnī*. 14 vols. Beirut: Dar al-Kutub al-ʿIlmiya, n.d.

Ibn Qutayba al-Dīnawarī. *ʿUyūn al-akhbār.* 4 vols. Cairo: Maṭbaʿat Dār al-Kutub al-Miṣrīya, 1349/1930.

Ibn Rajab al-Ḥanbalī. *Dhayl Ṭabaqāt al-ḥanābila.* 2 vols. Beirut: Dār al-Maʿrifa, n.d.

——. *Fatḥ al-bārī sharḥ Ṣaḥīḥ al-Bukhārī*, edited by Maḥmūd Shaʿbān ibn ʿAbd al-Maqṣūd et al. 10 vols. Madina: Maktabat al-Ghurabāʾ al-Atharīya, 1417/1996.

Ibn Rushd, Abū'l-Walīd. *al-Bayān wa'l-taḥṣīl wa'l-sharḥ wa'l-tawjīh wa'l-taʿlīl fī masāʾil al-Mustakhraja*, edited by Muḥammad Ḥajjī. 20 vols. Beirut: Dār al-Gharb al-Islāmī, 1404/1984.

Ibn Rusteh. *Les Atours Précieux*, edited by Gaston Wiet. Cairo: Publications de la Société d'Égypte, 1955.

Ibn Saʿd. *Kitāb al-Ṭabaqāt al-kubrā.* 9 vols. Beirut: Dār Ṣādir/Dār Bayrūt, 1377/1958.

——. *Kitāb al-Ṭabaqāt al-kubrā*, edited by Carl Brockelmann. 9 vols. Leiden: Brill, 1904.

Ibn al-Ṣalāḥ. *ʿUlūm al-ḥadīth*. Damascus: Dār al-Fikr, 1406/1986.

Ibn Shāhīn. *Nayl al-amal fī dhayl al-duwal*, edited by ʿUmar ʿAbd al-Salām Tadmurī. 9 vols. Ṣaydā and Beirut: al-Maktaba al-ʿAṣrīya, 1422/2002.

Ibn Sunayna, Muḥammad ibn ʿAbd Allāh. *al-Mustawʿib*, edited by Musāʿid ibn Qāsim al-Fāliḥ. 4 vols. Riyadh: Maktabat al-Maʿārif, 1413/1993.

Ibn Taymīya, Taqī al-Dīn. *Kitāb al-ikhtiyārāt al-ʿilmīya*, compiled by ʿAlī ibn Muḥammad al-Baʿlī. In *al-Fatāwā al-kubrā.* 5 vols. Cairo: Dār al-Kutub al-Ḥadītha, 1966.

——. *Majmūʿ al-fatāwā*, edited by Muṣṭafā ʿAbd al-Qādir ʿAṭāʾ. 37 vols. in 21. Beirut: Dār al-Kutub al-ʿIlmīya, 1421/2000.

Ibn al-Ukhuwwa. *The* Maʿālim al-Qurba fī aḥkām al-ḥisba *of Ḍiyāʾ al-Dīn Muḥammad ibn Muḥammad al-Qurashī al-Shāfiʿī known as Ibn al-Ukhuwwa,* edited and translated by Reuben Levy. E. J. W. Gibb Memorial Series, New Series, 12. London: Cambridge University Press, 1938.

Ibrāhīm Rifʿat Bāshā. *Mirʾāt al-ḥaramayn.* Cairo: Dār al-Kutub al-Miṣrīya, 1344/1925.

al-Idrīsī, ʿAlī ibn Maymūn. *Risālat Bayān ghurbat al-islām bi-wāsiṭat ṣinfay al-mutafaqqiha wa'l-mutafaqqira min ahl miṣr wa'l-shām wa-mā yalīhā min bilād al-aʿjām.* Princeton ms., Garrett 828H.

ʿImāra, Muḥammad. *al-Islām wa'l-marʾa fī raʾy al-imām Muḥammad ʿAbduh.* Cairo: Dār al-Hilāl, 1979.

al-ʿImrānī, Yaḥyā ibn Abī'l-Khayr. *al-Bayān fī fiqh al-imām al-Shāfiʿī*, edited by Aḥmad Ḥijāzī Aḥmad al-Saqqāʾ. 13 vols. Beirut: Dār al-Kutub al-ʿIlmīya, 1423/2002.

ʿIzzat, Hiba Raʾūf. *Al-Marʾa wa'l-ʿamal al-siyāsī: ruʾya islāmīya.* Herndon, VA: al-Maʿhad al-ʿĀlamī li'l-Fikr al-Islāmī, 1416/1995.

Jaddāʿ, Ismāʿīl Sulaymān. "*Dawr al-marʾa fī'l-ʿamal al-islāmī.*" Muslim Brotherhood Information Center, Syria. http://www.ikhwan.net/wiki/index.php, accessed April 4, 2010.

al-Jāḥiẓ. *al-Ḥayawān*, edited by ʿAbd al-Salām Muḥammad Hārūn. 7 vols. Cairo: Maktabat Muṣṭafā al-Bābī al-Ḥalabī wa-Awlādihi, 1356/1938.

——. *Rasāʾil al-Jāḥiẓ*, ed. Muḥammad Bāsil ʿUyūn al-Sūd. 4 vols. in 2. Beirut: Dār al-Kutub al-ʿIlmīya, 1420/2000.

al-Jamal, Sulaymān ibn ʿUmar. *Ḥāshiyat al-Jamal ʿalā Sharḥ al-Minhāj.* 8 vols. Beirut: Dār al-Kutub al-ʿIlmīya, 1417/1996.

al-Jaṣṣāṣ, Aḥmad ibn ʿAlī. *Aḥkām al-qurʾān*, edited by ʿAbd al-Salām Shāhīn. 3 vols. Beirut: Dār al-Kutub al-ʿIlmīya, 1428/2007.

al-Jazīrī, ʿAbd al-Qādir ibn Muḥammad. *ʿUmdat al-ṣafwa fī ḥall al-qahwa*, edited by ʿAbd Allāh ibn Muḥammad al-Ḥibshī. Abu Dhabi: Cultural Foundation Publications, 1996.

al-Jaznāʾī, Abū'l-Ḥasan ʿAlī. *Kitāb zahrat al-ās fī bināʾ madīnat Fās*, edited and translated by Alfred Bel. Algiers: Jules Carbonel, 1923.

Jenkins, Hester Donaldson. *Behind Turkish Lattices: The Story of a Turkish Woman's Life.* London: Chatto and Windus, 1911.

Johnson, Sarah Barclay. *Hadji in Syria: or, Three Years in Jerusalem.* Philadelphia: James Challen and Sons, 1858; New York: Arno Press, 1977.

al-Jurjānī, ʿAlī ibn Muḥammad. *Kitāb al-Taʿrīfāt* (*Le Livre des Définitions*), translated by Maurice Gloton. Beirut: Albouraq, n.d.

al-Kāsānī. *Badāʾiʿ al-ṣanāʾiʿ.* 10 vols. Cairo: Zakarīyā ʿAlī Yūsuf, n.d.

Khalīl ibn Isḥāq al-Jundī. *al-Tawḍīḥ fī sharḥ al-Mukhtaṣar al-farʿī li-Ibn al-Ḥājib*, edited by Aḥmad ibn ʿAbd al-Karīm Najīb. 9 vols. Cairo: Markaz Najībawayh, 1429/2008.

Khamenei, L'Ayatollah Ali. *Les principales fatwas*, translated from the Arabic and annotated by Fouad Noun. Beirut: Dar Albouraq, 1427/2006.

Khomeini, Ayatollah Sayyed Ruhollah Mousavi. *A Clarification of Questions, An Unabridged Translation of* Rasaleh Towzih al-Masael, translated by J. Borujerdi. Boulder, CO: Westview Press, 1984.

al-Khūlī, Al-Bahī. *al-Marʾa bayna al-bayt wa'l-mujtamaʿ*. Cairo: Min Rasāʾil al-Ikhwān al-Muslimīn, [1953].

al-Khurashī, Muḥammad ibn ʿAbd Allāh ibn ʿAlī. *Ḥāshiyat al-Khurashī ʿalā Mukhtaṣar sayyidī Khalīl*, edited by Zakarīyā ʿUmayrāt. 8 vols. Beirut: Dār al-Kutub al-ʿIlmīya, 1417/1997.

al-Kirmānī, Muḥammad ibn Yūsuf. *Ṣaḥīḥ Abī ʿAbd Allāh al-Bukhārī bi-sharḥ al-Kirmānī*. 25 vols. in 12. Cairo: Muʾassasat al-Maṭbūʿāt al-Islāmīya, n.d.

Kruse, Fr., ed. *Ulrich Jasper Seetzen's Reisen durch Syrien, Palästina, Phönicien, die Transjordan-Länder, Arabia Petraea und Unter-Aegypten*. 4 vols. Berlin: G. Reimer, 1855.

Lane, Edward William. *An Account of the Manners and Customs of the Modern Egyptians*. Cairo: The American University in Cairo Press, 2003.

Lang, Jeffrey. *Even Angels Ask: A Journey to Islam in America*. Beltsville, MD: Amana Publications, 1418/1997.

——. *Struggling to Surrender: Some Impressions of an American Convert to Islam*. Beltsville, MD: Amana Publications, 1415/1994.

Libois, Charles, S.J., ed. and trans. *Le Voyage en Egypte du Père Antonius Gonzales, 1665–1666*. 2 vols. Cairo: Institut Français d'Archéologie Orientale du Caire, 1977.

Lithgow, William. *The Totall Discourse of the Rare Adventures and Painefull Peregrinations of Long Nineteene Yeares Travayles from Scotland to the Most Famous Kingdomes in Europe, Asia and Affrica*. Glasgow: James MacLehose and Sons, 1906.

al-Maʿarrī, Abū'l-ʿAlāʾ. *Dīwān Luzūm mā lā yalzam*, edited by Kamāl al-Yāzijī. 2 vols. Beirut: Dār al-Jīl, 1992.

al-Maghrāwī, Muḥammad ibn Manṣūr. *Ghurar al-maqāla fī sharḥ gharīb al-Risāla*, edited by al-Hādī Ḥammū and Muḥammad Abū'l-Ajfān. Printed with Ibn Abī Zayd al-Qayrawānī. *al-Risāla al-fiqhīya*. Beirut: Dār al-Gharb al-Islāmī, 1406/1986.

al-Maḥallī, Jalāl al-Dīn Muḥammad ibn Aḥmad. *Kanz al-rāghibīn sharḥ Minhāj al-ṭālibīn*. Printed with *Ḥāshiyat Shihāb al-Dīn Aḥmad ibn Salāma al-Qalyūbī . . . wa-Shihāb al-Dīn Aḥmad al-Burullisī al-mulaqqab bi-ʿUmayra . . . ʿalā Kanz al-rāghibīn*. 4 vols. Beirut: Dār al-Kutub al-ʿIlmīya, 1417/1997.

Maḥmūd, ʿAbd al-Ḥalīm. *Fatāwā al-imām ʿAbd al-Ḥalīm Maḥmūd*. 2 vols. Cairo: Dār al-Maʿārif, n.d.

Makhlūf, Muḥammad ibn Muḥammad. "al-Fatāwā." In *Majallat al-Azhar*, 861–64. Ramaḍān 1376/[April 1957].

——. *Shajarat al-nūr al-zakīya fī ṭabaqāt al-mālikīya*. 2 vols. in 1. Beirut: Dār al-Kitāb al-ʿArabī, offset edition of first edition of 1349, n.d.

al-Makkī, Aḥmad ibn Muḥammad. *Ikhbār al-kirām bi-akhbār al-masjid al-ḥarām*, edited by Al-Ḥāfiẓ Ghulām Muṣṭafā. N.p.: Dār al-Ṣaḥwa, 1405/1985.

Malcolm, Colonel Sir John, K.C.B., K.L.S. *The History of Persia from the Most Early Period to the Present Time*. 2 vols. London: John Murray, 1815.

Mālik Ibn Anas. *al-Mudawwana al-kubrā*, transmitted by Saḥnūn ibn Saʿīd al-Tanūkhī. Beirut: Dār al-Kutub al-ʿIlmīya, 1426/2005.

——. *al-Mudawwana al-kubrā*, transmitted by Saḥnūn ibn Saʿīd al-Tanūkhī. 6 vols. Beirut: Dār Ṣādir, facsimile of Cairo, n.d.

——. *al-Muwaṭṭaʾ*. Vaduz, Liechtenstein: Thesaurus Islamicus Foundation, 2000.

al-Maqqarī al-Tilimsānī, Aḥmad ibn Muḥammad. *Nafḥ al-ṭīb min ghuṣn al-Andalus al-raṭīb*, edited by Iḥsān ʿAbbās. 8 vols. Beirut: Dār Ṣādir, 1388/1968.

al-Maqrīzī, Aḥmad ibn ʿAlī. *al-Mawāʿiẓ wa'l-iʿtibār bi-dhikr al-khiṭaṭ wa'l-āthār*. 3 vols. Cairo: Maktabat al-Madbūlī, 1998.

——. *Kitāb al-Sulūk li-maʿrifat duwal al-mulūk*, edited by Saʿīd ʿAbd al-Fattāḥ ʿĀshūr. 4 vols. in 12. [Cairo]: Dār al-Kutub, 1973.

al-Mardāwī, ʿAlī ibn Sulaymān. *al-Inṣāf fī maʿrifat al-rājiḥ min al-khilāf ʿalā madhhab al-imām al-mubajjal Aḥmad ibn Ḥanbal*, edited by Muḥammad Ḥāmid al-Faqqī. 12 vols. Beirut: Dār Iḥyāʾ al-Turāth al-ʿArabī, 1406/1986.

——. *al-Tanqīḥ al-mushbiʿ fī taḥrīr aḥkām al-Muqniʿ*. N.p.: al-Maṭbaʿa al-Salafīya, n.d.

al-Marghīnānī, ʿAlī ibn Abī Bakr. *al-Hidāya sharḥ Bidāyat al-mubtadiʾ*, edited by Muḥammad Muḥammad Tāmir and Ḥāfiẓ Āshūr Ḥāfiẓ. 4 vols. Cairo: Dār al-Salām, 1420/2000.

al-Marwazī, Muḥammad ibn Naṣr. *Qiyām al-Layl wa-qiyām ramaḍān wa-Kitāb al-Witr*, abridged by Aḥmad ibn ʿAlī al-Maqrīzī. Sangla Hill, Pakistan: al-Maktaba al-Atharīya, 1389/1969.

al-Māwardī, ʿAlī ibn Muḥammad ibn Ḥabīb. *al-Ḥāwī al-kabīr fī fiqh madhhab al-imām al-Shāfiʿī raḍiya Allāh ʿanhu wa-huwa sharḥ Mukhtaṣar al-Muzanī*. 19 vols. Beirut: Dār al-Kutub al-ʿIlmīya, 1414/1994.

——. *al-Nukat wa'l-ʿuyūn: tafsīr al-Māwardī*. 6 vols. Beirut: Dār al-Kutub al-ʿIlmīya, 1412/1992.

al-Mawṣilī, ʿAbd Allāh ibn Maḥmūd. *al-Ikhtiyār li-taʿlīl al-mukhtār*. 3 vols. Amman: Dār al-Fikr, 1420/1999.

al-Maydānī, Aḥmad ibn Muḥammad al-Naysābūrī. *Majmaʿ al-amthāl*. 2 vols. Beirut: Dār al-Kutub al-ʿIlmīya, 1408/1988.

Mažuranić, Matija. *A Glance into Ottoman Bosnia, or A Short Journey into That Land by a Native in 1839–40*, translated by Branka Magaš. London: SAQI and Bosnian Institute, 2007.

Menavino, Giovanni Antonio. *I costumi, et la vita de Turchi di Gio. Antonio Menavino Genovese da Vultri: con una Prophetia, & altre cose turchsche/tradotte per m. Lodouico Domenichi*. Fiorenza: Appresso Lorenzo Torrentino, 1551.

Mihailović, Konstantin. *Memoirs of a Janissary*, translated by Benjamin Stolz, historical commentary and notes by Svat Soucek. Ann Arbor: University of Michigan, 1975.

al-Miknāsī, Muḥammad ibn ʿAbd al-Wahhāb. *Riḥlat al-Miknāsī*, edited by Muḥammad Būkabūl. Beirut: al-Muʾassasa al-ʿArabīya li'l-Dirāsāt wa'l-Nashr, 2003.

Minutes of the Proceedings of the First Egyptian Congress Assembled at Heliopolis (Near Cairo) from Saturday 30 Rabi-al-Thani 1329 (29 April 1911) to Wednesday 5 Gamad-ul-Awwal 1329 (4 May 1911). Alexandria, 1329/1911.

al-Mizzī, Jamāl al-Dīn Abū'l-Ḥajjāj Yūsuf. *Tahdhīb al-Kamāl fī asmāʾ al-rijāl*, edited by Bashshār ʿAwwād Maʿrūf. 35 vols. Beirut: Muʾassasat al-Risāla, 1403/1983.

Molina, Luis, ed. and trans. *Dhikr bilād al-andalus li-muʾallif majhūl*. Madrid: Consejo Superior de Investigaciones Científicas Instituto "Miguel Asín," 1983.

Montagu, Lady Wortley. *The Letters and Works of Lady Mary Wortley Montagu, Edited by Her Great-Grandson, Lord Wharncliffe*. 3rd ed., edited by W. Moy Thomas. New York: AMS Press, 1970.

Moüette, Germain. *The Travels of the Sieur Mouette, in the Kingdoms of Fez and Morocco, During His Eleven Years Captivity in Those Parts*. London, 1710. British Library Eighteenth Century Collections Online, Range 10026. E-book.

Mujīr al-Dīn al-Ḥanbalī. *al-Uns al-jalīl bi-taʾrīkh al-quds wa'l-khalīl*. 2 vols. Najaf, Iraq: Manshūrāt al-Maṭbaʿa al-Ḥaydarīya, 1388/1968.

al-Muqaddasī, Muḥammad ibn Aḥmad. *Aḥsan al-taqāsīm fī maʿrifat al-aqālīm*. Leiden: Brill, 1906.

Muqātil ibn Sulaymān. *Tafsīr Muqātil ibn Sulaymān*, edited by Aḥmad Farīd. 3 vols. Beirut: Dār al-Kutub al-ʿIlmīya, 1424/2003.

Muslim Brotherhood. "The Role of Muslim Women in an Islamic Society [Official Translation]." http://www.jannah.org/sisters/ikhwom.html, accessed April 6, 2010.

Muslim ibn al-Ḥajjāj al-Qushayrī. *Ṣaḥīḥ Muslim*. 2 vols. Vaduz, Liechtenstein: Thesaurus Islamicus Foundation, 2000.

al-Nafrāwī, Aḥmad ibn Ghunaym. *al-Fawākih al-dawānī ʿalā Risālat Ibn Abī Zayd al-Qayrawānī*. 2 vols. Beirut: Dār al-Kutub al-ʿIlmīya, 1418/1997.

al-Nahrawālī, Muḥammad ibn Aḥmad. *Kitāb al-Iʿlām bi-aʿlām bayt allāh al-ḥarām*, edited by ʿAlī Muḥammad ʿUmar. Cairo: Maktabat al-Thaqāfa al-Dīnīya, 1425/2004.

al-Nawawī, Yaḥyā ibn Sharaf. *Khulāṣat al-aḥkām*, edited by Ḥusayn Ismāʿīl al-Jamal. 2 vols. Beirut: Muʾassasat al-Risāla, 1418/1997.

——. *Kitāb al-Taḥqīq*, edited by ʿĀdil ʿAbd al-Mawjūd and ʿAlī Muʿawwaḍ. Beirut: Dār al-Jīl, 1413/1992.

——. *al-Majmūʿ sharḥ al-Muhadhdhab*, edited by ʿĀdil ʿAbd al-Mawjūd et al. 27 vols. Beirut: Dār al-Kutub al-ʿIlmīya, 1423/2002.

——. *Rawḍat al-ṭālibīn*, ed. ʿĀdil ʿAbd al-Mawjūd and ʿAlī Muʿawwaḍ. 8 vols. Beirut: Dār al-Kutub al-ʿIlmīya, 1412/1992.

——. *Ṣaḥīḥ Muslim bi-sharḥ al-imām Muḥyī al-Dīn al-Nawawī al-musammā al-Minhāj sharḥ Ṣaḥīḥ Muslim ibn al-Ḥajjāj*. 18 vols. in 9. Beirut: Dār al-Maʿrifa, 1414/1994.

al-Naysābūrī, al-Ḥasan ibn Muḥammad al-Qummī. *Gharāʾib al-qurʾān wa-raghāʾib al-furqān*, edited by Ibrāhīm ʿAṭwa ʿAwaḍ. 30 vols. in 10. Cairo: Muṣṭafā al-Bābī al-Ḥalabī, 1386/1967.

Nicolay, Nicolas. *Dans l'empire de Soliman le Magnifique*, edited by Marie-Christine Gomez-Géraud and Stéphane Yérasimos. Mesnil-sur-l'Estrée, France: Presses du CNRS, 1989.

Nightingale, Florence. *Letters from Egypt: A Journey on the Nile, 1849–1850*. New York: Weidenfeld and Nicholson, 1987.

[d'Ohsson, Ignatius Mouradgea]. *Tableau Générale de l'Empire Othoman*. 7 vols. in 8. Paris: De l'imprimerie de monsieur Firmin Didot, 1788–1824.

Pardoe, Julia. *City of the Sultan; and Domestic Manners of the Turks, in 1836*. 3 vols. London: Henry Colburn, 1837.

Pedro'nun Zorunlu İstanbul Siyahati, translated by Fuad Carım. Istanbul: Güncel Yayıncılık, 1995.

Pidou de Saint-Olon, François. *The Present State of the Empire of Morocco, with a Faithful Account of the Manners, Religion, and Government of That People, by Monsieur de St. Olon, Ambassador There in the Year 1693*. London, 1695.

Pitts, Joseph. *A True and Faithful Account of the Religion and Manners of the Mohammetans, with an Account of the Author's Being Taken Captive*, in *Piracy, Slavery, and Redemption*, selected and edited by Daniel J. Vitkus and introduced by Nabil Matar. New York: Columbia University Press, 2001.

Pococke, Richard. "Travels in Egypt." In *A General Collection of the Best and Most Interesting Voyages and Travels in All Parts of the World; Many of Which Are Now First Translated into English*, edited by John Pinkerton. London: Longman, Hurst, Rees, Orme, and Brown, 1814.

al-Qabbāb, Aḥmad al-Fāsī. *Mukhtaṣar kitāb al-Naẓar fī aḥkām al-naẓar bi-ḥāssat al-baṣar li-Ibn al-Qaṭṭān*. Riyadh: Maktabat al-Tawba, 1418/1997.

al-Qalyūbī, Aḥmad ibn Salāma, and ʿUmayra (Shihāb al-Dīn Aḥmad al-Burullusī). *Ḥāshiyatā Qalyūbī wa-ʿUmayra*, edited by ʿAbd al-Laṭīf ʿAbd al-Raḥmān. 4 vols. Beirut: Dār al-Kutub al-ʿIlmīya, 1417/1997.

al-Qaraḍāwī, Yūsuf. *Hudā al-islām: Fatāwā muʿāṣira*. Cairo: Dār Āfāq al-Ghadd, 1401/1981.

al-Qarāfī, Aḥmad ibn Idrīs. *al-Dhakhīra*, edited by Saʿīd Aʿrāb. 14 vols. Beirut: Dār al-Gharb al-Islāmī, 1994.

——. *Kitāb al-Furūq (Anwār al-burūq fī anwāʾ al-furūq)*, edited by Muḥammad Aḥmad Sarrāj and ʿAlī Jumʿa Muḥammad. 4 vols. Cairo: Dār al-Salām, 1421/2001.

al-Qarāfī, Badr al-Dīn. *Tawshīḥ al-dībāj wa-ḥilyat al-ibtihāj*, edited by Aḥmad al-Shatyawī. Beirut: Dār al-Gharb al-Islāmī, 1983/1403.

Qāriʾ al-Hidāya, Sirāj al-Dīn ʿUmar ibn ʿAlī. *Kitāb Fatāwā Qāriʾ al-Hidāya*, edited by Muḥammad al-Raḥīl Gharāyaba and Muḥammad ʿAlī al-Zughūl. Amman: Dār al-Furqān, 1420/1999.

al-Qurṭubī, Abū ʿAbd Allāh Ibn ʿAbd al-Raʾūf. *Ādāb al-ḥisba wa'l-muḥtasib*, edited by Fāṭima al-Idrīsī. Beirut: Dār Ibn Ḥazm, 1425/2005.

al-Qurṭubī, Muḥammad ibn Aḥmad. *Tafsīr al-Qurṭubī (al-Jāmiʿ li-aḥkām al-qurʾān)*, edited by Sālim Muṣṭafā al-Badrī. 21 vols. in 11. Beirut: Dār al-Kutub al-ʿIlmīya, 1424/2004.

al-Ramlī, Shihāb al-Dīn. *Nihāyat al-muḥtāj ilā sharḥ al-Minhāj*. 8 vols. Cairo: Muṣṭafā al-Bābī al-Ḥalabī wa-Awlāduhu, 1386/1967.

Rauwolff, Leonhart. *Aigentliche Beschreibung der Raiss inn die Margenlaender*. 1583; repr., Graz, Austria: Akademische Druck- und Verlagsanstalt, 1971.

al-Rāzī, Fakhr al-Dīn. *al-Tafsīr al-kabīr*. 3rd printing. Beirut: Dār Iḥyāʾ al-Turāth al-ʿArabī, n.d.

Reland, Adrianus. "A Short System of Mahometan Theology." In *Four Treatises Concerning the Doctrine, Discipline and Worship of the Mahometans*. London, 1712. Gale Eighteenth Century Collections Online, http://gdc.gale.com.

Riḍā, Muḥammad Rashīd. *Fatāwā al-imām Muḥammad Rashīd Riḍā*, edited by Ṣalāḥ al-Dīn al-Munajjid and Yūsuf Q. Khūrī. 6 vols. Beirut: Dār al-Kitāb al-Jadīd, 1390/1970.

——. *Ḥuqūq al-nisāʾ fī'l-islām (Nidāʾ ilā al-jins al-laṭīf)*. Beirut: al-Maktab al-Islāmī, 1395/1975.

Roger, Eugène. *La Terre Sainte our Terre de Promission: Description topographique des Saints Lieux, avec un traité des nations de différantes religions qui l'habitent, leurs moeurs, croyances, cérémonies et police*, edited by Elias Kattar. Kaslik, Lebanon: Université Saint-Esprit, 1992.

Rūmī, Jalāl al-Dīn Muḥammad-i Balkhī. *Masnavi-ye maʿnawī*, edited by Qiwām al-Dīn Khurramshāshī. Tehran: Intishārāt-i Nāhīd, 1375/[1956–57].

Rutter, Eldon. *The Holy Cities of Arabia*. 2 vols. London: G. P. Putman's Sons, 1930.

al-Rūyānī, ʿAbd al-Wāḥid ibn Ismāʿīl. *Baḥr al-madhhab fī furūʿ madhhab al-imām al-Shāfiʿī*. 13 vols. Beirut: Dār Iḥyāʾ al-Turāth al-ʿArabī, 1423/2002.

al-Ṣafadī, Ṣalāḥ al-Dīn Khalīl ibn Aybak. *Aʿyān al-ʿaṣr wa-aʿwān al-naṣr*, edited by ʿAlī Abū Zayd et al. 6 vols. Beirut: Dār al-Fikr al-Muʿāṣir/Damascus: Dār al-Fikr, 1418/1998.

al-Sakhāwī, Muḥammad ibn ʿAbd al-Raḥmān. *al-Ḍawʾ al-lāmiʿ li-ahl al-qarn al-tāsiʿ*. 12 vols. in 6. Beirut: Manshūrāt Dār Maktabat al-Ḥayāt, n.d.

Ṣāliḥ, Suʿād. *Aḥkām ʿibādat al-marʾa fī al-sharīʿa al-islāmīya*. Cairo: Dār al-Ḍiyāʾ, 1406/1986.

Salīm, ʿUmar ʿAbd al-Munʿim, arr. *al-Masāʾil al-ʿilmīya wa'l-fatāwā al-sharʿīya, fatāwā al-shaykh Muḥammad Nāṣir al-Dīn al-Albānī fī'l-Madīna wa'l-Imārāt*. Tanta, Egypt: Dār al-Ḍiyāʾ, 2006.

al-Samhūdī, ʿAlī ibn Aḥmad. "al-Wafā bi-mā yajib li-ḥaḍrat al-Muṣṭafā." In *Rasāʾil fī taʾrīkh al-madīna*, edited by Ḥamad al-Jāsir, 95–179. Riyadh: Manshūrāt Dār al-Yamāma, 1972.

——. *Wafāʾ al-wafā bi-akhbār dār al-Muṣṭafā*, edited by Muḥammad Muḥyī al-Dīn ʿAbd al-Ḥamīd. 4 vols. Cairo: Maṭbaʿat Dār al-Saʿāda, n.d.

Al-Ṣanʿānī, ʿAbd al-Razzāq ibn Hammām. *Al-Muṣannaf*, edited by Ḥabīb Allāh al-Aʿẓamī. 11 vols. [Beirut?]: al-Majlis al-ʿIlmī, [1970?].

Sandys, George. *A Relation of a Journey Begun an. Dom. 1610*. London: Andrew Crooke, 1637.

Ṣaqr, ʿAṭīya. *Mawsūʿat Aḥsan al-kalām fī al-fatāwā wa'l-aḥkām*. 7 vols. Cairo: Maktabat Wahba, 1432/2011.

——. *Mawsūʿat al-usra taḥta riʿāyat al-islām*. 6 vols. Cairo: al-Dār al-Miṣrīya li'l-Kitāb, 1410/1990.

al-Sarakhsī, Muḥammad ibn Aḥmad. *Kitāb al-Mabsūṭ*, edited by Muḥammad Ḥasan Muḥammad Ḥasan Ismāʿīl al-Shāfiʿī. 30 vols in 15. Beirut: Dār al-Kutub al-ʿIlmīya, 1421/2001.

——*Kitāb al-Siyar al-kabīr*, edited by Ṣalāḥ al-Dīn al-Munajjid. [Cairo]: Maṭbaʿat Miṣr, 1957.

Sauneron, Serge, ed. *Voyage en Egypte de Jean Palerne, Forésien 1581*. [Cairo]: L'Institut Français d'Archéologie Orientale du Caire, 1971.

al-Ṣāwī, Aḥmad ibn Muḥammad. *Bulghat al-sālik li-aqrab al-masālik ilā madhhab al-imām Mālik*. 3 vols. Cairo: ʿĪsā al-Bābī al-Ḥalabī, 1978.

al-Ṣayrafī, ʿAlī ibn Dāwūd. *Nuzhat al-nufūs wa'l-abdān fī tawārīkh al-zamān*, edited by Ḥasan Ḥabashī. 4 vols. [Cairo]: Maṭbaʿat Dār al-Kutub, 1983.

Schiltberger, Johann. *The Bondage and Travels of Johann Schiltberger, a Native of Bavaria, in Europe, Asia, and Africa, 1396–1427*, translated by J. Buchan Telfer. London: Hakluyt Society, 1879.

Schweigger, Salomon. *Ein Newe Reyßbeschreibung auß Deutschland nach Constantinopel und Jerusalem*. Nuremberg, 1608; facsimile edition Graz: Akademische Druck- und Verlagsanstalt, 1964.

al-Shabrāmallisī, ʿAlī ibn ʿAlī. *Ḥāshiya*. Published with Shihāb al-Dīn al-Ramlī, *Nihāyat al-muḥtāj ilā sharḥ al-Minhāj*. 8 vols. Cairo: Muṣṭafā al-Bābī al-Ḥalabī wa-Awlāduhu, 1386/1967.

al-Shāfiʿī, Muḥammad ibn Idrīs. *al-Risāla*, edited by Aḥmad Muḥammad Shākir. N.p., n.d.

——. *al-Umm*. 8 vols. in 4. Beirut: Dār al-Maʿrifa, n.d.

al-Shaʿrānī, ʿAbd al-Wahhāb. *al-Ṭabaqāt al-kubrā li'l-Shaʿrānī*. Cairo: Maktabat wa-Maṭbaʿat Muḥammad ʿAlī Ṣabīḥ wa-Awlādihi, n.d.

al-Shāshī al-Qaffāl, Abū Bakr Muḥammad ibn Aḥmad. *Ḥilyat al-ʿulamāʾ fī maʿrifat madhāhib al-fuqahāʾ*, edited by Yāsīn Aḥmad Ibrāhīm Darādikah. 3 vols. Beirut: Muʾassasat al-Risāla/Amman: Dār al-Arqam, 1400/1980.

al-Shaybānī, Muḥammad ibn al-Ḥasan. *Kitāb al-Aṣl al-maʿrūf bi'l-Mabsūṭ*. 4 vols. Beirut: ʿĀlam al-Kutub, 1410/1990.

——. *Kitāb al-Ḥujja ʿalā ahl al-Madīna.* 4 vols. Beirut: ʿĀlam al-Kutub, 1983.

al-Shaykh ʿAlwān, ʿAlī ibn ʿAṭīya al-Hītī. *Asnā al-maqāṣid fī taʿẓīm al-masājid.* Beirut: Dār al-Kutub al-ʿIlmīya, 1424/2003.

——. *ʿArāʾis al-ghurar wa-gharāʾis al-fikar fī aḥkām al-naẓar,* edited by Muḥammad Faḍl ʿAbd al-ʿAzīz al-Murād. Damascus: Dār al-Qalam/Beirut: al-Dār al-Shāmīya, 1410/1990.

——. *al-Naṣāʾiḥ al-muhimma li'l-mulūk wa'l-aʾimma,* edited by Nashwa al-ʿAlwānī. Damascus: Dār al-Maktabī, 1420/2000.

——. *Nasamāt al-asḥār fī manāqib wa-karāmāt al-awliyāʾ al-akhyār,* edited by Aḥmad Farīd al-Mazīdī. Beirut: Dār al-Kutub al-ʿIlmīya, 1421/2001.

al-Shaykh al-Mufīd. *Aḥkām al-nisāʾ.* Vol. 9 of *Muṣannafāt al-Shaykh al-Mufīd.* N.p.: al-Muʾtamar al-ʿĀlamī li-Alfīyat al-Shaykh al-Mufīd, 1413.

al-Shaykh, Muḥammad ibn Ibrāhīm. *Fatāwā wa-rasāʾil samāḥat al-shaykh Muḥammad ibn Ibrāhīm ibn ʿAbd al-Laṭīf Āl al-Shaykh,* arranged and edited by Muḥammad ibn ʿAbd al-Raḥmān ibn Qāsim. 13 vols. Mecca: Maṭbaʿat al-Ḥukūma, 1399.

Shaykh-zādeh, ʿAbd al-Raḥmān ibn Mūḥammad. *Majmaʿ al-anhur fī sharḥ Multaqā al-abḥur.* 1328/[1910]; repr., Beirut: Dār Iḥyāʾ al-Turāth al-ʿArabī, n.d.

al-Shirbīnī, Muḥammad ibn Aḥmad. *Mughnī al-muḥtāj ilā maʿrifat maʿānī alfāẓ al-Minhāj.* 4 vols. Beirut: Dār al-Kutub al-ʿIlmīya, 2006.

al-Shirwānī, ʿAbd al-Ḥamīd, and Aḥmad ibn Qāsim al-ʿAbbādī. *Ḥawāshī al-Shirwānī wa-Ibn Qāsim al-ʿAbbādī.* 10 vols. Beirut: Dār Ṣādir, 1972.

Southgate, Horatio. *Narrative of a Tour Through Armenia, Kurdistan, Persia and Mesopotamia.* 2 vols. New York: D. Appleton, 1840.

Spencer, J. A. *The East: Sketches of Travel in Egypt and the Holy Land.* New York: George P. Putnam, 1850.

St. John, James Augustus. *Egypt and Mohammed Ali; or, Travels in the Valley of the Nile.* 2 vols. London: Longman, Rees, Orme, Brown, Green, and Longman, 1834.

al-Subkī, Tāj al-Dīn. *Ṭabaqāt al-shāfiʿīya al-kubrā,* edited by Maḥmūd Muḥammad al-Ṭanāḥī and ʿAbd al-Fattāḥ Muḥammad al-Ḥilw. 11 vols. in 7. Cairo: Hajar, 1413/1992.

al-Suyūṭī, Jalāl al-Dīn ʿAbd al-Raḥmān ibn Abī Bakr. *al-Ashbāh wa'l-naẓāʾir,* edited by Muḥammad al-Muʿtaṣim bi'llāh al-Baghdādī. Beirut: Dār al-Kitāb al-ʿArabī, 1407/1987.

——. *al-Durr al-manthūr fī'l-tafsīr bi'l-maʾthūr.* 6 vols. Beirut: Dār al-Maʿrifa, n.d.

——. *Isbāl al-kisāʾ ʿalā al-nisāʾ.* Beirut: Dār al-Kutub al-ʿIlmīya, n.d.

al-Ṭabarānī, Sulaymān ibn Aḥmad. *al-Muʿjam al-kabīr,* edited by Ḥamdī ʿAbd al-Majīd al-Silafī. 25 vols. Beirut: Dār Iḥyāʾ al-Turāth al-ʿArabī, 1422/2002.

al-Ṭabarī, Abū Jaʿfar Muḥammad ibn Jarīr. *Jāmiʿ al-bayān ʿan taʾwīl āy al-qurʾān.* 30 vols. in 15. Beirut: Dār al-Fikr, 1408/1988.

——. *Taʾrīkh al-umam wa'l-mulūk,* edited by Muḥammad Abū'l-Faḍl Ibrāhīm. 11 vols. Beirut: Dār al-Turāth, n.d.

al-Ṭabarī, Muḥibb al-Dīn Aḥmad ibn ʿAbd Allāh. *Ghāyat al-iḥkām fī aḥādīth al-aḥkām*, edited by Ḥamza Aḥmad al-Zayn. 7 vols. Beirut: Dār al-Kutub al-ʿIlmīya, 1424/2004.

al-Ṭaḥāwī, Aḥmad ibn Muḥammad. *Mukhtaṣar Ikhtilāf al-fuqahāʾ*, abridged by Abū Bakr Aḥmad ibn ʿAlī al-Jaṣṣās and edited by ʿAbd Allāh Nadhīr Aḥmad. 5 vols. Beirut: Dār al-Bashāʾir al-Islāmīya, 1416/1995.

——. *Sharḥ mushkil al-āthār*, edited by Shuʿayb al-Arnaʾūṭ. 16 vols. Beirut: Muʾassasat al-Risāla, 1415/1994.

Thackeray, William Makepeace. *Notes of a Journey from Cornhill to Grand Cairo*. New York: Charles Scribner's Sons, 1904.

Thenaud, Jean. *Le voyage d'outremer*. Paris, 1884; repr., Geneva: Slatkine Reprints, 1971.

Thomson, H. C. *The Outgoing Turk: Impressions of a Journey Through the Western Balkans*. London: William Heinemann, 1897.

Tott, François. *Memoirs of Baron de Tott, Containing the State of the Turkish Empire and the Crimea, During the Late War with Russia, with Numerous Anecdotes, Facts, and Observations, on the Manners and Customs of the Turks and Tatars*. 2 vols. in 1. 1785; repr., New York: Arno Press, 1973.

al-Tunbuktī, Aḥmad Bābā. *Kifāyat al-muḥtāj li-maʿrifat man laysa fī'l-Dībāj*, edited by Muḥammad Muṭīʿ. 2 vols. Rabat: al-Mamlaka al-Maghribīya, Wizārat al-Awqāf wa'l-Shuʾūn al-Islāmīya, 1421/2000.

al-Ṭurṭūshī, Abū Bakr Muḥammad ibn al-Walīd. *al-Ḥawādith wa'l-bidaʿ*, edited by Muḥammad Ḥasan Īsmāʿīl. Beirut: Dār al-Kutub al-ʿIlmīya, 1424/2003.

al-Ubbī, Muḥammad ibn Khalīfa al-Washtānī. *Ikmāl Ikmāl al-muʿlim*. Printed with Muslim ibn Ḥajjāj al-Qushayrī al-Naysābūrī. *Ṣaḥīḥ Muslim*. 9 vols. Beirut: Dār al-Kutub al-ʿIlmīya, 1415/1994.

al-ʿUkbarī, al-Ḥusayn ibn Muḥammad. *Ruʾūs al-masāʾil al-khilāfīya bayna jumhūr al-fuqahāʾ*. 6 vols. Riyadh: Dār Ishbīlīyā, 1421/2001.

[Villalón, Cristóbal]. *Viaje de Turquía*, edited by Fernando G. Salinero. Madrid: Ediciones Cátedra, 1980.

Wakīʿ, Muḥammad ibn Khalaf. *Akhbār al-quḍāt*, edited by ʿAbd al-ʿAzīz Muṣṭafā al-Marāghī. 3 vols. Cairo: al-Maktaba al-Tijārīya, 1366/1947.

Wānilī, Khayr al-Dīn. *al-Masjid fī'l-islām: risālatuhu, niẓām bināʾihi, aḥkāmuhu, ādābuhu, bidaʿuhu*. N.p., n.d.

al-Wansharīsī, Aḥmad ibn Yaḥyā. *Al-Miʿyar al-muʿrib wa'l-jāmiʿ al-mughrib ʿan fatāwā ahl ifrīqīya wa'l-andalus wa'l-maghrib*, edited by Muḥammad Ḥajjī. 13 vols. Rabat: Wizārat al-Awqāf wa'l-Shuʾūn al-Islāmīya li'l-Mamlaka al-Maghribīya, 1401/1981.

Warner, Charles Dudley. *In the Levant*. Boston: James R. Osgood, 1877.

——. *My Winter on the Nile*. 1876; repr., Boston: Houghton, Mifflin, 1900.

al-Wazzān, Amīn ibn Yaḥyā, arr. *al-Fatāwā al-jāmiʿa li'l-marʾa al-muslima*. 5 vols. Riyadh: Dār al-Qāsim li'l-Nashr, 1419.

al-Wazzānī, Abū ʿĪsā Sayyidī al-Mahdī. *al-Nawāzil al-jadīda al-kubrā fīmā li-ahl Fās wa ghayrihim min al-badū wa'l-qurā.* 12 vols. [Rabat]: al-Mamlaka al-Maghribīya, Wizārat al-Awqāf wa'l-Shuʾūn al-Islāmīya, 1417/1996.

Wellsted, J. R. *Travels to the City of the Caliphs, Along the Shores of the Persian Gulf and the Mediterranean.* 2 vols. London: Henry Colburn, 1840.

Wharton, Edith. *In Morocco.* 1919; repr., Hopewell, NJ: Ecco Press, 1996.

Wild, Johann. *Voyages en Egypte*, translated and annotated by Oleg V. Volkoff. Cairo: Institut Français d'Archéologie Orientale, 1973.

Yāsīn, Maʾmūn Maḥmūd. *al-Riḥla ilā al-Madīna al-munawwara.* N.p., 1407/1987.

al-Yūnīnī, Quṭb al-Dīn Mūsā ibn Muḥammad. *Dhayl Mirʾāt al-zamān.* 4 vols. in 3. Hyderabad: Dāʾirat al-Maʿārif al-ʿUthmānīya, 1374/1954.

al-Zabīdī, Muḥammad Murtaḍā. *Tāj al-ʿarūs.* 40 vols. in 20. Beirut: Dār al-Kutub al-ʿIlmīya, 1428/2007.

al-Zarkashī, Muḥammad ibn Bahādur. *Iʿlām al-sājid bi-aḥkām al-masājid.* Cairo, 1384.

Zayn al-Dīn al-ʿIrāqī. *Ṭarḥ al-tathrīb fī sharḥ al-Taqrīb.* Beirut: Dār Iḥyāʾ al-Turāth al-ʿArabī, n.d.

al-Zurqānī, ʿAbd al-Bāqī ibn Yūsuf ibn Aḥmad. *Sharḥ al-Zurqānī ʿalā Mukhtaṣar sayyidī Khalīl.* 4 vols. Beirut: Dār al-Kutub al-ʿIlmīya, 1422/2002.

SECONDARY SOURCES

ʿAbd al-Razzāq, Aḥmad. *al-Marʾa fī Miṣr al-mamlūkīya.* Cairo: al-Hayʾa al-Miṣrīya al-ʿĀmma li'l-Kitāb, 1999.

Abou-Bakr, Omaima. "Qirāʾa fī taʾrīkh ʿābidāt al-islām." In *Zaman al-nisāʾ wa'l-dhākira al-badīla: Majmūʿat abḥāth*, edited by Hudā al-Ṣadda, Sumayya Ramaḍān, and Omaima Abou-Bakr, 141–61. Cairo: Taḥrīr, 1998.

Abou El Fadl, Khaled. *Speaking in God's Name: Islamic Law, Authority and Women.* Oxford, UK: Oneworld, 2001.

Abulafia, David. "The Apostolic Imperative: Religious Conversion in Lull's *Blaquerna.*" In *Religion, Text, and Society in Medieval Spain and Northern Europe: Essays in Honor of J. N. Hillgarth*, edited by Thomas E. Burman et al., 105–21. Toronto, Ontario, Canada: Pontifical Institute of Mediaeval Studies, 2002.

Abu-Zahra, Nadia. *The Pure and Powerful: Studies in Contemporary Muslim Society.* Reading, UK: Ithaca Press, 1997.

Adang, Camilla. "Women's Access to Public Space According to *al-Muḥallā bi-l-Āthār.*" In *Writing the Feminine: Women in Arab Sources*, edited by Manuela Marín and Randi Deguilhem, 75–94. London: I. B. Tauris, 2002.

Aḥmad, Narīmān ʿAbd al-Karīm. *al-Marʾa fī miṣr fī al-ʿaṣr al-mamlūkī.* Cairo: al-Hayʾa al-Miṣrīya al-ʿĀmma li'l-Kitāb, 1993.

Ahmed, Leila. *Women and Gender in Islam: Historical Roots of a Modern Debate.* New Haven, CT: Yale University Press, 1992.

Ali, Kecia. *Marriage and Slavery in Islam.* Cambridge, MA: Harvard University Press, 2010.

ʿAlī, Muḥammad Ibrāhīm. *Iṣṭilāḥ al-madhhab ʿinda al-mālikīya.* Dubai: Dār al-Buḥūth li'l-Dirāsāt al-Islāmīya wa-Iḥyāʾ al-Turāth, 1421/2000.

Andrews, Walter G., and Mehmet Kalpaklı. *The Age of Beloveds: Love and the Beloved in Early-Modern Ottoman and European Culture and Society.* Durham, NC: Duke University Press, 2005.

Asad, Talal. *The Idea of an Anthropology of Islam.* Washington, DC: Center for Contemporary Arab Studies, Georgetown University, 1986.

Aston, Margaret. "Segregation in Church." In *Women in the Church: Papers Read at the 1989 Summer Meeting and the 1990 Winter Meeting of the Ecclesiastical History Society*, edited by W. J. Sheils and Diana Wood, 237–95. Cambridge, MA: Basil Blackwell, 1990.

Bano, Masooda, and Hilary Kalmbach, eds. *Women, Leadership, and Mosques: Changes in Contemporary Islamic Authority.* Leiden: Brill, 2012.

Baron, Beth. *The Women's Awakening in Egypt: Culture, Society, and the Press.* New Haven, CT: Yale University Press, 1994.

Bauer, Karen. "Room for Interpretation: Qurʾānic Exegesis and Gender." PhD diss., Princeton University, 2008.

Bayle, Pierre. *Dictionnaire Historique et Critique par Pierre Bayle, Cinquième édition de 1740 revue, corrigée et augmentée.* 4 vols. 1740; repr., Geneva: Slatkine Reprints, 1995.

Beck, Lois. "The Religious Lives of Muslim Women." In *Women in Contemporary Muslim Societies*, edited by Jane I. Smith, 27–60. Lewisburg, PA: Bucknell University Press, 1980.

Berkey, Jonathan. *Popular Preaching and Religious Authority in the Medieval Islamic Near East.* Seattle: University of Washington Press, 2001.

———. *The Transmission of Knowledge in Medieval Cairo.* Princeton, NJ: Princeton University Press, 1992.

Betteridge, Anne H. "Muslim Women and Shrines in Shiraz." In *Mormons and Muslims*, edited by Spencer J. Palmer, 127–38. Provo, Utah: Religious Studies Center, Brigham Young University, 1983.

Blair, Sheila S. "Islamic Art as a Source for the Study of Women in Premodern Societies." In *Beyond the Exotic*, edited by Amira El-Azhary Sonbol, 336–46. Syracuse, NY: Syracuse University Press, 2005.

Böttcher, Annabelle. "Islamic Teaching Among Sunni Women in Syria." In *Everyday Life in the Muslim Middle East*, edited by Donna Lee Bowen and Evelyn A. Early, 290–99. Bloomington: Indiana University Press, 2002.

Brink, Judy. "Lost Rituals: Sunni Muslim Women in Rural Egypt." In *Mixed Blessings: Gender and Religious Fundamentalism Cross Culturally*, edited by Judy Brink and Joan Mencher, 199–208. London: Routledge, 1997.

Brockopp, Jonathan. *Early Mālikī Law: Ibn ʿAbd al-Ḥakam and His Major Compendium of Jurisprudence.* Leiden: Brill, 2000.

Brookes, Douglas Scott, ed. and trans. *The Concubine, the Princess, and the Teacher: Voices from the Ottoman Harem.* Austin: University of Texas Press, 2008.

Brooten, Bernadette J. *Women Leaders in the Ancient Synagogue: Inscriptional Evidence and Background Issues*. Atlanta: Scholars Press, 1982.

Brown, Jonathan A. C. *The Canonization of al-Bukhārī and Muslim.* Leiden: Brill, 2007.

——. *Hadith: Muhammad's Legacy in the Medieval and Modern World.* Oxford, UK: Oneworld, 2009.

Buckley, R. P., trans. *The Book of the Islamic Market Inspector:* Nihāyat al-Rutba fī Ṭalab al-Ḥisba (The Utmost Authority in the Pursuit of Ḥisba) *by ʿAbd al-Raḥmān b. Naṣr al-Shayzarī.* Oxford, UK: Oxford University Press, 1999.

Calder, Norman. *Studies in Early Muslim Jurisprudence.* Oxford, UK: Clarendon Press, 1993.

Calderini, Simonetta. "Contextualizing Arguments About Female Ritual Leadership (Women Imāms) in Classical Islamic Sources." *Comparative Islamic Studies* 5 (2009): 5–32.

Choksy, Jamsheed K. *Evil, Good, and Gender: Facets of the Feminine in Zoroastrian Religious History.* New York: Peter Lang, 2002.

Commins, David Dean. *Islamic Reform: Politics and Social Change in Late Ottoman Syria.* New York: Oxford University Press, 1990.

Cook, Michael. *Commanding Right and Forbidding Wrong in Islamic Thought.* Cambridge: Cambridge University Press, 2000.

Cortese, Delia, and Simonetta Calderini. *Women and the Fatimids in the World of Islam.* Edinburgh: Edinburgh University Press, 2006.

Crawford, Patricia. *Women and Religion in England 1500–1720.* London: Routledge, 1993.

Creswell, K. A. C. *The Muslim Architecture of Egypt.* Oxford, UK: Clarendon Press, 1952; New York: Hacker Art Books, 1978.

Daniel, Norman. *Islam and the West: The Making of an Image.* Oxford, UK: Oneworld, 1993.

Dankoff, Robert. "Ayıp değil! (No Disgrace!)." *Journal of Turkish Literature* 5 (2008): 77–90.

Dannenfeldt, Karl H. *Leonhard Rauwolf: Sixteenth-Century Physician, Botanist, and Traveler*. Cambridge, MA: Harvard University Press, 1968.

Davis, Robert C. "The Geography of Gender in the Renaissance." In *Gender and Society in Renaissance Italy,* edited by Judith C. Brown and Robert C. Davis, 19–38. London: Longman, 1998.

De Maillet, [Benoît], and M. L'Abbé Le Mascrier. *Description de L'Egypte*. Paris, 1735.

Doumato, Eleanor Abdella. *Getting God's Ear: Women, Islam, and Healing in Saudi Arabia and the Gulf*. New York: Columbia University Press, 2000.

——. "Hearing Other Voices: Christian Women and the Coming of Islam." *International Journal of Middle East Studies* 23 (1991): 177–99.

D'Souza, Diane. "Women's Presence in the Mosque: A Viewpoints [*sic*]." In *Islam, Women and Gender Justice*, edited by Asghar Ali Engineer, 193–217. New Delhi: Gyan Publishing House, 2001.

Duval, Soraya. "New Veils and New Voices." In *Women and Islamization: Contemporary Dimensions of Discourse on Gender Relations*, edited by Karin Ask and Marit Tjomsland, 45–72. Oxford, UK: Berg, 1998.

Early, Evelyn A. *Baladi Women of Cairo: Playing with an Egg and a Stone*. Boulder, CO: Lynne Rienner, 1993.

Elewa, Ahmed, and Laury Silvers. "I *Am* One of the People: A Survey and Analysis of Legal Arguments on Women-Led Prayer in Islam." *Journal of Law and Religion* 26 (2010–11): 141–71.

El Guindi, Fadwa. *Veil: Modesty, Privacy and Resistance*. Oxford, UK: Berg, 1999.

El-Kholy, Heba Aziz. *Defiance and Compliance: Negotiating Gender in Low-Income Cairo*. New York: Berghahn Books, 2002.

Fadel, Mohammad. "Two Women, One Man: Knowledge, Power, and Gender in Medieval Sunni Legal Thought." *International Journal of Middle East Studies* 29 (1997): 185–204.

Faroqhi, Suraiya. *Pilgrims and Sultans: The Hajj Under the Ottomans 1517–1683*. London: I. B. Tauris, 1994.

Fernea, Robert W., and Elizabeth W. Fernea. "Variation in Religious Observance Among Islamic Women." In *Scholars, Saints, and Sufis*, edited by Nikki R. Keddie, 385–401. Berkeley: University of California Press, 1972.

Fiey, J. M. *Moussoul Chrétienne*. Beirut: Imprimerie Catholique, 1959.

al-Fihris al-shāmil li'l-turāth al-ʿarabī al-islāmī al-makhṭūṭ, al-Fiqh wa-uṣūlihi. Amman: Muʾassasat Āl al-Bayt li'l-Fikr al-Islāmī, 1421.

French, Katherine L. *The Good Women of the Parish: Gender and Religion After the Black Death*. Philadelphia: University of Pennsylvania Press, 2008.

Friedman, Mordechai A. "The Ethics of Medieval Jewish Marriage." In *Religion in a Religious Age*, edited by S. D. Goitein, 83–102. Cambridge, MA: Association for Jewish Studies, 1974.

Gerrard, Christine. *Aaron Hill: The Muses' Projector, 1685/1750*. Oxford, UK: Oxford University Press, 2003.

Goitein, S. D. *A Mediterranean Society*. Vol. 2, *The Community*. Berkeley: University of California Press, 1971.

Goldman, Karla. *Beyond the Synagogue Gallery: Finding a Place for Women in American Judaism*. Cambridge, MA: Harvard University Press, 2000.

Goldziher, Ignaz. "ʿAlî b. Mejmûn al-Maġribî und sein Sittenspiegel des östlichen Islam: Ein Beitrag zur Culturgeschichte." *ZDMG* 28 (1874): 293–330.

——. *The Ẓāhirīs: Their Doctrine and Their History*, translated by Wolfgang Behn. Leiden: Brill, 1971.

Golvin, Lucien. *Essai sur l'architecture religieuse musulman.* Vol. 4, *L'Art hispono-musulman.* N.p.: Éditions Klincksieck, 1979.

Grabar, Oleg. *The Illustrations of the Maqāmāt.* Chicago: University of Chicago Press, 1984.

Guthrie, Shirley. *Arab Social Life in the Middle Ages.* London: Saqi Books, 1995.

al-Ḥāfiẓ, Muḥammad Muṭīʿ. *Jāmiʿ al-Ḥanābila "al-Muẓaffarī" bi-Ṣāliḥīyat jabal Qāsiyūn.* Beirut: Dār al-Bashāʾir al-Islāmīya, 1423/2002.

Haider, Najam. *The Origins of the Shīʿa: Identity, Ritual, and Sacred Space in Eighth-Century Kufa.* Cambridge: Cambridge University Press, 2011.

Halevi, Leor. *Muhammad's Grave: Death Rites and the Making of Islamic Society.* New York: Columbia University Press, 2007.

Hallaq, Wael B. *Authority, Continuity and Change in Islamic Law.* Cambridge: Cambridge University Press, 2001.

al-Harithy, Howayda. "Female Patronage of Mamluk Architecture in Cairo." In *Beyond the Exotic: Women's Histories in Islamic Societies,* edited by Amira El-Azhary Sonbol, 321–35. Cairo: American University in Cairo Press, 2006.

Hattox, Ralph S. *Coffee and Coffeehouses: The Origins of a Social Beverage in the Medieval Near East.* Seattle: University of Washington Press, 1988.

Heyd, Uriel. *Ottoman Documents on Palestine, 1552–1615: A Study of the Firman According to the* Mühimme Defteri. Oxford, UK: Clarendon Press, 1960.

Hirschler, Konrad. *The Written Word in the Medieval Arabic Lands: A Social and Cultural History of Reading Practices.* Edinburgh: Edinburgh University Press, 2013.

Ho, Engseng. *The Graves of Tarim: Genealogy and Mobility Across the Indian Ocean.* Berkeley: University of California Press, 2006.

Hoffman-Ladd, Valerie J. "The Religious Life of Muslim Women in Contemporary Egypt." PhD diss., University of Chicago, 1986.

——. "Women and Islam: Women's Religious Observances." In *The Oxford Encyclopedia of the Modern Islamic World,* edited by John L. Esposito, 4:327–31. New York: Oxford University Press, 1995.

Höglmeier, Manuela. *al-Ǧawbarī und sein Kašf al-asrār—ein Sittenbild des Gauners im arabisch-islamischen Mittelalter (7./13. Jahrhundert): Einführung, Edition und Kommentar.* Berlin: Klaus Schwarz Verlag, 2006.

Holod, Renata, and Hasan-Uddin Khan. *The Contemporary Mosque: Architects, Clients and Designs since the 1950s.* New York: Rizzoli, 1997.

Hurgronje, C. Snouck. *Mekka in the Latter Part of the 19th Century.* Leiden: Brill, 1970.

al-Ḥusaynī, Suhayla. *al-Marʾa fī manhaj al-imām al-Ghazālī.* Cairo: Dār al-Rashād, 1419/1998.

Jackson, Sherman A. "*Kramer Versus Kramer* in a Tenth/Sixteenth Century Egyptian Court: Post-Formative Jurisprudence Between Exigency and Law." *Islamic Law and Society* 8 (2001): 27–51.

Jaschok, Maria, and Shui Jingjun. *The History of Women's Mosques in Chinese Islam*. Richmond, Surrey, UK: Curzon Press, 2000.

Kahf, Mohja. *Western Representations of the Muslim Woman, from Termagant to Odalisque*. Austin: University of Texas Press, 1999.

Kaḥḥāla, ʿUmar Riḍā. *Muʿjam al-muʾallifīn*. 4 vols. Beirut: Muʾassasat al-Risāla, 1414/1993.

Kalmbach, Hilary. "Social and Religious Change in Damascus: One Case of Female Religious Authority." *British Journal of Middle Eastern Studies* 35 (2008): 37–57.

Kamali, Mohammad Hashim. *Principles of Islamic Jurisprudence*. Cambridge, UK: Islamic Texts Society, 1991.

Kaptein, Nico. "Materials for the History of the Prophet Muhammad's Birthday Celebration in Mecca." *Der Islam* 69 (1992): 193–203.

Karim, Jamillah. "Voices of Faith, Faces of Beauty: Connecting American Muslim Women Through *Azizah*." In *Muslim Networks from Hajj to Hip Hop*, edited by Miriam Cooke and Bruce B. Lawrence, 169–88. Chapel Hill: University of North Carolina Press, 2005.

Katz, Marion. *The Birth of the Prophet Muḥammad*. London: Routledge, 2007.

——. *Body of Text: The Emergence of the Sunni Law of Ritual Purity*. Albany, NY: SUNY Press, 2007.

——. "The Corruption of the Times and the Mutability of the *Shari'a*." *Cardozo Law Review* 28 (2006): 171–85.

——. *Prayer in Islamic Thought and Practice*. New York: Cambridge University Press, 2013.

Keller, Shoshana. "The Struggle Against Islam in Uzbekistan, 1921–1941: Policy, Bureaucracy, and Reality." PhD diss., Indiana University, 1995.

Khalafallah, Haifaa. "Public Authority, Scriptures, and Islamic Law." In *Beyond the Exotic: Women's Histories in Islamic Societies*, edited by Amira El-Azhary Sonbol, 37–50. Syracuse, NY: Syracuse University Press, 2005.

Kugle, Scott. *Rebel Between Spirit and Law: Ahmad Zarruq, Sainthood, and Authority in Islam*. Bloomington: Indiana University Press, 2006.

Lachiri, Nadia. "Abū'l-ʿAlāʾ al-Maʿarrī wa'l-marʾa." In *Nadwat Abī'l-ʿAlāʾ al-Maʿarrī, Maʿarrat al-Nuʿmān, 24–7 Rajab 1418 A.H./November 24–27 (1997)*, 2:775–95. [Damascus]: Wizārat al-Taʿlīm al-ʿĀlī, al-Majlis al-Aʿlā li-Riʿāyat al-Funūn wa'l-Ādāb wa'l-ʿUlūm al-Ijtimāʿīya, n.d.

Lacroix, Stéphane. "Between Revolution and Apolicitism: Nasir al-Din al-Albani and His Impact on the Shaping of Contemporary Salafism." In *Global Salafism: Islam's New Religious Movement*, edited by Roel Meijer, 58–80. New York: Columbia University Press, 2009.

Lagardère, Vincent. *Histoire et Société en Occident Musulman au Moyen Âge: Analyse du* Miʿyār *d'al-Wanšarīsī*. Madrid: Consejo Superior de Investigaciones Científicas, 1995.

Lambert, Elie. "L'histoire de la Grande Mosquée de Cordoue aux VIIIe et IXe siècles d'après des textes inédits." *Annales de l'Institut d'Études Orientales* 2 (1936): 172.
Lange, Christian. *Justice, Punishment, and the Medieval Muslim Imagination.* Cambridge: Cambridge University Press, 2008.
Leder, Stefan, Yāsīn Muḥammad Sawwās and Ma'mūn Ṣāghirjī. *Mu'jam al-samā'āt al-dimashqīya: Les certificates d'audition à Damas, 550–750 h./1155–1349.* Damascus: l'Institut Français d'Études Arabes de Damas, 1996.
Le Strange, Guy. *Palestine Under the Moslems.* Beirut: Khayats, 1965.
Lévi-Provençal, E. "Documents et Notules: Les Citations du *Muqtabis* d'Ibn Ḥayyān Relatives aux Agrandissements de la Grande-Mosquée de Cordoue au IXe Siècle." *Arabica* 1 (1954): 89–95.
Lowry, Joseph E. *Early Islamic Legal Theory: The* Risāla *of Muḥammad ibn Idrīs al-Shāfi'ī.* Leiden: Brill, 2007.
Lutfi, Huda. "Manners and Customs of Fourteenth-Century Cairene Women: Female Anarchy Versus Male Shar'i Order in Muslim Prescriptive Treatises." In *Women in Middle Eastern History: Shifting Boundaries in Sex and Gender,* edited by Nikki R. Keddie and Beth Baron, 99–121. New Haven, CT: Yale University Press, 1991.
Mabro, Judy. *Veiled Half-Truths: Western Travellers' Perceptions of Middle Eastern Women.* London: I. B. Tauris, 1991.
al-Madanī, Muḥammad Mughayribī. *Firqat al-ikhwān al-islāmīya bi-Najd aw wahhābīyat al-yawm.* N.p., n.d.
Maher, Vanessa. *Women and Property in Morocco: Their Changing Relation to the Process of Social Stratification in the Middle Atlas.* Cambridge: Cambridge University Press, 1974.
Mahmood, Saba. *Politics of Piety.* Princeton, NJ: Princeton University Press, 2005.
Makdisi, George. *The Rise of Colleges: Institutions of Learning in Islam and the West.* Edinburgh: Edinburgh University Press, 1981.
Marçais, Georges. *L'Architecture Musulmane d'Occident.* Paris: Arts et Métiers Graphiques, 1954.
Marcus, Julie. *A World of Difference: Islam and Gender Hierarchy in Turkey.* London: Zed, 1992.
Marín, Manuela. *Mujeres en al-Ándalus.* Madrid: Consejo Superior, 2000.
Marlow, Louise. *Hierarchy and Egalitarianism in Islamic Thought.* Cambridge: Cambridge University Press, 1997.
Marmon, Shaun. *Eunuchs and Sacred Boundaries.* New York: Oxford University Press, 1995.
Martin, John. "Out of the Shadow: Heretical and Catholic Women in Renaissance Venice." *Journal of Family History* 10 (1985): 21–33.
Massignon, Louis. "La Cité des Morts au Caire." *Bulletin de l'Institut Français de l'Archéologie Orientale* 57 (1958): 25–79.

al-Mawsūʿa al-fiqhīya. Kuwait: Wizārat al-Awqāf wa'l-Shuʾūn al-Islāmīya, 1404–1427/1983–2006.

Mazumdar, Shampa, and Sanjoy Mazumdar. "In Mosques and Shrines: Women's Agency in Public Sacred Space." *Journal of Ritual Studies* 16 (2002): 165–78.

Meijer, Roel. *Global Salafism: Islam's New Religious Movement*. New York: Columbia University Press, 2009.

Melchert, Christopher. "The Meaning of *Qāla 'l-Shāfiʿī* in Ninth Century Sources." In *ʿAbbasid Studies: Occasional Papers of The School of ʿAbbasid Studies*, 277–301. Leuven: Uitgeverij Peeters, 2004.

———. "Whether to Keep Women Out of the Mosque: A Survey of Medieval Islamic Law." In *Authority, Privacy and Public Order in Islam, Proceedings of the 22nd Congress of L'Union Européenne des Arabisants et Islamisants*, edited by B. Michalak-Pikulska and A. Pikulski, 59–69. Leuven: Uitgeverij Peeters, 2006.

Melman, Billie. *Women's Orients: English Women and the Middle East, 1718–1918*. Ann Arbor: University of Michigan Press, 1992.

Mickelwright, Nancy. "Musicians and Dancing Girls." In *Women in the Ottoman Empire*, edited by Madeleine Zilfi, 153–68. Leiden: Brill, 1997.

Mitchell, Richard P. *The Society of the Muslim Brothers*. London: Oxford University Press, 1969.

Al-Musawi, Muhsin J. *The Islamic Context of* The Thousand and One Nights. New York: Columbia University Press, 2009.

Nadwi, Mohammad Akram. *Al-Muhaddithat: The Women Scholars in Islam*. Oxford, UK: Interface Publications, 2007.

Necipoğlu, Gülru. *The Age of Sinan: Architectural Culture in the Ottoman Empire*. London: Reaktion Books, 2005.

Nicholson, Reynold A. *The Mathnawí of Jalálu'ddín Rúmí*. London: Cambridge University Press for the Trustrees of the E. J. W. Gibb Memorial, 1934.

Pauty, E. "Communications: Le plan de l'Université de Qarawiyin á Fès." *Hespéris* 3 (1923): 515.

Peirce, Leslie P. *Morality Tales: Law and Gender in the Ottoman Court of Aintab*. Berkeley: University of California Press, 2003.

———. "'The Law Shall Not Languish': Social Class and Public Conduct in Sixteenth-Century Ottoman Legal Discourse." In *Hermeneutics and Honor: Negotiating Female "Public" Space in Islamic/ate Societies*, edited by Asma Afsaruddin, 140–58. Cambridge, MA: Harvard University Press, 1999.

———. "Seniority, Sexuality, and Social Order: The Vocabulary of Gender in Early Modern Ottoman Society." In *Women in the Ottoman Empire: Middle Eastern Women in the Early Modern Era*, edited by Madeline C. Zilfi, 169–96. Leiden: Brill, 1997.

Perlmann, Moshe. "A Seventeenth Century Exhortation Concerning Al-Aqṣā." *Israel Oriental Studies* 3 (1973): 261–90.

Pesle, O. *La Femme Musulmane dans le Droit la Religion et les Mœurs*. Rabat: Les éditions de la porte, 1946.

Pouzet, Louis. *Damas au VIIe/XIIIe s.: Vie et structures religieuses dans une métropole islamique.* Beirut: Dar El-Machreq Sarl Éditeurs, 1988.

Qāḍī, Widād. "Mafhūm al-fitna wa-ṣuwaruhā fī adab ʿAbd al-Ḥamīd al-Kātib." In *Fuṣūl adabīya wa-tārīkhīya li-majmūʿa min al-ʿulamāʾ wa'l-udabāʾ muhdāt ilā Nāṣir al-Dīn al-Asad*, edited by Ḥusayn ʿAṭwān, 337–61. Beirut: Dār al-Jīl, 1993.

Rapaport, Yossef. *Marriage, Money and Divorce in Medieval Islamic Society*. Cambridge: Cambridge University Press, 2005.

Reinhart, A. Kevin. "When Women Went to Mosques: al-Aydini on the Duration of Assessments." In *Islamic Legal Interpretation: Muftis and Their Fatwas*, edited by Muhammad Khalid Masud, Brinkley Messick, and David S. Powers, 116–28. Cambridge, MA: Harvard University Press, 1996.

Roald, Anne Sofie. *Women in Islam: The Western Experience*. London: Routledge, 2001.

Ro'i, Yaacov. *Islam in the Soviet Union*. New York: Columbia University Press, 2000.

Romano, Dennis. "Gender and the Urban Geography of Renaissance Venice." *Journal of Social History* 23 (1989): 339–53.

Sabra, Adam. *Poverty and Charity in Medival Islam: Mamluk Egypt, 1250–1517*. Cambridge: Cambridge University Press, 2000.

Sadeghi, Behnam. *The Logic of Law-Making in Islam: Women and Prayer in the Legal Tradition*. Cambridge: Cambridge University Press, 2012.

Safrai, Hannah. "Women and the Ancient Synagogue." In *Daughters of the King*, edited by Susan Grossman and Rivka Haut, 39–49. Philadelphia: Jewish Publication Society, 1992.

Sayeed, Asma. "Early Sunni Discourse on Women's Mosque Attendance." *ISIM Newsletter* 7 (2001): 10.

——. "Space: Mosques, Arab States (Excepting the Gulf and North Africa)." In *Encyclopedia of Women and Islamic Cultures*, edited by Suad Joseph, 4:549–50. Leiden: Brill, 2007.

——. "Women and Ḥadīth Transmission: Two Cases from Mamlūk Damascus." *Studia Islamica* 95 (2004): 71–94.

al-Shahrī, Muḥammad Hazzāʿ. *al-Masjid al-nabawī al-sharīf fī'l-ʿaṣr al-ʿuthmānī, 923–1344, dirāsa miʿmārīya ḥaḍārīya*. Cairo: Dār al-Qāhira li'l-Kitāb, 2003.

Shoshan, Boaz. *Popular Culture in Medieval Cairo*. Cambridge: Cambridge University Press, 1993.

Sirriyeh, Elizabeth. *Sufi Visionary of Ottoman Damascus: ʿAbd al-Ghanī al-Nābulusī, 1641–1731*. London: Routledge Curzon, 2005.

Smith, Jane I. "Old French Travel Accounts of Muslim Beliefs Concerning the Afterlife." In *Christian-Muslim Encounters*, edited by Yvonne Yazbeck Haddad and Wadi Zaidan Haddad, 221–41. Gainesville: University Press of Florida, 1995.

Stillman, Yedida Kalfon. *Arab Dress: A Short History from the Dawn of Islam to Modern Times*. Leiden: Brill, 2003.

Sule, Balaraba B. M., and Priscilla E. Starratt. "Islamic Leadership Positions for Women in Contemporary Kano Society." In *Hausa Women in the Twentieth Century*, edited by Catherine Coles and Beverly Mack, 29–49. Madison: University of Wisconsin Press, 1991.

Taft, Robert F. "Women at Church in Byzantium: Where, When—and Why?" *Dumbarton Oaks Papers* 52 (1998): 27–87.

Talmon-Heller, Daniella. "*The Cited Tales of the Wondrous Doings of the Shaykhs of the Holy Land* by Ḍiyāʾ al-Dīn Abū ʿAbd Allāh Muḥammad b. ʿAbd al-Wāḥid al-Maqdisī (569/1173–643/1245): Text, Translation and Commentary." *Crusades* 1 (2002): 111–54.

——. *Islamic Piety in Medieval Syria: Mosques, Cemeteries and Sermons under the Zangids and Ayyūbids (1146–1260)*. Leiden: Brill, 2007.

Tammam, Husam. "Yūsuf al-Qaraḍāwī and the Muslim Brothers: The Nature of a Special Relationship." In *Global Mufti: The Phenomenon of Yusuf al-Qaradawi*, edited by Bettina Graf and Jakob Skovgaard-Petersen, 55–83. New York: Columbia University Press, 2009.

Taylor, Christopher S. *In the Vicinity of the Righteous:* Ziyāra *and the Veneration of Muslim Saints in Late Medieval Egypt*. Leiden: Brill, 1999.

al-Tāzī, ʿAbd al-Hādī. *Jāmiʿ al-Qarawīyīn: al-masjid wa'l-jāmiʿa bi-madīnat Fās, mawsūʿa li-taʾrīkhihā al-miʿmārī wa'l-fikrī*. Beirut: Dār al-Kitāb al-Lubnānī, 1973.

Tetsuya, Ohtoshi. "Cairene Cemeteries as Public Loci and Mamluk Egypt." *Mamlūk Studies Review* 10 (2006): 83–116.

Thys-Şenocak, Lucienne. *Ottoman Women Builders: The Architectural Patronage of Hadice Turhan Sultan*. Aldershot, Hampshire, UK: Ashgate, 2006.

Tietze, Andreas. *Muṣṭafā ʿĀlī's Description of Cairo of 1599: Text, Translation, Notes*. Vienna: Verlag der Őesterreichischen Akademie der Wissenschaften, 1975.

Tillier, Mathieu. "Women Before the Qāḍī under the Abbasids." *Islamic Law and Society* 16 (2009): 280–301.

Torab, Azam. *Performing Islam: Gender and Ritual in Iran*. Leiden: Brill, 2007.

Tuğlacı, Pars. *Women of Istanbul in Ottoman Times*. Istanbul: Cem Yayinevi, 1984.

Turki, Abdel Magid. "Femmes privilégiées et privilèges féminins dans le système théologique et juridique d'Ibn Ḥazm." *Studia Islamica* 47 (1978): 25–82.

Tyan, Emile. *Histoire de l'organisation judiciaire*. Leiden: Brill, 1960.

Ukeles, Raquel Margalit. "Innovation or Deviation: Exploring the Boundaries of Islamic Devotional Law." PhD diss., Harvard University, 2006.

Vadet, Jean-Claude. "Quelques remarques sur la racine ftn dans le coran et la plus ancienne littérature musulmane." *Revue des Études islamiques* 37 (1969): 81–101.

van Doorn-Harder, Pieternella. *Women Shaping Islam: Reading the Qur'an in Indonesia*. Urbana: University of Illinois Press, 2006.

van Ess, Joseph. *Theologie und Gesellschaft im 2. und 3. Jahrhundert Hidschra*. Berlin: Walter de Gruyter, 1992.

Vitkus, Daniel J., and Nabil Matar, eds. *Piracy, Slavery, and Redemption*. New York: Columbia University Press, 2001.

Walther, Wiebke. *Women in Islam*. Princeton, NJ: Markus Wiener, 1993.

Watt, Jeffrey R. "Women and the Consistory in Calvin's Geneva." *Sixteenth Century Journal* 24 (1993): 429–39.

Weiss, Bernard G. *The Search for God's Law*. Salt Lake City: University of Utah Press, 1992.

Wensinck, A. H., and J. P. Mensing. *Concordance et indices de la tradition musulmane*. Leiden: Brill, 1965.

Wherry, E. M. *A Comprehensive Commentary on the Qur'an: Comprising Sale's Translation and Preliminary Discourse, with Additional Notes and Emendations*. 1882; repr., Osnabrück, Germany: Otto Zeller Verlag, 1973.

Yacoob, Saadia. "Women and Law in the Pre-Modern Middle East: Reconstructing the Lives of Female Jurists (faqihat)." Paper presented at the Middle East Studies Association annual conference in Washington, DC, November 24, 2008.

al-Yūbī, Laḥsan. *Al-Fatāwā al-fiqhīya fī ahamm al-qaḍāyā min ʿahd al-Saʿdīyīn ilā mā qabla al-ḥimāya*. [Rabat]: al-Mamlaka al-Maghribīya, Wizārat al-Awqāf wa'l-Shu'ūn al-Islāmīya, 1419/1998.

Zaghlūl, Muḥammad al-Saʿīd Basyūnī. *Mawsūʿat aṭrāf al-ḥadīth al-nabawī al-sharīf*. Beirut: Dār al-Kutub al-ʿIlmīya, n.d.

Zaydān, ʿAbd al-Karīm. *al-Mufaṣṣal fī aḥkām al-marʾa wa'l-bayt al-muslim fī'l-sharīʿa al-islāmīya*. Beirut: Muʾassasat al-Risāla, 1420/2000.

al-Zuḥaylī, Wahba. *al-Fiqh al-islāmī wa-adillatuhu*. Damascus: Dār al-Fikr, 1425/2005.

Zysow, Aron, "The Economy of Certainty: An Introduction to the Typology of Islamic Legal Theory." PhD diss., Harvard University, 1984.

INDEX

ʿAbd Allāh ibn Aḥmad ibn Ḥanbal, 117–18
ʿAbd Allāh ibn al-Mubārak, 50
ʿAbd Allāh ibn ʿUmar, 17, 52
ʿAbd al-Razzāq al-Ṣanʿānī, 22
ʿAbd al-Ḥamīd (jurist), 123
ʿAbd al-Malik (caliph), 146
ʿAbduh, Muḥammad, 178, 260–61
Al-ʿAbdūsī, ʿAbdallah, 126
Abou-Bakr, Omaima, 147, 166
Abou El Fadl, Khaled, 281
Abū Barza, 114
Abū al-Dardāʾ, 146
Abū Ḥanīfa, 65, 71–74
Abū 'l-Jawad, 136
Abū'l-Suʿūd, 87
Abū Shāma, 132, 152–53
Abū Shuqqa, ʿAbd al-Ḥalīm, 273–74
Abū Umāma (al-Bāhilī), 147
Abū Yaʿqūb Yūsuf, 124
Abū Yūsuf, 71–72, 74
Al-ʿAdawī, ʿAlī ibn Aḥmad, 35, 284
Al-ʿAdawīya, Maʿādha, 118
additions, to mosques. *See ziyādas*
adolescent girls, 107. *See also* age cohorts of women
adornment, 13, 220, 287. *See also* clothing; dress
adultery. *See zinā*
Africa. *See* Spain and North Africa
afterlife, 108–9, 175. *See also* paradise
age cohorts of women, 128, 249–50; significance of, 23–25, 63, 73–74, 89, 100–102, 106; significance of questioned, 41, 55–56, 63, 74–75, 96, 98, 103. *See also* adolescent girls; *ʿajūz*; *mutajālla*; old and young women; *shābba*
aḥkām (legal statuses of actions), 34; *ḥarām*, 34, 233, 236; *makrūh*, 235; *mubāḥ*, 37, 49, 91–92, 98
Ahmed, Leila, 2, 292
ʿĀʾisha bint ʿAbd Allāh ibn ʿĀṣim, 126
ʿĀʿisha report, 18, 50, 62, 64, 261; commentary, 84, 97; perfume and, 260

ʿ*ajūz* (old woman), 24, 71, 72, 102. *See also* age cohorts of women
Al-Albānī, Nāṣir al-Dīn, 281–85, 287
ʿĀlī, Muṣṭafā, 141
Ali Bey, 169
ʿAlī ibn Abī Ṭālib, 115
Āl al-Shaykh, Muḥammad ibn Ibrāhīm, 278
ʿAlwān, al-Shaykh (ʿAlī ibn ʿAṭīya al-Hītī). *See* Al-Shaykh ʿAlwān
amrad (beardless youth), 105–6
Andrews, Walter, 84
Al-Anṣārī, Zakarīyā, 70
Al-Aqfahsī, ʿAbd Allāh ibn Miqdād, 32
Al-Aqfahsī, Ibn al-ʿImād, 63, 137
Aqṣā Mosque, 166–71
ʿĀshūrāʾ, 130, 144, 194, 261, 332*n*76
Al-ʿAsqalānī, Ibn Ḥajar, 55–56, 59, 69, 137, 156, 195, 250
Aston, Margaret, 173
ʿAṭāʾ ibn Abī Rabāḥ, 22
ʿĀtika bint Zayd, 18, 23, 27
Al-Aydinī, 87
Al-ʿAynī, Badr al-Dīn, 84

Al-Bahūtī, Manṣūr ibn Yūnus, 96, 98
Baiqarā, Ḥusayn, *186*
Al-Bājī, Sulaymān ibn Khalaf, 30, 36
Al-Balāṭunusī, Muḥammad ibn ʿAbd Allāh, 66
balconies, 120, 182–83, *184*, 185, *186*, 187–88, 289, 292; in synagogues, 349*n*325. *See also* women's space, in mosques
Bale, Pierre, 175
Al-Baʿlī, Aḥmad, 96
Al-Bannā, Ḥasan, 266, 269, 275
Al-Bāqillānī, Abū Bakr ibn al-Ṭayyib, 33
baraka (blessings), 6–7, 131
barza (non-secluded woman), 96–97
Al-Barzanjī, Jaʿfar, 222
Al-Baṣrī, al-Ḥasan, 115
Bauer, Karen, 108
Al-Bazzār, Aḥmad ibn ʿAmr, 101
beardless youth. *See amrad*
beatific vision, 109
Beck, Lois, 296*n*8
Berkey, Jonathan, 136, 157–58
bidaʿ (innovations), 10, 12; books on, 112; Ibn ʿAbd al-Ghaffār on, 224, 226, 244–45; separate prayer rooms for women as, 285–86, 371*n*115
Black Stone, 217, 221, 239; kissing, 357*n*64
Blair, Sheila, 185
blessings. *See baraka*
blocking the paths. *See sadd al-dharāʾiʿ*
Blunt, Fanny, 191
boots, 50, 113, 151, 309*n*121
Boulden, James, 188
Al-Bukhārī (author of *Ṣaḥīḥ*), 23, 31, 58
Al-Bukhārī, ʿAlāʾ al-Dīn, 162–63
Burton, Richard, 278
Al-Burullusī, Aḥmad, 70
Al-Burzulī, 123
Al-Būṭī, Muḥammad Saʿīd Ramaḍān, 263–65

Cairo, Egypt: grave visitation, 139–45; ʿ*īd*, 129–30; *Jumʿa*, 133–34, 139; study sessions, 134–35; women preachers, 136; women's de facto presence in mosques in, 128–45; women's space in mosques, 134
Castellan, Antoine-Laurent, 187
Çelebi, Evliya, 187, 221, 255
changing of legal rulings with changing of circumstances. *See taghayyur al-aḥkām bi-taghayyur al-aḥwāl*

childbirth, 102; rituals, 7; seclusion after, 222
children: care for, as women's obligation, 263, 267, 268–72, 279, 286, 291; in mosques, 31, 97, 131, 133, 136, 159, 162, 171, 189, 193, 194, 261, 278
circumambulation area. *See maṭāf*
classical schools of law. *See madhāhib*
clothing, 62, 357*n*59; festive, 47, 131; humble, 29; inspection, 233; modest, 138, 266; ostentatious, 69; revealing, 130. *See also* dress; jewelry
coercion. *See kurh*
coffee, 201–4
coffeehouses, 6, 291
commanding right and forbidding wrong, 206, 247–48, 251, 329*n*50; conditions of performance, 233
concubine. *See umm walad*
conditions for women going out to mosques, 28–30, 53–54
congregational prayer. *See al-jamāʿa*
Cordoba, Great Mosque of, 24, 120–21, 122
Craven, Elizabeth, 188

dāʿiyāt (female preachers), 283
Al-Dajjānī, Muḥammad ibn Ṣāliḥ, 150, 170–71
Al-Damīrī, Sharaf al-Dīn Yaḥyā, 252
d'Andrea, Giovanni, 173
Dankoff, Robert, 255
Al-Dasūqī, Muḥammad, 35–36
Davis, Robert, 7
daytime, woman who goes out (or does not go out) during, 21–22, 107, 217, 324*n*324. *See also* times of day
de Amicis, Edmondo, 192–93
de Nicolay, Nicolas, 181
Dernschwam, Hans, 181, 182
de Saint-Olon, François Pidou, 144–45, 174
De Tott, Baron, 175, 182
dhikr (remembrance [of God]), 33, 35–36, 180, 196, 273
discretionary punishment. *See taʿzīr*
d'Ohsson, Ignatius Mouradgea, 181, 187, 191
Dome of the Rock, 167, 177
domesticity, 262–64, 266–67; duties, 269–70, 275, 280; Ḥanafīs and, 85–86; shift in theme of, 277
dress: adornment, 13, 220, 287; boots, 50, 113, 151, 309*n*121; conditions for, 261; footwear, 309*n*121; improper, 285; men's, 287; proper Islamic, 286, 290. *See also* jewelry
Du Fresne-Canaye, Philippe, 174
Duval, Soraya, 289

Early, Evelyn, 291
Edib, Halidé, 191
education, 4–5, 276, 277, 280. *See also* schools
Ellison Grace, 188
enclosures. *See maqṣūra* (pl, *maqāṣīr*); women's space, in mosques
eunuchs, 182, 222
European Council for Fatwa and Research, 271

Fabri, Félix, 137–38, 168–69, 173
Faḍl Allāh, Ayatollah Muḥammad, 290
Al-Fākihānī, ʿUmar, 29
farāʾiḍ (religious obligations), 282
Al-Farazdaq, 117
Al-Farrāʾ, Abū Yaʿlā ibn, 88, 93
Fāṭima bint ʿAbbās ibn Abīʾl-Fatḥ, 152

Fāṭima bint Sahl, 152
fat women, 303*n*35
Al-Fayyūmī, Aḥmad, 96
female preachers. *See dāʿiyāt*
festival prayers. *See ʿīd*
fire temples, 326*n*26
First Egyptian Congress, 262
fitna (sexual temptation), 34, 102–3, 307*n*98; de-emphasis, 280; development of concept, 323*n*307, 323*n*309; Ḥanafīs and, 73–75, 83–85; Ḥanbalīs and, 83–8588, 90–92; Ibn ʿAbd al-Ghaffār and, 226, 228, 232, 237–38, 240, 242, 246, 250–51, 255; legal doctrines development and, 3; Mālikīs and, 24–26; Muslim Brotherhood and, 266, 268; in Qur'an, 103–4; women's mosque attendance, sixteenth-century Mecca and, 216, 227; Ẓāhirīs and, 40–41
food, 114, 183; distribution, 145; preparation, 327*n*28; vendors, 170; wedding, 163
footwear. *See* boots
forbidden. *See aḥkām*; *ḥarām*
forbidding wrong. *See* commanding right and forbidding wrong
fornication. *See zinā*
Friday prayers. *See Jumʿa*
funerals, 35, 36, 113, 114, 145, 262, 325*n*2

garlic, 226, 228, 232
Garnett, Lucy, 189
Gauvain, Richard, 285
gender-inappropriate behavior. *See tashabbuh*
gender mixing. *See ikhtilāṭ*
generalization. *See taʿmīm*
Georgijevic, Bartholomej, 179–80
Gerlach, Stephan, 174
Al-Ghawrī (Mamlūk Sultan), 205
ghayra (jealousy), 41, 101, 109, 231, 282
Ghazāla, 115
Al-Ghazālī, Abū Ḥāmid, 51–53, 63, 69, 104, 135, 149, 150, 171, 268–71
Golvin, Lucien, 124
Gonzales, Antonius, 138–39
gossip, 228, 237–38, 239
Grabar, Oleg, 185
grave visitation, 67, 139–45, 164, 336*n*134
El Guindi, Fadwa, 8
gynaeceum (women's section), 187. *See also* balconies

ḥadīth (reports recounting statements and actions of the Prophet), 8
ḥadīth, specialists in. *See muḥaddithūn*
Al-Ḥāfiẓ, Muḥammad Muṭīʿ, 154
Hagia Sophia, 187–88, 190–91
ḥajj, 42–43, 90, 94, 284
Al-Ḥajjāj, 114–15
Al-Ḥalabī, Ibrāhīm, 86
Halevi, Leor, 113
Ḥamza, ʿAbd al-Laṭīf, 264
Ḥanafīs (legal school), on women's mosque attendance, 71–87
Ḥanbalīs (legal school), on women's mosque attendance, 88–99
ḥarām (forbidden), 34, 233, 236. *See also aḥkām*
harassment of women, 84, 209
Al-Ḥarīrī, 183, *184*
Harvey, Annie Jane, 190
Al-Ḥaṣkafī, Muḥammad, 86
Al-Ḥaṭṭāb, Muḥammad, 200, 202
Al-Haytamī, Ibn Ḥajar, 66–70, 106, 108, 199, 205–6, 212–15, 227, 237, 239–40, 243, 244, 246
Ḥijāz, 7, 22, 113, 222, 230

Al-Ḥijāzīya, Umm al-Khayr, 128, 331*n*72
Hill, Aaron, 174, 182
Hirschler, Konrad, 154
Al-Ḥiṣnī, Taqī al-Dīn, 64–67, 99, 166, 170, 198
Al-Hītī, ʿAlī ibn ʿAṭīya. *See* ʿAlwān, Al-Shaykh
Hoffman, Valerie, 262
Holod, Renata, 292
home, 48, 66, 266, 267–68; commitment to, 286; economics, 262; as mission, 268; women's worship in, 263, 268. *See also* domesticity
Al-Huḍaybī, Ḥasan, 267
Hunter, William, 175
Hurgronje, Snouck, 222
husband's permission (required for woman to attend mosque), 264, 272, 279, 282, 297*n*13, 351*n*354; Ḥanbalīs on, 95; Mālikīs on, 26–28; Shāfiʿīs on, 42–43, 45–46; Ẓāhirīs on, 60

Ibn ʿAbd al-Barr, 29–30
Ibn ʿAbd al-Ghaffār, Aḥmad: age cohorts and, 254–55; on *bidaʿ*, 224, 226, 244–45; biography, 200–201; on coffee debate, 201–4; on commanding right and forbidding wrong, 233; concept of *taʿmīm*, 232, 250; *fitna* and, 226, 228, 232, 237–38, 240, 242, 246, 250–51, 255; *istiftāʾ* and, 213–15; *Izālat al-ghishāʾ* and, 202, 211; legal analysis, 225–51; on Meccan women's behavior in mosque, 216–25; personal involvement in debate over women's access to mosque, 207–11; on punishment, 232–33, 247
Ibn ʿAbd Rabbih, 167
Ibn ʿAbd al-Wahhāb, Muḥammad, 278
Ibn Abī Jamra, 31, 37
Ibn Abī Shayba, 116
Ibn ʿAqīl, 132
Ibn al-ʿArabī, Abū Bakr (jurist), 37, 148–49, 167
Ibn ʿArabī (mystic), 41
Ibn ʿArafa, 33
Ibn ʿAsākir, 147–52
Ibn al-ʿAṭṭār, ʿAlī ibn Ibrāhīm, 57–58, 63
Ibn Baṭṭāl, 26, 30
Ibn Baṭṭūṭa, 151, 220
Ibn Bāz, ʿAbd al-ʿAzīz, 279, 282
Ibn Daqīq al-ʿĪd, 55–57, 60, 83
Ibn al-Ḍiyāʾ, 223–24
Ibn Fahd, 205, 238–39, 256
Ibn Farḥūn, Ibrāhīm ibn ʿAlī, 32
Ibn al-Ḥaddād, Abū Bakr, 77
Ibn al-Ḥājj, 5, 6, 10, 11, 31–32, 129–35, 137–44, 194, 198, 261
Ibn al-Ḥakam, ʿAbd al-Raḥmān, 120, 155
Ibn al-Ḥakam, Hishām, 121
Ibn Ḥamdān, 96
Ibn Ḥanbal, Aḥmad, 88–89, 95, 103, 117, 277
Ibn Ḥazm, 9, 38–41, 59, 62
Ibn Hubayra, 89–90
Ibn al-Humām, 82–83, 102
Ibn Jābir, ʿAbd al-Raḥmān ibn Yazīd, 147
Ibn Jamāʿa, ʿIzz al-Dīn, 220–21
Ibn al-Jawzī, 5, 90–92, 102, 117, 147, 150; hagiographical accounts, 166–67
Ibn Jurayj, 22
Ibn Kathīr, 61, 147
Ibn Khajjū, Abū'l-Qāsim, 125–26
Ibn Manẓūr, 20
Ibn Masʿūd, 113–14, 118
Ibn Maymūn, ʿAlī, 163, 165–66, 196

Ibn Māza, 76–77, 85
Ibn Mufliḥ, 96, 132
Ibn al-Mulaqqin, 70
Ibn al-Munāṣif, 122, 198
Ibn Muzayn, Yaḥyā ibn Ibrāhīm, 26
Ibn al-Naḥḥās, 159
Ibn al-Najjār, 96
Ibn al-Naẓẓār (or Ibn al- ʿAṭṭār, author of *Aḥkām al-nisāʾ*), 64, 66
Ibn Nujaym, Zayn al-Dīn, 86–87
Ibn al-Qāsim, 19, 22, 25
Ibn Qayyim al-Jawzīya, 95, 279
Ibn Qudāma, 92–93, 151, 155–56, 279
Ibn Rajab al-Ḥanbalī, 97–98, 105
Ibn Rushd, Abū'l-Walīd, 24–27, 35–36, 102, 104, 198, 247, 303*n*35
Ibn Saʿd, 20, 116–17
Ibn Shāhīn, Zayn al-Dīn, 133
Ibn Shuhayd, Abū ʿĀmir, 122
Ibn Ṭawq, 158–59
Ibn Taymīya, 93–95, 109, 152, 279
Ibn al-Ukhuwwa, 135, 150
Ibn ʿUthaymīn, 280–81
Ibn Zabāla, 120
Ibrāhīm ibn Aḥmad (Aghlabid sultan), 127
ʿīd (festival) prayers, 92–93, 129–30, 192, 275; discouragement from, 362*n*164; legal obligation to, 317*n*38
iḥtiyāṭ (pious precaution), 79
Iḥyāʾ ʿulūm al-dīn (Al-Ghazālī), 51–52, 149–50
ijtihād (legal reasoning), 236, 241–42, 248–49, 257, 261; engagement in, 305*n*67
ikhtilāṭ (mixing of men and women), 54, 208, 221, 266, 271–72
Ikhwān al-Muslimūn. *See* Muslim Brotherhood
ʿilla (rationale), 79, 80, 88, 240
illegitimate sexual intercourse. *See zinā*
imāma (ritual leadership), 9
imprisonment (*ḥabs*), 285
innovations. *See bidaʿ*
Iraq, 89, 112–19, 351*n*354
Al-ʿIrāqī, Zayn al-Dīn, 63
Al-Isfāhānī, Abū'l-Faraj, 117
ʿishāʾ (nighttime prayers): Ḥanafīs on, 71–72, 77; Mālikīs on, 22–23; Ramadan, 180, 191, 272. *See also tarāwīḥ*
IslamOnline website, 271
Istanbul, Ottoman: balconies, 183, *184*, 185, *186*, 187–88, 349*n*325; gender segregation, 175–76; *ʿīd*, 192; *Jumʿa*, 192, 198; Ramadan, 180, 190–91, 195; women's de facto presence in mosques in, 171–95; women's space in mosques in, 171–95
istiftāʾ (legal inquiry), 211; al-Haytamī, 214–15; Ibn ʿAbd al-Ghaffār, 213–15
Italy, Renaissance, 7
*iʿtikāf (*religious retreat*)*, 115–16, 167; Ḥanafīs on, 73; Syria, 147
ʿIyāḍ ibn Mūsā al-Yaḥṣubī (al-Qāḍī ʿIyāḍ), 27–28, 29, 31, 60
Iyās ibn Muʿāwiya, 118
Izālat al-ghishāʾ, 202, 211

Jackson, Sherman, 248–49
Al-Jāḥiẓ, 22, 100–101
al-jamāʿa (congregational prayer), 30–31
Jāmiʿ al-Jabal, 152
Jāmiʿ al-Muẓaffarī, 153–56
Jāmiʿ al-Nisāʾ (Women's Mosque), 168–69
Al-Jawbarī, 135
Al-Jazeera, 271
Al-Jazīrī, ʿAbd al-Qādir ibn Muḥammad, 200–201
Al-Jaznāʾī, ʿAlī, 124–25

jealousy. *See ghayra*
Jenkins, Hester Donaldson, 191
Jerusalem: Aqṣā Mosque, 166–71; celebrations, 170; enclosed space for women, 167, 169; *Jāmiʿ al-Nisāʾ*, 168–69; *Jumʿa*, 169–70; permanent retreats, 167; women's de facto presence in mosques in, 166–71
jewelry, 13, 28, 55, 165, 214, 219, 236
Johnson, Sarah Barclay, 177–78
John the Baptist, shrine of, 260
judge. *See qāḍī*
Al-Judhāmī, Ibn al-Fakhkhār, 126
Juḥā, 150
Jumʿa (Friday prayers), 5, 31, 242, 264, 275; Cairo, Egypt, 133–34, 139; Ḥanafīs on, 86; Ḥanbalīs on, 92; Iraq, 113–14, 116; Jerusalem, 169–70; Mālikīs and, 34, 37; Ottoman Istanbul, 192, 198; Qur'an on, 108–9; to renew religion, 366*n*46; Shāfiʿīs on, 43–44, 46; as social acts of worship, 267; Spain and North Africa, 121–22, 125; Syria, 148–49; women's mosque attendance and, 7–8, 292; Ẓāhirīs on, 54–55
Al-Jundī, Khalīl ibn Isḥāq, 30–31, 34
juristic analogy. *See qiyās*
juristic principles. *See qawāʿid al-fiqhīya*

Kaʿba, 16, 222–23, 228–30, 246
Kahf, Mohja, 174
Kalpaklı, Mehmet, 84
Al-Kāsānī, 75, 85
Kathīr ibn Murra, 147
Kemalpaşazadeh, 106
Khalīfa ibn Khayyāṭ, 115
Khalīl ibn Isḥāq al-Jundī, 30–32, 34, 252
Khan, Hasan-Uddin, 292
Khārijism, Ibāḍī, 9
khāṭiba (matchmaker), 159
Khawla bint Qays, Umm Ṣubayya, 20
Khāʾir Beg, 203–4
El-Kholy, Heba, 290–91
Khomeini, Ayatollah, 290
Al-Khūlī, al-Bahī, 267–68
Al-Khurashī, ʿAbd Allāh, 34–35
Kufa, Great Mosque of, 115
kurh (coercion), 236

Al-Lakhmī, 123
Lane, Edward William, 193–94
Al-Laqānī, Nāṣir al-Dīn, 252
lattice. *See shabaka*
al-layālī al-fāḍila (sacred nights), 223–24
Laylat al-Qadr, 132
de Maillet Benoît, 141
Leder, Stefan, 153, 155
legal inquiry. *See istiftāʾ*
legal statuses of actions. *See aḥkām*
Lescalopier, Pierre, 174, 182
Lithgow, William, 173, 189
locking mosques, 161, 354*n*17
Lufti, Huda, 10
Lull, Ramon, 172–73

Al-Maʿarrī, Abū'l-ʿAlāʾ, 148
madhāhib (classical schools of law), 277. *See also* Ḥanafīs; Ḥanbalīs; Mālikīs; Shāfiʿīs
maghrib (sunset), 217
Al-Maḥallī, Jalāl al-Dīn, 63, 70
maḥḍar (memorandum), 208
Maḥmūd, ʿAbd al-Ḥalīm, 264
majlis al-ʿilm (religious instruction), 78
makrūh (undesirable), 235
Malcolm, John, 176
Mālik ibn Anas, 17–18
Mālikīs (legal school), on women's mosque attendance, 17–38

maqāṣīr (enclosures), 167, 333*n*99. *See also* women's space, in mosques
Al-Maqdisī, Muḥammad ibn ʿAbd al-Wāḥid, 149
Al-Maqdisīya, Fāṭima, 155
Al-Maqdisīya, Ḥabība bint Ibrāhīm, 155
maqṣūra (enclosed space, pl. *maqāṣīr*), 120–21, 123–25, 167, 287–89, 333*n*99. *See also* women's space, in mosques
Al-Mardāwī, ʿAlī ibn Sulaymān, 96, 98
Al-Marghinānī, ʿAlī ibn Abī Bakr, 77, 83–85
market inspector and enforcer of public morals. *See muḥtasib*
Al-Marwazī, Muḥammad, 85
Masjid al-Bayāṭira, 153
Masnavī (Rūmī), 150
mass media, 275, 276
maṭāf (circumambulation area [around Kaʿba]), 207, 209–10, 217–18, 221, 223, 229
matchmaker. *See khāṭiba*
mature woman. *See* age cohorts of women; *mutajālla*
Al-Māwardī, ʿAlī ibn Muḥammad, 48–49
Al-Mawṣilī, ʿAbd Allāh, 75–76
Mazumdar, Sanjoy, 5
Mazumdar, Shampa, 5
Mecca, 15–16, 21, 146. *See also* pilgrimage to Mecca; women's mosque attendance, sixteenth-century Mecca
Mecca, Great Mosque of, 43, 68; access to, 201; coffee and, 204; custodians, 206–7; women's attendance in sixteenth-century Mecca, 15–16, 216–25, 249
Medina, 19, 22, 120, 153, 183, 200, 218, 222, 287–88
Melchert, Christopher, 2, 99, 113
memorandum. *See maḥḍar*
men, 7, 11, 191, 351*n*35; adornment and, 287; male authority, 4; male guardian, 21; maleness, 57; young man, 105–6. *See also* husband's permission; *ikhtilāṭ*
Menavino, Antonio, 180
menstruating women, 102, 284–85, 348*n*312
merit, 286; Mālikīs on, 36–37; Ẓāhirīs on, 38, 56–58
mīʿād (regularly-scheduled lesson), 157–58
Mihailović, Konstantin, 178
minor pilgrimage. *See ʿumra*
Misʿar ibn Kidām, 117
mixing of men and women. *See ikhtilāṭ*
Montagu, Lady Mary Wortley, 189
mosques: Aqṣā Mosque, 166–71; children in, 31; Great Mosque of Cordoba, 24, 120–21, 122; Great Mosque of Kufa, 115; Great Mosque of Qayrawān, 123–24, 127; legal procedures in, 118; locking of, 161, 354*n*17; men's attendance at, 11; range of functions performed in, 5–6; record keeping, 12–13; sacred functions performed in, 6; separate entrances for women, 364*n*12; shrines compared to, 6–7, 131; village mosques, 291; *ziyādas* and, 333*n*98. *See also* Mecca, Great Mosque of; women's mosque attendance; women's mosque attendance, modern developments; women's mosque attendance, sixteenth-century Mecca; *specific geographic locations*
mothers, 271; desexualized, 276

Moüette, Germain, 174
mubāḥ (permissible, legally neutral), 37, 49, 91–92, 98
Mudawwana, 19, 22
muḥaddithūn (scholars of *ḥadīth*), distinctive attitudes towards women's mosque access, 52–63, 81–83
Muḥammad. *See* Prophet Muḥammad
muḥtasib (market inspector and enforcer of public morals), 51, 121, 135, 150, 234, 237
Mujīr al-Dīn, 168
mukhaddara (secluded woman), 107, 108, 218, 324*n*324
Al-Mukhtār, 114
Muslim Brotherhood: *fitna* and, 266, 268; home worship and, 266; members, 289; mothers and, 271; origination, 265–66; thinkers, 274; training and deployment emphasis, 271; views, 282; women's mosque attendance, 265–77
Al-Mustanṣir, Al-Ḥakam, 121
mutajālla (mature woman), 19–21, 23–25, 30, 34–35, 301*n*12. *See also* age cohorts of women
*Muwaṭṭa*ʾ, 17–18
Al-Muzanī, 128

Al-Nābulusī, ʿAbd al-Ghanī, 169
Nadwi, Muhammad Akram, 136
Al-Nafrāwī, Aḥmad ibn Ghunaym, 34
Al-Nakhaʿī, Ibrāhīm, 114
Al-Nasafī, ʿAbd Allāh ibn Aḥmad, 78
Nāṣif, Malak Ḥifnī, 262–63, 277
Nāṣiḥ al-Dīn ibn al-Ḥanbalī, 151
Al-Nawawī, Abū Zakarīyā, 53–55, 63, 69, 104, 250
nāẓir (superintendent), 137
Necipoğlu, Gülru, 298*n*25
Nightingale, Florence, 176–77
nighttime, women's mosque attendance at, 22–23, 29–30, 77, 82, 158–59, 179, 207, 217–19, 239
nighttime prayers. *See ʿishāʾ*
nighttime prayers during Ramadan. *See tarāwīḥ*
Niṣf Shaʿbān, 132, 171, 196
non-secluded woman. *See barza*
North Africa. *See* Spain and North Africa

oaths, 21–22, 298*n*20
old and young women. *See* age cohorts of women; *ajūz*; *mutajālla*; *shābba*

Palerne, Jean, 138, 140–41
paradise: Islam and, 174–75; women's exclusion from, according to Western reports, 174; women's place in, 108–9. *See also* afterlife
Pardoe, Julia, 1, 175–76, 188, 189
Pedersen, Johannes, 2
Peirce, Leslie, 106
perfume: prohibited for women attending mosques, 55, 69–70, 260; used by Meccan women, 220–21
permissible, legally neutral. *See mubāḥ*
physical attractiveness, 46, 150, 309*n*120; grave visitation and, 142; old woman and, 35; public worship and, 47, 48–50, 52, 65, 160–61, 227
pilgrimage to Mecca, 16, 21, 356*n*54; minor pilgrimage, 222–23; Shāfiʿīs and, 42–43; women's mosque attendance, sixteenth-century Mecca and, 224–25
pious foundation. *See waqf*

pious precaution. *See iḥtiyāṭ*
Pococke, Richard, 141
political awareness, 276
postclassical stage, 249–50
postmenopausal women, 102
prayer. *See ṣalāt*
prayer leadership, 288, 330*n*63. *See also imāma*
prayer space. *See maqṣūra*; women's space, in mosques
preacher. *See wāʿiẓ*
preacher-storyteller. *See qāṣṣ*
preaching sessions: Ḥanafīs on, 78–79; Syria, 150–57, 165–66
Prophet Muḥammad, 2–3, 18; actions and statements, 23; birthday, 196; birthplace, 205–6; grave, 16, 222–23, 228–30, 246; guidance, 260; *ḥadīth* and, 8; innovations and, 39–40; permission and dispensation, 71; Shāfiʿīs on wives of, 44–45
punishment. *See taʿzīr*

qāḍī (judge), 203
qafaṣ (cage), 288. *See also* women's space, in mosques
al-Qaffāl al-Shāshī, al-Qāsim ibn Muḥammad, 50–51
Al-Qaraḍāwī, Yūsuf, 271–73
Al-Qarāfī, Badr al-Dīn, 200, 202
Al-Qāsimī, Jamāl al-Dīn, 260, 277
qāṣṣ (preacher-storyteller), 117, 158
Qaṭām ibnat al-Shijna, 115
qawāʿid al-fiqhīya (juristic principles), 241
Qayrawān, Great Mosque of, 123–24, 127
Al-Qayrawānī, Ibn Abī Zayd, 34
qiyās (juristic analogy), 62
Qur'an, 79, 161, 191, 264; *fitna* in, 103–4; on men's "degree" over women, 108–9
al-Qurṭubī , Aḥmad ibn ʿAbd Allāh ibn ʿAbd al-Raʾūf, 121
Al-Qurṭubī, Muḥammad ibn Aḥmad, 105, 228

Ramadan, 67, 117; Cairo, Egypt, 133; Ottoman Istanbul, 180, 190–91, 195; *tarāwīḥ*, 272; women's mosque attendance, sixteenth-century Mecca and, 223–24
Al-Ramlī, Shams al-Dīn, 70
Al-Raqqī, Hilāl ibn al-ʿAlāʾ, 118
rationale. *See ʿilla*
Raʾūf, Hiba, 274–75
Rauwolff, Leonhart, 179
Reformation, 173–74
regularly-scheduled lesson. *See mīʿād*
Reland, Adrianus, 174
religious instruction. *See majlis al-ʿilm*
religious obligations. *See farāʾiḍ*
religious retreat. *See iʿtikāf*
Riḍā, Rashīd, 261–62, 267, 277
Roald, Anne Sofie, 287
Roger, Eugène, 170
Rūmī, Jalāl al-Dīn, 150
Rutter, Eldon, 278
Al-Rūyānī, ʿAbd al-Wāḥid ibn Ismāʿīl, 51

sadd al-dharāʾiʿ (blocking the paths), 240, 242–44
Sadeghi, Behnam, 2, 75, 87
Al-Ṣāgharjī, Maʾmūn, 153, 155
Al-Ṣaʿīdī, ʿAlī al-ʿAdawī, 30
St. John, James Augustus, 193
Al-Sakhāwī, Muḥammad ibn ʿAbd al-Raḥmān, 135, 220
Salafism, 277–89
ṣalāt (prayer), 5, 6; congregational, 30–31; daily prayers, 206–7, 217, 219; men's prayers, 351*n*35; public prayers, 352*n*366. *See also ʿīd; ʿishāʾ; Jumʿa*

Sale, George, 175
Ṣāliḥ, Suʿād, 265
Al-Ṣāliḥīya (area of Damascus), 197
Salīm, Shaykh ʿAbd al-Majīd, 263
Al-Samdīsī, Shams al-Dīn, 251
Al-Samhūdī, ʿAlī ibn Aḥmad, 218
Al-Ṣanʿānī, ʿAbd al-Razzāq. *See* ʿAbd al-Razzāq al-Ṣanʿānī
Sandys, George, 182
Al-Sarakhsī, Abū Bakr, 73–74, 77, 83, 104
Saudi Arabia, 265, 281, 288
Saudi Permanent Council for Fatwas, 279–80
Al-Ṣāwī, Aḥmad, 35–36
Al-Sawwās, Yāsīn, 153, 155
Al-Ṣaydalānī, 63
Sayeed, Asma, 2, 264
Schiltberger, Johann, 178, 188
school precedent. *See taqlīd*
schools, 262
schools of Islamic law, classical. *See madhāhib*
Schweigger, Salomon, 174, 188–89
secluded woman. *See mukhaddara*
Selim (Ottoman sultan), 205
sexual temptation. *See fitna*
shabaka (lattice), 288, 369*n*95
shābba (young woman), 23–25, 36, 122. *See also* age cohorts of women
Shabīb ibn Yazīd, 115
Al-Shabrakhītī, Ibrāhīm ibn Marʿī, 35
Al-Shabrāmallisī, ʿAlī, 70, 71
Al-Shāfiʿī, Muḥammad ibn Idrīs, 25, 41–51, 65, 77, 90, 128, 141
Shāfiʿīs (legal school), 25, 41–71, 77
Al-Shaʿrānī, ʿAbd al-Wahhāb, 135
Al-Shāṭibī, Abū Isḥāq, 132
Al-Shaybānī, Muḥammad ibn al-Ḥasan, 71–72, 74
Al-Shaykh ʿAlwān, 66, 160–66, 198
Shaykh-Zādeh, 102
Al-Shayzarī, ʿAbd al-Raḥmān ibn Naṣr, 152, 159
Shīʿism, Imāmī, 9
Al-Shīrāzī, Abū Isḥāq, 49–50, 54
Al-Shirbīnī, Muḥammad, 70
shrines, 296*n*8; grave visitation and, 139–41; of John the Baptist, 260; mosques compared to, 6–7, 131; visitation, 278
Shurayḥ, 115
Al-Shuwaykī, Shihāb al-Dīn, 252
Sibṭ Ibn al-Jawzī, 152–53
Sind ibn ʿInān al-Azdī, 23, 26–27, 36
Sitt al-Wuzarāʾ bint ʿUmar ibn al-Munajjā, 136
Southgate, Horatio, 175–76, 188, 189, 192
space, women's. *See* women's space, in mosques
Spain and North Africa: *Jumʿa*, 121–22, 125; women's de facto presence in mosques in, 119–28; women's prayer space in, 120–27
storyteller. *See qāṣṣ*
study sessions, 134–35
Al-Sunbāṭī, Aḥmad ibn ʿAbd al-Ḥaqq, 252–53
sunset prayer. *See maghrib*
superintendent. *See nāẓir*
Al-Suyūṭī, Jalāl al-Dīn, 63, 109
Syria: de facto presence of women in mosques in, 145–66; preaching sessions, 150–58, 161, 165–66

Al-Ṭabarānī, Sulaymān ibn Aḥmad, 101
Al-Ṭabarī, Muḥammad ibn Jarīr, 114–16, 218–19
Al-Ṭabarī, Muḥibb al-Dīn, 218–19
taghayyur al-aḥkām bi-taghayyur al-aḥwāl (changing of legal rulings with changing of circumstances), 243

Al-Ṭaḥāwī, Aḥmad ibn Muḥammad, 72–73
Talmon-Heller, Daniella, 149, 183
ta'mīm (generalization), 225, 232, 250
Al-Ṭanbadāwī, Aḥmad ibn al-Ṭayyib, 253
Al-Tanūkhī, Saḥnūn ibn Sa'īd, 19
taqlīd (school precedent), 9, 248–49
tarāwīḥ (special nighttime prayers during Ramadan), 180, 191, 272
tashabbuh (gender-inappropriate behavior), 283
Al-Tatā'ī, Muḥammad ibn Ibrāhīm, 34
Taylor, Christopher, 143
ta'zīr (discretionary punishment), 232–33, 247
Temple Mount (Jerusalem), 167
Thackeray, William Makepeace, 190
Al-Thawrī, Sufyān, 50, 72
Thenaud, Jean, 140
Thévenot, Jean, 174
Thomson, H. C., 189
Time of Ignorance, 229
times of day, 77, 84, 246, 255. *See also 'ishā'*; nighttime, women's mosque attendance at; nighttime hours
travelers, Western, 6, 12, 15, 112, 124, 137, 139–40, 144, 171, 172–73, 182, 193
Turkey, 1, 172, 181. *See also* Istanbul, Ottoman
Al-Ṭurṭūshī, Abū Bakr, 132

al-Ubbī, Muḥammad ibn Khalīfa, 28–29, 37
Al-'Umarī, Ibn Faḍl Allāh, 168
Umar ibn al-Khaṭṭāb, 2, 18, 36–37, 116
Umm al-Dardā', 146–47
Umm Ḥumayd, 89
umm walad (concubine), 114
'umra (minor pilgrimage), 222–23
undesirable. *See makrūh*
Al-'Utbī al-Qurṭubī, 19–20, 24
'Utbīya, 26

village mosques, 6, 149, 183, 261, 291
Virgin Mary, 171
virgins, 23, 180, 332*n*298

Wahhābī movement, 278, 282
wā'iẓ (preacher), 151, 253, 260. *See also dā'iyāt*
Al-Walīdī, Rāshid ibn Abī Rāshid, 32–33, 126
Al-Wansharīsī, Aḥmad ibn Yaḥyā, 123
al-Waqā'i' al-miṣrīya, 261
waqf (pious foundation), 229
Warner, Charles Dudley, 193–94
weddings, 13, 163, 170
Wild, Johan, 138
women, 267–68; adolescent girls, 107; advocacy, 290; affluent, 220; aged, elderly, 72; categorization concerning, 3; chaste woman, 96–97; divorced, 301*n*8; fat, 303*n*35; free, 104–5; groups of, 250; *ikhtilāṭ*, 54, 208, 221, 266, 271–72; latter day, 31–32; learned and pious, 58, 63; menstruating, 102, 284–85, 348*n*312; postmenopausal, 102; prayer room, 125–27; preachers, 136; teachers, 146–47; women's space, 134; working-class, 291. *See also* old and young women
Women and Gender in Islam (Ahmed), 2
Women Between the Home and Society (Al-Khūlī), 267–68
Women's Mosque. *See Jāmi' al-Nisā'*

women's mosque attendance: debate in sixteenth-century Mecca, 199–257; Egypt: Cairo, 128–45; examples of historical practice, 111–98; Ḥanafīs, 71–87; Ḥanbalīs, 88–99; Iraq, 113–19; Islamic reform from the turn of the twentieth century, 259–65; Jerusalem: al-Aqṣā, 166–71; legal debates in classical schools, 17–109; Meccan women's usage of the Sacred Mosque, 216–25; modern developments, 259–93; the Muslim Brotherhood, 265–77; Ottoman Istanbul, 171–95; Salafism, 277–89; Shāfiʿīs, 41–71; Spain and North Africa, 119–28; Syria, 145–66; Ẓāhirīs, 38–41. *See also specific topics*
women's prayer rooms, in mosques. *See* women's space, in mosques
women's section. *See gynaeceum*
women's space, in mosques: in Alexandria, 177; in Aqṣā Mosque, Jerusalem, 167–69, 178; balconies and, 183, *184*, 185, *186*, 187–88, 287, 349*n*325; in Cairo, 133–34, 137–38; as a legal issue, 123–24, 285–86, 287–89; in Medina, 120, 287–88; in Spain and North Africa, 119–25; in Turkey, 179, 182–83, 187–88, 191

young man. *See amrad*
young woman. *See* age cohorts of women; *shābba*

Al-Zabīdī, Muḥammad, 96
Al-Zāhid, Aḥmad ibn Sulaymān, 135–36
Ẓāhirīs (legal school), 38–41
Zarrūq, Shaykh Aḥmad, 126
Zaynab bint al-Kamāl, 155
zinā (illegitimate sexual intercourse), 41, 165, 237–38, 240, 241, 244
ziyādas (additions, to mosques), 333*n*98
Ziyād ibn Abīhi, 115
Al-Zurqānī, 34